# THE DEAD ARE ARISING

# THE DEAD
# ARE ARISING

## THE LIFE OF
## MALCOLM X

# Les Payne
### and Tamara Payne

LIVERIGHT PUBLISHING CORPORATION

A DIVISION OF W. W. NORTON & COMPANY

*INDEPENDENT PUBLISHERS SINCE 1923*

FRONTISPIECE: Malcolm X smiling, ca. 1964. (Photograph by Ed Ford for *New York World-Telegram and Sun*, Library of Congress Prints and Photographs Division)

Copyright © 2020 by the Estate of Les Payne
Introduction copyright © 2020 by Tamara Payne

All rights reserved
Printed in the United States of America
First Edition

For information about permission to reproduce selections from this book, write to Permissions, Liveright Publishing Corporation, a division of W. W. Norton & Company, Inc., 500 Fifth Avenue, New York, NY 10110

For information about special discounts for bulk purchases, please contact W. W. Norton Special Sales at specialsales@wwnorton.com or 800-233-4830

Manufacturing by LSC Communications, Harrisonburg
Book design by Daniel Lagin
Production manager: Anna Oler

ISBN 978-1-63149-166-5

Liveright Publishing Corporation, 500 Fifth Avenue, New York, N.Y. 10110
www.wwnorton.com

W. W. Norton & Company Ltd., 15 Carlisle Street, London W1D 3BS

1  2  3  4  5  6  7  8  9  0

*To Violet, whose love and support are the foundation*
*upon which this work was completed.*

*To Tamara, whose tireless effort was integral in the completion of this work.*

*To the family—both nuclear and extended—whom I wanted to make proud*
*with all of my work and effort in the world over the years.*

*Les Payne*

*And in loving memory of the life and legacy of Les Payne.*

# CONTENTS

# PART III: 1946–1963

# PART IV: 1963–1965

# ACKNOWLEDGMENTS

*THE DEAD ARE ARISING* IS THE CULMINATION OF A TWENTY-eight-year journey. Les Payne's curiosity and his skills as an investigative reporter and writer are on full display. Les was sparked to write this book after learning of Malcolm's childhood from Malcolm's brothers Wilfred and Philbert.

As a son, as a grandson, and as a brother to siblings John Payne, Joseph Payne, Mary Ann Glass, and Raymond Johnson, Les understood the importance of those formative years. He would often say that "we did not come out of the womb fully formed." The family environment imprints on us early and is a constant influence throughout our lives. The unconditional love and support of Les's family throughout the years has been a steady presence during every stage of the journey to complete this work.

Special thanks go to:

Faith Childs, whose friendship, patience, professionalism, and steady energy throughout this journey have kept this project on course.

Robert Weil of Liveright/W. W. Norton, whose commitment and dedication in editing the manuscript made this publication possible.

Walter and Linda Evans, whose friendship, support, and generosity have been invaluable. Walter and Les grew up together in Hartford, Connecticut, and their friendship has only grown deeper.

Many others have supported the completion of this work along the way. Special mentions go to Paul Lee, Liz Bass, Peter Eisner, Ken Paul, Sallye Leventhal, Jamal Payne, Haile Payne, Alfred Muhammad, Royal Shariyf, Derrick Jackson, Frances Cameron, Henrietta Cameron-Mann, Marilyn Milloy, Bernestine Singley, Dr. Frances Brisbane, Randy Daniels, DeWayne Wickham, Drake McFeely, Julia Reidhead, Steven Pace, Bill Rusin, Peter Miller, Cordelia Calvert, Gabe Kachuck, Steve Attardo, Anna Oler, Nick Curley, Trent Duffy, Dr. Cynthia Barnes, Emory University, Nebraska State Historical Society, Newsday, the National Association of Black Journalists, the Trotter Group, and the Schomburg Center for Research in Black Culture.

# INTRODUCTION

## by Tamara Payne

WHEN MY FATHER, LES PAYNE, BEGAN HIS RESEARCH IN 1990 for *The Dead Are Arising,* Malcolm X was very much alive in the consciousness of the black community. Walking down Harlem's 125th Street, you would hear Malcolm's emphatic voice resounding from the speakers of sidewalk vendors selling his speeches and you would see his countenance emblazoned on T-shirts.

This generation of hip-hop embraced Malcolm X because he spoke directly to them. His messages provided clear, direct analyses of what was happening around them in their communities. Point by point, he outlined how state-sanctioned racism is not new, but a continuation of the coordinated destruction of black people in America. Malcolm changed the way they viewed themselves and gave voice to their struggles; numerous rappers and activists quoted Malcolm in their lyrics and interviews on radio and television.

Malcolm also changed the way Les Payne viewed himself. As a college student in 1963, he had heard Malcolm speak in Hartford, Connecticut. On that June night, my father came face-to-face with his own self-loathing. Malcolm X addressed the race issue head-on:

> "Now I know you don't want to be called 'black,'" he said. . . .
> "You want to be called 'Negro.' But what does 'Negro' mean except 'black' in Spanish? So what you are saying is: 'It's OK to call me 'black' in Spanish, but don't call me black in English."[1]

Later, in "The Night I Stopped Being a Negro," an essay that was first published in a collection titled *When Race Becomes Real,* Payne wrote that he had entered "Bushnell Hall as a Negro with a capital 'N' and wandered out into the parking lot—as a black man."[2]

Born in Tuscaloosa, Alabama, Payne had moved to Hartford with his mother and two brothers at age twelve:

> I'd never met a white person, South or North, who did not feel comfortably superior to every Negro, no matter the rank or station. Conversely, no Negro I'd met or heard of had ever felt truly equal to whites. For all their polemical posturing, not even Baldwin, Martin Luther King, Jr., or the great Richard Wright, with all his crossed-up feelings, had liberated themselves from the poisoned weed of black self-loathing with its deeply entangled roots in the psyche.[3]

The lightning strike of Malcolm's sword released the "conditioned sense of Negro inferiority" that was housed in the college junior's psyche. Hearing Malcolm's piercing analysis forced him to think about the Jim Crow South he was born into: remembering how he was told that Negroes were "just as good" as whites, but seeing Negroes rise only to janitors, cooks, cotton pickers—not to landlords or owners of lumberyards. By the end of the lecture, Payne was irrevocably changed. "Whites were no longer superior. Blacks . . . were no longer inferior,"[4] he wrote.

Always inspired by Malcolm X, Payne would reread his dog-eared copy of the *Autobiography* every five years. So he was naturally curious when his high school buddy Walter O. Evans, who had become a successful surgeon in Detroit, introduced him to Philbert Little, one of Malcolm X's brothers. Payne discussed this meeting with Gil Noble, a friend and fellow journalist who at the time hosted the weekly Sunday show *Like It Is* on WABC-TV in New York. In addition to his work as a renowned broadcaster, Noble was an admirer of Malcolm X. Every year, he dedicated episodes of *Like It Is* to the life and assassination of Malcolm X. Noble suggested that Payne also meet Wilfred Little, Malcolm's oldest brother and best friend.

At the time, Payne was an editor at *Newsday*, a daily newspaper on Long Island. He had won a Pulitzer Prize in 1974 as part of a reporting team investigating the international flow of heroin from the poppy fields of Turkey, through the French connection, and into the veins of New York drug addicts. He was renowned for his investigative persistence and his skill in obtaining the truth from reluctant sources. As he often told his three children—Jamal, Haile, and myself—he could not abide the phrase "We may never know."

After sitting down in Detroit with the two siblings, he was shocked to realize how much he did not know about the man whom he had admired and studied. For such a persistent seeker of the true story, the fact that so much remained unknown about Malcolm proved irresistible. It set my father on a journey that would last twenty-eight years, until his untimely death in 2018.

Tracing Malcolm X's steps—from the Nebraska cauldron he was born into and the family life that shaped him to the gunshots that would silence him forever—Payne traveled around the world, conducting hundreds of interviews with Malcolm's family members, childhood friends, classmates, buddies on the streets and in prison, as well as cops, bodyguards, FBI agents, drivers, informers, photographers, journalists, U.N. representatives, African revolutionaries and presidents, sworn enemies, fake followers, and the two men falsely imprisoned for shooting him dead.

As he tracked down how Malcolm became the person he was, he learned an extraordinary amount of biographical detail that was new. Even though much has been written about Malcolm in the years since Payne's investigation began, much that he found has never been told before or has been sketched only roughly, without the deeply reported detail and color that bring a life to life again.

Plying his Pulitzer-level skills as an investigative reporter, Payne was mindful that even though Malcolm X told his story well, his and other published accounts are neither fully rendered nor entirely accurate. Accordingly, the reader will discover that key trails explored in *The Dead Are Arising* are less well-trodden, and some—details of Malcolm's sit-down with the Ku Klux Klan, for example—were long considered unattainable. Through extensive interviewing and reporting, the reader is now brought in on this 1961 meeting around the kitchen table of Minister Jeremiah X* in Atlanta.

*The Dead Are Arising* sheds light on Earl Little's tragic death in 1931, and Malcolm's haunting, lifelong doubts about the official version are, after extensive investigation, squared with the facts. New details about the breakup of the family reveal the roles played by state institutions, an insurance company, and young Malcolm himself as his mother tried to care for her eight children during the

---

* In America the surname for black people usually is that of the slave owners and does not reflect their African family heritage. Therefore, members of the Nation of Islam change their surname to "X," which stands for unknown. If there is more than one person with the same first name in a Nation of Islam temple, or mosque, a numeral is placed before the "X" representing the number of people with that name that precede them, such as Charles 37X or Benjamin 7X.

harshest years of the Depression, in the end, crumbling in on herself. "Instead of being the happy person when our father was alive," said one son, "she was quiet. My mother stopped singing."

*The Dead Are Arising* also provides a new portrait of the young man known as East Lansing Red (long before he was dubbed Detroit Red), as Malcolm, starting at age twelve, hustled reefers from a neighbor's garden plot and then became a sneak thief by pilfering scarce cash even from his mother: "Malcolm never would deny that he stole," recalled one of his brothers, who had caught him red-handed. "He was not a liar." He was, however, reckless. And long before the Muslim days, Malcolm's craving for attention was chilling, as when he challenged a notorious Lansing cop holding a gun to his adolescent head: "Go ahead! Pull the trigger, Whitey."

This biography will show readers in often astonishing detail how Malcolm, as the Nation of Islam's great proselytizer, "fished" for converts and built a disciplined chapter, inciting a group of New England prospects to service in a cramped, housing-project apartment, while implicitly shaming the shorts-clad daughter of the house with his call to modesty. Away from media noise, the presence of ever wary cops, the muscling of rivals—and even the coaxing of the Nation of Islam's leader, Elijah Muhammad—we catch an early glimpse of how Malcolm would run things when left alone.

Finally, the book provides readers with a moment-by-moment account of the February 1965 assassination, which is reconstructed with unparalleled vividness. Les Payne's sources here include the undercover New York City policeman whose testimony might have cleared two men who were unjustly sentenced for the murder, and a member of the Nation's Newark "goon squad" who provides an insider's account of the planning and immediate aftermath of the murder.

This work, moreover, contextualizes Malcolm's life against the racial conflicts, violence, and aspirations of twentieth-century

America—all of this history richly rendered. Along the way, *The Dead Are Arising* provides portraits of the Marcus Garvey movement that shaped young Malcolm's early life, the Nation of Islam organization that gave him direction when he came out of prison, and the Ku Klux Klan that he saw at one time as the most honest face of white America.

Although Les Payne's investigative research revealed much that was new about Malcolm's life, his assessment of Malcolm's core message did not change. In a 1989 column, he wrote:

> More than any other leader of the 1960's, Malcolm moved blacks to consider who they were and whence they came, and to plan for what they could become. He saw his people as a brutalized class, who after centuries of slavery and oppression had been made to think of themselves—and to act—as inferiors, as "niggers."
>
> To correct this condition, the black man could either work on the outer manifestations of discrimination—as did Martin Luther King—or change himself from within, through transformation. Malcolm took the latter course, both in teaching and in his personal life on this planet. He underwent a dramatic conversion, from street criminal to devoted moralist and revolutionary.
>
> Along the way, Malcolm sought to upset the white man's grossly inflated sense of himself, his complacent arrogance and smugness. In rejecting the dominant society that had rejected him, he instructed his followers to reject the white man's ideas, values and above all, the way he looked down upon blacks as inferiors.
>
> King offered racists the other cheek, Malcolm the back of his hand. Freedom was so important to him that Malcolm counseled risking all, except one's sense of self-respect, in the

fight. Nonviolence, he taught, unduly narrowed an oppressed people's options. "We have to change our minds about each other," Malcolm said often to his followers.[5]

Even as he tracked Malcolm X, Payne was busy at *Newsday*. He wrote a weekly syndicated column, and as an assistant managing editor, he was in charge of the daily newspaper's state, national, international, and science coverage. During the years he worked on this book, he supervised reporting that won four Pulitzer Prizes: for coverage of genocide in Bosnia, U.S. friendly fire deaths in Iraq, Ebola in Zaire (now Democratic Republic of Congo), and the aftermath of genocide in Rwanda. Outside of *Newsday*, he participated in a weekly discussion panel on *Sunday Edition*, a popular CBS Sunday morning news show.

In 1975, he helped to found the National Association of Black Journalists, which was organized to "improve the number of black journalists over all in America. [To] improve the treatment of black journalists already in the profession. [To] improve the coverage of the black community and the third world community," explained Payne. "We had to organize and challenge the industry of journalism. Confront and demand these things because black people read newspapers. Black people watch television. Plus, a lot of the information the media puts out about black people is distorted." And then in 1992 he helped to found the Trotter Group of black columnists, named after William Monroe Trotter, a black journalist and editor of the *Boston Guardian*. Trotter was thrown out of the White House in 1914 for arguing with President Wilson against the policy of segregating federal offices. In addition to organizing black columnists, the Trotter Group met with both President Clinton and President Obama during their terms in office.

Some fifty years after William Trotter's White House incident, Payne started his career in journalism as a federal employee of a sort. After graduating from the University of Connecticut, he spent six years in the U.S. Army as a Ranger, serving as an information officer in Vietnam for General William Westmoreland, where Payne ran the army newspaper. In 1969, attired in his captain's uniform, he applied for a job at *Newsday,* where he stayed until his retirement in 2006, but at every stage of his life he confronted racism. "When I was a rookie reporter," he later recalled, "my young daughter asked why there were no blacks among *Newsday*'s 102 summer interns, in 1973, I shot off a note to management demanding an explanation. The reason I gave Tami, I wrote in my note to *Newsday,* was that her daddy worked for a 'racist newspaper.'"

As the young daughter cited here, I have worked on this book as a researcher since its earliest days. In a meeting with Faith Childs, his literary agent, Payne shared his experience of meeting the two Little brothers. He was intrigued by what he had learned from them. It was at this meeting he decided to write *The Dead Are Arising.* The title refers to Malcolm's description of conversion into the Nation of Islam. Before they joined the Nation of Islam, members were "dead" because they did not know their true selves. Elijah Muhammad's teachings—particularly those aimed at strengthening black communities through improving their diet and removing distractions of prostitution, gambling, drugs, and alcohol—enabled members to free themselves from the false sense of inferiority imposed by the larger society. Malcolm continued his work of eradicating this inferiority complex after he left the Nation of Islam, until his death. This work remains unfinished.

Embarking on this journey, Payne continued working at *Newsday. The Dead Are Arising* became one more project he had to manage. He hired Paul Lee, a professional researcher who has dedicated much of his career to archiving accurate records about Malcolm's life and work. Payne also brought on Elizabeth Bass, a longtime colleague and trusted friend, as an editor. Bass had worked for him as the science and health editor at *Newsday*. She also had served as *Newsday*'s deputy national editor and deputy foreign editor. Over the next twenty-eight years, this team worked with my father to bring this book together.

Les Payne's untimely death on March 19, 2018, left both his immediate and his larger family devastated. In my sorrow and disbelief, I knew that the final work—his life's work, as he would refer to this book—had to be completed.

Assisting in tracking down many of those who were interviewed for this book, I have also transcribed most of the interviews. My father had also brought me along on some of the interviews. Meeting Malcolm's associates and family members over the years and watching Les Payne's investigative techniques at work have been the unique reward of a lifetime for me. My many discussions with him about how this work was taking shape proved to be invaluable in the finishing of the manuscript. As the copilot and conavigator, I could confidently and successfully complete this part of the journey.

The manuscript was mostly finished by the time of his death. With the help and support of my family, Faith Childs, Elizabeth Bass, Robert Weil of Liveright/W. W. Norton, and countless others, I was able to bring the manuscript to the desired end. I was thankfully able to follow my father's lead, as he tracked Malcolm's steps, in his words, "from street criminal to devoted moralist and revolutionary."

# PART I

1925–1939

# CHAPTER 1

# Born Against the Current

THE METALLIC CLICKING OF HOOFBEATS ON THE GRAVEL ROAD drew five-year-old Wilfred to the small-pane window. His mother, wiping her hands, hurried to the front door as a group of horsemen with flickering torches rode up to their wood-frame home on the outskirts of Omaha, Nebraska.

"Little!" yelled one of the half dozen men.

Louise Little said that her husband was not at home. And with the tree leaves rustling in the evening breeze, the horsemen steadied their mounts in the front yard, and declared that they were the "knights" of the Ku Klux Klan.

"Get that nigger out here, now!" one of the strangers shouted.[1]

Haltingly, a young housewife,[2] precise in her West Indian accent, said that her family didn't cause trouble or bother neighbors, that they minded their own business. The excitement of the horses died down for young Wilfred as his mother folded her arms. Seen against the flickering kerosene light, she was a sight that, at least momentarily, might have given the white vigilantes pause. Light-complexioned, with thick hair flowing to her waist, Mrs. Little stood taller than the average man of her day, at more than five feet eight inches. And she was pregnant. "She was big," Wilfred said years later, "she was expecting at any time."

"Y'all" better get on out of town, said the man in front, exclaiming that they didn't tolerate "troublemakers." Bristling before the young family, the Klansmen clutched their shotguns by the trigger housing and made "all kinds of threats," aimed chiefly against the man of the house. The unfolding drama puzzled the eldest child of the household.

"I didn't know what to make of it," Wilfred recalled. "My mother was angry, so naturally, I'm angry too. My mother is challenging 'em, you know, verbally, she never used any profanity." Still, several of the men waved gun barrels toward the door as another spurred his horse forward, shaking his torch at the defiant Mrs. Little.

"My mother kept arguing," Wilfred said. "[The Klan leader] got mad. He took the butt of his rifle and knocked the front window out." Baby brother Philbert started crying in a back room and three-year-old Hilda tugged at her mother's housedress. If fear of the gunmen gripped Mrs. Little, her children detected no sign in her tone and body language, as Wilfred recalled the incident years later. The children, in fact, drew lasting strength from the manner in which their mother stood her ground that spring evening before the bullying white strangers on horseback. However, contrary to his initial impressions, Wilfred would conclude later that it helped greatly that his father was indeed not at home.

Eventually, the armed knights of the Klan jerked their horses around in apparent frustration, dipped their torches, and without firing a shot, galloped away as dusk turned into pitch darkness. Their memory of the standoff, dangerous and yet alluring to the youngsters at the time, would trouble them for the rest of their lives, especially the keenly observant Wilfred. After he learned that such Ku Klux Klan visits often ended with roped Negro bodies dangling from a tree, flashbacks of the terror would bolt him awake from youthful sleep some nights. And this eldest child of the Little family would later recount for the author poignant details about that fateful evening.

After the vigilantes rode away, the pregnant mother of three did not consider calling police to be a viable option because Negroes understood that city officials generally approved of such Klan activity. Instead, she sought help from prosperous acquaintances, using their two-piece, candlestick telephone to get word of the emergency to her preacher husband, some five hundred miles away in Milwaukee, Wisconsin.[3]

The Reverend Earl Little booked the next train back to Omaha. Having moved away from their first cramped quarters on the northern strip of city blocks designated for Negroes, the growing family now lived in a rented farmhouse—among white neighbors. In the Omaha of the 1920s, this exercise of open housing was a civil right reserved strictly for Caucasians; however, violating the policy was in keeping with the rebellious spirit of the pioneering, young Negro couple. Their breach did not go unnoticed by white residents, including the Klan. Upon discovering the "treachery" of the white property owners who had rented to the Littles, neighbors turned downright unneighborly—except for an immigrant Hungarian family who, despite icy stares of others, befriended the Littles even as they were openly harassed as "Negro troublemakers."

All across America, during the first half of the twentieth century, such was the treatment of blacks who dared exercise civil rights reserved for "whites only." In the North, the racial divide was de facto and maintained at key levels of society, including housing, education, employment, restaurants, nightclubs, hotels, bars, hospitals, and even church services. In the South, where racial segregation was de jure, Jim Crow laws codified by state and county governments posted dire "white only" warning signs everywhere and fielded brutal sheriff's departments to enforce the policy, with unofficial assistance from vigilantes such as the Ku Klux Klan.

Upon arriving back home in Omaha, Reverend Little paced the floor as his young wife detailed how she and the children had weathered the raid of the white knights. Dark-skinned and standing more than six feet four inches, the reverend had a glass eye from an accident back home in Georgia, when a nail had pitched up from an errant blow of his hammer and struck his left eye. Despite the lawlessness of the Klan ordeal, Reverend Little agreed that calling the Omaha police about the vigilante raid would have gone for naught. Already, the trek into town for household goods and services by borrowed horse and wagon had been risky for the isolated family. Now the Klan visit had rendered their very home unsafe.

Under this uniquely American cloud of racial dread, the Reverend Earl Little and his pregnant wife, Louise—the parents of daughter Hilda and sons Wilfred and Philbert—awaited the birth of their fourth child.

———

Louise Norton Little arrived by horse and wagon at Omaha's University Hospital and was signed in at the admission office as: "West Indian housewife." She was attended by Dr. W. A. Lear, a white obstetrician, as such state institutions of the day did not grant practice privileges to Negro physicians. After a routine delivery that Tuesday evening, Dr. Lear applied the requisite water solution to each eye of the infant and declared him alive and healthy. It was 10:29 p.m. on May 19, 1925.[4]

The parents named their baby boy Malcolm. This future icon of the global human rights struggle was the fetus that Mrs. Louise Little was carrying that night the Klan terrorized her family at the doorstep. Some years later, his brother Wilfred would render detailed recollections about the family to the author, many hours of which were tape-recorded over a period of five years, along with in-depth interviews with three younger siblings and telephone chats with two others. This material, including some closely held secrets, was supplemented by accounts from other relatives, neighbors, teachers, classmates, acquaintances, friends, enemies, as well as attributed accounts from *The Autobiography of Malcolm X*—all verified by official records where possible—and synthesized as the main body of the present story of this special son of a pioneering, Midwestern family who would become a major figure in twentieth-century American history.

Baby Malcolm was the seventh of Earl's children. The first three were offspring from a previous marriage in rural Georgia, where kinfolks, and father Earl occasionally, would boast that the birth sequence of this new boy-child placed him under a "good luck" sign. This charm-digit, as old as the Bible, was popularized by Negro folklore of the time, as it would be later in blues lyrics, such as the "Hoochie Coochie Man," who was said to have been born:

> *On the seventh hour*
> *On the seventh day*
> *On the seventh month*
> *Seven doctors' say*
> *He was born for good luck . . .*[5]

This fortuitous omen, however, did not attend baby Malcolm in Omaha because he was but the fourth child born to Earl and Louise. The infant did attract attention at University Hospital, where the offspring of Negro couples of extreme light and dark skin tones aroused curiosity among nurses and staffers on the ward. His paternal relatives in Georgia took pride in producing children tall in stature and dark of hue, and this despite the complexion of Earl's mother, Ella, who was light-complexioned with gray eyes. Word circulated on the University Hospital ward, however, that baby Malcolm looked like his own mother, Louise, with a milky complexion and "near-blue" eyes that matched his mother's when she was a child.[6]

In a more practical way, father Earl welcomed his new son as a pair of future hands for the plow and other chores around the farm-house. For the moment though, baby Malcolm was another mouth to be fed by parents who were eking out a living under the dismis-sive eyes of white neighbors, indifferent Omaha officials, and now, the gun barrel of vigilantes on horseback. Experiencing Klan terror firsthand was unnerving to the family, but the father had grown up hearing widely circulated accounts of deadly Ku Klux Klan lynching in the Deep South.

The father had been born Early Little, in Butler, Georgia, in 1890. He was the son of former slaves, whom only a generation earlier the state had forbade to be taught to read or write, subjecting violators to a $500 fine, lashings, and possible imprisonment.[7] Attending one of the few rural schools for postslavery children, young Early com-pleted the third grade, was subsequently trained as a carpenter and brick mason, and then entered the ministry as a Baptist preacher. His early schooling came just as the U.S. Supreme Court sanctified Jim Crow laws in its "separate but equal" *Plessy v. Ferguson* decision of 1896. It would be more than half a century before Georgia gover-nor Lester Maddox wielded an ax handle in defiance of the Court's 1954 decision reversing *Plessy* and outlawing school segregation.[8] Under the racist Jim Crow system, the education of Negroes was woefully thwarted by white government officials mandating grossly disparate and insufficient expenditures, as well as out-of-date books (castoffs from white schools), poorly trained teachers, and scant job opportunities after graduation. Accordingly, although quite ambi-tious, smart, and enterprising, Earl (as he was known outside of the family) and Negroes of similar stature, including key members of his family in rural Georgia, were not afforded much chance at formal education.

In the early twentieth century, most black southerners resided on land farmed for its white owners. Charged exorbitant rents, these "sharecroppers" were extended credit for household goods, food, and clothing, all charged against labor on the farm and in the kitchen. Harvesttime usually found the bookkeeping white landowners taking the hog's share of the crops. Disputes were put down by brute, white force that could all too often turn deadly. Saddled with unpaid bills on the ledgers, the sharecroppers were essentially tied to the tenant farms under a postslavery system of debt peonage. Word of such debtors skipping to the North brought down terror raids upon their families, as did other perceived slights.

Young Malcolm's paternal grandparents, John and Ella Little, were something of a rarity among Negroes in turn-of-the-century Georgia in that they owned land. They passed along their drive to own property to their son Early, and he to his children, most especially to Malcolm's older half sister Ella. Later, this anointed eldest child would recall how her traveling evangelist dad, ever enterprising, used to occasionally exhibit her at various churches to emphasize a preaching point from the Bible. "I'd have my little chair on the pulpit," Ella fondly recollected.[9]

During Earl's adolescence in Georgia, he was, it was said, quite reluctant to yield to the tradition of Southern etiquette that required Negroes to accede to total white dominance. State law defined the suppressed class as anyone with "any ascertainable trace of Negro blood,"[10] and the statutes segregated the races on public transport and in prisons, mental hospitals, barbershops, pool halls, and public schools. A poll tax made Negro voting almost nonexistent in their home state. Young Early's natural rebelliousness attracted the notice of local white merchants and—as was the the pattern of the day—he was tagged by the dangerous sobriquet "uppity nigger."[11] Later, when he was a young husband, Reverend Little's intransigence occasioned brushes with the law. This, coupled with frequent household squabbles with his first wife, Daisy Mason, placed him at odds with his more "servile" in-laws, according to his two sisters. Conflicts flared openly between the two families and rendered the marriage rocky throughout. Moreover, Earl's alarming tendency to back-talk to whites in public reportedly placed the "uppity nigger" preacher in danger wherever he traveled throughout the South.

According to relatives, Early's father, "Pa John"—conforming to the pattern of concerned Negro parents of the times—advised that his "uppity" son, for safety's sake, should gather his family and leave Georgia and, for that matter, the South.[12] Eventually the young father did just that, departing abruptly—although without his wife of almost ten years and their three children, Ella, Mary, and Earl Jr.

Landing a job in Philadelphia, the restless young, carpenter-preacher was soon exposed to the secular teaching of Marcus Garvey, whose Universal Negro Improvement Association (UNIA) sought to uplift the race globally. Reverend Little was deeply impressed. The message of the campaigning Marcus Garvey struck Earl as just the tonic for an independent-minded Negro in search of himself. It was not so much the UNIA's global outreach to Africa that finally persuaded the young preacher as it was the group's uncompromising tenet that the individual free himself from the strictures of the psyche imposed by white racist domination in America—and that Negroes demand equal treatment across the board.

The peripatetic Reverend Earl Little, separated from the family he had abandoned in Georgia, occasionally went to Canada to hear Marcus Garvey speak and once, when he was between jobs, sought a brief respite from U.S. racism as a UNIA camp follower. In the Commonwealth nation of Canada, the Caribbean UNIA members, as British subjects, could move about more freely. At a UNIA meeting during a visit to Montreal, Earl met a handsome, twenty-year-old* woman from the tiny Caribbean island of Grenada, Louise Helen Langdon Norton,[13] who worked as a seamstress and housekeeper for white families. She had migrated to this Quebec city in 1917 with her uncle, Edgerton Langdon, who had introduced her to the teaching of Marcus Garvey. The tall, light-complexioned Louise had attended a religious school under the English system that stressed geography, mathematics, and language skills. She spoke English with a Caribbean accent, as well as Spanish and a smattering of French. Never having known her Scottish father, Louise was raised by a stern grandmother, Mary Jane Langdon, and aunt, Gertrude, after her unmarried mother, Edith, died during the birth of her third child.

After a brief courtship, the twenty-nine-year-old separated father of three, who some relatives say never divorced his first wife, Daisy, took the younger Grenadian as his bride, in May 1919, six months after the war had ended in Europe. Soon after, the couple left Canada and settled in Philadelphia, where their first child, Wilfred, was born on February 12, 1920. A few months later, Earl, shifting among several jobs, took his young family to Georgia to meet his parents and siblings. Louise was in her second pregnancy. Relatives noted that Earl had landed a young beauty but assumed that the neatly dressed, well-spoken, Caribbean-bride-made-American-citizen, the product of five years of strict Anglican education, was a snob not much given to hard work. They were wrong in this assumption because Louise, as a youngster, had been entrusted with run-

---

* There is a discrepancy regarding Louise Little's age. When she was admitted to Kalamazoo State Hospital on January 9, 1939, her age was recorded as forty-two, making her birth year 1897, the date we use in the book. According to Erik McDuffie's 2016 essay on Louise Little (see note 2 for this chapter), her birth date on her baptismal records in Grenada is listed as January 2, 1894.

ning the household of her grandmother and aunt. Housework, responsibility, and authority, enforced with corporal punishment, were nothing new to the West Indian mother of a growing family. When mixing it up, especially with the womenfolk, Louise was careful to concentrate her talk on what they had in common, such as housekeeping, child-rearing, and racial discrimination. And she wisely did more listening than talking.[14]

In short order, Louise also rolled up her sleeves and cordially dispelled all notions of sloth with thoroughgoing housework that won over her husband's family—all except for the wife from Reverend Little's first marriage, and her family. The Masons were understandably livid that Early had the temerity to parade his pregnant new bride before the family he had abandoned for parts unknown. The first wife, according to their daughter Ella, threatened to stage a Daisy-Louise showdown during the family visit.

Once again, Early's father intervened to preserve peace at home and the family's reputation downtown. Just as when the son first migrated north, Pa John feared that his son's "uppity" rebelliousness was certain to attract local law enforcement, and possibly a visit from white vigilantes.[15] In due course, Early and his pregnant wife and son headed back north. And when his bachelor brother James landed a job at a large meatpacking company in the Midwest, where jobs were plentiful, Earl and Louise were invited to join him in Omaha. The migration of Negroes to the city was the largest on the Great Plains at the time. With 10,315 such residents, Omaha was second only to Los Angeles, in cities west of the Missouri River, in terms of black population.[16]

As a frontier settlement in 1854, Omaha had been named after a Native American tribe that the U.S. government restricted at the time to a reservation in northeastern Nebraska. In the Siouan language of the tribe, "Omaha" means "those going against the current."[17] The fate that had befallen this tribe stood as an ominous warning to residents who challenged the federal government. It's not a stretch, however, to note that the determined resistance of Earl and Louise to racist suppression matched the spirit of the Omaha tribe. Nor is it an exaggeration to suggest that the couple's fierce determination, against overwhelming odds, would be sharply reflected in their fourth-born child, Malcolm.

While constituting only 5 percent of the city population, the strictly segregated Negro community of Omaha supported forty small Protestant churches; some one hundred family businesses, including a few doctors, lawyers, and dentists; and two dozen elite, secret social clubs and organizations.[18] Feature stories about the activities of these groups, as well as news of the entire community, could be found in the weekly *Monitor*, the local Negro newspaper. And community activists had established, in 1912, the first chapter of the National Association for the Advancement of Colored People (NAACP) west of the Mississippi River. The civil rights group, however, was severely challenged as racial tension initially flared in Omaha when local meatpacking firms in 1917 recruited Negroes as strikebreakers, pitting these longtime Americans against immigrant workers from Europe. These Caucasians had not themselves been integrated as full-fledged white Americans. However, they had gained the upper hand in the workplace by controlling the unions as well as the crime syndicate in town. As white Americans on probation, these foreign-born Europeans, mainly Irish Catholics, cracked down brutally on incoming Negro citizens from the Deep South— as if such behavior would speed their acceptance by the dominant, native-born whites. In 1918, the Irish hold on the workplace was threatened when Edward Parson Smith, a reform-minded Anglo candidate, defeated the longtime machine mayor, who had been more tolerant of the unions and the criminal syndicate. These contending political forces—with Negroes trapped as the consensus underclass—created an explosive atmosphere in the city.

And the next year, when a frenzy of race rioting was sweeping the nation, a local killing was so gruesome that it got this Nebraska city featured on the "lynching" map under what historians labeled the Omaha incident.

———

As returning military veterans competed for jobs and housing amid major population shifts, including the Great Migration, in which some half a million blacks moved from the South to Northern and Midwestern cities, racial violence went full throttle. Having fought for democracy in Europe, where they were treated more equally, Negro soldiers pushed for their civil rights at home, thereby rocking the prewar status quo. Even before the signing of the Versailles Treaty, which officially concluded the war with Germany, a race riot led by U.S. sailors erupted in Charleston, South Carolina; during this melee on May 10, 1919, three Negroes were killed, with injuries on both sides. In Chicago that July, a weeklong explosion flared at a segregated beach, with thirty-eight deaths, some fifteen of them whites, as Negroes fought back.

"We return from fighting. We return fighting," wrote W. E. B. Du Bois in the May issue of *The Crisis*, the NAACP magazine.[19] The Windy City riot was part of a firestorm that hit some thirty-three cities, with mainly white mobs attacking Negroes, according to the U.S. Department of Labor. Hundreds were left homeless and about 175 were killed, including at least 76 Negroes who were lynched, 11 of them war veterans. Writer James Weldon Johnson dubbed this bloody conflagration the Red Summer, even though it flamed on into October.[20] Negroes campaigning for equality were said by some federal officials to be under the influence of the Bolsheviks, who had recently staged the Russian revolution, giving rise to America's first so-called Red Scare, which replaced anti-German sentiment among whites in the United States. "The American negro returning from abroad would be our greatest medium for conveying bolshevism to America," President Woodrow Wilson reportedly told his personal physician, Dr. Cary Grayson. "The French people have placed the negro soldier in France on an equality with the white man," Grayson wrote in his diary, adding that President Wilson stated, "And it has gone to their heads."[21]

The Red Summer spark that touched off the racial explosion in Omaha was more typical of a Deep South powder keg. In fact, the origins of this race riot were part of a familiar trope of American history. Nineteen-year-old Agnes Loebeck reported that she and her boyfriend were attacked walking home from a movie theater on September 25, 1919. A "Negro jumped out of the weeds at us," she said, and robbed the couple at pistol point. According to newspaper accounts, Loebeck claimed that the man "dragged me into the weeds by my hair and assaulted me."[22]

"I tried to scream," she said, "but he covered my mouth with his left hand," while adroitly holding the pistol on her "crippled" boyfriend, Milton Hoffman.*[23] As with other Red Summer allegations in the news, local authorities made little effort to check the validity of the white accuser's sketchy claims. "Black Beast" screamed the subheadline of the first-day story in the notoriously race-baiting *Omaha Daily Bee.* Its front-page story tagged the unconfirmed episode "the most daring attack on a white woman ever perpetrated in Omaha."[24]

The very next day, Will Brown, a Negro man of about forty with acute rheumatism, was pointed out as "suspicious" by a white resident who had observed that Brown, a packing house worker from Cairo, Illinois, was renting a room at a woman's home nearby.[25] Police officers brought Brown to Loebeck's residence as a possible suspect. Already, a raucous crowd, whipped up by the *Omaha Bee*'s yellow

---

* Newspapers reported the name of Agnes Loebeck's boyfriend as Millard for several days before correcting it to Milton.

journalism, had created a circus atmosphere outside the teenager's home, where she supposedly identified the startled, middle-aged black laborer as the "guilty man," although police and U.S. Army reports later indicated that the teenager did not make a positive identification of her alleged attacker.[26]

Straightaway, the 250 white residents camped outside the Loebeck home bolted into action. "Don't take that man to jail!" the white mob shouted, according to one newspaper account. "Let us have him. The courts won't punish him. We will!"[27] Bent on making the arrest, the city police called in reinforcements but barely managed to extricate Brown from a group attempting to loop a rope around his neck. Several men even landed a few blows about the heads and shoulders of the cops as others punctured the tires of their patrol cars. The officers finally managed to escort the Negro suspect to booking at court, and later to jail. Headed by the reform-minded Mayor Smith, city hall was despised by the mostly Irish mob, which had been lathered up by news reports, a local crime syndicate leader, simmering tension in the workplace, and deep-seated fear and hatred of Negroes said to be after their jobs—and now their women.[28]

The racial horrors of the Red Summer—played out in cities from Tuscaloosa, Alabama, to New London, Connecticut, and across to Texarkana, Texas—were so well rehearsed that the innocent Will Brown had already been convicted of a capital crime against white womanhood by the Omaha press. Indeed, local working-class whites pursued the meatpacking worker as a handy scapegoat for their own problems, to say nothing of their insecurities about black sexual prowess.

At 3:00 p.m. that Sunday, some "200 boys," aged fourteen to twenty, from the Bancroft School, which Loebeck had attended, were intercepted by detectives as they marched on the Douglas County Courthouse, according to "Omaha's Riot in Story and Picture," a twenty-six-page pamphlet reporting on the incident. One of the leaders reportedly rode a horse "from whose saddle hung a long rope." Within two hours, the "boys' brigade" was joined by thousands of white adults, mainly immigrants, who pushed one policeman through a glass door, assaulted two others, and rushed the courthouse. When policemen trained a water hose on the crowd, they countered with "bricks and sticks" and broke "nearly every window on the south side" as they "swarmed about the courthouse on all sides."[29]

"We are going to teach these Negroes a lesson," said one man, a local newspaper reported. The crowd was estimated at 10,000 to 20,000 people, angry, mainly Caucasian immigrant men and women. It seemed as if all of white Omaha, save authorities, was united in this bloodthirsty pursuit of a Negro American citizen innocent by every standard of a lawful society. The residents pillaged nearby hardware stores and pawn shops, stealing more than a thousand revolvers and shotguns, according to police records. As the sheriff and his deputies periodically dodged bullets themselves, the irate workers and idlers torched the lower floors of the courthouse with gasoline.

Inside the stately courthouse, Will Brown moaned to Sheriff Mike Clark, "I am innocent; I never did it; my God I am innocent," the more reliable *Morning World-Herald* told its readers. And a local reporter and attorney who interviewed Brown in jail agreed with a physical examination report that Brown was "too twisted by rheumatism to assault anyone."[30]

The white mob made clear its nonnegotiable demand: prisoner Brown was to be taken from the fifth-floor jail cell and handed over to them. When Police Chief Marshal Eberstein failed to quell the crowd, Mayor Smith, whom the immigrants in the mob blamed for their labor discontent with Negroes, emerged from the flaming courthouse at about eleven that evening and pleaded for order. Someone hit Smith "on the head with a baseball bat." Another man "slipped the noose of a rope around [the mayor's] neck," and the crowd dragged him away. Several "spectators . . . wrested the mayor from his captors and placed him in a police automobile." Within minutes, the crowd recaptured its victim, roped him once again, and managed nearly to suspend the body of Omaha's chief executive from a traffic signal tower.[31]

On the verge of strangulation, the dangling Mayor Smith was dramatically rescued by special agents driving through the throng in a "high-powered automobile." They rushed the mayor to the hospital—where, after two days on the critical list, he would recover. One not-so-lucky sixteen-year-old was shot dead while leading a gang to the fourth floor of the courthouse. A block away, James Hiykel, a thirty-four-year-old businessman, was shot dead by two stray bullets. Throughout the melee, "Negroes were dragged from streetcars and beaten,"[32] while other such unsuspecting pedestrians were chased down on sight. Well-meaning whites attempting to render aid were themselves battered about.

Meanwhile, the gasoline-fed flames lapped up the side of the five-story building, where policemen, court officers, and 121 prisoners had fled to the roof. Despite cries for mercy, the mob blocked all attempts to hoist rescue ladders, and they severed water hoses that firemen hooked up to nearby hydrants. As the roof weakened under the heat, the women prisoners were allowed to depart the building. However, the men trapped by the inferno yelled through the billowing smoke for help as some of the married officers reportedly placed goodbye telephone calls to their wives and families.

"Bring Brown with you," shouted one man, "and you can come down!"[33] The bloodthirsty mob had clearly regained its singular focus on "the Nigger." With human incineration a distinct possibility, trapped officials on the fourth floor tossed down three notes.

"The judge says he will give up Negro Brown. He is in dungeon," one piece scrawled. "There are 100 white prisoners on the roof. Save them." Another note read, "Come to the fourth floor of the building and we will hand the negro over to you." Then, with automobile spotlights trained on the burning courthouse, two nimble young men with a shotgun and a coil of rope scaled the west wall to the fourth floor to the accompaniment of thunderous cheering punctuated by a "fusillade of shots."[34]

A mighty roar went up from the crowd with word that "Will Brown had been captured," reported "Omaha's Riot in Story and Picture," which was published that year by the Educational Publishing Company. This most destructive riot by the lawless white mob was reported in the journal as having been sparked by "a boyish sense of mistaken chivalry." And in a mere eight-line paragraph, the pamphlet summarized what the mob did next to their Negro captive.

According to newspaper accounts, some eleven hours past church services, the white rioters, still dressed in their Sunday fancy, proceeded to beat Will Brown bloody as he proclaimed his innocence. Shredding his clothes from his torso, they mercilessly whipped the near-naked Negro, who pleaded for his life as the mob cheered. The captive was then dragged to the higher of two lampposts on the south side of the smoldering courthouse, where several immigrant attackers slid the knotted noose around the neck of this American citizen vaguely accused. Then, without so much as a rhetorical question about his guilt, they slung the cord over the arm of the pole and jerked the middle-aged, arthritic laborer off the ground. The abrupt snapping of live, human vertebrae, a sound like no other, brought a blood-chilling hush upon the crowd. The limp body of Will Brown began to spin rapidly from the centripetal force of the hoisting. It steadied only when gunmen fired a volley of some hundred bullets into the roped torso.

The eerie scene moved the white mob to rapture. No other word seems appropriate. Whooping catcalls rang out like hosannas in a church revival, with the accompaniment of wild gunfire resounding throughout the smoke-filled Omaha plaza at the approach of midnight.

In due course, a few rawboned young men lowered Brown's stiff body on the taut rope and tied it to the rear bumper of an automobile. A driver gunned the engine and what was left of the cadaver was driven through the wildly cheering throng of Omaha revelers, eager as hyenas at an antelope kill. At the intersection of rampage-cluttered Seventeenth and Dodge Streets, several other men hustled up kerosene from nearby danger-signal lamps used for street repairs. And in the autumn hush of midnight, a few pale, sweating attackers doused Brown's body on a woodpile with coal oil and set the corpse ablaze.

Dozens of sporty youths in peaked caps and sweaters, along with churchgoing men in wool suits, neckties, and felt hats, swaggered about the killing ground, posing for photographs with the shredded body of their victim. Wide-eyed and eager, white residents of Omaha were photographed in full celebration of their naked human sacrifice roasting on an open pyre.

The lynching of Will Brown was witnessed by one fourteen-year-old who would grow up to become a leading Hollywood actor, portraying quiet, "quintessentially American heroes." His movie roles included *Young Mr. Lincoln,* as well as the juror who saves a Latino man from an all-white jury's death sentence in *Twelve Angry Men.* Henry Fonda recalled that as a teenager he peered down at the handiwork of his neighbors that night from the second-floor window of his father's printing shop. "My hands were wet and there were tears in my eyes," the adult Fonda said of this incident of his childhood. Presumably, the youngster never left his perch for the hours-long lynching episode, reportedly standing the entire time alongside his father, William. "When it was all over, we went home . . . All I could think of was that young black man dangling at the end of [a rope]."[35]

By 3:00 a.m. on Monday, September 29, federal troops of the Twentieth Infantry restored order by setting up machine-gun and one-pound-cannon emplacements in the downtown business district and, as a precaution, in the "black belt" section of town. The troops were under the command of General Leonard Wood, who two decades earlier had led Theodore Roosevelt's Rough Riders during the Spanish-American War and had been a contender for the Republican presidential nomination in 1916. "Omaha is not ashamed, but Omaha is frightened," wrote *The New York Times,* which reported that "at least 2,000 negroes have left the city by railroad."[36] A headline that day in the Omaha *Morning World-Herald,* which would win a 1920 Pulitzer Prize for its editorial "Law and the Jungle," read:

## FRENZIED THOUSANDS JOIN IN ORGY OF BLOOD AND FIRE

### Crowds Search Through Streets Attacking Negroes Everywhere[37]

Unlike some of the Red Summer riots, or the lynching of Negroes in the South, the Omaha incident was complicated by the collateral loss of white lives and heavy damage to public property. Therefore, it could not be so easily dismissed by officials. Significantly, in the frenzy of seizing and torturing Will Brown, the largely immigrant mob had attacked local police and even the sitting mayor. Additionally, two white men were killed accidentally and fifty-six others injured, including policemen. The mob also had wreaked about $750,000 in damage to the stately Douglas County Courthouse alone, including the loss of property records, tax lists, and other documents. This lawlessness against white residents and public property necessitated that judicial authorities prosecute, or at least identify, the more culpable transgressors among the largely immigrant crowd.

Accordingly, under a federally authorized investigation, martial law authorities and police reportedly rounded up "many of the mob leaders," totaling some 120 persons, and held them for trial in state court. Of those indicted or jailed for involvement in the riot, none reportedly served prison time. However, "with the view of stimulating serious thought and a possible probe into conditions that seem to foster anarchy," authorities commissioned an investigation that, as previously mentioned, was printed as a twenty-six-page pamphlet. "The psychologist will be interested in the mental reactions of the mob to the circumstantial stimuli," it noted. "The layman will exercise a righteous curiosity in the hope of learning why law-abiding men and women become as wild beasts under the influence of the mob idea."[38]

The Omaha police later verified that the kingpin of the local Irish crime syndicate, one Tom "Pick-Handle" Dennison, had in several other instances paid whites in blackface to attack white women, not unlike Agnes Loebeck, in order to embarrass Mayor Smith and city hall. And a subsequent grand jury report stated: "Several reported assaults [reported in the *Omaha Bee*] on white women had actually been perpetrated by whites in blackface."[39] The authorities all but specified that the reported attack on a white woman that sparked the ghastly lynching was probably staged by white men in blackface. Once again, a Negro had been set up as the scapegoat of cold-blooded white residents who considered themselves civilized, superior even. And except for the incontrovertible fact of Will Brown's body having been incinerated at the center of the Omaha incident, no precise accounting was recorded of the damage wreaked upon black lives and property that hellish day and night. Nor was anyone ever convicted of the kidnapping, torture, brutal killing, and desecration of the victim, an innocent American citizen. What was left of Brown's body was buried in an unmarked grave in a potter's field while an interment log listed him as "Lynched."

Grisly photographs of Brown's body roasting on the pyre were sold as postcards at the time. And rope used in his lynching reportedly fetched ten cents a length as souvenirs. Such was the savagery of whites in Omaha and the barbarism in matters of justice for Negroes across America in the 1920s—and well beyond. As was the national pattern, the open-ended mob-lynching was dangled for years as a warning to migrating Negroes seeking jobs and justice on the Great Plains.

# CHAPTER 2

# Storms of Racism

THE TERROR GENERATED BY THE OMAHA LYNCHING, AS WELL as hundreds of other atrocities, had the intended effect of creating an indelible sense of fear and anger that suffused the consciousness of virtually every Negro American during the 1920s. However, faced with death threats in the Deep South—where local sheriffs openly assisted white lynch mobs, and where newspapers didn't consider such atrocities "newsworthy"—Negroes continued their Great Migration north by the tens of thousands. One of these Omaha job seekers was James Little, joined by his married brother Oscar. And with the racist threat growing worse, they were joined in Nebraska by their rebellious brother Earl and his wife. Despite the racist terror in Omaha, Earl and Louise would insist upon establishing a chapter of the Universal Negro Improvement Association (UNIA) in the city.

From this uncertain foundation on the Great Plains would spring a singular life that, even now, continues to give voice to people struggling for their human rights against powerful forces imbued with a false sense of white superiority. But to understand what brought forth this dynamic advocate for those conversely afflicted, often unknowingly, by a false sense of black inferiority, it is necessary not only to examine young Malcolm's childhood environment but also to detail relevant acts by white Americans that constituted barbarous, racist torts against Negro Americans of his day. Chief among these offenses was the daily violation of the Equal Protection Clause of the Fourteenth Amendment, among other broken contracts with citizens not deemed "free white males."

Shortly before Reverend Earl Little and his wife, Louise, arrived in the city, native-born white residents, as if envious of the European immigrants who staged the Omaha incident, invited the Ku Klux Klan to launch a local operation, according to an official of the Atlanta-based group. It was not coincidental that the Klan was closed to Catholics and non-Anglo European immigrants. Inspired nonetheless by the Will Brown lynching, locals in early 1921 established Klavern Number One, the first KKK unit in Nebraska, on Forty-First and Farnan Streets.[1] Despite petty squabbles over political turf and internal rivalries, Omaha whites, both foreign and domestic, stood united in suppressing Negro citizens as a permanent underclass. This kind of threat the parents of baby Malcolm would know well and were determined to resist as UNIA organizers.

A brief history of the Klan is useful to put into perspective the hooded knights of the 1920s who were sworn to "keep blacks in their place." The white-supremacist group was created immediately after the Civil War as an on-the-ground terror organization to help officialdom deny Negroes the fulfillment of promises made in the Thirteenth, Fourteenth, and Fifteenth Amendments to the Constitution, as well as those of the 1866 Civil Rights Act. The group's robed and hooded night riders, many of them bitterly arrayed as vanquished Confederate veterans, terrorized former slaves pursuing their constitutional rights as citizens. When the national Republican and Democratic parties beat back Reconstruction at the federal level—culminating with the Hayes-Tilden Compromise of 1877,

which withdrew federal troops from the South and permitted Jim
Crow laws to enshrine segregation and suppress Southern Negroes
as second-class citizens—the Klan faded from prominence.

In 1915, however, the white knights were widely introduced to
popular culture—and eventually reintroduced to real life—by director D. W. Griffith's movie *The Birth of a Nation*. Released on the fiftieth anniversary of the end of the Civil War, the silent film was based
on a pro-Klan novel, *The Clansman: An Historical Romance of the Ku
Klux Klan,* by Thomas Dixon. The three-hour film celebrates the
Southern Confederacy, damns the Yankees, and renders Negroes
as unspeakable hoodlums, political tyrants, and violators of white
womanhood. In something of an artistic foreshadowing of the real-
life staging of the reported sexual attack in the Will Brown lynching
in Omaha, the hapless black villains in Griffith's movie are mainly
white cast members in blackface. And the overall Klan message was
made more lethal on film by the technical innovations of director
Griffith and his attention to the minutest detail, which revolution-
ized the art of moviemaking. For example, there were three thousand
horses in the production, and a battery of two hundred seamstresses
labored for two months producing historically accurate costumes for
the eighteen thousand cast members.[2]

This Hollywood portrayal of the Klan as noble saviors of white
America was so popular that President Wilson, a native Virginian
with ingrained racist views, screened *The Birth of a Nation* in the White
House; it was the first movie ever shown there and a political nod
to Southern racist supporters. Negroes across the country staged
demonstrations against the film. William Monroe Trotter, a black
journalist who a year earlier had been removed from Wilson's White
House for protesting the president's segregation policies, waged an
even more strenuous campaign against Griffith's film. But the Southern director's "masterpiece," premiering to segregated audiences in
Atlanta, aroused white racists to arms for miles around. A notorious

former Methodist preacher, one William J. Simmons, retreated to Stone Mountain, Georgia, with at least fifteen other local firebrands, including the speaker of the Georgia legislature. Simmons, the son of a physician who had been a leader of the original Alabama Klan of the 1860s, presided over a squad of men shivering before a burning cross of pine boards. They placed a Bible on a jutting rock altar, along with an American flag, a canteen of water, and a sword, over which they swore allegiance to wage an armed campaign against Negroes seeking rights as full citizens of the United States.

During the night of fireworks on November 15, 1915, this band of fierce and fearsome Georgians reconstituted the Ku Klux Klan as a secret organization of native-born "Protestants, white, gentile Americans." And for generations the hooded, white horsemen would crack down brutally on Negro progress with such terror methods as firebombings, torture, abduction, castration, gang rape, and death by gunfire, drowning, and lynching. This revived group of self-described white supremacists expressed a stronger intolerance for Jews and Catholics than the original Klan. Despite its signature cross-burning ceremony—a visual innovation Hollywood gave the revised white knights—and its armed night raids on the homes of unsuspecting residents, the "secret" Ku Klux Klan also operated in full daylight, with faces unhidden. The reborn Klan became one of the most effective groups at influencing postwar American policy, campaigning vigorously, for example, for Prohibition and against non-Anglo immigration from Europe. With its largest klaverns outside the South in Indiana, Colorado, and Michigan, the national organization claimed a membership of some 3 million that included sheriffs, cops, district attorneys, mayors, and at least two sitting governors, not to mention hundreds of thousands of women. So encompassing was its sectional appeal that it also enrolled one future Supreme Court justice, Hugo Black of Alabama, who later described the Birmingham klavern as "a fraternal organization, really" but quit after two years. According to some historians, the Klan even attracted a subsequent U.S. president, Harry S. Truman, who as a candidate for office in Jackson County, Missouri, reportedly sought Klan backing but asked for his Klan dues back when ordered not to appoint Catholics to government positions. At the height of its political power, the Klan flexed its muscle when some forty thousand white-robed men and women waved American flags and proudly paraded down Pennsylvania Avenue in the nation's capital as onlookers cheered on August 8, 1925—a few months after local KKK vigilantes had terrorized Malcolm's pregnant mother, Louise.

Upon arriving in Omaha on the heels of the Brown lynching and months after the formation of the Omaha klavern, Reverend Little landed an industry job, and settled in initially with the Smiley family on the Negro side of town. Soon after, Louise gave birth to daughter Hilda, on October 22, 1921, then son Philbert eighteen months later. Scars of the Omaha incident were still visible downtown, and at barbershops, hairdressers, social clubs, and family gatherings, the Little family heard neighbors talk warily about how the Brown lynching had totally disrupted their lives. As if that were not terror enough, local Negroes now faced the better armed and organized menace of homegrown white-racist Klansmen. Straightaway, Klavern Number One launched separate youth branches for boys and girls, and a Women of the Klan auxiliary that expanded its Omaha rolls to eleven hundred, according to the *Monitor*. In due course, Klan officials would claim a statewide tally of forty-five thousand members of every age, gender, and social class, who regularly mounted street demonstrations, weekend parades, and cross-burning ceremonies in open fields.

Early on, local whites branded Reverend Little and his wife as troublemakers, in part because they had established the UNIA chapter. When a Klan letter was posted in the *Monitor*, Louise and her husband got the boastful missive reprinted in the UNIA journal, the

*Negro World.* "White supremacy is our slogan and we are going to rule this country without the aid or consent of the Negro," wrote the Klan leader. As a warning for families such as the Littles, the letter continued, "We are checking up on you [Negroes]. . . . Omaha comes next." UNIA leader Marcus Garvey used the Klan letter, along with the 1919 Omaha riot, to make his case that America would brutally defend white supremacy at all cost.[3]

Garvey's international group differed noticeably from its domestic rival, the strictly homegrown National Association for the Advancement of Colored People (NAACP). Both were nonviolently opposed to racial oppression, but the NAACP was at the time predominantly white. It had been founded in 1909 in New York City with some sixty charter members—only seven of whom were "colored." The organization that Malcolm's parents joined was exclusively black, and as community activists, they focused on the domestic group tenets counseling self-reliance, independent mindedness, and a fierce racial pride—all dangerous pursuits for Negroes in the United States. As their family grew, Earl and Louise would insist upon fairness for their children at school, just as they demanded it for themselves in housing and elsewhere. Again and again, they would pay a terrible price for their stance. Even before the Klan horsemen rode up to their door on the outskirts of Omaha in the spring of 1925, a white delegation had paid Earl's bosses a visit at the meatpacking plant where he earned his living. They demanded that the "uppity nigger" be fired—or else. He was let go.

So by the time Malcolm was born, Reverend Little was supporting his growing family with freewill offerings from churches and housing repair jobs he picked up as an independent contractor. "He'd drive around in the neighborhoods where he might see things that needed repair," Wilfred remembered. "He'd make them an offer; they agreed to it and he'd go ahead and repair whatever it was—or he'd build an outhouse, all kind of stuff."[4] Such repair work fell within the skill set of Malcolm's father, who had trained as a carpenter and mason back in Georgia.

⸺

Already, some two generations out of slavery, when statistically they had been three-fifths of a person, "Negroes" conducted an unrequited love affair with the republic that had, reluctantly at best, freed them in 1863. They fought in U.S. wars and paid taxes. They rendered cheap labor on railroads and docks, in factories, private kitchens, and cotton fields. Although fulfilling the *obligations* of citizenship, Negroes were systematically denied the *benefits*. White supremacy was certified and enforced as national policy by the full force of the Supreme Court, Congress, and the executive branch of the federal government, although in wholly different ways. The Court's 1896 *Plessy v. Ferguson* "separate but equal" ruling was a sham decision that froze in place an impregnable caste structure under legalized segregation. Negroes were repressed as a permanent underclass and were flagrantly denied equal access to housing, jobs, education, public accommodations, due process in the courts, and, despite the passage of the Fifteenth Amendment, the guaranteed right to vote. Even when American women were granted the vote in 1920, Negroes across gender lines were largely denied the franchise, especially in the South, where some 80 percent of them lived.

Even in the nation's capital, racial segregation was the law of the land, harshly enforced by no less authority than that of the president. In addition to mandating separate and less well-appointed and maintained cafeterias and toilet facilities for Negroes in federal buildings, Woodrow Wilson had allowed the Treasury Department and the Post Office to segregate black civil-service employees from whites by makeshift wooden partitions. One colored postal clerk, whose duties required regular contact with whites in the office, "had a cage built around him," according to a letter of complaint to President

Wilson from noted scholar W. E. B. Du Bois. When, as previously mentioned, William Monroe Trotter, the editor of the widely read Negro newspaper the *Boston Guardian,* took a delegation of Negro leaders to the White House to protest this segregated federal policy, President Wilson rebuffed them sharply.

"Segregation is not humiliating, but a benefit, and ought to be so regarded by you gentlemen," President Wilson told the delegation from the National Independent Equal Rights League during its November 12, 1914, visit. When Trotter disputed Wilson's claim that federal employees were racially separated to avoid friction, the president, as widely reported in *The New York Times* and elsewhere, cited Trotter's "tone" and dismissed the delegation leader. "Your manner offends me," Wilson muttered.[5] Despite street rallies defending Trotter, the federal government continued to segregate the races for decades.

When in early 1917 the president subsequently petitioned Congress to enter the war in Europe to make the world "safe for democracy," Negro leaders debated what their stance should be toward an administration that so egregiously denied them equal rights. Should they push for inclusion in American society and join the fight? After having supported Wilson's candidacy in 1912, Du Bois was appalled by the president's eager collaboration with racist Southern legislators. However, just as abolitionist leader Frederick Douglass had argued for blacks to fight during the Civil War, Du Bois urged them to join the ranks of Wilson's racially segregated army and drew sharp personal criticism for his support.

White military officers, however, were reluctant to field armed black GIs against the European soldiers of Germany, Austria-Hungary, and the other Central Powers. The Marines strongly opposed accepting Negro volunteers, and those the Navy accepted were restricted to noncombatant, menial posts as stewards or mess-hall workers. Still, some 2.3 million Negroes registered for the draft, with 370,000 inducted into the military. And despite heavy resistance from white officers and fellow soldiers, Negroes performed acts of battlefield valor that went largely unnoticed. Not until seventy-three years later—when a government review disclosed strong racial bias in the Army—would America award a Medal of Honor to a black combatant from World War I. In a 1991 White House ceremony, President George H. W. Bush presented the honor to the sister of Corporal Freddie Stowers, who had been recommended for it shortly after he died from wounds suffered when he led an assault on fortified German trenches.

In a postwar editorial in *The Crisis*, Du Bois, again like Frederick Douglass, urged Negroes to "close ranks" for full citizenship and to "marshal every ounce of our brain and brawn to fight a sterner, longer, more unbending battle against the forces of hell in our own land."[6] Later in 1919, Du Bois more specifically wrote: "For three centuries we have suffered and cowered. No race ever gave passive submission to evil longer, more piteous trial. Today we raise the terrible weapon of self-defense. When the murderer comes, he shall no longer strike us in the back. When the armed lynchers gather, we too must gather armed. When the mob moves, we propose to meet it with bricks and clubs and guns."[7] Despite the odds, Du Bois urged Negroes to make their armed stand in the land where their forebears labored and died as slaves.

The foreign-born Marcus Garvey was convinced otherwise and counseled not black fight but black flight, at least psychologically, and in some cases physically, from the presence and influence of the white men he considered irredeemably racist, too numerous, and far too well armed. In this conflict of perspectives, Garvey would capture the loyalty of both Malcolm's Caribbean-born mother and his rebellious father from Georgia. Earl Little, a restless man of prodigious energy (with a whispered reputation as a ladies' man), visited the homes of curious Negroes to ply his admixture of

Christian gospel and secular Garveyism. Africa was the homeland sure enough, but Garvey's group did not call for mass repatriation in the near term, and unless the specific question was raised, the third-grade-educated Reverend Little did not discuss global, pan-African repatriation at all.

Combating white dominance in the United States during the first quarter of the twentieth century broke down roughly along these two distinct, tactical lines pushed by the NAACP and UNIA, and spearheaded nationally by W. E. B. Du Bois on one side and Marcus Garvey on the other. Ironically, each man had been influenced early on by Booker T. Washington, the famed educator who started Tuskegee Institute in Alabama, and who published his influential autobiography, *Up from Slavery*, in 1901. However, the internecine battle between the two camps and their strong-minded leaders would rage for years even as Negroes continued their central struggle for equality.

Du Bois had posed the global parameters of the racial conflict, though not the solution, in his 1903 book *The Souls of Black Folk*: "The problem of the twentieth century is the problem of the color-line,—the relation of the darker to the lighter races of men in Asia and Africa, in America and the islands of the sea."[8] Garvey, agreeing that European colonialism was the dominant world force at the turn of the century, advocated that indigenous peoples in Africa, India, and the rest of Asia should rise up and reclaim their occupied homelands from the illicit white settlers—and leave them Europe, with the United States and the West Indies apparently to be shared with indigenous people of the American landmass.

The British colonization of Jamaica had been a key trigger for Marcus Garvey's program when, at the age of twenty-seven, he founded the UNIA and expanded it as a bulwark against white rule and racism in the West Indies, Africa, Europe, and elsewhere. Following his relocation to America in 1916, the skilled, self-assured promoter, a printer by trade, launched his organization in Harlem, the newly acclaimed capital of Negro America, almost fifty years after the Civil War. Offering his "up you mighty race . . . call to the colored citizens,"[9] which seemed more practical than the NAACP program, the Jamaican leader began barnstorming key cities of the North and also ventured as far south as Atlanta. "The Great West Indian Negro Leader," as Garvey was billed on promotional posters, directed his "message of inspiration to the 12,000,000 of our people in this country."[10] And during World War I, he found a surprisingly receptive audience among the thousands of Southern Negroes streaming north in search of industrial jobs at the start of the Great Migration, which would continue into the 1970s and total some six million persons.

Accordingly, Garvey skillfully went after the nonreading Negro masses in America with pomp, glitz, and ceremony. He staged colorful street parades complete with marching bands, Black Cross nurses in white dresses, and men of erect bearing decked out in military uniforms with medals, lavalieres, and swords. The lead touring car of this extravaganza showcased the "Honorable President," as Garvey was referred to, done up in a naval dress uniform with gold buttons, sash, silver saber, and a plumed cap befitting a crowned emperor. This pomp and circumstance was intended to improve blacks' self-respect. "We must canonize our own saints, create our own martyrs, and elevate to positions of fame and honor black men and women who have made their distinct contributions to our racial history," Garvey insisted.[11] During the postwar years, the UNIA met in its Liberty Hall site in Harlem with an initial membership mainly of West Indians, who constituted roughly a quarter of the nonwhite population in Upper Manhattan. In due course, Garvey also would attract homegrown Negroes streaming out of the South to work in the war industries of the North and the Midwest.

The group's first New York City convention, in 1920, packed

Madison Square Garden with some 25,000 blacks from throughout
the hemisphere. Boasting 4 million members by 1923, the UNIA
ultimately listed some seven hundred branches in thirty-eight states.
Insiders put the U.S. number at 20,000 to 30,000 dues-paying
members, with thousands more curiosity seekers, supporters, and
hangers-on. Garvey would turn out to be one of the most charismatic evangelists of the 1920s. The federal government zeroed in
on him as an "exceptionally fine orator, creating much excitement
among the negroes through his steamship proposition" and saw in
his appeal seditious potential.

The Black Star steamship line was a major fund-raising campaign
Garvey had launched to establish a shipping operation between
the United States and Africa. In a 1919 memo, the young J. Edgar
Hoover, head of the Special Intelligence Division in the Bureau of
Investigation (the predecessor of the FBI), specializing in deporting
"undesirable aliens," took note of Marcus Garvey as a "prominent
agitator" among Negroes. "Unfortunately," Hoover wrote Special
Agent Ridgely on October 11, Garvey "has not as yet violated any federal law whereby he could be proceeded against on ground of being
an undesirable alien." With an eye toward building a federal deportation case, however, Hoover noted that "there might be some proceed-
ing against him for fraud with his Black Star Line propaganda."[12]
Subsequently, in a pattern of domestic spying that would expand
ominously through the years and would eerily echo forty years later
in its surveillance of Malcolm X, the Bureau hired four Negroes to
work the case and had one of them infiltrate the UNIA and spy on
Garvey's every move in Harlem. Detailed memos were filed on all
meetings, official contacts, and the group's financial records.

Unaware of the government surveillance, Garvey stridently promoted Africa as the proud homeland of all blacks, and unlike Du
Bois and the NAACP, he countered claims of white supremacy by
proclaiming that, if anything, the Negro was superior. This clar-

ion message had no visible means of enforcement, but it was anathema nonetheless to the white population of early-twentieth-century
Omaha and the Midwest that baby Malcolm's parents encountered.
Nationally, the NAACP and its leaders, along with other racially
mixed civil rights groups, as well as mainstream Negro churches,
would differ with the UNIA over how exactly to combat the formidable superstructure of racism that had characterized the United
States since its very founding as a slave-holding republic.

Thundering against the Western view of the colonized "dark continent" as a basket case, the fiery Jamaican leader urged Negroes
foremost to work for the "total redemption of Africa" and to join him
in correcting this distorted image of the continent. "I want Mr. Du
Bois to know that all American Negroes are not ashamed of Africa,"
Garvey told a Liberty Hall audience, decades before an elderly Du
Bois would move to Ghana. "Why should we allow the Dutch, the
Boers and others to go down into Kimberly and possess the diamond fields. . . . Why should we allow the Belgians to go down into
the Congo and reap the profits of rubber? . . . We shall stand by the
slogan: Africa for the Africans." [13]

The global philosophy of the UNIA was summarized in Garvey's "Declaration of Rights of the Negro Peoples of the World," [14]
which he placed alongside the Bible as a guide for those who "with
confidence in ourselves" could "carve our way to liberty." [15] If Africans scattered throughout the diaspora were to progress as a people
anywhere in the world, Garvey declared that they must first reclaim
the birthplace of humankind as their "noble motherland." Broadly,
he asked, "Where is the black man's government? Where is his king
and kingdom? Where is his president, his country and his ambassador, his army, his navy, his men of big affairs?" [16] As part of a sym-
bolic response to these questions, Garvey designed a "black, red and
green" flag for his new republic and declared himself "Provisional
President." (The tricolors would subsequently be adapted by a few

African countries upon their liberation.) As a practical matter, however, the UNIA, short-term, was never the single-minded Back to Africa movement that outside critics claimed.

During these post–World War I years, Reverend Earl Little embraced Garvey while in Omaha but chiefly urged Negroes to organize and improve their lot here in the "white man's country." In this, Earl followed the lead of his other key hero, fellow southerner Booker T. Washington, whose *Up from Slavery* had inspired the teenaged Garvey himself. In his celebrated 1895 speech, dubbed "The Atlanta Compromise," Washington, born into slavery in 1856 in Virginia, had urged Negroes to acquiesce to the status quo and to advance in America by lowering their more lofty expectations. This plea for an apparent accommodation with segregation—including famously advising his followers to "cast down your buckets where you are"—earned him the embrace of white southerners and rendered Washington the most influential Negro in America.

While praising Washington, the "great sage of Tuskegee," as a mentor and even as the inspiration for the formation of the UNIA, Garvey geared his international group to move well beyond Washington's domestic plan of "industrial serfdom and industrial peonage." Garvey's group would demand a "place in the *political* sun . . . for "the 400,000,000 Negroes of the world." The UNIA leader blamed even Frederick Douglass, who had died in 1895, as well as Washington and contemporary Negro leaders, like W. E. B. Du Bois, "for not preparing the minds of the people for the approaching age. No, we won't make [that] mistake."[17]

As Garveyites, the parents of young Malcolm followed UNIA's policy of referring to Africa as the "homeland." Most Negroes, however, under the sway of Hollywood and prevailing public opinion, rejected the "dark continent" as a nation of savages and an unspeakable embarrassment. During America's long and genocidal history of slavery and suppression, Negroes had been conditioned—by state terror and brutal campaigns against aggressive leaders such as Nat Turner—into an apparent state of acceptance as a matter of survival. And under Booker T. Washington's counseling of group acquiescence, they felt not only inextricably bound to America but also strangely hopeful about their prospects. Thus Marcus Garvey's UNIA was increasingly challenged by homegrown interest groups, most especially the white-led NAACP and Du Bois, the erudite Harvard scholar. As a leading intellectual of his day, the Massachusetts-born son of a half-Haitian father[18] took great exception to the popularity of Marcus Garvey, the lightly educated autodidact from Jamaica.

In addition to their differences over "fight or flee" tactics, Du Bois and Garvey were separated by a more primal divide that could not be reconciled and that was keenly reflected among their followers. This shadowy ghost had plagued Negroes down through the generations as the group's nasty little secret: skin color.

Among individuals and families of Malcolm's childhood, for instance, many light-skinned Negroes judged the social fitness, intelligence, status, and the potential compatibility of others—within the race—by their admixture of white bloodlines. Those with lighter shades, along with softer hair texture and rainbow eye colors, were dubbed high yellows, red bones, or simply mixed-race, and, as such, they generally assigned themselves a superior status within the Negro race. "As your skin gets lighter, your future gets brighter" became a guideline of this prejudice, which, despite periodic ebbs, would survive into the twenty-first century. In most such instances historically, both in the United States and in the West Indies, the white parent or grandparent was paternal and almost universally was absent after the birth of the child, as was Louise's father back in Grenada. Having washed their hands of the matter, these fathers generally lived on in respectable denial with their white families across town. Still, despite laboring under the white-black oppression of slavery, Jim Crow, and persistent racism, some Negroes steadfastly embraced this intragroup color distinction as they grasped for a semblance of power.

Thus, a subcaste system among Negroes, attended by a discriminatory pattern of behavior, sprang up along skin-tone lines and has lingered over the generations as dirty linen in plain view. Negro leaders have generally not abstained or been spared. Early on, it was noted that Marcus Garvey's contempt for lighter-skin competitors was based on his experience with mixed-race Jamaicans back home and, in part, on what he perceived as skin-tone chauvinism among American-born Negro rivals in the NAACP, the National Urban League, "high-toned" churches, and other civic groups. Like Earl and Louise Little, their light-skinned son Malcolm had to contend with traces of this intragroup, skin-tone bias in dealing with key individuals and organizations throughout his life.

Scholars have traced this behavioral pattern back to the period when mixed-race slaves working within the plantation house would lord it over their brethren sweating in the fields. Whites generally looked on with stone-hearted indifference, if not denial, except when money was involved. Thus, all children of slave mothers were deemed by law to be chattel—no matter the race or circumstance of the father. President Thomas Jefferson, who held captive six hundred slaves, for example, reportedly fathered six children with slave mistress Sally Hemings. Those who lived past infancy were listed on the household ledgers as Negro chattel, the more hands for the kitchen the better. Nonetheless, a class distinction sprang up among chattel slaves, encouraged, perhaps, by some white holders as a method of appeasing bonded mulattos angling for advantages, no matter how slight.

Not all "fair-skinned" Negroes played along. The great abolitionist Frederick Douglass, a notable mixed-race offspring, for example, reacted to his circumstance by rebelling against white men in denial who condemned their very own children to an inferior state of captive existence. In his *Narrative of the Life of Frederick Douglass*, the exslave Douglass wrote:

> The whisper that my master was my father may or may not be
> true; and, true or false, it is of but little consequence to my purpose whilst the fact remains, in all its glaring odiousness, that
> slaveholders have ordained, and by law established, that the
> children of slave women shall in all cases follow the condition
> of their mothers.[19]

After the Reconstruction period, the U.S. census designated all ex-slaves simply as Negroes—and mistreated them as such. "One drop" of black blood made the case, as had been the custom for centuries. Mulattos or "mixed-race" types—save those secretly "passing" as Caucasians—were accorded the full range of racial suppression reserved for the Negro en masse. They were banned from jobs reserved for whites; segregated under federal, state, and local Jim Crow practices; restricted to inferior education, housing, and public accommodations; barred from major league sports; assigned to all-Negro military units—and more than a few were lynched without regard to their mixed-blood ancestry, straight hair, light-toned skin, or gray-green eyes.

Thus denied white privilege and rejected even by their paternal blood relatives, a determined segment of the mulatto subcaste resorted to mimicking the *petit* aspects of American racism toward dark-skinned Negroes. Over the years, with some exceptions, this rising so-called black bourgeoisie, including some civil rights organizers, maintained a *petit* caste system exercising economic, social, and psychological advantage over their darker Negro neighbors—and sometimes blood relatives, siblings even. The practice was most common among Negroes along the Tidewater basin of the Virginias, in the District of Columbia, in large swaths of the Carolinas, and in niches of the Deep South, such as Atlanta, and most especially in New Orleans, and patches of Louisiana; but it was not unknown in urban areas such as Chicago, Philadelphia, Baltimore, and even New York City.

Functionally, the "bright skin" Negro class screened out darker members of the race from prime enrollment at historically black colleges and universities, banning them altogether from certain Greek fraternities and sororities, and, for the most part excluding non-mixed blacks from leadership roles in clubs and secret societies and even as pastors and ranking officials in "high-toned" black Protestant churches. Whites of Malcolm's day, if they noticed at all, mostly looked on in bemused connivance, angling always to accrue the benefits of such divisiveness within the suppressed race. Still, over the generations, heroic and oft-times complicated struggles against Jim Crow racism were often conducted by such mixed-race men and women. Rejected by their white paternal relatives, these activists counterrejected those bloodlines and on principle threw in aggressively with their darker brethren. These staunch race men included Negroes such as Booker T. Washington, the journalists Samuel Cornish and William Monroe Trotter, the writer James Weldon Johnson, the poet Jean Toomer, and the physician Charles Drew, as well as mixed-race achievers such as the NAACP leader Walter White, the Reverends Adam Clayton Powell, father and son, Thurgood Marshall, Rosa Parks, and, indeed, W. E. B. Du Bois himself. Even while battling the imposition of an inferior status by white Americans, many of these mixed-race types held out for their subcaste advantages over their darker brethren. And thus, just as Negro leaders of Malcolm's childhood differed over how to combat exterior white racism, they also squared off among themselves over the interior matter of skin-tone chauvinism.

Unlike Du Bois, who considered himself a mulatto, Marcus Garvey was dark as a Senegalese and proud of it. At the time of his birth, the British Commonwealth census recorded Jamaica's population as 2 percent Anglo-Saxon, 18 percent mixed-race Euro-Jamaicans, and 78 percent Afro-Jamaicans. This multitiered register of the white-minority British settler colony foreshadowed the codifying of racial apartheid by the minority Boer government of South Africa. As in South Africa, the ebony majority in Jamaica was treated as a permanent underclass. They were looked down upon, if not despised, not only by the white settler colonialists on the island but also by mixed-race Euro-Jamaicans. (Unlike these countries, the United States, with a safe white majority projected into the mid-twenty-first century, has only recently seen demographers toying with population control devices that would fragment "minority groups" grounded by African Americans into such divisive categories as mixed-race, nonwhite Hispanics, "browns," "people of color," etc.)

As an unmixed Afro-Jamaican, Garvey abandoned all hope that whites and the mulatto class on the island, backed by the British empire, would voluntarily relinquish their privileged status. So the fiery UNIA leader set out to force this double-barrel issue of race and subcaste inequality at home as well as in the United States. Casting aside subtlety as in all matters of policy, Garvey drafted UNIA doctrine calling for a "pure black race just as all self-respecting whites believe in a pure white race," according to *The Philosophy and Opinions of Marcus Garvey*, compiled by his second wife, Amy Jacques Garvey. "I am conscious of the fact that slavery brought upon us the curse of many colors within the Negro race," Garvey stated, "but that is no reason that we ourselves should perpetuate the evil; hence, instead of encouraging a wholesale bastardy in the race, we feel that we should now set out to create a race type and standard of our own which could not, in the future, be stigmatized by bastardy, but could be recognized and respected as the true race type anteceding even our own time."[20]

Accordingly, Garvey notably disparaged even his Negro heroes such as Booker T. Washington, born to an enslaved cook and an unknown white man, and the great Frederick Douglass, citing their "unfortunate circumstance" of being "brought into the world through bastardy, the rape of one race upon the other . . . the abuse . . . of the mothers of one race by the men of the other." It did not escape notice that leaders of the UNIA were darker-hued than leaders of other Negro movements of the day. The NAACP, for example, fielded mainly light-skinned Negro officials. Its famed Walter White was indistinguishable from a Caucasian to the most discerning eye. Thus, the bold African palette of UNIA leaders shamed some Negro groups that, taking their cue from the integrated NAACP, branded themselves as "colored."

"The [UNIA] emphasis was on 'Black,'" recalled Thurgood Marshall, the nation's first Supreme Court justice of his race. When they "would parade up Seventh Avenue," Marshall recalled years later, "if my brother and I were out there in the street, we had to get off the street. Right in the middle of Harlem. I mean, no light-skinned Negro was allowed around."[21] The blunt-speaking jurist quite likely exaggerated a bit, but his recollections accurately reflect the clash of skin-tone cultures that proliferated within the Negro race, a tension that weakened its unity. For instance, when Garvey attempted to recruit William Pickens Sr. away from the NAACP, where he was an executive officer, the dark-skinned Phi Beta Kappa Yale graduate refused as a matter of principle and charged that "Garvey tried to draw the black Negroes of America away from those of lighter skin." It was an intragroup tug of war between officials on both sides.

W. E. B. Du Bois likely adopted the "high yellow" preference while an undergraduate at segregated Fisk College, where such prejudices were common. Already a national leader, he took Garvey's countermove against caste privilege as a personal affront. Within the pages of *The Crisis*, the NAACP journal that he had created a year after the group's founding, Du Bois campaigned against Booker T. Washington's call for black intellectual acquiescence, and he wanted no part of Garvey's Back to Africa movement. Along with slamming UNIA policies, the Harvard scholar also attacked the West Indian's caste, education, and physical appearance. "A little, fat black man" is how Du Bois described Garvey in *The Century* magazine in February 1923, "ugly, but with intelligent eyes and a big head." He followed up this caste put-down by drafting a bill of particulars against the fiery Jamaican for Negro readers. Garvey countered that Du Bois was "pure and simply a white man's nigger" who was "a little Dutch, a little French, a little Negro . . . a monstrosity." The "rabid mulatto," he said, deserves a "horse-whipping."[22]

In less personal tones, however, some disciplined followers of these two pillars of Negro liberation would submerge the skin-tone issue to a point of being a nonissue. Relatives of young Malcolm's father in Georgia, for example, were surprised to learn early on that Louise was just as devoted to Garveyism as her dark-skinned husband. While quite proud of her light skin, as well as of Malcolm's, Louise did not consider Garvey's color fixation a matter of personal consequence, choosing instead to work for the larger cause of black unity. "As far as the family was concerned," said Wilfred, "my mother was always making us see the importance of not making a color distinction. She told us, 'The reason I married your father was because he was dark. I wanted my children to have some color.' She always made us feel proud of our black father. She would never let you say anything derogatory about somebody because they were black.

"In those days there were many people who did make something out of color. The community would try to establish this caste system. There were the blacks, there were the browns, there were the yellows, and on down the line. They would make much out of that. We never got caught up in that sort of thing. . . . As far

as we were concerned, blacker was the best."[23] As in other matters of social grounding, young Malcolm's family stood out among
Negroes as something of an exception.

———

On the national scene, as played out in mainstream newspapers,
Negro civil rights leaders campaigned boldly, if not singularly,
against the white superstructure backed by absolute state power that
maintained the de jure and de facto segregation, which was everywhere clear, present, and oppressive. As a foreigner, Garvey had a
blind spot for American Negroes' strong drive to indemnify their
birthright in the United States, despite generations of death, pain,
and suffering inflicted by the armed might of the state and the vigilante terror of night-riding white racists. The UNIA push for a separate black path to empowerment ran counter to the NAACP's steady
petition for racial integration. Their debate over whether to fight or
to flee also attracted the diligent surveillance of the U.S. government.

By 1922, the federal government energized its case against Garvey as the UNIA was losing much of the funds investors had put up to
capitalize the group's business ventures, notably its shipping operation, the Black Star Line. With the assistance of the Internal Rev-
enue Service and undercover agents inside the UNIA, the Bureau
of Investigation pounced on bookkeeping missteps. On January 12,
1922, Marcus Garvey was arrested and held on $2,500 bond, await-
ing appearance before a federal grand jury on charges of mail fraud.
The case was whipped up into an international scandal. Once freed,
and awaiting trial, Garvey traveled widely. Yet the arrest had devastating results. The Black Star Line dissolved financially, Garvey's first
marriage fell apart, and his *Negro World* newspaper was confiscated
in some cities and banned in colonized Africa.

During this period, a most unlikely white supremacist group,
bent on exploiting Garvey's dire legal situation for its own ends,

reached out to the UNIA leader. Even during slavery, working-class whites were obsessed with deporting to Africa those Negroes not needed for the labor market. Garvey's voluntary repatriation pitch, coupled with his stout rejection of "race-mixing," had caught the attention of the Ku Klux Klan. In 1922, Imperial Kleagle Edward Young Clarke posted Garvey a telegram at UNIA headquarters, requesting a meeting with that "King George Nigger." Viewing the Klan as the mainstream white nationalist group that it was, Garvey accepted the Klan invitation, imagining, some speculated, that the group might assist him with the pending federal issue.

On June 25, the two leaders met for some two hours at Klan headquarters in Atlanta.[24] With an eye ever peeled for the spotlight, Clarke, the number-two national Klan leader, was the group's chief fund-raiser and public relations spokesman and was considered something of a whiskey-drinking renegade. The very idea of a sit-down with Negroes was viewed by puzzled grassroots Klan members as a "flagrant disregard" of Klan policy, if not flat-out betrayal.[25] And the sit-down loosed a wildfire among Negroes, with even UNIA staffers riling into open revolt. Tight-lipped about points of agreements, Garvey published his Liberty Hall speech about the meeting in the *Negro World*, the group's primary organizing tool.[26] Based in Harlem, the paper at its peak printed editions in English, French, and Spanish that circulated among chapters in Detroit, Chicago, and Los Angeles, as well as internationally in London, Cape Town, Havana, Panama City, and elsewhere.

"The Ku Klux Klan is really the invisible government of the U.S.A.," said Garvey, who, in addition to heading the UNIA as president-general, spoke as the "Provisional President of Africa." The self-proclaimed, exalted global leader thus framed the meeting with the Klan as a sit-down with a group representing "the spiritual and even the physical attitude of every white man in this country." Imperial Kleagle Clarke, he said, claimed that the KKK "is stronger in the Northern states than it is in the Southern states." And while the Klan "desires to make America absolutely a white man's country," Garvey told his audience that, similarly, "the UNIA wants to make [colonized] Africa absolutely a black man's country."[27] In response, Du Bois and other leaders, such as NAACP official William Pickens, took exception: they knew that the Klan had no influence whatsoever in Africa, whereas homegrown Negro Americans had invested heavily over the centuries in the liberation, defense, economic buildup, and continued expansion of the American republic.

"You say in effect to the KKK: All right!" Pickens wrote in a sharp rebuttal to Garvey. "Give us Africa and we will in turn concede you America as a 'white man's country!' In that you make a poor deal: for twelve million people you give up EVERYTHING, and in exchange you get NOTHING. For the Klan has nothing to 'give up' in Africa. It does not own or control one square inch of Africa. But the Negro American citizen has everything to give up in America. You might as well tell the Klan: We will give up all our homes, our rights, our lives, our past and our future in our native land, provided the Klan will give us a free and undisputed title to the *moon!*"[28]

Furthermore, Garvey claimed to have confronted the Klan leader about the touchy issue of widespread miscegenation that had produced generations of mixed-race Negroes during slavery and beyond. "What would be your attitude if a white man was to go into a colored neighborhood and . . . take advantage of the womanhood of our race," Garvey reportedly asked about this crime that Klansmen were known to commit during some of their nighttime terror raids. Again, taking the imperial kleagle at his every word, Garvey told his Liberty Hall audience that Clarke "would be against that white man" and would support Negroes who opposed it. And in a backhand slap at Du Bois and others he considered mixed-race Negroes, Garvey boomed, "The United Negro Improvement Association is carrying out just what the Ku Klux Klan is carrying out—the purity of the white race down South—and we are going to carry out the purity of the black race not only down South, but all through the world."[29]

In the post-Reconstruction bleakness of 1922 America, Garvey argued that Negroes could best devote their energy fighting for the decolonization of Africa to "clear out the white invaders," where the odds were on the side of the overwhelming black majority. Conversely, he posited that they should opt out of their struggle against white supremacy in the United States, where he declared that the odds of 95 million against 15 million were simply too great. "We wish liberty," Garvey said in this July speech. "We wish to be good American citizens; we want to be President of the United States; we wish to be Congressmen; we wish to be Senators; we wish to be governors of states; we wish to be mayors of cities; we wish to be police commissioners. It is a wish, all right, but the other [white] fellow wishes the same thing. Now, is he going to allow you to have your wish?"[30] Garvey said he checked off for the Klan leader each specific political post that Negroes envisioned achieving in the future as citizens.

The Negro "shall never be [president, governor, mayor, etc.] as long as there is one white man living in the United States of America," Imperial Kleagle Clarke responded, according to Garvey. Thus, taking Clarke at his word about "representing the sentiments of the entire white race," Garvey told his Liberty Hall audience and *Negro World* readers: "The white people of this country are not going to allow Negroes—ambitious and educated Negroes—to have their wish . . . the KKK interprets the spirit of every white man in this country and say 'you shall not pass.' . . . The odds are against you." The UNIA leader, of course, could not imagine that, generations later, blacks in America would overcome what appeared to be insurmountable odds. Ultimately, Garvey felt that he was doing nothing surprising. This assessment of Negroes' chances of empowerment as utterly hopeless was precisely the conclusion he had reached long ago. "Mr. Clarke did not tell me anything new," the Jamaican said. Indeed, Garvey observed, it was this very rock "that caused me to have organized the Universal Negro Improvement Association four and a half years ago."[31]

Garvey's second wife and confidante, Amy Jacques Garvey, supplemented his account, reporting that his "long talk with the Assistant Imperial Wizard," about "race relations in the West Indies and the northern states, finally of his efforts toward colonization in Africa," had "impressed the white listener, as a new and candid approach to the old question." Naïvely, Amy Garvey expressed surprise that her husband's Negro competitors would seize upon his Klan meeting to discredit him, mistaking her husband's "bravery," she concluded, for sheer "cowardice" and worse.

"Most of them were afraid even to visit relatives in the South," she related in her biography. "The implications were that he would encourage the Klan to brutalize Negroes, and cause them to want to leave America for Africa."[32] Denying such charges, Ms. Garvey repeated her husband's statement that he never planned a mass migration of Negroes to Africa but rather envisioned that U.S. Negroes and Africans could reconnect in a symbiotic exchange of properties and expertise, with a select settlement of wealthy Negroes establishing themselves over there to help build up the continent.

Although the UNIA and the KKK reportedly had agreed to release a jointly edited statement of agreement, no such document was ever published. Subsequent to Garvey's public statements, however, newspaper tycoon William Randolph Hearst reportedly acquired a memorandum on the meeting between the UNIA leader and the Klan.[33] Imperial Kleagle Clarke purportedly agreed to grant safe passage for Garvey to journey around the South to conduct business and raise money from UNIA members and Negro recruits. In exchange, Garvey was to cooperate in advancing Klan interests by continuing to do battle against groups like the NAACP that supported integration. He also invited a Klan representative to speak at a UNIA convention. There were outside speculations that, going in,

Garvey had hoped somehow that the Klan would use its contacts to ease the federal charges and keep him out of prison. But there is no record of discussion of this issue during the meeting.

In the end, Garvey's meeting with the Klan was a gift to Du Bois and others galled by the Jamaican's race-purity pitch and popularity among Negroes. These opposing leaders doubled down on their efforts to lure the masses, including West Indians, away from the UNIA. Alderman George Harris of Chicago, for example, denounced Garvey's meeting as misrepresenting the attitude of 100 percent of the "native-born [black] Americans and 75 percent of the foreign-born [West Indian group]."[34] And in an article in the magazine *The Messenger,* labor leader Asa Philip Randolph described Garvey as "a Supreme Negro Jamaican Jackass" and, for good measure, dismissed him as "the messenger boy of the Klan."[35] Pickens, the NAACP official whom Garvey had tried to recruit, slammed the UNIA as a "criminal organization" more "unfortunate to the American Negro than the whole Klan." Their joint sit-down, he said was "a menace to interracial tranquility."[36]

In a follow-up letter to Garvey, Pickens continued: "I gather from your recent plain utterances that you are now endorsing the Ku Klux Klan, or at least conceding the justice of its aims to crush and repress colored Americans and incidentally other racial and religious groups in the U.S."[37] Even Timothy T. Fortune, the otherwise loyal editor of Garvey's *Negro World*, wrote an editorial opposing the Klan meeting. The Florida-born Fortune, however, was persuaded to publish a letter from Garvey retracting his tough editorial. Still, the brilliant, independent-minded editor, who had long served as an advisor to his close friend Booker T. Washington, tagged his boss's letter with a note stating that the newspaper's opinion was written in "good faith," and that "I see nothing in [the editorial] to modify or retract."[38]

As for outside critics, the resolute Garvey challenged Du Bois and Pickens to a public debate "to settle this matter once and for all." When they declined, the UNIA leader issued a broadside stating: "I regard the Klan, the Anglo-Saxon Clubs and White American Societies as better friends of the race than all the other groups of hypocritical whites put together. I like honesty and fair play . . . potentially every white man is a Klansman."[39] Four decades later, echoes of this view would resonate in Atlanta with the Klan.

The noisy, internecine fights among Negroes delighted the Bureau of Investigation, as well as others in the white mainstream eager to see two divisive forces mitigate the potential power of the Negro voice. However, to the iconoclastic writer H. L. Mencken, who mocked the foibles of "Boobus Americanus," including its racists, the contest spilled over as tragicomedy. As the foremost social and literary critic of the day, the Sage of Baltimore wrote that he was "frankly amazed (and delighted)" that, as the most oppressed group in the United States, the "dark brethren" would be the "frankest" in criticizing one another without "weasel words" in their newspapers and magazines. "Certainly nothing of the sort is visible in any other quarter," Mencken wrote. "One seldom finds an article against Jews in a Jewish paper. . . . The Irish, when they contemplate themselves, are just as cocksure and humorless, and so are the Germans, the Italians, the Poles, the Swedes, and the rest."[40] Mencken's comment suggested that the white mainstream reveled in this internecine black warfare, eager to see these divisive forces mitigate the power of the Negro voice.

This infighting among Negro leaders played into the hands of the federal government, whose motives were far more sinister and destructive. With fixed intentions of exploiting existing divisions within the black community and stimulating others, J. Edgar Hoover drew up a plan that, on the one hand, sought to destabilize Du Bois's group efforts against segregation and, on the other, aimed to thwart all attempts by Garvey's UNIA to empower Negroes by other means.

With Garvey already indicted and pending trial, this government pursuit was willingly assisted by Negro leaders, including church pastors who complained loudly that Garvey preached race hatred. Competing directly with him for popular and financial support from the Negro masses, these officials felt increasingly threatened by the organizing genius of the upstart Jamaican immigrant who had acquired the sobriquet "Black Moses."

The ire of Du Bois and other black leaders was considered pure envy by Garvey, who dismissed it with a Caribbean island adage: "The thief does not like to see another man with a long bag." Nonetheless, these competitors continued to provide endless streams of gossip, rumors, and, occasionally, hard evidence to federal authorities who were tracking the "man with a long bag." Stepping up the attack, Du Bois branded Garvey "the most dangerous enemy of the Negro race in America and the world." He and other prominent leaders reportedly went as far as to cooperate with the federal government, which was bent on getting Garvey deported back to Jamaica.[41] Two NAACP officials sent a letter to the U.S. attorney general urging a speedy prosecution of the pending federal case against Garvey.

Throughout 1922, the UNIA leader loudly proclaimed his innocence, even blaming his legal problems on the NAACP, Du Bois, and other Negro leaders. As group funds dried up, the UNIA had difficulty paying the headquarters rent. When the "Garvey Must Go" campaign stepped up, a few defectors formed a competitive organization, sparking group squabbling, breakups of old friendships and at least one shooting in New Orleans, for which two Garvey supporters were convicted of murder. On May 18, 1923, the UNIA leader himself was put on trial in federal court in New York City. Acting as his own attorney, Garvey denied, resisted, and challenged all counts of the mail fraud case during the four-week trial. However, on June 18, he was convicted and sentenced to a five-year prison term.

As Garvey appealed his sentence, loyal UNIA supporters, including Reverend Little and his wife, Louise, defiantly persisted in maintaining that their convicted martyr had been railroaded by federal authorities. While out on bail, Garvey would visit the Midwest, and, on at least one occasion slipped into Wisconsin to meet secretly with key officials of his struggling organization. Earlier, he had visited Earl and Louise Little in Omaha. Arriving by day, he would work into the evening, but never would stay overnight, according to relatives.

"The reason Garvey came to our place was my mother took care of a lot of his correspondence," Wilfred said of Garvey's covert visits to the Little home in Omaha. "And there was international correspondence, I remember that. There were people who were coming around who spoke foreign, different languages . . . and my father was unable to take part in the conversation because of the language."

"Garvey was dark-complexioned," Wilfred said, "kind of stocky built but not that tall, very strong eyes, strong voice, always a matter of taking care of business; very businesslike, never wasting any time. And people who would come around when he was there was the same way, busy, busy, busy. . . . I remember they warned us, don't say anything to anybody about [his coming] to the house. And we wouldn't tell anybody that he was there."[42]

In February 1925, his appeal exhausted, Garvey was remanded to a federal prison in Atlanta—essentially, for a $25 mail fraud charge. After serving two years and nine months, he had his sentence commuted when—reportedly to avoid a strong case for prosecutorial misconduct—President Calvin Coolidge ordered that the "race martyr" be deported to Jamaica as an undesirable alien. Arriving in Jamaica in December 1927, Garvey was restricted in his travel by the U.S. deportation order and bail restrictions.

The imprisonment and deportation of its high-profile leader had a devastating effect on the UNIA and Garvey's drive in the United States to unite "all people of African ancestry around the world into one great country." This blow landed even as the whole of sub-Saharan Africa suffered under brutal, European colonization that exploited the continent for its oil and mineral wealth.

Decades later, it would be revealed that almost every Negro leader of consequence, some of them Garvey opponents, had been spied upon—and, in some cases, harassed openly by the federal government. When Du Bois emerged as a leading international voice advancing pan-Africanism, for example, he—not unlike Garvey—would be relentlessly pursued by Hoover, who built a nasty reputation for neutralizing effective black movements he considered radical. Later on, Du Bois also would be betrayed by Negro leaders and subjected to relentless government pressure for his avowed Marxist beliefs. Stripped of his passport, the brilliant scholar would slip into self-exile during his final days and, at age ninety-five, would die and be buried in 1963 in Accra, as a naturalized citizen of Ghana, twenty-three years after Garvey's death in 1940 in London.

As for the parents of young Malcolm, pride in Africa aside, they clung to the essence of Garvey's message even after his deportation, rejecting the racial submissiveness so widespread among Negroes. With self-assurance and a sense of equanimity, Earl and Louise Little steadfastly worked to instill in their children a key Garvey credo: "Liberate the minds of men and ultimately you will liberate the bodies of men." On a more practical level, Malcolm's father, never a pastor of a fixed congregation, increasingly used his access to churches in the Midwest as a proselytizer for the secular Garvey gospel and also as a source of extra cash. And the better-educated Louise boosted her husband's role as president of the local UNIA chapter in Omaha, serving as bookkeeper for the regional office as well as writing articles for the *Negro World*.

In the wake of that horrifying visit by the Omaha Klan in the spring of 1925, Reverend Little was persuaded initially to move his young family back to the concentration of Negroes in the city, where his brothers James and Oscar lived. In due course, however, the staunch Garveyite father purchased several lots in a rural area, three miles from downtown, in North Omaha, and started building a 600-square-foot cabin at the far north end of a 58-by-130-foot lot, at 3448 Pinkney Street. This would be Malcolm's first home. In addition to gardening, Earl hunted game with his rifle, as wild turkeys, deer, and other wildlife roamed through and around his property day and night.

"He was the hardest working man you ever saw," Wilfred said of his father. "He'd be up at sunrise, working that garden and getting the crops going. We always had our own chickens. Wherever we lived, we were quite independent in that sense. Especially in his situation, he had to be where we could continue to eat even if there was no employment. We usually raised everything we needed and had enough [vegetables and fruits] to can and carry us through the winter." Malcolm was yet a baby when his brother Wilfred started the first grade in rural Omaha. "These white teachers," he recalled, "were looking at us like we were something strange."[43]

Despite the stepped-up racist harassment, Malcolm's mother openly ran her byline, "Louise Little, reporter," on *Negro World* articles about "great work" of her husband's Omaha chapter. In the July 3, 1926, edition of the paper, she wrote about a meeting presided over by "E. Little," where "a [local] membership drive was launched for the coming week"[44] at Liberty Hall, at 2528 Lake Street. Such high-profile promotions created a broader demand for her husband's proselytizing efforts beyond Omaha and took him away from home more often. Potential UNIA recruits in Omaha, always scarce after Garvey's legal problems, were practically scared away after word of the Klan visit circulated about town.

Despite the best efforts of baby Malcolm's parents, the UNIA could not garner sufficient support among Omaha's working class of Negro janitors, hod carriers, cooks, porters, meatpackers, and maids. They were being asked to challenge an implacable white power structure that paid their salaries, policed the byways, and ran the government. And the local Ku Klux Klan was at the height of its power, having reportedly fielded candidates for county commissioner and city sheriff. "The Negro race does not want hundreds of Klansmen patrolling Omaha streets as special deputy sheriffs," editorialized the *Monitor*, the city's Negro newspaper. Both KKK candidates won their elections in 1926, and the creditable Omaha *Morning World-Herald* claimed also that the Nebraska governor owed his victory to the Klan. Having been targeted by such vigilante gunmen the previous year, Louise and Earl Little were well aware of the great danger that "frontier justice" posed for Negroes seeking protection of the law in Omaha.

The city of Milwaukee was beckoning, offering at least a larger regional Negro population for UNIA recruitment. Perhaps not coincidentally, it was the place where Reverend Little had received that terrifying call that his pregnant wife and children had been besieged by the KKK. Selling their home and two lots to a local family, Earl decided to move his family to Wisconsin. (Their Omaha homesite ultimately would be designated by the state of Nebraska as an official historical site.)

In December 1926, Earl and Louise Little booked rail passage for six to Milwaukee. "It was exciting," Wilfred recalled, although the children were sad to leave their cousins in Omaha. Earl's younger brother James and his wife, Grace, had children, and the two wives as well as their kids were close friends. "We all grew up around each other and shared with each other and played with each other. Everybody was crying because we weren't going to see each other again."[45]

On that final day, the family of baby Malcolm drove past the Douglas County Courthouse where Will Brown had been lynched. On the skyline they spotted the eleven-story, Romanesque revival Livestock Exchange Building, recently completed by the city as testimony to Omaha's booming livestock industry. This workplace juggernaut employed some 80 percent of the workforce but had slammed its door shut on Reverend Little for daring to preach a doctrine demanding fair treatment for Negroes.

"And then we went to the [Burlington] train station and took off," Wilfred recalled of that trip to Milwaukee. Taking turns holding baby Malcolm's bottle along the way, Wilfred and Hilda shared their home-cooked lunches and took in the scenery. "My mother had babies," Wilfred said. "We would hold Malcolm while she was taking care of [Philbert]."[46]

Adult white men, however, were determined to prevent such black children from growing up in freedom and prospering as equal citizens under law. These men ran Omaha as a model of white supremacy enforced by the massive power of the state—as well as by the managers of the lynching bee. The exodus of the Little family foreshadowed the life of escape and struggle that awaited the fourth-born scion of this proud, black Midwestern clan in twentieth-century America. Just as the Great Migration moved north, the Littles were fleeing eastward as domestic refugees, seeking a tolerable life in yet another American city—and riding along on the train with his milk bottle was eighteen-month-old Malcolm in diapers.

# CHAPTER 3

# The Anchor Is Lost

MILWAUKEE, THE DESTINATION FOR THE LITTLE FAMILY, FEA-
tured a large settlement of German immigrants, who had
started arriving in numbers in the 1840s. They had been joined by a
major influx from Poland, and lesser streams from Russia, Ireland,
Italy, and Sweden, as Milwaukee evolved from an agrarian outpost
with light industry to become the twelfth-largest American city in
the 1920s. With the blooming of the postwar economy, a trickle of
Negroes of the Great Migration began bypassing more hectic Chicago to seek jobs in the meatpacking, brickmaking, brewery, and
shipping industries of this city ninety miles farther north on Lake
Michigan. Upon the family's arrival, Reverend Earl Little reached
out to UNIA members who had promised to help him find employment and get established in the area.

Incoming Negroes initially rented flats on Walnut Street, dubbed
Chocolate Boulevard, and later, amid widespread housing discrimination, the area expanded into what locals called Bronzeville. Once
again Earl and Louise chose not to live in the designated Negro
area. Instead they rented a second-floor apartment over a shop in an

Italian neighborhood on Galena Street. The local Italians, as newly arrived postwar immigrants, many without proper papers, were themselves not yet integrated into then WASP-controlled Milwaukee. The "swarthy" newcomers of Mediterranean stock, not unlike the Irish back in Omaha, were undergoing something of a probationary period as "honorary" whites in waiting. Even among other European immigrants, who constituted nearly 50 percent of the city population, Italians were slurred with stereotypes, as had been widely publicized in the recent Massachusetts murder trial of Nicola Sacco and Bartolomeo Vanzetti. Italians were said to be much given to sloth, easy men of loose morals, with a strong predilection for organizing themselves into criminal syndicates, as suggested by no less an authority than the Immigration Commission, created by Congress in 1907, which stated in its final report four years later that "certain kinds of criminality are inherent in the Italian race. In the popular mind, crimes of personal violence, robbery, blackmail and extortion are peculiar to the people of Italy."[1] In Wisconsin in the mid-1920s, the locals also snickered that the Italians laced their food with smelly garlic and their hair with all too much grease.

The white Protestant majority was wary of the Italians as Catholics, a religious identity that also drew the ire of the rapidly expanding Ku Klux Klan. With the enactment of Prohibition, the Klan targeted the Italians as the kingpins of the bootlegging whiskey industry nationwide. Faced with such ostracism, the tight-knit, immigrant Italians threw off signs neither of passivity nor of nonviolence, and thus the Klan, and often law enforcement, generally left them alone.

"We had no problems with the immigrants even though they were white," Malcolm's older brother Wilfred recalled. "You lived together and shared together and you were all almost . . . the same." As their children grew older, however, the European immigrants blended their accents, submerged distinct ethnic traits, and aimed more toward integrating into the social patterns of the domestic white majority. This distancing, which seemed a prerequisite for Americanization, did not go unnoticed by young Malcolm's family.

"They were immigrants," Wilfred said of the Italians, "and accepted us. It wasn't until later, when we got into our teens, . . . that they realized it was better to go their separate way from us because they didn't want to be classed [with] our people."[2] As with the Irish, the "swarthy" Italians, their skin color generally in harmony with that of the white majority, grew increasingly adept at segregating themselves from Negroes in their adopted homeland where but two major caste factors mattered: white or black.

Upon their arrival in Milwaukee, Earl and Louise Little lost no time in reorganizing the local UNIA chapter. As early as January 2, 1927, the *Negro World* mentioned Earl's addressing a "mass meeting" to initiate a new "program." A subsequent dispatch reported that the Milwaukee unit considered "Elder E. Little," its new "spiritual adviser," to be "quite an asset." And with Garvey still imprisoned in Atlanta before his deportation, Earl continued his campaign to get the UNIA leader's case overturned. On June 8, 1927, he wrote directly to the White House, petitioning President Coolidge to "release Marcus Garvey from the five-year sentence without deportation," as "your priceless gift to the Negro people of the world." The letter was signed E. Little, president, of "The International Industrial Club of Milwaukee."[3]

As Malcolm's father struggled to get the family settled, Louise, who already had made clothes, began to use the small, rented shop below their apartment to display merchandise for sale. She made knickers suits for boys, dresses and matching bloomers for girls and layettes for babies. She also took measurements and tailored adult clothes to order. The income came in handy once Reginald, the fifth addition to the family, arrived on August 23, 1927. With her knowledge of Spanish, French, and patois, Louise could communicate with the Italian speakers who came to the shop. Her children picked up strands of their mother's West Indian accent to the extent that many customers, neighbors, and even schoolteachers considered the Littles to be a Caribbean family. This perspective dissipated whenever Earl arrived on the scene with his backwater Georgia dialect.[4]

Multilingual Louise continued her secretarial and reporting work for Garvey's UNIA, keeping records, writing correspondence, and drafting articles for the *Negro World*. Despite the UNIA's legal setbacks, young Malcolm's parents worked to reestablish the group's reputation and influence. "My father thought [Garvey] was an idol," Wilfred recalled. "In our family, we had two idols that my father kept before us all the time. There was Marcus Garvey and Booker T. Washington."[5] Washington, who had been born into slavery in Virginia, was long dead. But Garvey remained a live, if now distant, presence.

That same year, Reverend Earl Little was making his rounds for Garvey's organization in a sedan Ford "touring car" with curtains on the side and a canvas top. A column in the *Negro World* referred to him as the chapter leader in the Indiana Harbor neighborhood in East Chicago, an Indiana town some 125 miles away. That summer of 1927, the family spent time with relatives, friends, and other Garveyites on a farm near New Lisbon, Wisconsin. As their children got closer to nature, the parents commiserated over the issue of social advancement under racism. Knowledgeable about plants and herbs from her Caribbean upbringing, Louise would instruct her children in how to use them as folk remedies and, sharing know-how that would come in handy later, how to cook certain weeds for food.[6]

Although Earl was a Baptist preacher, the family did not attend regular Sunday church services. Saturdays were set aside for UNIA indoctrination, and high expectations were maintained for preschool Garvey children. Study was mandated, reading paramount. Youngsters were also drilled in American Negro history with an eye toward not only countering the scant version offered in school but also blunting all indoctrination of black inferiority—notwithstanding its reinforcement by government policy and practice throughout society. One Garvey group lesson stressed that Negroes, as axiomatic as it may sound today, had five fingers on their hands and a brain in their heads like everyone else, and that it was entirely up to each Negro personally to learn and achieve—despite the white obstacles society placed in their paths.[7]

In Milwaukee, the Little youngsters felt more comfortable around Negroes, but, as in Omaha, public schools brought them into contact with the broader immigrant community with its false notions of white supremacy. Already, Wilfred, the oldest child, a second grader, was beginning to experience the effects of Garvey home training that so grated against fellow students and teachers in the classroom. But after a short stay in Wisconsin, the family moved once again, this time to Michigan, where they lived with Earl's brother James, who had moved to the town of Albion from Omaha. After working briefly in a local foundry, Earl landed a similar position with a company in Lansing, the state capital.

Meanwhile, young Malcolm was drawing notice in the tight-knit family as a two-year-old with great "physical and mental energy," Wilfred said. "He was very alert, always searching into things."[8]

---

In January 1928, the family moved a third time in only a year, this time to Lansing, Michigan. Here, Negroes were concentrated in what whites, even in polite parlance, called the Nigger Section. An initial stay with friends in an overcrowded tenement led Earl and Louise to move the family into a more sparsely populated settlement on the white, east side of town. In addition to tending her growing family, Louise continued sewing and selling clothing as best she could. Earl quit the foundry job and drifted back to his carpenter craft with local construction companies. At home, he complained that local firms would hire him only as a carpenter's helper, denying him union scale. And as word spread of his UNIA activity, the plant bosses turned hostile. One Sunday morning, Wilfred recalled, a friendly contractor instructed Earl not to report for work the following morning. The boss explained that a local white delegation had paid him a visit. Labor groups commonly monitored workforces for signs of employers allowing Negroes to be competitive with white workers. Unless Earl was let go, the delegation reportedly warned of labor trouble at the plant.[9]

The pressured employer fired Earl, a valued worker, with apologies. He then explained, confidentially, how a skilled carpenter like Earl might canvass wealthy Lansing neighborhoods for independent jobs, a practice Earl had pursued on a smaller scale back in Omaha. Although not unfamiliar, the job loss was a setback. Once again the father had been fired at the behest of whites and was at the mercy of home owners daring to opt for a black carpenter, albeit a highly skilled one forced to accept lower, off-the-book payments.[10]

Lansing also posed other challenges. Baby Yvonne arrived as the sixth child, on August 11, 1929, and the family moved into a small but comfortable house west of the city, near the airport. The one-and-a-half story house, with outbuildings, stood on three lots. The residence was suitable but for one problem: Michigan state law mandated that it be occupied by white residents only.

The previous owner had violated the spirit and letter of the deed containing the racially restrictive clause by selling to Earl and Louise. Such housing clauses were common across the country, especially in Michigan. In fact, a Michigan case, *McGhee v. Sipes*, along with one from Missouri, *Shelley v. Kraemer*, finally would lead the Supreme Court in 1948 to rule restrictive covenants unenforceable. In 1922, however, the Supreme Court had ruled that such racially restrictive housing covenants were legal and that local authorities could indeed enforce them.

Malcolm's parents knew nothing of the racist covenant. Soon after they moved in, however, a few of their white neighbors came by to talk over this "problem" with Louise. In the presence of the children, they explained boldly that their neighborhood was not open to Negroes. The group offered to buy back the property from the Littles, at what, given the circumstances, would likely have been a reduced price.

"I heard the man say so," Wilfred recalled decades later. "My mother let 'em know that their house wasn't for sale. I could see that they didn't appreciate the way she spoke to them. When my father came home, she told him what had taken place."[11] Undeterred, the neighbors started legal proceedings as plaintiffs of the Capital View Land Company suit to get the "colored" family removed. Judge Leland W. Carr ruled that the Negro family could legally *own* the property but, under the terms of the restrictive covenant, they could not *live* in the house. Siding with the white neighbors, Judge Carr initiated court proceedings for the Littles to vacate their home.[12]

A few weeks later, in the middle of the night—at about 2:30 a.m., on November 8, a Friday—an explosion rocked the house and the entire family. Earl said later that he woke up, saw two men running off through the fields, and got his .38 Colt revolver to fire a shot in their direction.[13] "My father jumped up," Wilfred said. "My mother jumped up. All the children, we all woke up, and fire was everywhere. My mother was running around getting us out of the house. We didn't even have time to get our clothes. I'm standing outside barefooted in my pajamas. All of my clothes burned out; couldn't get back into the house to get anything."[14]

Angry and disheveled, Earl and Louise rushed about getting a frenzied head count of the children. Earl slipped on his trousers and shoes as the blaze leaped from the kitchen to the second-floor bedroom. With the fire starting from the back of the house, they rescued a few things through the front. Two aroused neighbors from adjoining houses assisted in removing the children and a few possessions. Once outside, they hedged about venturing back inside as the flames were leaping twenty feet high. Alerted by a knock on the door, the owner of a nearby gas station, Joseph Nicholson, called local firemen.[15]

The Lansing Fire Department refused to respond to the fire at the "colored" residence, according to testimony Nicholson later gave to the police.[16] In the crush, Louise panicked about her baby, Yvonne. "She couldn't find the baby . . . and almost went crazy," Wilfred recalled. "Then somehow or other, they realized that the baby was under the stuff she had brought out."[17] Absentmindedly, Louise had put Yvonne down on a pillow outside and then run around checking on the others. Tar paper and scorched beams of the house filled the cement basement with smoldering embers and ash. The recovery of Yvonne was the only comfort the family could savor as they went wandering about in the autumn night air of Lansing— burned out of their home.

One white family from across the street peeled away from the gathered knot of seemingly indifferent neighbors and offered the family shelter as the flames died down in the wee morning hours. Earl went into town and through a friend arranged for his clan to stay with a family called Walker in the Negro section of town until things were sorted out. Almost immediately, controversy swirled around the cause of the fire. Officials speculated from the start, without evidence, that Earl might have torched his own home—with his wife and six young children sleeping inside.

The following afternoon, authorities dispatched a police investigator named G. W. Waterman to check the likelihood of arson by the "colored" owners. One white neighbor told him that she was awakened that night by a mysterious "knocking" on the kitchen door before hearing an explosion; then she noticed that "the colored family's house was afire."[18] The investigator did not follow up on this prefire knock or any of the other curious details in his report, nor did he explain why exactly the fire department did not respond to the blaze at the "colored family's house."

Earl's account of firing his weapon at fleeing perpetrators appears to have drawn the sharp attention of the investigator but mainly with regard to whether the firearm in question was registered—and the .38 Colt was not. Earl had handed off the unlicensed pistol to a neighbor that night and told the investigator that the warning blast had been fired with a shotgun. The investigator focused his initial suspicion on the burned-out family. When details of Earl's account did not match exactly those given by his wife and son Wilfred, Officer Waterman leaped to the initial speculation by officials. "We decided to lock up Mr. Little for further investigation," Officer Waterman wrote in his report.[19]

"Hold Man During Probe of Blaze," screamed the front-page headline of *The State Journal*, with the subhead "Earl Little, Living West of City, Said to Have Paid for Insurance After Fire." The house and possessions were insured for $2,500 by two separate companies. A few hours after the blaze, Earl had indeed paid the regular premium for his $500 policy on family possessions in the house, apparently without mentioning the fire. Returning later with a friend, he filed his initial report of the destructive blaze that spread rapidly after he "heard two explosions."[20]

The newspaper's implication of suspicion notwithstanding, Earl's reaction appeared to have been that of a home owner surprised by a blaze destroying his family dwelling. After scurrying until dawn in search of shelter, he claimed to have realized that his insurance payment was due and took steps to secure the financial aid available for his family rendered homeless. The scheming arsonist envisioned by officials would more likely have paid up his insurance policy beforehand.

Still, Reverend Little was held in jail, on suspicion of arson, and under $500 bail. Investigators confirmed that his unregistered pistol had somehow been passed along for safekeeping to Nicholson, the gas station owner. One .38-caliber round had indeed been fired. The legal shotgun Earl told authorities he fired was never found. Almost four months after the fire, on February 28, 1930, the arson case against Earl Little—who had served crucial days of jail time away from his distraught family during the crisis—was dismissed. The ordeal had damaged his reputation even further on both sides of the racial divide in Lansing.

Neither the investigating official nor the newspaper reports took into account the long history of racial violence against Negroes in the area. Although the suit of the Capital View Land Company constituted legal action by several middle-class neighbors against the Little residence, hard-eyed white residents further down the social ladder were known to resort to violence at the mere presence of Negroes in their midst. Race tensions nationally had come to a boil as economic conditions had taken a sharp downturn.

Two weeks before fire destroyed the Little home, the New York City stock market had crashed on Wall Street. Even though fewer than 1 percent of Americans owned stock, the tailspin reverberated, plunging the U.S. economy into the epic Great Depression. And, in Lansing, far from the rigors of high finance, in the remoteness of a private disaster, the family of four-year-old Malcolm had lost everything.

———

The Littles spent the next month recovering in the Nigger Section of Lansing. The fire that had destroyed their home only reinforced the parents' drive to reside on land of their choosing. Trying to attain this primal element of the American dream of home ownership had cost them dearly as Negroes, both in Omaha and Lansing. Yet the couple, undeterred, purchased a six-acre parcel with a stream running through it, at 4705 South Logan Street, just south of the capital city.

"Our father was famous for moving into areas where we were the only black ones," Earl and Louise's eldest son, Wilfred, recalled of their harried childhood in three heavily segregated Midwestern states.[21] Among a sea of compliant Negroes in the region, young Malcolm's family stood out in bold relief. And the defiant Earl and Louise Little—as with Malcolm in years to come—would, despite a terrifying price extracted, continue to pursue the American ideals so flagrantly denied black citizens. This early influence is generally underestimated by chroniclers who overlook Malcolm's interaction with his parents, as well as with his siblings—most especially, Wilfred. Key markers are laid down during this developmental stage, psychologists note. Malcolm's *Autobiography* also downplayed this early family influence for the sake of crediting the whole of his development to the spiritual leader he would encounter postadolescence.

As has been described, American Negroes in the post–World War I years could not escape a bare-knuckled, state-enforced panoply of white supremacy at every turn. For the sake of sheer survival, parents generally felt compelled to groom acquiescence into their offspring, especially their male children. Earl and Louise, however, were separately predisposed quite naturally to rebel in their own way, and the Garvey doctrine provided a philosophical platform for resisting the systemic bigotry they faced. So from the cradle onward, the couple proceeded to imprint their children with a genuine sense of racial equality. This uncompromising conditioning would reverberate years later as the defining trait in the lifework of the adult Malcolm.

Upon acquiring the parcel of land, in December 1929, Earl dug a basement with a horse-drawn scoop and set to plying his carpenter skills. By Christmas, he had enclosed the walls and completed the tar-paper roof of the new family home. As time and money permitted, he would improve the structure in stages, while Louise continued cooking, housekeeping, and sewing clothes for sale.

As the Littles would discover, Michigan's capital city was predominantly white. Its 57,000 residents, according to the 1920 census, included roughly 700 Negroes, or 1.2 percent, a presence that would double a decade later. Most resided on the west side with a sprinkling of immigrants from Syria, mainly Christians. The core of this Negro group was stable, decidedly working class, consisting mainly of foundry laborers, janitors, cooks, and drivers. The sporty few gentlemen about town held down jobs as porters and hotel doormen, low waged, but showy in their gold-button uniforms with epaulets. This dime-store gentry recently up from the South had little appetite for any praiseworthy references to Africa, to say nothing of the broader UNIA pitch from Reverend Little. Toning down the "dark continent" references as a result of these suspicions, Malcolm's father struggled to expand his regional group beyond those loyal members retained from his Omaha and Milwaukee days.

Lansing was decidedly a less urban city, and the locals who might have lent an ear, if only out of curiosity, were generally warned away from the "uppity" preacher spreading a West Indian doctrine and living with his family on the outskirts of town. Local shunning of the Garvey doctrine drove Reverend Little to focus his secular proselytizing far afield. Although the UNIA remained a viable force, it did not help matters that Garvey had been convicted of federal mail fraud and deported two years earlier. For the few Lansing residents who dared express interest, Earl organized weekend trips to Detroit, driving the miles eastward in the organization's black Buick sedan with the curtains swaying at the back window.[22]

During these Depression years, Detroit contended with Chicago for supremacy as the most desirable Northern destination among Southern Negroes. Chicago had its slaughterhouses and meatpacking industries by the lake, while Detroit boomed with a burgeoning automobile industry at the center of a network of supplemental parts and service centers. In addition to immigrants flooding in from all corners of Europe, the Motor City attracted a steady flow of Negroes heading up from the Deep South with similar high hopes for a better life.

The Littles' new manse stood at a remove, in so many ways, from the home of the more typical newly arrived Negro family. The newly dug well on the family's six acres reflected an independent though challenging existence. The scrappy, fourth-born Malcolm was contending with Philbert, who was two years older, for the middle spot among the six siblings. "Malcolm and I were always together," said Philbert, "even at night when we would go to bed. He was afraid of the dark. When he had to go to the toilet to pee, rather than get up and go outside, or use the slop-jar, as they used to call it, he would pee in the bed. And I'd get blamed for wetting the bed."

A daytime tactic of the younger brother—perfected years later— had him tilting the odds his way with the threat of retaliation. "We'd fight," Philbert recalled. "Malcolm would always plant like a hammer or a stick or ball-bat, a club. And if you'd chase after him he'd reach and grab the bat. If he didn't have the advantage, he'd run. Children—I'm not trying to say we were monsters. We were close. So whatever trouble came up we were both usually in it."[23]

Not surprisingly, the frolicsome boys were caught at pranks, such as stealing fruit or melons in the fields, yet spankings were generally reserved for sly disobedience or sloth, and for botching assigned chores. Earl and Louise ruled with an air of absolute authority and did not spare the rod, visiting swift corporal punishment on occasion. Children were to listen and obey, period. Although Louise primarily did the spanking, she passed the more serious cases along to her husband, who would lash the children with a leather strap, wooden board, and "switches" from tree branches—in a pinch, his callused laborer's hand would serve the purpose. Occasionally the whippings had no discernible trigger and caught the child off guard.

On some dark evenings, not even Louise was spared her husband's wrath, their adult children later confided.[24] A moody man of shifting fortunes in the outside world, Earl could be quick with the backhand when his wife displeased him, and he would often follow up with sustained physical and mental battering. Historically in the United States, wife beating was not only common but enshrined in common law as the husband's "right of chastisement," a legal defense in the unlikely event that he was charged with assaulting her. By 1920, when women were first allowed to vote, that "right" was no longer legally recognized. But the all too common practice of spousal "chastisement" in farm families, black and white, remained a stark household reality of Malcolm's early childhood. With underlying differences in education, skin tones, and views on family regimen, the couple's disputes over Earl's travel plans, late nights, or simple household matters would flare into all-out domestic warfare. The color differential always loomed in the air, with Louise's lighter complexion a seeming advantage. During one stretch, Malcolm wrote in his autobiography: "My mother was usually either arguing or not speaking to my father."[25]

Among the siblings, the two middle brothers were dealt with differently. "My mother whipped Malcolm," Philbert said. "I don't recall my father ever whipping Malcolm. I don't recall why. He'd say, 'Louise,' and she'd get Malcolm and whip him."[26] Occasionally, his mother would allow Malcolm to fetch the "switch" from a sapling for his own whipping. When he obliged with a leafy shoot judged insufficient for the task at hand, his mother would order Malcolm back to the tree for a rod of a higher caliber.

Notwithstanding the absence of his father's heavier hands, Malcolm would not go quietly. Whenever his mother drew the assignment, he would stage a preemptive show for de-escalation. "I would open my mouth and let the world know about it," he wrote about the spankings. "If anybody was passing by out on the road, she would either change her mind or just give me a few licks."[27] As with so many childhood traits carried forth, a besieged Malcolm would grow to master as an adult the preemptive tactic of motion and commotion. Philbert was not so clever. "My father whipped me, but I was the active one," he said. "I was the mischievous one; everyone called me mischievous. I had determined that when I got older I was going to fight my father. Because when he whipped me, he whipped me so hard. He would hold me by my legs upside down. And whip me. He was a big, powerful man. My mother would admonish him: 'Earl, you're gonna kill that boy.'

"I say he was a monster, but he was just a father and in those days, particularly when a father was not highly educated, they'd beat you."[28]

The firstborn son somehow escaped much of the rough treatment. Wilfred was well suited for his role as the classic, eldest brother of a large, working-class family, which numbered seven children, with the birth of Wesley in 1931. Even-tempered and selfless, Wilfred matured early with an instinctive sense of responsibility. Because the peripatetic Earl was grievously absent, Louise relied upon Wilfred to help manage the growing brood, increasingly vesting in her dutiful son the authority of family adjutant.

While organizing the clearing of the garden and barnyard, Earl worked out a crop-sharing arrangement with a neighboring Hungarian farmer with a larger spread. Seasonally, their acres were planted in lots of corn, potatoes, spinach, peppers, string beans, and squash. The Littles had a cow and a goat for milk, and chickens were raised for eggs, along with geese and rabbits. They also harvested white walnuts from the thirteen butternut trees on the property and sold them by the bushel at roadside, along with other crops that truckers would pick up on Saturdays and take to market.

Malcolm's father usually rose early and worked the fields but, at times, his contracting jobs pulled him away from the farm. Without warning, he would drop everything and head off for unscheduled UNIA work, or places unknown. Suspicions arose occasionally over other unexplained errands, as the family routine put a heavy strain on Louise and the not yet adolescent children.

"My father believed in child labor," Philbert recalled vividly. "He thought that children were for nothing but work. Every one of us had a chore. When I was too young to go into that garden and hoe, without cutting up plants, I had to bring the water. Malcolm was younger than me. But he couldn't pick up a pail of water like I could, so he would bring the dipper. When we got older, we were working in the garden. We got up early in the morning. I had to bring in coal. I had to go in the woods and pull out the old dead branches and chop 'em up for firewood. We had an old potbelly wood-burning stove. Work started from the day you could breathe, and it started early in the morning."[29]

When Malcolm's older siblings started primary school in Lansing, they trekked two miles through woods and cow pastures and across wooden fences. As the only black students in their classes, they were viewed by many as curiosities. All the teachers were white, and many had never seen Negroes up close. In January 1931, when Wilfred attended fifth grade, Malcolm was enrolled in kindergarten at the Pleasant Grove Elementary School; he was five years old. The family, as one of few Negro families in town and one self-assured and at ease with itself, got along fairly well with children of European immigrants, such as the Italians and the Swedes, but Malcolm would occasionally get into spats with native-born "hillbilly" students over matters involving race. As for the normal rough and tumble of the schoolyard, with fist-fights and face-downs, Malcolm and his siblings earned a reputation for sticking together.[30]

*The Story of Little Black Sambo*, published in 1899 by the British writer Helen Bannerman, was a standard children's reader at Pleasant Grove. The illustrations of the dark Indian child caused derisive snickering among whites, but the "pickaninny" slur—along with the unrestrained bandying about of the term "nigger"—repulsed the Little children, who were taught at home to disparage such putdowns of the black race.[31]

As the taunts escalated, it was their mother, Louise, who conditioned Malcolm and his siblings not to overreact to the racial slurs. "We didn't like being called a nigger," Wilfred said. "But we would try to downplay it. My mother always told us that you can handle [racial slurs] in a way where you make them continue" or "you can let them think they're not hurting you. She would give an example: if you're throwing darts at a dartboard, there's a satisfaction you get when you hit the target; when you miss it, you get another feeling. Well, she said, it's the same way with white people when they're throwing darts at you by things they say and do. But if they don't hit the target, then they won't get that satisfaction—and eventually they'll quit. And usually, that's the way it worked."[32]

This psychological training for resistance to racial provocation was conditioned into the behavior of young Malcolm and his siblings. Their behavior earned grudging respect among a growing number of whites in their neighborhood despite—and, in some cases, because of—their adherence to Garveyism. Some in Lansing attributed this accommodation with whites to the Caribbean side of the otherwise "uppity" Little family. The West Indians in town indeed tended to band together. Louise and her children, for example, had established their strongest ties with Islanders such as the Lyons family, who lived in nearby Mason, and the McGuire family. "We felt at home with each other," Wilfred said. "One thing about the foreign black people, they were more aware of the international picture. When you get around other black people, [overseas affairs] sound strange to them."[33] The Littles' experience seemed typical, as it did not go unremarked upon that whites got along better with the West Indian families than with native-born Negroes up from the South. Indeed, Caribbean families like the McGuires—and like the Littles, owing to Louise—were said to be more open and more neighborly, less uptight, agreeable . . . different.

"Our attitude made a difference in how they dealt with us compared to some of the others [Negroes]," said Wilfred. "When white people find out that you don't have that inferiority complex, they deal with you at that level; it makes a difference. A lot of our problems we bring on ourselves by our own inferiority feelings sometimes. If you acted like you were inferior, that's the way they related to you. If you didn't act like you were inferior, then they would be forced to treat you as an equal. And this is the way we were."[34]

It was upon this rock that the social perspective of young Malcolm was built. And he would carry throughout his life this family-groomed sense of equanimity. The Garveyite struggle of his parents formed the foundation for what, after years of evasive wandering, he would manage to fashion into his life's work and, ultimately, his legacy.

In the America of the 1930s, black immigrants tended to be somewhat tone-deaf to racial slights directed at Negroes in their adopted country and thus slower to take offense. Growing up, they had been spared family anecdotes about murderous white policemen and civilian mobs, including the Ku Klux Klan, the kind of stories that American-born blacks got in horse-doctor doses at the dinner table from grandparents, aunts, and uncles. With slave ancestors arriving in chains in 1619, a year before the *Mayflower*, American-born Negroes, although disenfranchised in every way, felt fully vested—starting with some 250-plus years of uncompensated labor. While their country had no intention of ever paying the debt, the United States had indeed benefited from this staggering sweat equity—an investment that was compounding still. As for the recently arrived immigrants, whether black or white, the ledgers were free and clear. Entering the country voluntarily, they landed with fresh eyes, willing hands, and a keen openness about the vaunted promise of "freedom" for all who entered. This sentiment clashed with that of longtime descendants of American slaves, who were hardened by brutal treatment despite their legacy as original co-inhabitants of the republic since colonial days. With their unique, native sensibility, American Negroes were spared the illusions about the land of the free. Backed up against the wall for generations, they had been conditioned to expect the worst.

Earl and Louise were a microcosm of this divide. Malcolm's West Indian mother had arrived in Philadelphia with much higher expectations than her Georgia-born husband. And with her buoyant hopes, fair skin (owing to her Scottish father), and linguistic abilities, she moved about with less of the stereotypical Negro "baggage." The harsh suspicions, dread, and mistrust born of experience that shadowed her dark-skinned husband was not part of Louise's lifetime heritage. Her maternal ancestors had toiled in Grenada under the white-minority yoke of European colonialism, sure enough. However, as a majority population on the tiny island of sixty thousand residents, they had more access to the crafts, educational, and economic systems. Lacking exposure to America's toxic brand of racism, she was afforded a more hopeful outlook than her husband.

In New York City and the Northeast more widely, first-generation West Indians such as Marcus Garvey, a Catholic son of a stonemason father and grandson of ex-slaves, increasingly took leadership roles in organized Negro movements against racism. In the Midwest, the barricades yielded ever so slightly to pressure exerted by the likes of the McGuires, the Lyonses, and the higher expectation of Malcolm's mother, from Grenada by way of Canada.

Communal cross-pollination between black immigrants and American-born Negroes gave birth to a heightened sense of group engagement generally—as it did specifically in the marriage of Louise and Earl Little. The marriage blended her relatively blank-slate optimism as an immigrant West Indian with his rebellious, and quite unusual, sense of entitlement, something absent in many citizen-descendants of slavery. Then there was the Garvey doctrine, welding their otherwise divergent views and sensibilities. Yet even while advancing the cause of the UNIA, the dynamics within the marriage played out under constant tension. Although some outsiders considered Earl and Louise unevenly yoked, and the union indeed had its stormy periods, the couple settled into a stable merger of shared striving, despite Earl's reported outbursts of violence. More even-tempered than her husband, Louise steered the children through roiling times brought on by the Depression and Earl's occasional lapses into racial self-loathing, all too common in child-rearing of the day.

Louise, like other Creole "subjects" back home on tiny Grenada, had also grappled with issues of identity. But, in her adopted country of "freedom and equality," she came into motherhood hell-bent on ensuring all due rights for her children to attain a sound education and a life of accomplishment. Educated in schools that emphasized geography, mathematics, and language skills, Louise had attained an excellent education as compared, say, to her husband.

"I can't say that I have any evidence that my father believed in education," Philbert observed. "His conflicts with my mother [which often flared into physical violence] were because of her education. She knew grammar and she was emphatic about how she taught us. She didn't accept the term 'colored'; she said we are black people; she never allowed us to accept the term 'Negro.' My mother was serious, never jovial. She'd always get us to the facts of what we were talking about. She would sing to us: 'one and one are two . . . two and two are four. . . .' Then there were French songs she would teach us. My mother was the one who brought knowledge out of us." [35]

Along the way, Louise, ever the Garvey devotee, would sternly warn her children that white teachers could be counted on to distort African and Negro history in an effort to block their advancement and to make them feel inferior. "These white teachers didn't [seem] to like to see you too proud of your black self," Wilfred noted. "They would do little things to try and make you feel somewhat beneath [the other kids]. And if they knew you were one of these Marcus Garvey [kids], they would give you an extra dose of this kind of thing."[36]

Some students from Garveyite families were made to stand in class and explain the version of African and Negro history they were taught in the Saturday UNIA classes. Occasionally, they would be made to sing the Garvey anthem which referred to Ethiopia as "the land of the free; the land where the gods used to be." Upon hearing that white teachers would degrade her children in class, Louise would visit the teachers the very next day for a sit-down. She would reinforce her children's account of black history, giving the teachers an adult double dose of Garvey doctrine. "She would let them know," said Wilfred. "Don't be trying to make niggers out of her children."

Wilfred continued, "Usually, when she made a trip to the school, we saw a difference in the attitude of the teachers. We seemed to be the oddballs, not only in the white community but in the black community because of our difference in how we saw ourselves and our people. We had many blacks in those days that accepted this inferiority complex, went along with it; but we didn't."[37]

Throughout their hardships, the troubled parents managed to instill a sense of independence and racial pride in their children, especially Wilfred—who, as oldest brother and confidant, would exert a powerful influence upon Malcolm throughout his entire life.

———

As in many families, Malcolm's parents related to their children in a pattern of uneven words, deeds, and misdirection that disguised which child might have been their favorite, if indeed they made such a choice. Still, rivalries, as they always do, broke out among the seven siblings all vying for their parents' attention. Interviews with Malcolm's adult brothers and sisters did not resolve the "favorite" issue. "If anybody favored Malcolm, I think it was my mother," Philbert observed. "She talked about [his being] pale. She said that he was not as strong as me or the rest of the children because he was pale." And it did not escape Philbert's notice that their father, while heavy-handed with him, continued to subcontract corporal punishment of Malcolm to their mother.[38] Both Philbert and Malcolm sensed in this the seed of favoritism, but they disagreed upon the culprit. Malcolm later suggested that his dark-skinned father preferred him for his "lightest complexion."

All the children agreed that, even though their father was not as given to education as their mother, Reverend Little was dead set on instilling a work ethic and that, as a preacher-organizer, he possessed a sharp ear for glibness. In this latter case, he likely had a penchant for young Malcolm's gift for expressing himself verbally and otherwise. In his first marriage, Earl had promoted Ella as something of a seer, a prophetess, taking his oldest daughter on evangelizing trips to sit "on the pulpit" as he preached from the Bible.[39] Now, this second time around, Earl would take young Malcolm with him on proselytizing trips for Marcus Garvey. It was "only me" that our father would take to the "U.N.I.A. meetings which he held quietly in different people's homes," Malcolm noted in the *Autobiography*.[40]

This special, and primal, paternal bond was the enduring essence of Malcolm's childhood imprinting. Even before he reached the first grade, he was impressed with the potency of leadership as demonstrated by his father at the UNIA gatherings. "I remember seeing the big, shiny photographs of Marcus Garvey that were passed around from hand to hand," Malcolm wrote. Despite Garvey's imprisonment and deportation, Reverend Little was highly respected as a regional UNIA president. And Malcolm recalled his father closing the house meetings with two dozen or so followers by chanting: "Up, you mighty race; you can accomplish what you will."[41] The accomplishments envisioned by the UNIA, however, were nowhere in sight in 1931, as Negroes were the most severely hit by the Depression. More than 50 percent were out of work, and in some Northern cities, employers were reportedly pressured to fire Negroes so long as there were unemployed whites in the area. Labor unions in Michigan and elsewhere practiced such discrimination, and Negroes attempting to organize themselves in the workplace were often threatened by lynch mobs.

That same year, the Black Legion, a splinter group of the Ku Klux Klan, was established in Highland Park, Michigan, by largely unskilled, white Protestants up from the South. This secret vigilante group would expand to some twenty-five thousand members, including elected officials, and would get involved in several high-profile murder cases over workplace issues. Operating across the state, the terrorist Legions were based in the Detroit area, where Reverend Little continued to make regular weekend visits with groups of locals attending UNIA meetings.

Amid the Depression, Earl Little cut back his organizing efforts as Garvey's stalwart Midwest representative. Yet in the teeth of the economic downturn, the enterprising carpenter-farmer managed to keep his family essentially self-sufficient. As his children maintained the cow, chickens, and goats for milk, eggs and meat, the family seasonally rotated the fruits and vegetables that they sold, along with walnuts, to truckers for the market. The rabbits caged out back were also livestock but were sold directly to white neighbors for food, as Louise adhered to dietary restrictions of the Seventh-Day Adventists, serving up mostly fish, chicken, lamb, and beef for the dinner table. The children were strictly forbidden to eat pork or rabbit.

At harvesttime after school one day, the children busied themselves separating the foodstuff to be canned from the stock that
was to be sold roadside. On this Monday afternoon of September
28, 1931—twelve years to the day after the lynching of Will Brown
in Omaha—Reverend Little came in from the field, with a gathering of vegetables, and abruptly killed one of the rabbits out back
by chinning its neck. For the first time the older children could
recall, their father demanded that his wife cook the rabbit for
dinner. A heated discussion ensued with the reluctant housewife
insisting that neither she nor their children would partake in the
sacrilegious meal. As usual, the man of the house had his way. As
the begrudgingly prepared rabbit stew simmered on the stove, Earl
reportedly washed up hurriedly and changed from field overalls
into dressier street clothes.

It came as news to the children, and seemingly to the wife, that
their father was heading into town. Louise inquired, not exactly
politely, about her husband's vague intentions. Their eldest son, Wilfred, related distinctly that the timbre of his parents' discourse this day
was outsized for the matter at hand, and quite disturbing. Finally, the
mother pleaded with her husband flat-out. "She was telling him that
she didn't feel right about him going into town that night," Wilfred
said, "because something was going to happen that wasn't right."[42]

Viewed now in distant retrospect, it recalls Shakespeare's Calpur-
nia beseeching her husband Caesar:

> *Do not go forth to-day: call it my fear*
> *That keeps you in the house, and not your own.*[43]

But just as Julius Caesar made his way to the Senate that day in Rome,
Reverend Little dismissed his wife's petition and prepared his exit.

The older children disputed Malcolm's point in the *Autobiography* that concern about the Black Legion stirred the tension, as such racist threats hung constantly over the family. All agreed, however, that the gravity of their parents' singular confrontation that afternoon was momentous. The details were separately and steadfastly verified over the years by Wilfred, his sister Hilda, then nine, and Philbert, then eight. In his *Autobiography* Malcolm wrote, "My father was well up the road when my mother ran screaming out onto the porch. *'Early! Early! . . .'* For some reason, considering how angry he had been when he left, he waved at her. But he kept on going."[44]

"[My father] felt that he had to go anyway," Wilfred said. "He didn't take what she was saying seriously. There were times he would and there were times that he wouldn't. This night, for some reason, he wouldn't."[45]

As for her intuition, Louise prided herself in being gifted with a telepathic sixth sense beyond physical perception—a sense that also warned of danger. Some called her psychic, a term she rejected. However, beyond the youthful notion of ghosts and prowling holiday goblins, she softened her children to the possibilities of spiritual revelations, danger warnings, myths, and even the envisioning of personages not physically present. Most of Louise's children, including Malcolm and Wilfred, would subsequently claim to "see," up close and personal, the image of a deceased spiritual leader they had accepted as divine but had never met. Malcolm, under the persuasion of his mother, boasted of his intuition. "When something is about to happen, I can feel something, sense something. I have never known something [truly significant] to happen that has caught me completely off guard," he would say toward the end of his life, "except once. And that was when, years later, I discovered facts I couldn't believe about a man who, up until that discovery, I would gladly have given my life for."[46]

That Monday evening, as their father, Earl, made his way beyond earshot of his pleading wife, the children were struck by her lingering sense of dread, if not doom. "She was seldom wrong about what she had said she had seen, or whatever," Wilfred recalled. "And as he left, she was distraught. She just didn't like seeing him go. He was certain he had to go. I remember him going down the road and she stood there and watched him; and pretty soon she called him and wanted him to come back. She called to him, but he kept on going."[47]

Later that evening, an unusually quiet yet fidgety Louise boiled, washed, and wrung out a load of clothes, with help from the children, and hung them up to dry. At the appointed times, the family members went off to bed.

Around midnight, a Lansing police car with bright lights pulled up to the house and a young uniformed officer, along with his partner, knocked on the door. He told Louise that she should come with them to Sparrow Hospital because her husband had been injured. Dressing quickly, she left Wilfred, who had to attend school the next day, wide awake and somewhat worried. The others, including Malcolm, worried along with him, despite their various stages of childhood slumber.

Upon arriving at the hospital, Louise learned that her husband had been run over by the back wheel of a streetcar. Earl's left leg had been severed, his abdomen crushed, and there were severe gashes on his head. He had been alive, but barely, when the police officers went to get Louise. Contacted at the rail barn, the motorman reportedly said he didn't know he had run a man over. Subsequently, Earl's blood was discovered on the wheels of his car and on the tracks.[48]

When Louise returned home distraught, in tears and unable to explain herself, it became clear to Wilfred that the worst had happened. His forty-one-year-old father was dead. Young Malcolm, who slept through most of the events of the night, was six years old. Wilfred was almost twice as old and by far the sharpest witness who retained a vivid memory of that most horrible night of his life.

"When they brought her back," said Wilfred, "I remember when she got out of the car and this officer—it was a young officer—told her that a lady had called and told him that this man was out there on the streetcar tracks trying to get up. And that's what brought him to where he was. He was still alive when they found him. He was able to talk and told them where he lived, and for them to come and get [Louise]. And so they beat it out to get her, hoping they would be able to get her back before he died. They knew he couldn't live, the condition he was in.

"And he told her that [Earl] had told them that he had gotten on the streetcar—there were two streetcars. The first one he had gotten on and he reached for his money and realized he didn't have his coat. So he had to get off. He told the man he'd get off and catch the next one. He had to go back and get his coat." The streetcar made a scheduled loop around Lansing and came back around.

"So, on the next streetcar he did have his coat because when they found him he had on a coat. He said that he was running to catch that car because it was the last car. If he didn't catch that one he would have to walk all the way home. And he was running to get on the car and when he got almost to it—the bricks were a little wet—he slipped and fell and slid right under the car. Before he could get up, the trucks of the car ran over him.

"And that's how he told the police he got hurt."

"I looked right at this officer as he was talking, and I didn't see anything about him that made me have any doubt about what he was saying. He was young; he was very sincere. And I didn't see anything that would cause me to doubt what he said.

"My mother accepted it—for then. She was crying and she had

a hard time breathing. She was just sighing all the time. The thing that bothered her was the fact that she knew that something was going to happen and she couldn't turn him around from it—and he went on."[49]

The autopsy report of the Lansing coroner stated that Earl Little's death by "accident" at "11:50 P.M." was caused by a "M. E. R. Street Car" that ran him over. The married, "colored" victim sustained "internal injuries" and his "left arm and left leg were crushed." His occupation was listed as "Minister."[50]

In the wake of the tragedy, the Lyons and McGuire families, the Littles' closest friends in the Lansing area, provided what comfort they could. As the children grieved among themselves, George and Beatrice McGuire assisted Louise in notifying relatives and making the funeral arrangements. During one of the early family visits to the white-owned Buck Funeral Home—there were no Negro undertakers in Lansing—Wilfred sneaked into a back room and pulled the sheet away from his father's body naked on a dressing table.

"His left leg was completely off. [It was] just laying there with the rest of the body," he said. "On his head, he had a gash and a couple of big bruises. And he had a gash just behind his ear. And so I got a chance to uncover him and look at the body and see for myself what had happened to him. And it was gruesome."[51]

Wilfred was so caught up in the secrecy of his venture—investigating the mystery of it all—that he did not remember crying, as he had when he got word of the tragedy the night it happened. In the preadolescent's view, the condition of his father's body did not appear to be inconsistent with the official account of his being run over by a streetcar.

Reaching out to relatives, Malcolm's Uncle James invited relatives from Earl's first marriage, including Ella, to the funeral. The teenager came in from Boston to meet the Michigan side of her father's family. This eldest child had been considered Earl's favorite back in Georgia, so the two "special" children, Ella and Malcolm, separated by about ten years, met briefly—for the first time—at their father's funeral. The very large gathering at the funeral home on October 1 was attended by friends, neighbors, the curious (both Negroes and whites), and acquaintances streaming in from as far away as Detroit, where some members of the secular Garvey group made their affection known. After services, out-of-town relatives huddled with the widow Louise to arrange shipment of Earl's body back to Reynolds, Georgia, for burial.

In the crush of her husband's sudden death, Louise and her adjutant, her oldest son Wilfred, gathered themselves and the other children as best they could. The youngest, Wesley, had just turned four months. Hilda, Philbert, young Malcolm, and the others clung ever tightly to their mother and one another, not fully grasping the meaning of it all.

Among the children, Malcolm in particular felt deserted and, it appeared, doomed to wander the earth in search of a substitute anchor. Gone away forever were those joyful trips with his dad to secret, private homes where he was exhibited as a family showpiece before perfect strangers, stints that groomed young Malcolm for the stage—and for the barricades. Sitting through those evening Garvey meetings exposed him to recitations of glib African ditties, poetic Negro hymns, and to his father's spirited prompting of UNIA warriors to lift up the race. This favored child was left now with an emptiness that would somehow have to be filled someday.

Yet the precocious six-year-old first grader had much growing up to do in the shadow of his family's twin midnight tragedies: the incineration of their home and the death of their father on the capital's streetcar tracks.

Down through ensuing generations, the Little clan would appear to be haunted by the specter of death and disaster: house fires, prison, manslaughter, and arson, combined with race terror, feuding, mental breakdowns, and even murder. It was as if some curse of Shakespearean proportion had befallen this American family of pioneers out on the Great Plains—and most especially young Malcolm and his offspring down through the decades.

# CHAPTER 4

# Pulling the Family Apart

THE SUDDEN DEATH OF YOUNG MALCOLM'S FATHER LEFT HIS mother to eke out a living with her seven children during the worst economic downturn in American history. Seeping into the void left by the removal of Earl's iron discipline was a sense of relief combined with uncertainty and dread. Although the isolated farm family perceived no specific threats from whites initially, the Little clan was obliged to continue navigating the suppressive, anti-Negro practices entrenched in the school system, in law enforcement, in government policies, and in the marketplace of Lansing.

In that first dark autumn of 1931, thirty-four-year-old Louise and her fatherless children, the oldest not yet a teenager, held to the household routine as best they could. Their drafty, tar-paper-roof cabin was heated by a coal-burning potbelly stove. Electricity and indoor plumbing had not yet come to much of rural America in the 1930s, so that the Littles, like most of their neighbors, were at the mercy of a creaky, outdoor toilet, while they had to hand-pump water from the backyard well and carry it indoors in buckets for cooking, washing, and other household uses. Still under the sway of their father's training, the children continued to gather the crops on the six-acre farm, setting aside daily rations, preparing food-stuff to be canned, and selecting vegetables for the roadside sale out front.

Despite the warmest Michigan winter weather on record for decades, with temperatures averaging 34.4 degrees, Louise had to enforce belt-tightening measures. As instructed by UNIA principles, the fiercely independent matriarch struggled mightily to keep her family off government assistance. Putting her children to bed half hungry, she was nagged by the prospect of a meager breakfast the next morning.

Their daily disaster was being controlled unduly by commercial forces. As it turned out, Earl had meticulously sacrificed to pay insurance premiums so that a sudden disaster would not financially collapse his family altogether, yet his $1,000 life insurance policy had been bitten into by funeral costs and the burial trip back to Reynolds, Georgia. A second $10,000 accidental-death policy had been calculated to tide the family over just such a calamity as the unexpected death of the key breadwinner. However, payment by that larger policy covering accidental injury and death was stalled by the issuing company. Despite the ruling of the Lansing medical examiner,[1] insurance officials, as is their wont, steadfastly disputed family claims that their policy covered the circumstances of Earl Little's death. Against all existing knowledge of his zest for life—and with not a scintilla of evidence noted in the investigation of the incident—the insurance company ruled that Earl's death was likely a suicide. This shocking conclusion further distressed the widow with seven young dependents to feed and clothe.[2]

The facts explaining the father's death on the rail tracks appeared straightforward. Coverage of the accidental-death policy seemed clear, just as Louise had fully accepted the report of the young police officer who had spoken to her dying husband—sensing nothing that challenged the official account. Additionally, the medical examiner confirmed eyewitness accounts and the conclusion of the railroad investigation that Earl was accidentally run over by that streetcar. In the wake of these grisly findings, the widow reassured the children and informed relatives and close friends that her husband's death was a tragic accident. Yet, despite the overwhelming evidence and the agony of the widow, the insurance company refused to pay the $10,000 policy.

It is not altogether surprising but historically telling that someone of Earl's precise, at times fanatically detail-oriented, personality would have taken out an insurance policy for his family, something that he could barely afford. It was this kind of attention to detail and discipline that his son Malcolm would inherit as well. But the insurance then became an element in a larger tragedy that shadowed the black family. No matter how carefully, how providently, Earl tried to play by the rules and protect his brood, they were done in by the system—in this case, by the dishonest scheming of the insurance company, which exploited many unfortunate victims but no doubt felt as if it could do so with wanton malice against a hapless black widow and her seven children.

As if this corporate miscarriage were not enough, Earl's death would subsequently be dogged on the street level by wrenching, and apparently unfounded, conspiracy theories. Even as Louise protested the insurance company's persistent suicide claim, another—even more troubling—rumor emerged about the cause of her husband's sudden death.

"One night," shortly after the funeral, Wilfred recalled years later, "a white man came by the house and said that some of his friends had raised some money to give to my mother. And he told her, 'I want you to know that I didn't have anything to do with what happened . . . 'cause I don't believe in that kind of stuff.'" The remark caught Louise completely by surprise, notwithstanding that she had experienced Ku Klux Klan intimidation firsthand and was acutely aware of vigilante Black Legion terrorism against Negroes in Michigan and elsewhere. In light of the evidence, she had absolutely no reason whatsoever to believe that Earl had met "that kind of fate. After these other stories started coming around," Wilfred recalled, "my mother began to wonder. She began to wonder because white people were saying things. So when you've got all of this stuff going around, you don't know what to believe. Some [suggested] that he may have been beaten and put on the tracks before the streetcar came along."[3] The street rumors, as biting as they were unsupported, subjected the widow to a new round of cruelty and terror.

The eldest son sifted through the rumors coming his mother's way and weighed them against all evidence available to them. Despite the disturbing hearsay, Wilfred held firmly to his belief in the official version—as reported by the police and supported by the medical examiner in the death certificate. Throughout his life, this closest confidant of Malcolm—nearly twelve years old at the time of their father's death and earwitness to the original account—would never accept or describe the death of his dad as anything other than an accident. "It wouldn't be right to just spread things [claims of homicide] when you don't really know," he maintained.[4] Contrarily, as Malcolm grew older, he would feel quite differently about their father's death—and he would boldly express his view to the world.

No group or individual ever publicly took responsibility for killing Malcolm's father, and the signature of the Ku Klux Klan was not left at the scene, as would have been the case were it an act of their terror. The Black Legion, the offshoot of the Klan, was indeed operating out in Michigan in 1931, and rumors pointed to this white supremacist group as possible culprits in the alleged killing of Earl Little. Like the Atlanta-based Klan operating openly throughout the Midwest, the Legion was not shy about "teaching Niggers a lesson" with extreme brutality, including death—and then taking credit. At the time, such acts against Negroes by white Protestant terrorists stood little real danger of prosecution, either in the South or in Michigan.

Harking back to his days in Omaha, it was well-known that Reverend Little, as a UNIA leader, was marked by white racists with a bull's-eye target on his back. Thus the prevailing assumption was that sooner or later some murderous Klan-type racists would catch up with this "uppity" Garvey man. But just as investigators attempt to weed out groundless rumors, conspiracy theorists tend not to allow for bothersome coincidences. And it is not unlikely that some white racist decided to take advantage of an accidental death and began bragging about it as a supposed hit. Many would-be thugs in beer halls across the ages have stitched for themselves just such a whole-cloth reputation of publicized derring-do.

As the insurance company pressed Louise Little to prove that her husband's death was not a suicide, these other rumors challenged the family to prove that his death was not a homicide. The pressure to establish either of these negatives was nothing short of maddening for this besieged black mother.

Despite not squaring with available facts, the conspiracy theories about a possible lynching would flourish briskly for decades— and are still thriving today. Young Malcolm picked up recycled rumors of his father's "murder" from "several white children" at school, echoing "what their parents had said, namely that the Black Legion or the Klan" had committed the "lynching." Although family lore dismissed this account, this fourth-born man-child, with a deep yearning for his deceased father, convinced himself beyond doubt that white racists had killed and—thus martyred—his dad. At critical points in Malcolm's own life, similar flashpoints of violence would trigger specious claims of arson, attempted homicide, and other acts of foul play, whipped along by predisposed notions that were contradicted by available facts. But, as with rumors about homicide, no credible evidence whatsoever has surfaced to support the insurance company's outrageous claim that Malcolm's father died other than by accident under the steel wheels of a streetcar in Lansing.

One side effect of Earl's death, convenient to some, was that it abetted the efforts of those opposing his UNIA operations throughout the Midwest. The small Lansing office he had chartered for residents to contact and hire day laborers, gardeners, and cooks was soon closed down. A few associates attempted to revive other of Earl's activities in the city, but these feeble efforts soon withered away.

As for the family, Louise kept alive the spirit of the Garvey philosophy by passing its tenets along, chiefly through her eldest son. Wilfred's strong grounding in the positive perception of Africa withstood every negative, popular-culture bombardment of 1930s radio and Hollywood films about the dark continent—for example, how it was portrayed in *King Kong* and the series of movies based on Edgar Rice Burroughs's *Tarzan*. Each of the Little children responded differently, with the ever curious Malcolm proving the most susceptible to the negative media stereotyping of Negroes. Still, not even he could totally block out the seeds of the Garvey doctrine planted at the family hearth. This immunization against black inferiority continued to set the Littles apart from their peers, both white and black.

Foremost among the values the mother passed down was a staunch adherence to black independence and self-reliance. Accordingly, the family patronized black merchants for goods and services whenever possible, sometimes going miles out of their way. The children were also taught to challenge, and even to defy, schoolteachers who held low expectations for them as Negroes. This latter assignment was no easy task in Lansing. "If you wanted to take skill courses," Wilfred said of the entrenched educational system, "teachers would try to discourage you. If you wanted to get into machine shop, or printing, they'd say, 'Why do you want to take that? There's no jobs for Negroes in this field.' They would encourage you to take singing and entertaining. 'You people make good singers.' My mother would say, whenever they say that to you, tell 'em, 'Well, maybe I'll be going back to Africa some day and I can use [those skills] over there.' "[5] Increasingly, the children would simply keep their career ambitions to themselves or dispense with them altogether.

Surviving during the Depression placed great stress upon family values of pride and self-reliance, to say nothing of career planning. With Earl's insurance benefits denied, the gravity of his death loomed even larger. Gloom grew steadily to dominate the daily family routine as Mother Louise could no longer hide her desperation from the children.

<hr>

"My mother stopped singing," Philbert commented about the effect of the death and the Depression on the family. "Instead of being the happy person when our father was alive, she was quiet." The storytelling sessions around the winter stove became rarer and less a thing of joy. The descent was not relieved even by the fellow West Indian families, the Lyonses and the McGuires, who initially had brought comfort by trekking out to the farm with goodies and whatever help they could extend.[6]

Cash flow trickled to a near halt. Family members recalled this destitute period below the subsistence level as almost unbearable. "We were so hungry we were dizzy," Malcolm wrote in his *Autobiography*.[7] Heavily breaded hamburgers, stewed tomatoes, and raisinless bread pudding were staples when they could afford them. When they couldn't, Louise would fall back on her West Indian culinary enterprise and boil up "a big pot of dandelion greens." Neighborhood wags would mock the dish as "fried greens." Rumors spread, and not without evidence, that the family was pulling up and eating wild plants and weeds.

As winter turned into spring and back again during the bleakest years of the 1930s, the command structure that Earl had hard-wired into place for his intermittent absences now short-circuited with the absence of his paternal authority. The mother was in sole charge. And in her absence, Wilfred, the model, teenaged big-brother, became the surrogate disciplinarian and adolescent muscle around the house and in the barren fields on the six acres. Third in command of the struggling family was Hilda, the sister, who played a vital role in comforting the brooding widow.

Increasingly, the high-energy Malcolm grew more creative as he maneuvered among his adolescent brother and siblings running down to baby Wesley. Earl had spared Malcolm corporal punishment, sure enough, and favored him in other ways, but he now seemed strangely the most affected by their father's absence. Young Malcolm especially began to pay less attention to assigned chores around the farmhouse. Despite the chill of their unfinished cabin, he and Philbert began taking their playful sweet time gathering firewood and sacking the coal spilled along the railroad tracks that fed the cooking and heating stoves.

At fourteen, Wilfred was on the job market as a ninth grader looking for part-time work. For even the menial jobs available to Negroes, the reputation of the Little family as "uppity niggers" became a hindrance. After one interview, a supervisor let the applicant know flat-out that he was in no mood to hire a "smart nigger" (with the emphasis on "smart").[8]

"In those days," Wilfred said, "many of us" learned to play along with white expectations "for certain types of jobs. We'd laugh among ourselves as teenagers at how we went down and played the part of a dumb nigger with this old ignorant hillbilly in order to get a job." In the end, Malcolm's brother landed a job at a Polish family's store and supplemented Louise's pension and the minimal cash she brought in selling hand-made clothes. Driving about in the family's old Chrysler sedan, the fair-skinned mother would also hire out for jobs in the city but sometimes she encountered problems. On one occasion she was fired when the employer, who had not asked her race, discovered upon examination that Louise was officially nonwhite. Another time, one of the Little children exposed the mother's assumed white identity by showing up at the office. The shocked white employer immediately let the newly exposed Louise go.[9]

Ineluctably drawn back to religion, Louise blended rather easily with whites of the local Seventh-Day Adventist church. However, Negroes were reportedly kept away from all responsibilities except tithing and fund-raising, so she drifted off to a local Seventh-Day Sabbath Keepers sect. The Sabbatarians held certain doctrinal differences with the Adventist Church, and among her increasingly independent children, only Philbert, who remembered the sect being led by one Mr. Seaton, took to the Keepers service. "I went every time the door was open," he recalled.[10] Adhering to the vegetarian diet of the Adventist church, Louise generally avoided beef, certain fish and fowl, as well as rabbits—such as the one she balked at cooking for Earl that fatal night. It went without saying that pork was to be avoided at all cost. No one could say Louise was not consistent. Once during these lean years, a neighbor, a Mr. Doane, offered the family two pigs that might have been customarily slaughtered to grace the dinner table for a few days running. Louise flatly refused the offer. "I thought she was crazy myself (as hungry as I was)," said Malcolm years later.[11] Such dietary abstinence by his mother only reinforced the youngster's initial rejection of religion.

As women's job opportunities trailed off—and they were never promising except during wartime—the family struggled during the bleak years while the Depression deepened. Relying mainly on her small widow's pension, Louise was no longer able to provide for seven children and the six acres. Beginning in 1935, President Franklin D. Roosevelt enacted widespread public-assistance relief programs to assist Americans battered by the grave economic conditions. Crushed by the dire circumstances, Louise cast aside her husband's Garveyite prohibition and reluctantly accepted government welfare checks and food assistance. Garveyite Earl, some suggested, would have turned over in his grave.

The state posted a pesky white social worker on the family's case. Louise got asked probing personal questions, as her entire family was placed under random monitoring. Years later, Malcolm wrote of this intrusion: "The state Welfare people . . . acted and looked at her, and at us, and around in our house, in a way that had about it the feeling–at least for me—that we were not people. In their eyesight we were just *things*, that was all." [12]

The fifth-grader Malcolm and his siblings constituted the entire black student body in their school, situated a two-mile walk from the farmhouse. Spared the inferiority conditioning that most Negroes were put through, they all got along fairly well with the white kids, more or less as schoolyard equals. One glaring exception was that teachers and students referred to the siblings as "niggers," and so matter-of-factly that they seemed to bear no sign of malice in this utterance. Such was the etiquette of Midwestern white folks far gone in their denial about offensively stereotyping others. Occasionally, overt bigotry would inspire the rougher-edge white boys to pick fights with Malcolm, Reginald, or the girls. Such encounters would usually trigger heavy family reinforcements.

"Malcolm got along well with the white students," said Philbert. "If there was a problem, it would be from the hillbillies. Malcolm [who, even then, loved to provoke] would say something to make them angry. Then a fight would engender; we would have to [settle it] after school, out in the field. And I was always the one; Malcolm never fought. I was protecting my little brother. My brother Reginald—he was younger than Malcolm—would also fight for Malcolm. So the word got around that if you fight one of the Littles, you've got to fight the entire family." [13]

As the family struggled with raising crops and doing chores, a decided waywardness, or slackness, set in among the growing children. Discipline became a thing of the past. As they grew into adolescence, Malcolm and Philbert especially turned their eyes away from the planting fields and took to unassigning themselves housework. The slack was taken up by Hilda and Wilfred. The older duo also increased their roles in helping their mother pay bills, buy food, repair furniture, tend the crops, and sell the shrinking farm produce roadside.[14]

Meanwhile, their mother's relations with the other West Indian families, which had been fraying, were now in tatters. In her bitterness, Louise began to suspect that her Caribbean friends, so helpful at the time of her husband's death, were scheming to take away their six acres of land. Whispering to her children about the matter, she made it clear that the McGuire and the Lyons families were not to come around anymore. Increasingly, the preachers and church deacons who continued visiting after Earl died were also made unwelcome. When they persisted, Louise became more and more aloof. As she grew more isolated out on the farm, a close friend from Jamaica began to spread rumors in the community that Louise was going "crazy."[15]

During one stretch, the family took in a Negro boarder, a Lansing workman who shortened his weekday commute and whose rent money helped defray the family bills. Rumors inevitably sprang up that Louise had taken up with the married man as something of a part-time lover. Occasionally there were other boarders. One of the former friends from the old days, Edgar Page, continued to visit. The children noticed their mother brighten up whenever he came around.

"He looked just like my father," said Wilfred. "If someone didn't know my father was dead, and saw him at the house, they'd think it was my father. He was the same height, same color, same every-thing."[16] Also, unlike the others, the single and independent Edgar Page was quiet and a good listener, and he appealed to Louise by not making assumptions. "He got my mother's ear," said Philbert. "They talked and talked. He didn't put pressure on her."[17]

The word got out that Louise, a widow of six years, was "seeing someone." In due course, Louise became pregnant, and late in the summer of 1938, she delivered her eighth child: baby Robert. Malcolm was entering the seventh grade. Even as Louise became more distant, the West Indian families remained supportive, at least of the pregnancy. The children overheard the McGuires and the Lyonses commenting that Louise was a young woman when her husband died, and that "nature is nature." Like the friends, the children seemed not to oppose the relationship with Edgar Page or to resent the new out-of-wedlock baby. The welfare caseworker, however, turned venom-ous, telling Louise directly, according to Wilfred, that "she had no business getting pregnant and having another child. Sometimes my mother would give her an argument; sometimes she would just tell her: 'You get out of my house.' After the woman would leave, I would try to calm my mother down 'cause she would be very upset. When she got upset, she would sigh and change her way of breathing."[18]

As the strain on the family intensified, Malcolm's oldest brother dropped out of the eleventh grade at Eastern High School and took on the role of surrogate father to hold the family together. Wilfred worked full-time as a presser at a local dry cleaner, took evening courses when he could, and came home each night as exhausted as father Earl used to be in the old days. With her brother as the steady breadwinner, Hilda began to take care of the younger children—and increasingly, their mother. Years later, Malcolm would confess, in something of an understatement: "Philbert and I didn't contribute anything."[19]

The two brothers increasingly stayed away from the household. Thirteen-year-old Malcolm had taken to hitchhiking into Lansing, returning home in the wee hours. The three-mile return trek grew less frequent after he fell in with a group of idle city youths prone to late-night mischief making. Louise gave up pleading for her sons to come home nights as Malcolm's attendance at Pleasant Grove School became more that of an interloper. And his truant reluctance to bend to the discipline demanded by the white teachers earned him low grades, which he hotly disputed, until the principal finally slapped him with terminal suspension.

As for funding their forays into Lansing, the two enterprising brothers initially targeted the dutifully employed Wilfred who on paydays would tuck his money in a chest of drawers, retrieving it later to pay bills. "Philbert would come out there when I was at work and steal it—he wouldn't just take some of it, [he'd] take it all." Once, when Philbert's own pay from odd jobs didn't cover the cost of a sporty jacket he was eyeing in a store, he stole his brother's money for the final payment. Given to wild exaggerations about his family's economic status, Philbert was intent on impressing a particular girlfriend. When his older brother tracked him down in Lansing, Philbert broke away and ran—wearing the new jacket. Cornered, he swore everlastingly to Wilfred that he had not stolen his money.[20]

Malcolm took occasionally to pinching from his brother's cash drawer also. Unlike his older brother in crime, he would, when caught, neither bolt nor lie. "Malcolm never would deny that he stole," said Wilfred. When caught, Malcolm would shrug. If pressured, he'd concede with a promise to repay the loot. "That's one thing I give Malcolm credit for, he was not a liar. Philbert was one of the biggest liars you ever saw. But Malcolm would not lie. If you caught him, you just caught him, but he sure wouldn't lie. And my mother used to talk about that. She gave him credit. She said, 'Malcolm will not lie.' But she used to tell Philbert, 'You're such a prevaricator. You mix a little

truth with your lying and a person doesn't know where you're leading.' Then, half jokingly, she'd chide him about his lying by claiming,
'I don't know where you came from. I wonder if they gave me the
wrong baby in the hospital.' "[21]

The two rivals, Malcolm and Philbert, continued drifting, though
separately, into the streets of Lansing. The older sibling, Philbert,
had quick reflexes and would hustle up cash as a prizefighter, building quite a local reputation for his prowess in the boxing ring.

As Philbert, along with any other black youngster, was aware, the
1930s were the golden age of boxing, and among Negroes, it was the
platinum era, representing something larger than mere sports. One
of the most memorable events of that decade had come on June 22,
1937 (not June 27 as recorded in Malcolm's *Autobiography*). Joe Louis,
the famed Brown Bomber of Detroit, by way of Alabama, knocked
out Jimmy Braddock to become the heavyweight champion of the
world. Louis later earned international fame by knocking out Nazi
hero Max Schmeling in the first round at Yankee Stadium during
a rematch of a fight Louis had lost to the German puncher. "No
one else in the United States has ever had such an effect on Negro
emotions," wrote Harlem Renaissance author Langston Hughes. "I
marched and cheered and yelled and cried, too."[22]

The Negroes of Lansing, according to Malcolm's *Autobiography*,
"went wildly happy with the greatest celebration of race pride our
generation had ever known. Every Negro boy old enough to walk
wanted to become the next Brown Bomber."[23] The more cerebrally
inclined Malcolm was not one of them. Even by his own admission,
Malcolm lacked the reflexes and hand speed that took brother Philbert, a "natural," to major regional amateur bouts at the local Prud-
den Auditorium.

Tall, gangling, if not awkward, Malcolm tried his prowess at basketball. But he was not content to watch Philbert train in the gym, so
the thirteen-year-old went after a share of the family fame by hiking

his age to the requisite sixteen and signing on for a boxing tourna-
ment. Adding insult to a bloodied nose in one pivotal bout, Malcolm
was also decked numerous times. The winner had been so frightened
of his taller opponent initially that he overcame his fear with a whirlwind of haphazardly delivered but quite effective punches. Malcolm
demanded a rematch and brought along his brother Reginald to
cheer his anticipated vengeance taking. This second time, Malcolm
was knocked out cold almost immediately. The ensuing shame he
brought upon the black west side was made all the worse by the fact
that his teenaged opponent was white.

Most embarrassingly, Malcolm lost the respect of his younger
brother Reginald, who, without comment, transferred his pugilistic
hero worshipping to the lightning-quick Philbert.

Hired out during the day to work on nearby farms, Philbert continued his prizefighting on the side. There were side benefits to his
part-time work in helping a Hungarian neighbor, herding twenty-two
cows each morning, threshing hay during season, milking livestock,
and slaughtering pigs. "They'd ring the bell for that big chow line,"
recalled Philbert. "I was attracted more for the food than anything
else."[24] Not even the victuals were sufficient to attract the ever hungry
Malcolm. His loathing of farmwork, as well as other manual labor,
ran deep. And his aversion to bodily harm, especially with him on
the receiving end, occupied a special place. After getting punched
squarely in the face a few more times, he would shy away from boxing. Turned off by these encounters in the ring, young Malcolm set
his sights on making his way in the world not by gloved hands but
by sharpened wits. And along the way, he set to mastering the art of
winning friends and influencing people across the spectrum.

In short order, said his older and somewhat jealous brother
Philbert, "Malcolm was a leader among the black boys as well as
the white boys."[25]

Like many families during the Depression, the Littles were locked in a devastating downward spiral. Louise sewed clothes for sale but was overwhelmed by the demands of tending eight children at home. Her widow's pension and the welfare payments, were simply not enough to stem the tide of monthly bills. And the state contributed to the situation, continuing its probing inspections, with the Michigan welfare caseworkers constantly berating Louise on housekeeping matters. The infant Robert, whose father was no longer on the scene, was a special subject of derision. For Malcolm, cultivating a flashy front with downtown buddies, as adolescents are prone to do, required money for snacks, movies and popcorn. Accordingly, vagabond Malcolm would sneak back home and pilfer dollar bills when his mother cashed her monthly checks. "He knew what time of the month the check would come," said Wilfred. "And he'd look around where she hid [the cash] 'cause she knew he was stealing, too. He and Philbert both did that."[26]

In the spring of 1938, before Robert was born, Wilfred had been laid off from his dry-cleaning job when returning college students were hired for the summer. Undeterred, the dependable eighteen-year-old, hardly one to accept money from his mother, to say nothing of filching it, booked a Greyhound bus to Boston, where a job awaited him.

Years before, Earl Little had warned his second set of children to steer clear of his first family, headed by Daisy Mason, whom he had abandoned in Georgia. Following their separation, his first wife, Daisy, had joined the Great Migration of Negroes from the South, leaving their three children behind in Georgia with their grandparents. By 1935, however, two of Malcolm's half siblings, Ella and Mary, had moved north to Boston, along with their two aunts. After she had met her father's second family at his funeral in 1931, the more independent-minded Ella maintained friendly relations with them. By the spring of 1938, when she was twenty-four, Ella had married her second husband and was dabbling in real estate and engaging in street enterprises of the underground economy. Some six years older than Wilfred, she had now found her half brother work in the kitchen of a Boston hotel.

As one of the oldest cities in America, Boston had many distractions and advantages. It possessed the nation's first public school and its inaugural subway system. And, in 1938, it boasted a lineup of such formidable Red Sox stars as Jimmie Foxx, Joe Cronin, and Lefty Grove. Not unlike its major league baseball team, which would be the last to field a black player, in 1959, Boston earned a reputation of stark hostility toward blacks during the interwar era and for decades beyond. As such, Bean Town was not a key destination of the Great Migration. The city's 2 percent black population hailed chiefly from the West Indies and Cape Verde, and they were steered away from the white, urban center and into the darker neighborhoods of Roxbury and, later, Dorchester.

Tall, stern, and dark-skinned, Ella kept a neat and well-ordered household. However, as his father had once warned the family, and as Wilfred was discovering after Ella settled him into his room, the Mason side of the Little family tended to operate as something of a "criminal element." With their common father dead now seven years, Wilfred's life with his half sister was even more challenging than he had expected. The shadowy, transplanted Roxbury resident was putting her Midwestern, straight-as-an-arrow half brother through the paces. It was unsettling.

"Ella had her hustle going," Wilfred said. "She didn't work. She would go out and steal more in a day than you could earn working. She was a shoplifter. I don't know how she could get the stuff she would get: clothes, grocery, all kinds of stuff." Wilfred observed people "working with her" that summer and, with scant visible means of support, Ella dressed well, in perfumed silk and natural fabrics, and was a fixture at the neighborhood beauty parlor. She and her husband "lived in the high-class side of town." Frank, her more levelheaded, straitlaced husband, who held down an industrial job, resented Ella's street hustling, and he was unnerved by the periodic house visits by Boston municipal police.[27]

Always careful not to lose sight of his mission to Boston, the hardworking Wilfred focused on his hotel kitchen job, grabbing every available overtime hour as a dishwasher, busboy, and one of the other less visible roles to which management restricted Negro workers. Each week, the frugal teenager would dutifully mail home about twenty dollars of his thirty-five-dollar compensation. Unfortunately, he had no way of ensuring that the cash intended for family bills would reach his mother and his sister Hilda. Increasingly, throughout the summer, he grew uneasy during his downtime at home as Ella quarreled regularly with her law-abiding husband over her suspicious activities.

In the fall, Wilfred received an ominous letter from the McGuires informing him about rumors that his mother might soon be institutionalized. Packing up after payday, the eldest son headed home to Lansing. Upon his arrival, Wilfred immediately discovered that the cash he'd been mailing regularly throughout the summer had failed to reach its intended destination. His financial assistance had not made things better.

Brothers Malcolm and Philbert, "whichever one got there first, had been stealing the money," Hilda reported to Wilfred. "Once in a while she'd get it."[28] Usually, however, the two blood rivals would race each other to the mailbox, rip open the envelope from Boston addressed to their mother, and brazenly head back into town with the pilfered dollar bills.

The situation was far more perilous than Wilfred had imagined. Louise "was in hell," he discovered firsthand. "It was a pitiful situation because she couldn't make ends meet. Food was a problem, getting from meal to meal." Gone were the chickens, rabbits, the goat, and the cow. The basement, once stocked with canned fruit and vegetables over the winter, was now completely barren. Working with the knowledge Louise had imparted to her children about wild plants, she and Hilda had taken to pulling up edible weeds, roots, wild-growing berries and herbs, in an effort to put meals on the table for the younger kids.

"She had reached a point where she either had to commit suicide or just leave this world one way or the other—by just tuning it out," reported Wilfred. "And that's what she did. She just tuned out everything. She started living in a world of her own, not communicating except when she wanted to. At times she'd be very communicative."[29]

During these final years of the Depression, a two-pound loaf of bread cost fifteen cents. Thus, the money Wilfred was mailing back from Boston could have provided food and made acceptable headway with the expenses. But such marginal relief failed to materialize with his two younger brothers on the prowl. When confronted about the thievery, Philbert, characteristically, denied it. Malcolm shied away from discussing it with his older brother. Each played a significant role in accelerating the family's downward spiral.

The usually frank though not fully forthcoming *Autobiography of Malcolm X* makes no direct mention of his household theft: perhaps it was too painful. Years later, Malcolm got around to apologizing for his corrosive acts directed toward his mother, much as he would for gross misdeeds committed against other family members and friends during his heathen days. However, his adult contrition could do nothing to mitigate the desperate straits of his mother, who was getting pressured by a probate judge to sell the six-acre farm—presumably to the judge's family.[30] Her monthly welfare checks had been diverted to his office where, upon picking them up, Louise was told that if she got rid of the house, her family would receive larger welfare payments. Sometimes she was threatened with losing the welfare payments altogether. The harried and rapidly deteriorating mother took to dispatching Wilfred, her one reliable son, to pick up her checks.

"His secretary [at first] would say that he was not there," Wilfred recalled. He was instructed to return and wait in the office for the judge. Invariably, "he was back in the office with someone that had appointments with him. I was sitting there. Finally, he would come out with this sheepish grin on his face. Then he would give me the check, every month."[31]

Despite her struggle with the mortgage and other household expenses, Louise resolutely refused to sell the farm to the judge or anyone else. At the behest of various social workers, the state dispatched a doctor to review Louise's worsening condition. In an effort to forestall court action on commitment to a mental hospital, Wilfred took his mother to a private psychiatrist to independently assess how she was bearing up under the burden. "She's trying to carry too much," Wilfred remembered the doctor saying, "with all the children, and she can't pay her bills. Plus, she's undernourished. He said if she could go someplace where she would not be bothered with [the children, expenses, and other problems] for a period of time, where she'd get proper nourishment, proper rest and not have to worry about anything, she'd soon be all right.

"And he said that she doesn't need to be institutionalized. All she needs is rest, proper rest, proper nourishment, and an environment that's conducive to her peace of mind."[32]

Upon reporting these independent findings to the state doctor, the apparently sympathetic psychologist asked Wilfred where else exactly would his mother find the "conducive environment" he recommended. "Have you got the money?" he naturally asked. The family lacked in truth the funds either to remove their mother from her debilitative environment or to hire an out-of-town lawyer to fight the local bureaucracy, which was seemingly working hand in glove to remove Louise Little from the modest family.

⸻

Although the Depression was beginning to lift, the war clouds that would soon engulf Europe and Asia in a worldwide cataclysm were darkening in December 1938. While Japan proclaimed a new empire in Asia and the Nazis tightened their noose on German Jews, the British government began to construct air raid shelters. The situation was no less gloomy in Michigan, where on Friday, December 23, only two days before Christmas, the probate court of Ingham County ordered that Louise Little, "the mother of 7 minor children living at home," be committed to Kalamazoo State Hospital. On January 9, 1939, as an indigent patient, without property, and with "no one to pay for her care," the court ruled her "insane" upon the recommendation of two doctors.[33]

Pitching in as surrogate parents, eighteen-year-old Wilfred and seventeen-year-old Hilda carried on as best as they could. In that anguished month of January, these older siblings found employment to pay the mortgage and buy food. As neighbors cared for baby Robert during the day, the other children continued in school, except for Philbert and Malcolm, who remained enthralled by the flash of the streets of the city. Despite family attempts bravely to hold together on the farm, the social service agency ruled that the youngsters needed adult care, so the state of Michigan stepped in to break up the Little family, a once proud exemplar of Garveyite dignity.

The two oldest teenagers were allowed to remain in the house, while four-month-old Robert and nine-year-old Yvonne were placed with George and Beatrice McGuire, who had five children of their own. Eleven-year-old Reginald and seven-year old Wesley were placed with a family named Williams. Malcolm, now thirteen, was housed with Thornton and Mabel Gohanna, as was Philbert. The stoutly religious elderly couple took in boarders, and reportedly were raising a nephew named Dave "Big Boy" Roper, whom the two Little brothers had already befriended.

Not eager to trade a fractured domicile for an unfamiliar one, young Malcolm took to the streets part-time—on his own recognizance. Officially, he resided with the Gohannas, on the Negro side of Lansing, and was now enrolled in West Junior High School. This divided life, to say nothing of his increasingly criminal activity, was not the path that Earl had intended for this favored son.

# PART II

1939–1946

# CHAPTER 5

# East Lansing Red

A S PRESIDENT ROOSEVELT'S NEW DEAL EASED THE ECONOMIC crisis of the Depression, the map of Europe was being redrawn chiefly by *Time* magazine's 1938 Man of the Year, Adolf Hitler, who in September 1938 had met with Neville Chamberlain at the Munich Conference, inspiring the British prime minister to famously declare "peace for our time"—on the eve of an epic world war. None of these events, however, in this age before broadcast television, attracted the attention of the Little family in Michigan as Mother Louise spent her first week in the psychiatric ward of the Kalamazoo State Hospital in January 1939, while her eight fatherless children wandered about separately in Lansing, with teenagers Hilda and Wilfred working odd jobs to cling to their six-acre farm.

As he had during their mother's waning days in the household, thirteen-year-old Malcolm drifted about in the west side streets. He spent some days at the Gohanna household, a few overnights with friends or in a vacant car, and, in a pinch, he would retreat back to the family farmhouse. Along with Big Boy Roper, Malcolm had fallen in with a group of idle youngsters on the boulevards searching for fun in mischievous places. As the tallest but youngest of the group, Malcolm displayed a steely confidence groomed by his Garveyite parents, a trait that passed as a commanding presence on the mean streets of the west side. Even the older teenagers looked to him for guidance as he matched their urban muscle with rural moxie and enterprise. Having already looted family cash hidden from the Little cabin, Malcolm now began trafficking in swag generated out in the country, beyond the Lansing city limits. One such enterprise involved a farm near the Littles' spread south of town, where a portion of the cornfield had been set aside for growing marijuana plants.

After discovering this illicit patch, Malcolm got himself tutored in the art of harvesting the herb for street commerce. And in short order, he became adept at rolling the crushed, dry leaves of the marijuana plants inside common use tobacco paper as "sticks" to be inhaled by not so common cigarette smokers.

"He'd head for town with this stuff [marijuana] and make him some money," said Wilfred. Malcolm's farmland business venture was discovered by his older brothers. First Wilfred and then Philbert wandered upon the stash out by the backyard chicken coop. "One day he was rolling some of them," Wilfred recalled. Ever protective of the family's reputation, the astonished family adjutant implored Malcolm to desist from his lawlessness immediately. Caught red-handed, Malcolm characteristically slinked away without denial but making no promises. "Malcolm was more interested in selling it than smoking it. He'd smoke reefer mostly with a crowd in order to get in with them. He'd figure out who was using the stuff and how he could sell it to them," Wilfred surmised.[1] Malcolm was not altogether forthcoming in the matter with his upright family. And in his *Autobiography* he made no mention whatsoever of his possession, use, and sale of marijuana during the Lansing days. Yet, it is clear that upon discovering a market, he commenced to pinch a portion of the neighbor's marijuana crop, secreting the herb in a bag, and hiding it near the

Littles' chicken coop. As a back-up source of marijuana, Malcolm befriended immigrants up from Mexico who brought along their seeds and planted the weed in vacant lots along with noncommercial plants growing wild.

Strutting into town with a fistful of reefers made Malcolm a rising star on Lansing's west side streets. Even at this early age he had a penchant for the spotlight and a daredevil knack for taking risks. As with every such attempt since their father's death, the family's attempt to head off Malcolm's drift into criminal activity would fall short, because he opposed in principle the work ethic that Earl and Louise had successfully drilled into the other children. Now, even before qualifying for the legitimate job market, Earl's favored child was rolling up marijuana leaves instead of his shirtsleeves. Unlike his brother Philbert, to say nothing of the evangelical Gohannas, Malcolm was not concerned about morality or at all given to religion. "Slow money was in [doing] what is right," Wilfred said, "but the fast money is in [doing] what's wrong. And he wanted fast money, so Malcolm was involved in anything that would bring him fast money— other than hurting somebody."[2]

One early brush with the law, however, did involve a predatory act, even if Malcolm did not participate directly. On April 30, 1939, a local white woman walked past a house on Williams Street where Malcolm was sitting on the porch with three buddies. "They called her skinny legs and other names," according to the police account filed with the Juvenile Division of Ingham County Probate Court. Two of the youngsters reportedly gave chase, "grabbed her by the arm, felt of her breast and privates," and ran away when the woman threatened to yell for the police. The report did not cite Malcolm as an active participant, but it appears that the investigating officers, especially Patrolman William Knapp, took special note of the lanky, easy-to-spot, thirteen-year-old redhead whom the court had labeled a "delinquent child."[3] A court-ordered investigation into his "parentage and surroundings" disclosed that his father was deceased, his widowed mother was committed to an insane asylum, and that officials of the Pleasant Grove School, from which he had been permanently suspended, did not have a favorable view of the seventh grader.[4] "Malcolm Little is a general nuisance," the district superintendent's statement to the probate judge began. "He refuses to obey any commands, causes scraps on the playground, is extremely disrespectful to his teachers and others in authority, and in many other ways disrupts the morale of the entire school."[5]

The marks Malcolm scored on his seventh-grade report card backed up the superintendent's account of his deportment at Pleasant Grove. Of the thirteen grades recorded for the two semesters, there were four Cs (average), seven Ds (poor), and two Es (failure).[6] This clearly was not the glowing report referred to in the *Autobiography*: "My grades were among the highest in the school."[7] He possibly was referring to his scholastic standing in the eighth grade, when his marks did improve dramatically. When adults recollect their schooldays, especially when talking to offspring, they often tend to adjust their grades up while, inversely, adjusting temperatures down, as when the writer Thomas Wolfe had a character observe that his father recalled attending grade school only under polar conditions.

That troubled summer of 1939, Malcolm remained under the watch of the court—and Patrolman Knapp. Although his official address was still listed as that of the Gohannas, he was rarely there, and he continued to drop by the family farm to visit Wilfred and Hilda. These older siblings ran a strict household and the "bossy" discipline his sister laid down could approach that of his mother in her younger years. Nevertheless, Malcolm would occasionally spend a stretch of overnights, sometimes bringing along a friend from the city to keep him company.

Roaming the streets of Lansing during the summer months and beyond, Malcolm drifted more toward compatible youngsters who had slipped their parental leash and could spend nights away from home. For a while, he hooked up with John Davis Jr., a teenager three years his senior. Freshly arrived from Picayune, Mississippi, Davis was amazed at the difference between the South and the North: "It was like going into a foreign country." He had a rough landing, however, at the household of Northern relatives, and a frazzled aunt threw him out of the house in Lansing. "I had a chip on my shoulder," he conceded. Death threats down south had forced him to leave friends and family, he disclosed, and the displacement left him quite bitter. Now living on the streets, the seventeen-year-old newcomer first encountered Malcolm at a pool hall on Olds Avenue, and they took to hanging out together. "I was older than Malcolm," said Davis, "but he actually looked older because he was tall." Neither had a family holding him to a curfew. "We just roamed the streets, going around town, stealing, because at that time—with the [Wall Street] crash, if you didn't steal, you didn't eat. We never did any big crime," said the small-town southerner. The more serious capers Malcolm committed were with local buddies, such as Sam Williams and Big Boy Roper. "We would go downtown," Davis said, "and steal cigarettes, pop, candy, stuff like that."[8]

In short order, adolescent Malcolm and his somewhat more experienced new buddy struck up a lively social life, mainly on the west side. In addition to the local schools, the Lincoln Community Center provided educational and recreational activities for Negro residents, and while a serial absentee at West Junior High, Malcolm was a regular at the center. In addition to playing sports and games, Malcolm and Davis used the center as a place to bring girls they met at the high school and around the neighborhood. During one stretch, the teenagers dated two sisters living on their own, "but they only had one bedroom," Davis recalled. "So we would stay up in the pool hall until they closed around two a.m. Then we'd go up to the playground and if it wasn't too cold, we'd sleep on the bench. My cousin had a car, and most of the time he'd park it in the driveway. So we slept in that car quite a lot."

One evening after a debating session at the Lincoln Center, the Mississippian told his younger Midwestern buddy exactly why he had had to beat a hasty retreat north to Lansing. Angry with his girlfriend one day in Picayune, Davis said he refused for the first time to step off a dirt path and allow a white man to walk past him, as required by the Jim Crow etiquette of post-Reconstruction Mississippi. When the two strangers bumped into each other, the young white man flew into a rage, cursed him, pulled a picket from a fence, and attacked Davis as a Negro miscreant. White men imbued with a false sense of superiority, and backed by the full weight of Mississippi law and tradition, felt obliged to attack or otherwise admonish "uppity" Negroes who dared not yield them the unconditional right-of-way at all times, whether sitting on public transportation, awaiting service at a counter, or strolling on a dirt footpath. Having already offended Jim Crow policy by not stepping aside, Davis decided that day on his way to school to follow up with self-defense.

Disarming his white assailant, the teenager got the better of his attacker during ensuing fisticuffs, as he reported to a riveted Malcolm. The beat-down, unfortunately, was conducted in full view of white onlookers at a nearby sawmill. The victorious Davis turned back from school that day—dead certain that a Klan-like response would ensue almost immediately. White Mississippians did not tarry at assembling reinforcements in such cases and making self-appointed, vigilante raids to teach "uppity" Negroes a lesson. Such were the terror tactics of the supposed superior race. Already, as an eight-year-old, Davis had witnessed a neighbor lynched by a white mob as a lethal warning for Negroes to keep to their designated, inferior station—and not contend for basic civil rights, to say nothing of equality. Fearing a similar fate, the teenager dodged school for three weeks, hiding about the neighborhood. "I couldn't be seen in public," he said. Word was out, and the pressure grew intense as groups of white men "were just driving around town trying to catch me." Finally, relatives up north were informed of the grave danger the eleventh grader faced under the racial matrix of Mississippi. Accordingly, they agreed to give him shelter.

"I was put on a bus at twelve o'clock one Sunday morning and I came to Lansing," Davis recalled.[9] Engaged by the telling of his buddy's hair-raising escape, Malcolm expressed surprise only at the petty, right-of-way encounter that triggered the fisticuffs in Picayune that morning. He was not altogether unfamiliar with the perils of racism, of course. Not to be outdone, the ever competitive Malcolm countered with the story of how his family had been hounded by the Klan in Omaha and had their home burned to the ground by whites, not in the South, but up north in Michigan.

Furthermore, Malcolm told Davis that his father had been killed by the white racist Black Legion right in Lansing. Rumors reaching his mother to that effect had been reinforced in Malcolm's mind during the ensuing years by similar accounts repeated by white students. Unlike his siblings, he then fully accepted the whispered account of a homicide as gospel truth.

Davis took exception to Malcolm's account of his father's death as a "lynching," explaining rather casually that he had heard a different account. But Malcolm flew into a primal rage, questioning his friend's right even to have an opinion on the family matter. Not one to back down, Davis took pains to concede that while he had no vested interest in Malcolm's version of his father's death, he had simply heard a different account from a credible, local source. An elderly

Negro in the neighborhood, Davis reported, had claimed in his presence that he had been a rider on that streetcar on the fatal night of September 28, 1931. The man reportedly had witnessed Reverend Little getting struck accidentally by the wheels that killed him.[10] (In a follow-up telephone interview years later, relatives of this elderly man verified, for the author, his account of Reverend Little's death.)

At the time of Davis's rebuttal, Malcolm was not amused—despite the fact that the old man's account of Earl Little's untimely death was widely accepted by the Negro community. "Malcolm said that they persuaded [the eyewitness] to lie. So I didn't mention it anymore because when I brought it up—Malcolm just blew up!" Davis said.[11] So the two friends tacitly agreed to clear their agenda of the matter, and they never again discussed how Malcolm's father died.

Survival on the streets of Lansing during the Depression was an agonizing challenge for these roving young Negro outcasts. As a southerner with a drawl and a severe stammer, Davis was ridiculed by the locals upon his arrival. "I used to fight quite a bit," he said, thus establishing his reputation as one not to be bullied. Putting his prowess to better use, he even gloved his fists and fought in the local amateur boxing ring, along with Malcolm's brother Philbert, whom Davis remembered as "a tremendous defensive fighter. [Philbert was] hard to hit. I used to tell him, if you had an offense to go with that defense, Christ, you would be the world champion." Still, Philbert's pugilistic skill was not a family affair. "I never knew Malcolm to fight," Davis said. "He was more or less like a con man. He would talk his way out of things." Despite all, and with little chance of mainstream employment, the two teenage buddies continued to work the shady side of the street.[12]

In addition to stealing food from stores and fruit stands, the enterprising Malcolm developed a number of schemes with Davis and others to bring in cash for movies, carfare, clothes, and dates at local nightclubs and dance halls. One scheme drew on Davis's mastery as a checkers player, a skill he had developed back home in Picayune. First, Malcolm would stage losing matches for Davis in the barbershop and recruit onlookers to make side bets against him. Then the Mississippi whiz would step up his game and proceed, most often, to win the house. Similarly, Malcolm set up hustles with himself as a featured cardplayer. His skills fell far short of mastery, however, and besides there was a bountiful supply of card sharks on the west side. Consequently, Malcolm's handiwork at bid whist and poker reaped paltry returns, and then only rarely.

This personal insufficiency at card sharking was compensated by a more successful scam. It involved Malcolm writing his name on a twenty-dollar bill and sending Davis into a downtown store to purchase a few items and get change. About fifteen minutes later, Malcolm would make a purchase at the same counter with either a one- or five-dollar bill. Upon receiving his change, he would pivot open-handed and report that he'd handed over a twenty. When the clerk disputed the claim, Malcolm would mount a pitched argument, demanding quite dramatically that the manager be brought forth to settle the dispute.

Escalating his demand, the redheaded teenager would declare, "Look, I know I had a twenty 'cause I wrote my name on the bill." When the cash drawer was flipped open, *voilà*!

"Malcolm had a lot of guts, a lot of nerve," Davis said of his buddy.

Occasionally, during the dozen times the teenagers pulled the twenty-dollar caper at different stores across the city, the arguments with the manager "would get real fierce and the guy wouldn't give. They would be arguing back and forth. I would be ready to say, 'Ah, well, let's just forget it.'

"But Malcolm was resolute with the manager. 'No, no, no, this is my money and I want my money.' And he would always get it, always!"[13]

The manager would overrule his clerk and hand Malcolm his

ill-gotten profit. The score was a tidy sum for the duo in 1939, when a movie ticket cost twenty-five cents and a gallon of gas, a dime. It could not be ascertained how the store managers accounted for the subsequent cash shortage. However, Malcolm's heist usually was followed by dinner at Miss Matthews Restaurant, where a full-course meal cost a quarter, then by a weekend of wild partying with their girlfriends at west side nightclubs.

Such profitable schemes allowed Malcolm to land older girlfriends, often of short duration and usually by his choice. His boldness did not go unnoticed. Davis admired his courage and occasionally was startled when the good friend he called "Red" would suddenly act downright reckless—even with his own life at stake.

One such incident unfolded when Malcolm and Davis were chatting publicly with two white girls at a downtown corner. Two of the city's harshest patrolmen happened upon Malcolm's irregular, mixed-race scene downtown. Officer Knapp, who had previously been assigned to investigate Malcolm as a juvenile delinquent, was the fiercer of the two cops, having reportedly shot a white man dead on a Lansing rooftop. Upon spotting the lanky redhead and his buddy with the two white girls, Officer Knapp pulled his .38 revolver from his holster, cocked it, and pointed it directly at Malcolm's head, inches away. With all the terror of Jim Crow Mississippi flashing through his mind, Davis froze in his tracks, sweating uncontrollably, fearing that the end was near.

"Go ahead, pull the trigger, whitey," Malcolm told Officer Knapp, to the horror of his buddy from Picayune, Mississippi.[14] The good-cop partner, an officer named Griffin, stepped forward and grabbed the hand of his opposite number, slowly lowering Knapp's service revolver. "Ah, it ain't even worth it," Griffin said, consoling his partner. Downshifting to the routine of precinct procedures, the two-officer team commanded Malcolm and Davis to get their "black asses" back to the west side. The two girls were whisked off to safety.

En route to the west side, Davis, still shivering like a weeping willow, noticed that Malcolm was laughing giddily. When pressed about the potentially fatal encounter, he dismissed the run-in with the trigger-happy cop as a lark. Then Malcolm pulled out an irregular, crinkly, self-rolled cigarette and lit it with a wooden match. "Well, I thought it was roll-your-own tobacco," Davis said. "Then I smelled it. And he told me to take a puff. I had never heard of marijuana. But I noticed it left me high. And I'd say twenty seconds out of every minute I wouldn't know what I had said or what I had done."[15] (Curiously, in answering a series of juvenile charges filed against him in probate court later that summer, Malcolm was recorded as stating "that he has done some of these [offenses] and did not realize what he had done until after he had done them.")[16]

"That's the first time I knew Malcolm was on pot," Davis said. "He smoked pot every day. He was his best customer."[17] There were not many marijuana smokers on the west side. Cheap wine, not reefer, was the elixir the players and street toughs resorted to for an escape from the pain and harshness of their daily lives. Furthermore, as the illicit forerunner of cocaine and heroin, marijuana carried a stiff penalty for those caught selling it on Michigan streets. Decades past the statute of limitation, Davis would not flat-out admit that Malcolm actually sold reefers on the west side—as both Malcolm's brothers had confirmed. On the other hand, Wilfred doubted that his younger brother actually smoked marijuana himself.

It was apparent from Davis and other street buddies interviewed that, in his association with whites, Malcolm demonstrated none of the self-doubt, insecurities, or fears that Negroes commonly displayed during close encounters with members of the group dominating American society. This manner emanated from parental conditioning, reinforced by the Garvey philosophy and sustained throughout Malcolm's life, even in the face of clear and present danger, by his strong penchant for risk taking. Thus the teenager, by all accounts, looked whites of all stations straight in the eye as no less than an equal. By contrast, Davis displayed—and sometimes confessed to struggling with, not altogether successfully—a deeply embedded sense of racial inferiority vis-à-vis whites. Nevertheless, despite their different comfort levels with the opposing group, the duo, in a curious way, bonded over their shared perception of the true feelings of white Americans. Both faced an entrenched system that maintained Negroes on tenterhooks, with racial challenges ever before them, while it spared white beneficiaries such untidy intrusions, to say nothing of a sense of guilt or indebtedness. In this system, the dominating group is afforded the privilege of existing in a state of denial of racism, discussing it only when it is brought forth politely at a cocktail party or explosively in a newspaper headline.

Above all of their other exploits, Davis was most exhilarated by Malcolm's open rampaging with white women. The older teenager from Mississippi had grown up with the realization that such escapades were due cause for lynching in the Deep South, as indeed was the case in the incident he had witnessed as a child, involving a white Picayune woman claiming rape upon being discovered in a consensual, interracial relationship. The Negro, whose friends had reportedly warned him to "stop fooling around" with the white accuser, was hanged by the neck with a rope from a tree, "where all of us kids could see. They wouldn't even let anyone take him down. That was to throw fear into blacks, to let them know what they could and could not do."

Dating across the color line in Lansing of the 1930s was taboo as well, but not necessarily considered a capital crime. "If you went with white girls around here," Davis said, "you had to sneak. Malcolm and I sneaked, oh yeah." Admired as a con man with a great gift of gab, Malcolm talked his way out of tricky street situations—and into more than a few dandies. "The first time I heard the word 'pimp,'" Davis said, "and Malcolm took money from white girls. Both of us ran around with white girls. He'd always say that black women don't have anything; after all, they're struggling, too. But he said the white girls, even if she gives you all of her money, can always go back to daddy and get some more. He never took any money, or stole from a black girl's place, never, always from a white spot."[18]

Davis continued, "Malcolm and I had one thing in common: we hated white people"—for what they considered justifiable reasons. Both agreed, he said, that "the crackers" were murderous, blood-thirsty racists who treated Negroes as inferiors with absolutely no respect for their rights or their person. Despite this, the duo, perhaps not unlike slaveholders such as Thomas Jefferson and admitted white racists such as South Carolina senator Strom Thurmond, saw no contradiction in "sneaking" around and sleeping with women of the race they loathed. While Malcolm never discussed with Davis how he justified dating white girls given his expressed contempt for how their race treated Negroes generally, his Southern buddy drew his own conclusion. "I think that he was more or less trying to [hit] back after what [whites] had done to his dad. He took it out on the girls."

Davis explained: "Malcolm was mean to the white girls. He would actually slap 'em. He would take their money. He would curse. I never knew him to hit a black woman. He never took a dime from black women. But he was cruel, very, very cruel to white girls." This left a deep and lasting impression on the black youngster who had nar-rowly escaped a lynch mob back in Mississippi.

Aside from the bustle at the nightclubs and the idle pool hall discussions, Malcolm and Davis continued to visit the Lincoln Com-munity Center and would wander into the public library mainly to hang out, get warm and, sometimes even to thumb through news-papers, magazines, and occasionally books. As the older sidekick with an eleventh-grade education, Davis initially assumed that he was smarter than Malcolm on matters of books and reading. "I had a pretty good memory," he said. "I don't think that Malcolm knew that he had a photographic memory. I noticed that he could read a page and tell you almost word for word what was on that page. He was brilliant, brilliant."[19] While Malcolm's family acknowledged his brilliance as a potential high achiever, they had noticed also that he was not motivated academically, and thus he was not much given to studying or achievement in school. On one hand, the prodding rod of his mother had been removed and, on the other, the requisite reward, so vital a motivating force for student learning, had been greatly downsized, if not denied altogether, for Negroes during the Depression, when jobs were scarce for workers of all races.

"When he applied himself," Wilfred Little said, his younger brother could distinguish himself scholastically. "Malcolm was very intelligent, had a very high IQ. I don't know what it was. In those days they would give you a test for it, I think just about all of us came out high."[20]

Scholastic potential aside, Malcolm continued to draw attention mainly because of his activities on the streets with Big Boy Roper and others, even as the Gohanna home was listed as his official address. In addition to being watched by school officials and police, the teen-ager's behavior was occasionally being tracked and filed with the court. On August 17, 1939, Investigative State Agent Maynard D. Allyn filed a report with the juvenile court prescribing that unless Malcolm's conduct improved, he should face a stint in a hard-core reformatory. "Malcolm's conduct is real aggravating to anyone with whom he associates," the report began. "He seems to want to be the center of attraction wherever he is which makes me feel that his conduct is more an attention getting thing rather [than] vicious traits being manifested." Malcolm admitted some of the charges and promised to change. With the juvenile court concurring, Allyn rec-ommended that the fourteen-year-old be made a ward of the state and "placed in a boarding house."[21]

Malcolm's fate was sealed. The detention home in which he was to be boarded, under supervision, was twelve miles away, in the town of Mason. After departing the Gohanna home and the family spread maintained by Wilfred and Hilda, Malcolm faced his first clean break with family. This separation strained emotions and brought on sadness, if not tears. While en route to Mason that first day, he remembered Agent Allyn explaining the positive aspects of reform school. "He talked about what the word 'reform' meant—to change and become better." Allyn's casual style apparently impressed Malcolm, who praised "the white, state man" (referred to as "Allen" in the *Autobiography*) as "being nicer to me than most of the State Welfare people had been."[22] At this early stage in life, Malcolm still considered the tough-love counseling from a white authority figure as positive, albeit punitive and backed up by the intervention of state authorities. This initial brush with incarceration did not sentence him to be locked down with the more troublesome kids prone to run away. It was a tough, somewhat caring nudge intended to jolt the adolescent out of his downward spiral in the wake of the great tragedies of his life: his father's death, the collapse of family life, the commitment of his mother to an insane asylum, all followed by the splitting up of her eight children. But being sent to this institution was not altruism on the part of government officials; clearing the troubled and troublesome Malcolm out of town served the perceived benefit of the established order. There was also a fresh flow of federal social service money to spread around to private handlers, go-betweens, and boardinghouse owners, thanks to the funding streams of the New Deal programs that President Roosevelt had pumped up to ease the suffering of Americans in the Depression.

Over the years that the Littles resided outside the designated boundaries of Negro neighborhoods, Malcolm had attended school with white students and lived alongside their families, but never before had he actually lived *with* whites. Displaced from his siblings, he now faced the white world up close and personal for the very first time. Agent Allyn dropped him off in Mason as a ward of the state at the home of Jim and Lois Swerlein,[23] the couple who ran his assigned boardinghouse. "It was something Malcolm accepted," Wilfred remembered his sibling thinking. "He knew he had to go somewhere; he knew he'd be better off there than in a reform school. It was better than him being in the street, it would be some kind of discipline. He had to be in at a certain time. There was some kind of control on him."[24]

Malcolm noticed that whites at home talked differently than in public. He observed that they ate different food, far more lightly seasoned—they even had, he sensed, a different body odor. Despite the newness of it all, he quickly warmed up to the host family, discipline and all. "They liked me right away, too," Malcolm noted in his *Autobiography*. And he went about his assigned cleaning duties, manning mops, brooms, and dust cloths with a gusto that would have shocked his sister Hilda—until the day of his uprooting, she had failed miserably in rousing her younger brother to clean so much as a soiled coffee cup around the farmhouse. In hindsight—after a more critical indoctrination—he saw himself as having been perceived as a "mascot." "They would talk about anything and everything with me standing right there hearing them, the same way people would talk freely in front of a pet canary. They would talk about me, or about 'niggers,' as though I wasn't there, as if I wouldn't understand what the word meant. A hundred times a day, they used the word 'nigger.' I suppose that in their own minds, they meant no harm, in fact, they probably meant well."[25]

Good intentions notwithstanding, the slur back then was empowered by racist government sanction and vigilante night riding that rendered "nigger" as caustic as during any period in American history since slavery. Rolling off the tongues of the Swerleins, the slur directed just as much hurt and vitriol at Negroes as individuals as it would later on when uttered by the prison guards waiting down the line for young Malcolm. Since they made an exception for him—that he was not like the "niggers" of their conversation—young Malcolm was willing, in exchange, to grant the Swerleins a certain innocence on race matters. Occasionally, however, the white family would challenge even this generous assumption. Upon returning from a drive through the west side, where Malcolm continued to hang out when he could steal away on weekends, Jim Swerlein said, "I just can't see how those niggers can be so happy and be so poor." His wife chimed in, "Niggers are just that way." Firing directly upon his buddies, including Big Boy and John Davis, their observations moved Malcolm to write years later: "That scene always stayed with me."[26]

The adolescent Malcolm would be far less forgiving of the wealthy, influential movers and shakers of the region who came around as house guests of the Swerleins. Their seeming unwillingness to see the key role they played in oppressing the Negroes of Lansing as a permanent underclass puzzled Malcolm as they pivoted away to observe the results of their oppressive handiwork. Parading through the boardinghouse were some of the capital city's big-name politicians, judges, real estate agents, and county officials representing the collective, exercised power of the state. All of them boldly discussed, right in front of Malcolm, what seemed to be their favorite topic: lazy, shiftless "niggers." Everything about the striving of his parents, for example, contradicted these hostile putdowns. His father's attempt at black social and economic uplift had mainly brought down upon his family and its associates the collective force of this very segment of white society, starting with those terrible days back in Omaha. Still, it was perhaps Malcolm's soft spot for the Swerleins that allowed him all those years later to give his detention home family the benefit of the doubt, at least, when they uttered the word "nigger."

With a population of some five thousand residents, Mason would prove to be something of an oasis for this lone "general nuisance" black teenager recently accused of disrupting "the morale of the entire Pleasant Grove School."[27] Enrolled in Mason Junior High School, a rarity for a ward of the detention home, Malcolm repeated the seventh grade, where he made new friends and gained a fresh lease on life—and dramatically improved his grades. The attention was a motivating factor, and he had in his favor Lois Swerlein's standing in the community, plus his own novelty as a tall, redhead Negro, smart and wily, who despite being called "nigger" even by the teachers, got around campus with no discernible chip on his shoulder. And, as always, young Malcolm was charming.

Increasingly, the attention that Agent Allyn proclaimed that Malcolm craved came gushing his way at Mason Junior High. "It became hard for me to get through a school day without someone after me to join this, or head up that—the debating society, the Junior High basketball team, or some other extracurricular activity, I never turned them down," Malcolm wrote in his *Autobiography*.[28] As with all such accounts owing to memory, there are instances of exaggeration in this book and a vagueness on names, times, and dates; however, the *Autobiography* is verifiably solid in recording that, in addition to holding down a job washing dishes in a local eatery, the popular Malcolm did indeed engage in numerous school activities. He played on the basketball team and was considered something of an accomplished boxer, an assessment that would shock his brother Reginald, who remained disappointed by Malcolm's pugilism, especially up against brother Philbert, the bona fide regional lightweight contender.

The days spent in Mason, everyone seems to agree, were critical for Malcolm and generally positive for his adolescent development. Siblings, including Wilfred, his closest confidant and brother, concurred that after their father's death, the Mason years were likely the most stable and constructive in Malcolm's young life. In addition to schooling and his dishwashing job, he would hold several other jobs about town: as a houseboy, an errand runner, and a handyman for a local physician.

During his early Mason days, Malcolm chanced to meet his half sister Ella, whom Wilfred had lived with that summer before Louise Little was hospitalized. Upon visiting Wilfred in Lansing, Ella rounded up Malcolm and their father's other children from their respective foster homes and went to visit Louise in Kalamazoo State Hospital. Other than the sharp contrast between dark-skinned Ella and his "near-white" mother,[29] who smiled lovingly at the sight of her children, Malcolm recorded little about this family gathering. However, he was deeply impressed with the bold, take-charge approach of his half sister and made special note of her open invitation for him to visit her in New England. Subsequently, Malcolm commenced to write her in Boston with increasing regularity while resident in the Swerleins' boardinghouse, a circumstance Ella considered highly objectionable.

Not unlike their father, the gangling Malcolm attacked the challenges of life head-on and with prodigious energy. In the *Autobiography*, however, he quite naturally omitted key points that others may consider important. Massaging rough edges, the well-written, first-person account is not altogether forthcoming or well rounded, despite Malcolm's best efforts at recall and the gap filling by his co-writer, Alex Haley, as well as editors. During his years in Mason, a somewhat different picture understandably emerges from discussions with a number of white classmates, relatives, and acquaintances, touching on the impact that race had upon his life. In the present case, an assessment of these views was also matched against available records and played against the prevailing environment.

The popular images of Negroes in Mason when Malcolm arrived

were sustained by radio and Hollywood movies, a decade before television was widely available to the public. Black women were stereotyped as wide-eyed, sexless Aunt Jemima maids and nannies, and their men as lazy, cowardly, buck-dancing sneak thieves, who schemed on their own kind, trembled before the white "Mister Charley," and ran like lightning from imagined ghosts. During the 1930s, Malcolm was an avid moviegoer, and in addition to watching Buck Jones and Tom Mix cowboy movies at the Mason Theatre on Saturdays, he and his fellow junior high students were huge fans of films demeaning Negroes as caricatures. There were such Hollywood numbers as *Tarzan* and *Our Gang*, and a close friend and classmate of Malcolm, James Cotton, remembered that the on-screen portrayal of Stepin Fetchit as the world's laziest human "was a main star in the movies."[30] Watching the popular *Gone with the Wind* alone in the Mason Theatre as a fourteen-year-old, Malcolm would say years later that he had been acutely embarrassed. "I wanted to hide under the rug" when Butterfly McQueen, shucking all dignity and sense, played maid Prissy "as a squeaky-voice, panic-prone neurotic." The film's more sedate "Aunt Jemima" role was played by Hattie McDaniel, who was rewarded with an Academy Award for her portrayal of Mammy, the stalwart maid to Scarlett O'Hara.[31] Tradition and social customs trumped even Hollywood honors, however, as McDaniel was not allowed to attend David O. Selznick's premiere of his movie in an all-white movie house in Atlanta. The Peach State, of course, was the place where the modern Ku Klux Klan had been resurrected in 1915, soon after Hollywood released *The Birth of a Nation*, the silent film classic that vilified Negroes as plunderers and rapists and glorified as heroes these very same Klan vigilantes. Although a more benign race policy against Negroes was enacted in Michigan, the media nonetheless reinforced negative stereotypes with the radio drama *Amos 'n' Andy* voiced by white actors in vocal "blackface" reinforcing the audio stereotypes so omnipresent on the movie screen.

Thus, it was as the lone Negro teenager and a ward of the state that Malcolm engaged the student body of some three hundred white adolescents, who were reassured that his race was given to sloth, ignorance, and irredeemable inferiority. Despite being considered something of an oddball curiosity, Malcolm did not play to the stereotype form. The self-assured pride and equanimity with which Louise had imbued her children convinced fellow students early on, and some teachers down the line, that Malcolm was no adolescent Stepin Fetchit. Several white classmates interviewed decades later confirmed that he quickly shattered their home-tutored, Hollywood-reinforced preconceptions about their inaugural Negro classmate. However, their parents, teachers, and Mason adults in general, including the probate judges, court agents, and police, all kept in place the entrenched racial barricades against Negro progress and achievement.

In due course, Malcolm discovered, somewhat curiously, that those students who befriended him as an individual, much like the Swerleins, could still be biased against Negroes as a group. Often it went beyond simply a negative stereotype. After a touchy introduction, James Cotton, for example, remembered feeling a preordained superiority over Malcolm as a student in seventh and eighth grades, but not as a basketball player or tap dancer. Recalling, perhaps, Bill "Bojangles" Robinson in one of the contemporary Shirley Temple movies, Cotton once asked Malcolm if he could tap dance. Robinson was a dignified Hollywood hoofer who submitted to stereotyped minstrel review shows that had become popular among whites of the 1930s in a string of Shirley Temple movies, which played at the Mason movie house. Never one to shy away from attention, Malcolm said he could indeed tap, and Cotton bugged his classmate relentlessly until one day he finally put on a display, much to the delight of young Jim and other white students.

"I took tap dancing when I was a boy but never obtained the

skills that Malcolm had, by any means," recalled Cotton. "By the time I was in seventh grade, I was pretty much past that stage."[32] He did not initially consider Malcolm a peer beyond such stereotyped Hollywood theatrics. So it was with basketball, a sport Malcolm had played with mediocre results among Negro friends on the west side. At Mason, however, he was, on sight, anointed by whites as a highly gifted "natural"; the same thing happened with boxing. Malcolm played along with the positive athletic stereotype for the attention it brought him as a shining star at Mason Junior High. Students from all strata flocked to him.

"Malcolm played a leading role in installing the punching bag in our basement and was teaching me how to use it," said Rollin Dart, who grew up to become president of the family-owned Dart National Bank in Mason. "No one questioned Malcolm's credentials to teach people how to fight. We simply accepted that he could." Learning to box from a Negro mentor was an especially strong bonding point for young Rollin in this era of heavyweight champion Joe Louis, the successor of Jack Johnson, the world-renowned, pioneering black pugilist of the early 1900s. Anemic as a child, Dart had undergone an appendectomy and a mastoidectomy complicated by a heart murmur. His weakened physical condition attracted a swarm of school-yard bullies. Up to age twelve, he recalled, "I took beatings—got chased home from school—from a variety of boys, either my age or four years older. My size and condition gave me no choice but to take the beatings and keep a 'bloody' upper lip." However, "Malcolm came along, and we became friends at a critical time in my growing up. I was determined to pick off these bullies one at a time regardless of age or size, and have my just revenge, and my new friend was determined to be my mentor, advising me on strategy with each upcoming opponent."[33]

A half century later, Dart "vividly" recalled one particular vengeance match when Malcolm gave him advice in real time. The boy Dart was fighting "had me down and was sitting on top of me attempting to pin me. Malcolm was trying to tell me—amid all the hollering going on from the many that were there—just what to do at that moment, what hold I could use to remove myself from the spot I was in. And, standing above me, looking down, he put his body in such an agonized-appearing condition—trying to show me what to do from a position I could relate to. He was trying to show me what to do but was afraid that I would interpret it in a reverse manner because of our different positions. I shall never forget it."[34]

This anecdote from childhood might stand as a metaphor for the frustrations the adult Malcolm would later express about his attempts to communicate political, social, and even religious maneuvers Negroes should use to extricate themselves from holds that white America had locked on them over the centuries. Within Malcolm's adolescent world at Mason, his white classmates seemed to be peeling away negative stereotypes of Negroes as they related to him as a true friend. Malcolm was a year or so older, having repeated a grade. He was taller, streetwise and, now with regular meals at the Swerleins, heavier. Ever eager to please, the state-ward teenager felt accepted by his classmates and quite happy as the center of attention. Overall, Malcolm was just plain "special" to the white kids in the neighborhood who sought his friendship. "He had a very special way of throwing his head back and breaking out with that broad grin," said Rollin Dart. "He had a didactic way about him but only in the kindest, caring way. My mom liked him, and he was able to have dinner with us several times."[35] This was no easy concession back then for a prominent ruling-class family such as the Darts, who lived in a small, stratified society that was quite class conscious, aside from being overwhelmingly white.

Sometimes the friendships got competitive, as with Jim Cotton. "We were both doing well in school. If he wasn't the top guy, it often was me," said Cotton, the son of a local National Guard official.[36]

At least two reliable sources contended that Malcolm was definitely among the top five in his eighth-grade class, even though not all transcripts could be located. As is so often the case, however, this assessment may hint of adolescent male posturing, even in distant remembrance. A female student Malcolm cited as a third contender for "topmost scholastic honors" in his autobiography disavows any such acclaim for the trio. "I think that's a bit exaggerated," said Audrey Slaught, who recalled that she "was an average student" (her transcript supports that). Even if she was not contending for top scholastic ranking, Slaught was cited by some as vying among the girls for Malcolm's adolescent affection. She did not deny this charge. In fact, several decades later, Slaught proclaimed her admiration for the only Negro at her school. "I remember that Malcolm was a nice kid," she said. "It was not beyond me to associate with him."[37]

The mother of Audrey Slaught had recently been widowed, and she differed from most white parents in Mason, including Audrey's deceased father, who flatly forbade their children to associate with the new "nigger" at school. "Some people just wouldn't have anything to do with him because he was black," said Slaught. There was an unspoken prohibition against white girls dating Negroes, but as he had in Lansing, Malcolm stood willing to flout the rules if the female could evade the iron-clad resistance of her father—most of the girls who dared even associate with Malcolm had only a single parent, a mother. Slaught and a few other such girls and boys enjoyed Malcolm's company singly and in groups after school hours. "We would walk down the street with him, and classmates would ask: 'Why would you do that?' At that time in our lives, we couldn't figure why people were like that."

Slaught continued, "Malcolm was tall for his age, [and] I'm tall. I had to look up for him, which was unusual for me. There weren't that many tall boys around." School-yard rumors had it that Audrey was drawn to the lanky Malcolm for his size as well as for his smarts and charm.[38] In addition to his height, Jim Cotton noted pointedly that Malcolm was "handsome" and that "the girls liked him." Also, Malcolm's accepted athletic prowess, Cotton added, increased his popularity above that of most other students at school.

"I nominated Malcolm for class president," said Cotton, the Army brat, "then I campaigned for him. He was very popular, so it wasn't a problem." Malcolm won the election and Cotton recalled that "he had the smarts and the personality of a good leader. He was willing to serve, to give of himself—that's all part of leadership, too. Malcolm was popular in the study hall, on the playground, before and after school. He would have chores to do at home [with the Swerleins], he wasn't usually available at nights, but none of us were at that particular time, in this particular town."[39] As an adult, Jim Cotton would rise to the rank of colonel in the U.S. Army and would brag to fellow officers about growing up with Malcolm, even when his former classmate was widely branding all whites as "blue-eyed devils."

"Malcolm's natural leadership ability was prevalent from my first meeting him right on through," said his friend steeped in the military appreciation of skills. Years later, "I read about him 'as a national figure' in the *Stars and Stripes* [military newspaper]. I was not surprised."[40] While underscoring support of Malcolm's leadership qualities as eighth-grade class president, some of the women interviewed, like Slaught, were attracted by other qualities. "I liked him," said another Audrey, who became the wife of Jim Cotton, and who was in Malcolm's biology class. "I thought he was interesting. He was good fun."[41]

Asked if she agreed with her husband's assessment that the white Mason Junior High girls found Malcolm handsome, Audrey demurred. "I don't know how to answer that because to me he certainly was not ugly. I didn't see that many black people, so whether he was considered good-looking, I can't answer that." However, there was no question that Audrey thoroughly enjoyed his company. "We went to movies, but it was a very small town. We'd have parties with record players and invite the boys and girls over. We didn't have dance halls, but we had movie theaters. And we'd hang out at the drugstore [soda fountain], he liked that a lot. Malcolm talked a lot, but he listened, too."[42]

Sometimes the teenagers would repair to Slaught's house after school. "We had a piano; we'd play and we talked," Audrey Slaught recalled. "My mother had no qualms about that. That's why Malcolm would come; it was all right with her."[43] Within the small group of junior high students, the two were reported as something of an item as these things went back then among Midwest adolescents.

When pressed decades later, Slaught would admit to enjoying Malcolm's company most when they were one-on-one. "I was less comfortable when he was with a group of people. I remember that we had big discussions on all kinds of things. He liked to do that. He'd ask, 'Where do you want your life to lead you to?' I wanted to go to college and become an interior decorator; he knew that he could never fathom to go as far as further education."[44] Students in Mason, when questioned years later, conceded that society simply was racist, that it flatly denied Negroes the chance to achieve lofty goals that were routinely expected of white students. Faced with stiff adult resistance to professional careers for blacks, coupled with low expectations from their peers, it was not uncommon for Negro students either to trim their ambitions, often with the nudging of parents, or simply to keep them secret from associates—and even siblings.

Not one to follow the norm even at this early stage, Malcolm dared against the odds to dream of becoming a professional man of respect. He did not share this ambition with his good friend Audrey, or even his siblings for he likely saw no need to hear them laugh it off. Thus he reserved his career aspirations for those with a need to know and the means to assist. One such gatekeeper, in fact, approached him about whether he'd been "thinking about a career." So Malcolm shared his guarded, junior high ambitions with what he called a "natural-born 'advisor,'" his white English teacher, who had given the impression that he cared about Malcolm and who had given him good grades. According to the *Autobiography*, it did not go well.

In a classroom alone with this advisor (pseudonymously called Mr. Ostrowski in Malcolm's book), Malcolm said, "I've been thinking I'd like to be a lawyer." The mustachioed teacher looked surprised, if not shocked.

"Malcolm, one of life's first needs is for us to be realistic. Don't misunderstand me, now. We all here like you, you know that. But you've got to be realistic about being a nigger. A lawyer—that's no realistic goal for a nigger. You need to think about something you *can* be. You're good with your hands—making things. Everybody admires your carpentry shop work. Why don't you plan on carpentry? People like you as a person—you'd get all kinds of work."[45]

This kind of wing-clipping moment, experienced by bright black students with high aspirations, was almost universal in twentieth-century America. At the time, and even years later, Malcolm considered Mr. Ostrowski as white society's gatekeeper, much like the movers and shakers at the Swerleins who were charged to keep Negroes "in your place."[46] Accordingly, he wrote, "I doubt that he meant any harm." The teacher's racist rejection of his student's dream profession was made worse by the substitute suggestion. Carpentry had been the very craft his father Earl had struggled with during those years of job rejections, "Negro pay scales," union banning, and flatlining from the time of his son's birth in Omaha until his untimely death on the Lansing rail tracks some six years earlier. Mr. Ostrowski's comment would have come as no surprise to his older siblings, since their mother, Louise, had warned about misguided white teachers targeting them as dartboards for scholastic demoralization and a dead end.

Consequently, Malcolm did not discuss this dramatic encounter with his siblings, not even Wilfred, who had, of course, encountered similar dream-killing attempts almost as a matter of routine during his school days. Subsequently, upon hearing his account, his white buddies in Mason were not surprised at the cold-heartedness of Mr. Ostrowski, whose real name, Malcolm's classmates revealed, was Richard Kaminska.[47] Yet word drifted back to Malcolm from white classmates that the English teacher had been very supportive with them, and that he enthusiastically "encouraged whatever they had wanted" to pursue by way of further education or careers. White students remembered Kaminska as a tall, brusque, "Prussian-like disciplinarian" with strong opinions, who was feared and despised as an unrelenting "tyrant."[48] However, the influential teacher had clout in the community and his recommendations were informed and could not be taken lightly.

Although the Littles were not middle-class and Malcolm would have been the first to attend college, lawyers had been a vexing part of his family's wrangling with insurance companies, schools, and family court. His father's work with the UNIA in the Midwest had brought Malcolm in contact with a few Negro attorneys, although none came to his mind as a role model. However, the courtroom power and drama were just the kind of forces that would constantly attract Malcolm throughout his life. Nevertheless, despite Malcolm's smarts, class standing, grades, and his exceptional ability to beguile others, all the while expressing himself, Kaminska, this stalwart gate-keeper at Mason Junior High School, was forcefully counseling that his eighth-grade student shut down all such aspirations for the bar—because, alas, he was a "nigger."

Malcolm took it hard. A sense of dread and alienation began to roll in and blunt the young redhead's ambitions. "It was then that I began to change—inside," he reported later. Even the Swerleins, kind souls that they were, appeared as a part of the problem. Ulti-mately, an adult Malcolm, looking back, wrote that they were incapable of considering that he had the "same sensitivity, intellect, and understanding that they would have been ready and willing to recognize in a white boy in my position."[49] Already, he had followed up on his half sister Ella's invitation to visit Boston by writing her several times a week. Finally, the fifteen-year-old coaxed her into financing a trip to Boston in the summer of 1940. Wilfred might have offered further caution about their half sister, but they had fallen somewhat out of touch.

Upon Malcolm's arrival by train at Back Bay Station, Ella noticed that he appeared to have been crying "like a little boy," but he assured her that these were tears of joy. "He looked like a bleached-out blond," his older sister recalled years later. "He didn't look like anybody else in the family. They were darker. His hair was standing up all on his head, knotty, and red, yellow. I was looking for him to be congenial in every way, with his mind wide open. And we could do things together, work together, plan, use our brain together. And grow." During Wilfred's own Boston stay, he had been repulsed by Ella's "plan," but she held out hope for his younger brother. En route to her home, Ella's well-mannered brother jumped off the streetcar to return a pocketbook a stranger had dropped. "God is going to bless you," the white woman told Malcolm with a hug and a kiss.[50] Quickly falling into the household routine, the younger brother would get up early and walk Ella's dog around Franklin Park, admiring statues like the Crispus Attucks Monument on Boston Common, and the historic buildings of one of the nation's oldest cities. He made young friends about town and met the extended clan up from his father's hometown in Georgia.

The Lansing teenager was exhilarated by the neon lights of the New England city and the hip Negroes in fancy cars, partying into the wee hours in nightclubs, pool halls, and glitzy bars around Roxbury. It's a good bet that Malcolm caught sight of Ella's netherworld dealings about town. However, unlike Wilfred, he was swooning with "my mouth hanging open." Sizing Malcolm up that summer, Ella concluded that he was quite smart, open-minded, and frugal. She noted that "he would take a quarter and save it for weeks" and finally recalled, "I detected a young boy that wanted to fit into my world." Similarly, throughout his *Autobiography*, Malcolm gave his half sister a clean, though vague, bill of approval that first summer: "Ella was busily involved in dozens of things."[51]

Upon his return to Michigan, Malcolm was released from the foster care of the Swerleins and placed with the Lyonses, one of the two black families in Mason, who had five children of their own. While finishing eighth grade, he sneaked even more frequently into the west side of Lansing. It would be his last stint in school, his dropping out reflecting the pattern of the day, when fewer than 20 percent of Negro adults completed the eighth grade, according to 1940 census figures. Only 4 percent had finished high school and fewer than 2 percent were college graduates, with most of those having earned degrees from historically all-Negro colleges and universities, largely in the South.

Maturing faster than his peers, the tall and slender Malcolm, aglow from his Boston stay, projected an even greater maturity in chats with Philbert, still his key family rival. He took particular delight in boasting of a worldly, macho sexuality over his reserved and religious older brother, who noted this sharp change especially after the Boston visit. "Malcolm was always glad to show me he'd learned something I didn't know," Philbert recalled. "He was drawn to girls earlier than me." He would brag often that he "wanted to lay some pipe [have sex with a girl]. This wasn't even on my mind." And he would rattle off a string of naughty pickup lines, such as "I'm not the plumber or the plumber's son, but I can fill your hole until the plumber comes."[52]

Impressed by the boldness of it all, Philbert still doubted that his brother was as sexually active as he claimed. "In those days, sex among teenagers was not played up the way it [would be later]. You would talk to a girl, you would put your arms around her, and sex just wasn't a thing that happened. There was a lot of exaggeration. And sometimes Malcolm was a master of letting silence rule. If you were to say that 'so and so happened,' he knew just how to act to make you really think, well, that's what happened. He had a façade about him all his life."[53]

Philbert noticed another trait in his brother. Malcolm was "souring on black people," he recalled. "He would say that the only thing a black woman can do for me is to show me which way a white woman went."[54] The Lyonses had imposed a curfew on Malcolm, but he still spent most of his time back on the streets. Although they didn't see the wild behavior for themselves, word did drift back to the Lyonses that their foster child was flouting one of the city's most implacable rules: he was openly dating white girls, and even holding hands with them in public. The god-fearing couple, who appeared to fear white residents more, worked mightily to protect the reputation of their family from Malcolm's outrageous social behavior. A court petition followed, and Malcolm was shuttled to the home of a less subservient black family in Mason, a couple without children.

As the more restrictive walls of the Midwest closed in on fifteen-year-old Malcolm, he busied himself writing letters. He wrote Ella "every day" after the summer visit, "to tell me about himself." He had left a good impression. Ella thought "he would fit neatly" in "with my level of society."[55]

"Ella never liked the idea that Malcolm was in the hands of white people," said Wilfred, referring to the Swerleins. "She made arrangement with the court to release Malcolm to her." Malcolm was surprised and greatly delighted that state custody was transferred from Michigan to Ella's care in Massachusetts. Days before his impending trip, "Malcolm was all in the streets of Lansing," his brother remembered, "talking to everybody, saying, 'I'm on my way to Boston.'"[56]

# CHAPTER 6

# Lighting Out for His Territory

THE WINTRY LANDSCAPE UNFOLDED BEFORE YOUNG MAL-
colm, while he catnapped between cigarettes in the rear of the
Greyhound bus rumbling along the two-lane highways. As the driver
maneuvered the "Super Coach" on the dogleg route around Lake
Erie, headed for Boston more than eight hundred miles away, the
fifteen-year-old was thrilled about his own private Great Migration,
although saddened by the thought of leaving friends and family
behind. Interstate bus travel in the United States had only recently
surpassed rail traffic, and Greyhound had plowed some of the profits into nifty, new art deco stations dotting the scenic route. Freeing
himself from restrictive house rules back in Mason, the teenager was
brimming with aspirations for a fresh start with his high-achieving
half sister in New England.

The implosion of his dream to become a lawyer silently nagged
at him. The Midwest had frustrated his father and unnerved his
mother. For Malcolm, Lansing held out prospects only for a stint as
a Negro waiter, likely at a country club, or "some other menial job."
Smarter in some ways than his siblings, and undoubtedly bolder, this

fourth-born child of Earl and Louise Little remained determined to make his way in life not by his hands—but by his wits. Ella may have sensed this ambition: like Louise, she fancied herself psychic and was cocksure that, if properly guided, Malcolm was headed for greatness.

His west side friends had other ideas. Before Boston emerged as a possibility, they figured that Malcolm would someday skip down the road to Detroit. With his Michigan years not nearly as dull as the *Autobiography* might suggest, the redheaded risk taker had hit the Lansing streets at age twelve. Later, skirting detention-house rules in Mason, his derring-do was so great that even his older, hell-raising associates begged off some of his capers. It was not so much a doorman's job or a shoeshine stand that his buddies saw in Malcolm's future but rather the prison tier, and beyond that, most likely, they agreed, an early grave. With few lucky exceptions, that's just the way American life in the 1940s was engineered for bold, highly intelligent, fast-tick Negro men without a support system—even those who wanted to become lawyers. And Malcolm was nothing if not ambitious. "I thought that eventually he would get in big trouble," said John Davis, who ducked out of committing all but the lesser misdemeanors with his street pal. "I never committed any big crimes with Malcolm because I didn't have anybody to speak up for me. They may give me three or four days in jail if I was caught, and that'd be it."[1]

Hell-bent on attracting attention, Malcolm was a daredevil of the sort who, upon surviving a jump from the second floor, would mount the stairs for a leap from the third. In addition, beneath his veneer of antisocial conduct, Malcolm still harbored a family-inspired, Garveyite resistance to white folks who traduced the rights of Negroes. "Malcolm was game," said Davis, "and there was a lot of racism around here. I figured he would get tied up with that and eventually get killed here."[2]

Instead, Malcolm was headed to the family safe haven in Boston that he had peppered Ella Collins to provide. The Midwestern siblings he left behind worried that Malcolm might run astray as something of a prodigal son. They had had hopes for their brother's tenure in Mason and were concerned that the journey east would hamper his rehabilitation. Their apprehension was not without foundation, given Wilfred's experience, at age eighteen, with the Boston side of the family. Before Malcolm left, Wilfred warned him again about the lures of the Roxbury streets, and most particularly about the criminal bent of their half sister. "I let him know what Ella was into," Wilfred said, "but it didn't make no difference."[3] Wilfred had taken a job in Boston to help support his mother and younger siblings, but Malcolm made it clear that his East Coast sojourn would be altogether different. This Brer Rabbit was headed for the Briar Patch of legend, fraught with dangers for others but a natural habitat for the young man living by his wits.

"He told me that his reason for leaving Lansing was because he wasn't going to be a janitor, or no ditchdigger," Wilfred recalled. "He was going out there to see what the possibilities were. Guys from Boston and New York always had money and clothes. They always had some kind of hustle—meaning they were [working] something other than those nigger jobs. Malcolm said he was going to look things over and see what he could get involved in."[4]

Upon Malcolm's arrival in Boston, Ella welcomed him this second time to her flat at 89 Harrishof Street.[5] In 1941 the Massachusetts capital was strictly divided by neighborhoods, as mentioned earlier, and she gave her brother a few idle weeks to find his way around town, so that he could explore the rail system, the traffic and the rhythms of the Roxbury boulevards, as well as those of Dorchester and the forbidding Irish neighborhoods of South Boston. These latter enclaves were noted for their aggressive, territorial street gangs who would occasionally attack Negroes on sight if they wandered into the gangs' exclusive areas. In fact, the Irish Catholics themselves were still something of an outcast group. As Malcolm sized up the city, Ella took her own measure of her new house guest. She had her plans for this man-child of promise; Malcolm had his.

On previous occasions, Ella had paid train fare for relatives visiting from Georgia and introduced several of them to the shady side of the city. Wilfred, by happenstance, had managed to divert one such prospect by financing a cousin's trip to Boston himself. Upon discovering how little the hardworking relative earned in Georgia, Wilfred advised him to snip his debt-peonage ties to the white landowner. This cousin departed by bus on a Sunday morning, which was the escape pattern, so as not to alert the churchgoing white landowners about his departure. Otherwise, the sheriff would likely have been called in to apprehend and brutalize the sharecropper as an example to other hopelessly indebted Negroes daring to take their dirt-cheap labor north. After landing a job, this cousin sent for his wife and children, and later a brother and their mother; all of them sneaked away on a later designated Sunday. In due course, the transplanted Georgia family, Wilfred said, bought a three-family house in Roxbury, fared quite well, and, having escaped Ella's influence, lived within the law. "By getting my cousin out, I got all of them out," Wilfred said. "Every time I would come to Boston, you would have thought Jesus had come to town."[6]

Unlike these religious relatives, his little brother, Wilfred calculated, would hasten to the web of street hustling that Ella had spun during the worst of the Depression. At about the time Malcolm arrived, however, Ella was turning increasingly respectable. Even before Pearl Harbor, the onset of war abroad had created a domestic shortage of white civilian manpower—opening up jobs in the business and labor market previously denied Negroes. Ella's shadier dealings gave way, somewhat, to more legal pursuits. The underground economy became more an expediency than a full-time career. Always prudent with finances, she turned increasingly to real estate investments, starting with a new two-and-a-half-story home at 72 Dale Street. She moved in there and set Malcolm up with a kitchenette flat on the attic level, complete with a hot plate. Imbued with the real estate drive of their common father, Ella had recently bought this house in a predominantly Jewish section of Roxbury called Elm Hill, which the newcomers rechristened Sugar Hill, shortened in conversation to "the Hill." Longtime residents were just beginning their flight into exclusive Brookline. "I was on the Hill," Ella said of her Roxbury home. "Those [Negroes] who didn't live on the Hill were trying to get on the Hill. We had one goal in mind, 'conquer the Hill.'"[7]

During her scramble, Ella had maneuvered for divorce settlements from two gainfully employed ex-husbands, starting with her first, who reportedly was a physician. Along the way, she schemed to hold on to whatever portions of family inheritance that could be snatched away from inattentive relatives. The extralegal acts that she engaged in during Malcolm's time seemed likely to have been a matter of sustaining old habits, paying the help, or replenishing a downturn in cash flow. Nonetheless, with a keen eye for talent, Ella held high hopes for her ambitious half brother. Despite her own achievements, she had been unable to gain acceptance by the "proper Boston Negroes," who tended to be lighter-skinned and who sought white acceptance while looking down on darker-complexioned members of the race, especially the Southern-born. It did not escape Ella's attention that Malcolm was not only aggressively intelligent but also was light-complexioned like his mother, and like their common paternal grandmother, Ella.

Ella said that being light-skinned "was crucial if one was to appeal to most of Boston's so-called Negro society," wrote Rodnell Collins, Ella's son, in his book *Seventh Child: A Family Memoir of Malcolm X.* "No matter how committed and able a dark-skinned person was, he or she would find it extremely difficult, if not impossible, to appeal to most color-obsessed Boston Negroes."[8]

Throughout her life, Ella maintained that she initially saw her eighth-grade-dropout brother becoming a lawyer. But Wilfred and other family members say that more likely she saw a common spirit in the smooth-talking operator who—unlike her string of husbands—had the chutzpah to tie whatever licit or illicit loose ends were needed to close a big-time score for her in Boston.

As part of her embrace, Ella harped upon the folklore mystique attached to Malcolm as their father's seventh child. Wilfred dismissed her numerological doting as self-serving theatrics that cloaked strictly commercial ambitions. This seventh-child nonsense, he said, "was something special when she wanted to use that. Ella would use anything when she's trying to influence a person."[9] The older half sister left no doubt that she intended to bring Malcolm under her influence and mold him into a Sugar Hill man of respect within the parameters of what she—but not necessarily the law-abiding community (and by no means, the dreaded White Man)—considered respectable.

Malcolm, she calculated, would "fit in perfectly" with her level of society. "He looked like a Little, talked like a Little, and measured up to a Little in every way," Ella recalled years later, even though his light skin and red hair were unusual in her family. "I detected a young boy wanting to fit into my world. Why, I don't know." She said that "Dad wanted Malcolm to be a minister." Other family members, including Malcolm, knew nothing of this. Her world, of course, was not exactly of the religious life she imagined that their father would have preferred for each of them.

Early on, however, Ella did steer her brother toward religious services in nearby Roxbury churches, and he played along—at least until it was clear that his stay in Boston was permanent. As a committed disciplinarian, she attempted to lay down the law for her half brother who boarded in the clean, sparse room upstairs. "I had built up a list of duties for him to perform daily," Ella said. Eager to please,

Malcolm fell into the routine of housework, walking the dog, and washing the family car, and "he put that [those chores] before anything else," she noted.[10] Occasionally, Ella reportedly would send Malcolm out to shop for grocery and household goods—sometimes, as was her wont, without money.

At about the same time, Malcolm accepted a part-time job in an uncle's auto-parts shop, a deal that, as with most such family employment, entailed hard work and irregular pay. This would not do for the young thoroughbred already champing at the bit in his sister's home. Taking advantage of Ella's frequent out-of-town trips, Malcolm would throw house parties for a growing clutch of new friends. And, ever the inveterate scribbler, he would occasionally leave notes of apology for soiled rugs and broken dishes.

When recounting his Boston experience in the *Autobiography*, Malcolm describes his early interactions with a man named "Shorty." Upon retracing his steps and comparing the traits and actions attributed to this Shorty, it appears certain that the character was not a single individual but a composite of several persons whom Malcolm encountered during those days. Such shorthand devices, as well as the exaggerations, borrowed from the fiction genre used by Malcolm's coauthor, Alex Haley, but are applied in the *Autobiography* here to speed along the subjective recounting of real-life events. In Malcolm's case, the act of embroidery was so ingrained in his frenetic and not always sober life on the streets that artifice could hardly be filtered from reality. Multiple sourcing with participants and observers by fair-minded biographers also has its limits, of course, yet the current effort of double checking with primary sources, enhanced by official records where available, seeks to render a more accurate account of important matters during this and other key periods of Malcolm's life.

The man whom the Shorty character most embodied, at critical points along the way, was Malcolm Jarvis, a Boston native. Since childhood, Jarvis had played the trumpet, misidentified in the *Autobiography* as a saxophone, and he was indeed Malcolm's closest real-life street buddy and ultimate partner in crime. The Shorty character's name evolved not from Jarvis's height—he was a six-footer—but from slang of the day. As the lone car owner in the group, Jarvis drove Malcolm and other buddies around town in what was then dubbed a "short," as in "whose short are we taking?" Jarvis's late-model Ford, and later his Buick Roadmaster, made the buddies' trip "shorter." He said Malcolm told him, "I'm not going to use your name," but he first heard of Shorty upon reading the *Autobiography*. "He always called me 'Jahrvis,' with that Midwestern drawl," Malcolm Jarvis recalled.[11]

A secondary embodiment of the Shorty composite was a half brother whom Malcolm met immediately upon arriving in Boston. At six feet three inches, Earl Little Jr. was even taller than Jarvis. But he was similar to Shorty in age, in his suave, hip style, and in his conked or straightened hair. Earl Jr. was the third born of Earl's children by his first wife, Daisy Mason, and was Ella's younger brother. Both siblings exercised what Wilfred considered the criminal tendency their father had warned about.[12] By age sixteen, Earl Jr., for example, was serving his second stint in reformatory school. There he likely polished the skills that had him shuttling between prison and the streets in 1941, when, at age twenty-four, he met his half brother Malcolm, living in Roxbury on Sugar Hill with Ella.

A third contributor to the Shorty montage was Kenneth Collins, Ella's husband. Collins had known Malcolm's older brothers back in Lansing before he moved to Boston and married Ella in 1941. Like Collins, the pool hall Shorty was from Lansing. Thus it was likely Collins who, upon meeting Malcolm, greeted him as Shorty does in the book: "My homeboy! Man, gimme some skin! I'm from Lansing."[13]

As the lone trending outlaw from Earl's second family, Malcolm had, as described earlier, drifted off with the street element back in Lansing. His Midwest siblings felt that such straying contributed directly to the breakdown of their widowed mother. Wilfred, Hilda, and even Philbert, who did a bit of drifting himself, agreed whole-heartedly that Malcolm's break from the discipline of the Little household would not have occurred had Louise been backed up by the iron will, and the leather belt, of her husband. "You can bet" Malcolm would *not* have rebelled against "Dad," said Wilfred, with the finality of a locked gate.[14] Thus it seems certain that, more than with the other children, the father's death had a powerful, albeit negative, effect upon the early direction of this favored son.

In Boston now, under the gravitational pull of his half sister and half brother, Malcolm was primed to spin even further from the straitened orbit of his Garveyite family back in Michigan.

———

Much to Ella's disgust, her intended protégé began to hang out with Earl Jr., Collins, and Jarvis, all sporty young men-about-town who were considerably older than he was. Although he was living on Sugar Hill, Malcolm felt more at home in the "valley" below the Hill among the pool sharks, pimps, hustlers, and plain old hardworking Negroes, all pinching a bit of weekend escapism from the rigors of menial-class striving at such spots as the Hi-Hat, the Savoy, and Wally's Paradise. The bars, pool halls, nightclubs, barbershops, and beauty shops, along with some scattered storefront churches, made up the tight black ghetto community of Boston. One night early on at the Roseland State Ballroom, "Freddie the shoeshine boy," as he's called in the *Autobiography*, handed off his stand inside the second-floor men's room to young Malcolm. Freddie, who was said to have hit the number for a big score, was actually Kenneth Collins, Ella's husband. With the help of Freddie/Kenneth and Shorty/Earl Jr., Malcolm got his hair painfully conked—straightened with a burning lye-based poultice—a process dramatically described in the book. (Later, with the cash rolling in, Malcolm had his hair conked professionally at a barbershop on Tremont Street.) He also talked his way into an introductory tour of the Boston entertainment world. This was the kind of nightlife he had longed to savor and then master.

"At the far end, under the rose-colored lights, was the bandstand with the Benny Goodman musicians moving around, laughing and talking, arranging their horns and stands," Malcolm wrote.[15] Just as Goodman and Glenn Miller reminded Malcolm of the social rhythms of white Mason of his Michigan days, the Count Basie band took him back to the black west side of Lansing. Snapping off letters to friends back home on both sides of the racial divide, young Malcolm raved about having graduated from those house parties with 78-revolutions-per-minute wax recordings to up-close, in-the-flesh performances by the big-name jazz stars his schooldays crowd had lionized. And he made a point of ticking off the performers he'd seen.

"Boston is really 'jumpin.' Count Basie is here Thanksgiving nite, and Cab Calloway is here the following day," he wrote a girlfriend in Lansing.[16] "I'm working in a dance hall where all the large bands come, therefore I've seen quite a few of them," the sixteen-year-old wrote Zalma, a girlfriend in Jackson, Michigan.[17] "Since I left Mason," he told another, "I've seen Gene Krupa, Cab Calloway, Ella Fitzgerald, Glen [sic] Miller, Count Basie, 7 times, and I saw Tommy Dorsey and the Andrew [sic] Sisters."[18] The sporting side of Malcolm had him requesting photographs from the Lansing girls "to show the fellas out here that we have some fine girls in Michigan too."[19] Occasionally when writing street buddies, the teenager would brag slyly, and quite accurately, about the wild nightlife he was leading: "It's 3:30 a.m. and I just got in."[20]

Contrary to assertions in the *Autobiography* that before becoming a Muslim in prison, Malcolm "didn't know a verb from a house,"[21] the prose of his early 1940s letters was sharp and clear. Indeed, the teenage dropout was noticeably concerned about the syntax of his writing, the tone of his letters, and even his penmanship. "I hope you will be able to read this letter," he wrote to one friend, apologizing for his late-night scribbling, saying that "my writing will be poor & spelling wrong (funny line). . . . I will stop boring you now with this poor penmanship and bad spelling & sign off."[22] His stickler-for-language mother had laid the foundation starting in the first grade with Wilfred and her older children, and they had passed along her linguistic rigor to the younger siblings as a signature trait of the family.

Malcolm's steady shoeshine job was not exactly a respectable occupation in Ella's estimation. As he had with his mother and later with Hilda, he paid lip service to his big sister's iron rules and curfews, attending church spottily and even stooping to sing for a brief spell in the choir of the Townsend Street Baptist Church. This sop to Ella was in reality undertaken at the urging of Earl Jr., possibly as a way for Malcolm to round out his singing voice, which was not exactly a gift of beauty from the gods.[23] Ella thought otherwise. "He had a beautiful baritone voice," she recalled, one that could have "been developed into a great voice." His solo rendition of "The Lord's Prayer" she considered particularly moving. "A bunch of women in the choir, in the church were crying. The minister even referred to [Malcolm] as a 'woman crier.'"[24] His tear-inducing baritone, however, was not fit for solos on jazz standards, especially not when compared with Earl Jr.'s voice. So as one not given to singing backup, the unfulfilled soloist, whose heart was not really in it, dropped out of the Baptist choir and, in short order, gave up church altogether.

The gifted singer of the family, Earl Jr., performed as a nightclub jazz crooner under the stage name Jimmy Carlton. After Earl Jr. died of tuberculosis during Malcolm's first year in Boston, Malcolm would periodically attempt his act onstage. Although he never quite measured up, he adopted the crooner's surname, and sometimes went simply by "JC"—an alias he would use for the rest of his life.

Before any of that, however, this shoeshine boy began to slip out more and more to bars and nightclubs with Earl Jr. and Ella's husband, Kenneth. In addition to teaching his wife's half brother how to earn bigger tips by snapping the shoeshine rag like a firecracker, Kenneth showed Malcolm how a penny investment in a hand towel, to be passed at the faucet, could bring a nickel tip after he whisked the targeted customer with a cheerful brush. Embellishing such tricks with a little *Amos 'n' Andy*–style grinning with the whisk broom could earn extra coins, especially on nights featuring whites-only dances at the Roseland ballroom. On such nights, the sensuous voice of Peggy Lee, crooning over the melodic tones of the Benny Goodman Band, came wafting into the men's room during Freddie's other tutorials with Malcolm. The youngster mastered such finer points as buying shoelaces for a nickel and persuading white drunks on the stand that they needed a replacement pair for a quarter. Then there were the handy prophylactics for the guys who got lucky or the tipsy ones convinced that they just might.

Initially, Freddie avoided prepping Malcolm, who had been nicknamed East Lansing Red, on his postgraduate nightclub hustle that earned the big bucks. First, Malcolm had to blend in with the ballroom staff and learn how to distinguish the Boston street cops from legitimate potential customers. Freddie finally instructed Malcolm on how unescorted men desperately seeking booze and illicit reefers could invariably be talked into addressing another appetite. This pitch for sex, or for reefer for that matter, was not as unfamiliar to young Malcolm as he might have let on to Freddie. (He also withheld details of this experience from readers of his *Autobiography*.) On occasions back in Mason, white students, excited by the prospect of breaching this sexual taboo, had persuaded the glib teenager to proposition white girls, sometimes their own sisters. And Malcolm himself had escorted some of these same buddies into the netherworld of west side Lansing to experience another social taboo of the times: sex with streetwalking Negro hookers.

But Boston was a different matter.

Most of the dances at the Roseland were for whites only, but Negro shoeshine boys and band members were, by necessity, allowed in. Between shines, Malcolm took advantage of his exclusive access by collecting the phone numbers and addresses of roving pimps and slipping them along to white men in the club looking for "black chicks." His hustle as surrogate club pimp garnered him piles of greenbacks and, combined with his energy, earned him a reputation as a rising star on the illicit circuit. Social mixing of the two races was permitted at the Roseland on "Negro Night," when white men and their curious women would mingle with dusky nightclubbers until the wee hours. Most settled for the mere thrill of "slumming" with the "darkies," but, with the aid of alcohol, Malcolm would direct the more adventuresome of *both* genders to peel off with random escorts from across the color line. The white johns submitting to Malcolm's steering would often hit him up for a condom before heading off with a young, ebony lady to a secluded spot.[25]

The glamour of nighttime Boston swelled the teenager's head. It would nearly explode on star nights, when the freight train of global jazz luminaries came roaring by his shoeshine stand: Duke Ellington, click, Count Basie, clack, Lionel Hampton, click, Cootie Williams, clack, Jimmie Lunceford . . . Johnny Hodges . . . Jimmy Rushing, whooooo—weeee! And the shoeshine-boy hustler would meet many other such stars, including saxophonist Buddy Tate, Buck Clayton, and the inimitable Harry "Sweets" Edison.

Malcolm's half brother, Earl Jr., was his key connection to the stars. In his role as the tuxedoed singer Jimmy Carlton, Earl was a local standout. He often opened up the evening on stage for Billie Holiday and other touring jazz artists. According to his sister Ella, Earl had a fling with Lady Day whenever she performed in Boston. And of all the luminaries Malcolm met in this era of the big bands, he was most taken with Billie Holiday. The star was revolutionizing popular music with her tense and heartfelt rendering of jazz lyrics, none more explosive than "Strange Fruit," a bold protest poem against lynching. Despite family tales about the Klan terrorizing their pregnant mother and his belief that his father had been killed by racists, Malcolm gave little ear to the "blood on the leaves" lyrics of Holiday's 1939 hit. His favorite Billie Holiday tune was "All of Me," and when Earl Jr. introduced the famed jazz stylist to his younger brother, Malcolm was starstruck.[26]

In due course, the legendary jazz songstress would relate to Earl's younger brother from Lansing as family. When Malcolm later introduced his kid brother Reginald to Lady Day, she referred to Malcolm as "little brother" and thus helped erase Reginald's long held memory of Malcolm's embarrassing failure in the boxing ring back home in Lansing. Brother Philbert may have reigned in the ring, but Malcolm was king of the nightclub.

Once again, Malcolm was slipping the leash of the family curfew intended to get him home before midnight. Putting her foot down, Ella initially refused to allow Malcolm to go out. "He put on his crying act," his big sister recalled, saying "he's a fatherless and motherless child. And I let him go. That was the first and last time I tried to stop him."[27]

Occasionally, when Malcolm broke curfew, Ella would lock him out of his room, and he would spend what was left of the night downstairs with his aunt, Ella's sister Mary. When even this arrangement got out of hand, Ella would storm into nightclubs and sometimes wring him away from buddies like Malcolm Jarvis. More than once, his knot of associates included her own husband and brother. "I was really angry with Earl and Ken," Ella later told her son Rodnell Collins, who wrote *Seventh Child*. "They knew he was a minor, but they acted like two irresponsible teenagers themselves."[28] In his own book, Malcolm disguised the duo's identity to protect them, just as he draped Ella's illicit reputation in alleged respectability, keeping her illegal enterprises out of print. Despite all, Ella tried to steer Malcolm toward nice, respectable Sugar Hill girls his age. "Even before I came to Boston," he conceded, as the record clearly shows, "I had always felt and acted toward anyone my age as if they were in the 'kid' class, like my younger brother Reginald. They had always looked up to me as if I were considerably older."[29] So the man-child continued to sneak determinedly around Ella's objection and projected an older, much worldlier image.

As for Malcolm Jarvis, the dominant character in Malcolm's Shorty composite, the devoted jazz trumpeter housed no loftier ambitions than starting a band and playing the local Boston area. "I don't dig joining some big band, one-nighting all over just to say I played with Count or Duke or somebody," Shorty says in the *Autobiography*.[30] Unmentioned in the book is the fact that Jarvis was married to his childhood sweetheart during the entire time he and his buddy ran the streets together.

"Malcolm had quite a reputation," recalled Jarvis, who was two years older. "I had heard some of the teenaged girls up in Roxbury speak about this tall, light-skinned dude and how attractive he was. He didn't have his hair conked at that time."[31]

Jarvis had met Malcolm for the first time in a Humboldt Avenue pool hall. "He had on that herringbone black coat and a zoot suit on under it, and a wide brim hat," he recalled. The sky-blue suit, of the style worn by jazz singer and bandleader Cab Calloway, had been purchased on credit. It featured trousers fitted at the waist, some thirty inches wide at the knee and tapering severely to twelve-inch cuffs. Malcolm also sported a three-quarter length, single-breasted suit jacket extending to four inches above the knee. The suit was draped by a polished metal chain running from the waist, front and back, and curving at a point twelve inches from the ankle. "Malcolm wore these big clothes to fit a tall person, which made him look older than he really was."[32]

Unbeknown to Jarvis, the leather strap of his expensive Longines watch broke that first day, and the $125 timepiece fell to the floor. An onlooker scooped it up. "Being that Malcolm had a reputation for being slick," Jarvis said, "I accused him."

"Give it back," Jarvis commanded as he backed the sixteen-year-old against the wall. "Back in those days, I was pretty fast with my hands, a good fighter. Then somebody tapped me on the shoulder and said, 'Man, he doesn't have your watch; the cat that got it split.' Malcolm was taller than me, and thin. What he was going to do if I had hit him, I don't know. So I apologized, and that's when he and I became friends."[33] Although Malcolm cultivated the image of a tough guy, he remained as his family knew him early on: the guy who would defend himself when he had the advantage but would gladly leave the aggressive physical fighting to others. Jarvis's first impression as he pinned him against the wall was confirmed over the years as their relationship grew close.

"Malcolm was mostly a camouflage person," Jarvis said. "He portrayed an image that he could have underworld ties. That's the way he walked around Boston. People knew this cat was into something. Being so young, he got into the habit of talking with such a heavy voice to impress people that he was older. He had an expert choice of words. And he was not a violent man" out on the streets.[34] While Malcolm was certainly no choirboy, his earlier church experience in Boston, according to Ella, allowed him to associate with one fellow choir member who impressed her initially as a nice, proper Sugar Hill girl. Malcolm made no mention of this church connection in his book. Instead, he wrote that he met this "choir member" under entirely secular circumstances.

―――

After quitting the shoeshine stand (to the delight of his sister Ella), Malcolm landed a full-time job at the soda fountain of the Townsend

Drugstore, a few blocks from her home. Although he had performed such duties gleefully back in Mason, the soda jerk job title didn't sit well with him in Boston, at least not in retrospect. And he grew to resent the Sugar Hill Negroes putting on airs with their "black Bostonese." Having abandoned school himself, Malcolm did, however, notice a cute high school junior who came for a regular banana split that turned into a thirty-minute afterschool routine. This studious neighbor bore a resemblance to Malcolm's mother, Louise, according to Ella, which may have attracted Malcolm initially. She was also West Indian and seemed one of the more studious of the Sugar Hill girls. During the early weeks of their acquaintanceship, as she pored over the banana split and her textbooks, "heavy school stuff—Latin, algebra," Malcolm was moved to reflect on the fact that he "hadn't even read a newspaper since leaving Mason."[35]

The encounter with this Boston teenager inspired Malcolm so strongly that he would use her fictionalized name "Laura" as the one-word title of the fourth chapter of his autobiography. This respectable, long-haired, prim-and-proper girl reflected good breeding as well as a quiet determination to succeed. She was an honors student, who was being raised by a strict and pious grandmother following the breakup of her parents when she was a baby. No stranger to such a fate, Malcolm developed a fast relationship, strengthened by Laura's fondness for dance and Ella's great hope that he'd found himself a cultured Hill girl with high expectations. "I liked her," Ella confirmed. "He liked her. They had a lot in common. She had come here to [become] a nurse."[36] Jarvis remembered her as a cute "brown-skin" girl, whose complexion only deepened Ella's appreciation for the relationship. Early on, Laura tried bending the eighth-grade dropout her way, coaxing her older friend to return to school and pursue his stale dream of becoming a lawyer. Having none of that fondness for hard work and striving so reminiscent of his mother, Malcolm instead worked on pivoting Laura his way, easing her away from books, scholarship, and the rigorous pursuit of mainstream achievements.

Under Malcolm's influence, the college-bound student, who loved to dance, became looser laced and less studious. Lying to her grandmother, Laura began to sneak out and Lindy-hop the night away with Malcolm. Her redhead, soda-jerk partner was usually decked out in orange shoes and zoot suits of a voltage that slowed traffic on the Roseland dance floor, just as they did on the boulevards of Roxbury. The relationship of the star-crossed teenagers deepened, to the delight of Ella and the horror of the girl's grandmother. In due course, Malcolm grew wary of Laura and—as he had with his mother back in Lansing—flew the coop like the prancing rooster he longed to be. In his telescoped account in the *Autobiography*, they split up at the Roseland after a spirited dance tune. With Laura's lithe body flying in sync with his rhythmic feet, the spotlighted couple jitterbugged so triumphantly this one night that "even Duke Ellington half rose up from his piano stool and bowed."[37]

In the midst of the swirl, Malcolm wrote that he spotted a "fine blonde's eyes" leveling on him. Not one to procrastinate at such moments, his next dance was not with Laura but with the blonde, whom he called "Sophia" in the *Autobiography*. A few dances later, Malcolm reported rushing Laura home so he could return by taxi cab to the Roseland and take up with Sophia and the friend she was with. Malcolm ended up spending a great deal more private time with Sophia, at dance bars around Roxbury or parked roadside with nothing on "but the radio."[38] He would go on to maintain a four-year relationship with Sophia—in real life, Beatrice Caragulian, a dark-haired Armenian American—a relationship that would continue even after he left Boston and she got married.

Barely a further word was heard from Laura. She stopped dropping by the drugstore and fell completely out of Malcolm's social orbit. Estranged from her grandmother as a result of her enrapture with Malcolm, the confused teenager reportedly was rocked by the abandonment. The once college-bound bookworm experimented with hard liquor and drugs, subsequently rotating in and out of prison as a Roxbury prostitute, notorious man-hater, and, in Malcolm's words, "a wreck of a woman." This crash of the high school graduate, who had embodied the ambitions of his mother Louise, added to the wreckage that Malcolm was leaving in his wake. "One of the shames I have carried for years is that I blame myself for all of this," he wrote about Laura in his book.[39]

Similarly, his many childhood betrayals—including his having repeatedly stolen money that could have saved the Little family from severe poverty—were cited by his siblings as a factor in their mother's mental breakdown. Malcolm himself blamed "the Welfare [department], the courts, and their doctors" for crushing the family and institutionalizing his mother "as a statistic that didn't have to be." Louise would remain in the mental hospital until 1963, when she was released to live with family. She died in 1991, at the age of ninety-four. Still, the tragic collapse of Louise would remain a touchy matter throughout Malcolm's life. After 1952, he never visited her again. "I have rarely talked to anyone about my mother," he wrote, "for I believe that I am capable of killing a person, without hesitation, who happened to make the wrong kind of remark about my mother. So I purposely don't make any opening for some fool to step into."[40]

Upon learning of Malcolm's breakup with Laura, Ella blasted him for ditching the proper Hill girl—and most especially doing so for a Beacon Hill white woman. Her feelings about her half brother had soured. "I didn't like zoot suits," she said. "He was about six foot five and thin, very thin. He looked horrible in that monkey outfit. His hair was conked. He was a real honest-to-goodness mess. The crowds he was running with when he stayed off his job some nights were against the grain of what I thought he should be part of. I'd lost the battle."[41]

Indeed, all signs of the disciplined upbringing of his older siblings had dropped from the teenager, who was showboating for attention, as he shook off the telltale taint of the Midwest. Slipping the mooring of Ella's household, young Malcolm traipsed along the shadowy boulevards of Boston as if trying to fill some vacuum in his life, a void left perhaps by his mother—and most certainly by his father.

# CHAPTER 7

# Chased Out of Seventh Heaven

THE MENIAL JOBS THAT MALCOLM HAD RUN AWAY FROM IN Michigan caught up with him in Boston. The gig at the drugstore was soon followed by one bussing dirty dishes to the kitchen at the Parker House Hotel. This daytime job served to mask the teenager's illicit night hustling in pool halls and jazz clubs around town. But his host and sponsor, Ella Collins, was neither deceived nor amused. One Sunday morning her tardy-prone young brother reported so late to work at the hotel that he fully expected to get fired. Instead, Malcolm found the workplace rattled by global news reports blaring over the radio.

"The United States was suddenly and deliberately attacked by naval and air forces of the Empire of Japan," President Franklin D. Roosevelt said of the "date which will live in infamy."[1] The lives of all Americans were changed dramatically on December 7, 1941, as the nation entered World War II. Millions of men twenty-one years and older were drafted into military service to be dispatched to battlefields in Europe and Asia, where the Axis powers led by Germany, Japan, and Italy had been waging war against the Allied forces of the United Kingdom, France, Poland, the Soviet Union—and now the United States.

Despite his adult posturing, Malcolm was spared military conscription as a sixteen-year-old. The restless busboy found that the draft greatly improved his job opportunities. Shortly after the United States entered the war, Ella put aside her disappointments and contacted a friend, a real estate agent called "Old Man Rountree" in the *Autobiography*.[2] He was an official of the Brotherhood of Sleeping Car Porters, the railroad labor union organized in 1925 by A. Philip Randolph. Passing Malcolm off as a twenty-one-year-old, Charles Roundtree arranged a job for him on the New Haven Railroad. Ella hoped that this new position would get her half brother back on track and away from his nightclubbing crowd—most especially, her husband, Kenneth Collins, and the white woman Beatrice Caragulian.

The railroad job opened up new horizons for Malcolm, the most alluring being the chance to visit New York City, an impossible dream of his since childhood in Lansing. Friends of his father had regaled them with stories about Marcus Garvey extravagantly parading along the boulevards of Harlem, where his United Negro Improvement Association was headquartered. Photographs of throngs lining the uptown streets were splashed across black newspapers whenever heavyweight champion Joe Louis defeated yet another white opponent at Yankee Stadium. Malcolm had fantasized about Harlem as the fabled showcase for the jazz musicians whom his circle of friends idolized back in Michigan. Yet everything about New York City came with a prohibitive price tag for a lone Negro teenager squeaking by in Roxbury with odd jobs and petty street hustles. With this new railroad job, the unreachable star that was Harlem suddenly seemed within Malcolm's grasp. At first he loaded trains in the rail yard, but then he wangled a dishwasher job on the Colonial run to Washington, D.C., where on his few layovers, he toured the nation's capital.

But the rigidly segregated neighborhoods in this surprisingly quiet Southern town triggered no desire in him to make it his home base. Malcolm's heart was set on what the hipsters called the Big Apple.

————

The great day came with a temporary assignment as a sandwich man on the four-hour Yankee Clipper run to Grand Central Terminal— with a stay-over every other day in New York. Determined to make this job permanent, Malcolm catered to the mainly white travelers with the affected Pullman-porter manner of the pliant, ingratiating Negro, as popularized on radio and in the Hollywood films of the day. And just as he had when hawking shoelaces and marijuana at the Roseland ballroom, the teenager perfected a winning sales pitch, hawking snacks while gleefully bobbing up and down the aisles with a coffee urn on his back and a sandwich box about his shoulders. When the Yankee Clipper finally braked at Grand Central that first day, the neon swirl outside the station awakened within Malcolm the peripatetic spirit that had once animated his itinerant-minister father.

Along with a veteran cook from the train, Malcolm, decked out in his fresh zoot suit, taxied up to Harlem, where he absorbed the scene at the famed Smalls Paradise like the rush of a first hit of cocaine. The black gentry at play knocked everything he knew of barroom etiquette into a cocked hat. The Big Apple customers in conservative clothes sipped their cocktails in a "low murmur" instead of the "big noise" flash to which he was accustomed. Instead of bois-terous spontaneity, the Paradise crowd projected calm, calculating nonchalance. "They were not putting on any airs," Malcolm wrote in his *Autobiography*. "I was awed. Within the first five minutes in Small's, I left Boston and Roxbury forever . . . In one night, New York—Harlem—had just about narcotized me."[3]

On layovers during the following months, Malcolm explored the breadth of northern Manhattan, seeking out not only the strivers, the hip, and the fanciful, but also the staid, the city slick, and the dispossessed. Soon enough, he would discover Harlem's more lumpenproletarian brothers and sisters, by the tens of thousands, who were "just as loud and gaudy as Negroes anywhere else."[4] Buzzing the aisles of the Yankee Clipper like a salesman possessed, "Sandwich Red," as Malcolm was known on the railroad, secured his hold on his job with ease. Then he turned his eyes to what had been his main interest all along: Harlem.

A fairly recent development had turned central Harlem, with roughly a quarter million people, into a neighborhood that was 90 percent Negro. The area's borders, then and now, are Central Park and 110th Street on the south, the Harlem River on the north, Fifth Avenue on the east, and Edgecombe and St. Nicholas Avenues on the west. Although Negroes had resided in New York City as early as the seventeenth-century slavery days, they had been quartered mainly in the Wall Street area downtown. In the 1910 census, for example, central Harlem was only 9.89 percent Negro, and the dominant ethnic groups were Italian, German, and Jewish, the last from Russia and elsewhere. However, with the Great Migration of Negroes from the South, mixed with an influx from the Caribbean, Harlem demographics began to shift in tone and color. Driven north by terroristic lynchings in the South and by the search for jobs and better living conditions, black Americans streaming into New York City, which was then 98 percent white, were steered into upper Manhattan. As whites predictably began to move out, some power brokers attempted unsuccessfully to make a stand and stem the ebony tide. "The Negro invasion must be vigilantly fought, fought until it is permanently checked, or the invaders will slowly but surely drive the whites out of Harlem," read a July 1911 article in the *Harlem Home News*.

Starting in the 1920s, as the white flight of largely European immigrants yielded to the influx of Americans from the South, central Harlem began to experience a sustained cultural renaissance that defined a new and optimistic "black aesthetic." Writer and professor Alain Locke, the first African American Rhodes Scholar, became the architect of this largely literary "spiritual awakening" when he edited the 1925 anthology *The New Negro* and enticed the publishing industry to explore this "exotic" new market. Noted critic H. L. Mencken declared Locke's book of essays "a phenomenon of immense significance," with the Negro writers presented in *The New Negro* taking "a fierce sort of racial pride" in a declaration of independence.[5] Key writers of this intellectual movement, which became known as the Harlem Renaissance, included James Weldon Johnson, Zora Neale Hurston, W. E. B. Du Bois, Jean Toomer, Sterling Brown, Langston Hughes, Nella Larsen, and Countee Cullen. The fine-arts aspect of the movement was represented by such painters as Archibald Motley, Palmer Hayden and Aaron Douglas and the sculptors Augusta Savage and Richmond Barthe. And running parallel to the intellectual renaissance were the jazz artists who were staging their own creative, cultural movement.

By the time Malcolm arrived in Harlem, the intellectual renaissance had dimmed, but the continuing jazz scene was renaissance enough for the interloper from Boston. At the time, he was no more interested in black literature and the fine arts than he was in the *Daily Worker* newspapers that the Communist party hawked up and down the boulevards of Manhattan. This journal informed its readers about such issues as rent gouging, lynching in the South, civil rights, safe streets, rodent control, progressive politics, and questions of war and peace—all matters of substance that would be spared Malcolm's attention for another decade or so.

Increasingly, the teenager in the blazing zoot suit became a familiar figure at the Apollo Theatre, Smalls Paradise, the Theresa Hotel, and the Savoy and Renaissance Ballrooms, all uptown magnets. On overnight stays, he would rent a room at the 135th Street YMCA or at cheaper places farther uptown like Mrs. Fisher's rooming house. Roaming with a growing band of buddies, he explored upper Manhattan from "rat-trap apartment houses, just crawling with everything you could imagine that was illegal and immoral,"[6] up to New York's own Sugar Hill district, north of 145th Street, where Duke Ellington, Billie Holiday, Coleman Hawkins, and other stars resided. Throughout the war years, Malcolm moved between Harlem and Boston, occasionally skipping back to Michigan when things got hot. Hell-bent on flirting with depravity, he narrowly escaped death several times as a quasi-pimp, petty thief, cocaine hustler, and "traveling reefer peddler" for musicians on the road and junkies on the streets. Newspapers reported stories about bodies dropping all over the area that this fast and fearless risk taker covered. Some died from lethal weapons fire, knife fights, police shootings, or gangland abductions, while others succumbed to increasingly available cocaine and heroin.

After work on his railroad day job, Malcolm buzzed all smiles on the Harlem nightclub circuit, jitterbugging and Lindy-hopping his way to the very edge of the brightest of limelights. Working the clubs up front at the bar and the uptown theaters backstage, he cagily befriended jazz musicians and was edging in as a supplier of reefers in the city and on the road. Some of the artists he already had met in Boston, thanks to his half brother Earl Jr. and his musician buddy Malcolm Jarvis. But in Harlem, he noticed, everyone brought their A game, with stars such as Billy Eckstine, Sarah Vaughan, Billie Holiday, Dizzy Gillespie, Ella Fitzgerald, Dinah Washington, Lionel Hampton, Illinois Jacquet, and Dexter Gordon. One evening on 126th Street at the famed Braddock Hotel, Malcolm wrote, he tracked Dinah Washington into the night after overhearing that the star singer for Lionel Hampton's band was headed to her gig at the Savoy Ballroom, a Harlem spot "that made the Roseland in Boston look small and shabby by comparison." The Savoy was just the setting for Malcolm to dance a few rounds of Lindy-hop with girls from the crowd. About a third of its patrons were whites, who mostly stayed in their booths as observers. After a spirited rendition of Lionel Hampton's "Flying Home," Washington, a Tuscaloosa, Alabama, native, "tore the Savoy roof off" with "Salty Papa Blues." As he did with Billie Holiday, Malcolm would strike up a friendly relationship with Washington that attracted even more attention to the young Sandwich Red on the rise.[7]

"New York was heaven to me," Malcolm later noted in his *Autobiography*. "And Harlem was Seventh Heaven!" Less tuned to the Big Apple's virtues than to its wickedness, he wrote of a determination "to become one of the most depraved, parasitical hustlers among New York's eight million people."[8] And with purposeful exaggeration, he proceeded to make the case for depravity. Although on rocky terms still with Ella, Malcolm was most grateful for the railroad gig and sought ways to assuage his demanding sponsor. However, her maneuvering to get him to give up his Boston running buddies would meet with little success.

Initially, Beatrice Caragulian, his white Boston girlfriend, begrudged Malcolm's frequent out-of-town trips, but then she warmed to the idea under the misperception that the railroad job spared her supposed twenty-one-year-old lover from military service. Also, Malcolm began to invite Beatrice, an aspiring entertainer, to New York City on special occasions. As for Jarvis, their friendship preceded that of Beatrice, and it remained deeper and more solid. Jarvis, in fact, had been present the night that Malcolm had met the brunette Beatrice, who'd become the blond Sophia in the *Autobiography*. In a fuller, less dramatic, and somewhat different version of that first encounter—which actually took place in 1942 at the Savoy, a South End Boston Club, not at the Roseland—Jarvis remembered Malcolm making the first move, more typically the aggressor than the self-described respondent. When Beatrice pulled out a cigarette, Jarvis said that Malcolm rushed in to light it. Upon learning that she was an aspiring dancer-actress, Malcolm turned creative. "He's telling me that when we get back to Hollywood next week we're going to see Mr. So-and-So—to set this girl up for a screen test, talking like we're big Hollywood producers," Jarvis recalled. "This is jive, now. These girls were just sucking it up." Then Malcolm offered to buy Beatrice and her friend, Kora Mardarosian, a drink. "They sat there talking. That's how we met."[9]

Jarvis continued, "Malcolm was a sharp talker. The man was a con artist. He could talk you out of your last dollar and make you feel enthusiastic about giving it up. He had that charisma about him that was magnetic." That first night, however, the two young women were being escorted at the club by another man. "We didn't know they were with this singer, Charlie Harris. He's a light-brown-skinned dude," Jarvis said. After his last performance, Harris went across the floor to meet his date. But Malcolm and his pal ended up leaving with the young women. "We wound up taking the girls out of [the club]. And this guy Charlie was [steamed]," Jarvis said. "To this day he hasn't forgotten it." In fact, Charlie Harris discussed the incident decades later, confirming for the author that Malcolm indeed talked his girlfriend away from him at the club that night.[10]

"I followed Malcolm in my car over to [Beatrice's] house in Belmont," Jarvis said. "She had a nice car, a Cadillac. The woman had money." Beatrice was reportedly the stepdaughter of a Cambridge restaurateur. "She was one of those young, white girls out seeking adventure. . . . She had a gorgeous home. She had a beautiful playroom and a bar, downstairs. She gave us a nice wine and a couple cans of beer. Then Malcolm and I went home and left the girls there. And that's how it started out."[11]

The two Malcolms, Little and Jarvis, had by then struck up a lasting friendship. As with her brother and husband, Ella did not approve of Jarvis's influence; however, she admitted "he was successful. I couldn't change him as far as Malcolm was concerned."[12] A cousin, John Walker, who owned a parking lot, said, "They were very tight. You saw one, you saw the other." Each helped the other out in a pinch, Walker observed. "Malcolm worked for a while, had money coming in; he would split it with the other Malcolm. When the other Malcolm worked, he would share."[13]

As a chauffeur working for a union secretary, Jarvis had traveled around Boston with Malcolm to nightclubs collecting "traveling dues" from touring artists for Local 535 of the Boston Musicians Association. Jarvis's father, Clifford Jarvis, was a charter member of the union and the trumpet-playing patriarch of his Boston jazz family. (Jarvis's own son, also named Clifford, became an internationally known drummer, playing for such standouts as Herbie Hancock and Sun Ra.) The all-black Local 535 "took in half of downtown, all of Cambridge, Boston, Roxbury, Jamaica Plain," Malcolm Jarvis explained. "So any hotel like Ramada Inns, Holiday Inns, any ballroom like the Roseland, Taunton, Mass.—they had to pay us."

Jarvis said, "If there was any question about Malcolm entering a nightclub, he was a delegate of the union, coming in to oversee what's going on with the union, the money, to check their union cards. This is how I got Malcolm in these clubs for free. We used to go into ballrooms where Duke Ellington, Lionel Hampton, Count Basie, even Jimmy Lunceford were playing."[14]

After taking the railroad job, Malcolm stayed in touch with Jarvis when visiting Boston, and occasionally his buddy would visit him in Harlem. As for Beatrice, he passed up no opportunity to showcase her around Roxbury until the wee hours. Yearning for attention since his younger days in Mason, Malcolm had raised the bar for himself in Boston and Harlem. His wide-brimmed hats, orange shoes, and iridescent, loose-fitting zoot suits made him appear older and attracted sufficient attention. Beatrice, however, brought him a premium of another sort among the smart set, the "proper Negroes" of Roxbury.

Like his dark-skinned sister Ella, who despite her achievements and real estate holdings, had found it impossible to break the crust of Boston's Sugar Hill society, Malcolm, despite his hustling and his lighter skin tone, also felt walled out by the inner circle on the street. Squiring Beatrice around town three nights a week finally began to earn him "some real status in black downtown Roxbury." Walking into the bars with the wealthy young Bostonian, and with the word out that this Cadillac owner was "giving me the money I spent," Malcolm was set up at tables with drinks, patted on the back as Red, and essentially welcomed into the Roxbury Club by "the big, important black hustlers and smart boys—the club managers, name gamblers, numbers bankers and others." On his runs to New York City, Malcolm had to be content with the spectacle of his one-man zoot-suit parade—sans the Roxbury "status." "I'd go through that Grand Central Station afternoon rush-hour crowd and many white people simply stopped in their tracks to watch me pass," he wrote.[15]

On both ends of the four-hour commute, whether at Smalls Paradise, the Savoy or elsewhere, Malcolm claimed to ply himself with so much liquor and marijuana, on his $25 weekly salary (plus tips), that his behavior spun out of control. The jolly Negro acolyte had morphed into a wisecracking, often high, ill-tempered, railroad hawker precariously rustling a forty-five-pound coffee container through the rickety aisles. He was like an accident about to explode. The firing ax he had dodged on the day of Pearl Harbor now dangled over Malcolm's head at the New Haven job: "It was inevitable that I was going to be fired, sooner or later."[16] His release had been forestalled many times by a kindly, white steward from Maine named Pappy Cousins. But the growing list of complaints from customers and fellow staffers alike finally wore out the steward's patience, and seventeen-year-old Malcolm was fired in the fall of 1942.

As World War II intensified, the Selective Service System lowered the draft age from twenty-one to eighteen, and the mobiliza-
tion allowed only a short list of deferments: conscientious objectors,
men with young dependents, clergymen, and workers in jobs considered essential to national defense. Malcolm's older buddy Jarvis
hired onto such a job at the recently opened Bethlehem Hingham
Shipyard, which built destroyer escort ships and landing vessels for
the Navy. Malcolm, instead, began taking note of the medication,
the posturing, and the other ruses his otherwise military-eligible
buddies were devising to render themselves unfit either physically,
mentally, or morally. With no steady cash flow and despite having
been fired, Malcolm was still able to use his free-travel train privilege
on return trips to Michigan to visit his scattered family and to work
temporary jobs.

The younger siblings were still residing with their foster parents,
the McGuires and the Williamses, and except for four-year-old Robert, they were attending school. Hilda was working downtown and
still living in the Little family farmhouse; Wilfred had landed a job
with the Water and Power Commission and had been posted in Wilberforce, Ohio. Steadfast in his religious pursuit, Philbert was on the
brink of a short-lived marriage, and in addition to work, engaged in
regional prizefights in the boxing ring.

All the relatives, along with West Indian friends of the family as
well as street buddies such as Big Boy Roper and John Davis, verified
Malcolm's assertion in his *Autobiography* that "my conk and whole cos-
tume were so wild that I might have been taken as a man from Mars."
No eyewitness could be located, however, for the car crash Malcolm
claimed he caused when "one driver stopped to gape at me and the
driver behind bumped into him."[17]

It had been nearly two years since Philbert had seen Malcolm.
Although not one to underestimate his younger brother's drive for
attention, Philbert was nonetheless stunned by the sight. Sibling

rivalry always moved the younger brother to "show me he's learned something I didn't know."[18] In Boston and Harlem, Red had learned a lot and did not spare his brother the details. Friends on the west side were no strangers to former sidekicks visiting from big cities, but they were nonetheless rocked by this "Harlem Red." Even preschool Robert would recall the dazzle, decades later, along with the family talk about his half brother. It was not just the shoes, broad hat, and zoot suits running every color from red and wild yellow to sharkskin blue, it was Malcolm's jive, his new strut, the Boston accent, the cant of the cigarette, the looping handshake with the entreaty for "daddy-o" to "give me some skin."[19]

A couple of white friends in Mason recalled this Malcolm–as–Cab Calloway visit with studied insouciance, as if he simply had arrived at the endpoint that Hollywood had foreseen for such Negroes. Others—white and black, male and female—had been alerted by personal letters boasting of his wild life first in Boston, then in Harlem. All hopes that his letters exaggerated were dashed upon observing the corruption of their pal "Harpy" (as Mason classmates had dubbed him) up close. Upon visiting Lois Swerlein, for example, Malcolm got the impression that she was so shocked by the show-time flamboyance of her former state charge that she almost bolted from his presence in horror.[20]

One account of Malcolm's home visits got mixed up in the *Autobiography*. It stated that he visited Shorty's mother in Lansing and reported that her son would one day have his own band. Of the people who constituted the Shorty composite, the one from Lansing was Ella's nonmusical husband, Kenneth Collins; it was instead Boston-born and -bred Malcolm Jarvis who was the musician angling for his own band. The book doesn't mention employment during Malcolm's visits, but the record shows that he was briefly employed as a porter-messenger at Shaw's Jewelry Store in Lansing, and that he spent time in Flint, Michigan, during a four-month stay in the fall of

1942. Understated as well was Malcolm's visit to the Kalamazoo State Hospital, where his mother remained institutionalized.

As in life, Malcolm was not forthcoming about his mother in his book, writing, "She sort of half-sensed who I was."[21] Hilda and Wilfred suspected that Malcolm's reticence likely stemmed from a nagging suspicion that his prior treatment of their mother, including his theft of household cash, contributed to her mental breakdown. "Sometimes she would be down-to-earth and other times she would be completely in another world," said Wilfred, who visited Louise every two weeks. Twenty-two and unmarried, Wilfred had gotten a draft deferment when the power commission assigned him a Wilberforce College post teaching a defense-related trade to students. In one of her clear moments, Louise stared down her devoted son, told him he "looked out for everybody but yourself," and said it was time for Wilfred to get on with his life. "It kind of shocked me the way she did it," he said. "But I did start thinking about maybe getting married."[22]

Harlem Red, as Malcolm signed his autograph around Lansing, had no such intention. He had several girlfriends but did not envision himself investing in permanent bonding anytime soon. On his final day at home, he reportedly staged a rousing Lindy-hop session at a dance in a high school gymnasium. Flinging local girls in orbit about his lanky frame, Malcolm nearly stopped the band as the locals in attendance froze and gazed upon him "with their eyes like saucers."[23] Once again, Malcolm was where he longed to be, at the center of attention.

Easing back onto the railroad payroll, thanks to the severe manpower shortage brought on by the war, Malcolm landed a job sweeping out coaches and peddling pillows to weary customers on the Silver Meteor, a New York to Florida train. A few mishaps of temper and intolerance, however, got him fired once again. This time he got work where he long yearned to play: Smalls Paradise.

Unlike such menial jobs back in Lansing, Malcolm considered waiting tables at Smalls as "Seventh Heaven seven times over." The highly respected, no-nonsense Charlie Smalls* laid down strict rules against sloth, thievery, tardiness and the hustling of customers, especially military servicemen. Although Malcolm had violated each of these tenets on other jobs, he swore allegiance with all intention of making this Seventh Heaven proud. "Charlie Small had no need to caution me against being late; I was so anxious to be there," he wrote, "I'd arrive an hour early."[24]

Customers found Malcolm somewhat amusing as their table server in a waiter's jacket. Careful to groom good relations with the bartenders and cooks, the ambitious new waiter greeted diners with the solicitous embrace he'd adopted while serving white travelers on trains. And while he played by house rules at the start, Malcolm pricked his ears whenever smooth criminals in their cups would discuss their hustle on the streets. These "players" offered crash courses on the fine art of the Harlem numbers racket, "pimping, peddling dope, and thievery of all sorts, including armed robbery."[25]

The numbers racket pulled Malcolm in first as a player who sometimes bet his entire daily take in tips. This illegal urban racket was a well-organized operation, raking in millions of dollars mainly from poor residents hoping to make a big score. The winning number was determined each day by the last three digits of the stock market totals. In later years, "the number" was the last three digits of the total that bettors waged on given races at major racetracks. Such track results, called "the handle," were published in several city tabloids and would skyrocket circulation even among otherwise nonreaders. At day's end the few who "hit the number" were paid off at a rate of 600 to 1, for a nickel bet and higher. As in the state lot-

---

* Smalls Paradise was owned by Ed Smalls. Charlie Smalls was his brother. According to Malcolm's *Autobiography* (p. 80), Malcolm dealt only with Charlie.

teries established decades later, the few winners were widely touted
and thus losers by the tens of thousands were encouraged to play the
next day, and forever more.

This policy racket, dubbed the Italian lottery, or the "nigger
pool," was a fixture of the underground Harlem economy, employing a network of "look-out men and runners" who collected "policy
slips" from players; controllers who filed them with "bankers," and a
syndicate that bankrolled the operation. As early as 1925, according
to Francis Ianni's *Black Mafia: Ethnic Succession in Organized Crime*,
"there were thirty black policy banks in Harlem, several of them
large enough to collect bets in an area of twenty city blocks and across
three or four avenues."[26] All along the way, bribes were paid to officials ranging from the patrolman on the beat to fixers in the district
attorney's office. In addition to mobster figures, such as the Bronx's
Dutch Schultz, who muscled in for control of the multimillion-dollar
numbers racket, Harlem grew its own crop of black policy operators.
One of its better known gangsters was Ellsworth "Bumpy" Johnson,
who, after Schultz was assassinated in 1935, made a deal with Mafia
leaders to split proceeds from the lucrative policy racket.[27]

From his perch at Smalls Paradise, Malcolm became schooled in
policy racketeering with such men as "Black Sammy," "Bud" Hulan,
"King" Padmore, and "West Indian Archie." In addition to such
operators, he was beginning to meet big-name pimps like "Cadillac
Drake," "Dollarbill," and a hustler he got to know quite well, "Sammy
the Pimp." Born in Kentucky, Sammy McKnight was described in
the *Autobiography* as Malcolm's "closest friend" at the time. He would
select women to turn into prostitutes by reading their facial expressions when they danced. His stable of women, both blacks and whites,
"were about as beautiful as any prostitutes who operated anywhere,"
Malcolm wrote.[28]

Among other colorful characters of the Harlem streets, Malcolm
was intrigued by the lone operators who stealthily lifted goods and

prized objects from others. The aptly named "Jumpsteady" was a cat burglar who, while working his rooftop trade in white residential areas downtown, would daringly maintain his balance scaling the thinnest of ledges leading to windows of targeted apartments. Another larcenist Malcolm admired was a pickpocket named "Fewclothes," who had been forced into retirement by arthritis that snarled his fingers so severely that diners could hardly bear to look at his hands. Still, he was a regular at Smalls and, without begging, would attract free drinks and a meal, all while regaling bartenders and customers within earshot about the good old days. "An old wolf that had lost his fangs was still eating," Malcolm noted. He filed away other light-fingered tips for "later years when hard times would force me to have my own burglary ring."[29]

No longer able to afford the railroad-subsidized accommodation, Malcolm roomed at an apartment house at 805 St. Nicholas Avenue.[30] When schedules allowed, Beatrice would take a train down from Boston, and Malcolm would squire her around the clubs and afterhours Harlem joints such as Jimmy's Chicken Shack and Creole Bill's, most of them crowded with middle-class whites from downtown. As in Boston, he discovered that Beatrice, as a prim and somewhat proper white woman, brought him a measure of status around Negroes—especially jazz musicians. "They made a big deal over her," Malcolm wrote.[31]

A slew of rooms along the corridors of the apartment building were virtual shopping malls for stolen items and merchandise: everything from fur coats and pricey perfumes to firearms and cameras. One could even purchase automobiles. As one of the few men rooming in the apartment building during the war, Malcolm wrote that he was taken under the wings of the women, many of whom were engaged in prostitution or some other illegal racket. Years later, a religious conversion would instruct an adult Malcolm that the criminal operations all around him in Harlem reflected malice aforethought by the dominant white society that had mastered the art of repressive social engineering of Negroes. Racial exclusion from the mainstream economy, he later reasoned, meant that "almost everyone in Harlem needed some kind of hustle to survive, and needed to stay high in some way to forget what they had to do to survive. . . . In one sense, we were huddled in there, bonded together in seeking security and warmth, and comfort from each other, and we didn't know it. All of us—who might have probed space, or cured cancer, or built industries—were, instead black victims of the white man's America social system."[32] Such analyses would come later.

Meanwhile, Malcolm-the-waiter was fully engaged in probing not outer space, but the inner workings of the numbers racket and the street life of Harlem. And there was the matter of registering for the military draft on his eighteenth birthday, in 1943. Already the conscription letter had been mailed to 72 Dale Street, his old residence in Boston. Just as he had to learn how to distinguish Boston cops from regular customers at the Roseland, Malcolm was instructed at Smalls on how to spot undercover detectives as well as plainclothes military officials. Special agents frequented the club to check on the treatment of servicemen on leave; others searched for AWOL soldiers and draft-age civilians who had not registered for the Army. "Impairing the morals" of U.S. servicemen was a catchphrase that guided the treatment of soldiers in clubs such as Smalls. The owners had instructed Malcolm, the other waiters, and the bartenders that servicemen were absolutely not to be subjected to any overture or hustle that the military might interpret as irregular. Offending establishments were placed "off limits" for soldiers, and it could mean a loss of state liquor license.

Skirting house rules, Malcolm offered a lone Negro soldier the services of one of his prostitute friends. The potential john accepted the offer and the phone number, only to trigger legal action by alerting the police as the undercover military officer that he was. Malcolm was taken to the 32nd Precinct and made to listen as cops beat a genuine pimp in an adjoining room. Then he was released. This station-house scare did not stay Charlie Smalls's hand. Malcolm was fired on the spot. "I wish you hadn't done that, Red," he said upon barring Malcolm from Smalls Paradise.[33]

Getting fired from his "Seventh Heaven" sent Malcolm spinning between regular jobs and the Harlem rackets, often at the same time. The prostitutes buzzing the St. Nicholas apartment building initially embraced him as something of a "kid-brother." Several would befriend him over reefers in the morning and school him about the people on both sides of the trade. "It was in this house that I learned more about women than I ever did in any other single place," he wrote. One of his takeaway lessons was "to be distrustful of most women"—a lesson he would carry throughout life.[34] He applied this learning from the flats to relations he groomed on the streets. Boarding away from St. Nicholas, he pinched living and recreational expenses from women, both black and white. One quite wealthy woman from Long Island, a buddy said, seemed casual about spending extravagant sums on her Negro "arm-piece." And she seemed uncaring about rumors that she was not the only woman Malcolm was showing about the city.

Over choice marijuana, Malcolm sat through what passes on the street as job counseling from his pal Sammy "the Pimp" McKnight. On-the-job training was ruled out chiefly because both men concluded that "I had no abilities in that direction," Malcolm later wrote, "and that I'd starve to death trying to recruit prostitutes."[35] While skilled at the chase, and even the running to ground, Malcolm lacked the brutal tenacity to hold a stable of call girls in check night after night.

And one singular effort by Malcolm would falter and nearly cause a family scandal. Philbert's ex-wife, Mary Bibbs, encountered his younger brother in New York after the couple had gone through a bitter separation back in Michigan. Older siblings in Lansing found plenty to fault mendacious Philbert about for the breakup with Mary, starting with deception about almost every aspect of his life. As but one example, one sibling confided, the groom reportedly told his bride that he was the chief owner of the family's six-acre farm. Upon noticing in New York that the Midwestern woman was struggling with finances, Malcolm, who was not exactly flush with cash himself, urged her into the "profession" by introducing her to associates. After a few connections, if not dalliances, Malcolm spread the word that his plain and quite pleasant former sister-in-law worked on a string that he pulled. Always one to lord advantages, real or illusory, over Philbert, Malcolm allowed the boast to reach his brother that he had turned Mary, the wife who had spurned him, out as a prostitute. While Philbert said he was indifferent, their brother Wilfred excoriated Malcolm for committing such a deed with any woman. At any rate, the ordeal, whether consummated or not, was short-lived: Mary Bibbs escaped Malcolm's attempt at pimping and prostitution altogether. Wilfred reported that his brother's former wife, who returned to a respectable life, was never "cut out for that kind of thing"—and neither was Malcolm.[36]

Instead, Malcolm and his buddy Sammy McKnight settled on peddling reefers for his entry-level hustle in Harlem. He was not exactly a novice at this game, having sold weed as a thirteen-year-old back in Lansing. In short order, "Crazy Red" was supplying marijuana for the jazz bands traveling through town. "I sold reefer like a wild man," he wrote. "I scarcely slept," but then he was already a confirmed nocturnal wheeler and dealer. Now, as an eighteen-year-old rolling in dough, Malcolm considered himself "the peer of the other young hustlers I had admired."[37] Working nights, Malcolm spent his days at the movies, taking in pairs of double features and more in a single day, a habit he shared with Sammy, his sometime roommate. On his occasional visits from Boston, Malcolm Jarvis would marvel at the women in the stable of Sammy the Pimp, most especially his girlfriend Hortense. "She was the most gorgeous Portuguese-Indian woman I ever saw in my life. Sammy McKnight was one of those dudes that dressed like Dorian Gray, with the fedora hat," said Jarvis. "He would go to the movies and come out and live the part. Malcolm used to laugh at him." However, Malcolm was not above affecting the style of Humphrey Bogart himself, with a dangling cigarette, swaggering through his own Hollywood movie on the streets of Harlem.[38]

Another of the many steady jobs Malcolm used to cover his petty thievery and hustling was as a waiter at the afterhours Jimmy's Chicken Shack. The speakeasy employed another redhead, a dishwasher named John Sanford, who like Malcolm, was fast gaining a reputation on the streets. To distinguish the two hustlers, Sanford was dubbed Chicago Red[39] and Malcolm became known as Detroit Red, since few had heard of Lansing. After drifting in Chicago with a small band playing a washboard, Sanford was struggling to achieve his true calling as a standup comedian—which he managed years later as the nationally known Redd Foxx.

Already, Malcolm found Sanford "the funniest dishwasher on this earth." His assessment was warranted. Foxx would have a huge hit in the 1970s with his sitcom *Sanford and Son*, a series distinguished by its edgy racial humor and listed as one of *Time*'s "100 Best TV Shows of All Time." Born John Elroy Sanford in St. Louis, he occasionally did comedy with another future star, Melvin "Slappy" White. Sanford was three years older than his fellow pool-hall hustler Malcolm. And the two rising stars shared more than the kitchen during their days at Jimmy's Chicken Shack.

"Malcolm was about the same color as me," Sanford is quoted as saying in the book *Redd Foxx, BS (Before Sanford)*, a title that referred to his TV show. "We both had these conks, and our hair was red with a high pompadour, and we wore the zoot [suits]—just like the 'high drape pants' Billie Holiday used to sing about in her blues. Malcolm didn't have the show business talent, so he didn't give a damn what he got into. He'd take on anything to get some dough. He was a little more aggressive. I'd rather miss sleeping with a broad and go somewhere and do [some] comedy."[40]

The two hustlers on the make worked at least one caper together. A girlfriend of Foxx agreed to leave the back window of the dry cleaner where she worked open. "Malcolm and I went in that night and took a hundred suits off the racks and put them on the roof. We'd sell one or two of them a day off the roof."[41] The rooftop operation, which police never detected, was but one of a stream of capers Malcolm pulled during his salad days uptown, most of them down on the streets peddling reefers.

As he would for much of the rest of his life, Malcolm took to carrying a small pistol inside his belt at the center of his back, a handy spot least noticed by cops during routine pat-downs. When approached by alerted narcotics officers, Malcolm resorted to a childhood trick that he had used with his mother to avoid punishment, calling attention to himself in a loud voice, declaring that he had no contraband and beseeching officers not to plant any on him. When making his rounds he would employ a number of tricks, including carrying his stash under his armpits so that it could be easily jettisoned in an emergency, as well as secreting packages in prearranged locations. Still, as the police heat increased, the lanky, easily spotted redhead began to fall on troubled times. To relieve the pressure, Malcolm began using his old railroad ID pass to travel the East Coast without charge or hassle. He started a lucrative business peddling reefer to the bands traveling on the road, swinging up to Buffalo and even Boston, where he spent time with Beatrice and Jarvis. He also tried to patch things up with his sister Ella, occasionally gifting a wad of cash.

His younger brother Reginald, who had joined the Merchant

Marines, came to visit Malcolm in New York when his ship docked for repairs. Six feet tall and "self-possessed,"[42] the teenaged traveler seemed uncomfortable about the wild lifestyle on the street. In one all-night session, Reginald brought Malcolm up to date on their family back home. Yvonne, Wesley, and Robert were in school back in Lansing, while Malcolm already had the latest news on the others. Surrounded by colleagues he could never trust, Detroit Red was ecstatic about the possibility of his admiring brother joining him in New York. However, the young seaman did not respond to his older brother's suggestion that he leave the Merchant Marines, and Malcolm himself was facing problems with the Selective Service.

The blistering war in Europe had somewhat softened U.S. military policy against black citizens. Prior to 1941, the military's racism was so virulent that, for example, the Naval Academy refused to let its lacrosse team play a Harvard team unless Harvard banished its lone black player from the field. At the outbreak of war, the Army did not include a single Negro in its initial requisition, because of its strong bias against fielding such soldiers. With the furious escalation of the war in 1943, the military set a maximum "quota" for Negro recruits at 10.6 percent, matching their ascribed proportion in the general population. Segregated at every level, these Negro soldiers were quartered at separate and inferior training bases, supplied inferior weapons and equipment, restricted to segregated post theaters, and transported on Negroes-only military buses. As during World War I, the Navy assigned blacks as servants and mess-hall personnel. The Marines were all white throughout most of the war, and only when German forces threatened victory in the decisive Battle of the Bulge at the very end of 1944 were Negro troops used in other than token numbers in Army combat units. Even then, the military was careful that "no black officer was to outrank or command a white officer in the same unit," according to Jean Byers's *A Study of the Negro in Military Service*.[43] Secretary of War Henry L. Stimson flatly opposed training blacks as officers, observing in his diary on September 27, 1940, that "leadership is not imbedded in the negro [sic] race yet."[44] Four years earlier, Benjamin O. Davis, the first Negro allowed to matriculate at West Point in the twentieth century, had graduated 35th in his 1936 class of 276 cadets, despite enduring the "silent treatment" from white fellow students. These white future officers refused to room with him or sit next to him on a military bus or in the academy cafeteria, and they spoke to him only in the line of duty. Offending classmates included such future Army commanders as General William C. Westmoreland, who commanded forces in the Vietnam War and graduated 112th in the class, and General Creighton Abrams, Westmoreland's deputy in Vietnam, who finished 185th.[45]

Despite such blatant government racism, some 2.5 million Negroes clamored to join the Army and defend their country. Malcolm felt no such need to prove himself to whites who had rejected him, whether civilians or military. He wanted no part of the Army and its war overseas. The streets of Harlem, Brooklyn, and the Bronx provided sufficient excitement for the eighteen-year-old, complete with a body count—and personal close calls with police and armed fellow travelers. When Ella alerted Malcolm about the draft notice, he dutifully checked in with Local Board 59 of the Selective Service System and registered some two weeks after his birthday, on June 1, 1943, listing his employment as a waiter for the Chicken Shack, 763 St. Nicholas Avenue. Some seven weeks later he was classified 1A and scheduled to report to the induction center for a physical examination.

Malcolm sprang into action. In an engaging personal account in the *Autobiography*, he describes how he spun a web of deception and obfuscation for the draft board. He started by professing a desire to join the Japanese army whenever he spotted a suspected army spy on the prowl in Harlem. And he underscored his readiness by reading aloud from his draft notice, making sure that his full and proper name and order number were loud and clear. On the appointed day, he dragged out his zaniest zoot suit and yellow shoes and bushed up his conk. He then went "skipping and tipping" into the induction center in what one must imagine to have been a most effeminate, warmongering performance by a redheaded Negro gung ho about enlisting. What amazes about Malcolm's recruitment yarn is how, with all of his "daddy-o's," he was even able to keep a straight face. The psychiatrist, who likely had seen even splashier displays, remained "objective and professional" and, when able to get a word in, tactful. Tightening the screws, Malcolm brought his warmongering closer to home. After peeping under both doors, he informed the "daddy-o" examiner of his eagerness to "get sent down South. Organize them nigger soldiers, you dig? Steal us some guns, and kill us crackers!"[46]

The resulting 4F rejection notice from the draft board, dated October 25, 1943, saved Malcolm from military service. It was based on his physical examination at the induction station, which reflected "that the subject was found mentally disqualified for military service by the reasons of psychopathic personality inadequate [sic], sexual perversion and psychiatric rejection." Thus spared the battlefield, Malcolm resumed his increasingly dangerous hustles on the streets. While he was on the road with the bands, the narcotics agents cooled down their pursuit. However, when he pulled a pistol on a dealer at a card game among train workers at Grand Central Terminal, he was warned away from the station by narcotics agents. Banned by the New Haven Railroad as he had been from Smalls Paradise, Malcolm fell back on odd jobs, and started sniffing cocaine and reportedly staging robberies in adjoining cities. Wilfred Little said that he bailed out his brother several times after Malcolm got arrested in Michigan.

Another time when Reginald visited Malcolm, the two brothers partied until dawn, causing the young merchant seaman to miss his ship. Malcolm had rented a three-room apartment so the family could have a place in Harlem to call home. While increasing his own hustling, Malcolm set his AWOL brother up with a peddler's license so he could sell cut-rate goods to customers who took the items to have been stolen and of a higher quality. After a short run, Reginald took up with an older woman, worked occasionally, and made his way back to Boston, living with Ella's younger sister, Mary.

Spiraling on a downward course, Malcolm stepped up his cocaine sniffing and numbers playing as he moved from one job in the rackets to another. In the numbers game he worked as a runner for a banker who had been the secretary of mobster Dutch Schultz. Subsequently, he hooked up with a Harlem madam specializing in providing Negroes to wealthy white New Yorkers with "weird sexual tastes." His job entailed steering the customers to the "sin-den." During this run of rackets jobs, and lesser hauls with Sammy the Pimp, Malcolm occasionally had to lie low or leave town altogether when pressure from police or competing mobsters became too great. On one occasion, a Negro with a stocking mask, who roughly matched Malcolm's height and skin tone, robbed a Harlem bar of the cash intake for the day. Gunmen looking for the culprit kicked in Malcolm's apartment door. After talking his way out of the jam, an innocent Malcolm took off to visit the family in Michigan until Sammy notified him that the gunmen had settled their score. Another "tall, light-skinned" Negro with a stocking mask had robbed a crap game of Italian racketeers in the Bronx. Two Italian gunmen approached Malcolm in a telephone booth in a Harlem bar near the Polo Grounds, and he managed to escape only when a policeman walked through the door. "I never in my life have been so glad to see a cop."[47]

The most severe threat, however, was not one of mistaken identity. Early in 1945, West Indian Archie, the notorious numbers man, paid Malcolm $300 for a bet he claimed to have placed. Known for his photographic memory, Archie often paid cash when a numbers player claimed a "hit," and later he would check the record. Malcolm's claim did not square with Archie's policy record. Armed with

a long-barrel .32-20 caliber pistol, Archie stormed into Sammy's flat
and, despite Malcolm's denial, gave him until noon the next day to
repay his $300.

"No one who wasn't ready to die messed with West Indian
Archie," Malcolm wrote. "He truly scared me." Already the face-off
was broadcast on the street wire. The $300 misunderstanding had
pitted Archie, a sixty-year-old hustler who was convinced that he had
been cheated, against a youngster threatened with a deadline. The
law of the "sidewalk jungle world," as Malcolm saw it, was that neither could back down without losing "face" and "honor." In dozens
of such showdowns, he wrote, "one took the Dead on Arrival ride to
the morgue, and the other went to prison for manslaughter or the
electric chair for murder."[48]

Malcolm borrowed Sammy's .32 pistol and went out to all his
"usual haunts." He picked up his friend Jean Parks and took in the
Billie Holiday set at the Onyx Club. Sniffing cocaine and boozing
along the way, the couple ducked into one of his key stops, La Marr-
Cheri, on St. Nicholas Avenue. With his back to the door of the club,
he was approached by an armed, obviously high West Indian Archie.
Cursing and "floor-showing for the people," Archie reiterated his
threat at full volume. Thereupon his buddies calmed him down and
walked him away from Malcolm.

Rather than the detractors shooting each other in the crowded
bar, the street code called for the second man to follow the first
out the door for a shootout in the street. Malcolm paid his tab and
walked out without looking back. He then stood outside "in full view
of the bar, with my hands in my pocket, for perhaps five minutes,"
no doubt cradling Sammy's .32-caliber pistol. "When West Indian
Archie didn't come out I left."[49]

Once Archie's noon deadline had passed, Malcolm followed his
routine, making one drug delivery after another, inhaling opium
reefers himself, and downing Benzedrine. Rattled by events, he had

an altercation with a young knife-wielding hustler and a close encounter with cops. And, as far as he knew, the Italian mobsters from the Bronx were still gunning for this "tall, light-skinned" Negro. Sammy sensed Malcolm was about to snap from the pressure and called Malcolm Jarvis to come get Malcolm.

"I said okay," Jarvis remembered. "I was playing a gig at a Boston club that night. I left right quick. I drove down in that Buick Roadmaster, and hit New York City at about five thirty a.m. 'I don't know where Red is—he hasn't been here all night,' Sammy said at the door. Those hit men were moving back and forth watching the house. 'You [need] to cruise down there around LaMarr-Cheri, sometimes he hangs around there. You get him. Don't even come back for his clothes. Hit the road.' I drove around to La Marr-Cheri" on Edgecombe Avenue, where Malcolm sometimes stopped in for breakfast. "Sure enough, here's Malcolm with his gray hat and that big herringbone coat. He didn't have the zoot suit on this time."[50]

Malcolm picked up the story in his *Autobiography*: "When I heard the car horn, I was walking on St. Nicholas Avenue. But my ears were hearing a gun. I didn't dream the horn could possibly be for me. I jerked around. I came close to shooting.

"Shorty, from Boston! . . . I couldn't have been happier."[51]

"He got in the car," Jarvis recalled. "He knew they were after him. I guess he had been dodging them."

Jarvis recounted the conversation he had with Malcolm: " 'Man, am I glad to see you,' Malcolm said. 'Let's get out of here.' We got on the Merritt Parkway heading back up to Boston. He told me that he had messed up. He told me that he had hit the number . . . that Beatrice had come down that weekend. They [Malcolm and Beatrice] stayed at the Victoria Hotel. She had to go back [to Boston] because she was married. And I guess her old man was due back that Sunday." Malcolm's Armenian girlfriend had gotten married about a year earlier, in February 1944, to Mehran Bazarian, a soldier home on leave.

On this midmorning ride back to Boston in his buddy's Buick, "Malcolm was scared," Jarvis recalled, "nervous" and quite talkative.[52] The pattern of his life of pursuit and evasion seemed strangely intertwined with that of his rebellious father, who had been told to leave Georgia, and his immigrant mother, who had been harassed by night riders and eventually pushed off their land. Indeed, here was Malcolm, sweating away in a nocturnal daze after being chased out of his "Seventh Heaven."

# CHAPTER 8

# Luck Runs Out

MALCOLM SPENT HIS EARLY DAYS BACK IN BOSTON AS AN exhausted exile. After years as a night owl, he reacquainted himself with REM sleep, indulging "even at night," and spent time "laying dead."[1] He idled away his few waking hours listening to jazz on the 78 rpm record player in Malcolm Jarvis's apartment, several blocks from Ella Collins's Dale Street home. Later he would reflect on how far he had strayed from the high hopes of his parents, and even from the plans of his half sister, who had rescued him from state control back in Michigan.

"Ella couldn't believe how atheist I had become,"[2] Malcolm wrote in the *Autobiography*. Jarvis was not surprised because, after having introduced him to a Muslim friend from India, he had concluded that "Malcolm was not religiously inclined." Tall, rugged, and not quite as light-skinned as Malcolm, Abdul Hameed had first impressed his fellow jazzman with the twelve-foot Mason and Hamlin piano at his home on Windsor Street in Roxbury. He also attracted due notice on the street because "there was no one else walking around Boston with a black fez." When Jarvis introduced his buddies to each other, the Indian musician, as was his wont, spoke reverently about his Ahmadiyya Muslim religion. Malcolm, however, "didn't want to hear nothing pertaining to no spirituality,"[3] recalled Jarvis, who attended church more out of habit than commitment. What did surprise Jarvis about his formerly wide-awake buddy was Malcolm's steadfast somnolence upon his return from Harlem.

As World War II wound down in Europe in that spring of 1945, Jarvis drifted away from his shipyard employment, working odd jobs and scattered music gigs with his jazz band, happy as always to share his meager lifestyle with Malcolm. The two roommates talked far into the night during the idle hours of Malcolm's first few weeks back in Massachusetts. Their rekindled relationship was as close and as contentious as always—a pattern Malcolm had begun with brother Philbert and continued with adolescent pals back in Lansing, such as John Davis. "We didn't have anything in common," the insightful Jarvis said of his buddy. "We were like negative and positive in a lightbulb. That light is what made us blossom in friendship. We would explode at each other every time we were together."[4] Characteristically, the friction seemed only to strengthen the relationship. A hallmark of Malcolm's association with close friends, both male and female, throughout the remainder of his life was this pattern of sustained discordance.

When idling alone with his jazz, Malcolm would smoke marijuana at the apartment, daydream and conduct "imaginary conversations with my New York musician friends."[5] Reminiscing around Jarvis, he would exaggerate his exploits, just as he had with Philbert during childhood. His embroidery now was stitched together from the wardrobe of Harlem street depravities; it steered clear only of personal behavior that Malcolm considered repulsive, such as wanton violence, consorting with "queers," and, given his fear of needles, injecting heroin. Once back on the boulevards of Roxbury, he supplemented his reefer smoking with cocaine sniffing and regained his sense of "supreme well-being." Jarvis, however, like other street associates, dismissed as hyperbole Malcolm's claims in the *Autobiography* that he became a depraved monster of a dope fiend. In addition to occasional use of illicit drugs, "Malcolm liked to drink Johnnie Walker Black whiskey," Jarvis recalled. "He used to smoke marijuana, but he was no addict," at least not of the caliber that Jarvis was accustomed to as a jazz musician playing among the rowdiest of street hustlers, more than a few of whom died young from hard drug abuse. "You won't call a person who smokes a joint here and there a dope addict. But Malcolm used to make money at it. He'd buy some stuff, roll the joints, and bring them into Boston and sell them for a dollar a piece among these cats in the show business."[6]

Exiled from the Harlem nightclubs and from his other cash streams in New York, Malcolm resorted to his Armenian American girlfriend for drug money and food, as well as for his three-pack-a-day cigarette habit. The wealthy Beatrice (Caragulian) Bazarian apparently pinched funds from her unknowing husband, who had been discharged from the military and was working as a bicoastal salesman. "My demands on her increased," he wrote, "and she came up with more [money]." Malcolm's long-standing and characteristically contentious relationship with Beatrice was largely exploitative—sometimes even involving physical violence. "I would feel evil and slap her around worse than ever, some of the nights when Shorty [Jarvis] was away. She would cry, curse me, and swear that she would never be back. But I knew that she was never thinking about not coming back." Malcolm had seen his father backhand his mother sure enough, and this macho image had been reinforced by Hollywood tough guys such as James Cagney, as well as by Harlem pimps and the prostitutes tutoring him in the apartment building on St. Nicholas Avenue. However, it was housewives and other average women who Malcolm said moved him to be "very distrustful of most women." The battery, he justified, was something women of that day "need, in fact want." Furthermore, he added, "When they are not exploited, they exploit the man."[7]

Since early adolescence, Malcolm's libido seemed to drive him more toward amassing power than toward pursuing sex for its own sake. Since his Lansing street days, his take-it-or leave-it approach to sex distinguished him dramatically from his older fellow travelers, for whom chasing girls into bed seemed not only an endgame but their singular goal in life. As sought after as Malcolm was by women of both races and all ages, he did not routinely string along several girlfriends at a time, as did Jarvis or Sammy the Pimp, his Harlem roommate who maintained a harem. His envious buddies could not fathom why the worldly, handsome teenager behaved with such restraint. Even the critically observant Ella noticed her brother's tendency toward monogamy. "He had one girlfriend. I can truly say he wasn't chasing girls."[8] Nor, she noticed, did her other Midwestern half brothers, Wilfred, Philbert and the rest, in stark contrast to the urban men she knew, including her husband and her late brother, Earl Jr.

Women "just loved Malcolm," Jarvis recalled. "He could have taken his pick of any girl he wanted, the cream of the crop. He had some foxes after him in those days."[9] Instead, by employing self-control and what he called reverse psychology, Malcolm sought to maneuver women—especially those who had influence over other men—into his sphere, and thereby establish control. For instance, when approaching a beautiful girl accustomed to praise and flattery, he would show disrespect to trigger her curiosity. The targets of his seduction seemed chosen to benefit him materially or otherwise extend his power base.

Nor was Malcolm entirely monogamous. Through intimate engagements, he cultivated his power-game influence with several women about town. In addition to his affair with the married Beatrice Bazarian, he maintained relationships with other women in

Boston, as well as with others while on the road, some of short duration, including at least one other white suburbanite. One such affair
not mentioned in the *Autobiography*, but verified by others, was with
Margaret Shackleford in Boston. "She was a professional prostitute,
but she was very high class," said Jarvis. "You come to her by appointment. When that chick stepped out on the street, she had a thousand
dollars' worth of clothes from Bonwit Teller on her back. All of her
clients were well-to-do people. And she would go down to a [five-
star] hotel and sit at the bar and kiss them white salesmen coming in
and out of Boston, and go up to the rooms. That's where this chick
made her money. And then she'd do her little business and go back
home at two to three o'clock in the morning. And she was married.
Her husband knew his old lady was a prostitute. She was bringing
the money home to him. She was married to Lester Shackleford,
a trumpet player." Despite her marriage and her business affairs,
"Margaret was in love with Malcolm," said Jarvis, who was dating
her best girlfriend, a woman named Jackie. "She [loved] the ground
[Malcolm] walked on. She knew he was going with this white chick
from Belmont. Margaret didn't care. Malcolm used to get out there
with Margaret, you know, he got a little bit here and there. It was no
charge to him because the chick dug him. Yes, Margaret would give
Malcolm money if he needed it. Yes, she would. I've seen her put fifty
or a hundred dollars in his hand many a time."[10]

Despite such exchanges, Malcolm's buddy, like other street associates, insists that he was not a pimp. "A pimp is a dude who lives
solely by having a chick up there on the block working for him making money and bringing it back to him," Jarvis said. "This was not the
case with Margaret. She had a husband. And when she took her cab
home, she had her money. But if Malcolm had no money, you see she
liked him. She was married, but she was in love with Malcolm. Some
days when Lester would be out of town playing, Margaret would call
Malcolm and he would go over there and sit half the day drinking

beer in the summertime."[11] She lived around the corner from Ella, who apparently had no knowledge of the relationship.

According to Ella's son Rodnell Collins, his mother was deeply concerned about another middle-aged neighbor with serious designs on Malcolm. Jackie Massey, a physically attractive woman with a flair for dressing just so, and a fine hand for preparing tempting meals, was the bane of housewives in Roxbury, and she became a bone of contention between Malcolm and his sponsoring sister. "She frequently turned up at our house asking about something or the other," Ella is quoted as saying in Collins's memoir, *Seventh Child*. "What she really wanted was Malcolm."[12]

Concerned perhaps about her undying ambitions for her half brother, and her own dislike for the flirtatious Jackie Massey, Ella would offer Malcolm flat-out ultimatums against marrying this older woman. Even though she had been unable to prevent Malcolm from dating his white girlfriend, at least that liaison posed no marital threat. In private moments, Ella held out hopes still for young Laura, the brown-skinned West Indian whom Jarvis felt Malcolm had deeply loved, or for Evelyn Williams, a light-skinned woman he had dated for many months when he first got to Boston.[13]

Meanwhile, Malcolm continued his affair with Beatrice. He was grateful to Jarvis for hosting him in his Hollander Street apartment, but considered his co-tenancy there to be a godsend for his friend because his white girlfriend would come around. "I never in my life have seen a black man that desired white women as sincerely as Shorty did," Malcolm said in the *Autobiography*.[14] In something of a plea bargain, Jarvis explained decades later: "When I was a young man in my teens, I had a certain aberration for a white girl or a light-skin girl. I was a victim of the power of suggestion from society about color. I did not know the power of blackness. I believed that white was right and black had to stay back. So I imagine some of that could be true, but I was never overboard as far as white women were concerned."[15]

As for Malcolm, Jarvis said that he had a "complex for white people. I think it was bred in him out in [Michigan]. He had animosity in his heart for them, but he loved to mess around with their women. It wasn't so much getting even with them, but he hated the white man always. I think that's because of the death of his father. But he didn't have no great love for no white woman either. He used them."[16]

On the first night that Beatrice brought along her younger sister Joyce to the apartment, Malcolm claimed that both she and Jarvis went overboard—Joyce, because Jarvis was a Negro musician, and Jarvis, simply because Joyce was white. "Joyce was only sixteen. She was a very pretty, cute girl," said Jarvis. "Beatrice, I'd say, was about a year older than Malcolm. He was very protective of her younger sister, Joyce. He wouldn't let anybody get near her. And there was this other white girl named Kora [Mardarosian], Beatrice's girlfriend. Now Kora was more or less the one I was keeping company with. But the only person that was having sex with any of these white girls was Malcolm with Beatrice."[17] That's what Jarvis recalled, while noting that his four-year-old marriage was then on the rocks and his two children were living around the corner on Humboldt Avenue with his mother. The still married jazz musician had several girlfriends concurrently. One he dated on weekends, and another, "a housemaid for wealthy people," was available only on Thursdays, the "kitchen mechanics night," when off-duty maids and domestics partied in the Roxbury clubs with the regulars as more Negroes of the Great Migration landed in New England during the war.

On May 8, 1945, shortly after Harry S. Truman was installed in the White House following the death of Franklin Roosevelt, the German forces of Hitler's Third Reich surrendered to Allied forces. World War II thus ended in Europe, although the fighting in Japan would continue for three more months. Still residing in Boston on V-E Day, nineteen-year-old Malcolm periodically visited his family back in Michigan and occasionally ventured to Harlem for Billie

Holiday jazz concerts and reunions with street contacts while stocking up on contraband. Sometimes he would drive down with Beatrice or other friends and musicians. In addition to hanging with his old group, Detroit Red made plenty of new contacts, gambled at local parlors (both white and black), and struck up deals during ventures outside the Boston area, frequently peddling marijuana sticks and other hot items, even guns, to a fence on the underground market.

On one return trip from New York, Jarvis noticed his buddy carrying a .32-caliber revolver purchased from a guy up from Philadelphia. "The gun had probably been involved in a crime so Malcolm didn't want to keep it around too long," Jarvis said. "He brought it to Boston to sell, that's how he made his money. He'd turn things over, buy it for maybe ten dollars and sell it for maybe forty." In another case, Malcolm wrote about once relieving a sailor of a stolen machine gun he was trying to sell in the men's room of a local bar. After turning the tables, and the loaded weapon, on the potential gunrunner, he walked him up the stairs "the way Bill 'Bojangles' Robinson used to dance going backwards."[18] Armed robbery generally ran counter to Malcolm's taste, although he had pulled a few such jobs in Harlem with Sammy the Pimp when pressed for cash. While he deeply admired sneak thieves and second-story men such as Jumpsteady, burglary was also not Malcolm's game, at least not quite yet.

As tales about his derring-do in Harlem circulated more widely, the increasingly restless Malcolm felt challenged to back up his reputation on the streets of Boston. Some incidents detailed in the *Autobiography* cannot be independently verified; others were confirmed by eyewitnesses, reliable reports, associates, police accounts, or by Malcolm Jarvis who, when not playing a gig, happened along on most of Malcolm's street escapades. "We were inseparable," he said. One such incident, given short shrift in the book, occurred at a gambling den on Humboldt Avenue, between Munroe and Bower Streets. On previous occasions, George Holt, a well-known gambling parlor owner, reputedly backed by the mafia in Boston's North End, had vouched for Harlem Red, and had even advanced him card-game money. "Malcolm was a good poker player," Jarvis recalled, but this night, "he had killed a whole bottle of scotch, and he made some stupid moves and lost his money."[19] Despite his condition, Malcolm asked Holt for a hundred dollars to continue playing, as the organized crime figures backing the game looked on.

Noting Malcolm's heavy drinking, Holt whispered to him that he should not risk another hundred dollars, that he should drop out of the game. "Malcolm got mad," Jarvis recalled, kicked back his chair, "reached into his pocket, and threw a .25-caliber pistol on the card table." Placing his right hand on the back of his belt, where he carried a .38 caliber, the inebriated Malcolm shouted, "If I can't gamble in here tonight, there ain't nobody going to gamble. Let the baddest dude in here reach and pick that pistol up."[20]

As a surprised though willing backup, Jarvis bolted upright and shoved his right hand into his pocket as if he had a pistol. Their companion John Richmond, who indeed had a .45-caliber automatic, stood by the door and declared, "Ain't nobody getting out of here unless we let 'em." Jarvis explained: "We were just bad little thugs. If we had to we might, but we were not planning to hurt anybody." Nor were they staging a robbery. The tempest Malcolm unleashed that night was simple attention-grabbing. "So the white [organized crime] dude jumped up, scooped up his five thousand dollars, and put it in an envelope. He tells George, 'We don't want no trouble, man. We'll get lost.'" With his house game dramatically shut down, George Holt scolded Red as a hothead and banned him from packing firearms at future gambling sessions. Henceforth, Malcolm would check two pistols at the door; however, he bragged in his *Autobiography* about settling a subsequent poker game tiff at Holt's gambling parlor by pulling a third revolver from a shoulder holster.[21]

This macho display, reckless at times around whites, attracted attention, as it had from the Italian gangsters in Harlem as well as from the police in Lansing. It was not always nightclub showboating simply for attention. Jarvis recounted a Saturday evening incident at Wally's Paradise in the Little Harlem section of Roxbury, when cops arrived to squelch a disturbance. While ejecting an inebriated woman at the center of this turmoil, a white Boston policeman, known in the Negro community for his overzealousness, acted with a roughness that grated on Malcolm's sensibility. When the lone cop made a concerted second attempt to drag the inebriated woman headfirst out the door, Malcolm leaped into the fray and "shoved the cop," said Jarvis. Stepping back, he then "put his hands into the inside pocket of his jacket," where he carried a .38-caliber revolver.

"Look, if that was your mother, or your sister, you wouldn't handle her like that," Jarvis recalled Malcolm exclaiming. "So don't put your hands on her like that again." Both Jarvis and John Richmond eased into the scene, surrounding the officer, their hands at the ready. When the patrolman made a move for his weapon, according to Jarvis, Malcolm stopped him with a warning, " 'Oh, we've got more than that.' So the cop left the woman where she laid and ran to the corner to put the key in the box," Jarvis said. As he called for reinforcements, Malcolm rushed the woman into a cab, gave the driver ten dollars to take her home, and he and his buddies drove away. "Malcolm was a bold, brazen dude." [22]

Some two weeks after that confrontation, with word in the precincts that Malcolm and his buddies were heavily armed, the easily recognizable redhead was approached at the Savoy by Harvey Yates, a notorious Boston detective who wore a bulletproof vest, rare for the time, after getting shot at on several occasions. Upon spotting Yates at the door, Malcolm slipped his .32-caliber pistol to Beatrice, who concealed it in her Russian muff. "Yates walked right up to our table," recalled Jarvis, and said, "Hey, Red, stand up, I want to shake you down." The detective searched Malcolm and found him unarmed.

He then warned him sternly that he'd better "watch yourself around here from now on." Sweating through the search procedure, Jarvis said, "[I'll] never forget this. Man, this was close." And it wasn't just the men. "Beatrice was crazy in love. She wasn't going to let that cop take him. If those cops had attempted to take Malcolm out of there, she would have shot the cop."[23]

The perception of female devotion was but another image of power that daredevil Malcolm was able to project among his male cohorts on the Boston streets and beyond, as he ran the nightclub circuit and tripped through petit criminal scores with his buddies. He usually maintained a day job as well, as a ruse born of his ingrained work ethic, and the need to show community roots and a job address in case of apprehension for an illicit caper. Even when visiting the Midwest for months-long, cooling-off periods, Malcolm would hire out in local cover jobs, sometimes as a houseboy, service assistant, or temporary railroad worker. Additionally, he had once hired on for a Harlem summer gig as an entertainer. However, neither Malcolm's singing attempts nor his drum playing persuaded Jarvis to bring him onstage in Boston, even though he joked about his buddy's stage name of Jimmy Carlton—"JC," as in Jesus Christ. Malcolm's jobs in the Boston area also included stints as a handler at Sears, Roebuck, and as a salesman for a tailor with farmhands as customers.

In that sales venture, Malcolm worked with a Boston clothier selling men's suits to Southern Negro college students working summer jobs in the fields of Connecticut's tobacco valley, which produced outer wrappings for cigars. In 1944, during the wartime labor shortage, the summer hires from Morehouse College brought up to the Cullman Brothers farm in Simsbury included a prospective freshman by the name of Martin Luther King Jr. Startled by his initial exposure to a society not rigidly segregated racially, the fifteen-year-old Atlanta native wrote his mother that, in Connecticut, "[Negroes] go to any place we want to and sit anywhere we want to. . . . I never thought that a person of my race could eat anywhere."[24] Contrari-wise, young Malcolm, almost four years older, was already a fast fish in both racial streams, having grown up around whites since his infancy in Omaha.

Another Southern Negro student working the Connecticut tobacco fields was Charles Tisdale of Athens, Alabama, who recalled buying a forty dollar "Stein" suit from young Malcolm Little one Sat-urday at a Suffield tobacco farm. "They came over from Boston in a blue truck. Malcolm was the only black guy," said Tisdale. "Malcolm's thing was his spiel. He convinced you that the only thing you needed was a brand-new suit. He seemed to be so hip. Guys from the South my age were naturally drawn to that. Several of us bought suits from him." Tisdale, who years later became the publisher-owner of the *Jackson Advocate,* a newspaper that fought for civil rights in Missis-sippi, once spotted young Malcolm in a Boston nightclub, introduced himself, and reminded the sharp-tongued salesman that he had pur-chased the suit from him.[25] There is no evidence that the teenaged King and Malcolm actually met in Connecticut's tobacco valley dur-ing their concurrent visits there in the mid-1940s. Their separate, but equally powerful New England experiences would, however, pro-foundly change each of their lives, with King subsequently declaring, upon applying to Crozer Theological Seminary, that the exposure to racial tolerance in Connecticut left him with "an inescapable urge to serve society."[26]

Malcolm also worked as a temporary houseboy, as he had done in Flint, Michigan. In addition to affording a convenient employ-ment address, such jobs also provided opportunities to meet local power brokers and to case wealthy sites vulnerable to burglary. One of Jarvis's Boston-born buddies had strong contacts with such upscale premises through an employment agency that hired him out as a part-time waiter for catered estate parties. Frank Cooper was a short, light-skinned "pretty boy" type whom Malcolm dubbed

"Rudy" in his book. On the side, Cooper had a seamier hustle that reminded Malcolm of his days steering whites to the sin dens of Harlem. "Once a week, Rudy went to the home of this old, rich Boston blue-blood, pillar-of-society aristocrat," Malcolm wrote. "He paid Rudy to undress them both [Rudy and the aristocrat], then pick up the old man, like a baby, lay him on his bed, then stand over him and sprinkle him all over with *talcum powder*. Rudy said the old man would actually reach his climax from that."[27] This wealthy Bostonian, William P. Lennon, lived downtown near the Ritz-Carlton Hotel, said Jarvis, who confirmed Malcolm's account of Cooper's singular sexual dealings with the fetishistic Lennon.

In addition to Lennon, Cooper, under prompting, told Jarvis and Malcolm about other such clients in Boston high society. They were predominantly old white men "who had their private specialty [sexual] desires catered to by Negroes who came to their homes camouflaged as chauffeurs, maids, waiters, or some other accepted image," Malcolm explained in his book. While Rudy's encounters were mainly with individuals, Malcolm regaled him and Jarvis with stories about the "organized specialty sex houses" in New York City, the outer fringes of which he hustled as a steerer, and supplier of drugs.[28] In discussing the wild things he'd seen in the sex trade, Malcolm indicated that just as he avoided heroin in his drug indulgence, he, unlike Cooper, steered clear of same-sex encounters with men, regarding such behavior as anathema. Not that such assurances were needed with his closest confidant or even with Cooper: "Malcolm hated the homosexuals," said Jarvis. Ever the "camouflage guy," as Jarvis saw him, Malcolm was not above projecting false images for profit, as when he presented himself as a heroin dealer around strung-out musicians, or wrangled his way out of the military draft by playing a gay enlistee eager to kill "crackers." Back in Mason, he had attempted to use as references the influential, government-connected guests who visited the Swerlein home. Now in Boston,

Malcolm was ever alert for cultivating such friends of Ella, Beatrice, and Rudy, as well as other power brokers, whether gay or straight, who might assist him down the road.

The mixed-race quintet of Malcolm Little, Malcolm Jarvis, and the three Armenian girls increasingly found themselves in the company of Frank Cooper, John Richmond, and a third buddy named Sonny Brown. In various combinations, the friends frequented the nightclubs about town where Jarvis was playing with local jazz bands, as well as speakeasy joints and gambling dens after hours. Jarvis, as always, was delighted to hang with Joyce and Kora at his place, at Beatrice's home when her husband was out of town, or on the occasional trips out of town. While Malcolm was ever amused by his buddy's infatuation with the white girls, Jarvis noticed that he was always angling to impress them with his daring. During one trip to Harlem, on a nearly deserted stretch of the Merritt Parkway, Jarvis and Kora were driving directly ahead of Malcolm, who was behind the wheel of Beatrice's car, with Beatrice and Joyce as passengers. Shortly after midnight, Malcolm poked his pistol out of the driver's side window and fired a shot over the top of his buddy's Buick. Jarvis pulled immediately onto the shoulder with Malcolm trailing.

"Man, are you crazy?" Jarvis screamed through his side window.

"I had to clean my gun out," his younger buddy replied.

"Well, don't be firing at me because I might spit one back at you."

Such recklessness by Malcolm was initially attributed to plain devilishness. "We were young," said Jarvis, "and he had these stupid, foolish ideas. That's how kids get into trouble." At another level, Malcolm's "showing off" was viewed as an attempt "to gain the respect of the girls, so that they would fear him."[29]

As the job market tightened with soldiers returning from the war, Negroes were increasingly constrained by the racist hiring practices so widespread in the 1940s. With Malcolm's low-paying day jobs not much of a help with the rent, especially given his demands for cigarettes and reefer, and his occasional dabbling with powdered cocaine, he set about planning his own criminal enterprise. Gambling-house job offers had come his way, but, he dismissed them, as he had pimping, as too much of a drain on his temperament and lifestyle. Already the quintet had become something of a gang.[30] So Malcolm settled on organizing a burglary ring, relying initially on the contacts that Frank Cooper (Rudy) had in wealthy communities. Malcolm was thrilled that Cooper, no stranger to hustling, was eager to get on board with such an operation.

When Malcolm approached Jarvis with the vague outlines of his plan to field a burglary team, he found his longtime friend and roommate surprisingly willing. Almost immediately agreeing, Jarvis noticed that Malcolm was stepping up attempts to establish control for himself as the unquestioned leader of the ring.

"In any organization," Malcolm wrote, "someone must be the boss." Once when Cooper, Jarvis, and the three women gathered in Jarvis's apartment to discuss the nascent burglary operation, Malcolm staged a rogue Russian roulette stunt. Emptying the chamber of his revolver, he replaced one bullet, spun the cylinder and, according to his account, placed the muzzle of the pistol to his head. In what he described as a test "to see how much guts all of you have," he dramatically pulled the trigger. "We all heard it click." His two buddies and the women grew livid with concern and begged their friend to stop. Instead, according to the *Autobiography*, Malcolm pulled the trigger a second time, as hysteria fluttered about the room. Then finally, with the odds one in three for a bullet being discharged into his head from the five-round cylinder, Malcolm wrote that he pulled the trigger a third time. "I'm doing this, showing you I'm not afraid to die. Never cross a man not afraid to die . . . now let's get to work."[31] Heroics aside, Malcolm said later that he had palmed the lone bullet seemingly loaded into the roulette pistol.[32]

While not doubting that Malcolm pocketed the ammunition,

Jarvis disclosed a totally different account of the Russian roulette incident. With emotions surfacing even decades later, Jarvis detailed what happened that night "in my house." Yes, he confirmed, Malcolm seemingly loaded a lone bullet in the chamber, placed it to his head, and clicked the trigger. "He called himself being cute in front of the girls. He said, 'See, I know what I'm doing.' Then, he spun the cylinder without looking and pointed the gun at me," some three feet away. "Beatrice got scared. He pointed the gun at me and pulled the trigger—and it clicked!

"Man, was I mad. Mad! I reached in my hip pocket and I come up with a .38. I put it right into his—" said Jarvis, breaking off in emotions. "'Man, I'll tell you something, you ever do that to me again, I'll blow your brains out.' I wasn't joking. And he took one look in my face and he knew I meant business."[33] Jarvis's version is in keeping with the provocative Malcolm of childhood, who recklessly pushed brother Philbert and others to the extreme limits of their tolerance. And although a drug-high Malcolm might exhibit a willingness to die, his dealings with Officer Knapp in Lansing revealed the sober Malcolm would more likely demonstrate bravery not as a readiness to die but as a willingness to kill. In any case, the roulette game required yet another silent truce in the contentious relationship of Malcolm and Jarvis, who continued as fast friends. Neither Jarvis nor Cooper "ever mentioned it," Malcolm wrote of the Russian roulette ordeal. "They thought I was crazy. They were afraid of me."[34] As for the girls, the incident—in a foreshadowing of terror tactics to come—was said to have imbued in Beatrice and her sister a deep respect and awe, if not total loyalty, toward Malcolm.

By the fall of 1945, Malcolm and his gang were brought together under what is described in the *Autobiography* as a well-conceived plan. Initially exploiting Cooper's contacts as a caterer's helper, Malcolm groomed the girls to serve as "finders," scouting and casing other wealthy homes as pollsters or saleswomen. Upon perusing the layout of the locations for valuables, the girls would report back. Although they would go along on the nighttime ride, the actual breaking and entering would generally be left to the menfolk. In addition to storing loot in Jarvis's apartment, the girls rented an apartment in Harvard Square as a base of operation. Kept in the dark about key aspects of the master plan—indeed, Malcolm's "well-conceived" structure may well have been sketched only in retrospect for the book—Jarvis said it was seemingly hatched on the spot one night when the fellows were having beer and wine at Beatrice's house. "One of the girls, I think it was Joyce, said she was bored. These types of women are always out for excitement," said Jarvis, meaning wealthy, teenage white women who were brazen enough to associate on the sly with jazzmen and black hustlers in segregated Boston of the 1940s. "They want to do something daring, against the law, and get away with it. And somebody said, 'Let's break into a house.' You see, this is the way they think. We said, 'Yeah, that's a good idea.'"[35]

However the burglary spree got launched, it is clear that while the adventurous young women were out for thrills, the men were out for hard cash to sustain their lifestyle. Malcolm recorded that the very first job, based on Cooper's inside information, was pulled off at the home of William Lennon, the wealthy old white man who had hired Cooper to sprinkle his naked body with baby powder. Familiar with the premises and the immediate neighborhood, the gang made the score without a hitch. In fact, Lennon later discussed the robbery with Cooper and revealed that the Boston police were hot on the wrong trail chasing another gang operating in town.

As a Boston native, Jarvis was far more impressed with another of the gang's early scores. Beatrice happened to know that a member of the Gamble family, of the international Procter and Gamble corporation, had a home in her town of Belmont. "We didn't want to go into a house and hurt anybody. Malcolm, being the brain of the gang, suggested that we pick houses when nobody's home. It so happened, Beatrice knew at that time that Mr. Gamble had gone to Hawaii or someplace for the winter. We drove up in my Roadmaster. It was a fairly big house. First, Malcolm rang the doorbell. He was going to act as a salesman. When we were satisfied nobody was home, we took a crowbar and jimmied the window from the side and entered the house through a back window. We took a whole case of Johnnie Walker scotch. We had beer. We took all of the bed linen they had, like sheets and pillowcases, stuff we couldn't get during the war but rich people could afford. We threw them in the trunk and took them back across town."[36]

Another well-known spot that the gang burglarized in similar fashion was the suburban residence of an executive of Esterbrook Pen Company. Starting around Thanksgiving, the five-person burglary ring—occasionally reinforced by Frank Cooper, Sonny Brown, and John Richmond—hit residences in the suburbs of Newton, Walpole, Arlington, and Brookline, garnering a spread of portable loot: rugs, jewelry, lamps, sheets, blankets, and other household items. "We didn't bother with silverware or anything bulky like that," Jarvis said. Normally the gang was in and out in ten minutes or so, depending on how isolated the spot was. "Once we went in," Jarvis said, "the girls would come in. They never looked to take nothing. They found it more exciting than anything else. It was a thrill to them. We guys took the stuff and bring it back home and sell it to a fence. Malcolm knew everybody in Boston—the prostitutes, the fences, the queers, everybody."[37]

In confirming Malcolm's account of a close call, Jarvis detailed how one night, in the white suburb of Newton, the police spotted the gang in their car with the girls and a trunk full of loot. Jarvis said he took the advice of the gang's "quick-witted" leader and beeped the squad car, then got out and asked the patrolmen for directions back to Roxbury. "To keep them from checking us out," Jarvis said, "we checked them out." Things didn't always go so smoothly between the two "polar-opposite" roommates who admittedly "never agreed, never." One night as they left a burglarized house and headed for the getaway car, a neighbor, out walking his dog, spotted the team and hid behind a tree. "Malcolm leveled his gun off like he was going to take a shot at the tree. I don't think he was going to shoot and kill the man. I pushed his hand out, and said, 'Uh, uh, I'm not going to be no witness to no murder by accident or on purpose.' So we got in the car and split before the man went home to call the cops." On this and other points, Jarvis was "rebellious against [Malcolm's] way of thinking. But the girls looked up to him, especially Beatrice; she was submissive, she really loved him."[38]

The members of the crime ring held to their cover routines by day, as the wealthy girls tended to their household duties. In addition to working on the railroad, Jarvis played his occasional nightclub gigs, and Malcolm continued to cycle among temporary jobs while squiring the young Armenian women about town.[39] John Richmond and Sonny Brown, came along intermittently, as did Frank Cooper, who "never missed attending his sensitive old man [Lennon]."[40] During this period, the *Autobiography* renders Malcolm as a reefer-smoking playboy lying low when not on the prowl or partying with the team girls at a Jarvis jazz gig. In one bragging encounter, he stared down a black detective over a phone call from Beatrice in a club. In another story, Malcolm, high on cocaine, got rattled upon encountering a close, war-veteran friend of Beatrice's husband, Mehran Bazarian, sitting with the women in a Roxbury club. Later that night, when Malcolm had pitched up at the gang's Harvard Square apartment, this veteran entered the hideaway with his own key. After noticing the women's belongings spread about the flat, he confronted Malcolm, who had been hiding under the bed.

"I really got sick," Malcolm wrote. "It was less of a physical sickness than it was all of the last five years catching up."[41] Even though the *Autobiography* does not make the connection here, his

foreboding, his sense of the world collapsing, harks back to that
psychic sense attributed to his mother, Louise, a sixth sense that
Malcolm claimed to have inherited.

Up to this point, Jarvis tallied the burglaries pulled off at fewer
than a dozen in some two weeks. "All this started the first week of
December."[42] Then, short of cash after a card game at George Holt's
place, Malcolm short-circuited the fencing procedure and dropped
off a plainly initialed wedding band at a jeweler-pawnshop on Warren Street, along with an expensive watch, a heist from a Dedham
home, which he also asked to be repaired. When cash from the fence
came through, Malcolm returned to pick up at least the watch.

A trio of policemen this time was waiting for Malcolm at the Roxbury pawnshop, since the well-to-do owners of the ring had filed a
burglary report. When approached, Malcolm innocently raised his
hands and alerted the arresting officer about his pistol, but characteristically noted in his book that his first instinct, during a moment
of distraction, was to shoot the cop dead. As portrayed in the *Autobiography,* Malcolm's arrest was a lucky break: he wrote that Beatrice's
cuckolded husband, alerted by his war-veteran buddy, had concurrently stormed over to Malcolm's apartment with a gun and bad
intentions. Fortunately, the leader of the burglary ring had just been
whisked away downtown, where things were going a bit easier for him
at the Boston police precinct.

"The detectives didn't beat me," Malcolm wrote. "They didn't
even put a finger on me." This nonviolence, he surmised, was because
he had not attempted to "kill the detective,"[43] even though he'd been
caught red-handed and was outgunned. This passive reaction when
cornered was in keeping with a pattern that Malcolm had followed
since mixing it up as a child with his brother Philbert and the tough
guys at elementary school. The police found no reason to get beyond
the "good cop" stage. "He wasn't fresh at all," said Detective Stanley
Slack, who gave the prisoner two packs of cigarettes, according to the

*Boston Globe.* "He was more scared than anything else. He was only a kid, and we felt sorry for him." With due cooperation, the detectives got the names of the young women, as well as of Jarvis, Sonny Brown, and John Richmond. A follow-up search of the apartment in Cambridge turned up burglarized loot, such as jewelry, rugs, and fur coats, burglary tools, and a small arsenal of handguns. Malcolm wrote that Jarvis was pulled off the bandstand and arrested. In reality, however, he was arrested while working his railroad job as a waiter in the club car.[44]

A preliminary search of Jarvis's apartment turned up a bullet, raising the suspicion that he was armed. After his mother told police his train was heading back from New York, detectives boarded it, and at about nine in the evening of January 12, 1946, approached the waiter on a break.

"Is your name Jarvis?" they asked. "You know a guy called Malcolm Little? We have him at police headquarters, and we're arresting you for burglary."

When the detectives asked for identification, Jarvis reached into his pockets for his ID. "They jumped back. They thought I had a gun. They could have shot me dead right there." (Actually, his .38-caliber pistol was back at his mother's house, hidden under the piano lid.) The officers handcuffed Jarvis near the Framingham train stop and hauled him back to Boston.[45]

With arrest warrants outstanding for the gang in two counties, the women were released on bail. Richmond and Brown remained on the loose, while Malcolm and Jarvis were held on $10,000 bail at the Middlesex County jail awaiting trial for breaking and entering. They couldn't prove that Malcolm had been armed during the burglaries, and Jarvis had his father throw his hidden pistol into the Charles River. "They tried to get the girls to say that we had raped them," said Jarvis, "but the girls wouldn't do it. They threatened to give them a lot of time if they didn't cooperate with them on making these charges." And Malcolm remembered that the court clerks, the bailiffs, the public defender assigned to him, and, most especially, the social workers were more concerned that upper-middle-class white women were consorting with "niggers" than they were with the criminality of the case. One of the four detectives who arrested Jarvis told him in the waiting pen that "if we had you niggers down south, we'd lynch you."[46] Such was the racial climate in Boston during the postwar years.

Awaiting trial, the two friends once again were at loggerheads. Malcolm spent most evenings asleep, while in the cell across the hall, Jarvis was awake until the wee hours, reading the Bible his religious father had given him. "Praying like some Negro . . . deacon"[47] on his knees in the jail cell is how Malcolm recalled his buddy awaiting trial. "I was the one who started getting into this mind thing," Jarvis recalled. "I wanted to know if there is a Jesus, or God, why would He leave me in prison when I repented for everything I had done wrong in life." Prison life was very regimented. Inmates were let out of their cells at 8:00 a.m. for breakfast, taking their food tray with them. From nine until three in the afternoon, they were required to work in a workshop. They had an hour for recreation, when they could walk around the yard and exercise. Then they would line up for dinner, pick up their food tray, and return to their cell until the next morning. The two Malcolms lived on the tier at each prison starting with the Middlesex County jail. Malcolm and Jarvis saw each other every day. "I cursed him out, asking how in the hell did the cops get my phone number and address?" said Jarvis. "They threatened to beat you with a rubber hose and you got scared. I was mad. To keep them from beating your head, you told them who we were. He always denied that's the way it was."[48]

At their trial on February 26, 1946, at the Middlesex County courthouse, Malcolm and Jarvis sat on a bench within a cage reportedly reserved for defendants unable to make bail. Beatrice

Bazarian, her sister Joyce Caragulian, and Kora Mardarosian sat at the defense table with their attorney, Walter McLaughlin, who seemed none too pleased with his clients' relationship with the black codefendant Malcolm. Nor for that matter was Malcolm's sister Ella, who had long been embittered by Malcolm's clinging to his white girlfriend after abandoning first Laura, then Evelyn. Still, she attended her half brother's trial, but, as Malcolm's full siblings had when he was hauled off to detention back in Michigan, Ella reasoned that a modest jail stretch might "teach him a lesson."[49] Jarvis had his own lawyer.

Malcolm's legal guardian, however, left her brother's defense up to a court-appointed attorney, who, Malcolm said, muttered, among other indignities, "You had no business with white girls!" On this key nonjudicial point, Judge Allan Buttrick appeared to be in total agreement with both sides. Beatrice and the other white girls turned state's evidence, testifying through their attorney that they had been forced to participate in the burglaries. With the evidence overwhelming and the prosecutor trying to nail them with additional, unknown cases, both Malcolm and Jarvis pleaded guilty to those burglaries they had committed.

The judge commenced reading the sentence: eight to ten years for each charge on the state's bill of particulars, which he said would run "concurrently." Doing the math, Jarvis, who misunderstood the meaning of "concurrently," started "counting ten, twenty, thirty. . . . When I got up to a hundred years, I went berserk. I grabbed the cage and rocked it—I got strength from I don't know where. Why don't you find me guilty of murder and send me to the chair?"[50]

Jarvis's family, along with spectators, both black and white, rose from their seats and grew unruly. Ella understood "concurrently" precisely—it meant the sentence for all counts would be served simultaneously, so the total prison time would be eight to ten years—but nonetheless screamed, "You're sending my boy to prison."[51]

The judge ordered the courtroom cleared, and a marshal reached to usher Ella out.

"Ella was a big, strapping woman, over two hundred pounds," Jarvis recalled. "When he grabbed her arm, she shoved and bounced that cat off the wall. And the riot squad came in and ushered the people out."[52] The *Boston Daily Record* described the fracas as "one of the wildest demonstrations ever seen" in a Middlesex County courtroom.[53]

Both Kora and Joyce were placed on probation and released, while Beatrice ended up serving some seven months in jail. Stunned at the news that he would have to serve a minimum of five and a half years before there was any possibility of parole, Malcolm allowed himself to be quietly escorted out of the courtroom.

# CHAPTER 9

# Learning to Fight with Words

N O OTHER GATE ON EARTH SLAMS WITH THE FINALITY OF A prison gate. Malcolm heard that wrought-iron sound of horror on February 27, 1946, when he walked inside the Charlestown State Prison. He had served brief periods in jails, starting with juvenile detention back in Michigan and, most recently, in Boston for a larceny indictment in 1944 that drew probation. But now, handcuffed to Malcolm Jarvis, he walked into a notorious, maximum-security, nineteenth-century granite prison complex, which still possessed the electric chair that had frizzled out the lives of the Italian immigrants and condemned anarchists Sacco and Vanzetti, only nineteen years before in a notorious case protested around the world.[1] One of the oldest state prisons in the United States, it was modeled after the infamous Bastille and had been completed in 1805, some sixteen years after French revolutionaries, on July 14, 1789, stormed that medieval fortress in the center of Paris.

On his first day, Malcolm was photographed as a stern, hard-eyed inmate above his new identity as number 22843. He was twenty years, nine months, and eight days old. Nothing had prepared him for confinement in a narrow cell, the raw impact so unshakable that, as he wrote years later, the convict "never will get completely over the memory of the bars."[2] Upon being processed, both he and Jarvis whiffed the sickening fecal odor wafting throughout the tier from the wooden toilet buckets in each cell.

A cursory medical examination of Malcolm noted a heart flutter, not unusual for fresh "fish" (prison slang for a new inmate) arriving at maximum-security prisons in a high state of anxiety, confusion, and bitter resentment.[3] Spewing "filthy names" at officials and even the chaplain, who had heard it all before, Malcolm, as was his habit on the streets, defiantly offered up a stream of misinformation about addresses, jobs, and family matters, especially those related to his mother. The prison psychiatrist was keen on double-checking data provided about her confinement in the mental ward of the Kalamazoo State Hospital. One return-mail reply corrected the point that Louise Little was "colored," and not "white" as Malcolm had indicated.[4]

As the starkness of incarceration set in on the once happy-go-lucky street hustler, Malcolm's demeanor changed dramatically. Malcolm Jarvis recalled, "His extroverted life was taken completely away from him and his introvert part began to come forward. That's what he used to tell us." Malcolm was rocked not only by that fecal stench on the cellblock but also by his forced withdrawal from cigarettes and drugs. Straightaway, he started hustling, Jarvis said, "because he was still smoking and would make little deals trying to get cigarettes."[5] Smokes came easily enough on the tier, but marijuana and cocaine were initially well beyond the reach of inmate number 22843. Frantically, he launched a search for substitutes, starting with his cellmate, from whom he learned that nutmeg smuggled from kitchen workers could be mixed with cold water to produce the kick of several marijuana joints. This handy spice contains myristicin and safrole, two psychoactive compounds that in a dose of two tablespoons, toxicologists say, could indeed stimulate something of an "out of body experience."[6] But first, Malcolm had to acquire some cash or a hoard of cigarettes, which served as the medium of exchange in the cellblock and on the prison yard.

As he had during weeks of pretrial confinement, Jarvis continued to hound his partner in crime for ratting him out to police. Even as Malcolm rebuffed such claims, both inmates stewed over the severity of their prison sentences, which they attributed to their association with the white women, an affiliation that was quite legal but deeply resented by the forces of the law. Malcolm made peace with Beatrice's testimony against him and the gang at the initial trial, chalking it up to duress and pressure from her attorney and the prosecutor. And the burglary ringleader, naïvely, in Jarvis's opinion, steadfastly held out hope that Beatrice and her wealthy contacts would assist him still, as the gang's second trial loomed in a Dedham courtroom for the group of burglaries that had been committed in Norfolk County.

This second trial, some five weeks later, in April, was pro forma for Malcolm and Jarvis. Although the gang pleaded guilty to four additional burglaries, their previous eight-to-ten-year concurrent prison sentences were simply allowed to stand. As Jarvis noted, however, the attendant drama during the proceedings stripped Malcolm of all expectation that his beloved Beatrice would ever again come to his aid. Trial transcripts do not reflect discussions apart from the testimony, but Jarvis and a friend in attendance confirmed that a shouting match erupted in which Malcolm blasted Beatrice's claim from the witness stand that she had been "forced" to participate in the burglaries. Unhinged by his longtime girlfriend's testifying that it was not "love" but brute pressure from her Negro acquaintance that roped her into the crime ring, Malcolm flew into a rage of counterbetrayal and laid bare not only the modus operandi of the gang but also their intimate relationship as lovers. It was the wealthy

Belmont resident, he shouted, who had in fact selected and cased targeted residences for the burglary gang. And for good measure, Malcolm snitched, in the presence of her father, that the married Beatrice had pilfered family money for him and for the renting and maintaining of the gang's safe house in Cambridge.[7]

This courtroom ordeal was not detailed in the *Autobiography,* and Malcolm also withheld his sinking reaction to betrayal by the lover whom he had intimately associated with for some four years. Notwithstanding the omissions, the thunder in the Dedham courtroom that day likely altered Malcolm's hopes for personal interracial relationships, and it may well have set fault lines for the earthquake that would subsequently rattle his overall view of black-white group relations. Several months after this second trial, a disgruntled Malcolm and Jarvis eased their relationship back to its normal state of friendly contentiousness as tier mates at the Charlestown State Prison.

One of Malcolm's first visitors in prison was his sister Ella Collins, who later decried the severity of his sentence, which was far too cruel to serve as the nudge she had hoped might push her half brother onto a better path. "He didn't have to go and live in the prison with criminals . . . including murderers," Ella protested in blasting the sentencing judge. In a mood of self-criticism, she partly blamed the severity of the court ruling on her own wayward lifestyle, which she felt impelled to resort to under the racial circumstances of Boston. "I often believe that he was sent to prison because I raised so much hell."[8] This sentiment, however, was not apparent during that first visit as Ella stared in amazement at the 22843 stenciled on her brother's prison denims. "Neither of us could find much to say," Malcolm wrote. "I wished she hadn't come at all."[9] The feeling was apparently mutual, given Ella's widely spaced subsequent visits. And Malcolm resisted all her efforts to rein him in even as he managed to persuade his half sister periodically to slip him cash in the mail, which he spent on contraband items. Starting with matchboxes of nutmeg from kitchen helpers, Malcolm stepped up his mind-altering intake to include brand-name drugs, such as Nembutal and Benzedrine, from corrupt prison guards, as well as occasional reefers.

As the first member of his Midwestern family to draw a stiff prison sentence, Malcolm attracted a stream of mail and a trickle of visits from Boston-area relatives, including his other half sister, Mary; his brother Reginald; his sister Hilda, when she visited Boston; and cousins. Early on, however, Malcolm's lingering bitterness and his leveling of sharp resentment at the pious Christians alienated those relatives, such as his two aunts Sarah and Gracie Little, who counseled prayer and Bible reading. A boastful, jailhouse heathen, Malcolm profanely fended off Philbert's overtures for spiritual reform, as his brother's letters offered up prayers from his newfound, fundamentalist Christian church back in Detroit. Even the ever patient Hilda was put off initially by her younger brother's drug-fueled attitude in the reception center during her early visits to Charlestown Prison.

In his quest for attention and respect on the cellblock, Malcolm cursed the Bible and the very God of his mother and Baptist-preacher father during the intermittent highs he got from the nutmeg concoctions and stronger drugs he was able to use. He also spewed abuse at the guards, heaved items through the iron bars, staged sit-down tirades in the prison workshop, and otherwise disturbed the peace along with the best of the tray rattlers on the cellblock. But it was his sustained antireligious campaign that reportedly got him dubbed "Satan" among inhabitants who were not much given to worshipping the first estate, but who held their tongue—or even attended religious services—in hopes of better treatment by prison authorities and the parole board. Discussing it decades later, Jarvis said he considered Malcolm's alleged "demonic" reputation on the tier an exaggeration and claimed he was not privy to his being tagged "Satan" (but Malcolm's account in the *Autobiography* tells a different story).

The two served but six months together in Charlestown before the jazz musician was transferred to another state prison. Jarvis, however, pointed out that the 900-plus inmates in maximum-security Charlestown included convicted murderers, rapists, stickup men, and mob enforcers, with plenty of hard-core agnostics, atheists even, among them. Besides, there was only so much mischief that a twenty-year-old fish could make among such hardened criminals locked up some seventeen hours every day. Daily routine had the prisoners out of their six-by-twelve-foot cells at 8:00 a.m., to return food trays and to empty toilet buckets before reporting to their assigned workshops, where they remained until three in the afternoon. They were then granted one hour to walk around the yard before returning with supper trays to assigned quarters, at around 4:30. The cells were so tiny inmates could span the walls with their arms. In this era before commercial television, there was no radio in the cells. The prisoners' solitude was broken by a newspaper perhaps, the Holy Bible, and "lice running all over," said Jarvis. "Rats don't live inside granite— there's nothing for them to eat."

In contrast to American prisons today, about 85 percent of Charlestown inmates in the 1940s were white. "We separated ourselves from them guys" on the yard, Jarvis recalled. "When we stood in a circle talking, they would walk around us trying to read our lips. We used to bow our heads so they couldn't." [10] This pattern initially cramped Malcolm's lifestyle of talking to everyone without regard to race, class, or gender. "I really disliked how Negro convicts stuck together so much," he wrote. In the workshops where inmates shared common space, there was one light-skinned, middle-aged convict who caught Malcolm's ear because of the attention that he attracted from not only black but white prisoners, as well as from guards who otherwise "wouldn't think of listening to Negro prisoners' opinion on anything." [11]

A man called Bimbi in the *Autobiography* has been identified as

John E. Bembry, a well-read autodidact not at all impressed with the "daddy-o" street-jive talk of the young inmate Malcolm Little. After laboring in the license plate shop, the gruff-speaking though scholarly Bembry would ensnare all comers who, during domino games on the yard, dared dispute his prison-tier postulations on a variety of subjects. As a gifted gabber predisposed to attention-grabbing himself, Malcolm saw in Bembry a possible role model who clearly had the prison crowd beating a path to his better rhetorical mousetrap. While granting Bembry credit in the *Autobiography* for inspiring him to ponder ways of lifting his own rhetoric from the streets perhaps to the podium level, Malcolm noted that his primary attraction was to the idea that, even among the most reluctant cellblock audience, a person could fight and win respect "with his words."

This jailhouse encounter was akin to the revelation of Mississippi-born novelist Richard Wright, who as an eighteen-year-old discovered the powerful writings of H. L. Mencken, the master wordsmith. "How did one write like this?" Wright wrote in his autobiographical *Black Boy,* recalling his thoughts upon first reading *A Book of Prefaces.* "I pictured [Mencken] as a raging demon, slashing with his pen. . . . He was using words as weapons, could words be used as weapons? Well, yes, for here they were. Then, maybe, perhaps, I could use them as weapons." [12] Thus began the lifework of one of America's greatest twentieth-century novelists. And as young Richard Wright sought to master the employment of the written word in fighting demons plaguing him in the racist South, young Malcolm was inspired now to weaponize the spoken word as an instrument for gaining notice on the tier and respect on the prison yard.

Fighting the demons in his life would come later.

In addition to appreciating Bembry's rich vocabulary, Malcolm noticed, upon further observation, that the older inmate's prison-yard dialectic was based on a command of historical facts, statistics, and the writings of cited philosophers, experts, and scholars. It was not just words simply. And Bembry had a knack for rendering lofty ideas accessible to even the unschooled, as he ranged from Thoreau and human behavior back to the architecture of the state institutions where he had served time. A frequenter of the prison library, such as it was, Bembry, who had mastered Kant, Nietzsche, and Schopenhauer, seldom used curse words even when he memorably destroyed Malcolm's loudly extolled but thinly supported commitment to "atheism." Indeed, after Bembry severely undercut Malcolm's cocksure, antireligious stance, the would-be protégé began to wind down his vicious cellblock tirades against the church and its supplicants. His family would take notice in due course.

Despite the public putdown, Malcolm was not moved to ponder broader scholarly pursuits until Bembry offered a private appeal. The jailhouse scholar directly admonished the young inmate on the prison yard, saying, as Malcolm recalled: "I had some brains, if I'd use them."[13] This straightforward nudge from a relative stranger was precisely the message that Malcolm's siblings, Wilfred and Hilda chief among them, had been trying to press upon him since the death of their father and the institutionalization of their mother. Malcolm's entire Midwestern family had long considered him the most gifted of the clan, the truly anointed scion. Many working-class black families had such a chosen child, but this special status was always embraced as a silent recognition, never much emphasized, if uttered at all, and most assuredly not celebrated openly with the subject. It was as if by citing such a blessing the family would turn it into a curse. And there was always the risk of stirring up envy among brothers and sisters. Nonetheless, working-class parents, sometimes with the compliance of mature-minded, older siblings, would compound their silent hopes and invest what resources they could spare to clear the way for this singular offspring to find his way and make them all proud.

In Malcolm's case, the wayward years spent on the streets of Lansing, Boston, and Harlem had all but eroded Ella's initial faith in him. And they were also straining the silent devotion of his patient sister Hilda and his long-suffering brother Wilfred, who, in addition to bailing him out of Michigan jails numerous times, occasionally had come up with travel money to get him back on the road east. Just as the juvenile detention in Michigan had reformed young Malcolm to the point of his being elected president of his eighth-grade class, Wilfred and Hilda were hopeful that prison might ultimately steer this man-child back onto the narrow path, where he could apply his quite remarkable gifts toward making the family proud.

The prospects for Malcolm, however, appeared quite dim, if not dead-ended, in the eyes of associates and, increasingly, relatives. More and more, the family letters thinned out and the visits grew fewer and far between. Hilda reportedly swore never again to go see him after a few prison visits with her drug-hazy brother at Charlestown. However, Malcolm was finding it difficult to accept the possible loss of this older sister who—since their mother had been institutionalized—had become a surrogate authority figure in his life. After years of complaining about his postcards mailed from Boston, some written in an altered state, Hilda suggested in a stern letter from Michigan that Malcolm improve his penmanship and revamp his grammar with an English course. This simple entreaty in prior days would have been flatly rejected or humored away with feigned respect. But the young inmate who hopelessly fancied himself as "Satan" began to realize that the embracing arms he kept slapping away were finally turning away from him—that he had backed himself into a granite corner with no way out.

In the first glimmer of the prodigal son turning his secular eyes homeward, Malcolm took Hilda's motherly advice. "I did begin a correspondence course in English," he wrote in the *Autobiography*. "Some of the mechanics of grammar gradually began to come back to me."[14] Thus inspired by kith and kin, book learning—a core ingredient of his mother's child-rearing—took on a new urgency.

With the added spark from Bembry, Malcolm set out to pursue education, this time around not as a way to seek the approval of teachers, or even family, but rather as a way to distinguish himself and wield power among the hardened convicts on the tier.

Regaining a purpose for his mental pursuits, Malcolm set to prepare for the long road of study with the high energy and work ethic of his father, although without embracing manual labor. Repeatedly, he shunned assigned duties in the prison workshops. Never much given to half-measures, he methodically began to retool his reading skills to better understand the serious tomes that Bembry talked so much about. Characteristically, Malcolm exaggerated how far he had fallen, claiming, "I didn't know a verb from a house." [15] His pursuit of language proficiency over the next few years in prison was doubtlessly keyed by a recently published scholarly primer that methodically walked readers through the origins and connectedness of languages. The 1944 book that Malcolm later touted to Alex Haley, the coauthor of the *Autobiography*, was *The Loom of Language* by Frederick Bodmer. Like others over the years, Malcolm prized Bodmer's work not as a guide to learning foreign languages but as a Rosetta stone for mastering his own language, English. And, as suggested, he started anew by building a vocabulary from "alpha" in the dictionary and working his way to "zebra."

With Hilda's urging and under Bembry's tutelage, in due course, Malcolm would take to reading everything from the classics of Shakespeare to Aesop's fables, reportedly his favorite for the varieties of interpretations he could apply to life, family, personal conflicts, and everyday human beings, including guards at the prison, thugs on the streets, and government officials on the take. His verbal dexterity, long a staple of Malcolm's limited street rap, would be upgraded with metaphors, similes, and poetry into a veritable dynamo of persuasion. Within a few weeks, Malcolm enrolled in a Latin course and subsequently, using his photographic memory, devoted himself to studying Bodmer's *Loom of Language*. This didactic pursuit of linguistics, together with his street-tested argumentative style, eventually would arm Malcolm with a terrible swift literary sword that could slay just about any dragon in a debate on the prison yard or in a lecture hall. This would not be the last time that Hilda, in combination with Wilfred as surrogate parents, would lay hands on their imprisoned younger brother to point him toward fulfillment of his high promise.

Deep into the autumn of 1946, Malcolm began to see the influence of Bembry—though not that of his family—as somewhat self-limiting within prison walls. The jailbird philosopher was, after all, a hopeless recidivist, adrift in an indefinite sea, pursuing book learning as an end unto itself. In addition to scholarship, Bembry had introduced Malcolm to the world of "cellblock swindles," which had him hustling domino sessions for packs of cigarettes, betting on ball games and boxing matches, and trafficking in various forms of contraband. Prison-tier hustling was not exactly the pursuit that Malcolm's family had envisioned for its favorite son. Use your brain indeed, as Bembry had instructed him, but toward what end? Under the glow of the study lamp, the prodigal son was beginning to see the fog of incarceration lifting away. Malcolm began to think about a future beyond prison.

As it happened, one of Jarvis's early visitors at Charleston Prison was Abdul Hameed, the Muslim from India whose talk of spirituality had failed to impress Malcolm on the outside. Upon being reintroduced, however, to the Ahmadiyya Muslim in the visiting room, inmate number 22843 paid him more attention, even respect. "When Hameed walked into that prison," said Jarvis, "he shook that place up with that black fez. Many of these white people belong to the Masonic lodge. So they gave him respect. He had these people wondering who [Malcolm and I] were that someone would visit us that had an international reputation. They didn't want any international repercussions coming for the way they were treating blacks in prison."[16] Always on the lookout for power brokers, real or illusory, Malcolm perked up his ears, and if for no reason other than the attention it attracted, he fell in with Jarvis in adjusting their behavior and even their appearance, by allowing their beards to grow and requesting a cell facing east.

It was soon after this request that Malcolm Jarvis was transferred to Norfolk Prison Colony, where he continued his pursuit of spirituality with the guidance of Abdul Hameed. Meanwhile, Malcolm was discovering that the Charlestown library was as deficient in reading material as it was in modern plumbing. So inmate number 22843 looked toward another institution to step up his scholarly pursuit of empowerment. Jarvis recommended his new prison as a better venue for education. Malcolm was eager to transfer, but first he had to get back into the good graces of his sister Ella, who had lengthened the intervals between visits. In mid-December 1946, Malcolm wrote "My Dear Sister" requesting a pair of mittens, family pictures to "brighten up my suite," and a fountain pen to write the book he'd several times attempted to start. Work in the prison foundry was harder and dirtier, but "I don't have any of those prejudiced, narrow-minded instructors messing with me now." Still, it was a struggle for him to hold his temper: "One good thing you learn how to do in here, and that is how to use a little self-control." And with his partner in crime off to the "model prison" in Norfolk, Malcolm pestered his well-connected sister about getting "me transferred to Norfolk." If she did so, he promised, "I'll try and complete that whole book next year . . . my only reason for wanting to go is the library alone." He closed by doubling down with a spirited plea: "I only hope you don't stop trying to get me transferred to Norfolk."[17]

Less than a month later, in mid-January 1947, Malcolm was transferred, not to Norfolk, but to the smaller Concord Reformatory, about twenty-five miles from Boston. The medium-security prison was conceived in 1878 as a unit for younger inmates whose maximum term could be cut short with parole, after working a trade and convincing officials they had reformed. Although its library was not as well stocked as Norfolk, the Concord Reformatory surpassed Charlestown in that regard. Moreover, its cells had toilets instead of wooden buckets, and the inmates ate in a dining hall. Malcolm was assigned to the woodworking shop at his new jail; in addition to making furniture, he found time to design small pieces of handcraft such as jewelry boxes, a venture that likely had him reflecting on his eighth-grade teacher's advice that he pursue carpentry, as had his father. Among the Concord inmates, who were more his age, Malcolm, as always, worked to seem more adult, shirking duty and jumping lines, flashing an image of menace even as he pursued the books and bet on major league sports.

The opening Brooklyn Dodgers baseball game, on April 15, 1947, transfixed Malcolm and his buddies on the Concord prison tier, as Jackie Robinson made his debut as the first Negro in the twentieth century allowed to play this "white man's game" of major league baseball. Owners had restricted stadium baseball as a bastion of lily-white privilege for some sixty years. "I'll never forget the prison sensation created that day," wrote Malcolm.[18] Not only had World War II created a shortage of white athletes and fans, it also exposed the contradiction of the nation's dispatching Negroes to die in uniform on battlefields abroad while forbidding them to suit up and play baseball on city fields at home. Still, it was not white altruism that broke the baseball color line, which had barred all Negroes since Moses "Fleetwood" Walker was banished in 1887.[19] Negro League baseball was increasing in popularity and expertise, as the profits of the white major leagues remained stable, when the Dodgers finally broke the gentleman's agreement among white owners. The Boston Red Sox had tried out and rejected Jackie Robinson two years earlier, choosing instead to field a white alcoholic infielder, John "Jackie" Tobin, who played the season crippled by a broken thumb.[20]

On opening day 1947, it was the other team in Malcolm's adopted hometown, the National League's Boston Braves, who opposed Robinson's Dodgers. All-white teams of both leagues were generally staffed by boozers like Jackie Tobin, notorious Southern racists, and scores of mediocre players, most of whom had never seen the inside of a college classroom. Robinson, on the other hand, had been the first four-letter athlete at UCLA and had served as a U.S. Army lieutenant during the war.[21] Despite facing harassment on and off the field that season, not to mention in the Dodger dugout, he would be named the National League's rookie of the year.

"Robinson had his most fanatic fan in me," said Malcolm. "When he played, my ears were glued to the radio, and no game ended without my refiguring his average up through his last turn at bat."[22]

When not clocking Robinson's baseball progress, Malcolm was reading every book he could get hold of and writing letters far into the night. Medium-security Concord was an easier prison station than Charlestown, and as his attitude improved on the yard, the wayward son worked at improving his relationship with his family in Boston and back home in Michigan. Still, sibling rivalry surfaced once more when Philbert wrote a letter touting a newfound religion and beseeching Malcolm to "pray to Allah for deliverance." Having blasted the Christian overture from his religion-prone brother in a letter months earlier, Malcolm doubled down with his improved syntax on Philbert's "natural religion for the black man." The self-assured inmate, while easing out of his "Satan" persona, never gave religion another thought until he got a letter from his younger brother Reginald, whom Malcolm had long worked to impress, from those early days as a floundering boxer to their street hustling together in Harlem. Unlike Philbert, the less zealous Reginald knew how to bait his wayward brother with a bill of particulars. Should Malcolm give up smoking cigarettes and abstain from eating pork, he wrote, "I'll show you how to get out of prison."[23]

Starting with Hilda and now with Reginald, the siblings had finally gotten the attention of their rebellious brother, who was wasting his life in ruinous cellblock living. But what exactly was this "religion for the black man" that two of his quite different blood brothers had found cause to press upon him?

—————

Malcolm's family had stumbled upon this "religion" because their eldest brother, Wilfred, lived his life by the secular teachings of Marcus Garvey. As a devotee of the Univeral Negro Improvement Association (UNIA) doctrine of self-reliance, Wilfred would occasionally challenge management over unfair treatment of fellow Negroes at the Detroit furniture store where he worked. Several white male supervisors, for example, were confronted directly for harassing female employees by patting their backsides. " 'Suppose I was pulling this stuff with one of your women,' " Wilfred remembers asking the sexual predators. " 'What would you think?' And they would go and apologize."

In other cases, Wilfred noticed that when Negroes came due for raises or promotions, they, unlike whites, were targeted for intimidation that was staged by management, he concluded, to forestall their advancement. After observing yet another such worker, a delivery truck driver, being dressed down by management in the store, Wilfred levelheadedly confronted the white manager. " 'Why don't you leave this man alone?' I said. 'You know good and well that he deserves his raise. You're trying to intimidate him so he won't ask for it.' So they went on and gave him the raise."

Wilfred added, "Everyone thought that I was going to get fired, but they didn't fire me." Instead, the store manager took him aside and inquired whether Wilfred—who had made himself valuable with his skill and work ethic—was satisfied with his personal situation. Subsequently, to the surprise of those he had defended, Wilfred was promoted. Still, the one-man labor union—true to the Garveyite prompting of Negro assertiveness in matters of racial fairness—sustained his gentle but effective pressure even as a supervisor at the household furniture store. Such aggressiveness was indeed rare for Negroes in the American workplace of the 1940s, and Malcolm's older brother did not go unnoticed.

"You're a Muslim, aren't you?" asked David Farr, the driver whose pay raise Wilfred had salvaged from a reluctant management. "What is that?" said Wilfred, who had never heard of such a group. "What makes you think I'm a Muslim?"

"For one thing," Farr said, "you always straighten these white folks out around here when they're not right. You make them respect our black women when they come in here. You don't smoke. You don't drink. You're always trying to encourage black people to do what's best for them and things like that. And you make these white people improve our jobs for us and make them give us our raise when it's due." If Muslims taught and practiced such self-help, a curious Wilfred was interested. He asked the delivery driver, "Where do they meet?"[24]

The Detroit chapter of Garvey's UNIA, which Malcolm's father helped organize back in the 1920s, had dwindled to a small group of elderly pioneers holding on against younger members and outside competition. So Wilfred attended his first meeting of the Nation of Islam with David Farr in an apartment building on St. Ann Drive. Initially, he was turned off by the boastful emptiness of the Muslim speaker that first Sunday. But he returned the following week, when a more progressive message was delivered by one Minister Andrew to the Muslims at Temple No. 1, where the Nation of Islam had been founded by Fard Muhammad about a dozen years earlier. "They didn't have that many people," Wilfred recalled, but he sensed that "it had the potential of becoming much more than it had. I decided, well, I'm gonna get with this Nation of Islam and see if we can make something out of it."[25]

# PART III

1946–1963

## CHAPTER 10

# Birth of the Nation of Islam

T HE "NATURAL RELIGION FOR THE BLACK MAN"[1] THAT PHIL-
bert and Reginald were pressing upon their imprisoned brother
was the same Muslim sect that Wilfred had first stumbled across in
Detroit. Upon attending that Sunday meeting at the founding temple of the Nation of Islam, Wilfred learned that the group's headquarters was in Chicago, with a half dozen other temples, in such
cities as Milwaukee, Washington, D.C., and New York. The Muslims'
"uplift program" touted by his co-worker David Farr did indeed target black Americans as a "nation within a nation"; while seeking
its "separate state," members were discouraged from voting, attending public schools, or serving in the U.S. military. Despite the government attention that would be attracted by such policies, Wilfred
joined the Muslims as a religious sect compatible with his secular,
Garveyite upbringing—and he encouraged family members to join
as well.

Although the group was designed exclusively to ease Negro
oppression in postslavery, twentieth-century America, Nation of
Islam leaders insisted that it was strictly religious. And its founding

pattern indeed resembled that of scores of religious sects founded in nineteenth-century America by other earthbound spiritualists, who had targeted white people with specific yearnings. One such religion that even now has sustained itself, for example, is Christian Science, as empowered by Mary Baker Eddy, in New England in the 1880s. Among other remedies in this age before modern medicine, the chronically ill Reverend Eddy proclaimed to her followers that human sickness was illusory and that it could be permanently dispensed with by prayer alone.[2] An earlier homegrown religion was that of the Latter-Day Saints (the Mormons), created by Joseph Smith.[3] Smith, the prophet of this once polygamous sect, claimed that the dogmatic text of the Book of Mormon, written in a novel form of Egyptian hieroglyphics on golden plates, was delivered to him by an angel named Moroni, near Palmyra, New York, in 1823. Among other strictures, subsequent church leaders, starting with Brigham Young, barred Negroes from entering the Mormon priesthood and from participating in key ordinances such as marriage. Justification for such racial exclusion was attributed by white Mormon leaders to a curse concocted from the biblical account of a transgression by Ham against his father, Noah, that supposedly led to the punishment of the offender's son Canaan, who was said to be the father of Canaanites. (These restrictions were lifted in 1978 after Mormon leaders said they had received a divine revelation.)

It would also take decades for Mormons to concede that Joseph Smith took unto himself at least thirty-three wives, some of them as young as fourteen, others already married to other men.[4] While some might consider such behavior deviant, in many respects these homegrown religions follow the general pattern of those widely accepted as mainstream. Similarities are noted by scholars such as Harold Bloom, whose acclaimed critique *The American Religion*, details the idiosyncrasies of such mainstream U.S. religious sects as Jehovah's Witnesses, Pentecostalism, Southern Baptists, and the

Seventh-Day Adventists, the group that Malcolm's mother intermittently worshipped with back in Michigan.

Down through the ages, anthropologists note among humankind of all continents what amounts to a spiritual appetite that is fed by nascent religions served up by a wide range of local idealists, zealots, and dreamers, more than a few of whom were considered quite bizarre in their day. These spiritualists, history instructs, usually proclaim an innate power to influence supernatural forces and thus promote themselves as sacerdotal rainmakers who can singularly petition the gods to relieve their besieged people of some earthly suffering, spare them dangers seen and unseen, and ultimately grant believers a purposeful life of joy and gladness. Along the way, these spiritual founders, such as Joseph Smith, promulgate a set of religious rules governing believers' behavior, the violation of which would not only reap earthly punishment but often subject errant supplicants to unspeakable horrors in some specified hereafter. In addition to adapting ritualistic worship for the sect, these mystics conjure dogmatic myths that cannot be proven explicitly but must be accepted by followers as the spiritual "evidence of things not seen."[5] Such principles appear to have triggered the founding of the Muslim "religion for the black man," which, like the others, borrowed lushly from preexisting spiritual groups.

And as with other sects, the founding impulse of the black "Islamists" in the United States was grounded upon phantasmagorical aspects of a doctrine concocted by a mysterious man claiming to address the unfulfilled aspirations of a defined group. In this case, the group was postslavery Negroes laboring under the brutal yoke of Jim Crow racism. Just as Malcolm's parents took up early with the independence doctrine of Marcus Garvey, so too did an enterprising young man from North Carolina named Timothy Drew. Born a generation after the Civil War and four years before Earl Little, the young southerner likewise opposed Negro acquiescence to the inferior status mandated by U.S. law, which, as a by-product, conditioned a sense of self-loathing and group hatred among its black victims. Like young Earl Little—and like his son Malcolm, most certainly—Drew was a rebel, as Albert Camus depicts the character-type: the bold young man who says no to the absurdity of ironclad tradition. Unlike Reverend Little, the Baptist preacher, however, Timothy Drew also rejected the Christian dogma that whites used as an instrument to sanction slavery and tolerate Jim Crow strictures. Amid the Protestant trappings of a Southern upbringing, the sensitive young Christian apostate steadfastly yearned for a "religion for the black man."

Details of the early years of Drew's spiritual quest are sketchy, with each account as colorful as the next and just as suspect. One oft repeated version has him being born in 1886 to former slaves, abandoned and either adopted or simply taken in by other relatives. Another has him reared either by Cherokees or perhaps a Moroccan father, a relation that would explain his subsequent penchant for North Africa, Islam, and the Moors. As a youngster, Drew ran off with a circus, yet another version goes, supposedly as a magician who somehow made his way to Morocco and Egypt, where he was exposed to the Muslim religion.[6]

Upon encountering Islam by whatever means, Drew was soundly impressed with the appeal of the religion, initially. This ancient Middle Eastern religion attracted the North Carolinian with not only its strict moral discipline but also the modest way its worshippers dressed and the proud and sober manner in which they carried themselves. After reportedly coming under the influence of Muslim teachers, Drew came to view Islam as "the only instrument for Negro unity and advancement."[7] Lacking knowledge of the Arabic language as well as grounding in Muslim orthodoxy, he examined its dogma as best he could by probing the international faith with a keen eye out for remedies that would help Negroes relieve the sociopolitical pain and suffering they endured early in the twentieth century as an oppressed people in the United States.

The young black supplicant found no such balm in orthodox Islam. Also, he reasoned that Arabic dogma would be a tough sell to a generation of Negroes just out of slavery and barely literate in English. Most troubling of all, the Arab Muslims in the Middle East had a long and barbaric history of enslaving sub-Saharan Africans— indeed, they dominated this ruthless human trade in Morocco and Egypt. Additionally, the Moors were known to widely practice color-caste discrimination among themselves.

So how exactly could Timothy Drew be expected to accept this foreign Islam that indulged African slavery and oppression, after having rejected Christianity precisely for sanctioning such atrocities against Negroes at home? This conundrum backed Drew into a spiritual corner. However, unlike Negro Christians in the United States and African Muslims in Morocco and Egypt, this rebel felt free to fiddle with Muslim orthodoxy, just as the mystics Joseph Smith and Mary Baker Eddy had done with Christianity. And thus the double apostate set to mixing and matching what he considered sound and unpracticed principles of Islam with those of Christianity in order to design a hybrid "religion of the black man" in America.

Accordingly, in 1913, twenty-seven-year-old Drew founded the Moorish Science Temple in Newark, New Jersey, and beatified himself as Prophet Noble Drew Ali, supreme temple leader for life.[8] As a magnet for working-class migrants from the South, the handsome, self-assured and inspiring speaker displayed a theatrical knack for pomp and attracted enthusiastic Negro crowds to his modest gatherings. Subsequently, the cagey young organizer adopted the popular, uplift plan of the UNIA to complement his religious dogma. Marcus Garvey was cast as "John the Baptist," paving the way for Prophet Drew Ali's new, domestic brand of Islam. Despite its motto, "One Aim, One God, One Destiny," the UNIA was strictly secular, with a sociopolitical anchor, and therefore Garvey posed no competitive threat to the temple leader's religious efforts. Just as Malcolm's father, Earl, simultaneously preached Christianity and practiced Garveyism, Prophet Noble Drew Ali floated UNIA principles while proselytizing for his signature version of Islam. As with most messianic types, Prophet Ali designed a career for himself that was supported by followers attracted by a healthy dose of racial pride, moral uplift, namesake imprinting, and, like Garvey, an eye-catching display of pageantry.

In one key departure, Drew differed sharply from Garvey over the concept of sub-Saharan Africa as the "homeland" for Negroes in the diaspora. Instead, the self-anointed prophet rooted his religion in the north of the continent, the Maghreb.[9] This region surrounding Morocco was dominated by Arab Muslims and allowed the pragmatic prophet to brand his followers "Moors," a euphemistic ruse that tactically evaded the widespread Negro aversion toward sub-Saharan Africa: as a result of early Hollywood films, U.S. government propaganda, white Christian missionary reports, newspaper coverage, and overall societal conditioning, many Negroes in the early twentieth century looked down upon Africa as a pariah "dark continent" of unspeakable embarrassments.

Skirting this negative perception, Drew Ali generally avoided the direct use of the term "Africa" when addressing intended recruits. Instead, his Moorish Science Temple declared that its domestic, black followers originated in Canaan, as "Canaanites," and that the racial designation for the contemporaneous "Moors" was "Asians." In addition to the Asiatic nations, his makeshift flock included the Moors, Hindoos of India, the Turks, Egyptians, and the native people of North and South America. As "olive-skinned Asiatic people," the "Moors" of the Science Temple were instructed to drop the current terms "Negro," "black," and "colored" and even the sometimes favored "Ethiopian," which Drew Ali said meant "divided." "The

word 'negro' deludes in the Latin language to the word 'nigger,' "
he wrote in an editorial in the *Moorish Guide* newspaper. And, in
a slap at the newly formed NAACP, he added, "The word 'colored'
deludes to anything that is painted, varnished, and dyed. And every
nation must bear a national descent name of their forefathers."[10]
Going halfway with Garvey in linking Negro origins to a continental
landmass, Drew Ali idealized this vague mosaic as the "Asiatic black
man." And lifting from secret Masonic orders that had borrowed
from Muslims of the Ottoman Empire, the prophet instructed his followers to drop their "slave" surnames and substitute "El" or "Bey." As
for the temple lifestyle, adherents avoided pork in the diet, eschewed
alcohol and cigarettes, and preached against "frying," or processing
their natural hair.

While visiting Morocco and Egypt as a restless if not rebellious
Christian, young Drew was said to have been especially inspired by
the ascetic discipline and dietary abstinence of the Muslims, as well
as their regime of prayer five times each day. This moral combination, along with the striking new features topping the makeshift
tenets borrowed from Islam, seemed just the remedy, he argued, for
breaking the habitual passivity that had Negroes reeling back home
under legalized Jim Crow segregation.

In Newark, however, a local Arab linguist, referred to by several
aliases, reportedly took strong exception to Drew's appropriation
of Islamic nomenclature, to say nothing of his proclaiming himself
"Prophet of Allah." With an unchallengeable knowledge of orthodox Islam, this Muslim foreigner, of Ahmadiyya stock, relented in
his attack on the so-called Moors, and settled instead for recruiting
Negro followers away from Drew Ali to his own masjid, or mosque,
in Newark. Wary of a more formidable Muslim challenge from the
east—as well as from city officials angered by antiwhite references—
Prophet Drew Ali focused his organizing for Allah less on Islamic
orthodoxy, where he could not compete, and more on spiritually

reforming the workaday habits of black "Asiatics" in America. The doctrinaire challenge in Newark also inspired the enterprising prophet to take his customized Islam on the road. Straightaway, he set up his base of operation in Chicago, at 3140 Indiana Avenue, and by 1925—the year Malcolm was born—the gifted organizer had established temples in a dozen cities, including Milwaukee, Cleveland, and Detroit—the city to which Malcolm's father, Earl, was driving his few Lansing followers for UNIA meetings in the late 1920s. During this era of the Great Migration, the Motor City and Chicago were being transformed into something of a fertile crescent for burgeoning Negro movements, each one staking out its individual nationalist identities.

Toning down antiwhite rhetoric and adjusting his religious dogma primarily to challenge Christianity among Negroes, Prophet Drew Ali preached that the dependency of the black man in America was keyed to a shameful ignorance of his "Asiatic" homeland, and that this disorientation engendered a destructive self-loathing encouraged by white Americans. With the appended Garvey doctrine addressing the political uplift issue, the prophet stressed that dependency and sloth were disabling counterweights to black progress. He contended that the fight for justice and equality had to be waged by counterattacking Jim Crow power and white dominance and, most directly, by disavowing Christianity.

"We are Moors," Drew would tell his followers at rallies. "Rise up and take your heritage," he intoned. Following the quite lucrative Garvey model to finance temple programs, Prophet Drew Ali looked no further than his followers. Although of meager means individually, the loyalists as a group could amass an impressive treasury with their steady, collective flow of dimes, quarters, and low-denomination paper currency. Even after jazz age glitziness gave way in the early 1930s to the Depression, the sin dens of the so-called chitlin' circuit of black nightclubs, bars, and afterhour gambling and whiskey joints continued to rake in impressive hauls in urban cities. The Christian side of urban areas also attracted black refugees from the South, who were surrendering disposable income unto orthodox purveyors of spiritual uplift. Like the mystic upstarts, the reverend leaders and their families kept hold of much of the loot.

As Earl Little had noticed on his visits to Detroit in the 1920s, the city folks there still supported a growing circuit of religious swamis, so-called divine prophets, and other exotics peddling dreams for upward mobility and a better day. Protestant Negro churches proliferated, as did the ranks of self-proclaimed messiahs, and urban black princes and potentates, ranging from the stern and sober, if unorthodox, to the dazzling and downright bizarre. The secret orders also lined up at the trough with their sparkle, odd rituals, and handshakes—groups such as the dapper Prince Hall Masons and their distaff Eastern Star, all striving in the splendors of the sweet urban here and now of Northern cities. Borrowing lustily from religious as well as social and fraternal orders in England, the Middle East, and America, such as the Ancient Arab Order of Nobles of the Mystic Shrine, Prophet Drew Ali and his temple people adapted titles, honorifics, and rituals, ordering up a custom-made rainbow of ribbons, lavalieres, crests, buttons, gold piping, and boots. As finishing touches, they lifted from the Masons the ceremonial apron and from the Shriners the rakish fez. Temple supplicants turned out for services in colorful robes, headscarves, decorative sashes, high-topped boots, turbans, and fezzes. Their ceremony leaned heavily upon ancient stories and rote passages from the Christian Bible, which, of course, had borrowed from earlier Jewish tracts that had channeled even earlier religious myths and parables of the Babylonians.

The key religious principles of Prophet Drew Ali were outlined in a 1927 pamphlet, "The Holy Koran of the Moorish Science Temple of America." Lifted almost entirely, chapter and verse, from two other publications, Drew Ali's Koran substituted "Allah" for "God" and extended the biblical lineage forward to his "Asiatic black man." In October 1928, the group held its first annual convention in Chicago, boasting of fifteen temples—with Detroit ringing in as Temple No. 4—claiming some thirty thousand members. The convention poster featured the noble "Founder" decked out in a red fez and tassel, with a gold embroidered Islamic crest and scimitar, boots, white shirt, and a necktie under a Middle Eastern robe, and seated in a regal Moroccan wood chair.

In Chicago, city officials watched the Moorish temples first as a South Side curiosity, then as a nuisance. Later, with the Moors' numbers increasing, Prophet Drew Ali was arrested, threatened, and told to tone down the antiwhite component of his Moorish dogma, such as it was. During an internecine clash in Chicago in 1929, the little prophet reportedly stabbed and killed Sheikh Claude Greene, a rival, and was arrested. While in police custody, Drew Ali was beaten before being released on bail.[11]

Later that year, it was announced mysteriously that Prophet Drew Ali was deceased.

In the wake of Noble Drew Ali's departure, and some three years after Marcus Garvey had been deported back to Jamaica, chaos continued to reign among Science Temple rivals vying for leadership, including the chauffeur of the deceased prophet. In an uneasy succession not unfamiliar to urban cults of the day, a Middle Eastern–looking former associate named W. D. Fard stepped forward to head a breakaway rump Muslim group calling itself the Nation of Islam (NOI).[12] Just as the deceased Drew Ali had borrowed ritual, dogma, and nomenclature from Islam, this second Muslim religion on the streets of Detroit initially seemed almost a carbon copy of the Moorish Science Temple. Still, the core of temple followers remained loyal to Prophet Ali—and his Moorish movement would be kept alive for decades, not only in Detroit but also in other cities including Newark, Richmond, Chicago, and Hartford.

The offshoot Islam group under W. D. Fard also maintained common cause with Garvey's secular UNIA and signed up some of the temple members. Its mysterious leader—as with the creation of most new religions—set about generating his own unique version of the origin of man and the universe. And given the Muslims' special audience, the homegrown dogma was grounded on the issue of race. The story of the emergence of this second, domestic Islam group has been no less clouded by myths, falsehoods, faulty recollections, and gross misdirection, with some of the obfuscation quite intentional— even on the part of the founders. This present account has weighed available research, matched it against fresh findings, and double-checked it to the extent possible with early participants, available records, founding pioneers, and a few eyewitnesses interviewed at length and cross-examined.

One of the early observers of the founding of the NOI was Christopher C. Alston, a well-respected union leader with impressive skills as an organizer for civil rights. Born in Florida in 1913, Alston moved at age three with his parents to Detroit, where some of his relatives were founding pioneers of the Moorish Science Temple and witnessed the struggle between warring factions as the seventeen-year-old Islamic group splintered toward the end of 1930. One of several factions evolved directly from the temple as the new Islamic sect led by Fard Muhammad, as W. D. Fard now styled himself. Curiously, this man would subsequently claim, inaccurately, that the members of his new group were the first "black Muslims" in modern America.

It was indeed Drew Ali, the self-proclaimed prophet and black pioneer from North Carolina—and not Fard Muhammad—who first introduced Negroes of the early twentieth century to the concept of an Islamic religion from North Africa. "We knew Fard [Muhammad] for a couple of years in the neighborhood here, before he was

associated with the [Moorish Science] Temple," Alston said of the
man credited with founding the new NOI. "He sold rugs, carpets,
from samples that he brought around. Initially, he didn't have anything to do with this movement at all. He came to our house at 981
Leland, and other people's houses. He was a very nice guy. I remember him as a boy. My family bought a rug from him."[13] Other Detroit
residents remember Fard peddling silks and raincoats door to door,
memories confirmed by writers Arna Bontemps and Jack Conroy in
their book *Anyplace but Here.*[14]

In his sales pitch, the immigrant peddling carpets and silks
would link his exotic merchandise to a Negro "homeland across the
sea," according to C. Eric Lincoln in his 1961 study *The Black Muslims in America.*[15] As word spread, this pitch earned Fard Muhammad
entree to a wider band of Drew Ali's Negro followers eager to learn
more about their original "homeland," where people wore such fin-
ery. Initially, this "kind, friendly, unassuming and patient peddler"
would speak about his travels over refreshments and sometimes a
meal at the homes of customers. Later, he took to critiquing the
diet of his hosts who served pork and other "unclean" fare, which
he contended, contributed to "rheumatism, aches, and pains." The
tentative Fard seemed to become more aggressive with less-educated
Negroes from the South who were loosely attached to church or
political groups. In time, his house-to-house table talk expanded
to cover religion, with the familiar Bible as a departure point. Soon
enough, as Drew Ali was stepping up his Muslim pace in Detroit and
elsewhere, Fard grew bolder in attacking Christianity and, finally the
common-chord evils of the "white man."[16]

"My father knew Fard," Alston recalled. "He said this fellow has
been coming around to the temple. The temple was on Livingston
and Hastings Streets. It was called the Moorish American Temple
of Science. And they had rented a building or bought a building
from the [fraternal] Masons. They used the entire building, with

classrooms, an auditorium, and everything in it. [Fard] said he was from the Middle East. That's all he said. I don't know what he was. He looked Egyptian. Very sharp nose and light skin. He had straight hair. He was definitely [light-skinned]. He never denied that he was [black].

"Fard saw this group [Moors] expanding. They were preaching that 'Allah is God' and that sort of thing. He apparently decided that he was going to be a part of it. Now, he talked with Lomax Bey [governor of the Detroit Temple No. 4], I know that, and he talked with Nelson Bey, because Nelson was related to our family. And I think they asked him to go to Chicago. When Noble Drew Ali came to Detroit, Fard met him, talked to him, and cooperated with him. It was an honest thing. He wasn't trying to make a racket out of it. He was [supposedly] from the east, and Drew Ali was talking about an Eastern thought. So it all fitted, and it attracted him. They had large crowds. But Fard never appeared at these large crowds and said anything. He left the [spiritual] leadership to Noble Drew Ali and the others. He would appear, but he never tried to dominate the scene at all. He definitely had a relationship and was in contact with Noble Drew Ali. He was, like, following the [party] line."[17]

The autoworker father of Christopher Alston was a Methodist and a Garveyite in Detroit who got his "El" in the early 1920s as a spiritual member of Drew Ali's Moorish Science Temple. The son remembers Fard Muhammad as speaking without a foreign accent, despite his supposed Middle Eastern background. He was an "excellent listener," a good salesman, talking mainly about the problems of Negroes in America. "Incidentally, he was in favor of the Japanese [in World War II]. A lot of blacks were, too. And when World War II broke out, the federal authorities went after a lot of the Moorish Americans and said that they were spies [for the Japanese], but they weren't spies."[18] (Nonetheless, C. Eric Lincoln and others do cite possible probes that the Japanese made to exploit any Negro predilection toward them as enemies of their recognized racist enemy, the oppressive American white man.)[19]

"Noble Drew Ali used to come around and tell all of us youngsters stories about our heritage," said Alston. "His idea was that Morocco—that's why he called it Moorish—was the leader of Africa. That wasn't true, but anyway, he'd tell us stories about the great Moroccan armies, the great Moorish armies. He talked about Marcus Garvey and his Back to Africa movement, but the idea of Drew Ali was to give the story romance. And we youngsters just ate it up.

"He was a very quiet man, by the way, Noble Drew Ali—nothing fiery about him at all. He was a quiet minister. He spoke very soft, very quietly. You have to get close to him a lot of times, to hear. And he was a tremendous organizer. That fitted the personality of Fard also. They associated together at the Moorish Science Temple here in Detroit. That's where he started off, and it was logical. Noble Drew Ali was in Chicago and Detroit and other cities. He set up things [temples] all around, and Fard never tried to take control—now this I know of the organization. It was a spiritual thing. That's what Drew Ali wanted to be, and that's what he was."[20]

After Negro soldiers participated abroad in World War I, there was a spike in the group's expectation for civil rights at home. Much as Frederick Douglass had lobbied for enfranchisement and other rights after former slaves fought in the Civil War, key black leaders pressed the case to the federal government for equal opportunities following the first worldwide war for liberation. In Detroit, the Negro population grew restless over brutal treatment by the city police, racial job bias, and blatant discrimination. Increasingly, nationalist movements sprang up to oppose the municipal system dominated by white bureaucrats and so-called criminal justice enforcers of the law.

"Blacks at that time," said Chris Alston, "needed something to lift us out of the caretaker mentality. We needed something to tell us that we were somebody important. And there had been a whole period we had been told differently. I saw my first black teacher in Detroit. The Moorish temple hired her." W. D. Fard was not a member of the temple when young Chris Alston first attended "children classes," in the early 1920s, "He came later and would talk to us about life in the east," Alston said, adding, "And he did talk about life in Japan, too. He said he had been to Japan."[21]

As Fard reportedly watched the disintegration of the Moorish temple mainly from the sidelines, Alston remembers hearing about the fight breaking out in the Chicago temple, complete with a stabbing and shooting of Sheikh Claude Greene that led to the arrest of several members, including Drew Ali. When the prophet died in 1929, Alston and others maintained that the authorities were responsible for his death. "Anyone that was organizing blacks constructively, they want to bring them down," said the union leader.[22]

As the shadowy W. D. Fard emerged, he proclaimed that he was from the holy city of Mecca—and that his mission was to secure "freedom, justice and equality" for his "uncle," the Negro living "in the wilderness of North America, surrounded and robbed completely by the [white] cave man."[23] Fard appeared to have had some prior familiarity with the orthodox religion of Islam; where exactly he acquired it is not clear. He would tell some followers that he descended from the "royal dynasty of the Hashimide Sheriffs of Mecca,"[24] and others that he was a member of Prophet Mohammed's tribe of Koreish.[25] None of these claims of origin would square with orthodox Muslims, and Fard's appendixes of Muslim revisionism, contained in two manuals he wrote for the movement, would be dismissed by such authorities as downright bizarre.

Nonetheless, in the power vacuum left at headquarters by Prophet Drew Ali, the silk peddler came into the fullness of his authority—and on July 4, 1930, W. D. Fard set up his first temple of Islam, in Detroit. Previously, Alston and his family had considered Fard an obedient assistant and servant of Prophet Drew Ali. So they were surprised when the former disciple emerged for a brief time in Detroit, claiming to be "the spiritual reincarnation of Drew Ali." Alston recalled that "Fard didn't seem [previously] to seek this deification for himself."[26]

This would all change as the NOI leader recast this separatist Black Muslim religion in his image. The gaudy dress code favored by Prophet Ali was toned down and the group's signature fez disallowed, but Fard retained much of the Moorish group's strict diet, prayer discipline, and orientation toward the Maghreb, although not as Moors but as "Asiatic black men." Among the tenets Fard grafted onto his restructured Islamic teachings was the concept of the white man as "Satan" and a "blue-eyed devil." A key mythology supporting this conclusion held that the "white race" was created some 6,600 years ago by a black scientist named Yacub, who anointed these Caucasians as a "race of devils."[27] Another of his exotic teachings had a heavily armed "Mother Ship," manned supposedly by Japanese, circling the earth constantly.[28]

The obviously well-traveled, self-taught Fard was a dabbler in science and mathematics, and he promulgated a thick if not impressive binder of question-and-answer lesson plans. These NOI "lessons" were peppered with scientific facts such as the speed of light and the distance of the sun from earth. In addition to indulging his undernourished yen for science, these "tracts" were intended to acquaint his weakly educated Muslim followers, many former sharecroppers a generation out of slavery, with the rigors of study by rote. Rudimentary literacy, encouraged by problem solving, was a basic requirement for potential recruits to absorb written propaganda aimed at imbuing them with unquestioning religious loyalty and self-respect as the "Original Man" who once ruled the world.

The mysterious wanderer Wallace D. Fard used a plethora of aliases: W. D. Fard, W. D. Muhammad, Wali Farrad, Farrad Muhammad, Professor Ford, Wallace Ford, F. Muhammad Ali, and others.

As with Drew Ali before him, Fard was watched closely by Detroit police as a threat to white interests and privilege. Occasionally, the authorities threw the leader of the black religious group into jail for cooling-off periods. Rough treatment during such stints hardened Fard against the "white devil," and he stepped up his attacks against white society before his growing NOI audience, which local authorities estimated at about eight thousand followers.[29]

One of the stragglers who made his way to the temple was Elijah Poole, a migrant up from Sandersville, Georgia. Unlike Alston, Elijah Poole had not met Fard prior to the spring of 1931. Elijah, who would become Fard's lieutenant—and later his heir—was reared under the fundamentalist strictures of his preacher father, William Poole, and was himself a devout reader of Holy Scripture. Not unlike Timothy Drew, however, young Elijah, the grandson of a slave, resisted family pressure to devote his life to Christ. Elijah had twice seen the Ku Klux Klan lynch Negroes in his Georgia hometown, once reportedly watching the group's handiwork in the body of a dead Negro "swaying in the breeze on the limb of a tree." Each time, the bloodthirsty white terrorists worked under the Christian cross of the church and the self-proclaimed sanction of the Holy Bible. After a white employer insulted him on the job in Georgia, Poole moved to Detroit in 1923 with his wife and two children. Some six years later, with the onset of the Depression, the thirty-two-year-old resettled southerner lost his job as an autoworker at a General Motors plant. Unemployment bolted him, his wife, Clara, and their six children into a desperate state of uncertainty and hunger, similar to the Littles' situation in Lansing. The entire Poole family took to scrounging food off the street. Nathaniel, the second oldest son, has a childhood memory of picking up "an icy white piece of cake out of the garbage can," and devouring it. Yes, Nathaniel recalled in an interview, "We ate out of the garbage can."[30]

By his own admission, Elijah Poole took to heavy drinking and waywardness during this period as he and his wife were driven to the brink. "Times were hard," recalled Nathaniel, who said that his mother, Clara, considered "killing herself and their children because she didn't want to live that way." And "my daddy [Elijah] actually laid across the railroad tracks, tried to commit suicide." A "white man" who lived nearby "snatched daddy off the railroad tracks and brought him home. A white guy saved [the future Elijah Muhammad's] life," recalled his son Nathaniel. "It was the Great Depression. Times were hard. Not just for us, for everybody."[31] Only later would Elijah Poole encounter the Nation of Islam religion that, among other things, condemned all white men as devils. The details of just how Elijah Poole and his entire family came into the fold of Fard Muhammad's NOI were laid out by Elijah's younger brother, John.

"The first time I met Fard Muhammad was in '31," said John (Poole) Muhammad, who bore a strong resemblance to his brother Elijah. "It was in the [Garvey movement's] UNIA Hall. They called him the Man from the East."

John Muhammad recalled that he and his dad, a Baptist minister who had also moved north, were invited by a fellow worker to visit the temple of W. D. Fard. "My father had never heard anything about being a Muslim. I heard Fard quite a few times. He often would start at the black people by saying to them who God is: 'God is Allah.' So [Fard] says that Allah [suggesting a man other than himself] put the sun, moon, and stars in the universe. My father, being a Baptist preacher, said to him, 'If God is man, how did the sun get up there?' [Fard] said man put it there. [My father then asked Fard], 'How could he do it?' [Fard responded], 'God has the power.' [Fard] only speaks to the things that he wants. And when he speaks to [my father] and the word be, there it is.' And [Fard] says that 'he [has] a nation of people that he started there.' And my father came home and he tells us all about this man that had been talking to him."[32]

Reverend William Poole's older son, Elijah, made a few passes by Fard's temple. It was overcrowded and he did not attend services. It was instead his wife, Clara, who first visited the Detroit temple one Wednesday and persuaded her husband to visit that Friday. This is how Elijah Poole first met Fard Muhammad, according to family members. After Elijah praised Fard for his timely doctrine and adept handling of his Detroit followers, the NOI leader, according to Elijah, took to visiting the Poole home in Detroit, "almost daily and taught me about Islam" for some fifteen months. Fard reportedly described himself to Elijah as a member of the "Ahmadiyya," a religious sect founded in the late nineteenth century in India. The fair-skinned Elijah was subsequently taken on as a lieutenant, along with his brother Kallatt, and taught Islam in schools that the NOI ran for the children of its members.

These native-born American converts—who at first took the last name Karriem, then later, Muhammad—enjoyed full access to potential recruits who remained somewhat skeptical about the sharp-featured, straight-haired, foreign-born Fard. Within a few months, the Karriem brothers were traveling to Negro communities in distant cities as surrogate proselytizers to organize regional Muslim groups. Meanwhile, their exotic religious teacher wisely kept a low profile, even in his home base of Detroit.

"[Fard] looked like a white man," Nathaniel recalled. By all reliable accounts, in fact, Fard Muhammad, the founder of the Nation of Islam, was indeed a white man.[33] And he was not, as some said, an Arab, an ethnic group listed as "white" in U.S. census reports, with straight hair and dark eyes.

The stark antiwhite religious message repeatedly got key NOI leaders, including Fard Muhammad, hauled in by Detroit police for questioning. Occasionally, Fard would invite his prized minister, Elijah Karriem, into jail to witness his rough treatment at the hands of Detroit's dreaded turnkeys and interrogators. Fard was photographed and fingerprinted, and his criminal record was tracked back to the West Coast.

According to the FBI, this Muslim "messiah" was a white confidence man by the name of Wallace Dodd, born in New Zealand, or perhaps Hawaii, who had conned his way to the leadership of the Negro Nation of Islam cult. To back up its claims, the Bureau subsequently circulated Fard Muhammad's rap sheet complete with photograph and fingerprints. Despite J. Edgar Hoover's long-standing and devious police-state tactics designed to discredit civil rights leaders and black groups such as the Muslims, the fingerprints, photographs, and rap sheet all checked out. Other police records, including fingerprints, appear to confirm that the man with the aliases "W. D. Fard" and "Fard Muhammad," was, in fact, a white New Zealander with a criminal record, a man who had served time in San Quentin for selling narcotics.[34] Fard's familiarity with Japan and the Pacific Rim, as reported by Alston and others, matches up with the FBI's description of him as a man of the Pacific with roots also in Hawaii and the West Coast, a man of several aliases whose listed, stateside name was "Wallace Ford." However, as head of the offshoot Nation of Islam, W. D. Muhammad reportedly insisted occasionally, against any known evidence, that he was from Mecca, in Saudi Arabia. Despite his appearance and birthplace of record, he was vague about his race, especially when among black temple members.

The NOI leader, like the Moorish Science Temple, continued to attract intense pressure from Detroit police authorities. Raids were conducted on charges running from kidnapping to human sacrifice. The latter charge against Fard and others stemmed from a ritual that produced an actual corpse. On November 20, 1932, in a bizarre ritual murder, James Smith was slain by Robert Harris, a deranged man who was not a NOI member but rather belonged to an offshoot group called the Order of Islam. Nonetheless, Detroit police cast a wide net and rounded up all Muslim sect leaders, including Fard Muhammad, who was arrested on November 23. Declaring that he was "the supreme being on earth," with NOI groups in four major cities, according to Detroit newspapers, Fard was cleared of serious charges but authorities permanently banned him from Detroit.[35]

Despite being exiled, Fard, now operating under the name Wallace F. Muhammad, occasionally sneaked back into the city to administer the NOI and prepare his key minister Elijah Karriem—upon whom he bestowed the surname Muhammad—for on-the-ground operations in Detroit as well as in the field. Elijah's travel assignments put a strain on his pregnant wife, Clara, which was relieved somewhat when Fard reportedly blessed as a future leader the Muslim couple's—lucky digit—seventh child to be. He proposed, if not ordered, that it be named after him. Later that year, on October 30, 1933, a son was born and duly named Wallace Delaney Muhammad. In addition to counseling Elijah on family matters, the strict disciplinarian leader continued to tutor him in organizational management, methods of daily prayers and assorted skills he would need to inculcate into his largely uneducated followers, such as reading, penmanship, and even how to wash one's hands and face each day.

In due course, on May 25, 1933, the covertly operating Fard Muhammad was hauled in by police, under the glare of the *Detroit Free Press* headline: "Banished Leader of Cult Arrested." Police released a questionable transcript reportedly exposing Fard as an admitted con artist out for the money. Upon agreeing to depart the city under a second banishment, Fard was allowed to address his local temple for the final time; as he drove away, some loyalists wept and touched his sedan. There is evidence that Fard kept in touch with Elijah after this second banishment.

In one handwritten letter from the "South West Part of N. America," dated "December 18, 1933, 4 a.m.," W. D. Fard berates Elijah for the "terrible mistake" of taking unauthorized trips, including one to Birmingham, Alabama. "I have numbers of records of charges against you," he wrote in his stilted English, "but I not brought them to enforce knowing you have taken these steps with good intentions." And the demanding leader, very much in control of his organization, insisted that Elijah "write to me every day and tell me about your study."[36] In addition to being instructed to master the Qur'an, Elijah reportedly was given a list of 104 additional books to read and master.

In a rare glimpse into Fard Muhammad's stated goal of establishing the homegrown Muslim religion for Negroes, he wrote Elijah that "I am here to guide you to the right road [of Islam]." And he counseled that his minister use a low-key approach to recruiting members until he learns "the labor of Islam . . . 100%." Dispatching Elijah secretly to Chicago Temple No. 2, Fard instructed him to "give them a lecture and run over to MILWAUKEE . . . and inquire about Mr. Joe Bey," a man who was apparently a member of the Moorish Science Temple No. 3. "Give them a lecture or two and go back to Evanston and ask for Mr. Brown. Try to get acquainted there and start a station there . . . and start arising the dead."

Far from dormant, the banished NOI leader further directed his key minister: "Then from Evanston you can round Chicago again [secretly], then home, stop in these little towns on your way home and leave little wisdom everywhere; get around and get acquainted; caravan the territory between your home and Milwaukee; start stations everywhere you can. St. Louis and Kansas City will be your territory too but at present you can master the above said and later, I will tell you when to go there."[37]

In addition to issuing such travel orders in his run-on, vaguely punctuated writing style, Fard swore Elijah to secrecy about his "assignment" on his theory of the history of the universe. "Light travel 186,000 miles per second and the sun is 93,000,000 miles from the Earth," the NOI leader noted from his lesson plan of "actual facts."

And "if you divide the traveling speed into the distance it shall give you the time to strike the earth. Ha! Ha! This is a good [problem] for you," he wrote to Elijah, after complimenting his prize student on his study: "you are doing fine . . . do not be bashful to study."[38]

Much like Drew Ali's disappearance, the official departure of the NOI leader from public view was sudden and as clouded in mystery as the background of W. Fard Muhammad. "I asked my brother [Elijah] where did he go?" said John Muhammad. "And he said, 'Fard Muhammad directed himself back to the heavens.' He was returned back to his thrones and that was the heaven place. He was never seen again, that I know of."[39] Publicly, Elijah Muhammad described his leader's departure from the airport in Detroit as one of the "greatest tragedies" ever visited upon the Negro community. His son Nathaniel, however, said that his family kept in touch with the departed Muslim leader for years, stating that he was once known to be residing in Mexico even as Elijah continued to declare him vanished to the sky "until he can secure the kingdom."[40]

---

After Fard's ballyhooed disappearance, Elijah Muhammad skipped hardly a beat in declaring that he was his handpicked successor, stepping ahead of his brother Kallatt and others to assume command of the Nation of Islam. More surprisingly, Elijah claimed that when shaking Fard Muhammad's hand, early on, the NOI founder revealed himself as the one prophesied in the Bible as the second coming of Jesus, to be the son of man. Elijah would say years later that Master Fard whispered in his ear, "Yes, I am the One, but who knows that but yourself, and be quiet."[41] "He took me with Him for three years, night and day. He said, 'Here it is, Elijah, you can go now, and I can go.'"[42]

Synchronizing this transition of power, Elijah told the Muslim pioneers that their departed leader was actually Allah Himself. The holy man of mystery, who had in the presence of others eschewed lofty titles for himself, was beatified, in absentia, as the divine godhead! As bearer of this tiding of great joy, Elijah concurrently declared that the new Almighty had bestowed upon him the divine honorific as his "Messenger of Allah." The blessed news infuriated other key Muslim temple officials, who became his cold-blooded rivals as ambition turned their hearts and hands against Elijah. Some officials splintered away and started rival Muslim groups, while others stood their ground to fight. John Poole, the youngest and more compliant of the brothers, closely watched the escalating power struggle between his older siblings, Kallatt and Elijah.

Earlier, said John Muhammad, "we didn't call Master Fard 'Allah,' because we didn't know it. We called him 'Brother Fard.'" This squared with the account of Clara, Elijah's wife, who recalled to her son Wallace that "Fard told us not to even call him 'Prophet.' He said 'cause that is too big a title for him." Despite this humility, later "we called him Prophet Fard," said John. "And next we was calling him Master Fard Muhammad. Then later, the Messenger [Elijah Muhammad] told us that this man is not just an ordinary man to look at, he is God in person!"[43] In addition to Kallatt, other potential heirs to the throne reached for their knives at word of Elijah's bold and singular self-promotion. The FBI watched the Black Muslim infighting with interest as local police jailed both dissidents and hard-liners alike.

Key family members, including Elijah Muhammad's son Wallace, who was a baby at the time, would maintain over the years that the Messenger's version of his handoff from Fard Muhammad was pure fiction. (Wallace would succeed his father decades later and totally redirect the sect toward orthodoxy as a recognized Muslim leader in the United States.) This deification of Master Fard Muhammad as "Allah," a claim that orthodox Muslims added to their lists of blasphemous affronts by the NOI, was concocted by Elijah, according to Wallace, as a clever way for the formerly wayward son of a Georgia Baptist preacher to install himself at the godhead of the emerging Nation of Islam.

The nascent black Islamists were viewed by Muslims of the Middle East and North Africa not so much with contempt as with a sort of pious pity. It must be said, however, that the largely underdeveloped Muslim countries of the former Ottoman Empire, many of them occupied after World War I by France and Great Britain, were intrigued in the 1930s by the popularizing of their religious brand name, albeit in distorted form, in a highly industrialized America coming on as leader of the so-called First World.

As for the domestic Muslims, even Fard Muhammad, a white man with passing familiarity with orthodox Islam, looked down on the underclass Black Muslim practitioners as "babies." In a condescending letter from exile to Elijah Muhammad, Fard pitied Negroes for being a "long way from home [Africa]" and in a "cave of savages[s] . . . without any right[s] in regards to the rules and regulations."[44] The NOI founder told followers that he had taken upon himself the burden of raising Negroes from their slumber. Here, Fard consciously misstated the fact that it was indeed Timothy Drew, the black North Carolinian, who, some two decades earlier, had resurrected Islam as a religious refuge for Negroes suffering under white oppression in the United States.

---

Centuries of terrifying isolation under the strain of social engineering by American enforcers had instilled in the surviving Negro masses a psychic drift with a residue of fear, turmoil, and self-loathing. To address this collective malaise, first the Moorish Science Temple and then the Nation of Islam sought to reconnect the alienated Negro to the "Asiatic" homeland they dared not call Africa. Still, both spiritual groups inspired a relatively small but significant group of followers to reassert their dignity and organize to take their rightful place in the sun.

In early-twentieth-century America, the Islamists were not the only homegrown zealots creating breakaway religions for Negroes. Scores of pioneer cults, each as exotic as the next, sprang up across the country, with only a few managing to nurture their start-ups beyond the larval stage. Just as the black Islamists thumbed through the Qur'an for loopholes, dozens of their contemporaries perused the Old Testament and traced their lineage, not to Africa, but to the land of the biblical Israelites. In Harlem alone, for example, a half dozen such sects rebranded themselves in the 1920s as "Black Hebrews," according to Peter Hudson's account of the "Black Jews," in *Africana: The Encyclopedia of the African and African American Experience.* As with the Moors and the Black Muslims, these religious upstarts were rejected by the orthodox members of their adopted religion, in this case Judaism. Nonetheless, some of the more hardy of the practitioners endured over the decades; indeed, several sects have persisted well into the twenty-first century, chanting their scriptures on Manhattan streets and by light of the menorah on low-budget, local cable television broadcasts.

While the Black Muslim sects strike some outsiders as fanciful and irrational on the surface, their impact upon their supplicants and their broader racial group has been noteworthy. Irrationality, as noted by journalist I. F. Stone, a scholar of Greek classics and legendary skeptic of the last century, is a core ingredient of all religions of the world: "Elijah Muhammad's weird [Muslim] doctrine" with such touches as the Mother Ship, racial group superiority, and the "black genius named Yakub . . . is not really any more absurd than the Virgin Birth or the Sacrifice of Isaac" by Abraham in the Bible. And, with the Black Muslims, Stone added, "the rational absurdity does not detract from the psychic therapy" designed to shake off the "feeling of nigger-ness [in order] to be fully emancipated."[45]

In addition to uplifting the group psyche and counterrejecting white supremacy with black supremacy, the Black Islamists, said August Wilson, the Pulitzer Prize–winning playwright, are to be praised for contributing a signature creation story to African American culture. "We had no original [creation] myths," said the famed black dramatist, whom some critics consider a modern American Shakespeare. "Certainly Elijah Muhammad [popularized] that . . . to black American culture with the myth of Yacub. These things the culture was lacking and they are forever a part of us. Whether you agree or disagree, you could always say, 'This is how the world started.' [This is] important, if for nothing else than that."[46] As a young man, August Wilson joined the NOI in Pittsburgh, and credits its leaders for exerting a profound effect upon his grounding as an American artist.

Early pioneers of the black Islamist movements reasoned that it was no more unseemly to follow their prophets in Newark and Detroit than for Mormons to have taken up with Prophet Joseph Smith in upstate New York or Brigham Young in Utah. And just as Drew Ali borrowed text and ritual from existing religions, so did the Mormons and other homegrown white sects. In addition to declaring upstate New York as their New Jerusalem, the early Mormons declared that the Second Coming of Jesus Christ would take place in Independence, Missouri, their designated Land of Zion. Hounded by wary government officials, Prophet Smith was eventually assassinated by a mob in Carthage, Illinois. A key member of the Mormon leadership, Brigham Young, succeeded Smith as church president and, with a bit of tinkering himself, carried forward the Mormon mission into the wilderness of the Utah territory. Like Mormonism, each offshoot religion was denounced, if not vilified, by its orthodox parent faith. Correspondingly, the now mainstream parent faiths, Christianity and Islam, had themselves been vilified at the time of their separate founding in the Middle East.

The initial rolls of the Nation of Islam were filled by dissident ex-Christians, some of them stragglers from earlier attempts at a separate religious way, more than a few of them eyewitnesses, like Elijah Muhammad, to racist atrocities such as lynchings in the South. While most Negroes laughed away Muslim recruiters pushing a divine "Master Fard" and his barely literate "Messenger," some found tempting, if not persuasive, the NOI's broader social appeal for self-reliance as a counter to economic oppression by white America. And the nonreligious elements on the streets and in the barbershops were generally susceptible to the group's notion of self-defense as a stance against white terror. Negroes encountering Black Muslims in the community were silently impressed by their discipline, their manliness, and their sober, dignified carriage, which contrasted with the gaudiness of the crackling ghetto streets around them. So from early on, the self-respecting black Islamists were keen to display a tight-knit unity against white oppression, however minuscule their actual numbers.

As with the Moorish Science Temple, the NOI was initially beset by a weakly educated and barely articulate leadership that lacked mass appeal. Both groups also were hampered by a structural weakness hindering long-term sustainability in a growing post–World War I society. While the NOI had brought forth the black creation myth, the Yacub story that August Wilson later praised, it lacked a sustaining mythology of the hereafter for its downcast followers. More pressing still, neither group had a clear plan of succession upon the death or disappearance of its founding supreme leader. Unlike, say, Christianity, with its resurrection and open-ended second coming of the Messiah, both home-based Muslim groups were blatantly term-limited by the mortality of their founding leaders and assigns. This shortsightedness endangered each group as a sustainable religious movement. Accordingly, both Muslim sects seemed destined to tread their religious path down a blind alley—unless some enterprising adherent emerged to tinker with the dogma with a farsighted view toward survivability.

Just as the death of Prophet Drew Ali set off a wandering about of his Moors, the departure of Fard Muhammad ignited a confused and sometimes bloody scramble to challenge Elijah Muhammad's claim to the leadership post. In Detroit especially, the elevation of the slow-tongued though clever Elijah continued to inflame rival ministers and even close relatives—most especially, his brother Kallatt. Envy flared openly into threats: there were even reports of a $500 bounty being placed on Elijah's head. Moreover, the Detroit police continued to hound Nation of Islam officials for, among other offenses, keeping NOI children out of the public schools. The local harassment and intragroup anger combined to drive the self-appointed new NOI leader first to set up his headquarters in Chicago and subsequently, as danger mounted, to take to the road.

Traveling initially to Milwaukee, Elijah Muhammad eventually settled in Washington, D.C. Using the aliases Gulam Bogans and Mohammed Rassoull, he set up temples in each city, Temple No. 3 in Milwaukee and No. 4 in Washington. In the capital, Muhammad rented a room under the name Gulam Bogans and converted his landlord and neighbors to the teachings of the NOI. He continued to spread the teachings of Fard Muhammad, which included telling members of the NOI not to register for the draft or serve in the military in any way. Members in both Milwaukee and Washington were harassed and arrested by authorities. Elijah himself was arrested in Washington for sedition, sent back for trial to Detroit, and sentenced to five years in prison. He served three years in the federal prison in Milan, Michigan, starting on July 23, 1943.[47] Upon his release, on August 24, 1946, Elijah Muhammad told authorities that "he would continue his religious activities and try to inform his people."[48]

As Elijah was paroled to Chicago, twenty-one-year-old Malcolm Little was entering his seventh month in a Massachusetts prison. Closer at hand, in the Nation of Islam's founding city of Detroit, his brother Wilfred was beginning to explore the teachings of Elijah.

## CHAPTER 11

# Building Temples in the East

AFTER ATTENDING A FEW NATION OF ISLAM MEETINGS IN Detroit starting in 1946, Wilfred Little was invited to Chicago, where he met Elijah Muhammad and was impressed by the man and his program. Comparing Elijah's teachings with his own parents' Garveyism, Wilfred said, "There really wasn't that much difference, except there was a little more religion emphasized than Marcus Garvey had." With his customary energy and highly developed sense of responsibility, Wilfred set out to help the group attract more members. First, he said, he wanted to counter the public perception that the Nation of Islam was "just a bunch of ignorant people."[1] He brought Elijah NOI pamphlets that had been distributed on the streets to show how they were poorly written and full of misspelled words. Acknowledging that the handouts poorly represented the group, Muhammad presented all of the group's literature and asked Wilfred to correct it, so it could be reprinted correctly.

When he returned to Detroit, Wilfred said, he and his wife, Ruth, "looked for little things to help improve the situation that would make things go better." They improved the temple's bookkeeping system. He helped bring young people to the meetings when the temple had guest speakers. And he decided to get the temple moved out of its meeting hall on St. Ann Drive, where it was sandwiched between a barbershop and the apartment of a man who would get drunk and beat his dog.

Wilfred recalled that he talked openly about the terrible conditions in Temple No. 1. "I said, 'You see this place where we're meeting in. This place is nothing but a dump and you're acting like you're so proud of it.' I talked about the place like a dog because it was a mess."[2]

Elijah's brother John Muhammad and his wife happened to be in attendance. They wrote to Elijah, informing him that Wilfred was badmouthing the temple. On Wilfred's next visit to Chicago, Elijah Muhammad confronted his young follower, who confirmed what he had said and invited the Messenger to visit the temple. Elijah Muhammad had not been to Detroit since leaving prison in 1946, nor had he been invited to come to the temple. He accepted the invitation and instructed Wilfred not to tell anyone he was coming.

Driven by his captain, Elijah Muhammad arrived at Wilfred's home one Saturday, where he spent the night. On Sunday, when the leader of the Nation of Islam walked into the temple, Wilfred said, "Everybody was so shocked. They were surprised to see him. And they were glad to see him." Even decades later, Wilfred could recall vividly what happened next: Elijah started speaking, but it wasn't long before "the guy upstairs who's drunk went to beating his dog. The dog was yelping and running around and around up there, and then the guy went and flushed his toilet. Whenever he would flush his toilet, it would leak through into the place where we were meeting. So they had to go and get a bucket and set it right in front of the stage to catch the leak." The Messenger looked at the leak and kept talking.

Then a fight broke out in the barbershop downstairs. It was

"one of the biggest fights they ever had. You could hear the stuff being thrown around down there and cussin', coming up through the floor." Elijah Muhammad was still trying to talk over the disruptions. "Pretty soon the band started up next door, and, boy, they was having a time over there. So everything happened at the same time. Usually it was just one thing or the other, but all of it happened at the same time that day."

At that point, Wilfred remembered, Elijah Muhammad "stopped speaking and he looked all around. He says, 'What is this?' He looked around there at me. He says, 'I guess this is a dump. How can you call yourself bringing a teaching like this in here sandwiched in between all this filth?'" Then he directed them to "'get out of here and find someplace right now that we can meet in other than this.' That's how they decided to move out of there."

After the temple relocated, Wilfred became more involved and brought in his brothers Philbert, Wesley, and Reginald. "My wife and brothers alone made a big difference," said Wilfred, who eventually would become the minister of the Detroit temple. "We just helped turn that whole thing around, started bringing in a whole different group of people with a whole different mentality. We brought them in and that started things to rolling."[3]

———

Both Philbert and Reginald, as described earlier, had written to Malcolm in Concord Reformatory in 1947, urging him to join the "natural religion for the black man." But they could not include a lot of detail, for they knew letters were being read by prison authorities. Malcolm was interested, according to Wilfred, but had a problem accepting that "'the white man is a devil.' That was a problem for him. He couldn't accept that."[4]

Then in March 1948, Ella's persistent attempts finally paid off, and Malcolm was taken to Norfolk Prison Colony, the prison endorsed by his buddy Malcolm Jarvis. Soon after this move, Reginald visited Malcolm to share what could not be written in letters.

"He went out and got Malcolm to talking," Wilfred recalled, "and would take what Malcolm would say and then turn it around for him and show him a different way of seeing it. Until eventually Malcolm realized that maybe this white man could be the devil." One experience Malcolm held on to as an example of his friendship with whites was that he was paid a thousand dollars for handling suitcases of money for various white-run numbers places in Harlem. Reginald explained that if the people in charge were really his friends, they would divide the profits with him. Instead, they "were tossing you a penny in relation to what you are bringing back and forth," recalled Wilfred. Malcolm thought about it and realized that he was "just one of their flunkies."[5]

After Reginald visited several times, Malcolm started receiving letters and printed material from his siblings almost every day about "the Honorable Elijah Muhammad" and "the true knowledge." The "true knowledge" that he gleaned was that history had been "whitened in the white man's history books, and that the black man had been 'brainwashed for hundreds of years,'" Malcolm later wrote. The literature explained that the black man was the "original man" and had "built great empires and civilizations and cultures while the white man was still living on all fours in caves." The white man "had pillaged, murdered, raped and exploited every race of man not white." Through slavery, the white man cut "black people off from all knowledge of their own kind and cut them off from any knowledge of their language, religion, and past culture, until the black man in America was the earth's only race of people who had absolutely no knowledge of his true identity."[6]

He summed up his reactions in the *Autobiography*. "The very enormity of my previous life's guilt prepared me to accept the truth." Malcolm withdrew from his surroundings while contemplating what had been given to him. "I was going through the hardest thing, also the greatest thing for any human being to do; to accept that which is already within you, and around you."[7]

Encouraged by his family, Malcolm wrote directly to the Honorable Elijah Muhammad, who responded with a letter welcoming him to "the true knowledge" and expanding on the information Malcolm's family had sent. Every day, Malcolm wrote letters—to his siblings, to Elijah, and to government officials—but he soon became frustrated by what he could not express on the written page. "My reading had my mind like steam under pressure. Some way, I had to start telling the white man about himself to his face." While continuing to write letters, he joined the prison's weekly debate team and cultivated world-class polemical skills during face-offs in Norfolk prison with debating teams from the Massachusetts Institute of Technology, Yale, and Harvard. These verbal calisthenics with Ivy League wordsmiths pumped up Malcolm's dialectical prowess as a fierce and fearsome debater, a skill that would power his meteoric rise as a Muslim advocate in Harlem, New England, and the rest of the United States—and eventually the world—while also incurring envy within the Nation of Islam. "Debating, speaking to a crowd, was as exhilarating to me as the discovery of knowledge through reading had been," he later wrote.[8]

Malcolm Jarvis, who had transferred to Norfolk directly from Charlestown, had a front-row seat for Malcolm's transformation. "I saw the whole thing taking place," Jarvis recalled. He was writing letters long into the night. "If you read those letters, you could see where his mind was. He was very heavy into meditation and spirituality and getting into himself as an introvert."[9] In a letter to "Brother Bay," a friend named Bazeley Perry, Malcolm wrote:

I thought of you and must write and tell you of the True Blessings of being in the country. . . . Of being so free, and away from

the ever-imprisoning confusion of the city . . . here in the Natural Habitat of Allah . . . with His Sweet Breath forever flowing
about us. . . . keeping us aware of His Presence. . . . Making us
feel sorry for those souls out there in the street, who think they
possess life, and freedom.

I could not . . . would not . . . trade a moment of my life *now*
for any part of someone else's. The ambition and contentment
I used to know years ago . . . as a child . . . has [sic] returned
to me.[10]

In other ways too, Malcolm's behavior in prison began to prefig-
ure, and to prepare him for, his role as the Nation of Islam's most
gifted and successful proselytizer and demander of justice. After
converting several other inmates to his newly embraced religion, he
started agitating for Muslim religious rights in prison, such as food
that met dietary restrictions and cells that faced east to facilitate
prayer. And in an early instance of his internationalist bent, he even
threatened to appeal for help to the global community of Islam.
His quests brought newspaper coverage, which was unwelcome to
the prison authorities, and in March 1950 he was transferred back
to the hardship confines of Charlestown Prison.[11] In June of that
year, he drew the FBI's attention when he wrote a letter to President
Truman, opposing the Korean War and claiming to be a Communist who had tried to enlist in the Japanese army during World War
II. During this same period, in letters to Philbert, he signed himself "Malcolm X Little," apparently adopting for the first time the
Nation's X, which stands for unknown family names stolen by those
who enslaved Africans.

The two Malcolms were up for parole at the same time. In preparation for this, Wilfred visited his brother to counsel him on how to
successfully attain it. "[I] talked to him to make him aware of what
people on this parole board look for in a person and what they want

to hear in order to consider you for a parole," Wilfred recalled. "I encouraged him to read this book by Dale Carnegie, *How to Win Friends and Influence People,* which has some very good techniques in it for dealing with people." Malcolm Jarvis read it and put it into practice; Wilfred's younger brother did not. "He wouldn't even go look at it. He was gonna go down there and tell these folks off." When the time came for the two Malcolms to appear before the parole board, Jarvis "passed with flying colors and they gave him his parole," while Malcolm "went in there using his method and turned [the parole board] completely off and they turned him down. He had to do another year." [12]

During the next year, Wilfred was able to persuade Malcolm to reconsider his approach toward dealing with people. Malcolm was constantly quoting from the Bible. In a letter, Wilfred advised his brother to let *How to Win Friends and Influence People* "be your bible for a while. [I] said, 'If you want to make it in this world, you better learn how to get along with people. And how to deal with people.' So he did. He got that thing and started reading it and practicing it and then, he became an expert. Such a change came over him that they didn't know what to do with him. The guards and the warden and all, they couldn't believe that this was the same guy 'cause he had a whole different approach," Wilfred explained years later. [13]

When Malcolm was paroled in August 1952, Wilfred gave him a place to live and arranged for a job as a salesman in the Detroit store where Wilfred himself worked. Soon after Malcolm was settled in Michigan, the brothers, along with others, drove to Chicago to hear Elijah Muhammad, the Messenger, preach. Inspired, Malcolm returned to Detroit primed for "fishing"—reeling in converts, especially young ones, in encouraging numbers. One of his most notable converts was a homeless World War II vet, Joseph Gravitt, later known as Captain Joseph, who would serve for years as one of Malcolm's most reliable aides before becoming an implacable enemy. In

1953, when Malcolm's parole ended, he became assistant minister at Temple No. 1 in Detroit, and started working for the Nation full-time, while continuing to visit Chicago for religious instruction by the Messenger.

His living situation did not go as smoothly. Tension arose between Malcolm and Wilfred's wife, Ruth, so they found him a room with a NOI member named Moustafa (Robert) Hassain and his wife, Raushanah Hassain (Dorothy Warren); they had a new six-room house on Keystone Street in Detroit. They took him in as a family member and never charged him rent. "He would offer to give me money. I would tell him to buy some clothes," Moustafa Hassain said.[14] His wife had not intended to become a Muslim until she was moved by Malcolm's preaching. "You know when a chill can go up and down your spine with the way a person teaches," she recalled. "He could teach that type of way. The things that he would say would always be unique."[15]

Yet some within the Detroit temple resented Malcolm's insistence on strict standards of conduct, his penchant for calling others to account, and, perhaps most challenging, his energetic success in recruiting new members. Temple members who disliked Malcolm wrote to Elijah Muhammad to tell him that the Hassains were housing the young convert. During one of Moustafa Hassain's visits to Chicago, Muhammad asked him about this. "I said, 'Yes, sir. Is there anything wrong with that?' He said, 'No. These people here, they [are] kind of backward. Don't pay any attention to them. If this man acts right and he lives what I teach him, you will have no problem with him. If you want him to live in your house, it's all right for him to live in your house,' " Hassain recalled.[16]

Despite their friendship—the couple even took Malcolm to visit Raushanah Hassain's parents in Little Rock—the Muslim wife did find Malcolm too bossy about what they should and shouldn't do. He took NOI rules restricting women "too seriously," she said, insisting that she stay in at night, and wear longer skirts and lower heels.[17] Only recently released from prison, Malcolm also seemed to her obsessed with the idea that he would be attacked or surveilled; he refused to sit with his back to a window, and he searched motel rooms and bathrooms minutely when they traveled.

"If you did the least little thing off the rule, [Malcolm] would criticize you right then. He would do it in a way that would ruffle your skin," explained Moustafa Hassain, who liked this about Malcolm. "I like a man to keep you on your toes. I wanted to get everything out of my life that was supposed to come out. And he would help you do it."[18]

Hassain and Malcolm fished for new members together. Hassain would bring people to the house Saturday night. "I wouldn't say nothing. I would let Malcolm or Wilfred talk to them. Wilfred was a good teacher, too. Then Sunday we would carry everybody to the temple." Temple members would use this as evidence that Malcolm and Hassain were trying to take over the temple. "The Honorable Elijah Muhammad asked me about it. And I told him what [we were] doing. He said, 'All the Muslims should be doing that.' "[19]

Raushanah Hassain, who had been married twice before, had no children and had been told by doctors that she couldn't have any. Elijah Muhammad, however, told her confidently that she would have a child. "I said, 'If I have a baby—I'm so sure I won't have a baby—if I have a baby, I will join.' "[20]

Raushanah Hassain became pregnant and, true to her word, accepted Islam. Soon, however, a rumor was going around that Malcolm was the father. The couple and their boarder-friend protested to Elijah Muhammad about this false slur, and the person held responsible, a minister's wife, was punished for it, Raushanah said.[21] At the same time, however, some temple members, resentful of Malcolm's critiques of their behavior, were warning the Messenger that Malcolm was trying to take over. So, despite Malcolm's success in bringing in new members, Elijah Muhammad "sat Malcolm down" late in 1953 and told him to leave Detroit.

The Messenger, according to Moustafa Hassain, did not want Malcolm to speak in the founding temples, those with numbers lower than seven. Those primary temples—Detroit No. 1, Chicago No. 2, Milwaukee No. 3, Washington, D.C., No. 4, Cincinnati No. 5, and Baltimore No. 6—had been established by Elijah Muhammad with older pioneers of the movement and were to be guarded closely against the new winds Malcolm was kicking up elsewhere.[22] But seven East Coast temples remained weak and disorganized, often with fewer than a dozen wandering, undisciplined members. These included Boston, New York, and Philadelphia. Indeed, Malcolm's younger brother Reginald had been the chief minister at Harlem Temple No. 7 until the Messenger suspended him for committing adultery with the secretary at the New York mosque.[23] The Harlem operation dated back to the 1940s, when Elijah Muhammad passed through the Northeast and left behind a few devoted followers to carry on. Now, contemplating these weaker chapters, the Messenger offered Malcolm his pick.[24]

Initially, Malcolm revived the anemic group in Boston, where he served as the first minister. The operation was coming along so "wonderfully well" that by December 1954, Elijah Muhammad designated Boston as Muslim Temple No. 11. "Just think, a year ago, there was no temple there," Malcolm wrote his brother Philbert.[25] In his role as Northeast regional NOI organizer, Malcolm also boldly reorganized what became the larger Temple No. 12, in Philadelphia, with himself as minister. During 1954, he also became minister at Temple No. 7 in Harlem, making his home in East Elmhurst, Queens.

Although Harlem became his base, Malcolm, with his regional responsibilities, routinely made on-site visits to Boston and Philadelphia, as well as to Springfield, Massachusetts, Camden, New Jersey, and other cities. After nursing along a local group, he would, with Elijah Muhammad's permission, instruct followers to rent a meeting hall with an eye toward purchase. When recruits for the Fruit of Islam, the Muslims' security force, approached fifty, with comparable numbers for the Muslim Girls Training, a group for new female recruits, Elijah Muhammad would post a permanent minister to exact dues and establish an independent, local treasury. And with money flowing to Chicago, national headquarters would assign the group a temple number.[26]

Already, the weekly financial and membership reports Malcolm filed to Chicago quantified his regional temples as the fastest growing, and his Temple No. 7, in Harlem, as a chief moneymaker. Increasing the rolls of the Nation and fattening the coffers at headquarters, however, would have the unintended side effect of inspiring concern among some of Muhammad's children and envy among fellow ministers. At this stage, however, the Messenger did little but bide his time and watch the profits roll in. Publicly he praised the energy, loyalty, and drive of his ace proselytizer. Privately, he fielded the growing whispers among his blood relatives. Secretly, so did the FBI.

The dramatic NOI growth was recorded by the group's national secretary with enthusiasm—and by the FBI with alarm. Director J. Edgar Hoover instructed field offices to note each new "hate group" Muslim temple in their ledgers and at Washington, D.C., headquarters, with an eye toward infiltration and disruption. Accordingly, special agents budgeted petty cash to develop Negro sources inside NOI temples to supply wide-ranging details of Muslim goings-on. Malcolm's every contact with NOI headquarters was to be tracked, as well as his outreach to black civil rights leaders. This fiery organizer of Negroes, in Hoover's mind, and increasingly those of local police departments, posed a high threat to stability on urban streets and continued white dominance across the board.

The elusive Malcolm X was summoned for a personal interview with the FBI on January 10, 1955. While admitting that he was a Muslim, he denied agents' suggestions that he was the leader of the Boston, Philadelphia, or even the Harlem temple. Subsequently, he instructed subordinates contacted by the FBI simply to "state briefly that Islam is a religion of peace."[27]

One bulwark of Malcolm's recruiting efforts, a subject that matched his soaring rhetorical skills in gravity, was the record of white violence against blacks, especially lynchings. Malcolm had heard many lynching stories, starting with the one by his adolescent buddy back in Lansing, John Davis, from Mississippi. Reminders of this peculiar form of Southern terror increased his commitment to emphasize the self-defense tenet of Muslim doctrine. At Muslim bazaars and street rallies, the Harlem minister reinforced Elijah Muhammad's preaching against such attacks by promoting the sale and reading of Ralph Ginzburg's book *100 Years of Lynchings*. The book documented some "5000 Negroes lynched in the United States since 1859." Between 1882 and 1946, according to the Negro Yearbook, a minimum of 3,425 blacks were documented as having been lynched in America, a rate of more than one incident a week.

Antilynching had long been a staple of Elijah Muhammad's indictment of American racism. However, Malcolm typically finetuned the bill of particulars by marshaling statistics, quantifying patterns of abuse, and pointedly directing detractors and disciples alike to the published record and historical data. His airtight intellectual approach, here and elsewhere, rendered the Muslims, or at least Malcolm himself, more acceptable to middle-class Negroes and intellectuals. His masterly facility with words contrasted sharply with the limitations of his mystic leader, who, while an artist of nonverbal communication, appeared shy, reticent, and often barely literate.

At any rate, Malcolm stepped up his use of Klan lynchings as fodder for the recruiting mills of the Black Muslims. Depictions of a limp, black body on a rope continued as backdrop pictures for Muslim classes for the young and the uninitiated. Needing no prompting from headquarters, Malcolm skillfully employed the metaphors of the rope, the Klan bedsheet, and the flaming Christian cross to hammer away at state-supported vigilantism as an extension of the racist American judicial system. The brutal murder of young Emmett Till in 1955, an instance of white terrorism that received international attention, provided yet one more sickening example Malcolm could later call on as he recruited members.

On the East Coast, Malcolm was religious yet secular, street-smart yet intellectual, dogmatic yet tolerant of the culture and backgrounds of the local recruits. In Boston, for example, Malcolm was higher toned in the environs of Cambridge and tended to attract better-educated recruits, some with college degrees, a distinct rarity during Elijah Muhammad's old regime. Captain Joseph, who had followed Malcolm from Detroit, where he'd been the cook at Temple No. 1, considered the Boston temple far too populated with snobs and literate men. As soon as Malcolm was transferred to Philadelphia, Captain Joseph fled on the dead run to Springfield.[28]

With an eye toward attracting younger, more educated members in the mid-1950s, Malcolm would tinker with the tough Black Muslim discipline on such strictures as diet, dress codes, and cigarette smoking. Most of the visitors to the Springfield and Harlem temples, he noticed, were women, "especially the young ones." Malcolm informed the Messenger that he had not instituted dress codes that might "scare them away."[29] Already, it was an inside secret that Elijah Muhammad played loose with his own strict code of conduct. Rumored occasionally to eat bacon for breakfast, the Messenger of Allah was reliably—although not openly—known to indulge in other forbidden pleasures of the flesh, activities that got ordinary members expelled.

By contrast even to his leader, Minister Malcolm was considered throughout the entire NOI as the most ascetic young zealot for Allah imaginable. He was reported to be steadfastly loyal to every jot and tittle of what observers understood as "the teaching." His loyalty to Elijah Muhammad was just as rock solid. Early on, for instance, members of the "royal family" noted that when departing the spiritual leader's headquarters Malcolm would walk backward down the steps until he reached the sidewalk.[30] And the devoted minister strictly enforced a policy of zero tolerance upon members for the slightest moral deviation.[31]

To combat idleness and drift, Malcolm initiated a Tuesday night Bible class, "just like the Jehovah's Witnesses," to improve each member's public-speaking skills. He also adapted that group's field mission program as an outreach model for fishing for Muslim converts at barbershops, pool halls, and beauty parlors.[32] Upon discovering high-potential recruits, Malcolm would direct them to Chicago, where Elijah Muhammad would vet them for consideration as on-site ministers or assistants of a given temple. John Ali, an efficient assistant at the Harlem temple, was introduced to Chicago this way. Subsequently, Muhammad kept the Bryant College graduate at headquarters as his national secretary. Malcolm regretted the loss of Ali, and there would be others, with telling consequences.

Promising young, female recruits were also sent to Chicago for Elijah Muhammad to make judgment about the best use of their services. Several were suspiciously kept on at headquarters as the Messenger's personal secretaries. One of those diverted was Evelyn Williams, the attractive Bostonian who, although they had not been intimate, was especially close to the bachelor minister Malcolm. Rumors from Chicago reached Malcolm in the fall of 1955 that Elijah Muhammad was having extramarital affairs with some of these secretaries. Other tidbits would come his way from Evelyn Williams herself. However, the chief apostle was so far gone in devotion to his savior that—as with overzealous members of fanatical cults, no matter how smart and insightful they may be otherwise—Malcolm discarded the salacious raw data as heresy. He dared not even discuss it with his brother Wilfred or other confidants.

As Messenger of Allah and surrogate father, Muhammad was as close to being divine as Malcolm was capable of imagining at the time. "So my mind simply refused to accept anything so grotesque as adultery mentioned in the same breath with Mr. Muhammad's name," Malcolm would say years later in his *Autobiography*. "I totally and absolutely rejected my own intelligence."[33]

His response approximates what Danish theologian Søren Kierkegaard wrote about the biblical Abraham, blindly accepting God's instructions to kill his son Isaac. If the Almighty ordered such an otherwise sinful act—or committed one, as in the Messenger's case—the devout supplicant could undergo a "teleological suspension of the ethical." Kierkegaard construes Abraham's willingness to commit the heinous act of killing one's own son as a religious, and thus blameless, action, performed in the service of obeying divine will.

In Malcolm's case, he simply suppressed the unverified but credible rumors of the Messenger's adultery—initially. His private struggle with the "teleological suspension of the ethical" question concerning the Messenger would confront him further down the road. Meanwhile, the dizzying workload, constant travel, growing insularity among the faithful, and his committed celibacy kept Malcolm occupied as chief minister building the NOI under the direction of the Messenger of Allah himself.

The history of the Black Muslims—to say nothing of the race of Fard Muhammad, the godhead of a sect that steadfastly opposed white dominance—sometimes proved a burden for ministers like Malcolm X. In deifying Fard, Elijah Muhammad allowed that he was a part-white man from the Middle East.[34] However, while splitting hairs on Fard's race, the Messenger strenuously denied FBI claims leaked to the press claiming that Fard used many criminal aliases and had served prison time in San Quentin as a drug dealer.

Elijah Muhammad instructed his ministers to leave the details of the founder—promoted as Allah Himself—up to him. As the public face of the nation of Islam, Malcolm occasionally had to explain the handiwork of the Yacub myth and the voyaging of the Mother Ship. As an organizer, he much preferred to grapple with the "white devil" and turn his mind to the uplift of his Muslim converts and the Negro race by extension. His success in building up the temples already was drawing competitive fire from the Reverend Martin Luther King Jr., and he had to contend also with the mischief making of J. Edgar Hoover's men.

Aligning the Black Muslims with the historic Middle East religion was double damned since the major Islamic sects considered Elijah's claims not just false but a blasphemous libel against the Prophet Muhammad. As a young, relatively inexperienced minister, Malcolm turned to his leader for directions on fundamental questions of Elijah's version of Islam, which had been homegrown expressly for Negroes in America.

"Many of the Muslims are asking me information on RAMADAN," Malcolm wrote to Elijah Muhammad in 1954. "I'm not versed enough to answer their questions. Will you help me on it? Let me know what we do during that month and also why we always have it in December, and in the East it is another month."[35]

Ever the mystic, the Messenger retreated deeper into the fog of the lake with his finessed answers about the ethnic and religious origins of Fard Muhammad. The entire superstructure of the Nation of Islam likely would have crumbled had Elijah Muhammad, in the majesty of his office, admitted that the founder of the Black Muslims was a convicted felon—not to mention a white man.

Using the Bible and the English-language Qur'an, the Messenger argued that Fard Muhammad descended from a white mother and a black father, without ever clearly presenting any detail of evidence of "Allah's" connection to Mecca, as claimed. In the 1950s, as they are today, Arabs were classified by the U.S. Census Bureau as "whites," even though they were not Europeans. However, setting aside Fard Muhammad's murky ethnic origins, there is overwhelming evidence that the tenets and practices of the Black Muslims were stitched together, not in Mecca as claimed, but in Chicago and Detroit.[36]

Despite his successes as an organizer and his electricity as a speaker, Malcolm was little known at the time outside his sect (and such precincts as the FBI). That changed in July 1959, when *The Hate That Hate Produced,* a five-part documentary, was broadcast on WNTA, a television station in New York. Tipped off about the NOI by the writer Louis Lomax, newsman Mike Wallace scraped up $3,000 to produce the series for his evening *News Beat* show. After opposing the idea initially, Elijah Muhammad agreed to cooperate with the show, with the caveat that Muslims not be interviewed by white journalists. Thus, Louis Lomax, who was black, put the questions to Elijah Muhammad himself, who proclaimed on air that blacks were divine and that all whites in America were devils. During Malcolm's own interview, which he gave as the NOI's newly anointed national spokesman, agreeing with the "evil by nature" charge, he stated that there was no "historic example" of Caucasians ever doing anything other than evil toward blacks. This counterrejection of whites, he asserted, was also the Black Muslim method of reversing Negroes' ingrained sense of racial inferiority and self-loathing.

The documentary, considered shocking by late 1950s standards, depicted the menacing, quasimilitary Fruit of Islam soldiers undergoing karate and other self-defense training. Along the way, Malcolm took pains to excoriate nonviolent, pro-integration civil rights groups, such as the NAACP "that are supposed to be for us [but] the leadership, or the brainpower, or their political power [that] runs it, really is the white man."[37]

Despite the heated tone of the show, Mike Wallace introduced Malcolm positively as "a remarkable man" to thousands of viewers. This Muslim assertiveness caused such a word-of-mouth stir that the station took the unusual step of broadcasting the black-and-white documentary, in somewhat different form, a second time.

"Hundreds of thousands of New Yorkers were exclaiming, 'Did you hear it? Did you see it? Preaching hate of white people?' " Malcolm wrote in the *Autobiography*.[38] "Here was one of the white man's most characteristic behavior patterns—where black men are concerned. He loves himself so much that he is startled if he discovers that his victims don't share his vainglorious self-opinion."

Across the racial divide, Malcolm's put-down of the behavior of white Americans gave a psychic lift to Negroes, especially to young, urban students wary of nonviolent civil rights tactics. And Malcolm's reasoning jolted many black youngsters—including some who would become key leaders of the Student Nonviolent Coordinating Committee and the Congress of Racial Equality and founders of the Black Panther Party—to a more aggressive level of resistance.

It was clear that Malcolm's irrepressible charisma and his debating skills made him a magnet for the media, and one of the most sought-after speakers on college campuses across the country. His popularity drove up the Muslims' membership, although the increase was nowhere near as great as his public following suggested.

Typical was the response of one young, high-potential student from Birmingham, Alabama, Angela Yvonne Davis—who a decade later would make the FBI's most wanted list as a "black revolutionary." She was "mesmerized" by Malcolm's sociopolitical critique when he visited Brandeis University in 1963.[39] However, the Muslims' national spokesman could not sell the Marxist-leaning Davis or most other young admirers on his exotic religion.

Even in big cities, the adventurous ones who dared attend the local temples were unnerved by the Fruits of Islam body searches, separate gender seating, and strict discipline. Many a potential Harlem recruit bolted as soon as they caught wind of the inarticulate Elijah Muhammad, to say nothing of the Yacub myth, the Mother Ship "nonsense," and the straight-faced claims that Master Fard Muhammad was Allah, the flesh-and-blood God of the universe. Although attracted to Malcolm's social analysis and the psychic remedy of self-help, these younger would-be converts cringed at his mantra: "The Honorable Elijah Muhammad teaches us that . . ." Unwittingly, Malcolm's persuasive call to arms was widening the gap between his more global view and the dogma of Muhammad's sect, weighted down with hocus-pocus religiosity.

That gap was on display a year after the documentary, when Elijah Muhammad was angered by Malcolm's warm welcome of Fidel Castro during the Cuban president's trip to New York to address the United Nations General Assembly. Malcolm was one of Castro's first visitors at the Theresa Hotel in Harlem; it reportedly was his idea for Castro to stay there, in the heart of the African American neighborhood. That move brought crowds of well-wishers out on the streets, a public relations bonanza for the Cuban leader, who already had been targeted as an enemy by the U.S. government.[40]

The outsized media fame of the national spokesman would not go unnoticed by his Messenger in Chicago—and most especially by the Messenger's prospective heirs—despite the abundant financial benefits that Malcolm was dutifully passing along to the coffers of the "Royal Family."

# CHAPTER 12

# Hartford: "The Dead There Are Rising"

THE CAPITAL OF CONNECTICUT, HARTFORD, HAD SEEMED little more than a whistle stop when Malcolm worked as a sandwich man on the railroad in the 1940s. On a warm summer Thursday a decade later, in 1955, he gazed out at the tallest building in New England, the stark thirty-four-story neoclassical Travelers Tower; it punctuated the skyline of the city. America's two most important novelists of slavery—Harriet Beecher Stowe, who wrote *Uncle Tom's Cabin,* and Mark Twain, who wrote *The Adventures of Huckleberry Finn*—once had been next-door neighbors in Hartford. On the New Haven train run as a teenager, Malcolm had been amused by the Bostonian tongue of the conductor dropping his *r*'s before consonants, shouting out, "Haaatfod, next stop, Haaatfod!" His own jazzed-up, Harlem accent had matured now into a baritone rolling with the precision of the autodidact on the make. And while his smile no longer reached his gray-green eyes, dimmed by years of study under cellblock lighting, the bespectacled, thirty-year-old

Malcolm emitted a charm that could raise goose bumps on women and put high resolve in men.

During these early Eisenhower years, Malcolm was expanding the rolls of the Muslims much as his father had promoted Marcus Garvey in the Midwest during the Depression. Especially adept at fishing for converts on streets he had once prowled as a hoodlum, Malcolm was celebrated, even in headquarters, as a masterly proselytizer for Elijah Muhammad's Nation of Islam (NOI). In addition to heading Harlem's Temple No. 7, he oversaw expanding operations in Boston and Philadelphia, and was cultivating Springfield, Massachusetts, among other outlets. Still, the tireless organizer kept his ears ever pricked for word of new opportunities up and down the East Coast.

"A lady visiting a Springfield meeting asked if I'd come to Hartford where she lived," Malcolm wrote in his *Autobiography*. "She specified the next Thursday and said she would assemble some friends. And I was right there."[1] Details of this venture into Hartford—which would prove pivotal—were omitted from Malcolm's book, along with the name of the woman who invited him. She was, in fact, Rosalie Bey Glover, a mother of nine, who had taken to attending the Muslim temple in Springfield whenever the tall, itinerant minister from Harlem lectured there. And on a whim, she had extended the invitation that would allow Malcolm not only to cultivate a greater Muslim presence in staid New England but also to tweak the nose of Elijah Muhammad in a city that years earlier had stymied the recruiting efforts of the Messenger. Unlike his religious leader, Malcolm was familiar with the culture and sensibility of New England Negroes, as well as whites.

Since Malcolm's railroad days, Hartford had blossomed into the Insurance Capital of the World, a reputation amplified by the popular radio drama *Yours Truly, Johnny Dollar*, which featured a daring, insurance investigator traveling the world on a bountiful expense

account.[2] The industrial juggernaut also was home to the gun-
making factory Colt's Firearms, an Underwood Typewriter plant,
and a sprawling aerospace network anchored by Pratt & Whitney Air-
craft Company. In addition to these middle-class job magnets, the
tobacco valley where Malcolm had sold clothing continued to flourish on nearby farms in Windsor and Suffield. When the Immigration
Act of 1924 curtailed the human flow from southern and eastern
Europe, the slack in the tight Connecticut labor market called on
workers from Puerto Rico, "temporary" farm laborers and domestics
from the British West Indies, and Negroes from the Deep South.
The white population in Connecticut increased by 44 percent from
1940 to 1960; during the same period, the Negro population rose
by 229 percent.[3]

One of those migrants was Malcolm's hostess, Rosalie Glover,
who had been forced to leave Florida after a young neighbor was
lynched in the brutal style all too familiar to Malcolm and the Muslims. Her time in Hartford only increased Mrs. Glover's disenchant-
ment with white Christians, and even black ones. By the fall of 1954,
just months after the Supreme Court's historic *Brown v. Board of
Education* decision overruled the "separate but equal" doctrine the
Court had endorsed in 1896, she took to visiting the Muslim temple
in Springfield. Services there were anchored by Brother Osborne
X Thaxton, who had served time as a prison inmate with Malcolm.

Hartford had proved more resistant to the Muslims' appeal. The
Messenger himself had tried to set up a temple there during the
1940s—and failed—leaving no Muslim seedlings among the hardworking descendants of Southern sharecroppers, most of them from
his home state of Georgia. Some would set up storefront Protestant
churches in apartment buildings; the more prosperous of the faithful, such as the African Methodist Episcopal worshippers, would convert the gothic cathedrals of retreating white Christians and Jews.
The high-toned Union Baptist congregation, for example, took over

the stately-church home of white Episcopalians fleeing the oncoming Negroes of Main Street.

A few old-timers of Hartford's North End vaguely remembered Elijah Muhammad preaching his "white man is a devil" credo, which had fallen on deaf ears during the booming wartime years. Having fled a bare-knuckled, violent racism in the South that was unimaginable in New England, blacks were brimming with the migrant's sense of optimism in their adopted city, with its better-paying jobs and desegregated schools.

No doubt recalling his chilly reception there, the Messenger dismissed Hartford to his young Hotspur as a total waste of time. Nonetheless, Malcolm had pressed for permission to pursue Mrs. Glover's invitation. Muhammad had given the go-ahead more with a sense of indulgence than with any expectation for success in Hartford. After all, the Negroes of Hartford had essentially thumbed their nose at the Messenger himself.

The challenge was not lost on the highly competitive Muslim disciple on the move.

———

On that initial Thursday in 1955, Malcolm was lighting out for new territory. The fair-skinned and graying Mrs. Glover greeted him with an easy smile at the door of her spruced-up flat in the Bellevue Square housing project. Other than hearing the rumor that food and soft drinks would be served, some of the dozen or so invited guests had only a vague notion about the purpose of the gathering. A gentle curiosity hung in the air as Malcolm sized up the North End strangers and folded his lean frame onto the living room sofa. "Thursday," the *Autobiography* stated, "is traditionally domestic servants' day off. This sister had in her housing project apartment about fifteen of the maids, cooks, chauffeurs and house men who worked for the Hartford area's white people."[4] Reaching for the snacks, Mrs.

Glover's neighbors gazed upon the stranger from Harlem, easing into his riff about how divided Negroes were in America generally. Switching gears, Malcolm got local and pitched the need for those in Hartford to unite on social, economic, and, yes, religious grounds.

Suddenly, the teenage daughter of the hostess felt tricked. In clear and secular language, she had demanded that the family spare her all religious events—especially, any contact with preachers. Unlike her two younger sisters, this newly minted high school graduate had her own apartment, a few blocks away. As a nod to her mother, this namesake daughter, Rosalie, had stopped by after work from her job at Connecticut General Life Insurance Company. But as the visiting minister continued his opening volley, the independent-minded young woman smirked her way backward toward the door. Something about this tall stranger, however, stayed her hand from the door knob. At first it was his neat, starched persona, his Lincolnesque chin, his golden hue, the horn-rimmed gaze of his light-colored eyes that held no doubt. The bright-eyed nineteen-year-old had encountered no other Negro radiating such confidence.

Avoiding the intensity of his beam, young Rosalie peered at Malcolm from the side, coyly. He was stern yet gentle, "high-toned," she sensed, yet quite earthbound, and flat-out reasonable—for a minister, that is. Her girlish eyes wandered playfully along the entire length of his body. The reverse usually was the custom, with the eyes of the smooth-talking preachers of her acquaintance doing the initial body scanning—sometimes accompanied by their roving hands, in a young lady's unguarded moments. And now, here *she* was, struggling sheepishly to get herself under control.

Indeed, young Rosalie was fetched by the forbidding sensuality of the glib, lithe minister from Harlem. With only her tame high school experience as a guide, she picked up no incoming signal of interest, no traces, say, of the wanton lustiness of the Detroit Red of a decade ago. Although he was speaking easily about riding the New Haven rails through Hartford as a teenager, Malcolm skipped over his pursuit back then of the Gomorrah delights of Boston and Harlem.

As with Nation of Islam orthodoxy, Malcolm's Muslim pitch was tilted sharply from the perspective of a dominant Negro male. He gave no hint that rapprochement between the black man and the black woman would be readily achievable, or even desirable. As Malcolm sounded the clarion, Mrs. Glover nodded agreeably and seemed prepared to sacrifice all, straightaway, for the cause of Islam.

The mind of her namesake daughter was someplace else entirely.

Upon stressing that black men must respect and protect their women, Malcolm paused for dramatic emphasis as effectively as any stage actor. He then deadpanned, pointedly, that black women must *earn* that respect. Decked out in tight-fitting "short shorts," young Rosalie froze at this riff. A rush of modesty shivered her momentarily. Struggling to regain her composure, she fidgeted, she folded her arms, and she tugged as best she could at the scant hem of the trendy red shorts riding well above midthigh.

Never had she felt quite this shamefaced in public. Although no one looked her way, she felt exposed in the crowded room—and yet, somehow, she felt alone. Young Rosalie would remember the poignancy of that 1955 moment decades later. The chaste baritone Malcolm had shamed her.

Her mother went busily about offering refreshments to the guests, occasionally forcing a smile, cutting her eyes over the room for clues as Malcolm roared on. The restless men in the rear grew rapt. This puzzled young Rosalie. She knew two of them as good-time Charlies prone to sipping Johnnie Walker Red at the nearby Subway Club on Main Street and chasing available ladies far into the night. There was at least one out-of-wedlock child. Yet the more Malcolm damned such behavior as abhorrent to black group advancement, the steadier this duo leaned forward in nodding agreement. It all seemed a tad surreal.

After an intense hour, Malcolm eased up, mindful of ending this initial lecture with an informal tone. The room came alive with questions. Someone asked whether Malcolm's Muslims were affiliated with the Moors. As instructed by the Messenger, he assured the audience, somewhat inaccurately, that the NOI was not entwined with the Moorish Science Temple.

The tone of the visiting minister that day in Bellevue Square was strict, if not intimidating, to the carefree group. "He had a voice that could capture you," young Rosalie said years later. "What he was saying wasn't like anything I had heard before. I was really looking forward to him coming back again."[5]

That initial Thursday gathering in Hartford reminded Malcolm a bit of those times his father had hauled him around as a young lad to sessions held in Lansing, a similar capital city in the Midwest. Like his father, Malcolm dressed neatly, with his shoes shined to a high gloss. And while not balding as was Elijah Muhammad, Malcolm nonetheless took up his religious leader's habit of always wearing a hat outdoors, the custom for so many gentlemen in that era. Over the coming months, during his visits to Hartford, he was seen sporting dark fedoras and occasionally even a French beret.

"You've heard that saying, 'no man is a hero to his valet,'" Malcolm wrote in the *Autobiography*. "Well, those Negroes who waited on wealthy whites hand and foot opened their eyes quicker than most Negroes . . . every Thursday I scheduled my teaching there."[6]

As early as the second week, Lewis Brown, a local teenager, was approached by a white man in a dark suit with spit-shined brown shoes. He introduced himself outright as an FBI agent and asked young Brown about the Thursday night goings-on in apartment 14B, the Glover place.[7]

The agent made specific reference to a tall, light-skinned man in the area at the time of the weekly meetings. Although his mother had attended the first meeting, young Brown had little to offer. The youngster viewed the agent with no particular alarm or animosity; in fact, he was a fan of the radio drama *The FBI, in Peace and War.*[8] This popular show promoted a positive image of J. Edgar Hoover and the Bureau among Negroes, and it was a valuable tool for the recruitment of his white agents and staff.

During the first few Hartford meetings, Malcolm went light on the Messenger's tough remedies. In hardscrabble Philadelphia, where moral reform was shamefully lacking, he had clamped down hard. There, a longtime Muslim named Jeremiah X, along with some backsliding practitioners (several of whom had served hard time in prison), had been disciplined by Malcolm to one meal during a workday that began with prayer at dawn. He outlawed cigarettes and alcohol, cold turkey. And Malcolm punctuated the brothers' habits with the five daily Muslim prayers, arms folded, facing the east, petitioning Allah in gibberish Arabic.

Starting with a blank slate in Hartford, Malcolm saw no reason to throw the fear of Allah too quickly into the hearts of hardworking potential converts. The Yacub myth was kept in storage, for example, as were the teachings about the Mother Ship, which already had clocked several overhead sightings in the sky above the believers down in Philadelphia.

"Never give meat to a baby; always give them milk, and you'll never lose them," Malcolm had advised his brother Philbert on his method of recruiting Muslim followers. "That is the KEY in setting up new temples . . . one of the hindrances of the past in trying to propagate Islam, we over-taught the lost-found, giving them meat that they just could not digest, thereby making many rebellious and go back just because once we got them to open their mouths (minds) we started giving them too heavy a food that they could not digest (see) yet."[9]

Nevertheless, disciplining the faithful in Hartford taxed Malcolm's patience at the outset. Both Rosalie and her daughter relentlessly smoked, as did others in the apartment. Malcolm initially endured the heavy, carbon-nicotine haze in silence. When offered pork chops, he simply declined. (His famed, upchuck-inspiring lecture on the sins of eating meat from the worm-infested swine would come later.) Early on, he spared the candidates the full exposure that the advanced believers were subjected to in the Springfield temple. Cigarettes there were already forbidden; pork was banned absolutely as the devil's meat; and Malcolm had imposed a sedate dress code, and a daily mimicking of Arabic prayers facing east.[10]

Aside from ethical reform and Muslim submission, it was Malcolm's clarion call for black resistance to racism that pitched him beyond the outer reaches of Elijah Muhammad's strictly religious orbit. This very sociopolitical message stirred in Mrs. Glover a troubling memory of an encounter with the Ku Klux Klan back home. It was an incident she rarely discussed, even with her closest friends and associates.

Malcolm broke the ice one Thursday evening while discussing the recent news of another such tragedy: the widely publicized lynching of fourteen-year-old Emmett Till on August 28, 1955. Mrs. Glover broke down sobbing and described to Malcolm the incident that had driven her out of the South more than a dozen years before—and that made her a refugee fleeing her birthright religion of Christianity.

On Monday, May 12, 1941, Rosalie Glover heard gunshots in the distance. Such night sounds were not unusual in the hamlet of Quincy, Florida, where firearms were plentiful and hunting was a sport for some and the means of subsistence for many. The gunfire, however, was followed this evening by plaintive moaning. Neighbors in the wood-frame houses lit by coal oil lamps cracked open their doors.

The groans, clearly human, grew louder, attracting a few scouts, who passed along the word that someone had been shot.

Twenty-two-year-old A. C. Williams crawled into the arms of his neighbors. His shirt and trousers were caked with mud; and his body was oozing blood from indistinct portals. Tearfully, Williams said that he had been waylaid and shot; his eyes, wide with horror, said the rest: it was a crosstown attack.[11]

Mrs. Glover kept her children at a distance.

Quincy police had picked up Williams in town a couple of days earlier. The Gadsden County sheriff arrested him on suspicion of attempting to assault a twelve-year-old white girl. That evening, a group of four white men stormed into the county jail. It is not clear what transpired between the angry men and jail authorities. However, they left the building with Williams as their prisoner. Beyond the reach of the dim lights of town, they beat him bloody about the head and body; then they shot Williams several times and left him for dead at the side of the road near a tobacco field.

Somehow Williams survived the battering and the gunshots. Regaining consciousness, he writhed his way homeward, as if by rote. A neighbor of Mrs. Glover allowed the men to bring the severely injured Williams into her home. Innocently, she called the police.

Williams was promptly then rearrested by Gadsden County Sheriff Luten, as a fugitive—although clearly he had been kidnapped out of jail by the white men bent on lynching him. There is no record of the sheriff expressing interest in the men who kidnapped his prisoner. On the advice of a doctor, the sheriff sent the ailing Williams for treatment by ambulance—without guards—to a Tallahassee hospital, about twenty-five miles away. The sheriff who had allowed the original abduction was quoted in an article in a New York newspaper as saying that he didn't "anticipate any more trouble."[12]

En route to the hospital, however, the Negro ambulance driver, a Quincy resident named Will Webb, was forced off the road by "four or five [white] men." Webb reported, "One of them said they wanted the man and didn't want any trouble. I told them they wouldn't get any trouble out of me, because I didn't even have a pocket knife." The sweating mob, none too proud of its initial attempt, abducted Williams once again.[13]

Several hours later, the hideously bruised and bullet-riddled body of young A. C. Williams was found on a bridge over a creek five miles north of Quincy. Such vigilante action was not new to the area. Four years earlier, in 1937, two Negroes accused of stabbing a policeman in neighboring Leon County were taken from the county jail by a white mob and lynched.

The tortuous Williams killing bore the unmistakable signature of the Ku Klux Klan. Keeping Southern Negroes "in their place" through just such brutality was the chief mission of these so-called white knights. Systematically, as a teaching point, they would kidnap and torture an available Negro attached to a transgression against a white person; almost any charge, no matter how sketchy and unsubstantiated, would suffice. The vague "attempt to assault" charge against Williams was typical. The victim would then be ceremoniously tortured, often castrated, sometimes before large crowds in open fields. Sheriffs and police chiefs most often cooperated with the abductors and murderers, rarely detailing a report of the incident. When those in the civil rights movement later persuaded the federal government to press for a trial, which was rare, the all-white jury never failed to acquit the killers. Indeed, the white community was likely to salute them as hometown heroes.

In relating her story to Malcolm, Rosalie Glover said that the incident convinced her that she could not protect her children, especially the boys, anywhere in the South. So common was the lynching of Negroes in the "modern" South that a *Washington Post* story on January 2, 1954, reported the notable good news that for two years running, no one had been lynched in the United States. "End of Lynching" proclaimed the wildly optimistic headline in the *Post*.[14]

The following year, as if to compensate for the lapse, two white men in Mississippi abducted Emmett Till in the most notorious lynching of the era. The adolescent visiting from Chicago allegedly whistled at a white female clerk, Carolyn Bryant, in a grocery store and, according to his cousin, upon leaving said, "Bye, baby." The two, including the woman's husband, abducted and beat the youngster mercilessly, riddled his body with bullets, affixed a seventy-five-pound fan from a cotton gin around his neck with barbed wire, and threw his body into the Tallahatchie River—all for "talking fresh" to a white woman. Following the internationally publicized, open-casket funeral of the victim in Illinois, an all-white Mississippi jury freed Till's white killers on the strength of the twenty-one-year-old Bryant's testimony that the teenager had physically grabbed and verbally harassed her. "I was just scared to death," she said. Some six decades later, she admitted to a writer that her testimony that Emmett Till had made verbal and physical advances was fabricated. "That part's not true," she told Timothy Tyson, author of *The Blood of Emmett Till*.[15] Whipped along by the Soviets during the Cold War, the outrageous Till verdict was presented to the world as an example of just how racial justice was dispensed in America.

The accused men had publicly maintained that they did not kill Till. Double jeopardy prevented a retrial. So after the trial, the white killers of Emmett Till brazenly sold their story for $4,000 to author William Bradford Huie, explaining in cold-blooded detail exactly how they executed the act of terror. Huie, who wrote best-selling books about other such civil rights atrocities, published the confessions of Till's acquitted killers in *Look* magazine.[16]

The determined efforts of Emmett Till's mother and the timing of the case a year *after* the Supreme Court had outlawed school segregation rendered the Till lynching a major stimulus for the civil rights movement—and for the rise of young Reverend Martin Luther King Jr. The Southern-based Christian minister would provide the non-violent alternative to the self-defense posture of the Muslims pushed most aggressively by Malcolm X.

For Mrs. Glover, the 1941 Klan "message" killing in her hometown of Quincy was a threat to be heeded. She immediately loaded her two young sons and three daughters aboard a train and headed north to Connecticut. Four of her older children had already migrated to Hartford or other Northern cities

Despairing of the Holiness Church that had been her "rock of ages" in Florida, Mrs. Glover joined the Hartford branch of the Moorish Science Temple, which promoted a "return to Islam as the only means of redemption." Emphasizing African heritage, moral uplift, and economic self-help, the local temple was headed by a man named Sheik F. Turner El, who conducted meetings in a small hall over a shop on Albany Avenue. Glover and her husband also took their children to the group's 275-acre spread in Massachusetts.

Upon discovering that funds raised to pay the mortgage on the Great Barrington retreat were being misdirected, Glover and other followers lost confidence in the leadership. It was then that Mrs. Glover began visiting the Islamic temple, twenty-five miles away, in Springfield, Massachusetts.[17]

The Moorish temple dropout was determined to rekindle the Islamic fires that had been banked by corruption. Quite beyond the dogma about the Qur'an, such as it was, and the moral uplift, Rosalie Glover was captivated by the raw aggressiveness of the young captain whose message of social resistance was nothing short of a call to arms. She had finally found comfort in the young and apparently fearless Malcolm, a minister who preached self-defense and ignited among Negro listeners a resolve to resist.

The act of lynching had long been a standard motif of the NOI.

The image of a rope looped around the neck of a Negro was inscribed on backdrops of Muslim classrooms where ministers instructed students about this historic handiwork of the "blue-eyed devils." As a recruiting tool, the Muslims never tired of such anecdotes as Mrs. Glover's recounting of the lynching of A. C. Williams.

Malcolm was masterly at folding such accounts of terror—including the death of his father—into a bill of particulars against all white Americans. And he held that bill out as a score that one day must be settled, if only, as the Messenger instructed, by Allah Himself.

As in earlier days, this model city of Hartford became in the 1950s something of an oasis for Southern Negroes seeking jobs and a better life. The economy continued to boom, and Connecticut had just elected as governor a liberal Democrat, Abraham Ribicoff, the state's first Jewish chief executive, who was popular among blacks.

As with most challenges, Malcolm was quick to grasp the unique significance of the Hartford experiment. The primal drive of the son to surpass the father also drives the protégé to surpass his mentor—and thus to please him. Conversations with relatives and with long-time associate Captain Joseph suggest that Malcolm viewed Hartford as a defining chance to build a temple from the ground up—and thus secure his special place as an organizer and leader. Away from the intense rivalries, the police pressure, and the press coverage in cities such as New York and Philadelphia, the creation of the Hartford temple became a case study of Malcolm's signature technique and his impact as a young minister spreading his wings.

The recruits whom Malcolm was nursing to salvation became too numerous for Rosalie Glover's cramped apartment. So the Muslim operation was moved to the home of her oldest daughter, Alzea. Alzea and her husband, Eddie St. John, had a roomy duplex, at 40 Pliny

Street. The Thursday sessions featured Malcolm's stepped-up lectures on black unity and self-respect. He illustrated his points about how every other people in the United States—save the Negro—had developed businesses, jobs, and self-reliance. Robbed of their African names and mother languages, the "so-called Negroes" were yet begging their white enemies for jobs, education, and housing. The housing issue got traction among the nodding heads in the modest living room of the St. Johns.[18]

As in most Northern cities fielding black migrants, housing remained a pernicious obstacle in the 1950s. Suburban tracts constructed on a vast scale for soldiers returning from World War II— and backed by Federal Housing Administration (FHA) grants—were generally closed to Negro veterans. "Restrictive covenants" limited ownership to whites only, including recent immigrants from Europe. In developments like the 17,000 tract houses of Levittown, built on Long Island between 1947 and 1951, federally subsidized housing generated equity wealth and spawned a new generation of white middle-class Americans.

Shut out of Levittown—the prototype for postwar suburbia— and other such developments for decades, Negro veterans were belatedly granted lesser subsidies for scatter-site housing in generally depressed areas. Moreover, the government subsidized public housing for Negroes that were not owner-occupied—like the homes for whites in suburbia—but rented to low-income families in inner-city areas. These federally backed housing projects capped family earning for eligibility at little more than minimum wage. The U.S. government essentially ran a two-tier program, encouraging a permanent Negro underclass of renters while operating the FHA-backed suburban home ownership program to stimulate a dramatic growth of the white middle class.

Bellevue Square, where Malcolm held his initial Hartford meetings, was just such an inner-city housing project. It was subsidized by the federal government for 501 working-class renters, 100 percent of whom were Negro. Citywide, according to the 1950 census, some 90.4 percent of the 12,790 nonwhite residents were crammed into a small pocket of the deteriorating North End. A seven-part series on city housing published in 1956 in the *Hartford Courant* opened with a blunt admission:

> One of Hartford's largest builders laughed when he was asked whether he would sell any of his new houses to a Negro. He laughed with reason, for the question was a naive one. Negroes cannot purchase any of the builder's houses, nor would a real estate broker sell an older house to a Negro. Even should a Negro find himself in fortunate circumstances, after contriving a way to bypass or hurdle the first two barriers, his chances of obtaining conventional financing from Hartford's lending institutions are mixed . . . discrimination solely on the basis of skin color does exist in the city.[19]

Malcolm knew well that this pattern was nationwide and of long standing, and that it was not lacking in malice and aforethought. He related Hartford's housing bias to his parents' Midwest experience back in Nebraska, Wisconsin, and Michigan.

The all-white housing covenant that had prevented Malcolm's father from legally living on land he purchased in Lansing had, at least legally, been voided by the 1948 Supreme Court decision in the *McGhee* and *Shelley* cases. In addition to this national ruling, the Connecticut Civil Rights Commission had recently voted to include the state's real estate brokers under the fair housing provision of the Federal Housing Administration. However, Mrs. Glover and other Muslims informed Malcolm about housing discrimination resulting from a new dodge of the local realtors. The code of ethics of the Hartford Real Estate Board, for example, contained a specific, exclusionary provision that read, "A realtor should not be instrumental in introducing into a neighborhood a character of property or use which will clearly be detrimental to property values in that neighborhood."[20] That clause was used to restrict Negroes from living in white neighborhoods. Without proof—indeed, the evidence ran counter—prospective black home buyers were preemptively accused of "bringing down property values."

In the segregated city, where blacks constituted a small minority, they nevertheless grew to become the largest ethnic group in one elementary school and one of the three local high schools. In due course, as in urban areas generally, most Negro children would end up in predominantly black classrooms from kindergarten through twelfth grade. Malcolm, however, did not offer the Pliny Street group a strategy for contesting the practice of the Hartford public schools or the policy of the real estate board. The fight for inclusion was left to the leaders of the local NAACP and the National Urban League.

Changing the behavior of the "blue-eyed devils," Malcolm observed, following his instructions from Elijah Muhammad, was a nonstarter. Instead, Negroes had first to change their minds about white folk altogether. But most important, Malcolm argued that blacks had to change their minds about one another and about themselves. They alone held the key to their upward mobility, he taught repeatedly.

The white man, he said, is a devil in real estate as in all other earthly matters. "The Honorable Elijah Muhammad teaches us," Malcolm said, that whites' insistence upon keeping to themselves, "living among themselves," at all costs—often brutalizing Negroes—was as much an expression of their evil nature as barking was a part of a dog's nature.

This twin slap at segregation and integration usually drew a barrage of questions early on from the floor. Unlike the Messenger, whose tongue got tied answering tough questions, Malcolm fielded

Will Brown's body roasting on an open pyre, September 28, 1919.

Marcus Garvey, ca. 1924.

*(George Grantham Bain Collection, Library of Congress Prints and Photographs Division)*

W. E. B. Du Bois, ca. 1919.

*(Biographical File filing series, Library of Congress Prints and Photographs Division)*

The Little family 1930 census entry.

*(Library of Congress)*

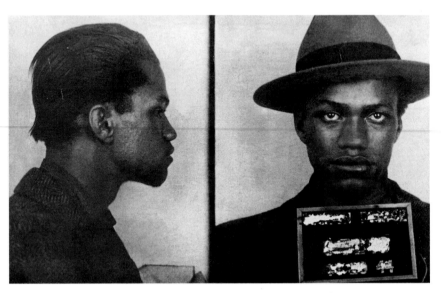

Malcolm Little, at age eighteen in 1944, was arrested for larceny
in Boston and was later released on probation.

*(Bettmann / Getty Images)*

(*above*) Elijah Muhammad, ca. 1964.

*(Photograph by Stanley Wolf, Library of Congress Prints and Photographs Division)*

(*right*) Rosalie Glover, founding member of the Nation of Islam Temple No. 14 in Hartford, Connecticut.
*(Courtesy of the St. John family)*

Rosalie Glover, ca. 1981.
*(Courtesy of the St. John family)*

Malcolm X (center) with Percy Sutton (left) and Hulan Jack (right)
at a Harlem rally, ca. 1962.
*(Photograph by O'Neal L. Abel)*

Malcolm X speaking at a Harlem rally, ca. 1962.

*(Photograph by O'Neal L. Abel)*

Malcolm X speaking at a Harlem rally, ca. 1962
*(Photograph by O'Neal L. Abel)*

Malcolm X standing at a podium next to an enlarged illustration
from *Muhammad Speaks* newspaper in Harlem, ca. 1963.

*(Photograph by Adger Cowans)*

Malcolm X with Captain Joseph (left of Malcolm), members of the Fruit of Islam, and assistant ministers at Harlem Unity Rally, ca. 1963.

*(Photograph by Robert Haggins)*

Malcolm X with Redd Foxx at Temple No. 7 Restaurant, ca. 1963.

*(Photograph by Robert Haggins)*

Malcolm with Benjamin Karim (center) at a protest rally
at Manhattan Criminal Court, ca. 1963.

*(Photograph by Robert Haggins)*

Malcolm X with Muhammad Ali, February 1964.
*(Photograph by Robert Haggins)*

Malcolm X being interviewed by a flock of reporters, ca. 1964.

*(Photograph by Marion S. Trikosko for* U.S. News & World Report *magazine, Library of Congress Prints and Photographs Division)*

Malcolm X and Martin Luther King Jr. meet in March 1964.

*(Photograph by Marion S. Trikosko for* U.S. News & World Report *magazine, Library of Congress Prints and Photographs Division)*

Malcom X waiting at a press conference, March 1964.

*(Photograph by Marion S. Trikosko for* U.S. News & World Report *magazine,
Library of Congress Prints and Photographs Division)*

Malcolm X visiting the home of Yuri Kochiyama, June 6, 1964.
*(Photograph by Yuri Kochiyama)*

Malcolm X with visiting Japanese scholars at the home of Yuri Kochiyama.
*(Photograph by Yuri Kochiyama)*

Malcolm X, Audee Kochiyama (left, front), and friends, June 6, 1964.
*(Photograph by Yuri Kochiyama)*

Exterior view of home of Malcolm X with charred furniture
remains in foreground, February 1965.
*(Photograph by Stanley Wolfson for* New York World-Telegram and Sun,
*Library of Congress Prints and Photographs Division)*

Circled bullet holes on stage after the killing of Malcolm X, February 1965.
*(Photograph by Stanley Wolfson for* New York World-Telegram and Sun,
*Library of Congress Prints and Photographs Division)*

Malcolm X at the United Nations, ca. 1963.

*(Photograph by Robert Haggins)*

each challenge smoothly. Still, his polished explanations, embroidered with wit, anecdotes, and historical data, left scattered clouds of unease among some—and flat-out rejection by others.

John Peoples, who worked on an assembly line at Pratt & Whitney, balked at every key point of Malcolm's lecture. Like others in the room, he was most uneasy with the teaching about the white man as an "evil devil" without hope. The aunt with whom he lived, for example, was married to a white man. "I could see the white man as being evil, but I didn't believe that his wife was just as evil," said Peoples. "I asked Malcolm, 'Do you mean to tell me that the white woman is just as evil?' Malcolm said that 'all of them are evil, brother, the fat ones, the skinny ones.' "[21]

Dutifully, Malcolm instructed that Elijah Muhammad's solution to the race problem was not to integrate with, but to separate from, the whites. Blockbusting to gain temporary entry into their Hartford neighborhoods was degrading, he taught. Instead Negroes should start developing their own neighborhoods, organizing businesses, and "doing for self."

Each week, Malcolm listened patiently to fresh anecdotes about racism at Hartford area jobs, in schools, and in housing. Such excesses, he insisted, only buttressed Elijah Muhammad's argument that blacks must separate themselves completely. As whites dismissed them as inferior, he counseled, Negroes should counterreject whites as irredeemable "blue-eyed devils."

Unease would rustle throughout the apartment, with more than a few potential recruits casting furtive glances over their shoulders. None, not even the interlopers from the Moorish Science Temple, had ever heard a Negro leader speak against white people as uncompromisingly as Malcolm did during these living room sessions. A few of Mrs. Glover's guests, who were mainly low-income workers and day laborers, admitted concern, if not outright fear of police authorities. Some fell away, only to be replaced by others. There was, as Malcolm suspected, a flow of attendees taking notes and, for payment, passing information along to the FBI.

Like Elijah Muhammad before him, Malcolm discovered that Hartford Negroes, in the main, had bought into the American dream. They held on to its promise, notwithstanding the numerous rejections they suffered daily. Malcolm steadfastly pointed out the contradictions. Yet even those who rejected the Muslim scenarios of whites as "blue-eyed devils," and America as a black man's hell on earth, were attracted to the irrepressible magnet that was young minister Malcolm.

As with the other temples under his tutelage, the Hartford group was composed mostly of women. They were pulled in by Malcolm's personal pitch, his charm, both verbal and physical, and his bold appeals to black pride, independence, and self-worth. The respect voiced for black women, at bottom, did not go unnoticed. His was an aggressive, macho approach, and he disparaged the nonviolent stance of Dr. Martin Luther King Jr. as cowardice pure and simple.[22]

Muslim's self-defense strategy demanded that if attacked, the Fruit of Islam, the Nation's security force, would not beg and crawl but would take "a life for a life." This point was not lost on the men in the room. It also reassured Rosalie Glover, whose experience back in Florida, was always on her mind. Sticking to the Messenger's basic recipe for a simple dose of self-help, Malcolm spiced it up with his own intellectual seasoning. American slave history, the failed Reconstruction, anticolonialism, and pan-Africanism pricked the ears of the scholars in the room. Occasionally, Malcolm would get drawn into geopolitical exchanges about the growing challenge to colonialism on the African continent as laid out in the writings of W. E. B. Du Bois, George Padmore, and C. L. R. James. Unlike his chief minister, Elijah Muhammad tended to avoid talking directly about sub-Saharan Africa, considering his followers "Asiatic black men."

Faithful to Muslim dogma in the main, and liberal with

attributions to "The Honorable Elijah Muhammad," Malcolm nonetheless stamped his unmistakable signature on each new temple
under his direct authority, most especially in Hartford.

In addition to menial workers and an ex-convict or two, the Hartford gatherings, in time, drew in upwardly mobile, working-class
nurses, machinists, and semiskilled factory jobbers. All were battling
racism in schools, housing, and the workplace, their upward mobility
stymied by the subtlety of the racial bias in Hartford. They surrendered their individual ad hoc coping mechanisms to the organized
self-help strategy of the Muslims.

Very few, if any, of the Hartford recruits had a stomach for violence, unlike followers in the Philadelphia, Newark, and New York
chapters, where head knocking had a broad appeal. The karate
sessions of the Fruit of Islam were a main attraction for the hard,
young recruits of Brooklyn, Harlem, and Philadelphia. In Hartford,
this manly art never got off the ground. Instead, Malcolm had the
recruits focus on other programs.

It was, for example, the self-help, economic aspects that pulled
in Eddie St. John, Mrs. Glover's son-in-law, whose larger Pliny Street
home became Malcolm's headquarters in the city. The thirty-year-
old homeowner, along with others, had earlier bolted the Moors
group when it drifted away from the teachings of its founder,
Prophet Noble Drew Ali. He saw the Nation of Islam as far less
given to corruption. "Malcolm was awfully convincing," St. John
recalled years later.

A post office worker, St. John was but one of the black Hartford
natives who burned with the entrepreneurial spirit. "Malcolm fos-
tered the economic program. He said we should do our own educat-
ing. We should open our own businesses and cooperate with each
other. We should help each other get on our feet and not be begging
the white man for handouts. Malcolm pointed out that in Chicago
the Muslims had their own school. They had a bakery. He pointed

out that New York [Temple No. 7] had begun to move in this direction. We were also caught up on that part of his message that stressed that we should be proud of our heritage."[23]

The message of white man as a "blue-eyed devil" did not sit well with St. John. He had worked odd jobs before landing at the post office and was taking an accounting course at local Hilliard College. After discussing his objection to the antiwhite emphasis, Malcolm told St. John to just overlook it and help with the economic aspects. "I never stated publicly to anyone else that I didn't go along with the 'white man is a devil.' I just kept that to myself."[24]

It was a different story with his wife. Unlike St. John, Alzea, the daughter of Rosalie Glover, was a southerner familiar with Jim Crow strictures. Given the Quincy experience, she, like the rest of her family, was exhilarated by the Muslims' casting of the white man as a devil. In the 1930s, Alzea's uncle had slapped a white man during a dispute, and he had to escape north in the dead of night.[25]

A similar incident had rocked the adolescence of John Peoples, the assembly line worker who joined soon after hearing his first Malcolm lecture. As a teenager in Barnwell, South Carolina, the future John X witnessed his uncle Adam arguing with a white man with a big truck over the price of a crop of watermelons his uncle was offering for sale. "Back then, you didn't argue with white folks," John recalled. "When they said, 'This is what I'm paying for the watermelons,' you said, 'Yes sir.'" His uncle made the mistake of trying to counter the white buyer's price in firm, commercial tones. The white man "pulled a pistol and shot Uncle Adam dead," Peoples said.[26]

John's father called the sheriff, who, upon encountering further arguments from the seventeen-year-old, advised that—for his own safety—John, the nephew of the victim, should leave town before nightfall. An example was to be made to local Negroes in order to reinforce the strict system of total white domination. "It was a common thing," John said fifty years later, breaking down in tears while relating the details of the shooting death of his uncle. "My father didn't like it, but there was nothing he could do. He didn't want to see the house burned down or see me lynched." The unwritten racial rules in such cases in certain parts of the rural South were such that if an individual Negro resisted, he had to be ready to kill or prepared to die. "I left town on the bus to Florida that night," John X said. "They had to see me getting on the bus; otherwise they would come around."[27]

Such acts of white vigilantism—sometimes ending with lynching—were commonly related by the Southern Negroes who formed the core of Malcolm's resolute Hartford group. These acts helped the Great Migration north after World War I, as documented by writers, scholars, and artists. Jacob Lawrence, in a sixty-part series of paintings, *The Migration of the Negro*, captured the pathos, strife, pain, and beauty of the dislocation, along with the injustice that forced it. One panel in the series—painted in 1941, the year Mrs. Glover left Florida—depicts a Negro sitting on a rock under a tree limb outfitted with a noose, with the caption "Another cause [of the Negro migration] was lynching. It was found that where there had been a lynching, the people who were reluctant to leave at first left immediately after this."[28]

The Glovers held out no expectation that the Quincy lynching would be documented, to say nothing of the crime being prosecuted. Mrs. Glover told Malcolm that she believed A. C. Williams, killed by the Klan in 1941, doubtlessly was yet another of those faceless black victims of Southern white terror—lost to history without a trace. However, factual accounts of the incident were clandestinely assembled, written, and—when no local newspaper dared touch the story—dispatched north. Indeed, they were printed in the pages of the then liberal *New York Post*, which had been founded by Alexander Hamilton in 1801. Since Dorothy Schiff had bought the *Post* in 1939, it held to its liberal bona fides as one of the few mainstream newspapers that paid attention to human rights violations against Negroes in the South of the 1940s.

Such newspaper stories, many of them investigated and verified by the NAACP, had been culled for *100 Years of Lynchings*, the book Malcolm touted. Unbeknown to Malcolm, this volume details the very lynching that drove Mrs. Glover out of Florida. It offered Malcolm an opportunity, apparently never pursued, to document for Mrs. Glover the episode that shaped the impulse which brought the Hartford temple into being.[29]

The toxic blending of religion, racism, and terror by Southern white Christians had long frustrated the sensitive Mrs. Glover. All Negroes were openly branded as inferior descendants of Ham, the allegedly cursed son of the biblical Noah. While both racial groups worshipped the same Christ Jesus, with an eye toward achieving the celestial heaven, postmortem, white churches in Florida barred blacks from entering their Christian sanctuaries on earth. Ushers and church deacons enforced this bias as rigorously on Sundays as the sheriffs' men did every day of the week. In escaping Florida, Mrs. Glover bolted also as a refugee from her religion.[30]

Soured forever on Christianity, Mrs. Glover accepted the Muslim religion as a road toward social and economic freedom for herself, her children, and Negroes in general. The pie-in-the-sky, by-and-by black Sunday preachers that she—and her namesake daughter—had encountered came nowhere close to the coping strategy that Malcolm offered up in his blistering lectures and follow-up.

Within the Nation of Islam, Mrs. Glover felt contentment for the first time since she had left Quincy. In Malcolm she saw a religious leader with the courage to demand a redress of grievances, the right to self-defense, and complete equality, a condition that blacks must hew out of the American circumstance with a fierce pride and their own blood, sweat, and tears. Those Hartford followers with no "Quincy experience" in their background looked to Malcolm's broader NOI promise of fellowship and a redemptive life of moral discipline, along with social and economic uplift for the group.

═══

Unlike bigger Northern cities, which were quite cosmopolitan, Hartford afforded Malcolm the opportunity to isolate recruits into a cocoon for intensified conditioning and indoctrination. Single male members were persuaded to live under a semicommunal system. John Peoples was assigned to rent out complete floors in adjacent North End apartment buildings. The initiates continued working their separate jobs about the city but withdrew from non-Muslim life after hours into something of a cultlike setting. They shopped, cooked, and ate cooperatively. Each one bathed, washed his clothes, and took care of his personal affairs in accordance with strict Muslim dictates.[31]

After months of struggling with anarchy among members of the Philadelphia operation, Malcolm was relieved to build a temple from the ground up. The barrackslike living conditions made it easier to instill discipline. Each man was assigned as his brother's keeper and enforcer of Muslim standards of diet, dress, socializing, and daily prayer.

A primary rule of the "barracks" was that all men must work. Malcolm did not tolerate sloth or allow members, or their families, to subscribe to public welfare. The half dozen bachelors studied Qur'an (in English translation) and secular books together, conducted meetings, and traveled to the temple in Springfield and elsewhere in the Northeast. Occasionally, they were called upon to provide security for Malcolm and visiting Muslim officials. In their withdrawal from the larger society, the young Muslims reinforced one another in a strict policy of no smoking and no drinking, as well as prayer five times a day, and a single daily meal consisting mainly of rice, fish, and large doses of milk. Malcolm was a frequenter of the nearby Lincoln

Dairy, where he indulged his great passion for ice cream, a pleasure the Messenger thankfully had not outlawed.

"We began to eat what Malcolm taught were the proper foods," said St. John. "The bean was a basic food; it was served in many different ways, bean soup, and bean pie. We were taught to eat more fish and eat the meat from the common animals like lamb, beef from the cow, chicken. We were encouraged to buy our meats from kosher markets where the meat was properly killed, properly taken care of."[32] In addition to banning pork, the Messenger's prescription for "eating to live" eschewed such other staples of the Southern "soul food" diet as collard greens, black-eyed peas, and corn bread.

No women were allowed in these communal Hartford apartments, which had to be kept neat and broom clean in case of a spot inspection by Malcolm or visits from out-of-town Muslim officials. Between work, housecleaning, study, meetings, and travel, the young Muslims had no time for courting—which was not allowed. Although not strictly arranged, marriages were usually announced within the community with the briefest period of association.

Malcolm made unannounced visits to the barracks and spoke with the men at length and, in a more relaxed way, about things he never mentioned to mixed audiences from the podium. In addition to discussing black history, slavery, Muslim dieting, and the early life of Elijah Muhammad, Malcolm revealed bits about his own criminal background and his days working the railroads and running the streets of Boston and New York City. "He would relate how he had been running numbers and doing things that the gangsters did, and how he had to go to prison . . . heard about Islam in prison," said Eddie St. John. "He explained how when he accepted Islam, it turned him from what he had been doing, led him to live an upright life. Once he came out, it made him devote his time and efforts to religion first of all and then talking to others and getting them involved.

"He would always give credit to Elijah Muhammad. He sort of swore our allegiance to Elijah Muhammad. He directed attention away from himself toward Elijah. But to me, I think he was the one creating the excitement, drawing the people to this religion of Islam in Hartford, mainly because of the way he presented it. And because he's such a convincing speaker."[33]

Malcolm emphasized furthermore that if a Muslim adhered strictly to the teachings and discipline of the sect, Allah would not allow anyone, or anything—not even a weapon—to harm the believer. "I and some of the other brothers didn't even believe that a bullet would hurt an observing Muslim," said John Peoples. (He later would be shocked to learn that Hinton Johnson, a devoted Harlem Muslim, had actually been wounded and hospitalized when shot by a bullet from a New York City policeman's revolver.) "The dignity that I saw in Malcolm gave me confidence in myself. He instructed me to pray to Allah to remove all fear. His teachings totally removed the fear of the white man from me. For the first time I was proud of being black." Such dramatic transformation was common among the male recruits.[34]

John Peoples, in fact, had been haunted by a sense of inadequacy. When whites ran him out of South Carolina over the watermelon incident, he feared down deep that he was a coward. The spirited, macho undertones of Malcolm's teachings against the "blue-eyed devil" hiked John's perceived sense of himself almost immediately.

"I had seen white people do some terrible things in the South," said Fred Forrest, an Army veteran, who had done his basic training and most of his two-year hitch at segregated Ft. Rucker, Alabama. "Malcolm made me feel like a man for the first time in my life."[35]

In Hartford as elsewhere, Malcolm followed Elijah Muhammad's instructions to have no dealings with the Moorish Science Temple sect. In accepting Mrs. Glover's invitation, he had organized his initiative to fish for converts not from among the Moors per se, but from among black Christians, whom the Muslims called the "lost-found" or the "dead." When the lost-found joined the Nation of Islam, it meant the dead were rising.

———

In Hartford, Mrs. Glover's namesake daughter, who had been so reluctant during Malcolm's initial visit, was the first charter member of the local temple. "Malcolm started coming around maybe in the summer and I know in the fall, I told my mother, 'I'm ready; I'm going to join,'" Rosalie, who would soon marry Fred Forrest, said. To be accepted as a member and be given X as a surname, an applicant had to submit an exactingly close handwritten copy of a headquarters form letter. "I wrote my letter [to Chicago, requesting her X] and mine passed right away, no problem." Mrs. Glover remained the driving force in the temple; however, she had problems getting her letter approved at headquarters. "My mother had a hard time with hers, because she wasn't an educated person, so her handwriting was not the best. I would sit down with her. We would have stacks of unlined paper. You couldn't erase."[36]

After several attempts, Rosalie Glover finally did get her X.

The letter-writing exercise had been started by Fard Muhammad as a way to force uneducated members to mount a difficult literacy barrier. Better-educated applicants had little trouble once they figured out what was required. Others, like Captain Joseph of the Harlem temple, cheated by holding the form letter up to a window and simply tracing it.

Meanwhile, Malcolm noted that his temples in Hartford and elsewhere on the East Coast had already outgrown the older temples, such as No. 3 in Milwaukee and No. 5 in Cincinnati, which had been set up by the Messenger himself. He bragged about his successes to his brothers back in Michigan, who had brought him into the Nation of Islam. At the same time, Malcolm had been angling for permission to return to Detroit and spend a month to "inject some life" into Temple No. 1, where Fard Muhammad himself and Elijah Muhammad had founded the NOI. In his zeal, Malcolm seemed unmindful of the Messenger's early measure of resentment that inspired the prohibition against his young disciple speaking in the older temples.

Awaiting permission to shake up Detroit, not to mention the Messenger's own Chicago headquarters, Malcolm was insensitive to the risk, and possible danger, posed by his aggression on the turf of his elders. In pushing against what he took to be apathy, if not sloth, he sincerely saw himself as promoting not himself—as insiders would charge—but Elijah Muhammad. Along the way, he sought, true enough, to make himself indispensable, as he had in every job he held since his days as a hustling sandwich man on the New Haven Railroad.

The Messenger "had to chastise me on some point during nearly every visit" to Chicago, Malcolm wrote of this period. "I just couldn't keep from showing in some manner that with his ministers equipped with the power of his message, I felt the Nation should go much faster."[37]

Shaped by his segregated Southern upbringing and narrow education, Elijah Muhammad's vision for his vanguard religious cult was too provincial to keep pace with Malcolm's more open-ended ambitions for building a truly national black movement. The Messenger once warned his young minister that speed, although perhaps desirable, could destroy an old car. On another occasion he sharply chastised Malcolm's critique of an inefficient though reliable Muslim minister, telling Malcolm, "I would rather have a mule I can depend upon than a racehorse that I can't depend upon."[38]

The FBI kept abreast of such fissures—in fact, the Bureau was eager to foment greater discord between Malcolm and Elijah Muhammad. In time, special agents, working out of the Hartford post office, recruited Bellevue Square residents to provide inside information in exchange for payments. These FBI informants attended Black Muslim meetings and then summarized Malcolm's lectures, listing the names of attendees and supplying schedules of all Nation of Islam events in the Hartford area.

These factoids began making it into Bureau memoranda, which were then filed by the Special Agent in Charge of the New Haven field office. Soon the file was full of such reports as the following:

On 1/24/57 and 1/28/57 MALCOLM X LITTLE was observed in Hartford, Conn., at the home of [redacted]. MALCOLM X was observed driving a 1955 yellow Chevrolet, 4-door sedan, N.Y. license 9678.[39]

MALCOLM X was surveiled [sic] to the home of [redacted] and also to the . . . Hartford RR station with [redacted] picked up trunks he shipped from Buffalo, New York, on 1/24/57.[40]

Unaware of this heavy federal and local police surveillance, Elijah Muhammad's national spokesman continued to dramatically increase the Hartford enrollment and to step up its overall educational level. The Thursday night group that Malcolm had nourished from the cradle up moved from the St. John home to a second-floor space over the Parsons Theater, then to a storefront on Albany Avenue. Finally the group purchased a building at 3284 Main Street, which also housed a bakery. Elijah Muhammad granted the Hartford Muslims the title Temple No. 14.

At the end of 1956, Malcolm proudly wrote Elijah Muhammad: "The East Coast has many rough spots (due to the newness of the Muslims). But overall the dead there are rising."[41]

# CHAPTER 13

# "Meet with Them Devils"

THE YELLOW WESTERN UNION ENVELOPE ADDRESSED TO THE "Black Muslims" caused a ripple of intrigue in the modest hall that the Atlanta temple had rented from the Odd Fellows Lodge. Up at the podium, Malcolm, who was visiting, worked through his sermon on the evils of the "white devils" in the New South as hands followed by whispers passed the telegram to the host minister up front. A quick read of the message, written all in capital letters and punctuated with "STOPs" for periods, moved Minister Jeremiah X to ease the cable into his jacket pocket and wait for a lull in the service.

The message had come from the Georgia Ku Klux Klan.

The white terror group was the worst nightmare of the audience listening raptly to Malcolm. Attendance at this Sunday meeting in the fall of 1960 had quadrupled thanks to the guest speaker from Harlem, whom Jeremiah X had heavily promoted as a firebrand celebrity in Buttermilk Bottom, a black neighborhood that would later be bulldozed to make way for the Atlanta Civic Center. Aware that his lecture was being recorded for *Mr. Muhammad Speaks*, a half-hour weekly radio show airing in several cities across the South, Malcolm had spiked his remarks so as not to disappoint.

"Our people here in the Deep South are ready for a change," Malcolm barked in his hoarse baritone.

> They want a religion that will give them a salvation which includes freedom, justice and equality, here in this life, right here on this earth. Realizing that the Christian church has failed them, they're turning back toward the religion of Islam, the religion of our forefathers. While we were members of the Christian church, we were rejected by the segregated churches of our slave masters . . . no one wanted us, we didn't even want ourselves.[1]

A chorus of "Teach, brother minister" rang up from the ranking Muslim congregants in the redbrick building on Auburn Avenue. Glancing at his scribbled notes, Malcolm anchored his exhortation by resorting to the Genesis, Samuel, and Job of the Old Testament— the font of Christians' belief in the Creation and in the efficacy of resolute patience in the face of suffering. He then launched a frontal assault upon the New Testament promise of the "hereafter" so widely accepted by Negroes, religious or not. Malcolm flatly dismissed all chances of human postmortem reward, proclaiming that there would be "no Heaven beyond the grave." A few in the audience gasped.

American Negroes, "the lost sheep," Malcolm thundered, would progress only when they forsook the Christian yearning for the hereafter and devote themselves to Muslim concerns for the right-down here and now.

> If you and I want Heaven, you have to listen to the Honorable Elijah Muhammad and come together right now and start to do something for yourself. You've got to pool your academic know-

how. You've got to pool your technical skills. You've got to pool
your education. You've got to pool your finances, your wealth,
get up and do something for yourself and your people right now.
If you don't, you'll never know what Heaven is.[2]

Such trips to the so-called Bible Belt stimulated in Malcolm the
same crusading zeal that had been central to Georgia-born Earl Little, his peripatetic Christian father. Malcolm's very first assignment
in the South, in 1955, had been to inaugurate the Atlanta temple
for Elijah Muhammad. The local contact, Brother James X, had duly
rented a funeral parlor for the meeting; Malcolm and his pioneers,
however, had to wait for a funeral service to end. Malcolm incorpo-
rated references to the family members of the departed loved one
and their Christian ritual into his remarks that day: "You saw them
all crying over their physical dead," he told the Muslim recruits. "Our
whole black race in America is mentally dead. We are here today with
Mr. Elijah Muhammad's teachings, which resurrect the black man
from the dead."[3]

Now, some five years later, at Temple No. 15, Malcolm held forth
in the famed Atlanta Lodge Hall, which had been dedicated in 1912
by Booker T. Washington. Christians among the curiosity seekers
relaxed only when the brash Muslim minister wrapped up his lecture
with a salute to the Honorable Elijah Muhammad.

As a perspiring Malcolm dismounted the platform, thirty-three-
year-old Jeremiah X rushed up and handed over the Ku Klux Klan
telegram, as if passing along a burning ember. The communiqué
caught Malcolm totally by surprise. It proposed a meeting between
the two groups and implied that they had a lot in common. Standing
carefully away from the windows, the two Muslim ministers read the
cable several times, probing the missive for motive. Who exactly was
this W. S. Fellows, who had signed the telegram? The inclusion of
his phone number, with an exchange that indicated he lived in the

Grant Park section of the city, suggested that he awaited an answer.
Was this a veiled threat? a setup? The Klan did not normally send its
messages to Negroes by day or post them in writing.

Unbeknown to Malcolm and Jeremiah, this initiative from the
most violent, self-declared "white racist" group in America was being
monitored by the FBI. Director J. Edgar Hoover had, of course, long
targeted both the Klan and the Nation of Islam (NOI) for surveillance, infiltration, and disruption. The more recent surge of the
civil rights movement had also attracted the Bureau leader's attention in the South. As many as two thousand paid FBI informers were
operating inside the Klan, it later would be revealed.[4] This penetra-
tion allowed the Bureau to control or influence one of every ten
members, or 10 percent of the Ku Klux Klan. This vast government
network may well have instigated the Klan's outreach to the Black
Muslims for Hoover's own ulterior motive, such as the desire to influence or get inside information about the NOI's plans.

The details of the Klan telegram, and the actions that resulted,
have never been fully disclosed. Each group determined that its
involvement in this cross-racial affair must be kept secret. Records
indicate that the FBI monitored the proceedings and kept its notes
classified for decades. It also kept secret whatever covert follow-up
action the Bureau may have taken against the Klan and the Black
Muslims, as well as against civil rights leaders. The original telegram
was thrown out, according to Jeremiah X (later known as Jeremiah
Shabazz). This account of the matter was pieced together from scattered government records, interviews with participants, group com-
muniqués and notes, personal diaries, and knowledgeable sources.

Race relations in America had been rocked by the 1954 *Brown
v. Board of Education* ruling, outlawing school segregation. Despite
the Supreme Court's caveat prescribing "all deliberate speed," the
decision inspired Negroes to accelerate the pace of desegregation—

against stiff white opposition from parents, school boards, governors and congressmen, sheriffs, and the terror tactics of the KKK. Spearheading the drive to enforce the ruling were such well-established organizations as the NAACP, the National Urban League, and the Congress of Racial Equality, as well as the newly formed Southern Christian Leadership Conference (SCLC), headed by the Reverend Martin Luther King Jr. In the wake of the 381-day Montgomery bus boycott that the SCLC had launched in December 1955, the Klan had stepped up its campaign against desegregation with night-riding attacks, lynching of blacks, and bombings of homes and churches. Cross-burning Klan rallies were staged in open fields—mostly on Friday or Saturday nights, to attract the largest working-class crowds, some bringing along their small children for the fireworks. The racist terror was intended to derail the civil rights movement led by King and other nonviolent leaders.

During these tumultuous days of racial confrontation, the Nation of Islam operated on a third rail, opposing integration from the black side of the race divide. Since the early years of the Depression, Elijah Muhammad, as described earlier, had preached that blacks should withdraw from mainstream America with its irredeemable devotion to de facto segregation in the North and de jure, or legalized, segregation in the South. The *Brown* decision had no impact whatsoever on the Messenger's drive to establish a separate black nation. Indeed, the "white man is a devil" doctrine had swelled the NOI ranks to some forty-nine temples in twenty-one states, due mainly to Malcolm's organizing efforts and the work of Jeremiah X in the South. At the same time that the Harlem minister drew national media attention with his oratory and caustic debating skills, Jeremiah was quietly consolidating small temples in Miami, St. Petersburg, and Tampa, Florida; Macon and Savannah, Georgia; Mobile, Alabama; and New Orleans and Monroe, Louisiana.

In Atlanta, Minister Jeremiah's fishing for converts attracted scant attention from the county sheriff, local media, or, for that matter, Negroes themselves. The temple's new seafood and poultry market drew in enthusiastic customers; only a few dozen, however, had dared pitch up at services with any regularity. The meager turnout was due mainly to fear of reprisals for the antiwhite rhetoric the Muslims preached so boldly. Moreover, Elijah Muhammad's followers were viewed as humorless, bow-tie-wearing "Black Mooselim" carpetbaggers from the North. They rejected Jesus Christ; didn't believe in heaven or hell; and, most unforgiving to Negro sensibilities, didn't permit music during worship services. "We were looked upon as freaks," said Jeremiah X. Despite being born in Georgia, as was Reverend King, Elijah Muhammad and his Chicago-based Muslims were considered creatures of the North. "It was all about Martin Luther King," conceded Jeremiah X. "We were not well-known among whites. Somehow, the Klan found out about us."[5]

With the white terrorists' telegram in hand, Malcolm got into Jeremiah's black Buick and headed to the Atlanta minister's rented, two-bedroom home in a working-class neighborhood. Jeremiah's home was a mere seventeen miles from Stone Mountain, the site where the Ku Klux Klan had been revived some forty-five years of mayhem ago. While the host minister drove the Atlanta streets, Malcolm rattled off details of his early life as if some sardonic force were closing the circle. He recounted for Jeremiah his family's lore about how, when he was yet in the womb, the Omaha KKK had harassed his pregnant mother. Subsequently, they killed his father, he told his host, leaving unstated that he alone among his siblings believed that their father had been murdered by a white racist group instead of having died in a streetcar accident. In any case, this paternal vacuum had triggered the wayward drift of this favored son, which had led him ultimately to the Honorable Elijah Muhammad.

It did not escape Malcolm's calculation that only blocks away,

Marcus Garvey, at the height of the Klan's power in 1922, had met with the Imperial Kleagle of the Georgia Klan, Edward Young Clarke. Garvey had sought, as previously described, white supremacist support for his UNIA movement, maintaining: "The Ku Klux Klan is going to make this a white man's country. They are perfectly honest and frank about it. Fighting them is not going to get you anywhere."[6] After his secret sit-down, the UNIA leader had been floored by a tonnage of Negro criticism led by W. E. B Du Bois, who wrote that Garvey was "the most dangerous enemy of the Negro race in America and the world."[7] This foremost hero of Malcolm's parents had been discredited by his flirtation with the Klan and, with the ghost of his father ever pacing in the shadow, Malcolm was determined to avoid a similar disaster. Yet itching as always for risky ventures, he stood eager to involve himself directly in the initiative, with an eye toward scoring big-time media points back in Harlem.

Upon arriving at Jeremiah's house, Malcolm unfolded the communiqué from the Klan. Straightaway, the two ministers reviewed their own group's flyers, which had circulated across the city, promoting Islam as "the True Religion for the Black Man" and attacking the white man's religion. A thinly veiled assault on Dr. King and the civil rights movement had stated that the visiting national spokesman would be delivering a wake-up call on the ills of integration. They concluded that this racial "separation" leaflet, so much a staple of the NOI, might have prompted the Klan's wire to the listed temple address.[8]

As NOI discipline demanded, Malcolm telephoned Elijah Muhammad in Chicago with the news, carefully summarizing the gist of the cable as a Klan invitation to God knows what. Never one to reveal surprise to his followers, the Messenger accepted Malcolm's report of the Klan outreach as if it were but another patch for the quilt he was sewing for Allah. The studied calm issued in part from Muhammad's wariness about telephone communications. All Nation officials had standing orders to speak on the phone for no more than three minutes, even on his private line, which was considered—inaccurately—to be secure from FBI wiretaps. Matters of significance were to be spoken directly into the Messenger's ear. This security procedure was sometimes breached by careless officials, and often by the Messenger himself. The precaution was hardly without foundation, given that on January 4, 1957, the FBI had secretly installed "technical" surveillance on five of Elijah Muhammad's private telephone lines at his eighteen-room residence at 4847 South Woodlawn Avenue in Chicago.[9] On June 9, 1960, the Bureau's Chicago Field Office installed a second wiretap system on a first-floor apartment at 8205 South Vernon Avenue, which it described as the Messenger's "office and hideaway." This redundancy was deemed prudent because the field office concluded that Elijah Muhammad, "feeling he is secure in his 'hideaway,' would converse more freely with high NOI officials and his personal contacts."[10] Already the Bureau was paying special attention to his phone conversations with other Negro leaders, with women friends, and especially with his national spokesman, Malcolm X.

Never the ambassador simply to await instructions, Malcolm curtly explained the Klan cable to his religious leader in such a way that follow-up planning would require Malcolm's personal touch. The Messenger summoned both ministers to Chicago. Jeremiah and Malcolm booked a flight the next day from Atlanta.

═══

En route to headquarters, Malcolm fine-tuned his plan to influence, if not dictate, the Muslim response to the Klan initiative. Jeremiah X, on the other hand, was not given to such strategizing, insisting instead that raw data be conveyed to the "Holy Apostle" without preemptive messaging. To Jeremiah, Elijah Muhammad's orders were to be executed, not analyzed. His assignment to Atlanta, in 1957, had baffled the then Philadelphia-based minister and distressed his wife, Elizabeth. Initially, Jeremiah was to be posted to the Los Angeles temple. However, when the Atlanta minister ran off to Dallas, reportedly with his secretary, the Messenger diverted Jeremiah south, "to straighten out that problem down there."[11] And despite never having set foot in the segregated South, the Philadelphian did not question the decision, much to the chagrin of his family. Consoling his wife as best he could, the wily Jeremiah arrayed himself to serve the Messenger of Allah in this strange and hostile place.

Now, three years later, as the seasoned and trusted overseer of the entire Southern region, Minister Jeremiah appeared to be the Messenger's most likely choice to handle the Klan initiative. Malcolm had other ideas, even as both men were ushered into the sterile Chicago headquarters with the usual brotherly greetings, prayer, and chitchat in the anteroom. They promptly repaired to the immaculate dining room, lined with two long tables, where the white lace mats and brocade curtains lent an air of high moment to the inner sanctum sit-down.

The Ku Klux Klan telegram was the sole agenda item.

Sweeping into the room with the majesty of a potentate, the Messenger acknowledged the greetings of his two supplicants. The slow-tongued "Holy Lamb" (another way Elijah's adherents referred to him) spoke sparingly, but his hold on his otherwise aggressive ministers was nothing short of mystical. The wattage of his "holy presence" relied not so much on words as on courtly gestures, cryptic signals, and nodding asides to attending aides. At the slightest challenge from an underling, however, Muhammad's balding head would bolt up and slightly backward, his cobralike eyes cutting a gaze that could freeze his toughest warrior. At tense meetings in this dining room, Muhammad had a way of speaking through his fingers, but as Malcolm read the Klan cable the elder man quietly tapped the tabletop. Probing for a motive, the officials recalled that a few weeks earlier, on September 11, 1960, the Messenger had visited Atlanta, in what the local press billed a "homecoming." Prior to the visit, there had been threats of Klan demonstrations, and NOI National Secretary John Ali had led a delegation of Muslim officials to negotiate safe passage with Atlanta Sheriff Herbert B. Jenkins. No white protests were mounted.

Addressing fifteen hundred followers from such distant temples as Boston, Los Angeles, and Chicago, Muhammad stressed that "separation" was the only solution for America's racial ills. Surrounded by the stern-faced Fruit of Islam, the Messenger was blistering in his attack on integration and, indirectly, the civil rights movement. Blacks, he preached, should get as far away as possible from the real devil. "The white man, as Allah has taught me . . . there is no good in the white man . . . All the whites are children of the devil," Elijah Muhammad had proclaimed. "We must separate ourselves as far as possible, for God did not intend for the two races to mix." In the poorly ventilated Magnolia Ballroom, the Messenger spoke for three hours, an hour of which was broadcast live across the state on a local radio station.

Despite a warm reception from followers in Atlanta, Elijah Muhammad harbored no "homecoming" illusions. And for a holy man so bold in his denunciations of whites, he revealed a cagey concern about his personal safety in the Deep South. When he inquired about living conditions during a visit to Minister Jeremiah's home, Elizabeth, Jeremiah's wife, reflexively answered that the family was coping "okay."

"How can you be doing okay—in Georgia?" Muhammad cut in with no attempt at humor. She held her tongue about security concerns as a young, black mother seriously troubled by the terror of her husband's Deep South assignment. Elizabeth quaked at the enforced customs that had her stepping off the sidewalk for white women, and getting overlooked by clerks at downtown stores even when she was the lone customer. The family had to contend with third-class service at all public facilities. Many a night, especially after hearing of a racial killing, a mob beating, or yet another Klan bombing, the young mother stayed awake with her young child, praying that her husband would return home unharmed. Even black Atlanta tended to isolate her family, and as a Philadelphian, she understood why. Their Muslim affiliation, although righteous, blocked the embrace of fellow Negroes, just as it had stemmed the flow of visitors to the local Temple No. 15. Above all, Elizabeth was appalled at how willingly Southern Negroes across the economic spectrum daily accepted the humiliating treatment at the hands of Southern whites at all levels. Elizabeth told friends, relatives, observers, as well as Minister Malcolm, that her years in Atlanta were pure hell.[12]

The Southern nightmare would not have been news to Georgia-born Elijah Muhammad had the wife of his Atlanta minister dared reveal it. Yet, much to Elizabeth's dismay, the Supreme Muslim Leader, who had ever so casually posted her husband in the South, now made it crystal clear that he dared visit his home state only during the daylight hours. Accordingly, his Chicago staff and security team pointedly executed their strict orders that under no circumstances whatsoever was their boss to spend the night in Georgia. The Messenger of Allah was whisked out of town by sundown.[13]

―――――

Now, in the fall of 1960, as the NOI leader and his two ministers discussed the Klan initiative in his Chicago dining room, he concluded that the telegram outreach was an olive branch. Malcolm likely accepted that the Muslims were no match in firepower for the Klan, to say nothing of the Atlanta cops and white Georgian civilians with guns. Still, it was unsettling to see that Elijah Muhammad's tough talk about whites apparently had been dismissed by the most violent terror group in the South as mere bluster intended for consumption by the Negro masses. Malcolm took comfort in the fact that the Klan olive branch had reached his hands quite by accident, while he was visiting Atlanta that Sunday. A direct appeal would have been a thundering insult, for Malcolm's abhorrence of the Klan was so deep-seated as to be downright prenatal. Given the circumstances, however, he still held out hope of crafting an aggressive response that would play in Harlem.

Initially, in the discussion at the table, Malcolm proffered that the Klan was obviously confused about the Messenger's stance on racial matters. Perhaps they misread his call for a "separate state." Malcolm drew a distinction between white supremacists in power excluding Negroes from every aspect of American society and their victims responding to such exclusion by striking out on their own. The whites' endgame of segregation was reprehensible; the Muslim response he viewed as a smart act of liberation. Negroes, however, should make the break independently, without conspiring with the "blue-eyed devil," in secret or otherwise. Such cooperation Malcolm dismissed as an unholy alliance completely out of the question—at least initially.

Yet the overture had to be weighed against the larger, national drama. For starters, the Supreme Court's *Brown v. Board of Education* ruling against segregated schools had thrown the Muslims' twenty-three-year-old demand for a separate state into disarray. The decision had placed the impossible dream of integration on the radar as achievable. Making peace with separation of the races, no matter how innovative the Muslim plan, now seemed a needless, if not cowardly, veering away from Negroes' core entitlement to rights denied for some centuries.

The most effective civil rights leader advancing this fresh possibility for racial integration was, of course, SCLC head Martin Luther King Jr. His campaign had been strengthened considerably by the historic 1960 election of President John F. Kennedy, a Catholic Democrat from Massachusetts. Aside from such pressing problems as the space race with the Soviet Union and the growing colonialist skirmish in South Vietnam, the administration was also challenged to resolve the domestic conflicts erupting in the Deep South over the issue of implementing racial desegregation as the law of the land.

On October 19, 1960, shortly before the election, Reverend King was arrested for protesting segregation at a snack bar in Atlanta. Chained up, he was secretly whisked to the Reidsville State Prison, 175 miles away. A panicked Coretta Scott King, who had met her husband in 1952 when he was a theology student at Boston University, reached out to a friend, Harris Wofford, who was working on the Kennedy campaign. Controversy over King's arrest also spurred baseball legend Jackie Robinson, a Republican, to appeal to his party's presidential candidate, Richard M. Nixon, who had met young Dr. King. The sitting vice president flatly refused to get involved.

During a campaign stop in Chicago, Senator Kennedy was privately approached by Wofford and Sargent Shriver, a key aide and Kennedy's brother-in-law, and persuaded to telephone Mrs. King, who was six months pregnant. "I know this must be very hard for you," the candidate said in a two-minute phone chat, as recalled by King's wife. "I understand you are expecting a baby, and I just wanted you to know that I was thinking about you and Dr. King. If there is anything I can do to help, please feel free to call on me." A grateful Mrs. King thanked the politician she had never met, adding, "I would appreciate anything you could do to help." The next day, Robert F. Kennedy, his brother's campaign manager, who had been initially reluctant to get involved, followed up with a phone call to Judge J. Oscar Mitchell, inquiring about bail. King was released that afternoon on a $2,000 appeal bond after nine days in prison. Dr. King said that the Kennedys' involvement made his release possible.[14]

Just days before the November election, the Kennedy gesture—

which had angered key staffers fearful of offending Southern voters and Dixiecrat segregationists, such as Georgia's Senator Richard Russell and Mississippi's Senator James Eastland—was leaked prominently to the national media and aggressively promoted among Negroes. The sympathetic act struck a nerve among civil rights leaders in Atlanta and Negroes across the country.

"I had expected to vote against Senator Kennedy because of his religion," said King's father at a hastily called rally at his Ebenezer Baptist Church in Atlanta. "But now he can be my president, Catholic or whatever he is," said Reverend Martin Luther King Sr. "It took courage to call my daughter-in-law at a time like this."[15]

Amid the simmering racial conflict, Kennedy's timely overture accelerated the sea change of Negroes away from the Republican Party of Abraham Lincoln. That movement had started during the New Deal of President Franklin D. Roosevelt, even though Negroes had been excluded from many of its benefits. King's father and many of the parents of his top aides were registered Republicans. Leaving no doubt about his personal newfound loyalty, the Reverend Ralph D. Abernathy, a cofounder of the SCLC, shouted for a frenzied Atlanta crowd of supporters to "take off your Nixon buttons."[16]

On election day, Negroes flocked to the polls and voted overwhelmingly for the junior senator from Massachusetts. In the previous presidential election, in 1956, about 60 percent of their vote had gone to the incumbent Republican, Dwight Eisenhower. This time, 70 percent of Negroes voted for Senator Kennedy—a decisive margin in five states—and helped provide him the slimmest popular vote margin of any president in the twentieth century: 118,000 votes out of more than 68 million cast, a winning margin of 0.17 percent. The abrupt switch was nothing less than historic, with implications that reverberate well into the twenty-first century.

The white South, with the Ku Klux Klan as its vigilante arm, branded President-elect Kennedy a presumptive friend of Negroes

and thus a serious threat to the policy and practice of white supremacy extending back to slavery. The powerful Dixiecrat wing of the
Democratic Party reasserted its allegiance to what incoming Alabama governor George C. Wallace would boldly declare in January 1963: "Segregation today, segregation tomorrow, segregation
forever!"[17]

The Klan proceeded to whip up hysteria against Kennedy, who,
at forty-three, was the youngest president ever elected. He was also
the first Irish-Catholic, another target of white Anglo-Saxon Protestant bigots. The Klan turned the Kennedy victory into a membership boon: by the time of JFK's inauguration in January 1961,
the KKK had doubled its sworn-in, dues-paying membership, to
around twenty thousand, since March of the previous year. Ral-
lying for a return to the barricades for a second Reconstruction,
white supremacists warned that the Kennedy administration would
impose "fanatic" legislation that would destroy white southerners'
"cherished way of life."[18]

Owing to Negroes' role in the presidential victory, the nascent
civil rights movement was motivated now by rising expectations that
centered on this newfound clout in the voting booth. A national
surge was spearheaded by Reverend King himself, the thirty-two-
year-old, Atlanta-based apostle of nonviolence. Despite Malcolm's
aggressive nationwide promotion of "the Honorable Elijah Muhammad" as the enfant terrible of Negro liberation, it was Reverend
King who caught the fancy of the Negro masses. And he struck
fear and loathing in the hearts of white southerners and even the
murderous Klan.

Increasingly, Malcolm faced claims on the lecture circuit that
his black-supremacist Muslims were but the flip side of the white-
supremacist coin of race hatred. The national spokesman usually
argued that America's hatred of Negroes was concocted for economic expediency, with no credible stimulus from the targeted

group, whereas the black resentment of their brutal oppressors sprang from clear and present provocation. Not only did Negroes have every human right to despise their powerful tormentors, Malcolm said, they also had the right to defend themselves against a barbarism that knew no bounds. Such counterrejection, at least in the short term, some psychiatrists have agreed, may well serve as an antidote to induced group self-loathing.

Unlike the civil rights movement, the Black Muslim doctrine was aimed not at whites, but at Negroes themselves. Malcolm popularized the notion that, despite centuries of bitter treatment, Negroes continued not only to love their white, racist, "Christian" enemies, but also to hate themselves. The Muslims, he preached, were determined to rid Negroes of such corrosive psychic impulses within the confines of a yet to be determined "separate black state." Meanwhile, Malcolm saw himself promoting a collective group pride—the raison d'être of the Muslims from the very beginning. "Elijah Muhammad teaches black people to love each other," Malcolm had told Louis Lomax on the 1959 TV documentary *The Hate That Hate Produced.* "And our love is so strong; we don't have any room left in our hearts for hate."[19]

In the Chicago headquarters meeting on that autumn Monday in 1960, as on the lecture trail, Malcolm downsized this "superior" white man as a coward, but a dangerous one with economic dominance, superior weapons, and the mechanisms of government behind him. The white man's legendary fear of competing openly with Negroes was not the action of a self-assured race, Malcolm calculated, but rather that of a man who suspected deep down that those he preemptively strapped to a board may well be his betters. Thus, this "superior race," went the Black Muslim analysis, cowered en masse to prevent all direct competition with the Negro threat, whether in education, sports, public transportation, lunch counters, libraries, the military, research labs, politics, the workplace, billiards halls, cemeteries, or, God forbid, the fluff of the boudoir.

"The desegregation decision and other types of legislation and Supreme Court decisions depend upon changing the white man's mind," Malcolm told a TV reporter in Harlem that same year. "We have to change our minds about ourselves [through] moral reformation, a knowledge of self. . . . The white man has brainwashed our people into believing in white supremacy so much that they don't think they're making progress unless they're living in a white man's neighborhood; have a seat in the white man's school; or a position in the white man's job; they even go so far that they think they're not successful in life unless they have a white woman for a wife."

This rejection of marriage between the races was one acre of common ground that the Klan and the Muslims both occupied. In addition to excusing slavery and Jim Crow restrictions as biblically proscribed, the Klan had indeed viewed Negroes as an ever increasing threat—especially to the keeper and preserver of the biological WASP seed, the white woman.

———

As the Muslim officials sat at the dining room table considering the Klan's telegram, they went over the role of the Klan in Southern white society. The lynching of waylaid Negroes was considered no mere punishment of the individual but rather a cowardly act of terror against all blacks in the republic. Preaching self-defense to counter such terror had been a founding principle of the black Muslims, starting with Prophet Noble Drew Ali. However, no official policy of lethal counterviolence against whites emerged until Fard Muhammad cryptically suggested in his early written lessons that members might kill "devils" and earn a button for their tunic and a pilgrimage to the holy city of Mecca. Rumors abounded that some ambitious acolytes had actually waylaid a white vagrant or two and brought in their severed heads in exchange for a tunic adornment and a Holy Land trip.

Elijah Muhammad, however, had long since downplayed as a gross misinterpretation Fard's suggestions of killing random "white devils." The cagey Messenger avoided any public resort to bloodletting across the color line, except to state that in some vague and distant future "war is inevitable between blacks and whites." No traceable order, direct or otherwise, was ever issued for spilling the blood of the "blue-eyed devils." Malcolm, on the other hand, slyly left violence against whites on the table. And the Harlem minister strongly dismissed passivity by such civil rights leaders as Reverend King as pure cowardice, stealing every opportunity to rattle the Muslim saber as a Qur'an allowance for self-defense.

"If someone puts his hands on you," Malcolm would tell an audience, "send him to the cemetery."[20] Turning their violence inward upon one another (say, on a Saturday night in their assigned ghettos), he counseled, would only sustain Negroes' conditioned inferiority complex. Internally, the Fruit of Islam was known to dish out corporal punishment and worse to wayward members. And Malcolm had ordered some head knocking himself during his early days at Temple No. 7 in Harlem.[21] Blacks, he felt, had a right to assert themselves through violence against all comers—blacks and whites—in defense of themselves, their families, and the Muslim religion.

Malcolm was ever alert for any table-talk hint from the Messenger that aggression might be deployed, or at least not ruled out, against whites—even against the likes of the Klan, if only someday down the line. Jeremiah held no such expectations. When the Muslims had been accused the previous year of rebelling against "law and order," Elijah Muhammad had told a Harlem audience, "We don't carry knife, gun, pistol, or nothing. We don't teach our followers to carry such things. . . . We come armed with nothing but the truth." Tough talking up to the line, the spiritual leader was careful as always not to cross over to action.

Fiery speeches on the road by the national spokesman brought regular chastisements from the Messenger. Bristling under the restraint, Malcolm wanted to order violent retribution several times against offending whites in law enforcement and elsewhere, but was curbed by Muhammad.

The tactics with the Klan being worked out that day were shaping up as a measure of the distance between Malcolm and Elijah Muhammad. The key question, laying aside violence and the pace of change, was whether the Muslims should bargain with or challenge this declared enemy of all Negroes. The discussion played against the deeper, long-standing question of whether Negroes should stand and fight for full inclusion in America, or take flight. This larger strategy, of course, was a settled matter with Muhammad, who was committed to abscond to some vague, yet to be determined "separate state."

Despite all, Malcolm held out hope that, given the Klan's bloody history of atrocities against Negroes, his religious leader would take the white group's invitation as an opening to cite irreconcilable differences.

On the matter of banning race mixing, the centerpiece of Klan doctrine, the Muslims had long stipulated that the KKK had lynched hundreds of innocent black men as human sacrifices upon this altar. Proof of a sexual encounter with white women, forced or otherwise, had seldom been presented against Negroes hanged and castrated for such alleged offenses. Contrariwise, the NOI had stipulated that white men, including the most avowedly racist, had, since the days of slavery, participated in widespread patterns of miscegenation, forced and otherwise, resulting in untold millions of mulatto and mixed-race children born to black women over generations. During terror raids on Negroes, in fact, Klansmen would sometimes "rape the female members of the household as a matter of course," according to Wyn Craig Wade in his authoritative book, *The Fiery Cross: The Ku Klux Klan in America.*[22] And unlike the Muslims, the Klan had a long and documented history of beating, torturing, and killing to put down the kind of race mixing it abhorred.

Underscoring the issue, Malcolm noted the Messenger's blistering public exchange of letters with a well-known, self-acknowledged Southern racist. Jesse Benjamin "J. B." Stoner had written the NOI convention, in Chicago in February 1957, that "Islam is a nigger religion" of "infidels." Stoner, the "Arch-leader and Imperial Wizard of the Christian Knights of the Ku Klux Klan"—who decades later would be convicted in the 1958 bombing of the Bethel Baptist Church in Birmingham, Alabama—boasted up front that "I believe in White Supremacy and the inferiority of all dark races."

Just as bluntly, Stoner, a trained attorney, outlined his case against racial "mongrelization." "Your desire for White [sic] women is an admission of your own racial inferiority. One reason why we Whites will never accept you into our white society is because a nigger's chief ambition in life is to sleep with a White woman, thereby polluting her. Every time a demented White woman marries a nigger, your newspapers brag about the sin. The day will come when no nigger will be allowed to even look at a White woman or a White woman's picture."[23]

Elijah Muhammad's lengthy response, which appeared in the *Pittsburgh Courier,* countered that, in addressing remarks to the Muslims about Negroes loving whites in general and their women in particular, Stoner had rung the absolute wrong doorbell. "The Truth [sic] of you will make all black mankind hate you, regardless of their color. . . . Who is to blame for this [race] mixing—black Africans or the White European devils?"

While attacking Stoner's "mongrelization" analysis, Muhammad claimed the higher ground of practicing what his black group preached about racial separation while exposing white men as shameless hypocrites. It was not Negro slaves who made "sexual love with their slave-masters' wives and daughters;" it was indeed the white man who violated black slave women, he wrote.

> We see you day and night after the so-called Negro men and women; whistling, winking your eyes, and blowing your car horns at them; making advances to every Negro woman that walks, rides, flies, or works for you in your homes, offices and factories. If YOUR women are so beautiful, why then do our "ugly" women attract you and your kind? . . . Your concern for the protection of your white women should have been prepared by your fathers, and self, by staying away from our women. YOUR race is still white, so what are you afraid of?[24]

Do you want your daughter to marry a Negro, went the race mantra of the Southern white man making his case against racial desegregation. The question was rhetorical, by Malcolm's reckoning. Laws against miscegenation and marriage across the color line had been enacted in thirty-three states. And, at bottom, Malcolm reasoned that white Americans' paralyzing fear of their women cohabitating with Negroes was essentially the phobia of a genetically recessive people. In prison, he had repeatedly read about Gregor Mendel's work in genetics and had reached the conclusion that "if you started with a black man, a white man could be produced; but starting with a white man, you could never produce a black man—because the white chromosome is recessive."[25] Thus, Malcolm preached that the white man lived in mortal fear that intercourse with black men of dominant physical traits would, over time, breed away those physical characteristics valued above all else among Caucasians: pale skin and a genetic tendency toward blond hair and blue eyes. Author James Baldwin, who would spend a session at Elijah Muhammad's dining room table the following year, turned the race mantra question on its ear. Marrying *your daughter* is not the fear, he retorted. We have been marrying white men's daughters for a very long time. It is *your wife's daughter* that is your concern.

On another front, J. B. Stoner's long letter, which accused Negroes of deep-seated self-hatred and dependency on whites, was suspiciously similar to what the Muslims preached in group sessions of self-criticism. The white racist's attack could well have been, and very likely was, in fact, lifted from Black Muslim tracts. "[Negroes] are ashamed of their race," Stoner wrote, in words that could have been penned by Elijah Muhammad. "If you aren't ashamed of your race, why don't you strive to keep it pure and preserve it and its characteristics?"[26]

For a quarter century, Muhammad had been preaching precisely this need to preserve black racial purity, within a separate black state.

Although the anti-integration perspectives of Muhammad and Stoner intersected at this and other points, the two leaders' groups were headed quite determinedly in opposite directions. Each claimed that its race was superior. Total separation, each organization believed, would spell the doom of the other—one according to the Old Testament, the other according to Allah. To the extent that blacks lacked self-pride and eschewed racial separation, Elijah Muhammad attributed it to "so-called Negroes educated and trained by" whites.[27]

"Who taught you to hate the texture of your hair," Malcolm would ask a black crowd in Los Angeles. "Who taught you to hate the color of your skin, to the extent that you bleach it, to get like the white man? Who taught you to hate the shape of your nose, and the shape of your lips. . . . Who taught you to hate the race that you belong to, so much so that you don't want to be around each other? Before you come asking Mr. Muhammad does he teach hate, you should ask yourself, who taught you to hate being what God made you? We [Muslims] teach you to love the hair that God gave you."[28]

Countering Stoner's "Christian" attack on Islam, Elijah Muhammad again claimed the higher moral ground in his return letter.

> Isn't it true that your Christian Party lynches and burns your
> black Christian believers there in your own state (Georgia)?
> Have you ever seen or heard of us Muslims lynching and burn-
> ing Negroes who believe or don't believe in Islam? . . . You beat
> and kill them [Negro Christian believers] day and night and
> bomb their churches, where . . . they are worshiping YOU, not
> Jesus. You even burn your own Christian sign (the cross) when
> you plan to kill or burn poor black Christian slaves.[29]

As when Marcus Garvey had met with the KKK thirty-eight years
earlier, Elijah Muhammad drew no distinction between the Klan and
other whites in America. The Klan of the Garvey era of the 1920s
was indeed a mainstream, white Protestant organization, whose mul-
timillion membership excluded Italians, Jews, Irish Catholics, and
other new immigrants. Its ranks included elected officials, public
and private power brokers, and law enforcement officers. Thus, as
the head of the "only exclusive Negro" organization, and the self-
appointed, "Provisional President of Africa," Garvey considered it
fitting to meet with the mainstream Klan—as one head of state with
another—at their headquarters in Georgia.

In the nearly four decades since Garvey's sit-down with the assistant imperial wizard, the Klan had devolved into a much smaller
racist, terror group on the margins of mainstream society. Still,
Muhammad drew no distinction between the hooded knights and
other whites, branding them all as irredeemable "blue-eyed devils."
If anything, both Garvey and Elijah Muhammad appreciated the
"honesty" of the white knights—and showcased the Klan as representative of all Caucasians.

A year before the dining room meeting in Chicago, when

responding to J. B. Stoner, the Messenger had shown an inclination to grant the Klan a public showdown in Harlem.

In a letter dated August 6, 1959, Stoner had warned the police commissioner of New York City that the Muslims were "much more dangerous to the white Christians of New York than you realize." To prevent Negroes from taking over the city, Stoner offered Commissioner Stephen P. Kennedy "the support of the Knights of the Ku Klux Klan."[30]

The Messenger responded, "I wish I could take him to [the U.S.] Congress, and he and I sit down face-to-face, with a mike, or a national hook-up, and let everybody see he and I talk together. We would pay $100,000 for every hour, or every half an hour, to get that kind of talk to show up that wicked one."

This exchange with the imperial wizard so inspired Malcolm that, on September 9, 1959, he read all of Stoner's August 6 letter at a NOI meeting at the Harlem temple. The challenge to debate the Klan leader had kindled in Malcolm the hope that the Messenger would allow his national spokesman "to show up that wicked one" down in Georgia. Such an extravaganza with the whole world watching would play well, not only in Harlem but across the nation. Northerners were usually impressed upon hearing the bold, antiwhite radio broadcast of *Mr. Muhammad Speaks* emanating from the Deep South.

With the Klan invitation to meet on the table, and with the hope that it could lead to a public debate, Malcolm struggled to land the role as chief debater, highlighting his media savvy and book-learned knowledge of American race history. To reassure his leader, he carefully reminded Muhammad that he embraced the Messenger's "separate state" policy, emphasizing an independent withdrawal, as well as an assertive Muslim-led resettlement.

Malcolm envisioned himself grabbing the Georgia Klan by the ear—and riding the wolf in its very own den, all at the behest of Elijah Muhammad. In addition to attracting national headlines, he thought, such a display of Muslim fearlessness would become a powerful recruiting magnet among restless young Negroes across the country. What better way to confront the media's nagging questions about reverse racism? Already, in a July 19, 1960, letter to his "Holy Apostle," Malcolm had cautioned Muhammad that even "Negro leaders" in Harlem "continued to class you as a Ku Kluxer."[31]

Once and for all, a squaring-off with the Klan leader could clear the slate on the thorny issues of the Muslim stances on integration, Christianity, mixed marriage, the Jews, miscegenation, and even violence. The unbridgeable racial chasm could be explained, and the need for the Messenger's "separate state" highlighted, all in a highly publicized, Atlanta extravaganza with the white knights—featuring Minister Malcolm X.

As Malcolm maneuvered for the key role at the Messenger's table, Jeremiah X listened quietly.[32] Elijah Muhammad appeared to have other ideas entirely. He struck a note nowhere near as assertive toward the Klan as Malcolm had hoped. As always, the mystic Holy Apostle cloaked his religious thinking in raiment tailored to advance his service to Allah, period.

Muhammad had no illusions about the dangers of dealing with the Klan, having spent his childhood in rural Georgia. At age ten, Elijah Poole had wandered upon the lifeless body of an eighteen-year-old acquaintance "dangling from a tree limb," as a crowd of whites from the town of Cordele looked on. Accused of, but never tried for, raping a white woman, the youth was roped by the neck, strung from a willow tree and, for good measure, riddled with bullets. Along with young Elijah, adult Negroes stopped by and viewed the lynching, but none dared intervene. "I cried all the way home," Muhammad was to recall years later. "If I ever got to be a man, I told myself I would find a way to avenge him and my people." Haunted by this menace, he was to witness another lynching before leaving Cordele for Macon at age sixteen.[33]

Throughout his life, the memory of Klan terror was never far from Muhammad's podium and dinner table talk. The lynching-bee relic was dangled before the faithful as a reminder of the satanic nature of the "blue-eyed devils" they were up against.

In Malcolm's *Autobiography*, which originally was intended to promote the divinity of his religious leader, he avoided any reference to young Elijah's tearful reaction to the Klan lynching. Instead, Malcolm said that, when he was twenty-five, Elijah Poole migrated to Detroit after he was cursed at by a "white employer," a final insult that drove him out of the South "to avoid trouble."[34]

It probably was adolescent brushes with the handiwork of the Klan and other crosstown humiliations that shaped Muhammad's adult fight-or-flight response to racist terrorism. His "separate state" scheme, at bottom, offered Negroes an escape from, rather than a stand-and-fight contest with, the ruling power structure of America.

Taking flight to avoid trouble was not Malcolm's pattern. Since childhood, friends and siblings alike confirmed, sometimes to their amazement, he seemed hard-wired against backing down. His libido for conflict had him staging dramatic showdowns with powerful figures, ranging from cops in Lansing, Boston, and New York to lethal thugs on the streets of Harlem, such as the numbers runner West Indian Archie.

Upon undergoing his spiritual conversion in prison, Malcolm had surrendered completely to the Messenger's religion—complete with its doctrine of racial avoidance. Still, on occasions such as the Klan matter, Malcolm's hunger for conflict would flare up and place him at odds with his spiritual leader.

The Messenger's apparent optimism about the South had been stirred by his recent visit to Georgia. After departing as a lowly railroad laborer, he had returned as the triumphant, so-called Maximum Leader of a 100,000-member sect considered the most fearless and fearsome black group in America. If nothing else, the civil rights movement had confirmed his belief in the growth potential in the South. The dawn of the 1960s seemed somehow ripe for his Muslim counterweight against Negroes' pursuit of racial integration.

Although Malcolm preferred the North, the Harlem minister voiced no reason to forfeit to Reverend King and his fellow integrationists the terrain occupied by the majority of Negroes. Despite sharp differences beneath the surface, Malcolm periodically offered up assurances that in this play of history, as in all matters, he would faithfully discharge every duty assigned him as national spokesman, both in deed and in spirit.

Dispassionate as usual when asserting NOI doctrine, Muhammad stated that his battle was not against whites but for the lost hearts and minds of Negroes. Both the Klan and the NOI, Muhammad summarized, opposed integration and race mixing. Each group was on record as opposing the goals of the Reverend Martin Luther King Jr., although for separate and unequal reasons. The Muslims viewed King as a chief rival. The Klan saw him as a dangerous threat to white hegemony. Moreover, Muhammad allowed for no "hierarchy" among Caucasians on the issue of white supremacy; from the sitting U.S. president to the imperial wizard, all were slammed as "white devils." Accordingly, the Messenger told his two ministers in Chicago that day that the Muslims and the Klan indeed had similar goals but with different shading. Finally, playing his fingers across his lips, Elijah Muhammad calmly instructed a restrained Malcolm and a resigned Jeremiah X: "You can meet with them devils."

"We want what they want," Jeremiah remembered the Messenger stating plainly. However, "let them know that you don't want segregation; you want separation. We want to be totally separated from you. Give us ours and you have yours. We want ours more or less free and clear. Give us something we can call our own. You just tell them devils that."[35]

Malcolm faced a major conflict of conscience. His hopes for

aggressive marching orders were dashed. Instead of sending his min-isters striding into the Klan meeting with their bow bent, the Messen-ger was dispatching them with a begging bowl. In a face-off with the most murderous "white devils" in America, the Nation's "separate state" program sounded like a plea rather than the assertion that Malcolm envisioned. Unable to dissuade his Messenger, however, he accepted the assignment.

Still, Malcolm could not shake the notion that Elijah Muham-mad's secret instructions to meet with the Klan, at bottom, pointed toward an unholy alliance. At a more personal level, he was deeply troubled by the possible effect of his mission on the memory of his very own father who had been killed, he believed, by this self-same terrorist group.

The Messenger's overture to the Klan began to tug at the cult leader's hold over Malcolm, like a crowbar prying loose a nail driven deep. It would prove to be a major turning point in the relationship between the two strong men, both reacting to a powerful enemy. Meanwhile, a shaken Malcolm decided to soldier on to the Atlanta meeting, determined to exploit every inch of wiggle room within the bounds of the Messenger's marching orders.

But the blind and faithful disciple had begun to doubt.

———

Muhammad instructed Malcolm and Jeremiah to pitch to the Klan that white America owed Negroes an allotment of land as partial payment for more than three hundred years of slavery and Jim Crow exploitation and that the inability of the two races to coexist would be eased by Elijah Muhammad's setting up of a black "separate state." Although a fixed amount of acreage was not specified, Malcolm was instructed to seek an opening to request Klan assistance in acquiring such designated land, or, at least, to negotiate a pact of noninterference with acquisition of land by other means. Also, as Garvey had done with Edward Young Clarke of the Klan, the two ministers were to bargain for free movement of Muslims throughout the South.

Coincidentally, in the wake of the election of President Kennedy, the Klan would begin to step up its bloody campaigns of murder and mayhem against Negroes throughout the South, and Reverend King and his nonviolent followers were on the front lines of this racial turmoil.

Malcolm was troubled that his religious leader had tactically conceded the power advantage to the Klan, that he would not be negotiating as an equal at the table in Atlanta. Muhammad's request to "Give us ours . . . free and clear" rested upon the hope that the Klan so despised Negroes that it would assist them in taking flight. This carrot was accompanied by no particular Black Muslim stick for exacting a consequence should negotiations flounder. Besides, this currying of favor from the very "white devils" who oppressed Negroes struck Malcolm as a fatal flaw in the Messenger's plan. Accepting the assignment would dog him for the remainder of his days in the Nation of Islam.

Elijah Muhammad, on the other hand, addressed the power inequality as he did most contradictions and Muslim myths: it was an article of faith that rested with Allah. In speeches and in books, Muhammad maintained, for example, that "war is inevitable between whites and blacks." When Louis Lomax asked him in *The Hate That Hate Produced* whether the race struggle would get bloody, the Messenger said yes, "According to the prophets of old and Fard Himself."[36]

Still, Malcolm was exhilarated by the idea of heading to the South as a good soldier to meet with the knights of the Ku Klux Klan. Jeremiah, the Atlanta minister, was assigned as a balancing, untroubled, loyal and imposing presence to keep Malcolm on track—and to report back to headquarters. Accordingly, playing the Klan meeting as a coup back in Harlem was nixed; it was not to be discussed even with family. Muhammad had sworn Malcolm to secrecy.

After a few days in Chicago, the two ministers were dispatched to Georgia by their religious leader, who bid them a fatherly "Be careful with them devils."[37]

Upon his return to Atlanta, Malcolm booked a room at a local motel where, in between time, he worked on the upcoming edition of *Muhammad Speaks*, the group's newspaper, which he'd recently launched back in New York. Ordinarily, he would have stayed at Jeremiah's home, but the couple was hosting the Messenger's father-in-law, who still lived in south Georgia.

The Muslim national spokesman also went fishing for converts in Buttermilk Bottom and among Atlanta's complex of five Negro colleges, including famed Morehouse, for men, and Spelman, for women. The pickings were slim, however, because students were cramming for final fall semester examinations, the worst time for collegiate proselytizing.

"I'm so well rested I almost feel guilty," Malcolm wrote in a letter that also critiqued local Muslim operations and sized up the black and white leadership of Atlanta. Writing to Elijah Muhammad, he praised the Muslims' new seafood and poultry market as "the most progressive move ever made in Atlanta" and recommended investing an additional five hundred dollars to advertise for more customers. "It will probably give us more converts and sympathizers in one week than a year of preaching." In an apparent request for karate-trained members of the Fruit of Islam, Malcolm wrote that given the magnitude of Muhammad's investment in the market, "you definitely need *experienced* protection."[38]

Malcolm's assessment of King's home base, after conversations with King's own SCLC staff and local black officials, was that the civil rights movement was disorganized. "The entire setup here insofar as the devils [sic] MAIN MAGICIAN (M.L. KING) is concerned is strictly a house built on sand," he wrote. Questions about King's nonviolent strategy, Malcolm said, would allow easy inroads for the Muslims. In something of an overstatement, he wrote the Messenger that "every [black] leader, whether it is a religious, political, or businesses [sic] leader, has the deepest respect, awe and even fear of you."[39]

As for the upcoming Klan meeting, Malcolm wrote that he would remain at least an extra day in Atlanta, depending "on what develops from the negotiations we are having (or contemplating) with these 'business men' about the possibility of getting some land . . . a county or two." Meanwhile, he honed his pitch to gauge receptivity to Elijah Muhammad's plan for establishing a separate state.[40]

Minister Jeremiah telephoned the Klan to set up the meeting.

Initially, W. S. Fellows, the Klansman who'd sent the telegram, suggested that he and Malcolm X meet at Klan headquarters across town in the Grant Park area. The cagey Muslim minister observed: "I don't think I'd be too welcome in your neighborhood."

Jeremiah counteroffered that they meet instead at his home in the Negro section of Atlanta. "Aww, hell, nigga," Jeremiah remembered Fellows saying, "we'll come to your place, I ain't scared."

The meeting date was set for January 28, 1961.[41]

══════

On the afternoon of the appointed Saturday, at the home of Minister Jeremiah X, Malcolm sprang to the living room window and peered through the venetian blinds. Some three dozen white men in civilian clothes sat bolt upright in a ten-car motorcade parking out front of his house. Each car held three or four men. Neighbors on adjacent porches and other Negroes strolling along the paved street scampered out of sight, some glancing back over their shoulders at the long column of four-door sedans. The Harlem firebrand and his Atlanta host kept unusually close to each other at the window.[42]

As the dust settled, a patrolman from the Atlanta police drove up to the lead vehicle and rolled down his window. After a brief and seemingly polite chat, the officer slowly drove his squad car away from the parked motorcade, and an eerie calm settled in on the usually bustling neighborhood. Suddenly, the convoy drivers all revved their engines nosily and sped off in the direction of the patrol car. Staring through the window at the dusty scene, a somewhat paler Malcolm seemed transfixed with mixed emotions. Finally, with upturned palms and a head nod, he reckoned that their meeting with the Klan had been short-circuited. Jeremiah concurred with a sigh. His wife, Elizabeth, who had prepared refreshments, seemed relieved.

Just as suddenly, the ten-car motorcade of white men rolled back into position in front of the house. A middle-aged passenger in the lead car got out abruptly, strode to the front door, and knocked determinedly. The short and scrawny stranger wore a black fedora with an unusually high crown, "like a witch's hat."

"Jeremiaaaah?" he called out.

"Yes, sir," answered the minister at the screen door. Canting his head to look around Jeremiah's shoulder, the Witch Hat inquired, "Are you that Malcolm X?" The reply rang just as determinedly, "Yes, sir."

"You'd lahk ta come in, sir?" asked Jeremiah, mouthing as much of a drawl as the native Philadelphian could muster. The cautious Witch Hat seemed not altogether reassured.

"I'm gonna tell you niggras something," said the diminutive white stranger as he gazed up at the lanky Muslim ministers, "If I'm not outta here in fifteen minutes, we're gonna burn this house down."

Glancing out at the parked convoy, Jeremiah assured his invited guest that such measures would not be necessary.

"Please, sir," he said, waving his arm backward, "just come on in. Everything is all right."

Stepping inside, the Witch Hat introduced himself as W. S. Fellows. After a brief sizing up of Malcolm and Jeremiah X, the lone Klansman hesitated, and then extended his right hand, exclaiming that it was the first time he'd ever shaken a "niggra's hand." But then, he added, with a quid pro quo grin, that the Muslims were the first "niggras" he'd met who didn't want integration.

Malcolm introduced Minister Jeremiah X as the local temple leader and himself as the national spokesman for the Nation of Islam, numbering some "175,000 followers"—the designated, but not quite accurate, NOI membership. He noted that Muslim doctrine indeed called for the "complete separation" of the races. Kicking the meeting into gear, Malcolm then gave a quick summary of NOI doctrine, emphasizing that everything he would say had been authorized by the "Messenger of Allah, the Honorable Elijah Muhammad."

"Oh, we know all about Ol' Lahj," said Fellows, pronouncing the Messenger's name with an extended vowel sound, connoting a belittling familiarity. "Ol' Lahj," the Klansman repeated. "He's a Georgia boah." The casual reference to their Holy Apostle rattled the two Muslim ministers more even than the Klansman's constant use of "niggra." Sticking to the mission, however, Malcolm suppressed such stylistic antagonisms. As for the substantive matters at hand, Fellows made it clear that in their push for separation of the races, the Klan considered "Ol' Lahj" as the "most sensible black man in America." Unlike Jeremiah, who had mastered the pretense as well as the kowtow, Malcolm visibly winced at such high praise of his spiritual leader coming from such low quarters.[43]

Sitting on the arm of the sofa, Fellows, who notably did not observe the Southern etiquette of removing his hat indoors, barked that the Klan liked what they'd heard about the Black Muslims' view on integration, sniping at the evils of "race mixing." While it was but a single, yet not significant, arrow in the Muslims' quiver, miscegenation—more specifically, sex between a white woman and a black man—had emerged as the primal fear triggering the white knights' decades-long lynching bee, which had killed thousands of Negroes.

As Fellows warmed to the key racial matters on his agenda, Elizabeth stepped into the living room and offered the three men refreshments. After a curt refusal, the white man noted that, unlike "Ol' Lahj," and despite Jeremiah's best efforts at a drawl, neither of the two Muslim ministers was from the South. A bemused Elizabeth shrugged back in the kitchen. Notwithstanding the hosts' trademark good manners and warm smiles, it did not escape the Klan leader that the self-assured Muslim men lacked the clammy deference that white southerners, especially the armed enforcers of Jim Crow stric-tures, had come to expect of Negroes they encountered, although granted, under quite different circumstances.

Malcolm had often proudly boasted that a sure sign of NOI con-version was a black man's ability to look a white man dead in the eyes without flinching. He had tested the faith of acolytes in Harlem by challenging them to attempt it on the job. Many were surprised and ashamed by their reflexive diverting of their eyes in the presence of white supervisors. "The Messenger had told me if you trust in Allah, the devil can do nothing to you," said Jeremiah. "He will take the fear [off] of you. I never was afraid of those crackers." Long before encountering Elijah Muhammad—as a child, in fact—Malcolm had been conditioned by his parents with a fearless sense of racial pride, combined with an assured equanimity. He had emerged as a leader among white students in Michigan, as well as on the streets of Har-lem and Boston, and even in prison. Still, following the etiquette of their Muslim sect, both Malcolm and Jeremiah addressed Fel-lows as cordially as they would whites and Negroes alike, seasoning their statements with "yes sir," "mister," and an occasional "with all due respect, sir."

On the other hand, Fellows threw off no sign of respect for his hosts, displaying no stomach whatsoever for racial parity. He dared even discuss rather casually his personal use of nonlethal violence against "niggras." Mindful, perhaps, of the agenda under discussion, the Klan leader initially steered clear of mentioning the use of deadly force against Negroes via lynchings in the South and elsewhere.

After some ten minutes, Malcolm took a distracted glance at his watch, in light of Fellows's initial threat and the three dozen Klansmen parked outside.

"Maybe," he interrupted Fellows, "you should go out there and let your friends know you're all right."

"Uh-huh, yeah," the Klansman muttered, clearly not used to fielding so much as a suggestion from a Negro. The agitated Fellows nonetheless arose from the sofa under the high crown of his witch's hat, walked outside, and chatted with his henchmen in the cars. Shortly afterward, he returned, accompanied by several lean, middle-aged Klan colleagues. One was a preacher from south Georgia outfitted in a gray suit and tie. The others were dressed more casually, including a rural politician in long sleeves. Although more nondescript than the diminutive Fellows, his buddies were no less tight-lipped and hard-eyed. At least one of the Klansmen was an FBI informer (a fact likely unknown to the other vigilantes, including Fellows). This undercover man would dutifully file notes on the Muslim meeting, dated January 30, 1961, with his control agent at the FBI Atlanta Field Office. Racial turmoil in the area had become a federal matter.[44]

Earlier that day, at two in the afternoon, about two hundred Georgia Klansmen had staged a parade a few miles away in downtown Atlanta. The "peaceful demonstration," according to the *Atlanta Journal and Constitution*, had "surprised thousands of shoppers." Several Klansmen, bristling in white robes, entered the Lane Rexall drugstore, on Broad and Alabama Streets, which was serving snacks to a few young whites and blacks. The drugstore lunch counter was hastily shut down.[45] Black college students had targeted such segregated lunch counters in their ongoing campaign against racial segregation throughout the South. The Klan staged counter-demonstrations to intimidate local business owners who, under pressure from civil rights protesters all across the Deep South, dared to serve both races. Seventy miles east in Athens, for example, the Klan stepped up activities in response to the recent desegregation of the University of Georgia. Almost three weeks before Malcolm met with the Klan, on January 10, 1961, following a long court battle, the historic admission of Negro students Charlayne Hunter and Hamilton Holmes had set off campus rioting, with thirteen white students suspended or expelled and sixteen arrested. Praising the arrested students as "patriots" and damning Governor Ernest Vandiver as an archvillain, Klan demonstrators promised a massive, downtown rally at an Atlanta theater later on that Saturday night, January 28.[46]

Unbeknown to Malcolm and Jeremiah X, the downtown Klan incident at the drugstore had triggered a citywide police alert. Despite this unfolding racial strife, Fellows and his Klansmen, for the sake of their mission, tried to steer clear of confrontation with their Black Muslim hosts. Each group, in fact, sounded a symbiotic tone of mutual convenience, keying in on the race-mixing issue.

The gray-haired Fellows, apparently more comfortable now that his buddies were in the room, removed his high hat and repaired with his hosts and associates to the kitchen table, which was spread with Elizabeth's sandwiches, cold drinks, and cookies. Probing for common ground on their terms, Fellows said that the Klan had gotten a bad reputation in the press. They didn't really "hate all niggras," he said, in an attempt to break the ice. There were "some good niggras," he said to the nodding grins of his colleagues. "Some work for me. Our problem is the bad niggras. You don't like bad niggras, yourselves." Fellows said flat-out that he had "beat a few of these bad niggras." One was a "lazy" worker bent on tardiness. "He kept coming to work late, so I took a stick and whipped that niggra," said Fellows. "He started coming to work on time after that." Fellows and his men didn't talk about any of the Klan's lethal handiwork against Negroes.[47]

After a round of sizing up and mutual jawboning, the two sides relaxed, and the Klansmen hit on what they took to be a mutual target: the Jews. It wasn't local "niggras" in the South causing the civil rights trouble themselves, Fellows said, but rather outside agitators and "the Jews." Left alone, "our niggras" would stay in their place, "I know that." They were, however, getting bad advice and good money from the Jews. Malcolm chimed in that the Honorable Elijah Muhammad maintained that the liberal Jews exerted undue influence on Negroes, north and south. Elijah said they headed most of the established black organizations, such as the NAACP and the National Urban League. He also said they were "using the Negro as a tool," a buffer for their own benefit in the pursuit of racial integration.[48]

Anti-Jewish sentiment was not a feature of Nation of Islam policy, and it was nowhere cited as a group practice under Elijah Muhammad, according to most observers, including the Anti-Defamation League of B'nai B'rith. In Muhammad's view, all whites were "blue-eyed devils," and Jews, varying only in small details of their somewhat belated integration, were perceived as white Americans. When singled out at all, especially in the South, Jews were usually cited by Negroes in their religious context, or as employers and businessmen of first resort. In contrast to the hard-core anti-Semitic views of whites, both in the South and North, including recent émigrés such as Italians and Irish, most Negroes generally considered Jews a better, more accessible, and acceptable group of white Americans.

Excluding a rare sour note blown out of proportion, these were the halcyon days of black-Jewish relations, in the opinions of leaders of both groups. Like other Americans, Negroes peppered their common jargon occasionally with the stereotypes of Jews as tight merchants with sharp practices, as dominant players in Hollywood and other media outlets, on Wall Street, and in the diamond and garment industries. But, in black hands, such stereotypes carried little of the venom of white bigots and certainly none of the competitive antagonism. In fact, Negroes did not consider these alleged group achievements objectionable. Indeed, if anything, their leaders, including Malcolm X, instructed followers to emulate what they considered the Jews' economic prowess and their aggressive pursuit of group self-interest.

Finding no preexisting anti-Jewish resentment among Negroes, Elijah Muhammad's homegrown Muslims neither drilled for domestic reserves of hostility nor expropriated the historical enmity between Jews and orthodox Muslims in the Middle East. A survey of references to Jews in Elijah Muhammad's published books and speeches found they related mainly to biblical references and contained no specific criticism of Jewish behavior or treatment of Negroes.

As was his wont, Malcolm, however, occasionally pushed the envelope for dramatic effect in Harlem on this issue. It was mostly during question-and-answer periods that he would single out Jews for criticism of their business practices vis-à-vis blacks. New York City contained a large, sensitive, and highly vocal Jewish population, somewhat entwined with the commerce and education of working-class blacks in Harlem, Brooklyn, and elsewhere. Thus, like politicians, activists, and writers, such as James Baldwin, Malcolm weighed in on the complex relation of Negroes with Jewish landlords, benefactors, shopkeepers, merchants, and schoolteachers. Such criticisms, often in generalized terms, earned him the label "anti-Semitic" in some Jewish quarters.

"We make no distinction between Jews and non-Jews so long as they are all white," Malcolm X said in a 1961 interview with C. Eric

Lincoln, reflecting more his leader's doctrine than his own stump views. "To do so would be to imply that we like some whites better than others." Malcolm had traveled in July 1959 to the Mideast, his first trip abroad, as an emissary preparing the way for the Messenger to visit Mecca. Following this trip, Malcolm became more vocal on the relationship between Jews and the State of Israel. "In America," he told Lincoln, "the Jews sap the very life-blood of the so-called Negroes to maintain the state of Israel, its armies and its continued aggression against our brothers in the East. This every black man resents."[49] The more provincial Elijah Muhammad curbed Malcolm's drift into foreign affairs, preventing him from traveling abroad again after that 1959 trip.

Now, at the Saturday Klan sit-down in Atlanta, Malcolm summarized the attacks on the Jewish influence on Negroes that he had expressed openly at lectures in Harlem, on radio and TV, on college campuses, and elsewhere. While his Klan companions appeared to relax, Fellows drew the contours of the Jews as a much larger threat. As if invoking a Klan version of *The Protocols of the Elders of Zion*, a widely circulated anti-Semitic fabrication, he stated that the Jews were about to fulfill their plans to take over the entire country. One of the other Klansmen, a middle-aged politician from south Georgia, weighed in to assert that his group had once lynched a Jew. The man seemed agitated, still so many years later, about "this little Jew who come down here" and had raped a white girl. Neither Malcolm nor Jeremiah X was familiar enough with the incident to comment.

The incident, it turned out, was the lynching of Leo M. Frank. Born in Cuero, Texas, Frank had grown up in Brooklyn, earned an engineering degree at Cornell University, and moved to Atlanta to manage his uncle's pencil factory. Following the 1913 rape and murder of thirteen-year-old Mary Phagan, who worked in the factory, Frank, who was then twenty-nine, was arrested and convicted on flimsy evidence, and on the testimony of a Negro janitor, who claimed that Frank paid him two hundred dollars to burn the body in the basement furnace. In a stormy one-month trial, punctuated by catcalls to the defense attorney of "Hang the Jew," Frank was given the death penalty. After several failed appeals, Governor John Slaton commuted the sentence to life in prison.

The unpopular decision touched off angry editorials and sporadic acts of vandalism against Jewish homes and stores in Atlanta and Marietta, Mary Phagan's hometown. Typically, *Watson's Magazine*, published by Thomas E. Watson, a prominent state politician, described Frank as a "typical Jewish man of business who lives for pleasure and runs after Gentile girls."[50] On the morning of August 17, 1915, Leo Frank was taken from his prison cell, with his hands tied in front, and was hanged barefoot from a tree limb in Marietta. Subsequent reports revealed that the kidnapping and killing were carried out by seventy-five men calling themselves the "Knights of Mary Phagan" and led by well-to-do white Georgians, including a former Georgia governor, several mayors, a judge, and several state legislators. The lynching of Leo Frank—who on March 11, 1986, would be granted a posthumous pardon by the Georgia State Board of Pardons—inspired the organization of the Anti-Defamation League. Along with the release of *The Birth of a Nation*, it also helped spur the Stone Mountain revival of the Ku Klux Klan, three months after Frank's lynching, led by William J. Simmons. A recruitment drive after Frank's death brought in the first ninety men to a Klan membership that grew steadily for decades.

Some forty-five years later, at the Klan-Muslim sit-down, the south Georgia politician insisted—bragged, in fact—that he had been present at the lynching of Leo Frank. Photographs of the grisly Frank lynching show prosperous white men, some in ties and neat straw hats, with plenty of young boys looking on. The boastful politician indicated that he was something other than a casual observer, uttering words Jeremiah X said he would never forget: "You should have seen that little Jew's eyes bulge when we pulled that rope."[51]

The other Klansmen cited the lynching of the Jewish victim apparently not so much to unnerve the two Muslim ministers as to strike what they believed would be a common chord. The bloody lynching ledgers of the white knights were replete with thousands of black victims across the South, yet the stringing up of white, Jewish Leo Frank was the only such incident the Klansmen felt comfortable enough to trot out at this meeting with the Muslims. It was as if they wanted to make a grisly case for their equal opportunity outlook, as they probed for mutual ground with the one black group that eschewed both nonviolence and integration.

Warming to this use-of-force challenge, Malcolm stated firmly that Muslims would do anything to defend their beliefs. Resorting to the cover of NOI doctrine, he implied that there would inevitably be violence between the races one day, especially if Negroes in America didn't acquire some land and separate from the white man. Preemptively, he announced that the Black Muslims were not in favor of the established, legal policy of Jim Crow segregation. At no point during the meeting did the Muslim ministers refer to whites as "devils," blue-eyed or otherwise, as was their usual practice. Still, the two races were said to be incapable of living together in peace. "God Himself" didn't intend for them to get along together as brothers and sisters "because we are two distinct people," and "therefore, the Muslims want complete, total *separation*," Malcolm stated.[52]

"The Honorable Elijah Muhammad teaches us" that after hundreds of years of slavery, the black man in America is entitled to some land, "free and clear," that he could develop and set up as a separate black nation, Malcolm said by rote. Exploring the opening, he then stated that his spiritual leader stood willing to accept the help of those white people, including the Klan, who would assist black people in obtaining this land to "maintain their own businesses and gov-

ernment." As ordered by the Messenger, the national spokesman of
the NOI requested directly that the Ku Klux Klan assist the Muslims
in acquiring a piece of land for blacks, perhaps a county for starters,
somewhere in the Deep South. It was pitched as something of a down
payment for blacks who stood absolutely opposed to integration with
their open "enemy, the white man," who hated them without cause.
Having officially placed Elijah Muhammad's pet proposal on the
agenda, Malcolm shifted into fervent, personal eloquence on a major
point of clarification: "We are in favor of complete separation of the
races—not segregation, *separation!*"[53]

This stark distinction seemed to puzzle Fellows and the other
Klansmen, who nodded quizzically to one another as Malcolm honed
more finely the Messenger's point. The Jim Crow segregation system
the Klan was hell-bent on preserving, Malcolm deadpanned, had to
date given Negroes the short end of the stick, and often no stick at all.
In abandoning their pursuit of integration, Malcolm stated, blacks
would need a nest egg so that they could strike out on their own with
a separate but appropriate share of the wealth they had helped accu-
mulate in America. Otherwise, civil rights integrationists would end
Negro and white progress, or at least shatter racial tranquility. The
time was ripe for revamping segregation so that it no longer fixed
blacks at an unacceptably low end of the totem pole. Instead of the
existing system, which exploited Negroes by rendering them totally
dependent upon the white man for food, clothing, and shelter, the
Black Muslims wanted a new permanent system that was more equi-
table and truly separate, politically, racially, and economically. It was
time for the white man in America to sever this Negro dependency
and allow the black man to separate and get out on his own.

As one, the Klansmen in the kitchen feigned to grasp the point
Malcolm struggled so painstakingly to register. But clearly the Klansmen considered their racial "segregation" and the Muslims' "separa-

tion" as amounting to a distinction without a difference over which the white knights need not quibble.

"It's all the same thing to us," Fellows said finally. "Whatever you niggras want, it's fine. Call it whatever you like. As long as you stay over there and you're glad to be black, good. We just wish all niggras would be glad to be niggras." His previously puzzled colleagues shook their head in firm agreement.

The Klansmen at the kitchen table were all working-class whites with no easy access to the amassed wealth of the South. Yet, they diddled with Elijah Muhammad's division-of-the-wealth proposition like so many day laborers contemplating the breakup, say, of the United Kingdom. Such geopolitical-economic matters were clearly beyond the grasp of the scrawny, poorly educated Klansmen—as well as the working-class Muslim ministers. With barely a college degree among them, each group worked through the sit-down as self-appointed diplomats for its entire race. The Klansmen, especially, bridled throughout the session, as they assumed the prerogatives of an ersatz ruling class.

"Malcolm was just being provocative" throughout the heady negotiations, Jeremiah recalled, "just leading them on to see where they were going." In matching wits with the dullard Klansmen ranged around the table, Malcolm trotted out verbal maneuvers from his prison days debating Ivy League scholars, and double entendre from his throwdowns in barbershops, pool halls, and churchyards. Adapting the tricky retorts that he shouted atop ladders and flatbeds trucks along Harlem's 125th Street, Malcolm set debate traps—debate ambushes, debate guillotines—for the Klansmen.

At the critical moment, however, the national spokesman restrained himself from pulling the trap door, laboring as he was under the strictures laid down by Elijah Muhammad—and with Jeremiah X taking note. After all, the assigned NOI mission was neither to score debating points nor to humiliate the Klansmen by smashing their credo to smithereens—as Malcolm forthrightly would have preferred. So those gaping holes that Malcolm blasted in the Klansmen's arguments, lapses that he normally would have exploited to guffaws and crackling applause before debate audiences, were instead left unexplored. In the warmth of Elizabeth's kitchen, Fellows and his Klansmen, thanks to the merciful Messenger, were thus allowed not only to save face but to carry on as if they were the embodiment of the sovereign state of Georgia, if not that of the Deep South.

Occasionally, the sly Hotspur within Malcolm compelled him to disobey his sovereign's orders that he humbly petition the Klansmen. After being allowed to ease away from the segregation-versus-separation stalemate, Fellows suggested, for instance, that the Muslims might operate as something of a Negro franchise of the broader Klan movement. "We can work together," Fellows said, "and put a stop to this integration." The direct offer brought a wicked smile across Malcolm's face that he just as quickly wiped away.

Still, he could not restrain himself. "Well, what do you mean, we can't join the Klan?" Jeremiah remembered Malcolm saying, wary of where the proposal was heading.

"We'll make y'all like a partner," Fellows explained—like an auxiliary.

"Are you going to get us some robes?" Malcolm deadpanned in a manner that had Jeremiah chuckling heartily, but only internally for the moment.

"Well, no, we can't let no niggra wear a white robe," the Klansman said, pondering alternatives as Malcolm leaned in over the tripod of his fingers.

"I tell you what, Malcolm," Fellows finally said, "we can get y'all some purple robes."

"Oh, no, no, no." said Malcolm, unwilling to let the opposing leader slip the leash. "We want white robes."

Returning to the stalemate over racial segregation versus separation, Malcolm chided the Klansmen that they shouldn't be able to segregate him and give him what they want to have, instead of what he should have. "If we are going to be partners in this thing, then give us a white robe like what you have."

"No, we can't let no niggras wear white robes," Fellows insisted, as he gazed back at the puzzled countenances of his colleagues at the table.

"Tell ya what," Fellows continued, "we'll bring some purple robes over here and you'll just have to make do with 'em."

Point made, Malcolm relaxed the purple-robe tension by allowing the matter to float away as a nonstarter. He then brought Jeremiah and the other Klansmen into the discussion on more general matters, focusing on the Nation of Islam's taking care of its black "hypocrites." Digressing somewhat from instructions, Malcolm stated that violence sometimes was indeed necessary, especially to defend one's people from those who would lead them astray. He then hinted darkly that if one of their people strayed from their religious teachings, "he would be destroyed." Elijah Muhammad taught, publicly at least, that such "hypocrites" would be chastised by Allah Himself. However, Malcolm knew of occasions when chastisement of said "hypocrites" was subcontracted to the earthly soldiers of the Fruit of Islam. The Klansmen's ears pricked. So did those of the FBI informer in the room who, according to a summary written by an Atlanta Field Office agent, filed a report that Malcolm said that if his people "were faced with the situation that white people in Georgia now face, that traitors, meaning those whites who assisted integration leaders, would be eliminated."[54]

With that opening for violence, Fellows shifted into an even more serious gear, repeating, "We can work together and put a stop to this integration." The provocative Malcolm again probed for Fellows to state his principal motive for dispatching the KKK telegram that convened the present meeting. Keying on their mutual disdain for race mixing, the Klansman attacked as wrongheaded the current student sit-in demonstrations by black and white "freedom riders" from the North. Seeking a point of agreement, Fellows extended an invitation for the Muslims to join the Klan in fighting this gathering "scourge of integration."

And then, revealing a key item on their agenda, Klansman Fellows expressed grave concern over the growing influence in the South of "Martin Luther Coon."

The mere mention of the thirty-two-year-old Atlanta-based civil rights leader shifted the mood of the room. The international media had made King a clear and present problem for Southern white segregationists, including the knights of the Georgia Ku Klux Klan. In discussing how "Martin Luther Coon" had excited Southern "niggras" to push for integration, Fellows could barely contain his anger, and his companions flashed tight grins. Elizabeth, observing from the sidelines, was not amused.

By January 1961, Reverend King had come to personify Negroes' relentless push for desegregation throughout the South. His Southern Christian Leadership Conference was considered the chief threat to white supremacy as steadfastly defended by the heavily armed Klan, along with White Citizens' Councils and many a Southern governor, congressman and county sheriff. Beginning with the 1955 Montgomery bus boycott and extending through the creation of the SCLC two years later, the Baptist minister had helped touch off a nonviolent blitzkrieg against segregation, that was beginning to gain results. Although King traveled widely throughout the nation lecturing and raising funds, he was based a few blocks away from the Odd Fellows Lodge, the site of the NOI's Temple No. 15, in the Sweet Auburn neighborhood of middle-class Negroes.

A hometown boy, King had been born in his grandparents' home, at 501 Auburn Avenue, a block away from his father's Ebenezer Baptist Church, at 407, where the son was an associate minister. The church was a relatively modest, redbrick building, by no means the largest such edifice in Atlanta, or even on Auburn, once dubbed "the richest Negro street in the world." However, because of King's growing national fame and his oratorical leadership of the civil rights movement, Ebenezer had eclipsed the more grandiose sanctuaries, such as "Big" Bethel Baptist, as the most important church in Atlanta.

On the lecture circuit, Malcolm himself had often attacked King as a patsy of the white man and a sellout, and he would do so again. Never had he imagined that this nonviolent Baptist minister, who preached Negro kindness and charity for one's enemies, could evoke such toxic venom, such genuine hatred from the very grassroots whites whom King continually encouraged his followers to love. And yet here was a group of local Klansmen plotting to stalk this nonviolent Negro leader toward no good end.

Fellows said they'd noticed in local media that the peripatetic Reverend King was irregularly traveling in and out of Atlanta a lot. Back in 1956, his Montgomery, Alabama, home had been bombed, and ensuing threats created a constant and justified fear for his life and safety. Although King and his family lived nearby, and Jeremiah saw him occasionally at Pascal's Restaurant and other dining spots, the internationally known celebrity had begun to move around his hometown stealthily and with security details. There were rumors that he had even taken on armed guards.

"We know he lives around here somewhere, but we don't know where," said Fellows, in a whisper. He asked Malcolm and Jeremiah directly if the Muslims would reveal exactly where King resided and supply the Klansmen a schedule of his habits and real-time movements when he was in town. Having read Malcolm's public attacks on King and other civil rights leaders who embraced nonviolence, Fellows had been led to believe that the Muslims saw King as an enemy they had in common. Initially, the Klansman did not state the intended purpose of the surreptitious surveillance—but he left little doubt.

The Klan request embarrassed Malcolm, according to Jeremiah and his wife, and it likely disheartened and shamed him as well. Also, it did not escape Malcolm's notice that, in contrast to the Christian Reverend King, the Black Muslims drew not a jot of ire from the one white group in America that was universally despised as devils by all Negroes, including Malcolm himself. In fact, the Klan was regarding him and Jeremiah, two key ministers of Elijah Muhammad's Black Muslims, as potential allies. Muhammad had warned his negotiators about Klan skulduggery, but not even the Messenger had anticipated such a cold-blooded request for a joint venture against King. The starkness of the request left Malcolm reeling.

In reply, Malcolm stated emphatically that the Muslims would not participate in any violence against Reverend King or any other action "hurting our own kind." Even though the Honorable Elijah Muhammad considered Dr. King to be leading Negroes astray, his national spokesman stated in as sharp and unmistakable words as Malcolm could muster that the NOI would in no way do physical harm to the SCLC leader. Each of the groups, he repeated, was to take care of its own traitors and hypocrites.

As a white man unaccustomed to black resistance, and with his Klan cohort cutting their eyes, Fellows maintained the air of a man who had every right to expect compliance. He assured the two Muslim ministers that his group would take care of the dirty work, that nothing would be traceable to their organization. "You don't have to kill him," Fellows said flat-out, according to an account Jeremiah subsequently gave during an interview with the author. "We'll take care of the violence."[55]

Doubling down, Malcolm made it clear that his objection to such collusion with the Klan was as stark and impenetrable as Stone Mountain. Still, like Elijah Muhammad's request for Klan assistance in land acquisition, the issue was left dangling. Neither representative at the table had the final say-so on such issues, and each was clearly unaccustomed to such incendiary give-and-take with members of an enemy race group. So the men slid along to lesser sticking points.

Throughout the two-hour-plus sit-down, Fellows and his Klansmen were as direct and self-assured as landlords sitting down with indigent tenants. As a Klansman of the protest march and the open fields, Fellows seemed unprepared for resistance, occasionally belittling, from a black man such as Malcolm. And the two Muslim ministers discovered that their unique views on segregation and other matters, in the mind of the Klansmen, was not simply talk but was backed by a force more muscular than even Malcolm realized. The instrument garnering the respect of the Klan was the Fruit of Islam, the Nation's security force.

Among hardened, urban street criminals, the Fruit of Islam was duly esteemed as a disciplined, karate-trained palace guard not to be messed with. This cadre consisted of hardy specimens chosen for their baleful prowess. The most cold-blooded of the bunch, some bordering on the pathological, were assigned to special security "goon squads." Some wore caps emblazoned "FOI" for Fruit of Islam, while the goon squads handled assignments involving heavy group discipline, beatings, the breaking of legs or kneecaps, and, occasionally homicide. The hand-to-hand combat featured in the documentary *The Hate That Hate Produced* was a tool for recruiting young, lethal, street toughs. And just as the special squads were a point of interest for the FBI, they also caught the eye of the Klan. Like most quasimilitary groups, the Klan judged friends and foes by the size of their arsenal and their willingness to use it. Respect for the Muslims, then, was helped along greatly by the FOI as a potent instrument of menace. Unbeknown to the Klan, however, the FOI conducted its violence almost exclusively against other blacks.

"I know you boys have your army, your Fruit of Islam," Fellows said. "Well, we have ours, too." Jeremiah took the gesture as ego tripping until the Klansman pulled out a card from his wallet and put it on the table. His cohort winced at this breach of security. Fellows said it was the first time they'd ever let a "niggra see this card." With the air of a fellow combatant, the Klansman told Malcolm, "This is our FOI. This is our secret army." Malcolm examined the card, which was inscribed "Brothers KLAW" and emblazoned with what appeared to be the fierce talon of a swooping vulture.

The cagey Jeremiah got Fellows's permission to keep a KLAW card for himself as a token for traveling on highways of the South. And sure enough, when an Alabama state trooper subsequently pulled the Muslim minister over yet again, Jeremiah X flashed his driving license, along with the KLAW card. "Nigger, where'd you get this card from?" the state trooper asked. "My boss man, sir," Jeremiah X replied, in the unctuous manner that infuriated his wife, Elizabeth.

"All right, nigger. Don't ya go so fast the next time, you hear me?"[56]

The Klan's respect for the prowess of the FOI caught Malcolm and Jeremiah off guard. Both, however, were relieved to learn that the scowling goon squads which intimidated Negroes had also earned the respect of the fierce white knights down south. Jeremiah filed away this lesson of mutual respect for future use, convinced that henceforth he would get saddled with the Atlanta follow-up to the Klan meeting. Residing with his wife and small child across town from the hooded knights, Jeremiah was eager to establish a nonaggression pact with the Klan, as the Messenger had instructed. To the embarrassment of Elizabeth, her husband had perfected a disarming, Uncle Tom persona, diverting the eyes, bowing at the waist, and peppering his affected laborer's drawl with a few "yes sir, boss"es. The performance could get the meanest redneck to help fix a flat tire on the highway, or to serve a meal at the side door of a "whites-only" restaurant. Sometimes Jeremiah would lapse into his Uncle Tom persona when escorting visiting Muslim officials to temples throughout the South. And he cautioned them to prune all mannerisms or even articles of clothing that might attract disfavor from state troopers. John Ali, the NOI national secretary, was once instructed, for example, to remove his sunglasses around Southern sheriffs.

"They don't like niggers wearing sunglasses down here," Ali remembered being told. "They want to see your eyeballs. They think you might be sneaking a look at some white woman." There had indeed been actual cases of black men in the South being charged with "reckless eyeballing," he cautioned the Chicago official.[57]

Throughout the Klan-Muslim meeting, Elizabeth busied herself in an adjacent room, keeping her ears pricked. Although her life as the wife of the chief Muslim organizer in the South was not without its heady moments of fulfillment, there were such days as this, with Klan members inside her home, that were heavy with uncertainty, anxiety, and sheer, unadulterated terror. Periodically during the meeting, she would screw up her courage and ply the guests with more cookies and juice, stealing a reassuring glance at Malcolm. She had known him during his budding organizing days as a skillful, mesmerizing debater in Philadelphia. Even now, though tense, she was spellbound as Malcolm probed the motives and intentions of the self-declared archenemies of Negroes across America—in her own kitchen. It was a tour de force.[58]

With Fellows glancing at his wristwatch, the two groups moved to adjourn. The secretive Klansmen suggested that they adopt an identification code for future contacts in Atlanta and elsewhere. Sly and provocative to the end, Malcolm, no stranger to numbers, assigned his Muslims the number 121 and, flashing his trademark warm smile with the steel teeth, coaxed the KKK into accepting as their code 666, the New Testament's number of the beast.[59]

———

The ten-car convoy took Fellows and his three dozen henchmen across town and emptied them out at the two-story Tower Theater at 583 Peachtree Street. The Atlanta showplace, with a sweeping marquee that had headlined such movie extravaganzas as Billy Graham's *Souls in Conflict*, was this night staging a massive anti-integration rally featuring the Knights of the Ku Klux Klan, Inc., as the nation's largest Klan group was officially called.

The Georgia imperial wizard, "Wild Bill" Davidson, unveiled a "secret weapon" to combat integration that included moving all of the Negroes in Georgia to a central location, Atlanta, "if necessary," according to the news account of the rally in the Sunday, January 29, 1961, edition of the *Atlanta Journal and Constitution*. Although details had not been hashed out, it was clear that Elijah Muhammad's request for Klan assistance in acquiring a parcel of land had figured somehow in the Klan leader's boast.[60]

"Resplendent in yellow robe," Davidson expounded upon his "secret weapon to the world," the *Journal* reported, by calling upon the robed and hooded members to: " '(1) Organize the youth into fighting young men and women who will not be touched by this brainwashing of integration, and rely on youth and the mothers of America to preserve segregation; (2) Boycott all white businesses which aid integration; (3). Move all Negroes to a central location, that location being Atlanta, the black jungle of the South.' The Klan has 'means and plans to do so if necessary,' " he said.[61]

The imperial wizard made no public mention of the secret meeting across town that Fellows had just concluded. It was discussed privately, however, with the FBI informant present, and plans were made to follow up with the local Muslims, headed by Jeremiah X.

Prominent among the Klan speakers were State Representative C. C. Perkins of nearby Carrollton and James Venable, a Klan leader and attorney whose family had owned Stone Mountain; they both rallied the hooded crowd to fight manfully against the "scourge of integration." Venable said the Communists, who, he asserted, first appeared in France in 1429, were "behind the nigger movement" that, among other recent villainies, had allowed those two black students to enter the University of Georgia. Perkins leveled his fire against Governor Vandiver, while praising the "patriots" who got themselves suspended and prosecuted in their riotous efforts to prevent Charlayne Hunter and Hamilton Holmes from desegregating the tax-supported state university.

The opening ceremony zeroed in on race mixing with a stage play attacking "amalgamation." It featured white girls holding hands with black boys (actually white students with their faces blackened). The mixed couples marched across the stage as Reverend E. E. George, a Klansman without his robes, preached that integration at the first-grade, hand-holding stage would eventually lead to teenage courtship, marriage, and the dreaded "mongrelization" of the white race.

As always, the Klan portrayed this unpardonable sin as a black male coupling with a white female.[62]

---

Back in Chicago, Elijah Muhammad expressed satisfaction with Malcolm's verbal account and his written report on the Klan meeting, congratulating his two ministers for their conduct of the mission. However, he did sense Malcolm's deep, underlying resentment of the manner in which he had been instructed to petition the Klan. The Messenger made it clear that the Klan sit-down be kept secret from all others, inside the NOI and outside. He pulled aside Jeremiah X to express his eagerness to exploit his new Southern strategy and essentially assigned him to coordinate follow-up NOI business ventures from his base in Atlanta. Moving swiftly on the initiative, Jeremiah X contacted several white officials in Atlanta, including James Venable, who promoted the idea that King and the civil rights movement were supported by Communist "Jews."[63]

Five weeks after the Atlanta meeting, on March, 5, 1961, police raided the Muslim temple in Monroe, Louisiana. Elijah Muhammad concluded that local Negro lawyers were afraid to defend the Muslims in court, so he summoned Venable to his Chicago dinner table. The Klan attorney was hired to represent the Muslims in the Monroe case. As a back-up, Muhammad dispatched two top officials from headquarters, Raymond Sharrieff, the supreme captain of the Fruit of Islam, and National Secretary John X (John Ali), to assist Venable in the defense of the Monroe minister, Troy X, and his temple members.

"We drove from Atlanta to Monroe with Venable in the front seat," said John Ali. "He was like any other Southern cracker, except he was there to make money from us. We flew down with $85,000 in bail money to get Minister Troy out." It would prove to be one of the most bizarre trial scenes in American history: the top Klan attorney in the South was petitioning the all-white court system to ensure justice for the Black Muslims. Hedging his bets, Venable sent a letter to Attorney General Robert Kennedy requesting that the Justice Department step in. The federal authorities declined, however, leaving Venable and an all-white jury to handle the fate of the Black Muslims in Monroe.

"The Messenger knew the die was set, but he wanted to do the best he could for Minister Troy and the other brothers," said John Ali. "Venable made a strong representation of our position. He said, 'Your honor, these niggras are nice niggras. They don't believe in race mixing like those other niggras.' The deputy sheriffs all stood in the courtroom and stared straight at us. It was quite an experience."[64] However, despite these efforts by—and the fat legal fee for—

the Klansman attorney, Minister Troy X was sentenced (under the name Troy Bland Cade) by an all-white jury to a ten-year prison term after two costly trials, convictions and the exhaustion of appeals. His crime of "criminal anarchy and flag desecration" stemmed from his temple's display of the standard Muslim backdrop, which featured the American flag, the image of a Negro hanging from a tree with a noose around his neck, and the caption "Slavery, Hell and Death." However, in 1963, the Louisiana State Supreme Court reversed the conviction and sentence. The case was remanded for a new trial.[65]

In addition to involving the well-known racist Klan lawyer in a Muslim cause célèbre, Jeremiah X, using Malcolm's designated code number 666, contacted Fellows to arrange an introduction to J. B. Stoner, the notorious imperial wizard of the Christian Knights of the KKK. He claimed that the reason he had written to Elijah Muhammad in 1957, as described earlier, was to attract publicity for his fledgling racist group. Meeting with the Messenger's poison-pen pal allowed Jeremiah X access to a wider circle of Klansmen in Atlanta and elsewhere. The Muslim minister even published a story about Stoner in *Muhammad Speaks*, the NOI journal, complete with photographs he'd taken of the Klansman in robe and hood, posing in Jeremiah's house, for a negotiated twenty-five-dollar fee.[66]

Aside from such personal relations, Jeremiah X developed long-term contacts from the 1961 Klan meeting that allowed him to begin negotiations with white businesses and farm owners. These contacts came, of course, at the expense of the Muslims' shattered relationship with mainstream Negro leadership in the South.

At times, as has already become apparent, the Muslims' cross-over connections with white racists took on elements of tragicomedy. Once, with the Klan in full regalia counterdemonstrating against civil rights marchers protesting the racial policy of a Lebanese-owned local restaurant, Jeremiah X showed up to take pictures and write a story for *Muhammad Speaks*. While photographing Reverends

King and Abernathy, as well as other leaders, sitting in and praying before the food establishment, the Black Muslim minister was courted on the scene publicly by the now familiar Klan.

"Jeremiah," he later recalled Klansman Calvin Craig shouting to him from across the street, "you don't belong over there with those integration niggras. You get over here with us." Out in the hot sun, Jeremiah X felt the pull not so much of journalistic objectivity as of shared oppression.

"Don't you go over there, Jeremiah, and be a traitor!" he remembered no less a light than Martin Luther King Jr. himself urging. With the civil rights leader speaking into his ear, the Muslim minister resorted to the teachings of his Messenger.

"I thought about it for a second," Jeremiah recalled, "There was another photographer on the scene named Dotson, so I said, 'Come on with me, Dotson, I want you to take a picture of me over here with these Klansmen.' Sure enough, Dotson trembling, we walked across the street. The Klansmen surrounded me, [suggesting] in other words, 'We got one of the integrators, and he believes like we believe.' So King's boys were across the street, yelling, 'Jeremiah, you're a traitor! You're a traitor!' I ignored them, dumb Negroes.

"I said, 'We'll get our separation before you get your integration.' So I stayed over there for a while and took some pictures after that, then I walked back across the street. They were more mad at me than [they were with] the Klan. Dotson took some incredible photographs."[67]

A few months after Malcolm and Jeremiah met with the Klan, Elijah Muhammad, who already owned farmland in the cold clime of White Cloud, Michigan, looked for real estate elsewhere. The FBI, which was closely monitoring the Muslim-Klan follow-up events, intercepted Muhammad's mention on the phone on May 9, 1961, that he was interested "in buying some land in the South." Jeremiah was assigned the task of exploring several possibilities. The Atlanta minister went to inquire about a $20,000 farm near Milledgeville, Georgia. As he approached the property, the white owner stormed to the front door, irritated that a Negro, even one wearing a suit and driving a shiny, new Buick, had dared come to the front of his sprawling farmhouse.

While being directed to the back door, Jeremiah X announced that he represented a religious group interested in purchasing the farm advertised for sale. "He changed right on the spot," Jeremiah X recalled. " 'Oh, come on in.' He invited me in the front door. This might be a big sale. He treated me real nice. We got in his pickup truck, and he drove all around the farm. I'll never forget the look on the face of this black farmhand, who earlier had tried to signal me to go to the back door. He was noticeably worried when he saw me riding in the truck with his boss. The white farmer said [to him], 'Nigger, you just mind your business. This is between me and this nigger here.' " Subsequently, Jeremiah forwarded his recommendation on the Milledgeville farm to Chicago, but the project was put on hold.[68]

Despite consorting with the Klan, Jeremiah X developed personal friendships with some of the more independent civil rights leaders, such as Medgar Evers of the Mississippi NAACP. Still, under Muhammad's orders, Jeremiah continued to cultivate commercial ties with Klan members, the White Citizens' Councils, and other openly racist white businessmen. There were stormy conflicts in the balancing act. When Medgar Evers was shot and killed outside his Jackson, Mississippi home by a Klansman on June 12, 1963, Jeremiah X, who had met with his good friend Evers two weeks earlier, rushed to the house to get the story for *Muhammad Speaks*.[69]

The following year, at a huge daylight Klan rally in Atlanta's Hurd Park, attended by most of the top leaders of the so-called Invisible Empire, including Imperial Wizard Robert Shelton, Minister Jeremiah X was recognized from the podium and singled out for praise.

His appearance there was particularly extraordinary because it followed the Klan's bold involvement in scores of violent attacks against the civil rights movement. Besides the assassination of Evers, these acts included bombing the homes of King and other black leaders; killing four black girls in the dynamiting of the Sixteenth Street Baptist Church in Birmingham, Alabama; and the slaying of civil rights workers Andrew Goodman, Michael Schwerner, and James Chaney in Neshoba County, Mississippi. "You're looking at the first and last black man to go to a KKK meeting in Georgia and come out alive," Jeremiah X bragged to a black gathering years later.[70]

Even at the behest of the Messenger, Malcolm X would never have agreed to establish such cordial ongoing relations with the Klan, Jeremiah X conceded. At the 1961 meeting, the national spokesman had finagled as best he could his direct orders to humbly petition the Klan for assistance in acquiring land and succor. Yet the experience still left Malcolm with a sense of having betrayed the very Negroes the NOI proclaimed to protect. Since Malcolm's religious conversion in the cellblock of Norfolk prison, Elijah Muhammad had managed a cultlike hold on him as the spiritual surrogate for his long departed father. Now, Muhammad's humbling outreach to the murderous Klan had served, finally, to open Malcolm's eyes. The Muslim-Klan alliance swept Malcolm back face-to-face with his upbringing by his Garveyite parents Earl and Louise.

It was not so much the sit-down itself that unhinged Malcolm, according to Jeremiah; after all, Marcus Garvey himself had met with the KKK's Imperial Kleagle Edward Young Clarke nearly four decades earlier in Atlanta. The flash point that likely irreversibly shattered Malcolm's blind devotion to the Messenger was more broadly his Southern strategy, which flowed out of the meeting. While this pact promised Klan-approved safe passage for Jeremiah and other Muslims in the South, it also committed the NOI to secret cooperation with the death-dealing white knights—who, among their contemporary atrocities, had even openly proposed killing Martin Luther King Jr. The willingness of Elijah Muhammad to overlook the long, bloody history, as well as the mounting terror, of the Klan struck his national spokesman on a deeply personal level. It was Malcolm, after all, who was the fetus being carried, back in Omaha, when those night-riding Klan horsemen terrorized his pregnant mother and her three older children in Omaha. And he had grown up convinced beyond all arguments that this same Ku Klux Klan had killed his father.

The resulting repulsion was primal. And in addition to ordering him to meet humbly with the Klan, Malcolm's spiritual leader had demanded that he relax his natural instinct to attack and not give ground. It was as if Malcolm had been forced to choose between Elijah Muhammad and the secular rock of his upbringing. Jeremiah had noticed the stiff resistance of the NOI spokesman to their Messenger from the very beginning. Unlike the petty recalcitrance of the past, he could see that this time it was quite serious—and Jeremiah knew that it would not go away.[71]

So, apparently, did Elijah Muhammad. He no longer trusted Malcolm to represent him in further negotiations with the white racist groups in the South. After praising Malcolm faintly for his handling of the Klan initiative, he damned him by abruptly banning him from the South altogether. All follow-up meetings were assigned to Jeremiah, who was instructed to break off communications with his old friend in order to execute the Black Muslims' Southern strategy.

As for the government informant in the room, it appears that the FBI was chiefly interested in recording any hints of Black Muslim violence, which could be used to discredit the group. The informant's notes disclosed to date no record of the death threat the Klan proposed against Reverend King. Such an oversight by the informant seems not just curious, but dangerous. It is possible, of course, that the informer himself, especially given his scant report on Klan maneuvers at the meeting, purposefully omitted this, along with other damning information, or, possibly, his account of the King threat resides in some yet undisclosed Bureau report. However, both Jeremiah X and his wife, independently, as well as confidants of Malcolm and other ranking NOI officials, confirmed that W. S. Fellows indeed requested that King be tracked so that his group, which had the motive and the means, could kill him.

Subsequently, ample FBI files have been released indicating that J. Edgar Hoover had reasons of his own to remove Reverend King from the scene. With extreme prejudice, the Atlanta FBI memorandum noted that the secret meeting between the Black Muslims and the KKK, if revealed, could be a possible source of embarrassment for the NOI. As for any hint of violence on the Muslim side, the summary noted that its unnamed source "advised that . . . MALCOLM X . . . stated that his people would do anything to defend their beliefs and promote their cause and in his opinion there would be violence some day."[72]

As for Malcolm, the meeting afforded firsthand insight into King's much greater state of danger vis-à-vis the Klan and the established order in the South. Nonetheless, the national spokesman continued to answer—although less blindly so—to a religious leader more willing to work with the Ku Klux Klan than with Negro leaders of the civil rights movement. This thundering contradiction began to raise serious doubt in Malcolm's mind about the efficacy of his cult leader's program and indeed his personal ethics and commitment. What facts the Harlem minister learned about the Southern strategy were gleaned from confidential sources in Chicago and Atlanta. Alerted about the probing and egged on by family members jealous of Malcolm's influence within the Nation, Elijah Muhammad grew increasingly wary of his young spokesman's trustworthiness.

Throughout the NOI-KKK relationship, Klan leaders, such as Venable and even J. B. Stoner, seemed always to get the better end of Muhammad's supposedly symbiotic Southern strategy, such as it was. They milked the Muslims for high legal fees, overcharged for real estate, and used the black group as poster children against integration. Double crossing the NOI was the ultimate feature of this unholy alliance: years later, their Klan cohorts poisoned Muslim cattle stocked at farms the Chicago-based group was developing in rural Georgia.

After getting expelled from the Muslims three years later, Malcolm would in passing attack the Klan from the podium. However, he never publicly detailed his meeting with the white knights at the kitchen table of Jeremiah X's house. He also kept what details he knew away from his wife, Betty, and even from his older brother Wilfred, with whom he ended up sharing almost every other dark secret of his risk-taking career. His published autobiography, originally conceived largely as a tribute to Elijah Muhammad, did not mention a single word about the secret 1961 meeting. One of the book's two mentions of the KKK addressed their possible involvement in the death of Malcolm's father, Earl. The other, an eerie foreshadowing, was the story relayed by Louise: "When my mother was pregnant with me . . . a party of hooded Ku Klux Klan riders galloped up to our home in Omaha, Nebraska, . . . [and] shouted threats and warnings at her that we better get out of town."[73]

Only toward the end of his life, after ridding himself of the "blind faith" hold of his cult leader, did Malcolm view the Klan sit-down as a shameful breach of his own better judgment. It was, he said, the disgraceful beginning of a "conspiracy between the NOI and the Ku Klux Klan that is not in the best interest of black people." With the zeal of a deprogrammed disciple, Malcolm doubled back on his contempt for Elijah Muhammad's poisonous relationship with the Klan that tortured and killed Negroes almost as a sport.

"The thing you have to understand about those of us in the Black Muslims movement was that all of us believed 100 percent in the

divinity of Elijah Muhammad," Malcolm would say in 1965. "We actually believed that God, in Detroit by the way, had taught him." [74] Malcolm left unstated what every follower, including his three brothers,
would strongly have attested to: that no one was more spartan-strict,
disciplined, and devout than Malcolm in laying down the law in the
service of the "Messenger of Allah."

In a memo dated three weeks before Malcolm's death, the FBI
noted that Malcolm's "next line of attack on MUHAMMAD and the
NOI" may be to expose that Muhammad is "in some way affiliated
with the KKK," beginning with the 1961 secret meeting. As with
other divisive counterintelligence moves by Director Hoover, the FBI
had held word of the secret meeting in reserve as a possible item of
blackmail, or embarrassment for the Nation of Islam.

"I know for a fact that there is a conspiracy . . . between the
Muslims and the [American] Nazis and also the Ku Klux Klan," a
newly bearded Malcolm stated publicly at the Audubon Ballroom
in Harlem only six days before his death in 1965. "The Ku Klux
Klan made a deal, or was trying to make a deal with Elijah Muhammad . . . in the home of Jeremiah X, the minister of Atlanta." They
were "trying to make a deal with him to make available to Elijah Muhammad a county-size tract of land in Georgia, or South
Carolina, where Elijah Muhammad could then induce Negroes to
migrate and make it appear that his program of a segregated state,
or separated state, was feasible. And to what extent those negotiations finally developed, I do not know because I was not involved
in them beyond the period of [January 1961]. But I do know that
Jeremiah . . . roamed the entire South and the Klan did not bother
him in any way, shape or form . . . nor would the Black Muslims
bother the Klan. . . . The attempts were made on my life because
I speak my mind and I know too much—and they know that I will
speak it whether they like it or not." [75]

And seven days before his death, Malcolm confessed that the Muslims "had to try and silence me because of what they know that I know. . . . There are some things involving the Black Muslim movement which, when they come to light, will shock you."[76]

His campaign against his former leader never advanced to the intended stage of exposing the full details of that 1961 meeting with the knights of the Ku Klux Klan. But fortunately, there were others present during the sit-down between the Klan and the Black Muslims who survived to talk about it.

# CHAPTER 14

# Malcolm, the Media, and Martin Luther King

Our goal has always been the same. The approaches are different . . . it is anybody's guess which of the "extremes" in approach to the black man's problem might personally meet a fatal catastrophe first—nonviolent Dr. King or so-called violent me.[1]

—MALCOLM X

DEEP INTO THE SPRING OF 1963, MALCOLM WAS WAGING A TWO-front campaign for the hearts and minds of Negroes across America. His training days as a barker for Muhammad on that Harlem ladder on 125th Street had paid off handsomely. The Muslim disciple was polished now and much in demand as the peripatetic national spokesman with the quicksilver tongue and the blistering retort. Crisscrossing the country, he proselytized on radio and TV as a celebrity and in lecture halls as a top draw.

Malcolm appeared to meet all the requirements of a black folk hero—except for the folks. Their sentiments, across the nation, did not swing to him but rather to a more traditional Christian embodiment of the black protest leader the Reverend Martin Luther King Jr. The Baptist minister presided at the head of a mass Negro movement that, despite its ragtag spontaneity, rolled through the South like a conventional army. His civil rights soldiers marched against the superstructure of racial segregation that rested on a foundation of white supremacy, three centuries old backed up by armed might and an entrenched Southern network of postslavery Jim Crow laws.

The state laws that King targeted had for generations separated the two races in the grand manner. Housing was segregated de facto and de jure, as were all jobs, schools, and churches, as well as access to finance, transportation, public facilities, and even cemeteries. Beneath this race canopy of the South, a crazy quilt of *petit* apartheid strictures regulated every stage of social contact between black and white individuals, from diapers to the shroud.

Each state also appeared to indulge its unique regional whim and bias. Alabama law, for example, categorically excluded white female nurses from assignments on wards or rooms in hospitals, either private or public, in which male Negro patients were present. Georgia did not allow merchants to dispense beer and wine to blacks and whites "within the same room at any time." In Florida, the state had to house white and black juvenile delinquents in separate buildings "not nearer than one-fourth mile to each other." White and black amateur softball players in Georgia were barred from playing on any vacant lot or baseball diamond within two blocks of one used by the other race. Louisiana had a thing about circuses, requiring that before the two races took their separate places under the Big Top, each had to be processed through a separate ticket booth, "with individual sellers" and that booths, "shall not be less than twenty-five (25) feet apart."[2]

King and his army of demonstrators sought to change all these segregation laws and reform the behavior of the Southern white men who ruled these states and municipalities. As Negro leaders attacked the absurdity and inhumanity of Jim Crow laws, their white detractors, from the statehouse to the lowliest tenant shack, defended segregation on the grounds that, at bottom, it was the will of their Christian god. Mixing of the races at any level, they maintained, was a sin against nature that would inevitably lead to miscegenation and intermarriage that would "mongrelize" the white race.

In light of this explosive charge, King and other civil rights leaders downplayed the Jim Crow laws against interracial marriages— especially since some of these men, such as James Farmer, the director of the Congress of Racial Equality (CORE), had white spouses. As late as 1963, thirty-three states still outlawed marriage between the races. Not all of these states were in the South, and some of them cast a wider, ethnic net. In Maryland, for example, the law forbade marriage between a white and a Malay, or a white and a Negro, or "a person of Negro descent, to the third generation, inclusive." In Missouri, marriages were disallowed between "white persons and Negroes or white persons and Mongolians." In Arizona, the marriage ban extended to "persons of Caucasian blood with a Negro, Mongolian, Malay, or Hindu." Wyoming bypassed Hindu, but targeted "Mulattos."[3]

Unlike King, Malcolm and the Muslims had no qualms about toying with the booby-trapped issue of miscegenation. Sex between black men and white women, Malcolm preached, was the white man's greatest nightmare. He took pains to note the fact that Southern white men had been fathering children by black women, almost as a matter of course, since the days of slavery. This particular version of miscegenation was never cited as a sin against God. This drive to preserve genetically the recessive white skin and, as the Muslims mocked, "blue eyes" was the primal reason that the white racist South had erected its citadel of segregation against the Negroes they preached would "mongrelize" them with one drop of blood.

The root of segregation, if not of racism itself, at one level rested upon the white South's perception of a need to prevent the procreative coupling of white women and black men at all cost. At another level, of course, segregation allowed the dominant white group, with access to national power, to deprive Negroes of their fair share of economic resources needed to reap the full benefits of citizenship.

The civil rights movement and the Muslims, Malcolm argued, disagreed in their approach to achieving economic empowerment with all the attendant rights of citizenship. King and his movement sought to remove all traces of racial apartheid and by the process of integration to gain fair access to the economy and full citizenship for Negroes. On the other hand, the Muslims totally rejected the possibility of integrating with whites, whom they considered incapable of living in peace with other than their own kind. Instead, as we've seen, Muslims sought to separate from white Americans and set up a black nation on land due them after centuries of slavery and exploitative low wages in the Americas. Although the specifics of the land issues were vague and changed over time, Elijah Muhammad was unwavering in his demand that blacks must separate from whites—physically, socially, spiritually, and in every way imaginable.

While pushing for economic empowerment, the Muslims ceded white southerners their demand to keep separate at every level, including the bedroom. For his part, Malcolm preached that the blind determination to forestall interracial marriage was the earnest—and immutable—sentiment of all whites. In light of this terminal white insularity, Malcolm counseled that Negroes in America should not waste their time pursuing integration with the very "blue-eyed devils" who were rejecting them as inferiors.

Instead, Malcolm derided the Jim Crow laws as proof positive of whites' incorrigibility as racists. And he wielded the issue of miscegenation as a double-headed battle-ax against whites who maintained segregation, as well as against Negroes who sought to integrate with them. In this he was especially tough on black civil rights leaders. At every lecture, he found an opening to lambaste them, as well as black celebrities married to white spouses, as examples of race traitors whose advice on all matters should be flatly ignored.

During a March 7, 1962, debate on "separation or integration" at Cornell University in upstate New York, Malcolm met the issue head-on with James Farmer of CORE. "Mr. X suggests that the Negroes in this country want the white man's women," Farmer said. He then noted that a recent issue of the Muslims' newspaper, *Muhammad Speaks*, had printed "that I myself have a white wife. And it was suggested that therefore I have betrayed my people in marrying a white woman." Farmer said that Negroes' virtues were not "so frail" that they could be "corrupted by contact with other people."[4]

Refusing to "get personal" with the civil rights leader, Malcolm broadened his miscegenation attack to include well-known black celebrities. "If you would have gone into Harlem a few years back you would have found on the juke box, records by [Harry] Belafonte, Eartha Kitt, Pearl Bailey. All of these persons were very popular singers in the so-called Negro community." Their popularity decreased, Malcolm told the Cornell audience, when these entertainers, as well as others like Lena Horne and Sammy Davis Jr., married white spouses. "They have a large white following, but you can't go into any Negro community across the nation and find records by these artists that are hits in the so-called Negro community. Subconsciously, today, the so-called Negro withdraws himself from the entertainers who have crossed the line. And if the masses of black people won't let a Negro who is involved in an interracial marriage play music for him—he can't speak for him!"[5]

Malcolm himself had married within his race and his religion, wedding Sister Betty X, a devoted member of his Harlem temple, in 1958. Georgia-born Betty Dean Sanders had grown up in Detroit and had attended Tuskegee Institute in Alabama before moving to New

York to study nursing. Malcolm described her in the *Autobiography* as "tall, brown-skinned—darker than I was. And she had brown eyes."[6] In keeping with Nation of Islam practice, there had been no courtship. Malcolm, who had been feeling pressure to marry amid unceasing attention from available sisters, had shown his brother Wilfred photographs of two women, Betty and another young woman named Betty Sue. "He said that he was trying to make up his mind which one of them he was going to marry," Wilfred recalled.[7] While stopping for gas at a Detroit filling station, Malcolm called Betty and asked her to marry him, according to the *Autobiography*. She immediately flew to Detroit, and they were married in Lansing, only two or three days after Malcolm had shown Wilfred his two candidates for wife. By the time of the Cornell debate in 1962, they had two daughters, Attallah and Qubilah, with a third, Ilyasah, on the way. Eventually, Sister Betty X (Betty Shabazz) would give birth to six daughters, including Gamilah, born in 1964, and twins Malikah and Malaak, born seven months after Malcolm's assassination.

Although Malcolm condemned interracial marriage, he did not subscribe to the Muslims' contention that segregation was ordained by God, a view that came straight from Elijah Muhammad and coincided with the view of white racists. Segregation, Malcolm maintained, was not ordained by God but created by white men. "The masses of white people don't want Negroes forcing their way into their neighborhoods, and the masses of black people don't think it's any solution to force ourselves into the white neighborhood."[8] The solution to segregation, he told the Cornell audience, was for blacks to separate—not segregate—themselves from the whites in America.

"Separation," Farmer countered, was hairsplitting; he accused "Mr. X" of making a distinction without a difference. "In saying that separation is the most effective solution to the problem, he makes a distinction between separation and segregation, saying that segregation is forced ghettoism while separation is voluntary ghettoism."[9] In rebuttal, Malcolm maintained that since Negroes had been rejected by the powerful white forces that ran the United States, blacks should counterreject them as the hopeless "blue-eyed devils" and establish a separate, independent nation that blacks controlled.[10]

Under the reins of Elijah Muhammad, Malcolm represented a vanguard religious sect that, instead of changing white folks' minds, concentrated on changing Negroes' minds foremost about themselves. Postslavery conditioning had reduced the psyche of the Negro to a shameful state of confusion, self-loathing, and cowardice. Malcolm told the Cornell students that the Muslims were determined to change all that.[11]

As the civil rights movement attracted national media attention in Southern cities, such as Montgomery and Birmingham, Alabama, and Albany, Georgia, the Muslims manned their solitary mosques in the dingy precincts of Harlem, Chicago, Boston, Detroit, Atlanta, and Watts.

King's early success with the Montgomery bus boycott in 1955 had caught the eye of the nation, and the media steadily warmed to the sight of his nonviolent army, which did not fight back when the sheriff's men attacked. King and his disciples quickly drew in the journalists who held out hope that their staged, nonviolent protests would flare into open violence and front-page news. Their expectations were often fulfilled with incidents of violence of a most brutal sort: a river would issue up the body of a civil rights worker; dynamite would splinter a church in the night; a Negro leader's home would get bombed; and occasionally, the press would be rewarded with a running news story, such as the murder by sniper fire of Mississippi NAACP leader Medgar Evers, in June 1963.

The unpredictability of this cycle of violence hooked the national media on a gothic civil rights drama that they unfolded on the evening news in the living rooms of America. Ambitious young journalists went south to make their careers, much as their predecessors had covered World War II, and as their successors would cover the Vietnam War and, later, the Watergate scandal that brought down President Richard M. Nixon.

In their fight against desegregation, the governors of Alabama, Georgia, and Mississippi rarely failed to put on a good show. A favorite was George Wallace, the "Bantam Rooster," who challenged the White House on desegregation by physically standing in a doorway to block U.S. marshals from escorting two black students to the University of Alabama. Headlines also emanated from the humorless knights of the Ku Klux Klan, who marched downtown in their bed ticks, by day, and worked the night with their dynamite, faggots, and shotguns.

At the center of media attention, of course, were the Negroes on the march for their civil rights. As bemoaned as they were bemused, these preacher-led proletarians endured police clubbing, high-powered water hoses, attacks by police dogs, and mass arrests in overcrowded jails. Faced with such police brutality, they were trained to eschew rage and wear acquiescence like a badge of courage. "We will overcome your ability to hate with our ability to love," King had promised. And his nonviolent army went forth and endured such violence as the whites served up.

As the Northern journalists made their rounds with requisite disinterestedness, they couldn't help being stirred by the heroic suffering of the Southern Negroes, the lay of the gentle landscape, and the relentless beauty of the freedom hymns rolling in a cadence so sweet and mournful that they rocked the very cradle of the coldest heart of the most irreligious reporter on the civil rights story.

Meanwhile, the Kennedy administration reached out increasingly to the Southern Christian Leadership Conference (SCLC) in an effort to maintain the peace and influence its confrontational leader. Within the civil rights movement itself, however, the winds were beginning to kick up against Reverend King. Young Turk student leaders were beginning to challenge the primacy of the protest impresario they had taken to calling "De Lawd."

King himself had emerged as a young minister during the Eisenhower years as a challenge to the old order. He was finally expelled from the prestigious National Baptist Convention in 1961 over the issue of civil disobedience. Along with Reverend Gardiner C. Taylor and other reformers within the established order of black Baptists, King helped form the Progressive National Baptist Convention, which worked to reform the Jim Crow laws. Now, on the secular front, King found himself being challenged more and more from within the movement over the efficacy of nonviolent resistance. The more radical of the college students working to register black voters throughout the Deep South were running short of patience. Black volunteers from such campuses as Howard University, where Malcolm had spoken on October 30, 1961, were especially growing weary of bearing up nonviolently under the brutal crackdown by Southern white sheriffs.

As this lightning flashed inside the movement, Malcolm continued to roll his thunder outside. Writer Alex Haley, soon to become the coauthor of Malcolm's *Autobiography,* pitted the Muslims squarely against the civil rights movement in his introduction to a long interview with Malcolm in the May 1963 edition of *Playboy* magazine.

"Today, [civil rights protesters] face opposition from not one but two inimical exponents of racism and segregation," Haley wrote, "the White Supremacists and the Black Muslims." The Muslims, he continued, "have grown into a dedicated, disciplined nationwide movement which runs its own schools, publishes its own newspaper, owns stores and restaurants in four major cities, buys broadcast time on 50 radio stations throughout the country, stages mass rallies attended by partisan crowds of 10,000 and more, and maintains its own police force of judo-trained athletes called the Fruit of Islam."[12]

As Haley saw it, the exposure of Black Muslims to the outside world had increased immeasurably thanks to Malcolm. Gone were the days when the young ex-convict lived a whirlwind life as a fanatic proselytizer within a tight cocoon of fellow ministers, captains, lieutenants, converts, and the ruling circles of the Nation of Islam. The stepped-up contact included publicized debates in the national media and exchanges with tough outside critics in the churches, universities, and the civil rights movement, including indirect skirmishes with King.

The rise of the Muslims, and Malcolm especially, made Reverend King all the more appealing to the white, mainstream power brokers. This point was not lost on Malcolm. Celebrity tours on campus had not won over the Negro masses. Although the fiery national spokesman radiated with black youth, even they tended to dismiss the Black Muslims as too scary, with their alien, anti-Christian religion, their intimidating Fruit of Islam guards, and the mystic Elijah Muhammad in Chicago. Despite this drag on the sect, Malcolm continued to fish for converts on his promotional national tours. His sales pitch would soar, then lose altitude when he reminded black listeners that he spoke not for himself—but for the so-called Messenger of Allah.

The growing popularity of King did not concern his fellow Georgian, Elijah Muhammad. After three decades in the vineyards, the Messenger had amassed impressive wealth, thanks largely to Malcolm, and was spending more of his time away from his opulent Chicago headquarters. He had envisioned his sect only as a vanguard religion among blacks, with no grand ambition for popular appeal across racial lines, and certainly not with the media.

The expansionist vision of the protégé had always been greater than that of his mentor. And, at thirty-seven, Malcolm had steadily outgrown his narrow organization. Television was the new medium-cool means of communicating with a national audience. And the charismatic minister was as skillful at exploiting it on the streets as President Kennedy was on the campaign trail. Once he had persuaded the Messenger to cooperate with *The Hate That Hate Produced*, the 1959 TV documentary, Malcolm seldom passed up an invitation for a TV interview. Since then, he had dramatically increased the Muslims' enrollment, reach, influence, and riches, beyond the highest aspirations of its national leadership in Chicago.

Still, while making his daily rounds, Malcolm bristled at the mounting, unfavorable media criticism of the Muslims, as well as praise for the relative effectiveness of King's nonviolent movement. At one level, Malcolm resented media insistence that there be but one national black leader of consequence; nevertheless, he invested in this widespread notion and worked to put Elijah Muhammad atop the heap.

In order to lead black America, Malcolm felt that the Muslims must seize the portfolio for the black masses and dominate the national Negro agenda. This external quest was the substance of one of his chief goals during the early part of 1963. At the internal—and increasingly dangerous—level, Malcolm sought to shake up the Chicago hierarchy of the Nation of Islam. His earnest intention was not to supplant the leadership but rather to make the Messenger proud by imbuing the temples of Chicago and Detroit with the spartan fires he had loosed on the East Coast from his base in Harlem.

As noted earlier, the Messenger purposely kept Malcolm from preaching in the first six charter temples that he had personally established, starting in the 1930s, with older pioneers. These temples, mostly in the Midwest, were jealously guarded against the more intense approach that Malcolm was using to wake the "dead" in the East.[13] It did not help that Malcolm bragged to his brother Philbert, who snitched to the Messenger, that his temples had outgrown those early six that the Messenger chartered and designated by numbers. Eager to "inject some life"[14] into the Chicago headquarters, Malcolm finally got permission to spend a month there during the Messenger's stay in Arizona.

His aggressive style stirred a nest of opposition among the sons of Elijah Muhammad and their powerful allies at Chicago headquarters. No matter how much the national spokesman paid homage to the Honorable Elijah Muhammad, Malcolm's fiery style attracted more national attention to himself at the expense of his retiring, inarticulate leader. This did not please the blood relatives of Muhammad, who fancied themselves the "Royal Family."

As long as the Messenger gave Malcolm his blessings, stability was maintained. However, Elijah Muhammad had a respiratory ailment, which was pulling him more and more now to the dry heat of Phoenix. In his absence, the Royal Family began whispering about succession—and worrying about the possibility of Malcolm's leap-frogging blood relatives.

Malcolm's interview in *Playboy* did not help matters, even though he had gotten the Messenger's permission to participate. In his introduction, Haley wrote of Malcolm: "The ambitious young man rose swiftly to become the Messenger's most ardent and erudite disciple, and today wields all but absolute authority over the movement and its membership as Muhammad's business manager, trouble shooter, prime minister and heir apparent."[15]

Despite Malcolm's efforts to give Muhammad the glory, the *Playboy* piece set Muslims' tongues wagging about the efficacy of his association with a "skin magazine" and the real motives and ambitions of the national spokesman. Haley's "heir apparent" reference confirmed the worst suspicions—and brought out the daggers. Thus, in Malcolm's campaign for the hearts and minds of Negroes across the country, this second front in Chicago would force him to direct more resources toward stabilizing his position from within.

Word of the looming power struggle within the NOI hierarchy did not quickly reach the membership beyond Chicago or the media. The FBI, however, had sources inside the headquarters, and listened in via telephone tapping as well. Increasingly, the Bureau covertly moved to stir dissension in an attempt to weaken the group from within.[16] Hoover's goals were to divide the Muslim leadership, limit Malcolm's influence, and ensure that the Muslims remained at war with King and the civil rights movement.

Malcolm informed his brother Wilfred, his closest confidant, that he had dangerously underestimated the opposition against him at Chicago headquarters. Now he worked furiously to find an "antidote" for what he increasingly took to be a poison spreading against him within the hierarchy of the Muslim leadership.[17]

Like his peripatetic Christian rival, Malcolm kept up a grinding schedule, with regular services at home mosques and irregular ones on the road. While presiding over the dozen Northeast regional temples, he regularly looked in on Chicago headquarters, with periodic stops to see the Messenger in Phoenix, all while jockeying with the "devils" on radio and TV, and lecturing on college campuses, at civil gatherings, and even in Baptist churches.

During Malcolm's swing through New England in the spring of 1963, any mention of the King juggernaut moved him to return a burst of fire. On his June 4 stop in Massachusetts, for example, he pointedly declared King's "foolish" nonviolent movement in the South a failure. "Negroes are in worse condition now than they were because the line is more tightly drawn," he said in a taped interview on WGBH, a Cambridge educational TV channel. "King is the best weapon that the white man, who wants to brutalize Negroes, has ever gotten in this country. . . . You're not supposed to fight or you're not supposed to defend yourself."[18]

Malcolm continued, "White people follow King, white people pay King, white people subsidize King, white people support King. . . . The masses of black people don't support Martin Luther King. . . . The majority of black people in this country are more inclined in the direction of the Honorable Elijah Muhammad."[19]

Publicly holding to the faith, Malcolm X persisted in casting his

Muslim nets in the heart of the ghetto, a lake stocked with fish more inclined toward the Christian lures of Dr. King. Over generations, Baptist fundamentalism had conditioned Negroes, many of them up from Georgia, Florida, and Alabama, to focus their attention on the hereafter. Here-and-now social movements usually found these Negroes taking their lead from their ministers who, north and south, favored their fellow Baptist prophet of nonviolence.

As Malcolm grew more to personify the Black Muslims, his notoriety fed the already entrenched envy among rival ministers and the so-called Royal Family. As if there could be but one black leader, the national media regularly contrasted Malcolm the black separatist with King the integrationist—leaving no doubt that they favored the nonviolent Southern Negro preacher.

The King comparison hung like cloud cover over Hartford, Connecticut, on the eve of Malcolm's June 5 lecture at Bushnell Memorial Hall. Amid the blizzard of his campus lectures across the nation in the spring of 1963, this one brought Malcolm back to the city where, eight years earlier, he had started his very first temple from scratch.

Once again, it was a pivotal time in his Muslim ministry.

Coincidentally, Reverend Martin Luther King Jr. had appeared in Hartford seven months earlier, on October 28, 1962, along with legendary gospel singer Mahalia Jackson. The civil rights leader attracted a massive crowd, according to press reports, "in behalf of two Negro churches burned in Georgia"[20]—2,500 people "overflowed" the house.[21] However, when Malcolm's appearance was announced in the same newspaper, the conservative *Hartford Times*, in June 1963, the seating capacity of the hall had been inflated by one-third: the *Times* asked, "Will the audience [Malcolm X] draws at the 3,300-seat Bushnell Memorial tonight be a fair measure of the strength of his movement?" It also suggested that Negroes stay away from the Malcolm lecture.[22] The Negroes of the Insurance Capital thus were primed to make a choice.

During an afternoon press conference before his lecture in Hartford, a wary Malcolm sensed a media trap. Knowing the habits of the press, Malcolm expected that reporters would try to push him into overestimating the attendance his lecture would draw. He sidestepped the temptation, telling newsmen wryly that if he "failed to outdraw the Reverend Martin Luther King," it would be due to poor press coverage.[23] Malcolm noticed that the atmosphere of the hourlong press conference was more intense than he expected, and the locals, although milder than the New York press, were tougher than usual. Rising to the occasion, he alternately charmed the journalists with his broad, warm smile and showed them his shark teeth.

"One should be nice," he deadpanned at one point, "to a man who is being shot at sunrise."[24]

It was just such a fate, of course, that Elijah Muhammad had predicted for all whites, whose time in North America, he preached, had run out in 1914 and would cease absolutely by 1970.[25] Malcolm had a way of disparaging whites in the vilest manner and yet not provoking individual reporters into taking it personally. He was effective at assuaging the feelings of white reporters in attendance—in fact, some journalists noted in their stories that the fire-breathing national spokesman for the Black Muslims had shown tolerance "of his white interviewers." The *Hartford Times* reporter wrote that the minister was "polite, urbane, even witty with the unfortunate victims of the [black man's] inescapable revolution."[26] As elsewhere, the media in Hartford were alternately repelled and attracted by Malcolm, like so many tourists gazing upon a king cobra.

Just prior to the lecture, Malcolm discussed the King factor in more measured tones while huddling with his local Muslim minister,

Thomas J. X, as well as with Abdel Krim X of the New Haven mosque. Malcolm scoffed at the *Times*'s embrace of his nonviolent rival and hinted that he would blast King in his speech that evening as a patsy for "white liberals."

Malcolm's topic that Wednesday night was "God's Judgment of America and the Only Solution to the Race Problem," a speech he had been polishing for some four months, since January 23, when he had appeared at Michigan State University in East Lansing, his onetime home.[27] Several of his childhood classmates had attended Malcolm's homecoming lecture, getting a glimpse of him for the first time since he had headed off as a teenager to Boston and the fast lane. His classmates had not known what to expect. These white Midwesterners were curious but not inclined to believe the more menacing facets of Malcolm's ferocious national image. One white classmate, Loretta Jones Bergen, from nearby Mason, left the hall in East Lansing that night puzzling over the disparity between the fierce orator at the podium and her gentle friend Harpy, the eighth-grade president.[28]

As with all his appearances before non-Muslim audiences, Malcolm had read up-to-the-minute reporting on local news, especially racial matters. While awaiting his cue to mount the stage, he clutched a section of that afternoon's *Hartford Times* that he had red-penciled for his opening remarks. The news story once again billed his appearance as something of a popularity contest between himself and the Reverend King. The separate editorial suggested that local Negroes, by boycotting Malcolm's lecture, should vote with their feet against the Muslims' "idea of apartheid translated from South Africa to America."[29]

Comparing Muhammad's vision of a separate black state with the South African apartheid system always frayed a nerve. Malcolm abhorred the brutal white racist regime, which he had so painfully studied while an inmate in Massachusetts prisons. During a heated debate the previous year, the civil rights leader Bayard Rustin cited a similar equation in the *Chicago Daily News*, which immediately had Malcolm snapping angrily at Rustin and the local newspaper.

> We don't feel that the *Daily News* is qualified to classify us as anything. . . . The people of South Africa left Europe and went into Africa, a continent which is not theirs and took it over from the black people. They are now there advocating white supremacy, which is a false doctrine. They are advocating black inferiority, which is another false doctrine. . . . If America gave the black man half of the country, they wouldn't be giving us anything. They worked our mothers and fathers 310 years with no pay.[30]

Now, in June 1963 in Hartford, the "apartheid" charge from the local paper had keyed up the spokesman for the Muslims for another hostile night on the hustings. Malcolm loped to the platform in the half-filled hall. He raised the *Times* aloft and straightaway began to pummel the white media for promoting the "nonviolent" King as a saint among blacks, while he himself was denounced as a "pariah." He cited the "popularity" issue and sketched the white press as a partisan force driving the fainthearted into the camp of his chief rival. He would, in time, get back to Dr. King, and his prepared remarks, but first Malcolm wanted to cut the legs from under the media so he could talk over their heads to the Negroes in the hall.*

Thundering against the more conservative *Hartford Times* in particular, Malcolm X asked rhetorically, "How can this white newspaper print the truth about black people when they don't employ a single

---

* Les Payne attended Malcolm X's lecture at Bushnell Memorial Hall on June 5, 1963.

Negro reporter on their staff?" Malcolm's query floated around the hall like a balloon sputtering helium. All Hartford knew the answer, although, no one—black or white—had dared pose the question. So it fell to the invited guest to surprise and shame the local folks. It was as if a stranger had pointed out a corpse in the closet that family members had agreed not to talk about. This was also the way many of Malcolm's revelations went on weightier issues bearing on the history of race relations. In the wake of his campus stops, professors were peppered with a battery of fresh questions about race, usually from aroused students, mostly Negroes, who had been shown their voice. Racism in the media was only the first—and, perhaps, the least troubling—of the revelations about racial unfairness that Malcolm had in store for his audience.

Yet when he posed the question, the audience erupted in applause, unaccustomed to such bold attacks on the venerable, albeit lily-white *Hartford Times.*

Neither the *Times,* an afternoon daily, nor the morning *Hartford Courant,* the nation's oldest daily newspaper (founded in 1764), had ever employed a black reporter. With 99 percent of the almost 1750 daily newspapers in the United States employing no black reporters, Malcolm knew that his charge against the *Hartford Times* had legs nationally. In his 1969 book *The Kingdom and the Power,* about the august *New York Times,* Gay Talese wrote that any blacks allowed on the editorial floor in the 1960s were most likely to be elevator operators.[31]

There was a sense in the auditorium that some, especially the mixed-race groups, who had entered the hall as observers from a neutral zone, were at risk of being pulled into the fray. Malcolm had that way of engaging an audience, and he was in fine form in a city with its own Black Muslim mosque, Temple No. 14. Malcolm continued storming against the *Hartford Times* as part of the "hypocritical" white media unworthy of sitting in judgment on any issue affecting black people. He rebuked that day's editorial, which had stated: "Other leaders among Negroes preach the Christian ethic of charity, they are more numerous and, so far, much more effective. . . . Chief among the majority is the Reverend Martin Luther King."

The initial pounding of the media was a tactic Malcolm employed increasingly in lectures away from New York. Such sorties seldom failed to bring the mixed audiences roaring to their feet. In media markets with slim black staffing, Malcolm would often dismiss the half dozen Negro journalists with major big-city dailies, such as *The New York Times*, and the three weekly newsmagazines, as "sellouts" under the lash of their white bosses. Almost every Negro interviewer got Malcolm's dismissive sign-off: "They're not going to let you print that."[32]

The few Negro reporters in mainstream daily journalism, when allowing themselves a preference, tilted toward Reverend King. Almost to the man they considered the Nation of Islam, and Malcolm X, an embarrassment to the race. Ted Jones, then a reporter for *The New York Times*, recalled that covering the Muslims was tough and forbidding duty. In addition to Malcolm rubbing their nerves raw, the Negro reporters covering the Muslims attracted dubious attention from their bosses and colleagues in the city room, and the beat seemed to hobble a black reporter's potential rise through the ranks.[33]

In polishing his attack against the white media, Malcolm developed the ironic knack of exhibiting a mainstream journal to buttress a point while attacking its credibility. During the Michigan State speech the previous winter, for example, he used *Time* magazine to promote his point that Islam was spreading rapidly:

Then *Time* magazine, heaven forbid I should mention that magazine [wild laughter], but *Time* magazine mentioned it, two weeks ago, that Islam is sweeping throughout the black people of Africa . . . it is sweeping throughout the black people right here in America. Only the one who's teaching it here in America is the Honorable Elijah Muhammad. He is the one who is spreading the religion of Islam among the slaves, ex-slaves, here in America.[34]

Wherever he was speaking, Malcolm got most of Muhammad's luggage through customs, including the full shipment of the "blue-eyed devil" contraband. "In 1963," he wrote in his *Autobiography*, "I was trying to cope with the white newspaper, radio, and television reporters who were determined to defeat Mr. Muhammad's teachings. I developed a mental image of reporters as human ferrets— steadily sniffing, darting, probing for some way to trick me, somehow to corner me in our interview exchanges."[35]

In Hartford that day, he reproached white liberals for "throwing crumbs to the bourgeois Negro," and reproved "moderate leaders like Martin Luther King for 'extracting tokens from the white man.'"[36] The King blast set press pencils scurrying.

The shadow of the Atlanta minister was extending now more and more across Malcolm's trail. In addition to spring protests in Danville, Virginia, and Albany, Georgia, King was focusing world attention on the Jim Crow South by dint of the starkly brutal images of unarmed young Negroes facing guns, police truncheons, dogs, and the high-pressure water hoses of fire departments. For example, in a series of events that would force President Kennedy to stand up for civil rights, Eugene "Bull" Connor, who ran the Birmingham, Alabama, police and fire departments, instructed his men to club Negroes under media spotlights before yielding the stage to an even more pugnacious defender of Alabama white supremacy, Governor George Wallace.

That June night at Bushnell Hall, Malcolm attracted a mainly non-Muslim, black and white crowd of adult Hartford residents, the socially concerned and progressive college students, and their professors from the region. Following his extemporaneous opening sorties against the media, he eased into his prepared remarks about Elijah Muhammad's tough remedies for the nation's race problem.

Categorically rejecting Christianity and any possibility of white morality and goodwill, Malcolm urged Negroes to strike out to their own territory. This Muslim prescription coincided more with the legacy of his parents' devotion to Marcus Garvey than to Jesus of Nazareth. In seeking to alleviate black children's growing sense of hopelessness and inferiority, Malcolm, unlike King, would no more have appealed to white "Christian and Jewish brothers" than he would have appealed to the Corinthians.

With a star and crescent, a symbol of Islam, pinned to the left lapel of his light gray suit, Malcolm spared no opportunity to highlight his differences with black Christians, especially ministers. "There is a strong anticlericalism among blacks," commented Reverend Gardiner Taylor, a Brooklyn pastor and a close friend of Reverend King, years after Malcolm's death. "There is a tendency even within the church for blacks to turn away from strong leaders. So Malcolm kind of [took advantage of] that for a time."[37]

In Malcolm's scathing view, the Reverend-Doctor Negro ministers were leisure-time lifers conning hardworking marks out of their pooled disposable income in order to meet their monthly notes for mortgages and Cadillacs. This barrage loosed a rustle of giggles among the churchgoers scattered in the Bushnell audience.

Malcolm held to this standard attack on Baptist preachers, despite the fact that the Bushnell event was cosponsored by a local church group headed by the Reverend James Earley, a Baptist minister who had recently moved to New York. Safely en route out of town, the reverend had conceived of the event as a moneymaker in which Muslims and he would go 60-40 on the $500 rental fee for the hall.

They would split the cost for advertising and insurance, charge $1.50 admission, and divvy up the profits 50-50. Instead, from his home in Phoenix, Elijah Muhammad instructed his Hartford mosque, Temple No. 14, to finance the advertising and pay Reverend Earley whatever he "puts into the meeting." By Muhammad's strict orders, no admission fee was to be charged. Instead, the Muslims, as was their custom, would pass around baskets for donations.

FBI phone taps of Elijah Muhammad's conversation were reduced to this notation on the meeting for the Bureau's Phoenix office files: "ELIJAH said he was against charging the people [of Hartford] to hear the truth."[38]

Accordingly, the public entered with no cover charge to hear a choir of ten-year-olds open the program, singing a medley of decidedly Negro spirituals for the Muslim minister. Although he would hold to the 50-50 split, Malcolm X despaired of Reverend Earley as promoter and scowled at the religious singers. The preliminaries were more apt for Reverend King than for the austere minister from an Islamic religion, albeit bastardized, that shunned music altogether.

The podium styles of Reverend King and Malcolm X, according to observers who attended each man's appearance in Hartford that year, were as different as their religions, birthrights, and body types. Malcolm approached the podium like a lean sprinter to his blocks. King, true to his surprising bulk, had ambled on months earlier as a priest escorting a condemned man to the gallows. Both men were masters of their stagecraft. Each created about him an air of podium expectancy, a trick of all the great orators. Hitler, it is said, would sometimes stand transfixed before his notes a full three minutes in silence before uttering a single sound.

King hadn't milked the silence, but in winding his horn, he took his own sweet, down-home Georgia time. With his text out of sight, he steadied his scanning, hooded eyes on the Bushnell audience. He then rocked his swept back head deliberately as he dropped in the quotes from Emerson, Hegel, Tillich, Paine, Mills, Locke, and an "old man I met once from Al-la-bam-maaa." Researchers would later document King's unfortunate habit as an author of borrowing lavishly, often without attribution, from the texts of less publicly known writers and scholars. However, at the Bushnell podium he seemed to have given each major contributor his due.

Unlike Malcolm's voice, King's was a Southern baritone rasped by country preaching, lacquered by Western philosophers, and disciplined by the classroom homiletics of a New England PhD program. There was something in King of the Oxford don but a much stronger trace of the preacher. He had long admired, and borrowed from, the style of black preachers, such as the legendary C. L. Franklin of Detroit, the father of singer Aretha Franklin. However, while King admired the gusto of folk preachers, his education and training as a preacher—and, most especially, his hopelessly mainstream father, Reverend King Sr.—would not permit him to whoop and heave in a grand manner. The decibel level was moderate, and the son acquiesced by limiting it further to project a sense of control and sophistication.

King looked leaner at the podium than he was. Likewise, Malcolm, who stood as erect as a Marine colonel, appeared even taller than his six-feet-three-inch frame. His voice was as raw as backwoods bourbon, and when uncorked, it was an instrument of stunning passion. His distinctive cadence, which he drilled into his ministers, had been conditioned by prison debate, and it rolled as unpredictably as mercury. Punctuated by slashing gestures and a wicked smile, the husky voice had all the range of a stage actor's: it could roar and bellow, then suddenly flutter and coo. As orators, both ministers could bring an audience as quickly to its feet as they could rouse it to its senses. As King was the preacher gone bookish, Malcolm was the hustler turned rebel.

By all outward appearances, Hartford, with its striving Negroes up from the South, was King territory. The Baptist minister, although not exactly a darling of the Kennedy administration, was receiving solid liberal support around the country and had made several fund-raising visits to the Insurance Capital, with good results. Andrew Young, a key aide who had attended Hartford Theological Seminary, had hooked up the business connections, while King's SCLC had also worked with union officials, pacifists, and organized black foot soldiers through local Baptist ministers such as the Reverend Richard C. Battles, of Mt. Olive, and Reverend Robert Moody, of Shiloh.

So it was to the cheering delight of some, and the distress of others in the Hartford audience, that Malcolm flogged Christianity up hill and down dale during his two hours on stage. Broadening his attack, he dismissed organized church enterprises as an insidious confidence game with a sad history of duping poor people the world over. He blistered high-living clergy for dressing in splendor while their parishioners struggled to put pork chops and collard greens on the table. The only edifices Negroes upgraded after buying from whites fleeing their community, he said, were ghetto churches that, instead, should be converted into centers for developing black economic power.

Malcolm spared Elijah Muhammad this criticism publicly— even though it had seeped into his mind that his Messenger had yielded to this temptation of the clergy. The spartan Malcolm could no longer suppress the realization that, like the Christian ministers he attacked, Muhammad and his Royal Family engaged in conspicuous consumption while presiding over a struggling, low-income, working-class flock.

Leaning into the Bushnell podium, and occasionally resting his jaw on the tripod of his left thumb and first two fingers, Malcolm launched into another favorite Muslim topic that might undercut his integration-prone rival: miscegenation. Increasingly now, he was hearing back from celebrity associates, especially friends of those he singled out as offenders with white spouses. Slashing with both edges of the knife, Malcolm sought to isolate these celebrities, many of whom had marched with King, and remove them as competitors and role models for potential supporters among the black middle class. He also sought to impugn their motives in the eyes of whites who used them as buffers and mouthpieces. The integration they sought, he said, led ultimately, if not singularly, to the bedroom. Away from the podium, he had encountered mixed-marriage surprises.

There was, for example, J. A. Rogers, the black nationalist author whom Malcolm praised highly and recommended widely, and who was credited in the *Autobiography* for opening Malcolm's eyes about "race mixing before Christ's time" in his three volumes *Sex and Race*.[39] During an unannounced visit to Rogers's cramped Harlem apartment on a steamy summer day, Malcolm was startled when, in the midst of a running conversation, the wife of his host, gasping for air, literally stumbled out of her hiding place in the closet. Later that night, Malcolm regaled his own wife, Betty, with a reenactment of this incident. Laughing uncontrollably, he detailed the stifling discomfort Rogers had put his wife through to conceal from Malcolm the fact that he, the famed black nationalist hero, was indeed married to a white woman.

By seeking to discredit such celebrities with the mixed-marriage charge, the Black Muslims seemed to march a few locked steps with Southern white bigots, including the Ku Klux Klan. This small parcel of common ground, together with the Muslims' general ideology of self-help and separation, also provided Elijah Muhammad an opportunity to break bread with the likes of American Nazi Party founder George Lincoln Rockwell, and reportedly even the far right-wing Texas oil billionaire H. L. Hunt. Just as Marcus Garvey saw no contradiction in meeting with the KKK in 1922, Elijah Muhammad sought to establish relations with hard-core, right-wing forces.

But now, two and a half years after Malcolm, at the Messenger's command, had himself sat down with the Klan in Atlanta, the national spokesman harbored deep, though suppressed, reservations about the Messenger's judgment and social instincts. Nevertheless, Malcolm, the faithful servant, continued to preach publicly hard and engagingly against miscegenation, although increasingly with private qualms.

Reverend King, vulnerable on this issue with both the Klan and Muslim listeners, usually sidestepped this potentially explosive component of his drive for integration. For Malcolm X, however, miscegenation was a face card some considered poisonous, so he didn't hesitate to play it for all it was worth in advancing Elijah Muhammad's call for black unity. He spiked his talk with attacks on such celebrities as Eartha Kitt, Ralph Bunche, and Harry Belafonte, and his comedic routine was as polished as a nightclub act.

Segueing to his miscegenation riff in his Hartford speech, Malcolm lapsed into his slick hustler voice wise to every secret lust. It was the voice that had served him so well on the streets of Harlem in the 1940s. He had specialized in steering white men to black prostitutes and black men to white hookers. Drawing on this experience, he primed the audience for his miscegenation attack on civil rights leaders. "Now these Negroes will tell you that they don't want your white women," he said, pausing for effect, ". . . but I know 'em." The hall shivered uneasily, then fluttered openly with snickers.[40]

Well versed on current events of New England, Malcolm X punctuated his address with witty slashes at local racial problems and capital city politicians. He drew sustained cheers, some even standing to clap, when he acidly contrasted Connecticut governor John Dempsey with Alabama's George Wallace. Seizing upon Dempsey's recent criticism of Wallace's public opposition to desegregation of Alabama public facilities, Malcolm dismissed the duo as an example of the mule-headedness of the South and the deception of the North. In his *Autobiography*, he wrote that as a "creation" of the Northern white man's attitude toward Negroes, his own life "mirrors this [Northern] hypocrisy." He would redraw a more pragmatic Mason-Dixon line, declaring, "The South to blacks means south of Canada."

With his right index finger darting over the podium, he stabbed at Governor Dempsey as a Northern liberal hypocrite: "How can the fox point the finger at the wolf?" [42] Venerable Bushnell Hall, built in 1930 as a home for the Hartford Symphony Orchestra and a show-case for opera and easy-listening pop singers, such as Perry Como and Johnny Mathis, had never seen its rafters shaken with anything so impolitic and sacrilegious.

Waging antiestablishment attacks on a half dozen targets, with an onslaught of metaphors, Malcolm stirred the college students in the audience as only the most legendary of their professors could have done. His tumbling of America's racial furniture was as shock-ing to them as those "Age of Reason" lectures were to freshmen fun-damentalists. Ranging over a vast landscape, Malcolm called into question the most entrenched of racial beliefs, some not even con-sciously acknowledged by many in the mainstream audience.

One intense white student in the audience, however, had indeed thought it all through. Brian Steinberg, a senior political science major at the University of Connecticut, was as serious a student of Marxist-Leninism as his land-grant, Yankee Conference college would allow. On a campus of racial insularity, where fewer than 1 per-cent of the students were Negroes, Steinberg dated a black coed from Oberlin College and played saxophone in his father's racially mixed rock 'n' roll band, the Deadbeats, known throughout New England. He had also trucked with left-wing radicals, having attended an international Socialist youth conference in Helsinki, Finland.

History and political science professors dreaded seeing Stein-berg's frame rise up on thin legs to question them as a prosecutor might cross-examine a hostile and insufficiently prepared witness. One professor would get so exasperated that he would rip off his eyeglasses and shake them at Steinberg. Another teacher, teary eyed on one occasion, heaved an eraser at him. As insurance against retaliation for his classroom heresy, especially in his political science major, the honors student took to writing two examination blue books, one with proper answers to the test questions, a second set with his own dissenting views.[42] Scorned behind his back as the "house commie," Steinberg was the roommate of a senior from Hartford whom housemates disparaged as a closet Black Muslim.*

The Cuban missile crisis of October 1962 had created a special challenge for Steinberg. The overwhelming majority of the students supported President Kennedy and viewed Premier Castro as a dangerous stooge of Moscow. Even with Nikita Khrushchev's decision to place Soviet missiles capable of carrying nuclear warheads in Cuba, Steinberg, as always, held to the party line as the atmosphere grew sullen, intolerant, and very dangerous.

With the threat of nuclear war in the air, anxious students marched around campus bonfires, phoned home, waxed patriotic in support of the U.S. blockade, and, of course, drank kegs of beer far into the night. At the peak of the crisis, Steinberg told all who would listen that Castro needed the missiles, nuclear tips and all, to defend against a United States angry over his government's treatment of the money interests of United Fruit and other avaricious U.S. corporations in Havana.

Shaking their heads in amazement after such night sessions with Steinberg, students wandered away from his room primed for the FBI agents who, unbeknown to him, were already investigating his campus activities. Students were paid to nose around Brian and his roommate, a cadet major in the campus ROTC, who although totally uninterested in Marxism, was zealous in his opposition to racism on campus and elsewhere.

---

* That roommate was the author, Les Payne.

Two FBI agents stopped by the office of Homer Babbidge, the university president, to inquire about the two roommates' leadership of the Northern Student Movement, a civil rights group that among other things tutored inner-city students and sent care packages and voter-registration volunteers to the South. The agents pressed Babbidge about the appearance on campus of a Communist Party USA member the group had invited to its campus program commemorating the centennial of the Emancipation Proclamation. Noting that the campus civil rights group had also invited representatives from the NAACP, CORE, and the Black Muslims, President Babbidge stood by the First Amendment in facing down the agents of J. Edgar Hoover.

Like most campus radicals, Steinberg was partial to Dr. King's biracial social activism. The white student and his Negro roommate waged heated debates on the competing approaches of King and Malcolm X to the race question. The roommate noted the contradiction between Steinberg's insistence on black nonviolence and his vigorous support not only for the nuclear arming of Cuba, but also for the rumble of Soviet tanks occupying East Berlin.

The two roommates had gone early to Malcolm's Bushnell lecture, primed and fully prepared to put the minister through a rough evening. With no stomach for racial sectarianism, Steinberg opposed the Muslims' exclusionary approach and dismissed many of their programs as so much hocus-pocus. His Negro roommate held grave and embarrassing reservations about the Muslim cult, its Yacub myth, the "blue-eyed devil" slur, and, most especially, its inarticulate Chicago leader in the bejeweled fez.

An hour into Malcolm's lecture, a restless Steinberg could not measure the bumpkin he expected. Malcolm's disarming display of wit, intellect, and agitprop had persuaded Steinberg to reevaluate the spokesman, if not the Muslims themselves. Steinberg had never witnessed such a formidable defense of what scholars, and whites of all stations, took to be patently indefensible. Fully expecting a religious fanatic, Steinberg found instead a facile polemicist whose rhetoric and reasoning reduced him to stroking his Lenin-like goatee, rocking attentively, laughing, and occasionally even nodding in agreement.[43]

When the question period finally arrived, Steinberg had been drained of his contempt for Malcolm. The political science major thought he had picked up signs not of a simple separatist but of a far more complicated black nationalist—if not a revolutionary. Still, putting on his stern classroom face, he gathered himself to hammer away at the heart of the message and at the Messenger, in absentia. As always with mixed groups, Malcolm X preferred questions from whites, seeking in the process to preserve as well as possible the illusion of black solidarity. The early questions, some from whites seemingly shell-shocked by his black boldness, pricked at the *petit* tenets of the Muslim doctrine.

One local white college student reacted sharply to Malcolm's biblical assertion that it would soon be "harvest time" when the goats, which he implied were whites, would be led to the slaughter. Accordingly, Malcolm had stressed the impracticality of "woolly haired sheep [blacks] lying down with straight haired goats."[44] How could Malcolm X, the student asked, speak so bluntly about blacks as sheep and whites as goats when his light complexion clearly indicated that he himself had mixed blood? Flashing that impish smile, the minister canted his head, ran his right hand slowly over his close-cropped hair and said, "I still have a lot of sheep in me."[45]

Finally, Steinberg rose and proceeded to tell, as much as ask, his question. Marxist in content, his attack had been shaped by a conversation the student had with James E. Jackson, the editor of the *Daily Worker* and a high-ranking member of the Communist Party USA. Given what Malcolm had described as the "white devil's" nature, Steinberg asked how the Black Muslim could reasonably expect to be given any worthwhile land to form a separate state without first going to war—a war that, he implied, Negroes could not possibly win. The glibness had gone out of the minister by this time. He ran through his nonanswer more now by rote than an attempt to convince logically.[46]

A black student[*] rose and feebly asked that if, by some miracle, the federal government could be pressured to grant Negroes a separate state, wouldn't the granted lands be as inhabitable as those the Indians got from the white man under treaty? He had in mind the Hopi reservation near the lip of the Grand Canyon, but he pinched off the details of his scribbled question.

Both questions Malcolm X had heard before, but, unbeknown to the Hartford audience—and even his closest disciples—the national spokesman had lost the blind faith he once had in Elijah Muhammad's call for a "separate state." This unraveling was part of a much larger eruption that had moved Malcolm to question other key social, religious, and moral tenets of the nation of Islam—and its leader, Elijah Muhammad.

———

A week after Malcolm's Bushnell appearance, Governor George Wallace made his historic stand in the doorway of the University of Alabama on June 11, 1963, to prevent Negro students from registering under federal court order. President Kennedy had introduced civil rights legislation to Congress and had thrown his full weight behind it with a deeply moving, televised Oval Office address. The president told the nation:

> It ought to be possible . . . for American students of any color to attend any public institution they select without having to be backed up by troops.

---

* Les Payne, again.

It ought to be possible for American consumers of any color to receive equal service in places of public accommodation, such as hotels and restaurants and theaters and retail stores, without being forced to resort to demonstrations in the street, and it ought to be possible for American citizens of any color to register and to vote in a free election without interference or fear of reprisal.

It ought to be possible, in short, for every American to enjoy the privileges of being American without regard to his race or his color. . . .

The fires of frustration and discord are burning in every city, North and South, where legal remedies are not at hand. . . .

A great change is at hand, and our task, our obligation, is to make that revolution, that change, peaceful and constructive for all.[47]

Prodding the White House by telephone, in letters, and through news coverage on the front page of *The New York Times*, Reverend King came on as a nonviolent knight, leading a desperate struggle against the entrenched fire dragons of racial segregation.

From the Northern ramparts, Malcolm had managed, by the strength of Muhammad's organization and the force of his own oratory, to project the Muslims as a potential, though not so patient, alternative to the Negro leadership of the civil rights movement. In making his high-profile rounds of lectures, speeches, and interviews, Malcolm was in effect offering himself—not his exotic Messenger—as a viable option should King's handling of racial matters falter, as the Muslim spokesman eloquently, although not quite accurately, predicted it would.

The white mainstream looked on, and the White House took note. Attorney General Robert F. Kennedy undoubtedly had Malcolm X on his mind when he asked James Baldwin to assemble a group of Negro artists, entertainers, and intellectuals to discuss civil rights issues. The group that Baldwin gathered at Kennedy's New York City apartment included singers Harry Belafonte and Lena Horne, playwright Lorraine Hansberry, psychologist Kenneth Clark, and an assortment of members of Baldwin's retinue. The attorney general brought along two aides from the Justice Department, Burke Marshall, who headed the Civil Rights Division, and Ed Guthman, the press secretary.

When someone in the group suggested that the Kennedy administration should move faster, the president's brother warned that "Negroes were listening to dangerous extremists such as the Black Muslims, who could cause real trouble."[48] Jerome Smith, a young CORE worker at the meeting who had been beaten and arrested in the South, dismissed the Muslims as passive observers of the civil rights struggle who refused to participate.[49]

Indeed, Elijah Muhammad, according to sources for this book and subsequently verified in the FBI files, had specifically ordered Malcolm X not to assist civil rights demonstrators in any way.[50] Jeremiah X, the minister of the Atlanta temple, had indeed simply stood on the sidelines in Birmingham and watched while black children faced Bull Connor's fire hoses and German shepherds.[51]

The larger picture, of course, was even more damning, as Malcolm well knew. Elijah Muhammad had allowed George Lincoln Rockwell, head of the American Nazi Party, to attend a Black Muslim meeting on June 25, 1961, at which Malcolm had been the main speaker.[52] The following year, Rockwell had been allowed to speak before thousands of Muslims gathered for Saviour's Day, an annual celebration of the birthday of Fard Muhammad. As we've seen, Malcolm and Jeremiah X, under Muhammad's orders, had met secretly in Atlanta with members of the Ku Klux Klan in 1961.[53] Following that initial sit-down, as described earlier, Muhammad sensed that Malcolm was too headstrong—and principled—to fol-

low orders to negotiate with the Klan and other avowed white racist leaders. Sworn to secrecy about the Klan meeting, Malcolm was
barred from any further NOI business contact with whites in the
South, while Jeremiah X established a secret working relationship
with unelected Deep South white leaders, including the Klan and
the White Citizens Council.[54]

Malcolm could not avoid the growing sense that the Muslims
talked tough but refused to act unless a Muslim was involved. Even
then, as when California cops shot and killed his friend Ronald X
Stokes outside the Nation of Islam mosque in Los Angeles in 1962
(an incident discussed in more detail in the next chapter), the Messenger would not allow the Fruit of Islam (FOI) to move against
white transgressors. As he boiled over the Stokes incident, Malcolm
began recounting his secret Atlanta meeting with the Klan. It likely
moved him to question the contradiction of Muhammad's policy of
nonengagement with other Negroes while he worked out business
deals with murderous Southern racists.

Shortly after the meeting between Bobby Kennedy and Baldwin's
group of Negro luminaries, Malcolm dismissed the gathering as a
sham exercise. "As long as they have interviews with the attorney general and he takes Negroes to pose as leaders, all of whom are married
to white men or white women, you'll always have a race problem," he
told one of the attendees, psychologist Kenneth Clark, a professor at
City College of New York. "When Baldwin took that crew with him
to see Kennedy, he took the wrong crew. And as long as they take
the wrong crew to talk to that man, you're not going to get anywhere
near a solution to this problem in this country."[55]

Still, the national spokesman was losing faith in the Messenger's
prescribed solution. In addition, Malcolm was losing hold over the
more aggressive young, karate-trained men of the Fruit of Islam,
who yearned for some action. Malcolm continued privately to view
Muhammad's overall program vis-à-vis whites as mainly talk, com-

mercialism, and narrow self-interest; meanwhile, he kept up the front publicly, mainly before the TV cameras and on the podium.

It had not escaped Malcolm's notice that King's nonviolent reputation had grown by leaps even as Malcolm gained prominence as an uncompromising firebrand, albeit one tethered to a religious leader riddled with contradictions. More and more he described himself to civil rights leaders, and even to such King aides as the Reverend Wyatt Tee Walker, as a black alternative that made King more acceptable to the establishment. "King had the benefit of middle-class rearing and the best of education, which altered his sense of rage," said Walker, who as a close associate ghostwrote many of King's newspaper columns. "Malcolm X didn't have that; his rage was right there on the surface." Despite this, Walker conceded many years later that both black leaders exerted great influence upon their generation.

"Malcolm X galvanized a quarter of black life—the unchurched masses—which up til that time had no interest in liberation matters," Walker said. "He became a voice for them because they had no voice. Those [blacks] in the organized religious arena had ministers and Martin [King] and the rest of us speaking for them. The people in the streets did not."[56]

Within white America, a few of the sharpest observers, not excluding the FBI, noticed that—despite surface differences between King and Malcolm on the ultimate goals of black progress—the two leaders were, as the writer Murray Kempton concluded, "alike in the feelings that count." While the media generally limited Malcolm's adherents to the disenchanted and King's to the upwardly mobile, Kempton knew better, observing, "I do not know a Negro so completely adjusted that some part of him did not respond to what Malcolm X was saying, just as I do not know a Negro so entirely alienated that some part of him does not respond to what Martin Luther King is saying."[57]

In the civil rights chiaroscuro of the early 1960s, the Muslim leader sought to deepen his apocalyptic tones, which contrasted all the more with King's bright optimism. In the minds of the masses, this study in contrasts, courtesy of the media, always seemed to favor Reverend King.

———

In this stellar period in a brilliant civil rights career, King, by dint of his oratory, held together the warring, disorganized factions of the movement in the South. In addition to fund-raising, he recruited celebrities, such as Belafonte and the comedian Dick Gregory, and young volunteers to energize the massive March on Washington of August 28, 1963, which would generate the substance and energy of global credibility. In addition to getting White House phone calls and earning world headlines, King received *Time* magazine's 1963 Man of the Year award on January 3, 1964. Such fame was but a prelude to the most coveted of all international trophies. Citing his eloquent oratory and nonviolent leadership, the Norwegian Nobel Committee awarded King, at age thirty-five, the 1964 Nobel Peace Prize. At the time, he was the youngest person to have been so honored. The twenty-hour days were paying off, and the Atlanta minister would go on to write a couple of books, travel some 325,000 miles, and make more than 450 speeches on behalf of the Negro struggle for civil rights.

Although Malcolm and King were considered archrivals in some quarters, they shared a much more insidious archnemesis. This sinister force was made all the more dangerous because of his single-mindedness, his meticulous stealth, and the awesome power and resources of the United States government. J. Edgar Hoover, the director of the FBI, stepped up his electronic snooping backed by technology, while continuing the provocative bulldogging with which the Bureau had harassed Elijah Muhammad in the 1930s,

Malcolm in the 1940s, and King since the 1950s. To attract Hoover's heavy investigative surveillance, a black leader—going back to Marcus Garvey in the 1920s—needed only to show signs of becoming effective at gaining an audience.

Reverend King had committed the unpardonable Bureau sin of criticizing the FBI by suggesting that its agents were complicit with Southern sheriffs and politicians in defending outlawed segregation. Publicly Hoover slammed King as the "most notorious liar" in the country.[58] Clandestinely, he stepped up the pursuit of King as the latest in a long list of black leaders to be "neutralized" or "destroyed."

The FBI placed at least eight wiretaps and sixteen electronic listening devices on telephones or in rooms Dr. King used during his travels across the country and abroad. Giving King the code name Zorro, the FBI relentlessly tracked and dirty-tricked him, beginning in October 1963, according to a Senate Intelligence Committee report. Under the guise of searching for Communist influence, Hoover successfully pressured Attorney General Kennedy to approve wiretaps "on King at his current address or at any future address to which he may move." James Adams, then the assistant FBI deputy director, told the Senate committee that the Bureau had discovered approximately twenty-five incidents of harassment of King by Hoover's agents for which there was no "statutory basis or justification."

The global accolades pouring in for King at the height of the civil rights struggle appear to have stirred in Hoover not so much a concern for national security as one of the seven deadly sins: envy. Hoover responded like a man countering a personal affront, according to some historians who have studied the FBI records. In several cases, the director's responses to King's triumphs were reminiscent of the dialogue of comic book villains. He tried, among other things, to block prestigious kudos, such as an honorary degree from Marquette University in Milwaukee, or to prevent King's visit to the Vatican. Upon reading an FBI document quoting a UPI wire service account of King's citation as *Time*'s 1963 Man of the Year, Hoover scribbled on the memo: "They had to dig deep in the garbage to come up with this one."

The Nobel Peace Prize—which Hoover coveted for himself— was the last straw![59] The enraged director was determined to use any means necessary, not only to prevent the civil rights leader from accepting the prize in Oslo but also to destroy him in the process. Already in clear violation of his own bureau's regulations, Hoover leaked damaging wiretap information on King's personal life to the national press. Focusing on the Nobel campaign, Hoover had his agents brief all ambassadors in Britain, Scandinavia, and the rest of Europe on the unflattering aspects of King's "Personal Conduct" that the agency had picked up on its phone taps and electronic surveillance of the civil rights leader's hotel rooms.

The ultimate secret plan to stop King from getting the Nobel Prize was a psychological operation with a lethal goal. Scrutinizing *Time*'s profile of King, which called him "the unchallenged voice of the Negro people,"[60] Hoover took serious note of its assertion that King, in his preteen years, had twice attempted suicide by jumping out of a second-story window. Weeks before King was to receive the prize, Hoover ordered that an obscene surveillance tape and a scurrilous letter be sent anonymously to the minister's Atlanta office. The thinly veiled suggestion in the error-strewn letter was that King should commit suicide.

> King, there is only one thing left for you to do. You know what it is. You have just 34 days in which to do (this exact number has been selected for a specific reason, it has definite practical significance). You are done. There is but one way out for you. You better take it before your filthy, abnormal fraudulent self is bared to the nation.[61]

King did not receive this package until January, well after the FBI's target date. The surveillance tape angered his wife, Coretta, and it did throw him into a depression—but not one quite as severe as Hoover had hoped.

The Muslims were by no means neglected. Throughout the spring of 1963, the FBI was keeping close informant and electronic watch over Malcolm X and Elijah Muhammad. As with the failed suicide plot, Hoover wasn't content simply to gather intelligence on black leaders. He aggressively sought ways to use this information to discredit these leaders, to strip them of organizational and even spousal support, to turn them against comrades, and, where possible, to clandestinely promote fratricidal bloodletting. This last ploy of Hoover's agency was headed toward fruition within the Muslim camp.

The FBI's counterintelligence program against black nationalist groups (part of COINTELPRO, which targeted domestic political groups) would not be officially promulgated until 1968, when the Bureau formalized covert operations long in practice against black leaders, going back to the days it had harassed Marcus Garvey. In plain English, the secret program outlined Hoover's plan to disrupt "the coalition of militant Black Nationalist groups," to "prevent violence on the part of Black Nationalist groups," and to mount a campaign of "discrediting" those black groups and their leaders. The FBI implored its agents to "prevent the rise of a 'messiah' who could unify, and electrify, the militant black nationalist movement."[62]

This counterintelligence program would cite Malcolm X posthumously as "the martyr of the movement." It also chillingly would refer to Dr. King—exactly one month before his assassination—as one of those who "aspire to this position" of messiah.

In 1963, however, the Southern Baptist minister was crisscrossing the nation, organizing support for the March on Washington planned for August. On Good Friday, as part of the high-profile campaign to integrate stores and public facilities in Bull Connor's Birmingham, King was arrested and decided to forgo bail in favor of a cell in the Birmingham jail. It was a lesson he brought away from his 1955 Montgomery boycott days when, after 125 other Negro demonstrators were arrested, he accepted bail and left his followers in jail. "I should have stayed in prison," he said later. "It would have nationally dramatized and deepened our movement even earlier and more quickly aroused America's conscience." Lesson learned, the civil rights leader, writing around the edges of a copy of the *Birmingham News* on April 16, 1963, penned his powerful twenty-page epistle, which would endure as the defining treatise on his Southern civil rights struggle.

A "Letter from Birmingham City Jail" became King's siren call to "my Christian and Jewish brothers" to join his fight against de jure segregation. Jarred by a local headline that stated "White Clergymen Urge Local Negroes to Withdraw from Demonstrations," King had scribbled the letter during his nine-day Easter-season stint in the jailhouse of the city that movement folks had come to call Bombingham and had it smuggled out of solitary confinement. Alone in a stone and metal cell with no mattress, sheets, or pillow, King wrote: "What else is there to do when you are alone for days in the dull monotony of a narrow cell other than write long letters, think strange thoughts, and pray long prayers?"[63]

Malcolm X, of course, was no stranger to the monotony of the prison tier. However, the scholarly purpose King made of his stint as a political prisoner had not been imaginable twenty years earlier when Malcolm began serving his six and a half years as a convicted burglar in a Massachusetts institution. As a wayward teenager from a broken family, Malcolm X, unlike King, was a late bloomer in matters intellectual. Whereas Malcolm Little would come to find his lifework in prison, King had discovered his as a newly minted twenty-seven-year-old pastor at the Dexter Avenue Baptist Church in Mont-

gomery. As early as the mid-1950s, E. B. Nixon, the head of the local
Pullman porters union, telephoned King to use his church to mount
a bus boycott after a forty-two-year-old seamstress, Rosa Parks, was
arrested on December 1, 1955, for refusing to give up her seat to a
white rider. The 381-day boycott catapulted King into the forefront
of what became the civil rights movement of the 1960s.

As a well-born child of Atlanta's black bourgeoisie, King had
become during his college days a practiced composer of the open
letter. Malcolm, by contrast, was born into an itinerant working-class
family, which was devastated by the death of the father in 1931 and
fell solidly upon hard times. When the prison gate slammed shut on
him at nineteen, he had evaded high school and claimed, with some
exaggeration, that he could barely read and hardly write. Under the
influence of a prison mate, as described earlier, and the tutelage
of Elijah Muhammad—who stressed penmanship along with his
pseudo-Islam—he retreated to his cell, dimly lit by a lamp, to study.
Evolving from his life of crime to one of spartan piety, Malcolm X,
unlike Reverend King, lost all confidence in white America and its
institutions. He saw himself as a man-child in what his Garveyite
father, and now Elijah Muhammad, taught him was a white man's
land without promise.

In his "Birmingham Letter," King had attempted to rally the
civil rights movement by bringing in "white moderate" Christians
and Jews. The heart of his integration plea for coalition building
reflected the unbridgeable chasm between his tactics (although not
necessarily his goals), and those of Malcolm X, the fiercely independent Muslim minister.

Holding up a mirror to the South, the SCLC leader chose to
write off as totally hopeless the largest white Christian group in the
region, the 12-million-plus-member Southern Baptist Convention.
"If they had opposed segregation," maintained Wyatt Tee Walker,
a close aide to King, "it would have ended the following morning."

However, the Convention, which had broken from Northern Baptists in 1845 over its ironclad support of slavery, would generally not even allow black worshippers to enter their edifices.

Born into this world of stifling segregation, King rebelled. Speaking to an interviewer in 1965, he recalled an indelible moment: "When I was fourteen, I [won] an oratorical contest . . . my subject was 'The Negro and the Constitution.' [On the bus home] the white driver ordered us to get up and give the whites our seats. We didn't move quickly enough to suit him, so he began cursing us, calling us, 'black sons of bitches.' I intended to stay right in that seat, but [my teacher] finally urged me up, saying we had to obey the law. And so we stood up in the aisle for the ninety miles [from Dublin, Georgia,] to Atlanta. That night will never leave my memory. It was the angriest I have ever been in my life."[64]

That experience in all likelihood was the call that turned the teenage King toward some larger, uncertain struggle, where he would wield his skills, oratorical and otherwise, like a shining sword. Born into a lineage of Baptist ministers, he knew throughout the days of his education at Morehouse College and Boston University that he would preach, as had his father, his grandfather, and his great-grandfather. In his young days as a minister, nonviolence as a personal philosophy was no more a part of his makeup than celibacy. As other Negro ministers did, King applied for a pistol permit, but was denied one as a young pastor in the capital of Alabama. By the time the boycott ended, he had settled irreversibly on Mahatma Gandhi's pacifist marches, which helped win independence for India, as an effective tactic for the South.

The pragmatic components of the King method fell into place on the night of January 31, 1956, when his Montgomery home was bombed. Although King was attending a meeting, his wife and children lived through this attack on their house. King strode through angry Negroes and wary white policemen to stand before the cameras and microphones and speak to the world. "He who lives by the sword will perish by the sword," he stated.[65]

The Voice had found its message. Upon stepping down from the porch of his bombed house, King set his feet on a path history has well documented. In November 1956, he and his Montgomery followers would win a Supreme Court ruling outlawing bus segregation. They then took on—and would finally pull down—the entire Jim Crow superstructure, bringing the South back fully into the union.

"All segregation statutes are unjust," King said often, "because segregation distorts the soul and damages the personality. It gives the segregator a false sense of superiority and the segregated a false sense of inferiority."

Malcolm did not disagree with this last sentiment. While it could be said that King dedicated his lifework to hammering away at the segregator's "false sense of superiority," Malcolm, under the influence of Elijah Muhammad, worked single-mindedly to help Negroes, the segregated, overcome their "false sense of inferiority."

# PART IV

1963–1965

# CHAPTER 15

# The Split

AFTER MALCOLM HAD SPENT NEARLY A DOZEN YEARS AS A disciple of Elijah Muhammad, it became evident that he was beginning to experience doubt about his faith. Whenever it had crept up previously, as during his 1959 trip to the Mideast, he had beaten back shivers of skepticism with prayer, fasting, and a renewed aggressive defense of his religion. Grounded in the black American experience, this homegrown version of Islam had turned Malcolm's life around after his satori-like conversion in prison. Since then, he had maintained a tough, analytical approach to all matters except those pertaining to the teachings of Muhammad of Chicago.

As a fiercely effective defender of the faith, this master salesman had become the public face and mouthpiece of a Muslim sect that otherwise had limited appeal. Under the sugar coat of Malcolm's witticisms and street savvy, the bitter pill of Muslim dogma had been easy to swallow for a surprising range of Negroes of every station. The Nation of Islam (NOI) had entered the 1950s as a shrinking band of aging, largely uneducated, pioneers up from the South. However, under Malcolm's influence, the group was continually being infused with younger members, some with high school educations, a few with college degrees. These were people who held down stable jobs and had marketable skills (some, albeit, picked up in prison workshops). In the Northeastern mosques under his direct jurisdiction, Malcolm skillfully applied the carrot and the stick to enforce the tough discipline and strict moral code of the religion. Violators, including top lieutenants such as Captain Joseph, the longtime associate who had come with Malcolm to Harlem from Detroit, were swiftly punished and sometimes suspended or expelled. The national spokesman had a fearsome reputation as a tough minister who laid down the law and did not spare the rod.

Although Malcolm never shrank from enforcing and obeying the rules, it was rumored, as we've seen, that high officials in Chicago—and even the Messenger himself—strayed from the strict Muslim codes governing everything from a non-soul-food diet to marriage and praying five times a day facing Mecca. Elijah Muhammad, for example, was reportedly observed eating bacon, but followers would dare not speak openly of such a forbidden indulgence. Minister Malcolm for his part would no more have eaten pork than he would have danced the jig at New York's Audubon Ballroom. His fanaticism, aided perhaps by the mysticism of his Christian parents, especially his mother, had Malcolm defending even the odd touches of his religion, such as the sightings of the Mother Ship in the night sky. And he led the way in refining the case for the infallibility of the Messenger. While Elijah Muhammad was likely to have prescribed the deity of Fard Muhammad expediently for his own purposes, Malcolm erected the saintliness of the Messenger essentially as an article of his faith. In his early years of allegiance, Malcolm saw himself as an Apostle Paul to the Messenger as Christ, believing in Elijah Muhammad as deeply as his parents back in Michigan had believed in Jesus of Nazareth.

As with all such devout believers, Malcolm had walled himself in against any inherent contradictions of his religion that were obvious to those outside the temple of the faith. The genealogy of the Nation, for example, was so bizarre that even Malcolm often deferred to the Messenger for teachings on the details. Yet, it could be argued, as Malcolm occasionally did, that such Muslim trappings as the Yacub myth and even the Mother Ship were common to all religions.

In such beliefs, Malcolm likely saw himself in step with Reverend Martin Luther King, for example, as a minister of faith constrained as a believer to accept the substance of unseen spiritual evidence that strained the imagination of the nonbelievers. The NOI credo, it was argued, was no more preposterous than, say, Reverend King's acceptance of the Old Testament account of a burning bush speaking to Moses, or Mormon founder Joseph Smith's receiving his religious orders from those gold plates, or fundamentalist Christians' literal belief in the biblical story that man was created on the sixth day and placed in the Garden of Eden.

Malcolm was prepared to deal with skeptics. Through his stepped-up schedule of speeches and debates, he increasingly encountered not only local white reporters, but big-name journalists, such as Mike Wallace on television, Irv Kupcinet and Barry Farber on radio, and M. S. Handler of *The New York Times* in print. Along the way, the national spokesman attracted younger, more outspoken white students as he lectured more on college campuses and faced down critics on radio and television.

A more immediate challenge to Black Muslim doctrine, however, was coming from inside the larger Negro community. Scholars, as well as blacks in barbershops and beauty parlors, were more boldly questioning the secular and religious groups they saw as being hopelessly rooted in the past. As always, Malcolm prepped for the opposition. As soon as nonfiction books on black topics were released, he would hit Michaux's National Memorial Bookstore on 125th Street in Harlem. In addition to treatises on Africa, on Asia, and on religions, he read the works of such writers as James Baldwin, Lerone Bennett, Frantz Fanon, and Kenneth Clark; the historians E. Franklin Frazier and John Hope Franklin; and the autodidactic John Henrik Clarke, his Harlem friend, among others. Malcolm also studied the liberal white social critics who wrote with a practiced disinterestedness, and from a great distance. The emerging black scholars, he found, offered up books and essays seasoned with experience and rich with the passion of the insider.

This new wave of black writers and public intellectuals slammed the American social order that had ensured a prevailing sense of domestic tranquility without providing justice and fair play for the Negro. Although they may have agreed with parts of Malcolm's diagnosis of the problem, these social critics did not square with his prescriptions for remedy. They had an impossible time dealing with Muslim ideology and with Elijah Muhammad's rendering of the white man as a "blue-eyed devil."

In critiquing white America's history of "inhumanity" to black citizens, social critic Louis Lomax, for example, warned blithely of his "prayer that white men will remove the reason to shoot before black men get something to shoot with." Malcolm had closely read Lomax's *The Negro Revolt*, and in conversations and running public debates with the author, he took exception to Lomax's prescription for racial harmony. As a Muslim minister, Malcolm held out no such hope that whites were capable of heeding such warnings and thus judged offering them up as a grand waste of time. Instead, Malcolm held to Elijah's notion, dismissed by Lomax, that Negroes should unite with Africans on the African continent, as well as with other nonwhites, because a global war—an Armageddon—between whites and others was inevitable, which the black man would win.

Increasingly, Malcolm paid close attention to the younger generations he viewed as restless and misguided in a Kennedy-era society in the throes of transition. These black youngsters despaired

of the straitjacket of King's nonviolence, as well as the noninvolve-
ment of the Black Muslims in broader societal change. Some of these
men, more than a few of them ex-convicts, found their way into the
ranks of the Muslims. These Fruits of Islam (FOI) rookies, along
with police informers, no doubt, gave rise to a grumbling criticism
within the ranks. While gaining strength on the stump from defending his religion from the heretics, Malcolm discovered that dealing
with criticism from within the Nation was a thorny endeavor.

The Ronald Stokes affair in 1962 had left its mark. On April 27,
two Los Angeles police officers confronted two Muslim men near
Temple No. 27, an encounter that quickly escalated into a battle
between dozens of police and Muslims from the mosque. During
the melee, police shot seven Muslims, killing one: Stokes, a mosque
stalwart and friend of Malcolm, who was shot in the heart, allegedly
while his hands were raised. (A coroner's inquest would rule it justifiable homicide.) In synch with the young Turks who were hungry for
revenge, Malcolm wanted to direct a little action at the Los Angeles
policemen who had killed his friend and fellow Black Muslim. An
eye for an eye was the doctrine long taught, and if a Muslim were
attacked, Malcolm preached that it would be "a head for a head, and
a life for a life." Such teachings had been the magnet for a loose cadre
of hard-core, action-oriented men. They suffered through the hours
of classroom sessions on religious dogma for the thrill of the whack
and tumble on the karate mats. These specially trained FOI squad
members enjoyed the discipline of cracking heads when the word
was given. Such orders, for the most part, had been restricted to dish-
ing out corporal punishment to members who abused their spouses,
misappropriated group funds, or otherwise violated temple rules.

The goon squad expected the word to be given after the Stokes
affair. With a half dozen Muslims injured and Ronald Stokes dead at
the hands of the Los Angeles police, special FOI squads eased into
action. Quite on their own, several had acquired the address of one

of the cops involved and started plotting his movements about the city. The word never came from the only man who could have given it, Elijah Muhammad. In fact, the Messenger ordered Malcolm to refrain from any appearance of retaliation by his followers. This put Malcolm on the spot and caused him to lose face in front of the men he had conditioned for an eye-for-an-eye code of revenge.

The inaction of the Messenger in the Stokes affair struck Malcolm as indifference, if not cowardice. He reasoned that it was not strictly speaking a religious issue. So he bit his tongue and soldiered on, publicly claiming an empty piece of vengeance by Allah when an airliner loaded with tourists from Georgia crashed near Paris.

> I got a wire from God today—well, somebody came and told me he had really answered our prayers over in France. He had dropped an airplane out of the sky with over 120 white people on it—because Muslims believe in an eye for an eye and a tooth for a tooth. Many people have been saying, well, what are you all going to do and since we know that man is tracking us down day by day to try to find out what we're going to do so he'll have some excuse to put us behind bars, we call on our God—he gets rid of 120 of them in one clop and now we challenge them to put God in jail.[1]

The Stokes affair nonetheless loosed a string of temple disaffection by younger men longing for action. Faced with charges that the Muslims talked tough but did not act even when police killed their followers, Malcolm increasingly talked even tougher as he made his rounds. Peppering his speeches with fewer remarks like "the Honorable Elijah Muhammad teaches us . . . ," he sometimes sounded more like the black nationalist revolutionary the FBI made him out to be. Gone were the cocksure assertions of the Muslim faith as droplets of doubt began to appear. Negroes, he now maintained, were only "inclined in the direction of" Elijah Muhammad. Still, Malcolm kept up the front even as he empathized with the perplexed men who began to fall away from the rolls of the Nation.

The internal contradiction brought on by the Stokes affair was a key turning point in Malcolm's move away from unquestioning adherence. Keen associates, such as Captain Joseph of the Harlem mosque, took notice. "The reason Malcolm began to have a problem with Mr. Muhammad was because Malcolm wanted to force Mr. Muhammad to send troops out there," said Captain Joseph.[2] Shortly afterward, Joseph, who was close to Malcolm in the Harlem temple, noticed a drift in the minister's loyalty to Elijah Muhammad. Upon noticing a corresponding shift in Malcolm's intensity, he confronted his minister outside the Muslims' restaurant on Lenox Avenue.

"In the early years when I listened to you speak," Captain Joseph remembered saying, "from the Holy Qur'an and the Bible, or history or whatever, it would send chills through me because it was so true. But now, I don't feel that anymore. And I think that there is a problem somewhere."[3]

Malcolm dismissed his top aide's complaint. Privately, however, he wrestled with the entire NOI organism—including the infallibility of Elijah Muhammad. The once sacred tentacles increasingly had the feel of a grip rather than an embrace. Months after the Stokes trauma, which had challenged Malcolm's secular beliefs, he would receive an even more devastating blow—this time spiritual.

This trauma to his faith occurred during a long discussion in February 1963 with Elijah's son Wallace D. Muhammad. During an extended visit at Chicago headquarters, Malcolm had picked up sustained chatter about low morals and high living among the Royal Family, including the Messenger. These transgressions could no longer be restricted to his private thoughts. Malcolm turned to Wallace because he knew that, more than any other member of the Royal Family, it was Wallace who, since birth, had been said to wear the spiritual mantle of heir apparent.

W. D. Fard, the NOI founder and designated savior, reportedly had instructed Elijah Muhammad to anoint Wallace at birth with the spiritual leader's name. The occasion inspired legend within family circles that this namesake son, Wallace Dean,* had been selected to succeed his father as leader of the Nation of Islam. Preparation for the golden child had included tutoring by Arabic scholars who, in addition to language instruction, exposed him to the tenets of the orthodox Sunni variety of Islam, which was more than a thousand years old. The bastardized, Detroit-grown Islam—with a Georgia-born Negro as the Messenger of Allah—made for interesting sessions indeed for these Middle Eastern tutors, whom Elijah Muhammad referred to as Asiatic black men.

The impact of true Islam upon the adolescent mind of the son of Elijah Muhammad was as profound as it was confusing. Although instructive in the ways of the Qur'an, it was corrosive to the teachings of his father's religion. In time, the son rebelled against his father, periodically stormed out of the household, and eventually spun out of the orbit of the Black Muslims altogether. As with his older brother, Akbar, Wallace also wandered into that older, Middle East tradition of orthodox Sunni Islam. While he struggled to find his spiritual way, Wallace strayed into and out of favor with his father, the Messenger, who had a tradition to maintain and his very own religion to run.

During these irregular exiles, Wallace was periodically approached by the FBI. Early on, the Bureau viewed the Nation as an exotic cult worthy of scrutiny mainly because it eschewed the U.S.

---

* Born with the middle name Delaney, as an adult Wallace published books under the name Wallace Dean Muhammad.

military draft. In time, especially because of Malcolm's influence, J. Edgar Hoover's agency viewed the Muslims as a much larger threat to tranquility among Negroes. Agents tried with limited success to establish a sympathetic relationship with Wallace, the wayward son. It was not lost on the Bureau that Muslim believers had accepted on faith that Wallace was ordained by Allah as the heir apparent of Elijah Muhammad.

Wallace Muhammad was thus viewed as a possible key to the FBI's long-term plans to neutralize the Nation of Islam and steer it away from the drift to black nationalism, to which Malcolm X was inexorably taking it. Neither Wallace nor Malcolm revealed to the other any knowledge of this clandestine piece of covert FBI planning. Specifically, the Bureau wanted to disband the FOI, the Muslims' fearsome karate-trained elite guard, which all new male recruits were required to join; to open up membership to whites; to tone down its rhetoric on violence; and generally to move the sect to a position within the nonviolent black mainstream.[4]

When Malcolm met Wallace in February 1963, the two men explored at great length the human side of the Messenger. Malcolm came with questions, rumors, and suspicions fed by his nagging doubt now about Elijah Muhammad. For his part, Wallace was as open and confident as any son groomed to entitlements.

Malcolm was particularly keen to hear Wallace's account of his father's personal behavior. Aware of palace rumors about philandering, as well as the ease with which he could have verified them, Malcolm had long considered such speculations not only dangerous but also blasphemous, and therefore unthinkable. Still, he knew second-hand about Sister Evelyn Williams. As a teenager, he had dated her during his pre-prison days in Boston. Later, after bringing her into the temple, Malcolm remained very fond of Evelyn and sent her from Boston to work as a secretary for the Messenger. She had given birth to an out-of-wedlock child and, as custom demanded, was expelled from the Nation. Rumors floated about in Chicago headquarters that Elijah Muhammad had fathered this child of the young lady whom Malcolm early on had considered marrying.

During their conversations, Wallace confirmed the rumors about Evelyn, rumors Malcolm had dared not allow himself to entertain. With these illicit relations confirmed by the chosen son of Elijah Muhammad, Malcolm could no longer suppress his inner pain. His natural questioning stance, so long suspended for matters pertaining to his religion, came to the fore. Under probing from Malcolm, Wallace disclosed rather cavalierly that the Messenger had also fathered children by several of his other young secretaries. Malcolm trembled at hearing this shocking account of Elijah Muhammad's infidelities. The details from Wallace were not only proof positive; to Malcolm, they became a smoking gun against Elijah Muhammad and a call for action.

The exact details of the encounter between Wallace and Malcolm are somewhat murky. The accounts from the two men differ, and it is clear that each realized the dangerous consequence of shouldering responsibility for exposing such information about the Messenger— no matter how truthful it might have been.

As for Malcolm, his account—as jolting as that of a cult member undergoing the early shocks of deprogramming—cannot be fully trusted. It is not so much that he intentionally lied about the process as that his perspective after a dozen years of blind devotion was perhaps too emotionally charged. The mind of the devout, no matter how sophisticated otherwise, is a tricky mechanism. This is especially true during the deprogramming phase, as experts will verify. With the mounting evidence Malcolm was attempting to free himself with virtually no outside help, now confronting a final gaggle of contradictions between the Messenger he had worshipped and the immoral entity he had discovered Muhammad to be.

Curiosity about the loose morals charges against the Messenger doubtlessly had driven Malcolm to Wallace, the one source who would know the truth about what the minister had come to suspect. Employing the guile of his street days, Malcolm worked his source as he once had worked his marks during his time as a confidence man. Although he already had heard some of the facts and was seeking confirmation from Elijah Muhammad's chosen son, Malcolm shrewdly managed to elicit the details as a cold revelation. Yet with suppression and denial so much a part of the psyche of the religious convert, it is impossible to know just what Malcolm consciously already knew about the transgressions of his leader and exactly when he realized they were true.

Still, this revelation about Muhammad's illegitimate children, as shocking as it was, did not constitute the full weight of the wrecking ball that Wallace slammed against the superstructure of Malcolm's Black Muslim faith. A more significant revelation, which Malcolm had suppressed even more deeply, would ultimately break the back of his belief in the religious sect.

Malcolm would later recall the shock of learning that the Nation's founder and savior, Fard Muhammad, was not God.

> [Wallace] said that he didn't believe that Allah was a man! [He said] that the Messenger in teaching that Allah came in the person of Master F. D. Muhammad knew that Allah Himself was not a man and that the Savior never taught that he was Allah. He said that it was the Messenger himself who started teaching that the Savior was Allah, but that the Messenger knows that the Savior himself wasn't Allah, per se . . . [Wallace] said that Allah is infinite . . . he frightened me with this![5]

The belief that Fard was Allah Himself and Elijah his Messenger was as fundamental a religious tenet for the cult as the holiness of Jesus is for Christianity. Despite his intelligence, judgment, and worldly past, Malcolm believed in this godhead as devoutly as any novice member—and perhaps even more devoutly than Elijah Muhammad. Since his conversion in prison, Malcolm had found great solace in Elijah both as a divinely influenced leader and as a replacement for his earthly father, whom he'd lost at the age of six.

Now, the worthy son of his Maximum Leader had rocked him on both fronts. Wallace had clocked Elijah's failure both as a religious leader and as an upright secular father. On the former front, the son said his father had faked his own religious credentials as Messenger by elevating Fard Muhammad to the rank of Allah Himself. On the latter front, Elijah, as just noted, had fathered several children out of wedlock, refused to acknowledge their paternity, and even had the mothers, who worked as his secretaries, expelled from the Nation of Islam for adultery.

En route home from Chicago, Malcolm changed his airline ticket to lay over for a few hours in Detroit to discuss this shattering development with the only person he could trust on such a matter: his brother Wilfred. "I never saw him ever in such bad shape," Wilfred would recall. "He was pale and just disconcerted. Then he started telling me what Wallace had told him. I let him talk because he needed it. He looked like he was completely out of it. It had knocked all the wind out of his sails. All this stuff was weighing on him and he's trying to sort it out. He was trying to figure out how he could get taken like this. When he told me what he had found out, I told him, 'Well, it's true.' He said, 'You mean to tell me that you knew?' I said yeah, the FBI had been spreading it all around. Friends of mine not in the mosque came and told me what was going on. I said people know about it. He said, 'Well, how come you didn't tell me?' I said, 'If I had told you, you would have went right on back and told Elijah Muhammad what I had said.' He said, 'You know what, you're probably right.'

"He told me what Wallace had told him about these children that all these secretaries were having. Wallace had said, 'Look, those are my brothers and sisters.' Malcolm just couldn't believe that he had been taken in so. He talked about how sharp he had been all his life, how nothing got past him.

"Now he was thinking about all these people he had led into the Nation. His conscience bothered him about that, you see. He was in bad shape."[6]

As an NOI minister, Malcolm had religiously informed his Messenger of every detail that remotely concerned the sect. And so he wrote the patriarch about Wallace's grave revelations about his half siblings, who had been born from the Messenger's adultery. Malcolm avoided mentioning the fact that his own older brother, Wilfred, had confirmed these blasphemous charges. FBI mail cover, electronic listening devices, and the Bureau's top informer in the Chicago hierarchy often relayed such sensitive information to the Special Agent in Charge even before it reached Elijah Muhammad in Phoenix. A meeting followed between Malcolm and Elijah Muhammad, in which the Messenger reportedly likened himself to the Bible's adulterous David, drunken Noah, and incestuous Lot, saying, "I have to fulfill all of those things." Malcolm could not yet bring himself to reveal that the anointed heir apparent had gone so far as to reject his very father as the Messenger of Allah along with the entire godhead of the Nation of Islam. Blasphemy was one thing; heresy, punishable by the caustic breath of hellfire, was quite another.

In the privacy of a hotel room a year later, in February 1964, Malcolm would secretly tape-record his recollections of his conversations with Wallace and read verbatim some of his own letters to the Messenger.[7] With one eye on posterity, Malcolm also had in mind the possible use of evidence in the future. At any rate, he composed portions of a chronology detailing the beginning of his fall from Muslim grace. He informed his brother Wilfred of this reel-to-reel recording and later forwarded him a copy for safekeeping. (Wilfred

later discussed with the author the entire range of the tape recordings, issues that the brothers had discussed in private meetings.)

Malcolm was never one to sit Hamlet-like, brooding too long
about pressing matters. So with his faith in free fall, Malcolm dropped
adultery from the list of unpardonable sins he railed against at the
podium. It was his first official public adjustment to the Messenger's
frailty as a human being. Privately, however, Malcolm set to discussing Elijah Muhammad's illicit relations with East Coast associates. In
time, the grapevine began to vibrate with chatter about Malcolm's
whisperings.

The Royal Family in Chicago sensed an opening and they too
decided to act. The word was given for Richard Durham, the non-
Muslim editor of *Muhammad Speaks,* to curtail its coverage of Malcolm's official activities, and his photograph was not to be run in
the journal. When East Coast regional writer Joe Walker resigned in
April, Durham accepted it with a sigh. Chicago, Durham said, had
derided the writer as Malcolm's "secretary," whose New York stories
did not give proper credit to the Honorable Elijah Muhammad.

As Malcolm became a nonperson within the pages of the Muslim
national house organ, the newspaper that staff members referred
to as *Speaks* cranked up even higher the wattage of its praise for its
Maximum Leader. Lacking all other discernible context, feature
stories favoring polygamy in African and Islamic countries began
to appear within the pages of the cult's weekly journal. Herewith,
in a nation where even bigamy is illegal, *Speaks* was promulgat-
ing a scriptural defense for Elijah Muhammad's weakness of the
flesh, a defense that Malcolm had discussed with his leader but had
not convincingly enough brought himself to put before the masses
and the media.

The external combat with Dr. King was finally yielding to a threat
looming within the hierarchy of the Nation of Islam. It was targeting the very Muslim who, over the past dozen years, had done the

most for the sect. Within his own community, Malcolm was in serious trouble.

Then, on November 22, 1963, President Kennedy was assassinated in Dallas. It was a shock no American alive at the time would forget, and it augured a series of political assassinations that would shape the future of the nation. Nine days later, on December 1, after delivering a speech in Manhattan, Malcolm was asked about the killing. He replied that it was an instance of "chickens coming home to roost"—in effect, payback for Kennedy's "twiddling his thumbs" at the murder of South Vietnamese president Ngo Dinh Diem only weeks before. "Being an old farm boy myself, chickens coming home to roost never did make me sad; they've always made me glad," Malcolm was quoted as saying.[8] Elijah Muhammad, who had forbidden NOI leaders to comment on the Kennedy assassination, immediately suspended or "silenced" Malcolm, ostensibly for ninety days.

Even after this blow, Wilfred recalled that "for a long time [Malcolm] thought that he could get things straightened out with Elijah Muhammad and they could save the Nation. He felt it was worthwhile saving if possible, because it was doing so much good for our people. He still had confidence that he could work out something.

"But [NOI officials] knew that they had no intention of him ever coming back. They wanted him out of the way. It wasn't long before they made it known that they wanted him dead. Several members of the family were saying it."

During Malcolm's exile, Wilfred would secretly visit him, flying from Detroit to spend some weekends at Malcolm and Betty's house in Queens. "It took him a while to realize that they wanted him dead. He even wrote a letter to Elijah Muhammad and told him that if you give the order for them to leave me alone, they will. The order never came down."[9]

In March 1964, Malcolm announced he was leaving the Nation of Islam.

# CHAPTER 16

# The International Stage

E VEN WHILE MALCOLM LEFT THE ORGANIZATION THAT HE felt had saved his life, and that now threatened to end it, the former national spokesman advised other members to remain within the Nation of Islam. But, within days of his decision to leave, Malcolm and some who had followed him out of the Nation established a new group, Muslim Mosque, Inc. (MMI),* which would inevitably be seen by the NOI as a rival, and a further reason to remove him from the scene. The agenda of the group was still to be formulated, but clearly it would free Malcolm to explore the orthodox Islamic beliefs, prayer, and rituals practiced by millions of people around the world, but not within the precincts of the Chicago-based Nation.

That same month of March 1964, Malcolm began planning a second group, the Organization of Afro-American Unity (OAAU), which would allow him and his followers to engage in activism and enter the civil rights arena in ways that the NOI, frustratingly, had

---

* Incorporation papers for Muslim Mosque, Inc., were filed on March 16, 1964, in New York City.

not allowed. This would be a purely secular effort with a political mission: to strengthen black Americans' struggle for equality by linking it with Africans' struggles for freedom from colonialism. Unlike most major civil rights organizations—but like the Garvey movement that had guided his parents, his siblings, and Malcolm himself in his early years—this movement would strongly encourage black Americans to embrace Africa and find strength in unity with black people around the world. As Malcolm was well aware, that world had changed mightily since Garvey's day, in promising ways. In the 1920s and 1930s, virtually all of Africa was under white colonial rule. Now more than two dozen African nations had been liberated, including Ghana (in 1957), Nigeria (1960), Tanganyika (1961), Zanzibar (1963), and Kenya (1963). In April 1964, two of these newly independent nations merged to become the United Republic of Tanganyika and Zanzibar, which renamed itself Tanzania six months later. That June, when Malcolm publicly announced the formation of the OAAU, its namesake, the Organization of African Unity (OAU), was only a year old and had thirty-two independent countries as members. In 1964, it appeared, Africa might be a source not only of pride and heritage, as in Garvey's day, but of strategic ideas and political power.

The struggle of black Americans for freedom and equality must be internationalized, Malcolm argued. Under a global light, racial oppression would no longer be seen as an internal U.S. issue of civil rights, but as the violation of international human rights it was. As such, it should be condemned by the United Nations, whose Universal Declaration of Human Rights, adopted in 1948, proclaimed that all people—regardless of race, color, sex, nationality, or political opinion—have a right to equal treatment. In the final, transformative year of Malcolm's life, when he spent months traveling in the Mideast and Africa, one of his main goals was to get at least one African nation to charge the United States with human rights violations in the United Nations.

Although pan-Africanism and orthodox Islam came to the fore in Malcolm's last year, these currents were hardly new in his thinking. For years, as mentioned earlier, Malcolm's preaching had trod lightly around such unorthodox NOI beliefs as the Mother Ship and Yacub. Now, with the help of Wallace Muhammad, he had freed himself from its central pillar—its contention that one man, Fard Muhammad, was Allah and another man, Elijah Muhammad, was his Messenger.

While he had been suspended from the Nation, Malcolm attended Juma, Friday prayers, at the Islamic Cultural Center's Sunni mosque in a town house on Riverside Drive in Manhattan, where the learned Dr. Mahmoud Youssef Shawarbi, an Egyptian, was the director. Malcolm had been in contact with Shawarbi and other Sunni scholars for years, and after prayer Malcolm would stay to talk about the Islamic religion. Ahmed Osman, a Sudanese student at Dartmouth College, took part in these discussions; he had kept in touch with Malcolm since they had clashed, cordially, over doctrine the previous summer.

That encounter occurred when Osman was showing New York to a friend who had missed his plane back to Sudan. With only half a Sunday to spend, they headed straight to Harlem, because, as Osman explained, "if you go to Sudan and they know that you went to New York, they will ask you, 'Have you been to Harlem?'" At Temple No. 7, Malcolm was speaking, as he often did, in "electrifying" fashion. During the question period, Osman respectfully introduced himself as a brother Muslim but said some of Malcolm's talk was "contrary to the Islam I believe in." Color, race, and nationality have no standing in Islam, said the young man from Sudan, so a blanket condemnation of whites was anti-Islamic. "The crowd was mad at me when I said this," Osman said. "But Malcolm really quieted them down. He said, 'Look here, let him speak of his mind.'" Malcolm told the young stranger that the Qur'an condemns the white man. "I told him, 'Brother Malcolm, I challenge you. Show me.'" So Malcolm opened an English translation of the Qur'an, and Osman recalled, "He read for me a verse, which in Arabic says that on the Day of Judgment, the unbelievers—it doesn't say white—it says the unbelievers would be put in hell and out of fear, their color would be like blue. . . . So he tells me that this blue means the 'blue-eyed devils,' " Osman recalled, laughing. "I said, 'No, brother. This is a misinterpretation.' So he invited us for dinner."

The crowd of five hundred, Osman said, was amazed that a young stranger had challenged Malcolm on his home ground, and that Malcolm let him speak openly even though he denied the "white devil" tenet that seemed to be one of Malcolm's core beliefs. Pressed for time, Osman turned down the dinner invitation that evening but kept in touch, sending Malcolm scholarly books and pamphlets about Sunni Islam, the predominant form of Islam worldwide. "And he wrote me back saying that he was very much impressed with these books." [1]

Now that Malcolm was out of the Nation, Osman, Shawarbi, and other orthodox Muslims urged him to take his open mind and make the *hajj*, the pilgrimage to Mecca that is a religious duty for all Muslim adults who are able. For funding, he turned to his big sister, Ella Collins, who was now about fifty and still living in Boston. Ella had become a Sunni Muslim after leaving the Nation of Islam in 1959, and she gave Malcolm the money she had been saving for her own *hajj*. Dr. Shawarbi provided the approval that Malcolm needed to enter Mecca, where only Muslims were allowed; he also provided high-level contacts to smooth the way.

Amid threats to his life and his home—the Nation had ordered the family to vacate their NOI-owned home in East Elmhurst, Queens—Malcolm left his wife and young daughters and flew out of New York under the name Malik El-Shabazz on April 13, 1964. First, he spent a few days as a tourist in cosmopolitan Cairo, where he was impressed with the modern schools, roads, and housing being built under Gamal Abdel Nasser, its anticolonial, pan-Arab president. Then he flew into Jeddah, Saudi Arabia, where he found himself stuck for days in a dormitory for pilgrims; Dr. Shawarbi's note apparently was not enough to persuade the religious authorities that the American was a true Muslim. Finally, Malcolm called one of Shawarbi's contacts. He happened to be the brother-in-law of a son of Prince Faisal, the regent of Saudi Arabia. From then on, Malcolm was treated royally, an experience he described with relish in the *Autobiography.*

As a Black Muslim minister, Malcolm had preached that Islam is a black man's religion and that whites were barred from Mecca. After his pilgrimage, in letters sent to family and friends for wider distribution, he presented himself as having had a revelation:

> During the past eleven days here in the Muslim world, I have eaten from the same plate, drunk from the same glass, and slept in the same bed (or on the same rug)—while praying to the *same* God—with fellow Muslims, whose eyes were the bluest of blue, whose hair was the blondest of blond, and whose skin was the whitest of white. . . . We were *truly* all the same (brothers)— because their belief in one God had removed the "white" from their minds, the "white" from their behavior, and the "white" from their attitude.[2]

Malcolm said he had seen "a spirit of unity and brotherhood that my experiences in America had led me to believe never could exist between the white and non-white." This experience, he wrote, "has forced me to re-arrange much of my thought-patterns previously held, and to toss aside some of my previous conclusions."[3]

The evidence indicates that, going back years, both Malcolm and Elijah Muhammad had known Muslims from the Mideast who were, by American standards of appearance, white. But the Black Muslims did not regard Arabs as white, no matter how light their skin, said Dr. Sam Hamod, whose father, also named Sam Hamod, was a light-skinned immigrant from the Mideast. The elder Sam Hamod had founded a Sunni mosque in Detroit, and he met Elijah Muhammad at Elijah's Temple No. 1 multiple times in the 1940s and 1950s. The son often accompanied his father. The son recalled that the Nation's rejection of whites "was against the Europeans. It was not against the Arabs. Arabs, we were not white. He [Elijah Muhammad] never thought of us as white."[4]

By publicly celebrating the existence of blond, blue-eyed Muslims, as he did in his reports from Mecca, Malcolm was breaking with a decade of his own preaching. Perhaps the enormity of the color variations among Muslims did not hit him until he saw them on thrilling display during his *hajj*. Perhaps his lightning-bolt report from Mecca was an eloquent narrative to accommodate mainstream Sunnis, who had objected to non-Islamic elements in the Nation's doctrines. Malcolm had heard those objections, his brother Wilfred said. "They said that stuff you been talking doesn't mean anything over here."[5] In any case, Malcolm's revelation in Mecca not only aligned him with mainstream Islam but gave him greater political flexibility, allowing the possibility of political alliances with, as he himself described them, whites who had removed "the 'white'" from their attitude.

"Despite my firm convictions, I have always been a man who tries to face facts, and to accept the reality of life as new experience and new knowledge unfolds it," Malcolm wrote after his pilgrimage. "I have always kept an open mind, which is necessary to the flexibility that must go hand in hand with every form of intelligent search for truth."[6]

After leaving the spiritual center of Islam, and stopping in Lebanon, Egypt, and Nigeria, Malcolm arrived in the spiritual center of pan-Africanism, Ghana. His week there would prove transcendent, reorienting him to the Africa-oriented Garveyism of his youth. Ghana, he knew, had been the first sub-Saharan African nation to gain independence. Its president, Kwame Nkrumah, had led it to freedom from British colonial rule in 1957 and played a leading role in founding the OAU. A student of Marx, Lenin, and Garvey, and a proponent of "scientific socialism," Nkrumah promoted African culture and liberation struggles, blasted notions of white supremacy, and put forth a vision of a strong and politically united Africa. In person, he "exuded quicksilver intelligence, genuine humanity, and reserves of energy," wrote historian David Levering Lewis, an American who was teaching in Ghana at the time and would later publish a towering biography of W. E. B. Du Bois. "He appeared larger than his trim, rather delicate frame. His eyes were startlingly bright."[7]

As the center of gravity of pan-Africanist aspirations, Nkrumah attracted black political refugees and expatriates from many nations, including a vibrant community of Americans. Sick of racism at home, they had been inspired by the Ghanaian struggle, and by Nkrumah in particular. "They went there to say, what could they do? They had certain skills," said Vicki Garvin, who was one of them. "They wanted to be a part of the development."[8]

The unofficial leader of the American expats was Julian Mayfield, a writer and activist who edited a magazine and wrote speeches for Nkrumah. Others filled a range of roles in the young nation. Garvin, a labor organizer, taught English to the embassy staffs of China, Cuba, and Algeria. She shared a house with Maya Angelou (then known as Maya Make), who worked in the University of Ghana's theater department, years before she published *I Know Why the Caged Bird Sings,* and with Alice Windom, a witty social worker and social scientist, who taught and worked as a secretary to the Ethiopian ambassador. Julia Wright, the daughter of Richard Wright, worked as a journalist and translator. Dr. Preston King, an exile charged with draft evasion in Georgia, taught political philosophy at the University of Ghana. Dr. Ana Livia Cordero, a Puerto Rican physician who was married to Mayfield, ran a health clinic in a country with few doctors. Robert and Sara Lee, both dentists, had brought their skills to Accra, Ghana's capital, years before independence and stayed permanently; Drs. Bobbie Lee and Kwame Nkrumah had been friends when both were students at Lincoln University in Pennsylvania. The most venerated of the expatriates was W. E. B. Du Bois, who had been invited to Ghana by Nkrumah himself. Du Bois had died in 1963, at age ninety-five, the summer before Malcolm arrived, but his widow, the writer Shirley Graham Du Bois, was director of Ghana's national television operation, an administrator in the state publishing house, and a trusted advisor to the president.

"Like only a very few others in the country, they had a direct line to the President, as well as intimate associations with some of his key advisors," expat Leslie Alexander Lacy wrote in a 1970 memoir, describing these Americans. "The President used their skills, including their literary talents, for speech writing; took their advice rather seriously."[9]

The welcome for Malcolm from these accomplished and politically aware African Americans could not have been warmer. Although they had heard he was coming, they didn't know the exact date and gamely met three planes at the airport, only to be disappointed each time. According to Lacy, "Fifty of us slept in at Julian's place, hoping to greet him."[10] Meanwhile, they started arranging lunches, dinners, speeches, soirees, a press conference, and meetings with officials from Ghana as well as from China, Cuba, and Algeria. Malcolm called Mayfield on Monday, May 11, the day after he arrived, and immediately began a hectic schedule that some nights ended with talk into the small hours.[11] He had been traveling alone, but in Ghana, Mayfield and the three housemates, Angelou, Garvin and Windom, accompanied him virtually everywhere. That Monday evening—"refugee night," Alice Windom called it—forty to fifty

Afro-Americans crowded into Mayfield's house to hear a relaxed-seeming Malcolm talk about his experience in Mecca and his plans.

Asked about the supposed change "from A to Z" in his attitude toward white people, Malcolm denied he was giving all white people a pass. Garvin remembered him saying, "We had some [good white] people, we had John Brown, who had the guts to take up a gun. We also had some Quakers when we were going through this Underground Railroad. They were exceptions. I found on my trip to Mecca that there were more people outside of the United States who could identify with us without the badge of skin color or racism. And so I think I'm going to give them a chance, but they have to prove something to me."[12]

In Windom's view, Malcolm was seeking to move beyond the mainstream media's obsessive focus on his opinions about white people. "He was trying to build his own mosque as well as his political organization. He needed a way to use the media to communicate with black people around the country. He could not use the media if the only thing they wanted to hear is, 'Do you hate white people, Mr. X?' . . . So the easiest way to [get them off that subject] is, 'I have seen the light, I know the white people are not all devils. . . . Now, can we discuss something else?'"

The expats also wanted to know more about Malcolm's split with the Nation. In a six-page letter to a friend about Malcolm's visit, Windom said the former NOI minister had declined to discuss the reasons for the split: "He intends to lend his talents to the building of unity among the various rights groups in America, and told us that, in his view, no useful purpose could be served by exposing all the roots of dissension." But in interviews with the author, both Windom and Garvin said Malcolm told them Elijah Muhammad's transgressions with young women in the Nation were the major reason for the split. Garvin also cited Malcolm's desire to engage in political action.

Although Malcolm was fiery in his public talks, he seemed

relaxed and open in private. "He listens, really listens to all that is said—sorting out, accepting valid suggestions, exploring, criticising confused thinking—with a working awareness that each person's thoughts have some value, and that even in disagreement the loser must not feel he has been destroyed," Alice Windom reported in her letter to friends. "Listening to him is a pleasure. His conversation is sprinkled with parables and analogies which illustrate and drive home his points in easily understood language, or politely obscure the fact that he does not want to give a direct answer."[13]

In his public talks, Malcolm vividly detailed racist oppression and violence in the United States and continued to push back against a sunnier picture of progress being purveyed by American diplomats. During a speech to a mixed audience of blacks and whites at the University of Ghana, Windom reported, Malcolm "addressed the whites in terms few Africans have heard used directly to whites in West Africa, accusing them of hypocrisy, murder and subversion. He said, 'I've never seen so many whites so nice to so many blacks as you people in Africa. Afro-Americans are struggling for integration in America. They should come to Africa and see how you grin at Africans. . . . But can you tell the Africans that you grinned at black people in America? . . . You don't like Africans but you do like the minerals Africa has under her soil.'"[14]

At a reception at the Ghana Press Club, where Malcolm stood "in a circle of admiring women," David Levering Lewis asked him a challenging question. "He had spoken emphatically of his determination to promote unity among the various civil rights organizations in the United States. But how, I asked Mr. X, could such a rapprochement come about between himself, an advocate of retaliatory violence, and Martin Luther King, Jr., the apostle of nonviolent passive resistance, without fundamental changes to his or King's beliefs, or both? His piercing eyes met mine. His tone was indulgent. I think he may have said something about mistaking appearances for realities, but the hiss rising from the audience was unnerving, and my concentration faltered so badly that I heard almost nothing."[15]

Students responded to Malcolm enthusiastically. But to pursue his quest to make U.S. racism an international issue, it was crucial for Malcolm to meet with President Nkrumah. Shirley Graham Du Bois, with her access to the president, was asked to set it up. "She said no because she was not going to take any riffraff to see the president," Windom recalled. "She didn't know anything about the Nation, except what she had seen in the press, which would be all criticism."[16] That week, however, Shirley Du Bois met Malcolm—razor sharp, well informed, and charming—at a reception. She pulled him aside, and they talked for at least an hour. When they were done, Du Bois announced, "This man is brilliant. I am taking him for my son. He must meet Kwame. They have too much in common not to meet."[17] Windom said, "They just fell in love right away. Then she arranged for him to meet with Nkrumah right away. She was comfortable once she had met him."[18]

In the *Autobiography*, published the following year, after his death, Malcolm presents a warm but vague account of his meeting with Nkrumah amid the impressive security of the president's office in Christiansborg Castle.* Nkrumah, he said, was well informed about Afro-American problems and "agreed that Pan-Africanism was the key also to the problems of those of African heritage."[19] Afterward, however, Malcolm seemed downcast. "When we picked him up after he met with Nkrumah, he was very somber," Windom recalled. "And we didn't feel like we could even ask him what had happened." Malcolm said nothing about it. Nkrumah, who had spent ten years in the United States as a student, was sympathetic to Afro-Americans' struggle, but he was not going to seek international action on their behalf. Kojo Botsio, a longtime close ally of Nkrumah who was then

---

* President Nkrumah by this time had survived several assassination attempts.

foreign minister, summed up the president's views: "We don't like what's being done to the African Americans, but it doesn't seem wise to raise, say, in the United Nations that sort of thing." Meddling in U.S. internal affairs would invite other countries, including the United States, to interfere in the affairs of Ghana. "Certainly, Kwame would say it. I mean, he wouldn't hide his feelings on that issue," said Botsio, who was not present at the meeting.[20]

Before he left Ghana on May 17, accompanied to the airport by an entourage of officials from friendly embassies, Malcolm experienced a smaller, more personal rejection. The young boxer Cassius Clay, soon to become Muhammad Ali, one of the world's most famous men, had been Malcolm's friend. In January, when Malcolm was suspended from the Nation but not fully detached from it, Clay was training for his bout against heavyweight champion Sonny Liston. The challenger invited Malcolm, his wife, Betty Shabazz, and their three daughters down to Miami; it was said to be the only vacation Malcolm and Betty ever took together. After upsetting Liston and becoming champion at age twenty-two on February 25, 1964, the young boxer made clear his adherence to the Nation of Islam and accepted his Muslim name from Elijah Muhammad, only days before Malcolm's exile from the Nation became permanent. Now, as Malcolm, the NOI apostate, left his hotel on the way to the airport, he crossed paths with Ali, the NOI true believer. Malcolm greeted the younger man, but Ali walked on. Years later, he said that snubbing Malcolm was one of the great regrets of his life. "I wish I'd been able to tell Malcolm I was sorry, that he was right about so many things," Ali wrote in a memoir published forty years later. "But he was killed before I got the chance. He was a visionary—ahead of us all."[21]

After leaving Ghana, Malcolm stopped in Senegal and Algeria before arriving home in New York on May 21. He would have only a seven-week sojourn before he left again for Africa. In that brief period, his relationship with the NOI became radioactive. He had previously spoken respectfully in public about Elijah Muhammad. Now he unloaded in speeches and media interviews with his charges about the Messenger's illegitimate children, whom he numbered at six. The attacks came as he fought eviction by the NOI, testifying in court amid heavy police protection because of death threats. At the same time, he announced the formation of his Organization of Afro-American Unity and tried to lay its foundation; he made plans for his next trip, and he saw his family grow, with the birth of a fourth daughter, Gamilah Lumumba. "And mainly I was trying to stay healthy and alive," he told a friend, noting "a *variety* of factions trying to get a shot at me so they could blame it on someone else."[22]

With civil rights protesters coming under attack in Southern cities, including Nashville, Tennessee, and St. Augustine, Florida, and police brutality sparking riots in Northern cities, including New York and Philadelphia, Malcolm continued to emphasize black people's right to self-defense. But he also sought connection with the nonviolent civil rights movement. At a secret meeting of civil rights leaders at the actor Sidney Poitier's house in June, he presented his idea of internationalizing the struggle by taking it to the United Nations. In a report to J. Edgar Hoover about the meeting, the FBI's New York Field Office stated that Clarence Jones, who was in attendance and authorized to speak for a jailed Martin Luther King Jr., considered this "the best idea presented."[23] The report, marked "urgent," was to be shared with the State Department and the CIA. The New York office followed up a week later with a report informing Hoover that Malcolm was meeting with various individuals "for the purpose of bringing American racial situation before the United Nations."[24]

A month later, Malcolm was back in Cairo, pressing his "best idea" at the African summit, the second meeting of the OAU, where delegates from more than thirty nations gathered. After several days of lobbying, he was awarded observer status to the meeting— apparently the only citizen from a non-African country to be given a floor pass—and was allotted a place on the *Isis*, a yacht housing free-dom fighters from around the continent. "We, in America, are your long lost brothers and sisters, and I am here to remind you that our problems are your problems," he wrote, beseeching African lead-ers to seek a U.N. investigation into the abuse of Afro-Americans. "Your problems will never be fully solved until and unless ours are solved. You will never be fully respected until and unless we are also respected. You will never be recognized as free human beings until and unless we are also recognized and treated as human beings." Using a favorite metaphor, Malcolm argued that in racial matters the United States was worse than South Africa, whose apartheid regime the OAU had condemned and targeted with sanctions. "South Africa is like a vicious wolf, openly hostile towards black humanity. But American is cunning like a fox, friendly and smil-ing, but even more vicious and deadly than the wolf. And if South African racism is not a domestic issue, then American racism also is not a *domestic* issue.

"We pray that our African brothers have not freed themselves of European colonialism only to be overcome and held in check now by American *dollarism*," he lamented. "Don't let American racism be 'legalized' by American dollarism.' "[25]

Despite Malcolm's lobbying, the OAU did not take the kind of strong action he sought. It did, however, pass a resolution deal-ing with U.S. racial practices. While "noting with satisfaction" the recent passage of the Civil Rights Act, it pronounced itself "deeply disturbed" by persistent racial oppression in the United States and urged the U.S. government to "intensify [its] efforts" to eliminate discrimination. The resolution and indeed the entire African sum-mit go unmentioned in the *Autobiography*, and the resolution gets only a passing reference in the published version of Malcolm's diary: clearly, it fell far short of his goal. Even its wording—it referred to "Negro citizens of the United States" rather than to "Afro-

Americans"—could be read as implying this was a U.S. domestic issue rather than an international one. But given the difficult
agenda of the OAU, which had to deal with border disputes, divisions over plans for a "United States of Africa," and requests from
liberation movements closer to home, it can be seen as an achievement, and a step toward something stronger.[26]

In a letter dated August 5, 1964, Malcolm told Betty he needed
to stay in Africa at least another month so he could try to persuade
leaders individually when they were back in their own countries.
"The enemy has successfully alienated most African governments
from wanting to get directly involved in the problems of the American Negro, and thus it takes personal diplomacy to show them that
our problems and failures are also theirs, and that they can make no
progress until we make progress."[27]

In the end, Malcolm stayed abroad a total of four and a half
months, despite getting reports of "some dissatisfaction" back home
and wondering "if I'm overplaying my hand (gamble) by staying
away too long."[28] First, he worked on strengthening his credentials as
an orthodox American Muslim, in sharp contrast to Elijah Muhammad and his ministers. During more than a month in Egypt, he
studied, spent time with Dr. Shawarbi, and was certified by Sheikh
Akbar Hassan Mamoun, the rector of Al-Azhar University, as being
qualified to teach Islam and spread the faith. In Alexandria, at a
grand rally with eight hundred students from around the world,
the Cairo-based Supreme Council on Islamic Affairs announced it
would give Malcolm scholarships so twenty Muslims from America
could study at Al-Azhar. "This affair impressed me even more than
my trip to Mecca: youth from everywhere, face [sic] of every complexion, representing every race & every culture . . . all shouting the
glory of Islam, filled with a militant, revolutionary spirit & zeal," Malcolm wrote in his diary.[29] In Mecca, the Saudi-based Muslim World
League endorsed his plan to establish an Islamic center in New York

and offered to accept fifteen scholars from Malcolm's group. The league also arranged to send a black Islamic cleric to New York to work with MMI, Malcolm's newly formed religious group, and teach the true faith. This not only would prevent further religious error; it also would free Malcolm to focus on his political arm, the Organization of Afro-American Unity (OAAU), with its work of linking black Americans to Africa.

From Mecca, Malcolm sent letters denouncing Elijah Muhammad personally as a "religious faker" and, with stark vehemence, proclaiming his own identity as an orthodox Muslim. This ax blow was delivered in a story in *The New York Times* of October 4 that reprinted long sections of one of the letters:

> For 12 long years I lived within the narrow-minded confines of the "strait-jacket world" created by my strong belief that Elijah Muhammad was a messenger direct from God Himself, and my faith in what I now see to be a pseudoreligious philosophy that he preaches. . . .
>
> I shall never rest until I have undone the harm I did to so many well-meaning, innocent Negroes who through my own evangelistic zeal now believe in him even more fanatically and more blindly than I did. . . .
>
> I am a Muslim in the most orthodox sense; my religion is Islam as it is believed in and practiced by the Muslims here in the Holy City of Mecca.
>
> This religion recognizes all men as brothers. It accepts all human beings as equals before God, and as equal members in the Human Family of Mankind. I totally reject Elijah Muhammad's racist philosophy, which he has labeled "Islam" only to fool and misuse gullible people, as he fooled and misused me. But I blame only myself, and no one else for the fool that I was, and the harm that my evangelic foolishness in his behalf has done to others.[30]

As September ended, Malcolm's efforts shifted from the Mideast to Africa, from the religious to the political. Throughout what remained of his life, Malcolm kept working to mobilize an African diplomatic charge against the nation he saw as a bastion of antiblack oppression. Traveling alone and with only the thinnest of organizations behind him, he won access to the leaders of Africa and practiced high-level diplomacy. Malcolm presented himself as speaking for 22 million Afro-Americans, and generally was treated as such. He made speeches, gave interviews, addressed parliament members, lobbied politicians, and met with many national leaders, including Jomo Kenyatta of Kenya, Gamal Abdel Nasser of Egypt, Sékou Touré of Guinea, Julius K. Nyerere of Tanzania, Nnamdi Azikiwe of Nigeria, and Milton Obote of Uganda, as well as Nkrumah. Sometimes he was treated as a head of state himself. In Guinea in November, he stayed in the president's home. "I'm speechless. All praise to Allah!" he wrote in his diary. "They gave me three servants, a driver, and an Army officer."[31]

For young, radical Africans, Malcolm "became the measuring rod" for all Afro-American activists. John Lewis, the civil rights leader and future congressman, was traveling in Africa that fall of 1964 with other members of the Student Nonviolent Coordinating Committee (SNCC). He found that even politically aware young people there knew little about the American civil rights movement, but they knew about Malcolm. "As soon as we were introduced to someone, the first thing he would ask was 'What's your organization's relationship with Malcolm's?'"[32]

*The New York Times* reported that U.S. officials had begun to pay attention to Malcolm's African campaign: "Officials said that if Malcolm succeeded in convincing just one African Government to bring up the charge at the United Nations, the United States Government would be faced with a touchy problem."[33] Faced with the new African nations' own pressing issues, and the economic and political power of the United States, Malcolm never did find an African champion to carry Afro-Americans' banner to the United Nations. But his international campaign caused unease in the U.S. State Department. In Kenya in October, he met with Dr. Njoroge Mungai, a cabinet minister and the personal physician to Jomo Kenyatta, who had helped lead Kenya to independence less than a year earlier and would soon become its first president. Mungai, who had done his medical training at Stanford and Columbia Universities, was familiar with U.S. racial politics. The cabinet minister said Malcolm wanted help getting meetings with African heads of state so he could build a bridge between black people of America and Africa. "He wasn't talking any violent means. He was building something big, which was admirable."[34]

A day later, Malcolm was seen with Kenyatta, who was past seventy and revered as a national father figure, during a celebration of Kenyatta Day, honoring those who had so recently won Kenya's independence. The next day William Attwood, the U.S. ambassador in Nairobi, chewed out Mungai for associating with an "undesirable person." Mungai recalls replying, "He is not an undesirable to me or to my government."[35] Attwood then met with Malcolm, accused him of being a racist, and "alerted other posts of his arrival, suggesting they enlighten their Africa friends in advance" about "who he really was."[36] Malcolm himself portrayed this encounter as a valuable learning experience. He said the ambassador and he "both agreed that American society makes it next to impossible" for people to relate as humans, without regard to race or color. "That discussion with the ambassador gave me a new insight—one which I like: that the white man is *not* inherently evil, but America's racist society influences him to act evilly."[37]

Again and again, Malcolm spoke about how his experiences in a postcolonial, politically active Africa broadened his understanding and his scope. He had stopped describing himself as a black nationalist after returning from his trip in the spring. In Ghana, he said, the Algerian ambassador, a revolutionary who was white, had asked, "if I define my objective as the victory of black nationalism, where does that leave him? Where does that leave revolutionaries in Morocco, Egypt, Iraq, Mauritania? So he showed me where I was alienating people who were true revolutionaries, dedicated to over-throwing the system of exploitation that exists on this earth by any means necessary."[38]

Instead, Malcolm had begun to talk about capitalism as the enemy. "The last bulwark of capitalism today is America," he told a New York audience in May, when he was just back from his *hajj*. "It's impossible for a white person to believe in capitalism and not believe in racism. You can't have capitalism without racism." If you meet a non-racist white, he added, "usually they're socialists."[39]

When Malcolm returned to Ghana for a brief visit in November, he seemed different, said Dr. Robert Lee, the expatriate dentist. "He was a bit more analytical. He talked about poverty and talked about poor people and rights of people. Not so much black people and white people."[40] John Lewis, then chairman of SNCC, ran into him in Nairobi that fall. "He talked about the need to shift our focus, both among one another and between us and the white community, from race to class. He said that was the root of our problems, not just in America, but all over the world." Lewis said Malcolm "seemed very hopeful. His overwhelmingly positive reception in Africa by blacks, whites, Asians and Arabs alike had pushed him toward believing that people *could* come together."[41]

Malcolm also was putting greater emphasis on women's roles. "In every Middle-East or African country I have visited, I noticed the country is as 'advanced' as its women are, or as backward as its women," he would write the following year, a week before his assas-sination. "Thus, in my opinion, the Muslim religious leaders of today must re-evaluate and spell out with clarity the Muslim position on education in general and education for women in particular. And then a vast program must be launched to elevate the standard of education in the Muslim World. An old African proverb states: 'Educate a man and you educate an individual; educate a woman and you educate an entire family.' "[42]

Along with his hopefulness, however, Malcolm also had "a great sense of alarm, a great sense of anxiety," Lewis recalled. He believed he was being watched and followed. He never sat with his back exposed. "In a calm, measured way he was convinced that somebody wanted him killed."[43]

Malcolm finally returned on November 24 to New York, where, according to the FBI, he was greeted at the airport by members of his two organizations, the religious Muslim Mosque Inc. (MMI) and the political Organization of Afro-American Unity (OAAU). So much had changed since his last homecoming in May. In July, President Lyndon B. Johnson had signed the Civil Rights Act into law, ostensibly outlawing racial discrimination in voter registration, education, and public accommodations, although Malcolm called it a deceptive propaganda tool. Johnson ("the fox") had beaten Barry Goldwater ("the wolf") in the presidential election. Martin Luther King Jr. had won the Nobel Peace Prize. A judge in Queens had ruled in favor of the Nation of Islam, saying Malcolm and his family had to be out of their home by the end of January. And there was dissension and disarray in Malcolm's two organizations, which had been without his leadership for months.

Nonetheless, in the next few months, Malcolm kept up a heavy speaking schedule, with travel to London, Oxford, Boston, Toronto, and Chicago. In Los Angeles, he met with two former NOI secretaries who were bringing paternity suits against Elijah Muhammad. On February 4, demonstrating solidarity with civil rights protests led by Martin Luther King, he spoke to young civil rights activists at a church in Selma, Alabama, and had a brief one-on-one discussion with Coretta Scott King. At the time, black citizens in Selma were demanding the right to register to vote and were being beaten and arrested. King was in jail there at the time.

Meanwhile, the threatening episodes, like a quickening drumbeat, escalated: Malcolm's car was tailed at high speeds in Los Angeles, police had to scare off attackers in Chicago and New York. Nonetheless, Malcolm left for his final trip abroad on February 5, 1965. He spoke at the first Congress of the Council of African Organizations in London before heading to Paris to talk to the Federation of African Students. At the Paris airport, however, he was not allowed to enter the country. He was told that the French government found his presence "undesirable." In light of such global incidents, Malcolm shifted his view of the master plan behind his planned assassination, no longer believing that only the Nation was targeting him. He returned to London, and finally arrived back home on Saturday, February 13, to his wife, now pregnant with twins, and their four young daughters. The next day, Valentine's Day, he was due to speak in Detroit. And on Monday, there was to be a hearing in Queens in hopes of delaying the family's eviction from their home.

# CHAPTER 17

# The Week Before: A Dry Run

G ENE ROBERTS REPORTED EARLY ON MONDAY, FEBRUARY 15, 1965, for his guard post at the Audubon Ballroom in Harlem, where Malcolm was to address his two fledgling groups. Front rostrum guards stood sentry, backs to the speaker, and scanned the audience for potential trouble.[1] This final line of defense, a holdover from Nation of Islam days, demanded that Roberts be alert, poised, and sure.

Roberts could handle himself in a fair fight, although the handsome bank-clerk-type was a departure from the image of Muslim guards, who were typically picked as much for showing a fierce mien as for their ability to deliver a swift karate kick. With his curly hair combed forward into a "top-notch," Roberts looked more like Floyd Patterson, the gentle former heavyweight boxing champion, than, say, Sonny Liston, the close-cropped challenger who had mercilessly dethroned him in 1962 and who, with his baleful, ten-yard glare, could have been a poster boy for the Fruit of Islam rostrum guard.

Since Malcolm's expulsion from the Muslims in 1964, he was moving away from employing scowling security men and pat-down searches at the doors of nonreligious public meetings. Old-timers considered the shift ill timed, if not eerie, especially given that his East Elmhurst home in Queens had just been firebombed the previous morning.

Malcolm had flown home from London on Saturday, and had worked late into the early hours of Sunday, typing out answers to a series of questions posed by the Islamic Centre of Geneva. One query asked why Elijah Muhammad had turned against him after he commented on President Kennedy's assassination. He replied that the Kennedy comments were merely a convenient pretext. "Elijah Muhammad," he wrote, "allowed himself to become insanely jealous of my own popularity which went even beyond his own followers and into the non-Muslim community, while his own prestige and influence was limited largely among his immediate followers." Moreover, Malcolm wrote, "At the time they announced I was to be suspended and silenced for 90 days, they had already set in motion the machinery to have me completely ousted from the movement, and Elijah Muhammad himself had already given the order to have me killed because he feared I would expose to his followers the secret of his extreme immorality."[2]

At 12:30 a.m., with a page still in the typewriter, Malcolm broke from his work to go to bed, Two hours later, arsonists from Temple No. 7 threw Molotov cocktails through the windows of Malcolm's family home in Queens. A daughter's scream awakened Malcolm and he managed to escort his pregnant wife, Betty, and their four daughters to safety in the frigid night.

Still, Malcolm maintained that the body searches at public events too much resembled harassment and might turn off the younger, better-educated, non-Muslim crowd he intended to attract to his secular, black nationalist Organization of Afro-American Unity (OAAU). Leaders of Malcolm's religious branch, Muslim Mosque, Inc. (MMI), had vigorously opposed this withering away of the heavy security presence at public gatherings. They stressed the violent threats to Malcolm's life that had emerged from his former comrades in the Nation of Islam.[3]

The risk of violence remained ever present. Elijah Muhammad himself had spoken of his impatience with Malcolm, his former national spokesman. In a top-secret September meeting with his most trustworthy captains, the Muslim cult leader had complained that "the chief hypocrite" had "mudwashed" the Messenger of Allah and should be "made to go away."[4]

Already, Nation of Islam assassins had made several bold attempts on Malcolm's life, in Boston, Los Angeles, Philadelphia, and New York, as well as in Chicago. Upon returning to his hotel during a trip to the Windy City that January, Malcolm and his party were joined by Chuck Stone, a journalist who was tagging along for an interview. Stone, formerly editor of the *Chicago Defender*, later became a columnist for the *Philadelphia Daily News*. When they got off the elevator, Stone was first to turn the corner on Malcolm's floor.

"There was a short, black guy in a three-quarter length coat, standing in the corridor with a sawed-off shotgun," Stone later recalled. "It scared the shit out of me. When he saw me, the gunman turned around and ran down the steps. If Malcolm had been first around the corner. . . ."[5]

These near hits were not appreciated at Chicago headquarters, least of all by some Royal Family members who were waiting for the deed to be done. As these blunders continued into the winter, a sense of urgency went out on the wire. An absolute deadline was set. The schedule was known only to the most trusted Muslim ministers— and, likely, the FBI. The former minister known as Malcolm X was to be eliminated during the ten days immediately before Saviour's Day, February 26.

The hit order itself was the worst-kept secret in Muslim circles, but word of the specific deadline was tightly held among trusted officials. Aware of the constant danger, the savvy MMI officials who had followed Malcolm from the Nation vigorously opposed his scaling down of security. One expert security man, a specialist in explosives and sidearms, had thwarted several attempts on his leader's life. Never much given to Islam, this secular expert was baffled that Malcolm would consider reducing security at the very time that the Muslims had obviously stepped up their plans to eliminate him.[6]

The latest, most dangerous attempt had been the firebombing of the family's home early Sunday morning, February 14. After keeping his scheduled speaking engagement at Cobo Hall in Detroit later that day, Malcolm returned to New York on Monday, planning to address the Muslims' arson attack when he spoke that evening at the Harlem auditorium. Security men around Malcolm staged as much a show of force as they could muster under the extraordinarily tense circumstances.

Gene Roberts was studiously aware of the internecine conflict between Malcolm and the Nation, but since joining the OAAU ten months earlier, he had been kept on the periphery. Malcolm's ruling circle consisted of Muslims he had known for years, men who came over with him or had proven their trustworthiness in direct fashion. Roberts was not a Muslim and thus could not be fully trusted. He had cultivated some of Malcolm's followers while hanging out at the Chock Full o'Nuts coffee shop on 135th Street and Lenox Avenue.

The glue that bound Roberts to the OAAU was his interest and proficiency in the arts of self-defense. He had been introduced to hand-to-hand combat during basic training in the Navy. His karate skills, however, were greatly intensified under the mat training of James 67X, an accomplished black belt who was also Malcolm X's top assistant and man Friday. "James was our martial arts instructor," Roberts said. "Sometimes I'd go one-on-one with him. He taught me a lot." James had recently brought in a mysterious karate master, Sensei Takahara. The tall Asian instructed a small group of Muslims in an extraordinary high level of *qigong*, a major component of martial arts. The contact with James 67X and the specialized training had earned Roberts his Monday night spot on the front-rostrum security detail.[7]

There was more, much more, to Gene Roberts than met the eye of Malcolm and his Harlem followers. James 67X was leery of Roberts from the very beginning, even though he could not quite say why. Early on, he had visited a Chase Manhattan Bank branch to verify the new member's reported place of employment. The bank vouched for Roberts. It was also verified that Roberts was born in Virginia, had grown up in the Bronx, and had served in the Marine Corps. Military service was no indication of anything special. Unlike Malcolm, many of the Muslims, especially those without prison records, had served, including James 67X himself. Still, there were the Florsheim wingtip shoes, the quiet reserve, the way Roberts kept much about himself away from the OAAU and the more prying eyes of the MMI. For example, although he was married, with a wedding band on his left ring finger, Roberts never talked about his wife and daughter or brought them around. While such secrecy was very much street Harlem, where men made ends meet with side hustles, the Muslims were accustomed to openness within the communal embrace of their religious cult.[8]

Besides, Gene Roberts was one of the guards handpicked to protect Malcolm this night from further attempts on his life. While lacking the fierce mien of the old Muslim guards, Roberts had the subtle style, discipline, and cunning that made him the master of those smash-face intimidators. Roberts was considered a thinking-man's guard who checked avenues of escape, a trained mental note taker who was quick to size up an audience and detect danger. He was willing, sure, and prompt, and was judged to know how to keep secrets.

Gene Roberts was also an undercover New York City police officer.[9]

What few black cops there were on the force were generally known about town, so the police department was then recruiting Negroes fresh out of—and in some cases still in—the military. Roberts joined the police upon his discharge from the Navy, and the rookie was rushed directly onto the streets of Harlem to infiltrate Malcolm's organizations. He had been covenanted to the Bureau of Special Services and Investigations (BOSSI), an intelligence unit that had recruited him to spy on Malcolm and the small knot of men who ran his operations during his constant travels.

"I had no weapon, no ID," Roberts recalled. "I was neither fish nor fowl. Nobody in the department probably knew who I was, except my control officer, Lieutenant Bernard Mulligan, and the other officers I was dealing with. I worked for BOSSI. . . . I read [police] rules and procedures. And I was told, 'Don't report anything that didn't happen.' I said, 'Hey, I ain't gonna do that anyway. I was taught better. I'll give you what's there. And if it ain't there, it ain't there, case closed.'

"I was just coming back from the military. I had heard a couple of Malcolm X's speeches when he was in the Nation. And I didn't particularly care for him. I was one of those middle-class blacks that had a half-ass education. I wasn't political."

Although Roberts had not penetrated Malcolm's inner circle, his feigned loyalty was sufficient to have gained him entrée. He had gotten close enough for his government work. What details he learned about Malcolm's movements, the young cop dutifully reported each night to his handlers at police headquarters downtown.[10] BOSSI shared its information with FBI Director J. Edgar Hoover, who had an even greater interest in Malcolm after his split from the Black Muslims.

Because his house had been bombed the day before, Malcolm was expected to set off some polemical fireworks against Elijah Muhammad at the Harlem meeting at the Audubon Ballroom.

As usual, Gene Roberts was prepared to assume his front-rostrum guard duties, carried out in thirty-minute, rotated shifts. As the crowd milled in, the former navy corpsman, along with five other MMI security men, marched into position, facing the audience with their backs to Malcolm. Their assigned duty was not so much to protect the speaker as to keep the audience at bay, to pinpoint the unruly, and to suppress any disruption in the audience.[11] With the New York newspapers blaring headlines about Malcolm's troubles, a crowd of five hundred had been attracted to his OAAU meeting that Monday night.

Malcolm did not disappoint, even though he began slowly. He appeared dazed when he came to the rostrum, tieless and wearing a suit reeking of smoke. After the firebombing and the quick trip to Detroit, he had taken a doctor-administered sedative in order to rest before the speech. Uncharacteristically halting and apologetic at first, he sketched out what had happened in the Sunday morning attack. He then got back on course with a scathing critique of U.S. misbehavior in the Congo and other parts of Africa, where countries were fighting European colonialism supported by American planes and matériel.

Then Malcolm sharpened his declaration of open warfare on Elijah Muhammad's group. As fiery as he'd ever been, he blasted Captain Joseph, the man he had brought with him from Detroit to Chicago a decade earlier, for claiming that Malcolm had bombed his own home with his wife and sleeping babies inside.

"Now, they are using the same tactics that's used by the Ku Klux Klan," Malcolm declared. "When the Klan bombs your church, they say you did it. When they bomb the synagogue, they say the Jews bombed their own synagogue." The reference to the white knights, so much the terror still of blacks in the South, was a calculated tactic employed to expose the broader, secret relationship that Elijah Muhammad had established over the years with the Klan. At Elijah's direction, Malcolm himself, as we have seen, had conducted a Muslim meeting in Atlanta in 1961 with the murderous white racist organization. Now, by alluding to those negotiations with the KKK, Malcolm was expressing his personal shame and was also lambasting Elijah Muhammad for secretly dealing with the acknowledged enemy of black progress in America.

That potentially explosive connection was but one of the deep and dangerous secrets Malcolm was privy to, one that he had increasingly hinted at exposing more fully at the proper time. Not only had Muhammad dealt with the Klan and with American Nazi leader George Lincoln Rockwell, Malcolm told the Audubon audience, but Elijah Muhammad also had armed his soldiers with a sword that drew only black blood. Instead of torching Malcolm's house, he said, "they could have thrown that bomb in a Ku Klux Klan house."

The Nation of Islam has been violent, Malcolm said, "violent from coast to coast. Muslims, in the Muslim movement, have been involved in cold, calculated violence. And not at one time have they been involved in violence against the Ku Klux Klan. They're capable. They're qualified. They're equipped. They know how to do it—only to another brother." [12]

In a broader sense, Malcolm was charging that Elijah Muhammad had struck a deal with white America. In addition to avoiding the civil rights struggle, his men, while capable, would do no tangible harm to white interests. Malcolm added that he knew full well what he was doing by revealing such damning details for the first time about Muhammad's links with violent, right-wing white groups in America. He indicated that he intended to step up the attack in the coming weeks, naming names, but acknowledged that such an indictment could have a dangerously high price: "Now, I am well aware of what I'm setting in motion by what I'm saying up here tonight. I'm well aware. But I have never said or done anything in my life that I wasn't prepared to suffer the consequences for." [13]

In fact, Captain Joseph had given the orders to torch Malcolm's Queens home on February 14. Some published reports, working from fire department accounts, said that one bottle of flammable liquid was found upright on a dresser, implying that Malcolm X had set fire to his own home. That charge had so incensed Malcolm that, during his Sunday speech in Detroit, he had flown into a rage and, for one of the few times in a public speech, had cursed uncontrollably.

For years, the Fruit of Islam (FOI) chief denied having ordered the firebombing and maintained that Malcolm likely had set fire to his own house.[14] However, the day before his death in 1993, Captain Joseph confirmed that it was he, clearly acting on orders from NOI officials in Chicago, who had ordered the firebombing. According to a close confidant, who implicated himself in the arson, Captain Joseph actually supervised the early morning arson hit himself. "No, sir, Malcolm definitely did not burn down his own house," Joseph said, asserting that "you can take my word that you can be absolutely sure in writing that."[15]

A week before this telephone confession, while walking across a Harlem street on a wintry day and clearly suffering from a debilitating bout with diabetes, Captain Joseph—the man informed Muslims all say knew the details of the assassination—surprised this writer by naming key participants in the murder of Malcolm X. He said that the Harlem temple was under direct orders from Chicago to harass Malcolm and—after the secret meeting Elijah Muhammad held in September—to do him "terminal bodily harm."[16] At this joint meeting of ministers and captains, held in Michigan, one of the key officials was Jeremiah X, the Muhammad confidant who set up Muslim temples throughout the South. On his deathbed in a hospital in the Germantown section of Philadelphia in 1998, Jeremiah X, who had for decades refused to discuss the issue, also confirmed that the top leadership in Chicago had ordered Malcolm X to be killed by Saviour's Day, February 26, 1965.[17]

On February 15, 1965, as he stood on the rostrum guarding Malcolm, Gene Roberts didn't know all that, but he was on sharp alert. With high tension in the air, he scanned the room for signs of danger in his dual role as a Muslim guard and as a cop gathering intelligence. He stood ready to suppress trouble and to pass any hint of it along to his bosses at police headquarters.[18] Malcolm's denunciatory speech was punctuated by applause and sprinkled with the naming of names to be catalogued and remembered. Then, toward the end of the speech, Roberts's guard-tower gaze froze on a section of the animated Audubon audience. A lone man, clean-cut, with a red bow tie, walked down the aisle as if heading for the stage. The crisp, electric atmosphere immediately changed. Roberts's eyes narrowed.

"I'm a Muslim, for which I am proud," Malcolm was saying. "And in no way has that changed, my being a Muslim. My religion is Islam . . ."[19]

At the same time, Roberts noted the sound of heckling off to one side. The words were inaudible; a tape recording later failed to reveal the words clearly. But the disturbance was distracting enough to draw the attention of Malcolm, the nearby audience, and the rostrum guards.

"What's up?" asked Malcolm, interrupting his speech. "Okay. Y'all sit down and be cool," he said to some laughter in the audience. "Just sit down and be cool."[20]

Gene Roberts moved away from the stage and intercepted the man in the red bow tie who had continued down the aisle. Roberts sized up the man as a Muslim regular. "I went toward him. He took his seat. No problem. Malcolm was still speaking. I'm keeping my eye on [the stranger]. My attitude was the way he was dressed: he was from the Nation, but hey, I don't know. I was basically a rookie cop, and I had good instincts."

After Roberts in his role as a guard helped Malcolm diffuse the disruption, he reported in his role as a police officer. "When I came back home, I called the police department," he said. "I told my staff people that 'I just think I saw a dress rehearsal for this man's assassination.' I told them I think it's going to go down."[21] One of Roberts's supervisors confirmed his warning to the department and the account became another of the clear warning signs—unheeded.

———

For years afterward, the more Roberts pondered the "rehearsal" incident at the Audubon, the more it sent shivers through him. He could not shake what rocked him most about the setup of Malcolm's murder. After the young cop's warning about Malcolm's imminent assassination, the police department reacted by sharply *reducing* the uniformed presence in front of the ballroom. Roberts would be even more troubled a week later by the inordinately long time the department took to answer the emergency call to take Malcolm to Columbia Presbyterian Hospital.

# CHAPTER 18

# The Hit

A S MALCOLM MADE HIS WAY TO THE AUDUBON BALLROOM ON Sunday, February 21, 1965, a sense of dread crackled among all those around him. Sara Mitchell, the coordinating secretary of the Organization of Afro-American Unity (OAAU), had arrived early, at around one in the afternoon. She was working in their small office backstage, something of a waiting room for the support staff to set up the program for what already promised to be an afternoon of disappointments for their leader.

A former Miss Black Georgia, Mitchell worked during the week as a receptionist at *The New Yorker* and aspired to one day break into the market as a writer. The Macon native had caught Malcolm's attention after writing him a letter about the OAAU. Between trips abroad, Malcolm had personally recruited her in June 1964 to work with other young non-Muslims who were launching the activist, political organization.[1]

Throughout the week, Malcolm had promoted this big Sunday meeting as only he could, by word of mouth on the street, at college lectures, and in spirited radio interviews. Ever since the bombing of his home a week earlier, he had been intimating that he would go even further than he had the previous Monday night in naming names. Moreover, in that February 15 speech, he had outright promised that the OAAU would make a great leap forward with a programmatic launch that would unfold with accompanying entertainment before a packed house of rainbow people and politics.

> We're going to have a rally here this coming Sunday at two o'clock in the afternoon . . . at which time we will give you the program of the Organization of Afro-American Unity: what our aims are; our objectives are; what our program is; whether or not you want to be identified with it, and what active part you can play in helping us to straighten Harlem out. Nobody's going to straighten out Harlem but us. Nobody cleans up your house for you. You can clean it up yourself. Harlem is our house; we'll clean it up. But when we clean it up, we'll also control it. We'll control the politics. We'll control the economy. We'll control the school system and see that our people get a break.[2]

It was vintage Malcolm, with that P. T. Barnum touch of the showman honed during his days with the Nation of Islam (NOI). The customary supporting cast, however, was no longer in place.

Malcolm had, for example, expected to have a completed draft charter that would jump-start the OAAU, but the document was not yet forthcoming from the appointed committee. His domestic group was to be patterned after its namesake, the newly formed Organization of African Unity (OAU), a coalition of African nations whose goals included eradicating colonialism on their continent. Malcolm's group was to have a board comprised of representatives from every black nationalist group in the United States. College-trained staffers, such as Peter Bailey and Muriel Gray, had been given responsibility for drafting the OAAU charter, while Sara Mitchell was charged with applying the final editing touches. These assigned administrative details had not been dutifully executed on time.[3]

Malcolm, the former minister of the highly disciplined, quasi-military NOI, was discovering, not unlike General Dwight D. Eisenhower upon entering politics, that his suggestions to the staff no longer constituted commands. There was much confusion in the leadership of the fledging OAAU about exactly who was to supervise whom, and what they were supposed to do toward whatever purpose. There were also ego battles over who was the boldest revolutionary, the best organizer, the one bathing in the warmest glow of Malcolm's confidence. The efficiency, to say nothing of the discipline, that Malcolm had built into Muslim temples over the years was nowhere present among his new, idealistic followers. As for the charter, they were hardly sure, given their conflicting signals, of exactly what Malcolm wanted the document to be.[4]

And there were intragroup turf battles. The new energy Malcolm dedicated to the OAAU came at the expense of his commitment to the Muslim Mosque, Inc. (MMI), according to several of the brothers. There were irreconcilable differences about religion, discipline, lifestyle, and the role of women in the group. Although the NOI, for example, idealized black women as mothers, daughters, and sisters to be protected, women were not given much of a role outside the home and they certainly were not to be allowed to run organizational matters. "Women were playing such a large role in the OAAU," said James 67X. "The younger brothers could accept this. Those of us who had been in the Nation with Malcolm could not."[5]

That Sunday at the Audubon Ballroom, the services began in earnest at around 2:00 p.m., when Gene Roberts, the undercover cop in his dark suit and four-in-hand tie, met Malcolm near the front door and escorted him with a trio of security men to the stage area. Then Malcolm retreated into the back office.

James 67X was present in that room but had shrunk from his

previously lofty position as Malcolm's most trusted assistant. After
several threats, the brilliant secretary had tendered his resignation,
and Malcolm had reluctantly accepted. The year of service James had
promised Malcolm was nearing an end, and he was disenchanted
over how things were going with MMI and the younger, undisciplined OAAU. Additionally, the man Friday had encountered irritat-
ing inquiries from Malcolm's wife, Sister Betty.[6]

Malcolm had shut his wife out of the loop of his ministerial
duties. As the pregnant mother of his four daughters, with heavy
household responsibilities, Betty constantly had to petition his inner
circle about his whereabouts and other tidbits of information. Since
his expulsion from the NOI, James 67X often found himself caught
in the middle.

"It is not ever easy to relate to the wife of a powerful person
because they feel that the power of the husband rubs off on them,"
said James. "And it seldom does in an organization like ours. I had at
times to call Malcolm to task about Betty. I said, 'Well, brother, you
have to make up your mind. Am I working for you or am I working
for your wife?' She would ask me, 'Where is my husband going to be
Thursday night?' I have to say, 'Why don't you ask him?' "[7]

James 67X showed up that Sunday troubled and uncertain just
how, or if, his relationship with Malcolm would survive the day. If
things fell apart, James was fully prepared to simply move on. Relations with Malcolm became even more tense after James received
a call about a cancellation on the program for the Sunday event.
The loose plan for the OAAU program had called for guest appearances by the Reverend Milton Galamison, an activist campaigning
for school desegregation in the city, and by Ralph Cooper, a well-
known Harlem DJ, who was to bring a singing group along with
him. The Muslim brothers who normally introduced Malcolm had
no stomach for frivolity, especially the music, so Sara Mitchell, a
singer of sorts herself, was scheduled to emcee the soft prelude to

Malcolm's speech. However, Reverend Galamison's secretary had called James the day before to say that neither man could attend. James knew that Malcolm had spent the night in a New York City hotel, but didn't know which one. So he reflexively called Malcolm's home number and relayed the information about the schedule change to Betty.[8]

But Malcolm hadn't received the message from Betty, and James 67X had to deliver the news about Cooper personally just as the event was about to begin. Malcolm tensed.

"Why didn't you tell me?" he asked.

"I called your wife and I told her," James replied.

"You know better than to tell her anything," Malcolm exploded. "You should have told me." The vein that appeared in the middle of his forehead whenever he got angry was never more prominent. "Get out, get out," Malcolm's other aide, Benjamin 2X, the assistant minister, remembered their boss shouting.

That last-minute change only added to Malcolm's irritation about the lack of organization. He was already annoyed that an acceptable draft of the group's charter was not ready; as always, he was time conscious and especially didn't like the idea of having to appear to be disorganized before the expectant crowd gathering at the hall.

After Malcolm's explosion, Benjamin 2X, who normally introduced Malcolm at the Audubon, instead went and sat across from Brother Hussein, an elderly Sudanese sent by a Sunni group in the Middle East to instruct the MMI in the tenets of orthodox Islam. Visibly disturbed, Hussein shook his head.

"He saw an ominous sign in this," Benjamin 2X said. "He said, 'This wonderful.' But by his not understanding English, I said, 'You mean this is terrible.' He said, 'Yes, this is terrible.'" Hussein tried to stress the point that it was a matter of the very deep place Malcolm's anger was coming from. "It was not a surface kind of anger."

Malcolm's outburst may well have been a bad sign. For the moment, however, his anger, like a crackling dry summer storm, momentarily cleared the pregnant air.

Sara Mitchell was now asked to have Benjamin 2X return and prepare to open up the session, and then introduce Malcolm. With none of the invited guests attending, the afternoon program was skimmed back to the basic MMI format.

"I asked him, 'What do you want me to say?'" Benjamin recalled. "Usually, he would say, 'Follow your mind.' But this time, from the mood he was in, I thought it was best to ask him to see what kind of feedback I got. So he asked me, 'How are you going to open up?' So I told him that what I would do was to prepare the mind of the audience to accept the fact that we don't have the OAAU charter.

"You can prepare an audience, or a group of people, to accept almost anything without telling them the thing that you want them to accept. It's like plowing, opening up the ground. You can plant almost any seed in the ground. It will grow in that climate. This is the same manner in which you can seed an audience.

"So anyway I felt something that was ominous in the air. I had never felt that way before in opening up for him. It was like an invisible weight sitting on my shoulder, on my back."[9]

The initial four-man front-roster guard, with Gene Roberts at the flank, had moved into position for its thirty-minute posting as the hall continued to fill. Charles 37X Kenyatta, who had been "sat down" for insubordination, took a seat near the back on the right side, all dressed in black.[10] Yuri Kochiyama, a Japanese American human rights activist, took a seat in the third row on the left side with her sixteen-year-old son.[11] Betty Shabazz, who had been driven to the Audubon by a family friend, shouldered her way onto her bench with her four neatly groomed daughters.

As he had done so often, Benjamin 2X walked out to the plywood rostrum to open up. "I began talking about a captain of a ship heading toward the destination. And he has a certain time to get there at the rate of speed he's traveling. But then sometimes a storm will come up, or something unexpected that he may have to ride the storm; or he may have to go around the storm; which was my way of preparing an audience to accept the fact that things had come up unexpectedly, which is why the charter wasn't ready.

"So I went on in that manner. And I didn't know he had walked out on the stage and had sat behind me. The minister had a way of walking, as tall as he was, that was real softly in leather-soled shoes.* Really, he could tip. And you wouldn't hear him unless a board had creaked or something. So as I looked down to check my notes, I was very nervous inside, very nervous.

"I saw these two brothers sitting there—dark-skinned brothers. I knew they were Muslims, it was something about them. And they had their coats folded over their arms. And the thing that attracted me about them was their silence. It was like a silence within a silence."

Of all the people in the Audubon Ballroom, Benjamin 2X had the most accurate instinct. As it turned out, he would be the person who got the best look at the gunmen. During his twenty-odd-minute warm-up, he scanned the audience repeatedly, his eyes falling back warily on the two dark men near the front with the coats slung over their arms. Although he knew them to be Muslims by their appearance, he did not recognize them.

"[For] some reason, I kept glancing at them and glancing away; it wasn't unusual for Muslims to be there, because Malcolm said, 'Let any Muslim in who wanted to enter.' But I kept glancing at them. I don't remember seeing them before, but I knew they were Muslims." Sect members had their ways of sensing one another out, and Benjamin was as sharp at this as anyone.

---

* West Indians call this distinctive style Malcolm's "tiger-boy" way of walking.

"Malcolm reached for a piece of paper that was lying in the seat next to the one he was sitting in, which was slightly to my right. I saw his hand [and] that's when I first realized that he was there. He must have sensed that I had sensed that he was sitting there. So he said, 'Make it plain.'"[12] This expression was the signal Malcolm always made to let his warm-up speakers know that he was ready to go on, and that they should wrap up their introduction.

"Strange, when I introduced him, brought him to the podium, I said, 'I now introduce to you a man that would give his life for his people.' Well, he got up and I turned to sit where he had just arisen from. And he stopped me briefly, and he said, 'Go in the back and tell them to let me know the minute that Reverend Galamison comes in.'" Already, Malcolm had dispatched Peter Bailey to wait at the front for the popular minister, even though Malcolm knew he had canceled. Clearly, he wanted the stage cleared behind him.

Puzzled that he was not allowed to remain on stage as he usually did, Benjamin 2X nonetheless headed backstage. "Among Muslims, whenever the minister gave you an order, it was carried out immediately. . . . If Minister Malcolm said, 'Go and bring my car,' even though ordinarily he would speak for a while, I wouldn't sit there and wait for fifteen minutes. I would go at that moment, or any Muslim, not just me, would have gone at that moment and carried out that order."

The dismissed lieutenant walked back to the rear office and told James 67X and Sara Mitchell that "'the minister said to let him know when Reverend Galamison comes in there.' Let me tell you something, I never felt so weird, and I had begun to perspire while I was talking. It was just beading; but when I had got into that room, water began to pour down my face. I mean just like you had taken a glass of water and poured it over my head. And I sat down, just briefly, all these things in just seconds."[13]

Benjamin 2X never did return to the stage.

Malcolm stood alone at stage center.

After watching her husband move to the rostrum with that grace-ful, tiger-boy stride, Betty quieted their four daughters and settled down uneasily. Ordinarily, the warm-up speaker would have returned to the seat adjacent to the one Malcolm had vacated. This day, how-ever, the chief minister cleared the stage with a nod and backhand gesture to a hesitating Benjamin 2X, who had just brought him on as a "man who would give his life for his people."

Shuffling his note cards as Goodman walked off stage, Mal-colm gathered himself against the dim backdrop of a faded pasto-ral scene that must have been scenery for another event. He had his three-by-five cards and did his usual shifting before speeches. To his chastened aides in the back room, this opening pause seemed a few seconds longer than normal.

Finally, the hoarse voice, more weary than usual, crackled into the dry microphone hooked into a reel-to-reel tape recorder.

"As-Salaam Alaikum . . . ," he said, drawing a scattered response of the requisite "Wa-laikum Salaam."

Suddenly, two men bolted up in a tussle four rows back and to the left, one shouting, "Get your hands out of my pocket." Sharon 6X Shabazz, who was in the audience that day, took it as the outburst of "some rowdy drunks."

Near the back, a man struck a match and lit a strip of photo-graphic film protruding from a rolled-up sock. He heaved it under-handed, like someone losing a bar of soap in the shower. A woman screamed nearby as the mock smoke bomb fizzled to the floor in noxious smoke. The disjointed sights and sounds lent an eerie feel to the hall of some four hundred onlookers.

Malcolm snapped his attention to the ruckus in the aisle. Two security men in front of the stage rocked on their heels and moved toward the disturbance—deserting their post. The audience turned its attention toward the noise—but three sets of eyes stayed focused on the podium. Malcolm—as erect as he had been at the Monday night meeting—appeared immediately concerned and moved to impose order in the hall. With arms raised, he exposed the full length of his body, stepped from behind the plywood lectern and said:

"Now, now, brothers break it up . . . hold it, hold it, hold it . . ."

In an instant, William 25X, a member of the Newark mosque who was also known as William Bradley, charged the stage in a slight crouch from the fourth row, locked his eyes and aimed his sawed-off shotgun dead level at the chest of Malcolm X. He paused, tensed, and jerked the trigger. The blast lifted Malcolm backward off his feet and the force of gravity folded his arms over his chest as he fell to the right over two wooden chairs. Seven of the buckshot pellets seared his jacket and shirt and dug an angry pattern of craters running five inches above the navel to an inch above his left nipple. One piece of hot shrapnel tore the web between his thumb and index finger. The main villain pellet punctured the wall of Malcolm's aorta.

The tape recorder on the podium caught what it could of the drama before the physics of the blast shut down its revolving reels as a bullet passed through the microphone.

Backstage, as Benjamin 2X Goodman was passing along the word about Reverend Galamison, Sara Mitchell heard a "terrible sound." Just as quickly, "James and Benjamin hit the floor," she said, "I ran behind a radiator. I stayed there until people started running in from the ballroom. I didn't go out there because there was nothing I could do. I didn't want to see."[14]

Malcolm hit the scuffed oak floor so hard that the jarring loosed his folded arms. "I heard this crash!" said Goodman. "I knew exactly what had happened on the stage; I knew, because the feeling—that weighty feeling that I had—just left.

"Then someone ran through the room, went through the door, the door flung open and I saw him. I saw Malcolm lying there, I knew that that was it. It's strange. It's hard to transmit that to someone else. I knew that that was his time to leave, I couldn't see him going any further. I was just sitting there. I saw that his eyes were fixed, you know open. And his mouth was like he was slightly gasping. And those people were trying to revive him, but I knew it was no use. I just knew it. I didn't want to go out there." [15]

The thumb on Malcolm's left hand folded between fingers, flung down at a 45-degree angle. The hand of his twisted right arm grasped at his belt in a defiant street pose. The fight now was all internal and molecular as Malcolm's pale skin went sallow and his eyes rolled back under his horn-rimmed spectacles, which somehow had remained hooked behind his ears.

The assassin's snap of the second trigger of the 12-gauge double-barrel had splintered the five-foot plywood lectern. And with this roar of his shotgun, William 25X had imposed a ghastly disorder in the hall.

Executing the next phase of their rehearsed performance, two other men with drawn pistols dashed three steps to the rim of the stage. Malcolm was flat on his back as this second wave arrived, one man brandishing a 9-mm, the other a .45-caliber automatic. Squeezing their triggers, this duo sensed that their hit-team assault was nonessential to the deed at hand, but orders were orders. Jerking his head away from his barking .45-caliber, the youngest of the trio, twenty-two-year-old Thomas Hayer, shot the prostrate and agonized Malcolm in the left ankle. The third gunman, Leon Davis, pumped one 9-mm Luger round into his victim's right thigh and another into the left thigh, four inches up from the knee. Each gunman squeezed off a few insurance rounds.

Jarred from her trance as empty cartridges rained to the floor, Betty Shabazz, pregnant with twins, dove beneath nearby chairs, shielding her four young daughters as best she could. With bedlam rippling all around, she shouted as if from the folds of a death chamber: "They're killing my husband; they're killing my husband. . . ."

Shrieking onlookers broke for cover: some belly flopped to the floor, while others took refuge behind their upturned hands. The backbenchers went bounding down the stairs, feeling their way as if by braille, and out onto Broadway. Only then did they dare risk inquiring about the terror unfolding.

The shotgun man, William 25X, dropped his warm, sawed-off weapon, wrapped in a brown suit jacket, on the stage. Leon Davis, who had fired the 9-mm, also stuck to the plan and dropped his automatic pistol. Thomas Hayer, the least experienced in these matters, held nervously on to his heavy, black pistol, revealing his role in the shooting to the world.

Wheeling, while still not fully erect, the trio of gunmen faced the chair-scattering crowd, and exploded into full retreat mode. The shooters maintained a military crouch and headed for the rear exit, two hundred feet away.

The plotters of the deed had drafted an escape for the killers through the tumult of the crowd.[16] As anticipated, few in the hall dared risk a head-on look at the gunmen. This cautionary lapse would sow confusion during the identification phase of the investigation. The lowered profiles also reduced the likelihood of the assassins getting hit with return fire from Malcolm's men. Despite their seemingly reckless execution before a packed ballroom, the gunmen had counted on escaping through the panicked audience.

Far from considering the Audubon onlookers as a hindrance to the escape, the Muslim official in Newark who drafted the plan had advised the hit team that "the crowd will be your getaway."[17]

As the three men picked their way toward the rear exit, Hayer nervously brought up the rear, squeezing off rounds from his .45 automatic. Already a .32-caliber pistol had struck up a dialogue with return fire. Another of Malcolm's fit security men, this one unarmed, stood his ground near the exit. Low-running through the stampeding sheep, the three wolves headed toward this lone fox disinclined to retreat. Gene Roberts appeared to keep his head as Malcolm's other defenders were losing theirs. He had just been relieved of his thirty-minute post at the stage up front and was taking a break in the back of the hall when the shooting started.

The two careers of Gene Roberts, activist and cop, came converging headlong down the aisle of the Audubon Ballroom. The former Navy corpsman had earned his NYPD salary by spying on the Harlem leader who now lay perforated with bullet holes and was bleeding to death. Juggling the separate calls of his counterfeit role and his official duty, Roberts braced for his next move. An adrenaline rush suddenly focused his attention: his own life was on the line. "I saw the three gunmen coming up the middle aisle," Roberts said years later, repeating what he had reported to his superiors at the time. "It was like a blur. I had never seen them before in my life.

"One of the gunmen I met face-to-face, maybe four, five feet away," Roberts said. "I found out later it was Hayer. He was running and he pointed his handgun right at me; it looked like an automatic. When he pointed it, I turned sideways. I was still looking at him face-to-face, I turned my body. As soon as I turned my body, he fired. He took a shot at me! I had a chair in my hand. I threw it at him. I knocked him down. He got up. I stood there for a moment frozen—I just knew I was hit! And I looked at myself, there was no blood. I was not hit."[18]

Roberts's quick reaction with the chair was attributable to the rigorous karate training he had recently undergone—not with the police department but with the Muslims he spied on. His martial arts skills notwithstanding, Roberts also chalked up his survival that Sunday to Hayer's errant marksmanship, along with his mother's prayers and plain old good luck. "The bullet didn't hit me. I had on a suit coat because we always dressed conservatively, suit and tie. No bow tie; Malcolm didn't like bow ties. The bullet went through my suit jacket, in the hip area. I just stood there for a while. I saw [Hayer] get up and stumble [toward] the door."[19]

Some of Malcolm's men were known to be armed, but their return fire, such as it was, seemed all to be coming from Reuben Francis, the chief of security. Within the echoing din of gunfire, the much vaunted Muslim security detail, save for Francis and one other armed brother, reacted rather passively. Like a cop chasing bank robbers through a crowded mall, Francis yelled for everyone to hit the deck, but no one listened. He figured that was the only way to get clear fields of fire at the crouching gunmen shielded by the crowd.

One eyewitness reported that Francis, an Afro-Cuban American, chased Hayer and others while firing his .32-caliber pistol with the vengeance, if not quite the accuracy, of Alan Ladd in the classic Western *Shane*.[20]

In the counterattack, Reuben Francis's relatively small caliber pistol managed one true shot. Thomas Hayer, the fleeing .45-caliber gunman, was hit in the right thigh. At least two other bystanders were hit by stray bullets in the melee, one in a foot, the other in a leg.[21] One of the wounded men was hustled away in a police squad car, leading to early media reports that two gunmen had been captured at the scene.

Floored by Roberts's chair and winged by Francis's bullet, Hayer was separated from his pistol and exposed to the attention of the crowd. Straightaway his troubles thickened. The determined, free-wheeling gunman hopped out the door on his good leg and into the angry fists, elbows, and feet of Malcolm's riled-up supporters. "We saw four or five Negroes come running out. They were chasing this other man," said Sergeant Alvin Arnoff of the nearby 30th Precinct, who was on the block with his partner. "They were pummeling him and kicking him, screaming, 'Kill the son of a bitch.'"

Hayer was yelling, "I've been shot. Help me."[22] This predatory fish had been trapped in a most unfriendly sea. Gathering itself, the milling crowd tightened into an angry net around the disarmed gunman, smashing him.

Finally Sergeant Arnoff and his men wrested Hayer away from the avengers, bundled him into a squad car, and drove him to a nearby hospital. Hayer's head was bloodied and swollen with a purple welt running across his face.

After several misses, one bullet fired by Malcolm's security men hit a telephone booth in the back of the hall, nearly smashing the face of Chuck Moore. The freelance reporter was dictating the unfolding story to the Sunday news desk at *Newsday*, a daily newspaper on Long Island. Barely able to breathe in the cramped phone booth, the 250-pound Moore closed his eyes and prayed. Another freelance reporter, Gene Simpson, had sprinted to an adjacent phone and called his Harlem apartment in search of a tape recorder to cover the story.[23]

Quicker to the telephone and more purposeful than the two journalists, however, was another set of eyewitnesses with a different reason for eagerly getting the word out. "Malcolm X has been shot and I think he's dead," was the cryptic message that one informer in the ballroom relayed to the FBI Field Office in New York.[24] FBI Director J. Edgar Hoover was fast in the loop on this one. And he would almost immediately relay the word to President Johnson.

In addition to undercover detective Gene Roberts, two uniformed NYPD officers were present nearby. At least one BOSSI officer, on his day off, was conducting secret surveillance at a nearby candy store, and several paid FBI informers worked the assassination scene with the expectation of a bonus from the U.S. government. The FBI had key sources within the Harlem Temple and in Newark, and had advance knowledge of the unfolding attempt on the life of Malcolm X.

Hoover was no stranger to internecine warring within the Nation of Islam. His FBI, as we've seen, had been tracking Elijah Muhammad since the days when the group's founder, Fard Muhammad, disappeared in the 1930s, back when Malcolm was a young lad in Lansing. The FBI director took more public interest in Martin Luther King Jr. because King's more visible and more influential civil rights movement had openly challenged the laws and policy of the federal government. However, Bureau agents were heavily involved with the Black Muslims and had nurtured—and worked hard to stimulate—the split between Malcolm and his Messenger, Elijah Muhammad.

FBI officials viewed Malcolm as posing a much greater threat since he had left the Nation. His recent travels abroad and his plan to file human rights charges against the United States before the United Nations had drawn the active attention of the State Department. The CIA, meanwhile, had sharply intensified its surveillance of the black leader's international contacts, his specific plans, and his movement.

Police agencies raced to collect the fullest, most favorable account of the rapidly developing conflict between Malcolm and the Muslims. Still, with something of a competition between the FBI and the CIA, as between the Bureau and BOSSI, coordination among the competing investigating agencies sometimes suffered. Each had key informers inside both groups, none of them known to the other. Accurate disclosure of the unfolding events, and even the subsequent prosecution—and nonprosecution—of the attackers would be sacrificed to the police agencies' determination to cover their trails and protect their undercover assets.

———

Betty Shabazz wandered dazed through the Audubon hall, while a small knot of women friends and strangers milled about her fallen husband. One of the women passed Malcolm's youngest daughter,

along with her baby bottle, to Yuri Kochiyama, who had been sitting
with Betty.

"They looked so frightened," said Kochiyama, a spirited woman
who had once hosted Malcolm at a meeting of Japanese writers at
her Harlem apartment. Once someone else relieved her of her nursing duties, Kochiyama, with her hesitant yet determined will for
order, asked a woman standing nearby to comfort Sister Betty and
keep her and the children back from the wounded Malcolm, who
was still lying on the floor.[25] The woman was Gene Roberts's wife,
Joan, who was present for her very first Muslim event. But when Joan
Roberts approached, Betty seemed to instinctively shun and push
her away, even though she had no way to suspect Joan was the wife
of a police informer.

Others present were either in shock or operating toward hidden purposes. Some were tainted with suspicions that they were
police informers or assets for government intelligence agencies. Earl
Grant, a close associate and professional photographer, calmly took
photographs. Charles 37X, once so close to Malcolm and now suspended, surveyed the devastation as if from a great distance.

Malcolm's loyal assistant James 67X slumped in the back office.
Benjamin 2X was frozen there, too. Sara Mitchell, the OAAU secretary, kept her private counsel in a room nearby. Others thought to
be security men simply disappeared.

Kochiyama made her way to Malcolm. "There were only a few of
us who were right around him," she recalled. "For a while I had him
cradled . . . sitting on the floor, I had his head in my lap."[26]

As she sat with Malcolm, Gene Roberts approached. Moments
after eluding Hayer's gunshot, Roberts had made his way back up
the aisle and jumped onto the stage to attend his fallen leader—and
target. In all the scurrying about, precious little medical attention
had been paid to the world-famed black leader felled in the vortex
of the bloody fusillade.

Eerily still, Malcolm lay on the stage outstretched on his back. His mouth was locked open in a slack expression somewhere between a grimace and a plea. Relatively little blood was visible on his fresh white shirt, but his chest cavity was flooding within. His small, maroon appointment book was still nestled in his breast pocket, pierced through by shotgun pellets. The lined pages were soaking in droplets of deep red, freshly oxygenated blood.

As Kochiyama continued to hold Malcolm's head, Roberts reached down to open his tie and ripped open his shirt. "And I saw these little holes in his chest. So I rolled him over a little bit. There were no exit holes that I saw. So I felt his pulse. It was still there . . . weak and rapid. The weird thing is that there was not that much blood. So I started giving him mouth-to-mouth resuscitation."[27]

The former Navy corpsman pulled a white handkerchief from his right rear pocket, cupped his long fingers around Malcolm's mustache and goatee, and then blew air between his pale, cold lips. Roberts turned Malcolm's head to the side and inhaled. He then repeated the process. As Malcolm's supporters and security men milled about haplessly, the kneeling undercover NYPD cop blew breaths of air into their leader's mouth and down his phlegm-clogged throat. After a few repetitions, tiny air bubbles of blood began to rise and fall over the shotgun holes in Malcolm's chest.

Exhaling, Roberts ministered to Malcolm like a true disciple. Inhaling, he rendered his service unto a modern-day Caesar. The cop also scoured the ballroom for tidbits of intelligence that might be useful in his written report to headquarters. He took mental note of every face around him. Inhaling, he looked around for weapons. Exhaling, he replayed Malcolm's plan to name names that day.

"While Malcolm was lying there," Roberts said, "I looked for those papers in his pockets. He was supposed to have a list of the [five] people who were supposed to kill him. I didn't see anything when I opened his shirt and tie. I didn't see any [such] papers in his pockets. I don't know whether he just had this [idea] in his head. I didn't see any papers removed. I didn't see Betty with anything."[28]

Gene Roberts had remained loyal—not to Malcolm X, his supposed black-nationalist leader, but to the New York City Police Department. The Negro cop monitored Malcolm's final breaths—while riffling through his pockets. Details of Roberts's frisking, along with almost everything else he observed, would be duly reported in his oral and written reports to the New York police department. Yet his care for Malcolm in his last moments would later get the young cop in trouble with his superiors at headquarters.

"Why did you give him mouth-to-mouth resuscitation," his commander later thundered.

"This is a human being," Roberts remembered answering in defense. "I don't care what his ideology is or his philosophy is. This is a human being gunned down in front of his family."[29]

The rookie cop cited his oath as a policeman sworn to defend property as well as human life. For good measure, he also referenced his prior training as a Navy medical corpsman conditioned to preserve the lives of fellow Americans. His handlers at headquarters, whom Malcolm had often criticized for brutalizing blacks, were unmoved. They chastised Roberts sternly for trying to save the life of this particular black leader.

Although they would deny any involvement in Malcolm X's assassination, New York police officials disassociated themselves from Roberts's attempt to save him. This cold-blooded fact—not previously reported—raises stronger questions about charges that the police could have prevented the attack had they heeded Roberts's warning that an assassination attempt appeared to be imminent.

At any rate, the transgression of Roberts's resuscitation procedure would be duly noted at police headquarters. "The strong inference from my superiors [at police headquarters] was that I should *not* have given Malcolm mouth-to-mouth resuscitation," he recalled.[30]

Roberts, waiting for assistance, worked over Malcolm for what seemed like ten minutes. "I still had a pulse," Roberts said. No other movement, just a faint pulse. Malcolm's eyes were closed. There was little movement of his exposed chest except the blood bubbles. The resuscitation efforts made Roberts faint, but he continued. A feeble gurgling sound started deep in Malcolm's throat rolling to the surface. Then, suddenly, with unexpected force and power, there burst forth between his bared lips a sharp, violent rush of air. "uuuuuUhhh . . . AAAAAhhhhh!"

"When I heard that gasp of breath," Roberts said, "I knew it was over."[31]

———

Roberts stood up and turned toward Betty Shabazz, who was crying. He feigned dizziness and asked that someone else take over and try to keep Malcolm alive. "I didn't have the heart to tell her," Roberts said.

Malcolm's stare was fixed. His shoulders relaxed. The cold, gray ash of death worked its way onto his bared lips and over his pallid face. Summoning her training as a nurse, Betty Shabazz fumbled into action. Through tears, she worked her husband's forearms in an effort to revive his breathing. It was a rusty attempt at the outmoded Schaeffer method.[32] No movement ensued save the faint oozing of blood bubbles from the bullet holes. Betty broke down, weeping uncontrollably as her role as nurse lost out to wife, then wife to widow.

———

The police deception onstage by Gene Roberts was only a prelude to a broad pattern of official cover-ups that has allowed the assassination of Malcolm X—one of the most notorious U.S. crimes in the latter half of the twentieth century—to go unresolved for more than fifty-five years.

Roberts's fruitless search for a list of killers was not the only frisking Malcolm would undergo as he lay dying on stage. Luqman Raheem, a resolute associate also known as Anas Luqman, who had vigorously advised Malcolm to have everyone searched at the door of the Audubon, paced nearby. His first thought upon watching Malcolm hit the floor was that the pistol he had given Malcolm might likely be on his seriously wounded person—with Raheem's fingerprints. He waited for a chance to search Malcolm's waistband and make sure. Wearing a light gray suit and camel-hair topcoat, he paced nervously at the periphery of Roberts's search-and-resuscitation effort. He was fixated on the damaging piece of evidence on Malcolm's body that might easily be traced to him. Like so many of those who had flocked to the inner circle of Malcolm's new organizations, Raheem was something of a mystery man with a shadowy background. Unlike some of the others, he did not pose as a devout Muslim and showed no interest in the minutiae of policy. Raheem was a weapons and explosives expert and had served abroad as a mercenary in Mexico and North Africa. His arrangement with Malcolm was mainly as a security man.

Several times Raheem had helped save Malcolm's life from attempts by Nation of Islam hit teams vastly less skilled in the dismal art of tracking down and killing a target. In the wake of the firebombing of Malcolm's house on February 14, Raheem was baffled by his leader's decision to forgo security searches at the door of the Audubon Ballroom. The relaxation of "body security," he argued, "placed Malcolm at grave risk." While some OAAU aides were supporting and even encouraging the idea, the security specialist had confronted Malcolm about the decision a couple of days before the event, at the apartment of Earl Grant.[33]

Raheem recalled, "Malcolm said that the body searches turned away more people than they attracted. 'It makes people think they're in an atmosphere of danger. We're trying to get away from that image,'" especially in the OAAU. It was particularly ominous, Raheem observed, that Malcolm had acknowledged that he had erred in stating that only the Nation of Islam had been gunning for him. He had expressed second thoughts about his Monday night tirade accusing Elijah Muhammad and Captain Joseph of ordering the firebombing of his house. He said that the Muslim officials would not have tried to hurt "women and children."

"None of them is that way," one staffer recalled him saying.[34] Malcolm speculated that someone else, likely a government agency, had bombed his home to set up the Muslims. At any rate, Malcolm said that he wanted to defuse the situation by refusing to fight them openly. Thus he instructed his security men not to carry their weapons, or to search visitors at the door.

"No matter what," Malcolm said, "people are just to be allowed to come in. And I'll be among my people."

Raheem argued quite the contrary. "I got mad, and pissed off about his attitude about security. Finally, I said, 'You know, you're a dead man.' Malcolm said, 'So be it.'"[35]

With gunmen still prowling for him, Malcolm had been persuaded to relax security as a means of attracting more non-Muslims to his public meetings at the Audubon. His reluctance to be swayed by others moved Raheem, who enjoyed his confidence on security matters, to attempt one last time to change Malcolm's mind. However, in their face-to-face, Malcolm stood his ground even after Raheem said that, after a year with Malcolm, he saw no further need for him to stick around and offer advice.

"I said, Look, if you don't want security, you'd better, at least, take my piece because you need it more than I do."[36] After his house was bombed, Malcolm, who had been photographed holding a carbine at his window, let it be known that he had applied to the 28th Precinct for a pistol permit.

After a bit of spirited and respectful arm-twisting, Malcolm agreed for his personal protection to take Raheem's pistol. Unlike the carbine, however, it required a city permit that he did not have and, as a convicted felon, was not likely to be granted. The two men repaired to Raheem's Harlem apartment for the weapon and ammunition. "He and I went up there and that's where I handed him the gun and some loose bullets."

It was a dark, snub-nosed, five-shot .38-caliber Chief Special, with a 2½-inch barrel and a cozy, thumb-sized handle. The holster of the revolver had an inside clip designed to be easily concealed without the bulge, say, of the six-shot Colt special of the same model. Raheem told Malcolm that the Chief Special was accurate up to twenty-five yards with good stopping power for a weapon its size. Before the two men departed amicably, the security man turned over more ammunition, three boxes of bullets, and showed Malcolm how to conceal the loaded pistol on his belt in the small of his back. "I told him that [giving him the pistol] was the best I could do, under the circumstances, because he was a dead man," Raheem said.[37]

Raheem had stopped by the Audubon that Sunday even though he no longer felt any obligation to Malcolm for security matters. Like everyone else that day, he walked in without being checked. He took a seat in the center section, about ten rows from the front. The armed assault and the ensuing crowd panic exploded all around him. With Malcolm dying on the Audubon stage, his thoughts turned to his .38 Chief Special.

"This man is going to die," Raheem thought. "He's going to go to the hospital. My gun is on him. My prints are all over it. I don't need this. I was debating whether to grab his legs and drag him off to the side behind the curtain and disarm him. All these cameras were there and running. I went back up to the stage, because I realized that Malcolm had my piece on him—and I had to get it! I knew he had it."

Those cameras later supplied TV news footage that survives in

the CBS archives and that did indeed catch Raheem moving purposefully up to Malcolm lying sprawled on the stage. "I had on a
camel-hair coat. So I pulled it off and spread it over Malcolm's [waist]
and slid my hands under it." Gene Roberts was in the midst of admin-
istering mouth-to-mouth resuscitation.

"I reached underneath Malcolm, felt along his belt," Raheem
said. "It was still there in the small of his back. It had never been
touched. Gene Roberts was still working on him. I lifted the gun
and holster up and put it in my pocket. People saw me doing this but
didn't know what I was doing."[38]

While some might speculate about the onstage interaction
between Raheem and Roberts, police investigators pieced the story
together with details from other informers, not from Roberts.
Although he was the closest to the action, Gene Roberts said he was
unaware of what Raheem had done and filed no account of it in his
report. Seeing the removal of the pistol from Malcolm's body would
have been a bonanza for the police, if not for Roberts.

Detectives, hot on the investigation trail, interrogated Raheem
about the pistol. They even swore out a warrant and searched for
the weapon in his apartment days later. They narrowly missed the
.38 Chief Special, which he had hidden in a box of Kellogg's Corn
Flakes. When they departed, he said, he ground the weapon into
powder on a rigged emery wheel.

During his appearance before the grand jury reviewing Malcolm's murder, Raheem also was questioned about removing the pistol from Malcolm's waistband and its whereabouts. "The grand jury
knew everything about that gun," he recalled years later. "I didn't
admit to taking it off him. They couldn't prove it, I knew, because
they didn't know what was with the gun. They couldn't reconstruct
it. Everything was gone. They knew what had taken place, but they
couldn't prove it."[39]

Like so much else surrounding the assassination, the truth about the existence of the .38 special—which never surfaced—would have been significant.

Ironically, both the government and Malcolm's supporters could have used the existence of the gun to their own advantage. The U.S. government—clearly no friend of the pan-Africanist leader who so effectively discredited it in black eyes the world over—would have preferred the notion that Malcolm X was armed at the podium where he died, and perhaps even fired an illegal pistol. Instead, he became a martyr, gunned down trying to restore calm in the hall. It is likely that police were aware beforehand that Malcolm was armed and, by some accounts, may have expected a shoot-out between Muslim gunmen and the black leader.

Malcolm's supporters continue to honor him as a martyr cut down by the white establishment, albeit by black gunmen. Yet some still persist in believing, without proof, that Malcolm, ever their warrior, would have preferred facing his executioners, even black ones, with a gun in his hands and perhaps going down in a blaze of glory. "Malcolm had the gun and he would have used it on stage that day if he had time," said Raheem. "He just didn't have time. We rehearsed it. I'm not saying that we knew the shooting would go down that day. But we rehearsed how to use the weapon if something like that should have gone down."[40]

Raheem, in any case, had not been thinking at the moment of how history might judge Malcolm's assassination. He simply wanted to recover his .38 Chief Special and remove evidence linking him to a murdered man he had tried to protect.

As with every scrap of new information, the disclosure of the .38 special also could have fed an assassination conspiracy. What if the police even had planted the weapon? Either way the authorities could have won. A shoot-out between Malcolm and his attackers would have brought a bloodbath with culpability on both sides. Even innocently gunned down as he was, Malcolm could have been discredited if the police or grand jury revealed that he had been armed with an illegal handgun.

Police authorities, working the media, would likely have vilified an armed Malcolm as a black nationalist leader who lived by the gun and died by the gun. Instead, the actor and activist Ossie Davis, in eulogizing him as "a prince—our own black shining prince," could ask, "Was he ever himself associated with violence or any public disturbance?"[41]

Cheated of being able to declare the death of an armed Malcolm X, authorities were left to solve the murder of a black martyr they despised. This task was complicated by a long-standing secret—the illegal FBI and police surveillance of Malcolm, including the handiwork of agent Gene Roberts. Although he had key information bearing on the murder, Roberts was not called to testify at the ensuing trial of Malcolm's alleged killers. With his up-close look at Hayer retreating with his .45-caliber, Roberts could have been effective before a jury. "I could positively identify Hayer," Roberts said. "I had no problems with that because he had almost blew off my hip [sic]."[42]

Roberts was sure he had never before seen the three shooters at the Audubon. His testimony—that the shooters were complete strangers to a trained police observer—could have dispelled the prosecution's charge that the other shooters were Norman 3X Butler and Thomas 15X Johnson, both members of the Harlem mosque whom Roberts knew. At the trial, several other witnesses testified against Butler and Johnson, and both men were convicted along with Hayer. Butler served twenty years in prison, and Johnson twenty-two years, for Malcolm's murder. Although Roberts gave eyewitness accounts to his superiors at police headquarters, he was never called to testify at the murder trial. Instead, he remained undercover to spy on several other black nationalist groups in New York City, including the aforementioned Black Panthers.

By this and other covert means, the government convicted only one of the three actual shooters: Hayer. The other two shooters, along with the conspirators who threw the smoke bomb and helped distract Malcolm's attention by shouting a ruse, never came to trial. The prosecution of the case was itself a distraction from the truth about the murder of Malcolm X. It was a case study in covering the tracks of the police, the federal government, and the FBI—a whitewash.

———

As soon as Malcolm's body hit the floor, an FBI agent, watching an NBA basketball game in his comfortable home in Montclair, New Jersey, got a call from one of his informers. "Malcolm X is shot and I think he's dead."

Aubrey Lewis, a former all-American running back at Notre Dame, was one of the first two black agents to undergo training in 1962 at the FBI academy at Quantico, Virginia. Following a brief stint in Cincinnati, where he worked a horse-thief case, he got his dream assignment, to the FBI's New York Field Office. Among about twenty special agents in the office, Lewis was the only black and had but a small piece of the NOI harassment and surveillance case.

White agents ran the secret Malcolm X operation. Its paperwork flowed directly into FBI headquarters, and during the pan-African leader's seven months of foreign travel, the Bureau coordinated heavily with the State Department and the CIA. Special Agent Lewis's main case involved tracking the Revolutionary Action Movement, a black radical group that allegedly plotted to kill NAACP director Roy Wilkins and to blow up the Statue of Liberty.

"I wasn't personally working that Sunday," Lewis said, "but I had an informer in the Audubon Ballroom."

His spy was indeed quick to the phone and offered good information. He was not, however, the informer Lewis had just planted inside

Malcolm's OAAU. The OAAU informer was attending the Audubon meeting as his first FBI assignment and, in something of a breach of policy, he had brought along his wife. When the shooting started, the couple spent a considerable time crawling around on the floor, holding each other's hands and praying. More than twenty-four hours would pass before Lewis's rookie spy could find his voice and weigh in with his telephone account of events.

"Informers are trained for this moment," said Lewis. "Everybody [every agent] wants to be first with the information in your field office—and get it to [FBI Director] Hoover. When something like this happens, you want to get it before the media get it. The Bureau likes to have an answer ready if the president calls and says 'so-and-so happened, what are you going to do about it?' You don't want Hoover to be caught by surprise."[43] Lewis dressed down his tardy, though prayerful, informer, noting that bringing one's wife on such an assignment was considered bad form. Only reluctantly did Lewis grant the confidential paid informer another chance to spy on black radicals in Harlem.

Lewis's piece of the Harlem Muslims case involved keeping track of Captain Joseph, once Malcolm's trusted aide.[44] Upon Malcolm's unceremonious dismissal from Temple No. 7, he had become the hunted quarry of his former captain and protégé. As the head of the Nation's karate-trained Fruit of Islam on the East Coast, Captain Joseph ordered his special team men to harass his "hypocrite" former mentor and his new recruits. Two of his top strongarm men, Norman 3X Butler and Thomas 15X Johnson, had been loyal Malcolm disciples, known to Betty Shabazz and other Muslims who had followed him out of the nation. Still, the two musclemen harassed the couple with telephone death threats at all hours of the night, and by day, they cruised by OAAU gatherings in bold attempts to intimidate and issue warnings. It was not all talk.

Chicago's hit order—from the highest possible authority—had

FOI teams from temples around the country vying to kill Malcolm X. "These hit teams started competing with one another in Boston, Chicago and Philadelphia," said Luqman Raheem. "Malcolm was a prime target. Whoever got him would be rewarded in whatever way the [Muslim leadership] reward people. The hit teams had some very close calls, by some very capable people. But some very capable people went along with Malcolm; this was the only reason he lasted as long as he did. It was not until he relaxed body security that they would be able to approach him in a successful way."[45]

Home-turf responsibility for Malcolm's elimination fell finally to his old Temple No. 7, and thus to Captain Joseph, the regional FOI commander. Extraordinary pressure from Chicago was exerted on Captain Joseph, mainly by Elijah Muhammad Jr., one of the Messenger's sons, accompanied by John Ali, the national secretary, and Raymond Sharrieff, the supreme captain of the FOI. Captain Joseph responded by talking the talk, but killing his former mentor, whom he had grown to despise but yet respected for having turned his life around, was not an order he yearned to carry out. Harlem as home turf was at a decided disadvantage. Malcolm had trained the FOI there and knew their methods and the few men capable of executing such a hit order.[46]

Although Captain Joseph's FOI enjoyed a numerical advantage, Malcolm's skilled security men were better armed. A year earlier, in 1964, Luqman Raheem had been tasked by Captain Joseph with the job of wiring Malcolm's Oldsmobile with explosives. Raheem had instead tipped Malcolm off and switched over to his side.[47] Charles 37X Kenyatta had defected with Malcolm and for his first ninety days guarded his mentor with a blind devotion and a .38-caliber. James 67X, the right-hand man who also had a black belt in karate, kept a loaded .357 Magnum that had been given to him by Sensei Takahara, who had continued to train Malcolm's men in the advanced level of *qigong*, which he had also taught to Gene Roberts.[48]

Malcolm had spoken increasingly in public about blacks laying in shotguns and forming rifle clubs ostensibly to protect themselves. Additionally, there were rumors that Malcolm's followers had escalated the arms race between the two groups, stockpiling rifles, pistols, and shotguns at caches around Harlem.

During Malcolm's extended absences in Africa and the Middle East the previous year, some of his associates—notably, Luqman Raheem, Charles Kenyatta, and Sensei Takahara—had made connections with weapons suppliers at various locations around upper Manhattan. Various intelligence units were aware of this arms buildup and, in some cases, actually may have made the connections. Malcolm had carefully couched his discussion of violence in a context of self-defense and gave no indication that he wanted his men to stockpile arms.

In one instance, for example, Kenyatta said he had made contact with a Korean for a shipment of arms that were stored in an apartment building. Malcolm excoriated Kenyatta for the risky venture after learning about the weapons upon his return from abroad. A daring and not particularly savvy risk taker, Kenyatta, unlike the highly skilled Raheem, seemingly invited police scrutiny with his bold plans for stockpiling arms to counterattack the Nation. In a private conversation with Malcolm, he even suggested that a preemptive strike might be made against Elijah Muhammad himself. "Malcolm told me," Kenyatta remembered, "that I had lost my religion."[49]

The police and the FBI, who may have actually controlled the supply of weapons, were greatly interested in this small-arms buildup. It was considered as a possible endgame in which they could prosecute the black militant groups out of existence. "My supervisors definitely wanted to know about guns," said Gene Roberts. "They wanted to know if Malcolm's people were armed. I think that was the real deal, because every time I made my report, they would ask, 'Is there any guns there?' No, there were no guns there."[50]

The Fruit of Islam, meanwhile, had largely forsworn firearms to avoid arrests, but had nonetheless attained its brutal but self-limiting capacity for violence. Its karate-trained "special squads" were experienced mainly at cracking down on wayward, backsliding temple members. Violating mosque rules, such as those against smoking marijuana or beating one's wife, or the serious crime of not selling enough *Muhammad Speaks* newspapers, brought down the wrath of the FOI.

"If you were a brother in the temple and weren't selling papers, we'd go to your house," said Thomas 15X Johnson, a key enforcer in the Harlem mosque since the days Malcolm was the minister, and one of the trio charged with Malcolm's murder. "We'd come up the stairs and hear babies crying and smell a little weed. The wife would come to the door and say, 'He ain't here. He can't pay his bills; he can't sell those papers; they're stacked up in the closet.' We'd bust on in the house and if he's in the house, we'd touch him up. A lot of guys got their bones broke. We didn't play around about that."[51]

In addition to such routine disciplinary head knocking, the Harlem FOI teams, extending back to Malcolm's administration, occasionally went beyond breaking members' kneecaps and smashing their shinbones on sidewalk curbs. Only a month before Malcolm's assassination, a Harlem hit team had botched an attempt on the life of Benjamin Brown, a renegade who left after Malcolm was expelled. Brown, a corrections officer, had established a separatist temple in the Bronx ostensibly under the auspices of the Nation. A five-man hit team approached Brown at his storefront temple, where he was instructing young recruits, with a picture of Elijah Muhammad on the wall. The five regulars threatened Brown as a "hypocrite" and sternly warned him to take down his posters of the Messenger.

"I told him to take down the picture of Elijah Muhammad," said the FOI lieutenant in charge that night. After some routine intimidation, several of the team members were dismissed. The lieutenant opened fire on the corrections officer with a .22 rifle he brought along for the occasion. Brown was wounded but survived. Both Thomas 15X Johnson and Norman 3X Butler were arrested in this botched shooting and were out on bail at the time of Malcolm's assassination.[52]

The Benjamin Brown shooting was but the latest bloody clash between Muslim regulars and renegade "hypocrites" pursued as loyal to Malcolm X. As demonstrated in Brown's case, the Harlem FOI expertise at street executions remained amateurish and unreliable.

When high Muslim officials decided that rough treatment, including murder, was called for, they looked not to Harlem, but to the temples of Philadelphia and Newark to carry out such work.[53] Jeremiah X, who'd moved back north to become the minister of Philadelphia's Temple No. 12, was considered by law enforcement, the local media, and even the Angelo Bruno organized crime family, as the head of the so-called black mafia. Newark's Temple No. 25, for its part, had been founded by a tight-knit element engaged in prostitution, grifting, and other street crimes. Instead of reform, a hard core of the Newark leadership graduated to extortion, armed bank robberies, and, later, drug dealing.

The temples of Philadelphia and Newark also boasted proficient hit teams.

Ever since Elijah Muhammad's secret death order, the Chicago Muslims had been working mightily to make it so. It certainly was not news within the goon squad of the Newark temple—where the deadly plot was hatched.

Malcolm had concluded that the Muslims were motivated by their own narrow interests, with greed and envy fueled by a personal vendetta. A larger, concentric government interest in Malcolm's elimination, as discussed earlier, also existed. Indeed, the federal government had stimulated the split between Malcolm and Elijah Muhammad, monitored its development, and encouraged its escalation. Thus it was not inconsistent with official priorities that New York police authorities would ultimately chastise Gene Roberts, their undercover agent, for attempting to save Malcolm's life.

Roberts had been assigned to work only a small piece of the puzzle. However, the cop's instincts afforded him a glimpse of a larger pattern. Roberts had seen clearly the fake Monday night distraction in the audience that drew the attention of Malcolm and his podium security men as a dress rehearsal for an assassination. He duly reported this intelligence to his superiors. As he would discover when getting chastised for giving Malcolm mouth-to-mouth resuscitation, the department was not particularly interested in keeping the black nationalist leader alive.

An ambulance finally arrived. After Malcolm's body had been carried out of the hall to the hospital, Benjamin 2X and Sara Mitchell made their way out of the back room. Mitchell and several other women rounded up Malcolm's four young daughters and took them home.

In the end, Thomas Johnson and Norman Butler were convicted along with Thomas Hayer (also known as Thomas Hagan) in the killing of Malcolm X.

Many people, however, knew that Butler and Johnson had not been at Audubon that day. For instance, Benjamin 2X knew both men and was certain of that. "We were raised up in the FOI by Malcolm," he said. "We were like brothers together, Butler and Johnson. We knew each other just as you would know people you work with every day."

Malcolm's assistant minister had been with him since 1957 and had supervised Butler and Johnson for years. However, after Malcolm had been expelled from Harlem Temple No. 7, and Benjamin had defected to him, the four men had undergone a decided falling-out. Always brutal head knockers on the FOI security team, Butler and Johnson became Captain Joseph's main intimidators against Malcolm. They cruised about Harlem, shaking their fists at Malcolm's men. Butler was thought to have fired shots at another Malcolm follower. Johnson had participated in the bombing of Malcolm's home, and after both men approached "renegade" Muslim Benjamin Brown about a month earlier, Johnson had stuck around to shoot him. "They were both treacherous as far as violence against Malcolm was concerned," said Benjamin 2X. Malcolm, his wife, and his followers would have considered Butler and Johnson the two people in all of New York most likely to try to kill him. "Now those two brothers we would have searched if they had gotten the nerve to even come to the door. They weren't there, period."[54]

Benjamin 2X knew that Butler and Johnson were not present in the ballroom when Malcolm was assassinated. But in the charged atmosphere following his mentor's murder, and with the men of Temple No. 7 celebrating the hit, Benjamin 2X was evasive during police questioning, allowing the two enemies who had been indicted to twist in the wind. He was the one man who could have positively stated whether or not Butler and Johnson were in the hall. The district attorney did not call him to testify—nor did the defense.

# CHAPTER 19

# Back at the Mosque

WHEN THE CADILLAC CAME SCREECHING AROUND THE corner of Springfield and South Orange Avenues in Newark, Talib* knew that the driver, William Bradley, was one of the gunmen who had just killed Malcolm X. Despite the February afternoon chill, sweat poured from Bradley's troubled brow and down his angular jaw. The engine still running, he dashed out of the car and bounded up the steps, where he was met by the captain of Temple No. 25 and another ranking Muslim official. Four men rushed from the temple and all seven men made their way around the corner, where they parked a safe distance from the mosque.

William Bradley excitedly briefed the Muslim officials about the events at the Audubon Ballroom. Chief among their concerns was the fact that Thomas Hayer had been shot and captured, and thus would not be making it back to Newark.

***

* A pseudonym.

Word of the Harlem shooting and Hayer's capture had first reached Temple No. 25 by telephone.

All day the atmosphere at the mosque had been electric, with high-ranking out-of-town Muslim dignitaries bunching at the cramped temple on Springfield Avenue. This seemed most unusual to one lowly secretary, especially given that the sect's massive celebration of Saviour's Day was less than a week away. Ministers, captains, and all other ranking officials, she knew, would ordinarily have been in Chicago steeped in heavy preparations to receive the tens of thousands of worshippers who flocked each year from across the nation to the Windy City to celebrate the birth of their Messiah, Master Fard Muhammad, on February 26.

The row of five offices and two anterooms in the rear of the mosque was abuzz all afternoon with an expectant air that the sister secretary could not quite pinpoint. Sunday afternoon, running up to Saviour's Day, usually found the support staff working, serving food sometimes, as the members milled in the halls to and fro, requesting forms, appointments, and last-minute transportation to Chicago. On this day, however, unbeknown to the members, the bewitching hour was approaching. The staff, which in winter months hung around the mosque until 8:00 p.m., was frantically being asked to depart without explanation. Officials rushed away the two women who manned the bank of telephones as if they expected some urgent call too precious for their ears. Although obedient to orders, the women were slow in vacating their accustomed posts.

"Y'all gotta go," one stern Muslim official yelled. "Come on, y'all, leave!"[1]

Around three in the afternoon, several Muslim officials crowded into one of the small anterooms where the telephones were: Captain John, from the Newark mosque; Minister John Nash; two officials from Harlem Temple No. 7; an unidentified national representative from Chicago; and, milling nervously with four aides and body-guards, Minister Louis X (Louis Farrakhan).

Farrakhan, the once proud and presumed loyal protégé of Malcolm X, was the minister of the Boston mosque and a rising star with East Coast responsibilities. Although he had visited Newark on occasions, his presence that day was highly secret. Except for a small knot of insiders, it would remain so for years.

Farrakhan himself did not publicly admit to his possibly incriminating presence until some twenty-five years later.[2] He cloaked his Newark appearance, however, as a chance substitution for James Shabazz, the minister of Newark's mosque, who had spoken that Sunday at Temple No. 7, Malcolm's old Harlem home mosque. Even so, as late as the summer of 2000, some of those present at the gathering refused out of fear to admit that Farrakhan had been in the Newark temple that day.

The critical placement of Farrakhan that day in Newark, according to Minister Jeremiah Shabazz, was Elijah Muhammad's maneuver to position this protégé of Malcolm's directly in the loop of his mentor's assassination, not so much as a fully trusted NOI official but rather as someone on probation whose complicity in the homicide at the Audubon Ballroom would ensure his silence, if not his trustworthiness.

"The Messenger was like that," said Jeremiah Shabazz, one of the craftiest insiders in the Nation's leadership, a valued organizer who enjoyed Elijah Muhammad's unstinting respect. The Philadelphia minister, who established most of the early mosques in the South, earned a reputation as one of the shrewdest, most cold-blooded operators within the Nation or anywhere else. And he was a man who knew how to keep secrets.[3]

While Farrakhan was definitely on the scene—and being closely watched—he was not, as Jeremiah and every other knowledgeable Muslim official we spoke to confirmed, a decision maker in a command position sufficient to issue an order for Malcolm to be killed. That sentiment had to issue directly from *them*, and the direct order for the plan of execution had to come from blood-family members very much higher up the chain of command.

On that Sunday, as the regular administrative staff was rushed out of the Newark office, two curious and cagey secretaries lagged behind long enough to overhear the hotly awaited telephone call, which came in shortly after 3:10 p.m. One actually caught snatches of the call on an extension. "As they were rushing us out," she recalled, "the call came, and it was shock time."[4]

The plan had called for a ranking member of the hit team to telephone the Newark office as soon as Malcolm was killed. He was not an armed assailant; "he didn't have a piece," she said. "Nothing that would put him in jeopardy," except as the man in charge of the operation on the ground. "The person who telephoned was not the one who [under the assassination plan] was supposed to call. The official on the [mosque office] phone was questioning why [that person] didn't call."

As the officials passed the phone around, it became clear to the two women nearby that the Muslim officials, including Farrakhan, were not at all surprised that Malcolm X had been killed. This realization panicked the secretaries. One of them was still deeply, though secretly, committed to Malcolm, even after he had been expelled and declared a pariah. The part of the telephone report that shocked the Muslim officials in the Newark office was that one of the shooters had been caught at the scene. "They didn't know which one," she said. "They went into alert!"

One junior member of the group from New York, relaying instructions from the rest of the assembled Muslims, said to the person on the other end of the telephone: "You know where you're supposed to go."

A great sigh seemed to seize the Muslim officials after they hung up the telephone. There had been a hitch, but the big deal had gone down. The secretary remembers the group of officials, including Farrakhan, stealing a look over their shoulders, and then joyously issuing themselves a congratulatory "All Praise Be to Allah!"[5]

―――

William Bradley—the man with the shotgun—had made it to the Newark mosque about forty-five minutes after the telephone call.

Talib, the first to spot Bradley wheeling back to headquarters, was himself a member of the goon squad of the Newark mosque. Talib figured that he narrowly had missed drawing some on-the-scene part in the Harlem assignment. As it developed, he was held back at the mosque as a sentry for the anxious officials.[6]

The Newark goon squad was considered one of the toughest bunch of FOI enforcers in the Nation of Islam, second, perhaps, only to Philadelphia. "Newark and Philadelphia always provided the real muscle for the Nation," said a knowledgeable Muslim historian for the group.[7] As mentioned earlier, the FOI security group in the City of Brotherly Love was headed by Jeremiah Shabazz, the so-called godfather of the black mafia. Although he denied his association with the black mafia to grand juries and the *Philadelphia Inquirer* over the years, Shabazz acknowledged his leadership in the FOI and its awesome power during a series of extensive interviews he granted in the hospital before he died of congestive heart failure in January 1998.

Backed by the image of the disciplined forces of the FOI, Shabazz had conducted several meetings with Angelo Bruno and negotiated a deal. The FOI organization wrested street control of heroin and prostitution in South Philadelphia from the Italian mob. In turn, the mafia was guaranteed peace and a cut of the action, while holding on to most of the major rackets in the rest of the city, as well as the lucrative illegal numbers racket in the black communities.[8]

Meanwhile, in Newark, some twenty hard-core members of the FOI goon squad dished out punishment, under the captain's orders, to selected targets. "If someone had to be taught a lesson," Talib said, "then it was up to the goon squad." Members had varying skills for applying trauma and, in extreme cases, killing their victims. Several of the brothers were proficient with lead pipes; another was highly skilled with an ice pick, keeping several in his glove compartment at all times. During an interview in a Newark restaurant, this goon squad soldier said casually, "I have an ice pick in my glove compartment right now."[9] The Newark mosque had distinguished itself, even beyond the scope of the Philadelphia group, with a roster of accomplished bank robbers who had access to caches of pistols, rifles, and shotguns.

William Bradley was the most cold-blooded of all on the Newark squad. Street legend had it that he was trained as a killer when he served as a Green Beret in the Army. As recently as the beginning of the twenty-first century, Bradley still enjoyed a reputation on the streets of Newark as a "lethal" man with a silent ferocity to be avoided at all cost. One ranking correction officer in the New Jersey prison system confirmed, based on confidential sources and records, that William Bradley was indeed the triggerman with the shotgun that killed Malcolm X. "I know him," the source said. "He's been through my jails. He was a head crasher, working out of Newark. He was a big tough guy, crafty and cunning."[10] Like Jeremiah Shabazz in Philadelphia, Bradley was reputed to have gone to the Italian mob in New Jersey with the supposed backing of the Muslims, demanded a piece of the local criminal action, and gotten it.

Malcolm X had never been a favorite in the Newark mosque. Even as national spokesman, Malcolm, working across the river in Harlem, was considered more a rival than a representative. Not surprisingly, his open criticism of Elijah Muhammad evoked great anger among members of Newark's FOI goon squad, said Talib. "Once Malcolm was labeled a hypocrite, we in the goon squad all had a little thing for him. We love the Honorable Elijah Muhammad, right. When Malcolm started talking against the Messenger, about [the babies he had with his secretaries], I was realistic enough to know about that. It didn't shock me. Master Elijah Muhammad had three wives to my knowledge.

"When Malcolm started blasting that he was going to expose the Messenger, that was his big mistake."

The order to kill Malcolm X thus was well-known among members of the goon squad. Talib had heard the words fall directly from the lips of Newark minister James Shabazz. First, Shabazz had let drop a few blunt hints at the end of his teachings at the Wednesday night meetings. "We should take that hypocrite's head on a platter to the Messenger," Talib remembers the minister saying earlier that winter.[11]

As Saviour's Day approached, James Shabazz upped the ante on Malcolm's head. "I'll tell you what," he said a few weeks before the hit, "anyone who kills that hypocrite wouldn't ever have to worry about a thing in their life. They would be well taken care of."[12]

This declaration by Minister Shabazz, not considered a man of empty promises, got Talib and other goon squad members to wondering—and likely inquiring—about how exactly the Muslims could ensure that the killers would escape prosecution. Unlike the mafia, the Muslims had no heavy influence within the criminal justice system, with no payoffs going to judges, politicians, or cops on the beat. Newark politicians and the nearby docks in Jersey City were deeply in the pockets of the Italian mob. Newark mayor Hugh Addonizio would subsequently be indicted on sixty-seven criminal counts involving such corruption linked to the mob.[13]

The Muslims had no such reach, yet James Shabazz was clearly promising protection requiring government connections. "I'm thinking," Talib said, "who in hell is going to take care of some of us for killing Malcolm?"[14]

Talib asked that question more than once. Other than Thomas Hayer, who was captured at the scene, none of the actual, on-the-scene participants in the assassination of Malcolm X—the shooters and drivers from Newark* and the look-outs and the ballroom distractors from Harlem[15]—have spent a single day in jail for the murder of Malcolm X on February 21, 1965.

The FBI and other government agencies are known to have had heavy involvement in discrediting Malcolm X and smashing his organizations, according to documents released under the Freedom of Information Act. It has not been lost on Talib—and specialists on government excesses against Malcolm, Martin Luther King Jr., and so-called black hate groups—that government influence is a certainty.

Weeks before Malcolm's Sunday appearance at the Audubon, Talib said, James Shabazz spoke for the first time of a specific date for moving against Malcolm. The minister met with the goon squad in person, one of his few such appearances—such team sessions were usually conducted by the captain or lesser officials. Now, after a regular Friday night temple meeting, the goon squad broke off and went across the street to the mosque restaurant. Only members of Shabazz's security were allowed to stand close to him. Malcolm X's foreign and domestic travels had made it difficult to monitor his recent movements. But now the Newark minister took note of the February 21 Harlem appearance.

"It'll be a good time to kill that hypocrite," Talib remembers Shabazz telling his squad.[16] As was his custom in speaking to small gath-

---

* Two of the shooters lived in Paterson, but all members of the hit team were members of Newark Temple No. 25.

erings, the minister spoke to the goon squad with his right hand over his mouth, a habit he had picked up in prison. The trio who would be the actual gunmen, William Bradley, Leon Davis, and Thomas Hayer, were not at the meeting. Bradley, a street tough who picked up jobs as an enforcer, seldom attended mosque meetings. However, a Paterson mosque official had already volunteered to take charge of the operation and was responsible for the three men. That official was present and paying close attention.

"James gave them the idea that Friday night," Talib said. "He said, 'You get there early, two brothers sit down in the back and the other three that are going to shoot, sit down in front. He outlined that the brothers in the back were to create a disturbance soon as [Malcolm] walked out. 'Make sure everybody turn their heads. Then, that's when you hit him. And the crowd will be your getaway.'

"Now I'm standing and hearing all this. There were ten or twelve brothers at the restaurant. The four volunteers weren't there. But there was a brother who was in charge of them, there."[17]

The bold daylight assassination plan, which some have surmised intended some additional sinister message, was basically a matter of expedience. Elijah Muhammad's deadline for Malcolm's death—by Saviour's Day—was fast approaching. As has been described, numerous attempts had been made—in Los Angeles, Chicago, Boston, and once at around 11:00 p.m. at Malcolm's home in Queens. Like the firebombing at Malcolm's home, all had failed. Each time, the FOI assailants were foiled by Malcolm's bodyguards, by his own evasive action, or by the presence of police.

The harassment campaign of late-night phone calls to Malcolm's home also had failed to get results.[18] Whatever the motive, harassment had not worked.

Time was simply running out. After berating Captain Joseph for his failed attempts, Chicago officials turned to the Newark mosque, which had both the means and a strong motive. It was no secret that James Shabazz, the Newark chief minister, personally despised Malcolm X.

"James [Shabazz] planned the whole thing," said Talib. The goon squad had even done a successful dry run on a target who had been hard to locate and pin down, Talib asserted; he himself had participated in that hit.

"This particular brother, a lost-found (we called them lost-found because he was not a Muslim), took his penis out at a Muslim sister working at a dry cleaner." Angry over his cleaning bill, the disgruntled customer exploded at the cashier, exposed himself, and said, "Suck on this." After the woman reported this disturbing incident to her mosque officials, the FOI said, "We've got to get this bastard." The job was passed on to the goon squad for action.

"The sister was a Muslim cashier dressed in Muslim garb; that was totally disrespectful," Talib explained. The goon squad "looked for him at night but couldn't find him." The squad favored running up on their victims after dark because attackers were more difficult to identify at night, and it was easier to get away. Finally, after vengeance was not taken, the Muslim sister told squad members where the man who insulted her hung out in the city every day.

" 'Don't wait for the night,' James instructed them, 'get him in the daytime.' " The plan was hatched to approach him in a small crowd by first creating a distraction.

"There were three of us," Talib said. "He knew we had to be Muslims because we were dressed up. And he knew what he had done to the Muslim sister. We saw him in the street where he hung out. We waited until he walked away from the ones he was talking to. We jumped out of the car and I started yelling, 'I told you to stay from my wife!'

" 'I don't even know your wife,' " the man pleaded.

"By that time, while I'm hollering, another brother hit him with a lead pipe on the shins of both his legs. He went down and they did him in. They beat him nearly to death. And we got back into the car and left. Nobody moved to help.

"It was brilliant the way James planned the whole thing: 'hit him in the daytime; let the crowd protect you.' In the past we'd only get people at night. It was the only daytime job I was ever on. It was something of a dry run for a much bigger action months later. James set up the [daylight] plan for Malcolm the same way."[19]

Minister James's envy of Malcolm was long-standing. Although James Shabazz had strong ties with Elijah Muhammad dating back to their prison days together, Malcolm had far outdistanced him as a magnet for helping the Messenger to build the Muslims into a national force. Although James, known as the "Son of Thunder," had an impressive speaking voice, he lacked Malcolm's charisma on the podium and off, as well as that mastery of the English language that made the national spokesman irrepressible before any audience, black or white, learned or unlearned. Watching Malcolm work a Muslim crowd, one Newark official overheard James Shabazz jealously comment, "Look at him, he's nothing but a Hollywood actor."[20] In addition to their disparate personal traits, the two ministers took different approaches to their religious leadership practices. While Malcolm was a born-again ascetic who insisted upon strict personal and group adherence to Islamic tenets as Elijah Muhammad passed them down, Shabazz played fast and loose with the rules. His Newark mosque was a base camp for bank robbers and strong-arm men.

Seldom had Malcolm visited the Newark mosque since Shabazz had been installed, and vice versa. And with Malcolm's expulsion, there was no love lost with Minister Shabazz. Next to the Royal Family living high in Chicago, he had the most to lose were Malcolm somehow to manage to work his way back into favor, as rumors persisted he was trying to do, up until the time of his death. So as Minister Farrakhan worked to prove to Chicago that he could be trusted, James Shabazz moved to take over the high-profile Harlem Temple

No. 7. One of his tactics, as the minister temporarily in charge of New Jersey and New York, was to discredit Malcolm as he attempted to take over what Malcolm had built.

"The effort of the press to cite Malcolm as a 'leader' is disgusting," he wrote in a bylined article in the October 9, 1964, edition of *Muhammad Speaks.* "Negroes never have experienced such a traitor, double-crosser, as Malcolm Little. I believe the name 'Little' is what he is trying to outrun. However, he has to learn that—in spite of calling himself 'Big Red,' the pimp, seller of black women to white men, pusher of drugs to demoralize the youth and corrupter of society— he has met one he can't outrun."[21]

This was no idle boast, as Talib watched the Newark minister boldly escalate the assassination plot. While he understood that James would not have passed along such orders without the consent of Chicago, Talib was confused when he read in *Muhammad Speaks,* in Elijah Muhammad's column, that the Messenger said that no harm should come to Malcolm. Muhammad was always careful in public to cloak whatever projection of harm that might come to Malcolm as being the handiwork of "Allah's chastisement."

"I was having second thoughts," Talib said. "I was with the group that Saturday [February 20, 1965] before that Sunday. I had finished selling my *Muhammad Speaks.* I went up to the mosque to check and see if [Malcolm's assassination plan] was still on. I asked a brother who was in the know and he said: 'If he shows, that's his ass!'

"I went home not knowing how it was going to come about. We had never had this kind of hit before. I had pictured that we would stand at attention [at the regular goon squad formation]; we used to line up. I thought they were going to line us up and ask for volunteers. I said I definitely won't be the first to volunteer, but if push come to shove, I'll give it a try, because I know I'm going to get away. That was my positive thinking.

"I stayed awake all night. I had car trouble that Sunday morning. It was the first time I'd ever had trouble with my '63 Chevy. The squad inspection at the mosque was at eleven a.m. My instructions were to get there an hour and a half early—that meant nine thirty a.m. for the goon squad. I got there at about ten a.m.

"When I got there, one of the brothers in charge said, 'They just left, but I got a post for you. I want you to sit in that car and listen to the radio.' It was someone else's car, the radio was already tuned to radio 1010 WINS. In those days, you might sit in anyone's car, if they got permission to use it for post. Normally, when you're on post, you don't play no radio. They'd jack you up for that. But he said, 'Keep the radio on—and listen!' Shortly after three ten p.m. the news broke.

"WINS broadcast that Malcolm X has been shot down and he's been rushed to the hospital! I admit that when I heard the news, I got out of the car—proud. Damn! We did it again! At that moment I was proud because we were something to be reckoned with—Temple Number 25.

"I went on in the temple and reported it. The captain was scared to death. Sweat started pouring down his face. He pulled out a hand-kerchief and kept wiping away the sweat. He said: 'Keep your eyes open! Keep your eyes open!' He was in charge. I went back and sat in the car. I had already learned the names of the five goon squad members that left the Newark mosque. I knew them all.

"After about forty-five minutes at the most, one of the five came shooting across Springfield Avenue. I found out later that he came back to tell them that one of the brothers didn't get away." Following the brief huddle, the word was secretly carried to the top officials inside Temple No. 25.

Minister James Shabazz reportedly had purchased airline tickets to Chicago and hotel room reservations for all five of the Newark men directly involved in the Malcolm murder. At any rate, during Saviour's Day celebration the following weekend, Talib spotted the gunmen.

"I went to Saviour's Day in Chicago," he said, "and the four brothers were there. They didn't talk. They just looked at me and winked. Like the cops do when they kill one of us, they give each other the wink.

"The hit against Malcolm X was never discussed, but the shooters gained great respect in the goon squads."[22]

# Epilogue

His repeated acts of self-creation spoke to me; the blunt poetry of his words, his unadorned insistence on respect, promised a new and uncompromising order, martial in its discipline, forged through sheer force of will.

—BARACK OBAMA[1]

SINCE HIS DEATH, MALCOLM X'S LIFE AND WORK HAS BEEN A major influence in the United States and has grown steadily around the world. Youth around the globe were exposed to Malcolm through the spread of hip-hop music and culture during the 1990s. And with the release of Spike Lee's *Malcolm X* in 1992, Malcolm was brought alive again, this time in color.

Not surprising, then, that Malcolm's messaging has been adopted by youth groups fighting their own identity struggles in many nations. The Arab European League of Belgium emerged in 2003, led by Dyab Abou Jahjah, warning Belgian officials that European Muslims would get their rights "by any means necessary!"[2] In 2005, the Natives of the Republic Party (Indigènes de la République) formed in France with a broader view of "defending the rights of all post-colonial populations, not just Muslims and Arabs."[3]

Malcolm's image has been utilized around the world. In 1984, Iran issued a postage stamp with Malcolm's image in honor of World Struggle Against Racial Discrimination Day. The United States honored Malcolm with a stamp in 1999 as part of the post office's Black Heritage series. Malcolm's truth telling has influenced many who have left their mark on this nation of America, including writers August Wilson and Audre Lorde; Black Panther Party founders Huey Newton and Bobby Seale; rap artists Chuck D, Ice Cube, and Kendrick Lamar; former Attorney General Eric Holder—and Barack Obama, who became the first black president of the United States.

At its core, Malcolm's message spoke to people of every rank: white people are not superior, and black people are not inferior. While black people have been conditioned by generations of oppression to feel a false sense of inferiority, Malcolm's core messaging provides tools to move from this self-loathing to self-acceptance with the hope of redirecting oppressed people's energy toward self-determination and community success. He reframed the oppression of black Americans from a civil rights issue to a human rights issue.

With his appreciation of the power of words, Malcolm helped change the very names people called themselves, turning "black" from an insult among so-called American Negroes—fighting words, in many cases—to a proud affirmation. Later, after his sojourn in Africa and his conversations with black American expatriates there, he helped popularize the term "Afro-American," embracing an Africa that had been seen only as an embarrassment by the Nation of Islam, as well as by many Christian Negroes. "You can't hate the roots of a tree and not the tree," he would say as he directed African American eyes toward Africa. "You can't hate Africa and not hate yourself."[4] These words speak directly to today's youth across the

United States as they challenge the media's beauty standards to be more inclusive.

Through his international travel, during which he saw oppression similar to that of black people in the United States, he fully understood the need to overcome the shackles of colonialism and gain control of natural resources. While speaking with students at the American University in Beirut on September 29, 1964, he advised that if they wanted to empower themselves, they needed to use their resources—especially oil—as a weapon, according to Dr. Azizah al-Hibri, one of the student organizers of this event. "Nobody had talked about that before," Dr. al-Hibri recalled a half century later. "Nobody. He laid it out so completely and so clearly, by the end of the lecture, I think the whole place was on fire."[5]

In 2015, fifty years after his death, a fictional Malcolm returned to the American University in Beirut to speak to students again, in a performance of *Malcolm X Speaks*. This dramatization was written and directed by Tariq Mehmood, who was born in Pakistan and raised in Britain. Growing up, he experienced "white boys who would rub their fingers on your skin to see if the dirt came off. In a sense you began to hate each other. . . . What racism did to people like myself was that it opened the door that there is something fundamentally wrong in the world in which we live. What Malcolm X did was give us a key to understand that there is something far far bigger, beyond that door. Beyond the darkness. We can negate the world in which we live. For me, he was a teacher. He was a comedian. He was a storyteller."[6]

Although Malcolm lived only to age thirty-nine, his cultural and political legacies are so far-reaching that to do them justice would require a reexamination of the last fifty-five years, which is well beyond the scope of this book. Instead, this brief epilogue will outline what became of those close to him.

In the days after Malcolm's assassination on Sunday, February 21, 1965, major media outlets routinely described the deceased as gifted but evil—a twisted, distorted, embittered fanatic who was fascinated with violence and who, as a result, was destined to become its victim. A *New York Times* editorial pronounced its judgment in terms that brought to mind Malcolm's own "chickens coming home to roost" comment about President Kennedy's murder. "Yesterday," the *Times* said, "someone came out of that darkness that he spawned, and killed him."[7]

El-Hajj Malik El-Shabazz, the name under which he was buried, was as fervently mourned as he was reviled. More than twenty thousand people waited in the cold of a harsh February day to file past the body as it lay in repose in a bronze casket in a Harlem funeral home. At his funeral in the Faith Temple Church of Christ in Harlem on February 27, Ossie Davis, the actor and activist, eulogized Malcolm as "our living black manhood" and crowned him with what has become a lasting title, "our own black shining Prince." Malcolm's political organization was not as durable, especially in the ominous climate that surrounded his assassination. Without his inspirational presence, and faced with the cloud of police investigations and death threats, many of Malcolm's followers dispersed, and his infant organizations, Muslim Mosque, Inc., and the Organization of Afro-American Unity (OAAU), faded into obscurity.

The enmity between Malcolm's followers and the Nation of Islam outlived the man. Two days after his assassination, Harlem's Temple No. 7, where he once preached so mesmerizingly, was firebombed and destroyed in a towering blaze of apparent retribution. Three days after that, on February 26, 1965, the Nation celebrated its annual Saviour's Day, the holy day that had been chosen as the date by which Malcolm should die. A crowd of twenty-five hundred in Chicago listened to expressions of unity and praise for Elijah Muhammad from Malcolm's own brothers, Philbert and Wilfred.

Soon, however, the eldest brother began looking for a way to extricate himself from the Nation "because," as Wilfred said years later, "I was in a precarious position myself, being Malcolm's brother." He added that he had to move "slow and easy"—"you know, when you're in a cage with a snake, you can't move too fast"—and he gradually withdrew from his role as minister of Temple No. 1 in Detroit. As his exit strategy, Wilfred ceded the temple's leadership to Philbert (Abdul Aziz Omar), who was favored for his deep religious commitment to Elijah Muhammad and the Nation's doctrines.[8] Philbert's formal ministry ended around 1980, and he worked for several years as a furniture salesman, before dying in 1994 at age seventy.[9]

Wilfred, after extracting himself from the Nation, went to work for a phone company, Michigan Bell, where he became a manager. He retired in 1988 and died ten years later, in 1998, at age seventy-eight.

Malcolm's half sister Ella Collins, who had given him money to make the *hajj*, came down to New York after his death and assumed control of his OAAU, claiming that had been his intent. She organized the annual May 19 birthday pilgrimages to Malcolm's grave, which continue today. When his key followers left, however, she returned to Boston and died there in 1996 at age eighty-two. Of Malcolm's siblings, the last survivor was his sister Hilda Little, who was ninety-three when she passed in 2015.

Malcolm's wife, Betty Shabazz, widowed at thirty, with four young children and twins on the way, received support from friends and allies. Eventually she moved her family to Westchester County, just north of New York City. While raising her six girls, she earned a bachelor's degree, a master's degree, and, in 1975, a doctorate in educational administration from the University of Massachusetts at Amherst. She worked for many years as an administrator at Medgar Evers College, a branch of the City University of New York named for the slain civil rights leader. In 1997, when her twelve-year-old grandson, Malcolm Shabazz, was living with her, he set fire to her apartment. Dr. Betty Shabazz suffered third-degree burns over 80 percent of her body, and three weeks later, at age sixty-three, she died. She was buried next to her husband, Malcolm, in Ferncliff Cemetery in Hartsdale, New York. Malcolm and Betty are survived by their daughters, Attallah, Qubilah, Ilyasah, Gamilah, Malikah, and Malaak. They all continue the work of and protect the legacy of their parents.

The Nation of Islam continued on under Elijah Muhammad until 1975, when the Messenger died at age seventy-seven. Then the leadership passed to his son Wallace, who over the next few years transformed the Nation into an orthodox Sunni Islamic group, which eventually would be called the American Society of Muslims. Wallace changed his name to Warith Deen Muhammad and assumed the traditional title of imam, rejecting the idea that Fard Muhammad was Allah and that his own father was a prophet. He disbanded the Fruit of Islam, invited whites to join the group, and honored Malcolm, another convert to Sunni Islam, by turning Temple No. 7 in Harlem into Malcolm Shabazz Mosque (Masjid Malcolm Shabazz). Many Nation members, including Muhammad Ali, followed their imam into orthodoxy. But not all did. Most notably, the powerful minister Louis Farrakhan (Louis X), who had been Malcolm's protégé before becoming his enemy, quit the group in 1977 and began resurrecting the old Nation of Islam, using the doctrines Elijah Muhammad had preached. Since then, the Honorable Minister Louis Farrakhan has continued to lead this reconstituted Nation of Islam.

———

Despite all the changes Malcolm experienced in his personal, spiritual, and political lives, he remained constant to the end in his central commitment to pursuing equity and respect for black Americans. In the closest thing we have to a deathbed statement, Malcolm typed out answers to a series of questions posed by the Islamic Centre of Geneva. A week before his murder, and just two hours before his home was firebombed, he had been responding to Question 7, about why he focused on black people when Islam spans all races. He wrote:

> As a Black American I do feel that my first responsibility is to my 22 million fellow Black Americans who suffer the same indignities because of their colour as I do. I don't believe my own personal problem is ever solved until the problem is solved for all 22 million of us.[10]

# APPENDIX

## Malik Shabazz (Malcolm X):
## Some Questions Answered

*The following is the text of the questionnaire Malcolm completed for the Islamic Centre of Geneva. His responses were completed shortly before his death. The beauty of this document is that it clearly shows where Malcolm's mind was at the end of his life with regards to Islam and Muslims, the role of women in society, and the importance of the black liberation struggle in America.*

## ON THE EVE OF HIS TRAGIC ASSASSINATION, MALCOLM X WROTE . . .

Malcolm X, the martyr of Islam, was good enough to dedicate one of his last trips to an exclusive visit to the Islamic Centre of Geneva. A few days after his departure, and before his tragic assassination, the Director-General of the Centre sent him some questions which he promptly answered in the characteristic openness, brightness and genuineness of his history-making leadership, whose immortal glow is still very much alive even after his shocking death.

Malcolm's answers were the last he wrote in his short but challenging great life that marvellously excelled all contemporary lives of American claimants to greatness: be they Negro, or White, or double-crossers playing over the heads of both—whatever false titles they choose for their game.

Of the following answers, the last two (as had been stated by the grieved widow, Sister Bahiyyah [Betty] Malcolm X) were edited and typed by Malcolm until late in the evening of Saturday, February 20, 1965, or rather after midnight when he so exhaustedly retired to sleep. On the morning of Sunday the 21st, he was treacherously killed raising a world-wide stir that marked historic image. He was then only 38 years old.

May God bless Malcolm's great soul.


## INTRODUCTION

More than any other man, the Muslim Malcolm X has had a revolutionary influence on contemporary American culture. He is quoted as authoritative by sociologists and politicians. He is honored by black nationalists and white liberals. He is acclaimed by socialists, rightists and leftists. He is revered by Christians, Muslims and people with no religion at all. But what, really, was the mission he attempted to accomplish?

It is certain that Malcolm's name is misused today by those who quote him in support of a variety of causes. A man of tremendous energy and mental alertness, he left the "Black Muslims" toward the end of his vigorous life and accepted Islam. He no longer preached the doctrines of racial extremism and black nationalism. "This was about the point where Malcolm X had started calling for 'human rights' as against 'civil rights' and striving 'to live the life of a true Sunni Muslim'" (*Impact,* London, 11–24 Feb. 1972).

Malcolm the Sunni Muslim is overlooked or misinterpreted by the majority of Western writers. Who was this new Malcolm? What insights on religious, social and political strategy did he gain from Islam? How did these change the emphasis of his struggle?

What positive role did Islam play in his plan to internationalize the struggle of the black American? How did Islam as a revolutionary way of life enhance Malcolm's own revolutionary outlook? What beneficial relations did he hope for between Afro-Americans and the Muslim/Arab world, both of which are victims of Capitalist and Zionist exploitation?

The answers to such vital questions are available only in the later writings and speeches of Malcolm X. As a unique service, the very last written words of Malcolm X—Hajj Malik Shabazz, *Shaheed*—are presented herein, to provide authentic signposts to his viewpoints as a Sunni Muslim.

S. S. Mufassir

## QUESTION 1

The Black Muslim Movement is one of the most controversial movements in the United States. Having been for a considerable period its main organizer and most prominent spokesman, could you kindly give us some concise first hand picture of the background of this Movement, its history, its main ethics, and its actual strength?

## ANSWER 1

The Black Muslim movement (which calls itself officially "The Lost-Found Nation of Islam") was founded in 1930 in Detroit, Michigan by a Mr. Fard Muhammad, who claimed he had been born in Mecca, and that he had come to America for the sole purpose of teaching the Supreme Secrets of Islam to the Black Americans exclusively, who he said were actually the people referred to in the Old Testament of the Christian scriptures as the "lost sheep." Elijah Muhammad was one of the first to be converted from among these "lost sheep," and Elijah taught us to refer to him as "the first begotten," or the "lamb of

God." Elijah also taught us that Mr. Fard was Allah in the Flesh, and that this Mr. Fard (God in Person) had been born in Mecca for the sole purpose of coming to America and teaching his secret Supreme Wisdom of Islam to the American Blacks, and by this he meant that this secret wisdom of Islam had been hidden even from the eyes and ears of the wisest and holiest men in Mecca and had been preserved specifically to be revealed by Allah Himself in Person to the American Blacks at the "end of time." Elijah said that the real Supreme Truth that had been kept a secret was that the white race was a race of devils that had been artificially created by a mad black scientist 6,000 years ago. They would rule the World for 6,000 years and then be destroyed at the "end of *their* time" by the Blacks. He said the whites were devils by nature and the Blacks were Gods, and Judgement Day means only that at the "end of time" the Gods (Blacks) would destroy the entire white race (devils) and then establish a Paradise (nation) on this earth ruled forever by the Blacks (GODS).

Elijah taught us that Mecca was a symbol of Heaven itself. He said that since whites were devils by nature they could not accept Islam, and therefore no whites could be Muslims. He taught us that Mecca was forbidden to all non-believers, and that whites could never enter the Paradise (heaven) that would be established by the Gods (Blacks) here on this earth after the destruction of the whites. He taught that "doom's day" refers to the "doom of the white race."

Mr. Fard taught in Detroit from 1930 until 1934 and then he disappeared. It was only after Fard's disappearance that Elijah then began teaching that Fard was Allah, Himself, that he had returned to Heaven, but would come back again to destroy the white race and America and then would take all the American Negroes (lost sheep) who had become Muslims back to heaven (Mecca) with him, and that he would then rule the entire world from there with an iron hand. He never did teach us that we would return to Africa. He shrewdly ridiculed the culture and the features of the Africans.

From 1934 until 1952 Elijah could only gather a handful of people who would follow him, which by 1952 numbered less than 400, most of whom were old people whose education was limited. No Arab or Asian Muslims were ever permitted in his temples or places of worship. In fact, his doctrine is as anti-Arab and anti-Asian as it is anti-white.

Until 1963 his followers practiced iron discipline, mainly because all of us believed in the infallibility and high moral character of Elijah himself, but when his own son Wallace Muhammad exposed Elijah Muhammad as a very immoral man who had deceived and seduced seven of his young secretaries, fathering at least 10 illegitimate children by them, the moral discipline of the entire movement decayed and fell apart.

From 1952 until 1963 over one million American Blacks have accepted Elijah's distorted version of Islam. But today he has less than 5,000 actual followers. Despite the fact that many have left him, no matter how disillusioned they have become even after learning the truth about his personal moral weaknesses and the fallacies of his doctrine, still they never return to the church, they never return to Christianity.


## QUESTION 2

What were the reasons behind Elijah Muhammad being against you immediately after the assassination of Kennedy, and then behind your breakaway from the Movement as a whole?


## ANSWER 2

Elijah Muhammad allowed himself to become insanely jealous of my own popularity which went even beyond his own followers and into the non-Muslim community, while his own prestige and influence was limited largely among his immediate followers. While I was still in the movement and blind to his faults by my own uncompromising faith in him, I always thought the jealousy and envy which I saw constant signs of was stemming mainly and only from his immediate family, and it was quite shocking to me whenever members of his own family would warn me that it was their father (Elijah Muhammad himself) who had become almost insane with jealousy.

When Elijah learned that his son Wallace had told me how his father had seduced his teen-age secretaries (by telling them that he was the Prophet Muhammad, and making each of them think she was to be his favorite and most beautiful wife AISHA) Elijah feared that my position of influence in the movement was a threat to him and his other children who were now controlling the Movement and benefitting from its wealth. Because they feared my popularity with the rank and file Muslims, they were careful about any immediate or open move to curtail my authority without good cause, so they patiently waited until after they felt that my statement about the late President Kennedy's assassination would give them the proper public support in any kind of action they'd take to curtail or remove me.

At the time they announced I was to be suspended and silenced for 90 days, they had already set in motion the machinery to have me completely ousted from the movement, and Elijah Muhammad himself had already given the order to have me killed because he feared I would expose to his followers the secret of his extreme immorality.

## QUESTION 3

Should these differences be of a basically ethical nature and on essential matters of faith? What, in your opinion, are the prospects of radical reform within Elijah Muhammad's followers now or in the future?

## ANSWER 3

No, Elijah Muhammad himself will never change. At least I doubt it. He's too old, dogmatic, and has already gone too far in teaching that he is a greater prophet than Muhammad Ibn Abdullah. He is too proud to confess to his followers now that he has deliberately taught them falsehood. But as his well-meaning followers become exposed to the True Religion of Islam they themselves will leave him and practice Islam as it should be. This is why it is so important for Centres to be established immediately where True Islam can be taught. And these Centres should be located at this time primarily in Black Communities because at this particular time the American Blacks are the one showing the most interest in True Religion.

## QUESTION 4

Have any of Elijah Muhammad's followers left the Movement with you, and do you think that your breakaway from the Movement has affected its main body in any considerable way?

## ANSWER 4

Yes, many of Elijah's followers could not go along with his present "immorality," and this opened their eyes to the other falsities of his doctrine. But we have not been able to regroup and reorganise them as we should. It takes finance, and we left all treasuries and properties with Elijah, and he uses this wealth that we ammassed [sic] for him to fight us and keep us from getting organised. He is fanatically opposed to American Negroes hearing True Islam, and has ordered his own well-meaning followers to cripple or kill anyone of his followers who wants to leave him to follow True Islam. He fears that True Islam will expose and destroy the power of his false teachings.

## QUESTION 5

Do you plan to just stop at voicing your opposition against Elijah Muhammed and his group or do you have any course of action in mind towards establishing some new organisation in the field? If so, on what basis and for what specific near or distant goals?

## ANSWER 5

With what little finance we could raise, we have founded the Muslim Mosque, Inc. with headquarters here in Harlem. Our sole interest is to help undo the distorted image we have helped spread about Islam. Our Mosque also is for those who want to learn how to live the life of a True Muslim.

However, since we live as Black Americans in a white racist society, we have established another organisation which is non-religious, known as the Organization of Afro-American Unity (OAAU), and which is designed to unite all Black Americans regardless of the religious affiliation into a group that can fight against American racism and the economic, political and social evils that stem from white racism here in this American society. With the Muslim Mosque we are teaching our people a better way of life, and with the OAAU we are fighting on an even broader level for complete respect and recognition as human beings for all Black Americans, and we are ready and willing to use any means necessary to see that this goal is reached.

## QUESTION 6

What have you been actually doing since you broke away from Elijah Muhammad's Movement?

## ANSWER 6

I have travelled to the Middle East and Africa twice since leaving
Elijah Muhammad in March of 1964, mainly to get a better understanding of Islam and the African countries, and in turn to give the
Muslim World a better understanding of problems facing those of us
here in America who are trying to become Muslims. Also, in Africa
to give our people there a better understanding of the problems confronting Black Americans in our struggle for Human Rights.

## QUESTION 7

Is it true that even after your breakaway from Elijah Muhammad you
still hold the black colour as a main base and dogma for your drive
under the banner of liberation in the United States? How could a
man of your spirit, intellect and worldwide outlook fail to see in
Islam its main characteristic, from its earliest days, as a message that
confirms beyond doubt the ethnological oneness and quality of all
races, thus striking at the very root of the monstrosity of discrimination. Endless are the texts of Qur'an and prophetic sayings to this
effect and nothing would testify to that more than the historic fact
that heterogeneous races, nations and linguistic entities have always
mingled peacefully in the homeland.

## ANSWER 7

As a Black American I do feel that my first responsibility is to my
22 million fellow Black Americans who suffer the same indignities
because of their colour as I do. I don't believe my own personal problem is ever solved until the problem is solved for all 22 million of us.

Much to my dismay, until now the Muslim World has seemed to
ignore the problem of the Black American, and most Muslims who

come here from the Muslim World have concentrated more effort in trying to convert white Americans than Black Americans.

Editor's Annotation

I had arrived back in the States from London at 4:30 p.m. on February 13, and had worked until 12:30 . . . just after midnight . . . on the above. I got very tired at midnight, decided to leave the above pages in the typewriter and finish early in the morning. I retired at 12:30 and exploding bombs that were thrown into my home by would-be murderers rocked me and my wiffe [sic] and four baby daughters from sleep at 2:30 a.m. Only ALLAH saved us from death. This is only one of the many examples of the extremes to which the enemies of Islam will go to see that True Islam is never established on these shores. And they know that if I was so successful in helping to spread Elijah Muhammad's distorted version of Islam, it is even easier for me to organise the spread of True Islam.

There are two groups of Muslims in America: (1) those who were born in the Muslim World and migrated here, and were already Muslims when they arrived here. If these total over 200,000, they have not succeeded in converting 1,000 Americans to Islam. (2) American-born persons who have been converted to Islam are 98% *Black* Americans. Up to now it has been only the Black American who has shown interest even in *Sunni* Islam.

If a student of agriculture has sense enough to concentrate his farming efforts on the most fertile area of his farm, I should think the Muslim World would realize that the most fertile area for Islam in the West is the Black American. This in no way implies discrimination or racialism, but rather shows that we are intelligent enough to plant the Good Seed of Islam where it will grow best . . . later on we can "doctor up" or fertilize the less-fertile areas, but only after our Americans who already show signs of receptiveness. Was it not Bilail, the Black Ethiopian, who was the first to receive the Seed of Islam from the Prophet Himself in Arabia 1,400 years ago?

## QUESTION 8

Now that you have visited and revisited many Muslim countries, what are your major impressions regarding Islam and Muslims both in the present and in the future?

## ANSWER 8

We are standing at the threshold of the Nuclear Age. Education is a must, especially in this highly Technical Era. In my opinion, Muslim religious leaders have not stressed the importance of education to the Muslim communities, especially in African countries. Thus when African countries become independent, the non-Muslim areas have the higher degree of educated Africans who are thus the ones best qualified to occupy the newly created positions in government. Muslim religious leaders of today need a more well-rounded type of education and then they will be able to stress the importance of education to the masses, but oftimes when these religious leaders themselves have very limited knowledge, education, and understanding sometimes they purposely keep their own people also ignorant in order to continue their own personal position of leadership. They keep the people narrow-minded because they themselves are narrow-minded.

In every Middle-East or African country I have visited, I noticed the country is as "advanced" as its women are, or as backward as its women. By this I mean, in areas where the women have been pushed into the back-ground and kept without education, the whole area or country is just as backward, uneducated and "underdeveloped." Where the women are encouraged to get education and play a more active role in the all-around affairs of the community and the country the entire people are more active, more enlightened and more progressive. Thus, in my opinion, the Muslim religious leaders of today must re-evaluate and spell out with clarity the Muslim position on education in general and education for women in particular. And then a vast program must be launched to elevate the standard of education in the Muslim World. An old African proverb states: "Educate a man and you educate an individual; educate a woman and you educate an entire family."

## QUESTION 9

Africa seems to have captured most of your attention and eager concern. Why? And now that you have visited almost every part of it, where do you think Islam actually stands? And what, in your opinion, could be done to save it from both the brainlessness of many or rather most of those who are considered to be the champions of its cause and from the malicious, resourceful alliance of Zionism, atheism and religious fanaticism against Islam?

## ANSWER 9

I regard Africa as my Fatherland. I am primarily interested in seeing it become completely free of outside political and economic influence that has dominated and exploited it. Africa, because of its strategic position, faces a real crisis. The colonial vultures have no intention of giving it up without a fight. Their chief weapon is still "divide and conquer." In East Africa there is a strong anti-Asian feeling being nurished [sic] among the Africans. In West Africa there is a strong anti-Arab feeling. Where there are Arabs or Asians there is a strong anti-Muslim feeling. These hostilities are not initiated by the above-mentioned people who are involved. They have nothing to benefit from fighting among themselves at this point. Those who benefit most are the former colonial masters who have now supplanted the hated colonialism and imperialism with zionism. The zionists have outstripped all other interest-groups in the present struggle for our Mother Continent. They use such a benevolent, philanthropic approach that it is quite difficult for their victims to see through their schemes. Zionism is even more dangerous than communism because it is made more acceptable and is thus more destructively effective.

Since the Arab image is almost inseparable from the Image of Islam, the Arab World has a multiple responsibility that it must live up to. Since Islam is a religion of Brotherhood and Unity those who take the lead in expounding this religion are duty-bound to set the highest example of the Brotherhood and Unity. It is imperative that Cairo and Mecca (The Supreme Council of Islamic Affairs and the Muslim World League) have a religious "summit" conference and show a greater degree of concern and responsibility for the present plight of the Muslim World or other forces will rise up in this present generation of young forward-thinking Muslims and the "Power Centres" will be taken from the hands of those that they are now in and placed elsewhere. ALLAH CAN EASILY DO THIS.

# NOTES

## INTRODUCTION

1. Les Payne, "The Night I Stopped Being a Negro," *When Race Becomes Real* (Chicago: Lawrence Hill Books, 2002).
2. Ibid.
3. Ibid.
4. Ibid.
5. Les Payne, "Taking the Measure of Malcolm and Martin," New York *Newsday*, May 14, 1989.

## CHAPTER 1: BORN AGAINST THE CURRENT

1. 1 Wilfred Little, interview with Les Payne, April 26, 1991.
2. Erik S. McDuffie, "The Diasporic Journeys of Louise Little: Grassroots Garveyism, the Midwest, and Community Feminism," *Women, Gender, and Families of Color* 4, no. 2 (Fall 2016): 165n2.
3. Wilfred Little interview.
4. Malcolm Little, Birth Certificate (#A19357), University Hospital, Omaha, Douglas County Health Department, Omaha, Nebraska.
5. Willie Dixon and Don Snowden, *I Am the Blues* (New York: Da Capo Press, 1990), 6–7.
6. Wilfred Little interview.
7. Tara D. Fields, comp., "A Brief Timeline of Georgia Laws Relating to

Slaves, Nominal Slaves and Free Persons of Color," February 14, 2004; http://files.usgwarchives.net/ga/court/lawsfreed.txt.

8. *Was Lester Maddox the South's Most Racist Governor?*, GPB Education documentary, published November 21, 2017, on YouTube; https://www .youtube.com/watch?v=sHNR5GRKCqg.

9. Transcript, Ella Collins, interview with CBS News for "Malcolm X: The Real Story," produced by Brett Alexander, aired December 3, 1992.

10. Pauli Murray, *States' Laws on Race and Color* (Athens: University of Georgia Press, 1950), 90.

11. Wilfred Little interview.

12. Rodnell P. Collins and A. Peter Bailey, *Seventh Child: A Family Memoir of Malcolm X* (Secaucus, N.J.: Birch Lane/Carol Publishing, 1998), 33.

13. McDuffie, "The Diasporic Journeys of Louise Little," 153. Louise sometimes used the surname of her father, Edward Norton, but dropped the name completely after her marriage. Her given name was spelled Louisa on her birth certificate.

14. Philbert Little, interview with Les Payne, November 15, 1990.

15. Collins and Bailey, *Seventh Child*, 35.

16. U.S. Bureau of the Census, *Fourteenth Census of the United States, 1920*, vol. 3, *Census of the Population: 1920* (Washington, D.C.: Government Printing Office, 1922), 609; https://www.census.gov/library/publications/1922/ dec/vol-03-population.html, accessed November 21, 2019.

17. Chris Peters, "Omaha Tribe Members Trying to Revitalize an 'Endangered Language,'" Omaha *Morning World-Herald*, February 15, 2015.

18. Works Progress Administration, *The Negroes of Nebraska* (Lincoln, Neb.: Woodruff Printing Co., 1940), 28–37.

19. W. E. B. Du Bois, "Returning Soldiers," *The Crisis* 18, no. 1 (May 1919): 14.

20. Cameron McWhirter, *Red Summer: The Summer of 1919 and the Awakening of Black America* (New York: Henry Holt, 2011), 13.

21. Excerpt from the diary of Dr. Cary T. Grayson, Sunday, March 9–10, 1919, in Arthur S. Link et al., eds., *The Papers of Woodrow Wilson*, vol. 55, *February 8–March 16, 1919* (Princeton, N.J.: Princeton University Press, 1986); available at https://rotunda.upress.virginia.edu/founders/WILS-01-55 -02-0342, accessed November 21, 2019.

22. "Escort Held at Bay as Girl Assaulted," Omaha *Morning World-Herald*, September 26, 1919.

23. Ibid.

24. "Negro Assaults Young Girl While Male Escort Stands by Powerless to Aid Her," *Omaha Daily Bee*, September 26, 1919.

25. George Ross Leighton, "Omaha, Nebraska—The Glory Is Departed: Part Two," *Harper's Monthly Magazine*, August 1938, 319; Nicholas Swiercek,

"Stoking a White Backlash: Race, Violence, and Yellow Journalism in Omaha, 1919" (paper presented at the 3rd Annual James A. Rawley Graduate Conference in the Humanities, "Imagining Communities: People, Places, Meanings," Lincoln, Neb., April 12, 2008); available at https://digitalcommons.unl.edu/historyrawleyconference/31.

26. "Girl Identified Assailant: Officers Keep Mob off Negro," *Omaha Daily Bee*, September 27, 1919; Orville D. Menard, "Lest We Forget: The Lynching of Will Brown, Omaha's 1919 Race Riot," *Nebraska History* 91 (2010): 155.

27. "Girl Identified Assailant."

28. Menard, "Lest We Forget," 155, 157.

29. "Omaha's Riot in Story and Picture" (Omaha: Educational Publishing Co., 1919).

30. Leighton, "Omaha, Nebraska," 319. See also Menard, "Lest We Forget," 157–58.

31. "Omaha's Riot in Story and Picture."

32. Ibid.

33. Ibid.

34. Ibid.

35. Henry Fonda and Howard Teichmann, *Fonda: My Life* (New York: New American Library, 1981), 25.

36. "General Wood Orders the Arrest of Omaha's Rioters," *New York Times*, October 1, 1919, pp. 1, 3.

37. "Frenzied Thousands Join in Orgy of Blood and Fire," Omaha *Morning World-Herald*, September 29, 1919, p. 1.

38. "Omaha's Riot in Story and Pictures," 20, foreword.

39. Menard, "Lest We Forget," 163.

## CHAPTER 2: STORMS OF RACISM

1. Michael W Schuyler, "The Ku Klux Klan in Nebraska, 1920–1930," *Nebraska History* 66 (1985): 235.

2. "The Birth of a Nation" brochure (New York: Epoch Producing, 1915), 15.

3. Marcus Garvey quoted these passages from the anonymous KKK letter in his "Editorial Letter by Marcus Garvey" of June 27, 1922, which was printed in *Negro World*, July 1, 1922; reprinted in Robert A. Hill, ed., *The Marcus Garvey and Universal Improvement Association Papers*, vol. 4, *1 September 1921–2 September 1922* (Berkeley: University of California Press, 1985), 681–82.

4. Wilfred Little, interview with Les Payne, April 26, 1991.

5. Stephen R. Fox, *The Guardian of Boston: William Monroe Trotter* (New York, Atheneum, 1970), 180.

6. W. E. B. Du Bois, "Returning Soldiers," *The Crisis* 18, no. 1 (May 1919): 14.

7. W. E. B. Du Bois, "Let Us Reason Together," *The Crisis* 18, no. 5 (September 1919): 231.

8. W. E. B. Du Bois, *The Souls of Black Folk* (New York: Penguin, 1989), 1.

9. Marcus Garvey, "Look Up, You Mighty Race," *Black Man* 2 (September–October 1936): 3–4.

10. Poster of UNIA meeting in Atlanta, ca. 1917, in Hill, ed., *The Marcus Garvey and Universal Improvement Association Papers*, vol. 1, *1826–August 1919* (Berkeley: University of California Press, 1983), xli.

11. Marcus Garvey, "African Fundamentalism," *Negro World,* June 6, 1925, in Hill, ed., *The Marcus Garvey and Universal Improvement Association Papers*, vol. 6, *September 1924–December 1927* (Berkeley: University of California Press, 1989), 161.

12. J. Edgar Hoover memo to Special Agent Ridgely, Washington, D.C., October 11, 1919, in Hill, ed., *The Marcus Garvey and Universal Improvement Association Papers*, vol. 2, *27 August 1919–August 1920* (Berkeley: University of California Press, 1983), 72.

13. Marcus Garvey, "All Negroes Not Ashamed of Africa" (speech), in Hill, ed., vol. 4, 40.

14. Marcus Garvey, "Declaration of Rights of the Negro Peoples of the World," in Hill, ed., vol. 2, 571–80.

15. Marcus Garvey, "Editorial Letter by Marcus Garvey" of September 7, 1920, in Hill, ed., *The Marcus Garvey and Universal Improvement Association Papers*, vol. 3, *September 1920–August 1921* (Berkeley: University of California Press, 1984), 10.

16. Marcus Garvey, "The Negro's Greatest Enemy," in Hill, ed., vol. 1, 5.

17. Marcus Garvey, "The UNIA Has Counted the Cost," in Hill, ed., vol. 4, 847.

18. David Levering Lewis, *W. E. B. Du Bois: A Biography* (New York: Henry Holt, 2009), 18.

19. Frederick Douglass, *Narrative of the Life of Frederick Douglass: An American Slave* (1846; repr., New York: Signet, 1968), 23.

20. Marcus Garvey, "Purity of Race," in *The Philosophy and Opinions of Marcus Garvey, Or Africa for the Africans,* comp. Amy Jacques Garvey (Dover, Mass.: Majority Press, 1986), 37.

21. Mark V. Tushnet, ed., *Thurgood Marshall: His Speeches, Writing, Arguments, Opinions and Reminiscences* (Chicago: Lawrence Hill Books, 2001), 421.

22. W. E. B. Du Bois, "Back to Africa," *The Century* 105, no. 4 (February 1923): 539.

23. Wilfred Little interview.

24. Marcus Garvey, "Cable by Marcus Garvey to Chairman, Liberty Hall," June 25, 1922, Atlanta, in Hill, ed., vol. 4, 679.

25. William Pierce Randel, *The Ku Klux Klan: A Century of Infamy* (Philadelphia: Chilton, 1965), 196.

26. Marcus Garvey, "Honorable Marcus Garvey Tells of Interview with Ku Klux Klan," in Hill, ed., vol. 4, 707–15.

27. Ibid.

28. William Pickens to Marcus Garvey (response to invitation to UNIA Convention), July 24, 1922, W. E. B. Du Bois Papers (MS 312), Special Collections and University Archives, University of Massachusetts Amherst Libraries.

29. Garvey, "Honorable Marcus Garvey Tells of Interview with Ku Klux Klan," in Hill, ed., vol. 4, 707–15.

30. Ibid.

31. Ibid.

32. Amy Jacques Garvey, *Garvey and Garveyism* (New York: Collier, 1970), 100.

33. Garvey, "Cable by Marcus Garvey to Chairman, Liberty Hall," in Hill, ed., vol. 4, 680n2.

34. Marcus Garvey, "Speech by Marcus Garvey," July 16, 1922, in Hill, ed., vol. 4, 719–20.

35. Asa Philip Randolph, "A Supreme Negro Jamaican Jackass," *The Messenger* 5, no. 1 (January 1923): 561.

36. Pickens to Garvey, July 24, 1922.

37. Ibid.

38. Marcus Garvey to Norton G. Thomas, August 14, 1925, in Hill, ed., vol. 6, 228n2.

39. Marcus Garvey, "The Negro, Communism, Trade Unionism and His Friend: Beware of Greeks Bearing Gifts," in Garvey, comp. *The Philosophy and Opinions of Marcus Garvey*, 71.

40. Henry Louis Mencken, "Notes on Negro Strategy," *Mencken's America* (Athens: Ohio University Press, 2004), 143.

41. Lewis, *W. E. B. Du Bois*, 149–52.

42. Wilfred Little interview.

43. Ibid.

44. Louise Little, "Omaha, Neb.," *Negro World*, July 3, 1926.

45. Wilfred Little interview.

46. Ibid.

## CHAPTER 3: THE ANCHOR IS LOST

1. U.S. Senate, *Reports of the Immigration Commission: Emigration Conditions in Europe*, 61st Cong., 3d Sess., doc. 748 (Washington, D.C.: Government Printing Office, 1911), 209.

2. Wilfred Little, interview with Les Payne, April 26, 1991.

3. Earl Little to President Calvin Coolidge, June 8, 1927, in Robert A. Hill, ed. *The Marcus Garvey and Universal Negro Improvement Association Papers* vol. 6, *September 1924–December 1927* (Berkeley: University of California Press, 1989), 561.

4. Wilfred Little interview.

5. Ibid.

6. Ibid.

7. Ibid.

8. Ibid.

9. Ibid.

10. Ibid.

11. Ibid.

12. Capital View Land Company and James W. Nicoll v. Earl Little, Louise Little and Cora I. Way, Ingham County Circuit Court, docket 14215, dated October 12, 1929. The Little family was referred to as "colored" throughout the documents in this lawsuit.

13. Michigan State Police Report, filed by Officer G. W. Waterman, Bureau of Criminal Investigations, case 2155: suspected arson of the Little family home on November 8, 1929. Courtesy of the Ingham County Probate Court, Lansing Office.

14. Wilfred Little interview.

15. Waterman, Michigan State Police Report, case 2155.

16. Ibid.

17. Wilfred Little interview.

18. Waterman, Michigan State Police Report, case 2155.

19. Ibid.

20. "Hold Man During Probe of Blaze," Lansing *State Journal*, November 11, 1929, 1.

21. Wilfred Little interview.

22. Ibid.

23. Philbert Little, interview with Les Payne, November 15, 1990.

24. Wilfred Little interview; Philbert Little interview.

25. Malcolm X and Alex Haley, *The Autobiography of Malcolm X* (New York: Ballantine, 1992), 7.

26. Philbert Little interview.

27. Malcolm X and Haley, *Autobiography*, 7.

28. Philbert Little interview.

29. Ibid.

30. Wilfred Little interview.

31. Philbert Little interview.

32. Wilfred Little interview.

33. Ibid.

34. Ibid.

35. Philbert Little interview.

36. Wilfred Little interview.

37. Ibid.

38. Philbert Little interview.

39. Transcript, Ella Collins, interview with CBS News for "Malcolm X: The Real Story," produced by Brett Alexander, aired December 3, 1992.

40. Malcolm X and Haley, *Autobiography*, 6.

41. Ibid., 6, 7.

42. Wilfred Little interview.

43. William Shakespeare, *The Tragedy of Julius Caesar*, II:ii.

44. Malcolm X and Haley, *Autobiography*, 9.

45. Wilfred Little interview.

46. Malcolm X and Haley, *Autobiography*, 9.

47. Wilfred Little interview.

48. Ibid.

49. Ibid.

50. Earl Little, Death Certificate (register 545), Michigan Department of Health, September 30, 1931.

51. Wilfred Little interview.

## CHAPTER 4: PULLING THE FAMILY APART

1. Earl Little, Death Certificate (register 545), Michigan Department of Health, September 30, 1931.

2. Malcolm X and Alex Haley, *The Autobiography of Malcolm X* (New York: Ballantine, 1992), 11.

3. Wilfred Little, interview with Les Payne, April 26, 1991.

4. Ibid.

5. Ibid.

6. Philbert Little, interview with Les Payne, November 15, 1990.

7. Malcolm X and Haley, *Autobiography*, 13.

8. Wilfred Little interview.

9. Ibid.

10. Philbert Little interview.

11. Malcolm X to Philbert Little, December 12, 1949, Lot 2162.

12. Malcolm X and Haley, *Autobiography*, 12.

13. Philbert Little interview.

14. Ibid.

15. Ibid.

16. Wilfred Little interview.

17. Philbert Little interview.

18. Wilfred Little interview.

19. Malcolm X and Haley, *Autobiography*, 11.

20. Wilfred Little interview.

21. Ibid.

22. Langston Hughes, *I Wonder as I Wander: An Autobiographical Journey* (New York: Fang Hill, 1993), 315.

23. Malcolm X and Haley, *Autobiography*, 23.

24. Philbert Little interview.

25. Ibid.

26. Wilfred Little interview.

27. Ibid.

28. Ibid.

29. Ibid.

30. Ibid.

31. Ibid.

32. Ibid.

33. "Petition for Admission Mentally Diseased," December 22, 1938, in State of Michigan, Ingham County Probate Court, file B-4398, Louise Little.

## CHAPTER 5: EAST LANSING RED

1. Wilfred Little, interview with Les Payne, April 26, 1991.

2. Ibid.

3. Police report, May 8, 1939, in Malcolm Little Juvenile Division (file 4053), Ingham County Probate Court, State of Michigan.

4. Report of Malcolm Little's family circumstances, August 17, 1939, in ibid.

5. Superintendent's statement to Probate Court, October 21, 1938, in ibid.

6. Robert E. Lott of Lansing School District to William T. Noble of the *Detroit News*, January 17, 1966. This letter, responding to the newspaper's request, includes Malcolm Little's grades at Pleasant Grove schools during the 1938–1939 school year.

7. Malcolm X and Alex Haley, *The Autobiography of Malcolm X* (New York: Ballantine, 1992), 31.

8. John Davis Jr., interview with Les Payne, September 1, 1993.

9. Ibid.

10. Ibid.

11. Ibid.

12. Ibid.

13. Ibid.

14. Ibid.

15. Ibid.

16. Report of Malcolm Little's family circumstances, August 17, 1939.

17. John Davis Jr. interview.

18. Ibid.

19. Ibid.

20. Wilfred Little interview.

21. Report of Malcolm Little's family circumstances, August 17, 1939.

22. Malcolm X and Haley, *Autobiography*, 25.

23. U.S. Census, 1940, entry for Jim G. and E. Lois Swerlein, Mason, Michigan.

24. Wilfred Little interview.

25. Malcolm X and Haley, *Autobiography*, 26.

26. Ibid., 26–27.

27. Superintendent's statement to Probate Court, October 21, 1938.

28. Malcolm X and Haley, *Autobiography*, 28.

29. Ibid., 34.

30. James Cotton, interview with Les Payne, June 20, 1992.

31. Malcolm X and Haley, *Autobiography*, 32.

32. James Cotton interview.

33. Rollin Dart, interview with Les Payne, 1992.

34. Ibid.

35. Ibid.

36. James Cotton interview.

37. Audrey Slaught, interview with Les Payne, June 7, 1993.

38. Ibid.

39. James Cotton interview.

40. Ibid.

41. Audrey Cotton, interview with Les Payne, June 1992.

42. Ibid.

43. Slaught interview.

44. Ibid.

45. Malcolm X and Haley, *Autobiography*, 36.

46. Ibid.
47. James Cotton interview.
48. Slaught interview.
49. Malcolm X and Haley, *Autobiography*, 37.
50. Transcript, Ella Collins, interview with CBS News for "Malcolm X: The Real Story," produced by Brett Alexander, aired December 3, 1992.
51. Malcolm X and Haley, *Autobiography*, 34; Collins interview.
52. Philbert Little interview.
53. Ibid.
54. Ibid.
55. Collins interview.
56. Wilfred Little interview.

## CHAPTER 6: LIGHTING OUT FOR HIS TERRITORY

1. John Davis Jr., interview with Les Payne, September 1, 1993.
2. Ibid.
3. Wilfred Little, interview with Les Payne, April 26, 1991.
4. Ibid.
5. Reginald Little posted a letter to Malcolm at this address. The postmark is May 22, 1941.
6. Wilfred Little interview.
7. Transcript, Ella Collins, interview with CBS News for "Malcolm X: The Real Story," produced by Brett Alexander, aired December 3, 1992.
8. Rodnell P. Collins and A. Peter Bailey, *Seventh Child: A Family Memoir of Malcolm X* (Secaucus, N.J.: Birch Lane/Carol Publishing, 1998), 67.
9. Wilfred Little interview.
10. Collins interview.
11. Malcolm Jarvis, interview with Les Payne, December 9, 1992.
12. Wilfred Little interview.
13. Malcolm X and Alex Haley, *The Autobiography of Malcolm X* (New York: Ballantine, 1992), 44.
14. Wilfred Little interview.
15. Malcolm X and Haley, *Autobiography*, 46.
16. Malcolm Little to Johnny Mae Horton, n.d. (Saturday; c. 1941), courtesy of Walter and Linda Evans, Savannah, Georgia.
17. Malcolm Little to Zalma Holman, November 18, 1941, courtesy of Walter and Linda Evans.
18. Malcolm Little to Mary Jane, n.d., courtesy of Walter and Linda Evans.
19. Malcolm Little to Holman, November 18, 1941.
20. Malcolm Little to Horton, c. 1941.
21. Malcolm X and Haley, *Autobiography*, 154.

22. Malcolm Little to Horton, c. 1941.

23. Collins and Bailey, *Seventh Child*, 39.

24. Collins interview.

25. Jarvis interview.

26. Ibid.

27. Collins interview.

28. Collins and Bailey, *Seventh Child*, 61.

29. Malcolm X and Haley, *Autobiography*, 42.

30. Ibid., 45.

31. Jarvis interview.

32. Ibid.

33. Ibid.

34. Ibid.

35. Malcolm X and Haley, *Autobiography*, 60.

36. Collins interview.

37. Malcolm X and Haley, *Autobiography*, 66.

38. Ibid., 67.

39. Ibid., 68.

40. Ibid., 22.

41. Collins interview.

## CHAPTER 7: CHASED OUT OF SEVENTH HEAVEN

1. Elsie Freeman, Wynell Burroughs Schamel, and Jean West, "'A Date Which Will Live in Infamy': The First Typed Draft of Franklin D. Roosevelt's War Address," *Social Education* 55, no. 7 (November–December 1991): 467–70.

2. Malcolm X and Alex Haley, *The Autobiography of Malcolm X* (New York: Ballantine, 1992), 70.

3. Ibid., 73, 75.

4. Ibid., 73.

5. H. L. Mencken, "The Aframerican: New Style," *The American Mercury* 7, no. 26 (February 1926), 254–55.

6. Malcolm X and Haley, *Autobiography*, 76.

7. Ibid., 74, 76.

8. Ibid., 76, 75.

9. Malcolm Jarvis, interview with Les Payne, December 9, 1992.

10. Bazeley Perry, interview with Les Payne, February 27, 1993.

11. Jarvis interview.

12. Transcript, Ella Collins, interview with CBS News for "Malcolm X: The Real Story," produced by Brett Alexander, aired December 3, 1992, p. 32.

13. Transcript, John T. Walker, interview with CBS News for "Malcolm X:

The Real Story," produced by Brett Alexander, aired December 3, 1992, p. 19.

14. Jarvis interview.

15. Malcolm X and Haley, *Autobiography*, 68, 78.

16. Ibid., 78.

17. Ibid., 79.

18. Philbert Little, interview with Les Payne, November 15, 1990.

19. Malcolm X and Haley, *Autobiography*, 79.

20. Ibid.

21. Ibid.

22. Wilfred Little, interview with Les Payne, April 26, 1991.

23. Malcolm X and Haley, *Autobiography*, 79.

24. Ibid., 80.

25. Ibid., 83.

26. Francis A. J. Ianni, *Black Mafia: Ethnic Succession in Organized Crime* (New York: Simon & Schuster, 1974), 111.

27. Ibid., 118–19.

28. Malcolm X and Haley, *Autobiography*, 87–88.

29. Ibid., 89–90.

30. Malcolm X, FBI file.

31. Malcolm X and Haley, *Autobiography*, 93.

32. Ibid., 91.

33. Ibid, 97.

34. Ibid., 91.

35. Ibid., 98.

36. Wilfred Little interview.

37. Malcolm X and Haley, *Autobiography*, 99.

38. Jarvis interview.

39. Malcolm X and Haley, *Autobiography*, 96.

40. Joe X. Price, *Redd Foxx, B.S. (Before Sanford)* (Chicago: Contemporary Books, 1979), 109–10.

41. Ibid., 110.

42. Malcolm X and Haley, *Autobiography*, 104.

43. Jean Byers, *A Study of the Negro in Military Service* (Washington, D.C.: Department of Defense, 1950).

44. Henry L. Stimson, Diary (entry of September 27, 1940), Henry Stimson Papers (MS 345), Yale University Libraries.

45. "Ranking of Cadets of 1936 Class at United States Military Academy Announced," *New York Times,* June 9, 1936, 27.

46. Malcolm X and Haley, *Autobiography*, 106.

47. Ibid., 125.

48. Ibid., 126, 127.
49. Ibid., 130.
50. Jarvis interview.
51. Malcolm X and Haley, *Autobiography*, 132.
52. Jarvis interview.


CHAPTER 8: LUCK RUNS OUT

1. Malcolm X and Alex Haley, *The Autobiography of Malcolm X* (New York: Ballantine, 1992), 134.
2. Ibid.
3. Malcolm Jarvis, interview with Les Payne, December 9, 1992.
4. Ibid.
5. Malcolm X and Haley, *Autobiography*, 134.
6. Jarvis interview.
7. Malcolm X and Haley, *Autobiography*, 135.
8. Transcript, Ella Collins interview with CBS News for "Malcolm X: The Real Story," produced by Brett Alexander, aired December 3, 1992.
9. Jarvis interview.
10. Ibid.
11. Ibid.
12. Rodnell P. Collins and A. Peter Bailey, *Seventh Child: A Family Memoir of Malcolm X* (Secaucus, N.J.: Birch Lane/Carol Publishing, 1998), 65–66.
13. Ibid.
14. Malcolm X and Haley, *Autobiography*, 135.
15. Jarvis interview.
16. Ibid.
17. Ibid.
18. Malcolm X and Haley, *Autobiography*, 138.
19. Jarvis interview.
20. Ibid.
21. Ibid.
22. Ibid.
23. Ibid.
24. Martin Luther King Jr. to Martin Luther King Sr., June 15, 1944, in Clayborne Carson, Ralph E. Luker, and Penny A. Russell, eds., *The Papers of Martin Luther King, Jr.*, Vol. 1, *Called to Serve, January 1929–June 1951* (Berkeley: University of California Press, 1992), 112–13. King also wrote to his mother on June 1, 1944, about his experience in Simsbury, Connecticut.
25. Charles Tisdale, interview with Les Payne, May 15, 1994.

26. Admission Application to Crozer Theological Seminary, dated February 1948, in Carson, Luker, and Russell, eds., *Papers of Martin Luther King, Jr.,* 1:144.

27. Malcolm X and Haley, *Autobiography,* 140.

28. Ibid.

29. Jarvis interview.

30. Ibid.

31. Malcolm X and Haley, *Autobiography,* 142, 143.

32. Jarvis interview.

33. Ibid.

34. Malcolm X and Haley, *Autobiography,* 143.

35. Jarvis interview.

36. Ibid.

37. Ibid.

38. Ibid.

39. Ibid.

40. Malcolm X and Haley, *Autobiography,* 145.

41. Ibid., 147.

42. Jarvis interview.

43. Malcolm X and Haley, *Autobiography,* 149.

44. Jarvis interview.

45. Ibid.

46. Ibid.

47. Malcolm X and Haley, *Autobiography,* 151.

48. Jarvis interview.

49. Collins interview.

50. Jarvis interview.

51. Bill Cunningham and Daniel Golden, "Malcolm: The Boston Years," *Boston Globe Magazine,* February 16, 1992, 30.

52. Jarvis interview.

53. Untitled clipping, *Boston Daily Record,* 1946.

## CHAPTER 9: LEARNING TO FIGHT WITH WORDS

1. Bruce Watson, *Sacco and Vanzetti: The Men, the Murders, and the Judgment of Mankind* (New York: Viking, 2007), 76, 82, 254–55, 308.

2. Malcolm X and Alex Haley, *The Autobiography of Malcolm X* (New York: Ballantine, 1992), 152.

3. Ibid.; Charlestown State Prison medical report, February 28, 1946.

4. "Massachusetts State Prison Psychometric Report (of Malcolm Little)," May 1, 1946, prison file of Malcolm Little.

5. Malcolm Jarvis, interview with Les Payne, December 9, 1991.

6. Leon Gussow, M.D., "Toxicology Rounds: Kitchen Toxicology: Nutmeg (the Hallucinogen)," *Emergency Medicine News* 33, no. 5 (May 2011): 16; https://journals.lww.com/em-news/Fulltext/2011/05000/Toxicology_Rounds__Kitchen_Toxicology__Nutmeg__the.7.aspx?WT.mc_id=EMxALLx20100222xxFRIEND. See also Deborah Blum, "A Warning on Nutmeg," *New York Times*, November 25, 2014.

7. Jarvis interview.

8. Transcript, Ella Collins, interview with CBS News for "Malcolm X: The Real Story," produced by Brett Alexander, aired December 3, 1992.

9. Malcolm X and Haley, *Autobiography*, 152.

10. Jarvis interview.

11. Malcolm X and Haley, *Autobiography*, 153.

12. Richard Wright, *Black Boy: A Record of Childhood and Youth* (New York: Harper & Brothers, 1945), 218.

13. Malcolm X and Haley, *Autobiography*, 154.

14. Ibid.

15. Ibid.

16. Jarvis interview.

17. Malcolm Little to Ella Collins, December 14, 1946, courtesy of Walter and Linda Evans, Savannah, Georgia.

18. Malcolm X and Haley, *Autobiography*, 155.

19. William C. Rhoden, *Forty Million Dollar Slaves: The Rise, Fall, and Redemption of the Black Athlete* (New York: Crown Publishers, 2006), 80.

20. "The Boston Red Sox and Racism: With New Owners, Team Confronts Legacy of Intolerance," National Public Radio, October 11, 2002; http://www.npr.org/programs/morning/features/2002/oct/redsox/, accessed April 10, 2008.

21. "The Name. The Legend. The Man," UCLA History; alumni.ucla.edu; Jules Tygiel, "The Court Martial of Jackie Robinson," *American Heritage*, August–September 1984.

22. Malcolm X and Haley, *Autobiography*, 155.

23. Ibid.

24. Wilfred Little, interview with Les Payne, April 26, 1991.

25. Ibid.

## CHAPTER 10: BIRTH OF THE NATION OF ISLAM

1. Malcolm X and Alex Haley, *The Autobiography of Malcolm X* (New York: Ballantine, 1992), 156.

2. Mary Baker Eddy, *Science and Health* (Bedford, Mass.: Applewood, 1875).

See also Georgine Milmine, *The Life of Mary Baker G. Eddy* (New York: Doubleday, 1909).

3. http://www.mormonnewsroom.org/article/joseph-smith; accessed June 25, 2017.

4. Peggy Fletcher Stack, "New Mormon Essay: Joseph Smith Married Teens, Other Men's Wives," *Salt Lake Tribune*, October 22, 2014, updated February 20, 2017; http://www.sltrib.com/lifestyle/faith/1733664-155/plural -marriage-essay-smith-church-joseph, accessed June 25, 2017.

5. Hebrews, 11:1.

6. Peter Lamborn Wilson, *Sacred Drift: Essays on the Margins of Islam* (San Francisco: City Lights, 1993), 15; Michael A. Gomez, *Black Crescent: The Experience and Legacy of African Muslims in the Americas* (Cambridge: Cambridge University Press, 2005), 203; Fathie Ali Abdat, "Before the Fez: Life and Times of Drew Ali, 1886–1924," *Journal of Race, Ethnicity, and Religions* 5 (2014): 1–39.

7. Arna Bontemps and Jack Conroy, *They Seek a City* (Garden City, N.Y.: Doubleday, Doran, 1945), 174–77.

8. C. Eric Lincoln, *The Black Muslims in America* (Boston, Mass.: Beacon Press, 1961), 51.

9. E. U. Essien-Udom, "The Nationalist Tradition," *Black Nationalism: A Search for an Identity in America* (Chicago: University of Chicago Press, 1962), 46.

10. Ibid., 47.

11. In the July 27, 1929, issue, the *Chicago Defender* stated, "It is believed that the ordeal of the trial together with the treatment he received at the hands of police in an effort to obtain true statements are directly responsible for the illness which precipitated his death."

12. Arna Bontemps and Jack Conroy, "Registered with Allah," *Anyplace but Here* (New York: Hill & Wang, 1967), 177.

13. Christopher C. Alston, interview with Les Payne, September 19, 1993.

14. Bontemps and Conroy, "Registered with Allah," 217–18.

15. Lincoln, *The Black Muslims in America*, 10.

16. Ibid., 11.

17. Alston interview.

18. Ibid.

19. Lincoln, *The Black Muslims in America*, 26.

20. Alston interview.

21. Ibid.

22. Ibid.

23. Lincoln, *The Black Muslims in America*, 12.

24. Larry Murphy, ed., "Voodoo Cult Among Negro Migrants," *Down by the Riverside: Readings in African-American Religion* (New York: New York University Press, 2000), 210.

25. Lincoln, *The Black Muslims in America*, 12.
26. Alston interview.
27. Elijah Muhammad, "Mr. Muhammad Speaks: The White Man's Claim [sic] to Divine Superiority," *Pittsburgh Courier,* July 4, 1959, 14.
28. Claude Andrew Clegg III, *An Original Man: The Life and Times of Elijah Muhammad* (New York: St. Martin's, 1997), 65.
29. Fard Muhammad, FBI file.
30. Nathaniel Muhammad, interview with Les Payne, September 27, 2015.
31. Ibid.
32. John Muhammad, interview with Les Payne, September 18, 1993.
33. FBI Files, Airtel, SAC, Los Angeles, to Director, FBI, Interview with Hazel Barton Ford Evelsizer, October 18, 1957. Vault website: Fard Muhammad, part 2 of 7, pp. 9–14.
34. FBI Files, Airtel, SAC, Los Angeles, to Director, FBI: includes summary of information on Wallace Don Ford, January 13, 1958. Vault website: Fard Muhammad, part 2 of 7, pp. 34–88.
35. "Cult Killer Bares Plot on Mayor," *Detroit Evening Times,* November 23, 1932, 1–2; "Leader of Cult Admits Slaying at Home 'Altar,'" *Detroit Free Press,* November 21, 1932, 1–2.; "Leader of Cult Called Insane," *Detroit News,* November 22, 1932, 4.
36. Fard Muhammad to Elijah Muhammad, December 18, 1933.
37. Ibid.
38. Ibid.
39. John Muhammad interview.
40. Nathaniel Muhammad interview.
41. Clegg, An Original Man, 22.
42. Elijah Muhammad, "The Knowledge of God Himself: Saviour's Day, February 26, 1969," *Our Saviour Has Arrived* (Chicago: Muhammad's Temple of Islam No. 2, 1974), 35.
43. John Muhammad interview.
44. Fard Muhammad to Elijah Muhammad, December 18, 1933.
45. I. F. Stone, "The Pilgrimage of Malcolm X," *In a Time of Torment* (New York: Random House, 1967), 112.
46. Jackson R. Bryer and Mary C. Hartig, eds., *Conversations with August Wilson* (Jackson: University Press of Mississippi, 2006), 128.
47. FBI Files, Report, January 27, 1958, pp. 56–79, Title of Case: Elijah Muhammad (with a list of his aliases), Character of case: Internal Security—NOI. Vault website: Elijah Muhammad, part 2 of 20. See also Report, August 6, 1942, pp. 49–59, Title: Gulam Bogans with aliases, Character: Sedition Selective Service. Vault website: Fard Muhammad, part 1 of 20.
48. FBI Files. Vault website: Elijah Muhammad, part 2 of 20, p. 61 of 100.

## CHAPTER 11: BUILDING TEMPLES IN THE EAST

1. Wilfred Little, interview with Les Payne, April 26, 1991.
2. Ibid.
3. Ibid.
4. Ibid.
5. Ibid.
6. Malcolm X and Alex Haley, *The Autobiography of Malcolm X* (New York: Ballantine, 1992), 162.
7. Ibid., 163, 164.
8. Ibid, 184.
9. Malcolm Jarvis, interview with Les Payne, December 9, 1992.
10. Malcolm Little to Bazeley Perry, August 5, 1949, courtesy of Walter and Linda Evans, Savannah, Georgia.
11. "Four Convicts Turn Moslems, Get Calls Looking to Mecca," *Boston Herald,* April 20, 1950, 3.
12. Wilfred Little interview.
13. Ibid.
14. Moustafa Hassain, interview with Les Payne, June 8, 1996.
15. Raushanah Hassain, interview with Les Payne, June 16, 1996.
16. Moustafa Hassain interview.
17. Raushanah Hassain interview.
18. Moustafa Hassain interview.
19. Ibid.
20. Raushanah Hassain interview.
21. Ibid.
22. Moustafa Hassain interview.
23. Philbert Little, interview with Les Payne, November 15, 1990.
24. Moustafa Hassain interview.
25. Malcolm X to Philbert Little, December 9, 1954, courtesy of Walter and Linda Evans.
26. Yusuf Shah (aka Captain Joseph), interview with Les Payne, October 9, 1992.
27. Clayborne Carson, *Malcolm X: The FBI File,* ed. David Gallen (1991; repr., New York: Skyhorse, 2012), 107–15.
28. Shah interview.
29. Malcolm X to Elijah Muhammad, November 11, 1954, courtesy of Walter and Linda Evans.
30. Nathaniel Muhammad, interview with Les Payne, September 27, 2015.

31. Moustafa Hassain interview.

32. Ibid.

33. Malcolm X and Haley, *Autobiography*, 295.

34. Dr. Abdul Salaam, *Is the White Man Still the Devil? Myths vs. Realities: An Islamic Perspective* (Victoria, BC: Friesen Press, 2013), 103, "It was important, said Elijah Muhammad, for Fard Mohammad to look like a white man. Only his mother, again according to the teachings of Elijah Muhammad, who had been especially chosen and prepared to birth him so that he could travel easily among both white and black with minimum suspicion, was white." In addition, an FBI memo dated July 30, 1963, addressed to Mr. W. C. Sullivan, re: Nation of Islam (25-330971), filed in Nation of Islam—LA 25-330974-25, and in W. D. Fard 105-63642, clarifies that the information in the article in the *Los Angeles Herald Examiner* dated July 23, 1963, called "Black Muslim Founder Exposed as a White," is not new to the FBI. The memo also states that "the NOI has been successful in contributing to the mystery of Fard's origin claiming that his father was a 'devil' (white man) while his mother was one half 'original' [other than white such as Negro, Chinese or Indian)."

35. Malcolm X to Elijah Muhammad, November 11, 1954.

36. Nathaniel Muhammad interview.

37. *The Hate That Hate Produced*, Mike Wallace and Louis Lomax, producers, July 13–17, 1959, WNTA-TV, Channel 13, New York.

38. Malcolm X and Haley, *Autobiography*, 238.

39. Angela Davis, *Angela Davis: An Autobiography* (1974; repr., New York: International Publishers, 1996), 126.

40. Rosemari Mealy, *Fidel and Malcolm: Memories of a Meeting* (Melbourne: Ocean Press, 1993), 35, 38–40.

## CHAPTER 12: HARTFORD: "THE DEAD THERE ARE RISING"

1. Malcolm X and Alex Haley, *The Autobiography of Malcolm X* (New York: Ballantine, 1992), 222.

2. The radio drama *Yours Truly, Johnny Dollar* aired on CBS Radio from January 14, 1949, to September 30, 1962.

3. Franklin J. Watson, "A Comparison of Negro and White Populations, Connecticut: (1940–1960)," *Phylon Magazine* 29, no. 2 (1968): 142–55.

4. Malcolm X and Haley, *Autobiography*, 222.

5. Rosalie Forrest, interview with Les Payne, April 14, 1993.

6. Malcolm X and Haley, *Autobiography*, 222.

7. Lewis Brown, interview with Les Payne (notes), 1994.

8. Ibid.

9. Malcolm X to Philbert Little, March 19, 1955, courtesy of Walter and Linda Evans, Savannah, Georgia.

10. Rosalie Forrest interview.

11. Ibid.

12. "Florida Negro Kidnaped and Lynched: Shot to Death—Accused of Assault on Girl, 12," *New York Post*, May 13, 1941, 7.

13. Ibid.

14. "End of Lynching," *Washington Post*, January 2, 1954, 6.

15. Timothy B. Tyson, *The Blood of Emmett Till* (New York: Simon & Schuster, 2017), 6.

16. William Bradford Huie, "The Shocking Story of Approved Killing in Mississippi," *Look*, January 1956; https://www.history.com/this-day-in-history/emmett-till-murderers-make-magazine-confession, accessed May 23, 2018.

17. Eddie St. John, interview with Les Payne, August 14, 1993.

18. Ibid.

19. Robert Rotberg, "Where Can a Negro Live? A Study of Housing Discrimination in Hartford" (part 1 of 7), *Hartford Courant*, August 19, 1956, 1.

20. Quoted in ibid. (part 4 of 7), August 22, 1956, 6.

21. John Peoples, interview with Les Payne, August 1993.

22. Group interview with several founding members of the Hartford temple (Rosalie Forrest, Eddie St. John, Paul Sturges, Johnnye James, etc.), August 1993.

23. St. John interview.

24. Ibid.

25. Ibid.

26. Peoples interview.

27. Ibid.

28. Elizabeth Hutton Turner, ed., *Jacob Lawrence: The Migration Series* (Washington, D.C.: Rappahannock Press, 1993), 73 (#15 of the Migration Series).

29. Ralph Ginzburg, *100 Years of Lynchings* (1962; repr., Baltimore: Black Classic Press, 1988), 235.

30. Rosalie Forrest interview.

31. Peoples interview.

32. St. John interview.

33. Ibid.

34. Peoples interview.

35. Peoples interview.

36. Rosalie Forrest interview.

37. Malcolm X and Haley, *Autobiography*, 222.

38. Ibid., 223.

39. FBI Files, SAC, New Haven, to SAC, Buffalo, "RM-MCI," January 31, 1957.

40. Ibid.

41. Malcolm X to Elijah Muhammad, December 21, 1956, courtesy of Walter and Linda Evans.

## CHAPTER 13: "MEET WITH THEM DEVILS"

1. Malcolm X, speech at Temple No. 15, Atlanta, 1960, cassette in author's collection.

2. Ibid.

3. Malcolm X and Alex Haley, *The Autobiography of Malcolm X* (New York: Ballantine, 1992), 223.

4. Richard Gid Powers, *Secrecy and Power: The Life of J. Edgar Hoover* (New York: Free Press, 1987), 413.

5. Jeremiah Shabazz (aka Jeremiah X), interview with Les Payne, January 1997.

6. E. David Cronin, *Black Moses: The Story of Marcus Garvey and the Universal Negro Improvement Association* (Madison: University of Wisconsin Press, 1960), 189.

7. W. E. B. Du Bois, "Lunatic or a Traitor," *The Crisis* 28, no. 1 (May 1924): 8–9.

8. Jeremiah Shabazz interview.

9. FBI Files, Memorandum, SAC, Chicago, to Director, FBI, "Justification for Continuation of Technical or Microphone Surveillance," October 30, 1959. File 105-24822 (Elijah Muhammad), Serial 56X.

10. FBI Files, Memorandum, SAC, Chicago, to Director, FBI, "Recommendation for Installation of Technical or Microphone Surveillance," June 9, 1960. File 105-24822 (Elijah Muhammad).

11. Jeremiah Shabazz interview.

12. Elizabeth Shabazz, interview with Les Payne, February 1, 1997.

13. Ibid.

14. Steven Levingston, "John F. Kennedy, Martin Luther King, Jr., and the Phone Call That Changed History," *Time*, June 20, 2017; http://time.com/4817240/martin-luther-king-john-kennedy-phone-call/.

15. Michael O'Brien, *John F. Kennedy* (New York: Thomas Dunne/St. Martin's, 2015), 487.

16. Taylor Branch, *Parting the Waters: America in the King Years, 1954–63* (New York: Simon & Schuster, 1998).

17. George Wallace, inaugural speech, January 14, 1963; https://www .npr.org/2013/01/14/169080969/segregation-forever-a-fiery-pledge -forgiven-but-not-forgotten.

18. Wyn Craig Wade, *The Fiery Cross: The Ku Klux Klan in America* (New York: Simon & Schuster, 1987), 309.

19. *The Hate That Hate Produced*, Mike Wallace and Louis Lomax, producers, July 13–17, 1959, WNTA-TV, Channel 13, New York.

20. Malcolm X, "Message to the Grassroots," in *Malcolm X Speaks,* edited by George Breitman (1965; repr., New York: Grove Weidenfeld, 1990), 1.

21. Yusuf Shah (aka Captain Joseph), interview with Les Payne, October 9, 1992.

22. Wade, *The Fiery Cross,* 76.

23. J. B. Stoner, "White Filth Crusader Aims Guns at Moslems," *Pittsburgh Courier,* March 23, 1957, 6.

24. Elijah Muhammad, "Mr. Muhammad Responds to White Filth Crusader," *Pittsburgh Courier,* March 30, 1957, 6.

25. Malcolm X and Haley, *Autobiography,* 175.

26. Stoner, "White Filth Crusader Aims Guns at Moslems," 36.

27. Elijah Muhammad, "Mr. Muhammad Responds to White Filth Crusader," 37.

28. Malcolm X, speech at Los Angeles, May 5, 1962; https://www.youtube .com/watch?v=18Ern-fNEb4.

29. Elijah Muhammad, "Mr. Muhammad Responds to White Filth Crusader," 37.

30. J. B. Stoner to New York City Police Commissioner Stephen P. Kennedy, August 6, 1959, courtesy of Walter and Linda Evans Archives, Savannah, Ga.

31. Malcolm X to Elijah Muhammad, July 19, 1960, courtesy of Walter and Linda Evans Collection, Savannah, Georgia.

32. Jeremiah Shabazz interview.

33. Wallace H. Terry II, "Black Muslim Elijah's Lowly Start" (part 2 of 6), "Cult of Hate" series, *Washington Post,* December 11–16, 1960; reproduced at the National Archives, Washington, D.C.

34. Malcolm X and Haley, *Autobiography,* 206.

35. Jeremiah Shabazz interview.

36. *The Hate That Hate Produced.*

37. Jeremiah Shabazz interview.

38. Malcolm X to Elijah Muhammad, January 23, 1961.

39. Ibid.

40. Ibid.

41. Jeremiah Shabazz interview.

42. Ibid.

43. Ibid.

44. Clayborne Carson, *Malcolm X: The FBI Files*, ed. David Gallen (1991; repr., New York: Skyhorse, 2012), 203–4.

45. FBI Files, Atlanta Airtel and LHM to Bureau, "U.S. Klans, Knights of the Ku Klux Klan, Inc., aka, Racial Matters," February 2, 1961. Copy in Files MX/NY-2174 and 21-73 (Malcolm X).

46. Ibid.

47. Jeremiah Shabazz interview.

48. Ibid.

49. C. Eric Lincoln, *The Black Muslims in America* (Boston, Mass.: Beacon Press, 1961), 166.

50. Editorial, *Watson's Magazine* 20, no. 3 (January 1915); available at https://nationalvanguard.org/2015/01/tom-watson-the-leo-frank-case/, accessed January 4, 2020.

51. Jeremiah Shabazz interview.

52. Ibid.

53. Ibid.

54. Carson, *Malcolm X: The FBI Files*, 203–4.

55. Jeremiah Shabazz interview.

56. Ibid.

57. John Ali (aka John X), interview with Les Payne, February 28, 1998.

58. Elizabeth Shabazz interview.

59. Jeremiah Shabazz interview.

60. FBI Files, "U.S. Klans, Knights of the Ku Klux Klan, Inc., aka, Racial Matters," February 2, 1961.

61. Ibid.

62. Ibid.

63. Jeremiah Shabazz interview.

64. John Ali interview.

65. State of Louisiana v. Troy Bland Cade, Supreme Court of Louisiana; https://law.justia.com/cases/louisiana/supreme-court/1963/244-la-534-0.html.

66. Jeremiah Shabazz interview.

67. Ibid.

68. Ibid.

69. Ibid.

70. Ibid.

71. Ibid.

72. Carson, *Malcolm X: The FBI Files*, 203–4.

73. Malcolm X and Haley, *Autobiography*, 1.

74. Malcolm X, "Educate People in Politics," (Ford Auditorium, Detroit, February 14, 1965), *February 1965: The Final Speeches*, ed. Steve Clark (New York: Pathfinder, 1992), 103.

75. Malcolm X, "A Worldwide Revolution," (Audubon Ballroom, Harlem, February 15, 1965), ibid., 128.

76. Malcolm X, "After the Bombing (Detroit, February 14, 1965)," in Breitman, ed., *Malcolm X Speaks*, 211.

## CHAPTER 14: MALCOLM, THE MEDIA, AND MARTIN LUTHER KING

1. Malcolm X and Alex Haley, *The Autobiography of Malcolm X* (New York: Ballantine, 1992), 377.

2. Jim Crow laws in various states can be found on the National Parks Service website, https://www.nps.gov/malu/learn/education/jim_crow_laws .htm, accessed June 7, 2018.

3. Ibid.

4. "Separation or Integration," debate between Malcolm X and James Farmer, Cornell University, Ithaca, N.Y., March 7, 1962. A transcript of this debate was printed in *Dialogue* 2, no. 3 (May 1962): 14–16, and reprinted in Ronald F. Reid, *American Rhetorical Discourse*, 2d ed. (Prospect Heights, Ill.: Waveland, 1995).

5. Ibid.

6. Malcolm X and Haley, *Autobiography*, 227.

7. Wilfred Little, interview with Les Payne, April 26, 1991.

8. "Separation or Integration."

9. Ibid.

10. Ibid.

11. Ibid.

12. Alex Haley, "Playboy Interview: Malcolm X; A Candid Conversation with the Militant Major-Domo of the Black Muslims," *Playboy*, May 1963, 53–63.

13. Raushanah Hassain, interview with Les Payne, June 16, 1996.

14. Malcolm X to Philbert Little, December 9, 1954, collection of Walter and Linda Evans, Savannah, Georgia.

15. Haley, "Playboy Interview: Malcolm X," 53–63.

16. FBI Files, Airtel, SAC, Chicago, to Director, FBI, "Nation of Islam, IS-NOI," March 11, 1963. Copy in File MX/NY-3429 (Malcolm X).

17. Wilfred Little interview.

18. "Malcolm X Says: Passive Resistance Has Failed in South," *Hartford Courant,* June 5, 1963, 14.

19. Ibid.

20. Ron Spencer, "Mahalia Jackson, Dr. King Draw 2,500 to Integration Benefit Here," *Hartford Times,* October 29, 1962, 7.

21. "Muslim Here Voicing Whites Doom," *Hartford Times,* June 5, 1963.

22. Ibid.

23. Ibid.

24. Ibid.

25. Jeremiah Shabazz (aka Jeremiah X), interview with Les Payne, January 1997.

26. "Muslim Here Voicing Whites Doom."

27. Ibid.

28. James Cotton, interview with Les Payne, June 20, 1992.

29. "What Can We Expect When Equality Rules," *Hartford Times,* June 5, 1963.

30. Interview with Malcolm X and Bayard Rustin, by James Donald, January 23, 1962, WBAI Radio studio, New York City. This is just prior to their debate "Separation or Integration" at the Community Church in New York City.

31. Gay Talese, *The Kingdom and the Power* (1969; repr., New York: Random House, 2007), 326.

32. Ted Jones, interview with Les Payne, September 1992.

33. Ibid.

34. Malcolm X, "God's Judgment of America and the Only Solution to the Race Problem" (speech given at Michigan State University, January 23, 1963); https://www.youtube.com/watch?v=4RC4oSHikak (at 35:29).

35. Malcolm X and Haley, *Autobiography,* 269.

36. "Malcolm X Spoke Theme in State Often," *Hartford Times,* February 22, 1965, 12.

37. Gardiner C. Taylor, interview with Les Payne, August 1993.

38. FBI files.

39. Malcolm X and Haley, *Autobiography,* 175.

40. Les Payne's own recollection.

41. Don O. Noel Jr., "Black Muslim Leader Gets Faint Support Here," *Hartford Times,* June 6, 1963.

42. Brian Steinberg, interview with Les Payne, December 1993.

43. Ibid.

44. "Malcolm X States Creed of Muslims at Bushnell," *Hartford Courant,* June 6, 1963, 35.

45. Les Payne's own recollection.

46. Steinberg interview.

47. John F. Kennedy, address to the American people on civil rights, June 11, 1963, John F. Kennedy Library and Museum, Boston; https://www .jfklibrary.org/learn/about-jfk/historic-speeches/televised-address-to -the-nation-on-civil-rights, accessed July 15, 2019.

48. Taylor Branch, *Parting the Waters: America in the King Years, 1954–63* (New York: Simon & Schuster, 1988), 810.

49. Ibid.

50. FBI Report dated November 15, 1963, by the New York office, Title of Case: Malcolm K. Little aka, Character of Case: IS—NOI, filed in New York (105-8999), 27.

51. Branch, *Parting of the Waters,* 810.

52. Sam McPheeters, "When Malcolm X Met the Nazis," *Vice,* April 16, 2015; https://www.vice.com/en_us/article/dpwamv/when-malcolm-x-met-the -nazis-0000620-v22n4, accessed September 15, 2019.

53. Jeremiah Shabazz interview.

54. Ibid.

55. "Perspectives; Negro and the American Promise: The Malcolm X Inter- view," June 24, 1963, WBGH-TV, Boston; WGBH Media Library and Archives, http://openvault.wgbh.org/catalog/V_FE25740F38E943A098 6F93AD4A03E425, accessed June 11, 2018.

56. Wyatt Tee Walker, interview with Les Payne, June 1994.

57. Murray Kempton, interview with Les Payne, June 1992.

58. "Hoover Calls Dr. King 'Most Notorious Liar,'" New York *Daily News,* November 19, 1964, 3.

59. Curt Gentry, *J. Edgar Hoover: The Man and the Secrets* (New York: Plume, 1992), 568, 571.

60. Ibid., 571.

61. Ibid., 572.

62. FBI Files, Airtel, Director, FBI, to SAC, Albany, "Counterintelligence Pro- gram Black Nationalists–Hate Groups Racial Intelligence," March 4, 1968.

63. Martin Luther King Jr., "Letter from Birmingham Jail," *The Atlantic Monthly,* August 1963, 78–88.

64. Alex Haley, "Martin Luther King Jr.: A Candid Conversation with the Nobel Prize Winning Civil Rights Leader," *Playboy,* January 1965, 65–78.

65. Joe Azbell, "Blast Rocks Residence of Bus Boycott Leader: No One Injured After Bombing of King Home," *Montgomery Advertiser,* January 31, 1956, 1, 2A.

## CHAPTER 15: THE SPLIT

1. Malcolm X, statement at a meeting held at the Garden of Prayer Baptist Church, Los Angeles, Calif., June 3, 1962. Transcript obtained at the National Archives, Washington, D.C.
2. Yusuf Shah (aka Captain Joseph), interview with Les Payne, October 9, 1992.
3. Ibid.
4. FBI Files, Airtel, SAC, Chicago, to Director, FBI, "Nation of Islam, IS-NOI," March 11, 1963. Copy in File MX/NY-3429 (Malcolm X). See also FBI Files, Airtel, SAC, Chicago, to Director, FBI, "Afro-Descendant Upliftment Society, aka IS-Miscellaneous," December 31, 1964. Copy in File 100-441765 (Muslim Mosque, Inc.).
5. Malcolm X recorded his thoughts and observations of incidents leading up to his suspension from the Nation of Islam. The recording is dated Thursday, February 13, 1964.
6. Wilfred Little, interview with Les Payne, April 26, 1991.
7. Malcolm X, recording, February 13, 1964.
8. "Malcolm Scores U.S. and Kennedy," *New York Times*, December 2, 1963, p. 21
9. Wilfred Little interview.

## CHAPTER 16: THE INTERNATIONAL STAGE

1. Dr. Ahmed Osman, interview with Les Payne, August 2016.
2. Malcolm X and Alex Haley, *The Autobiography of Malcolm X* (New York: Ballantine, 1992), 340.
3. Ibid.
4. Dr. Sam Hamod, interview with Les Payne, January 1995.
5. Wilfred Little, interview with Les Payne, April 26, 1991.
6. Malcolm X and Haley, *Autobiography*, 340.
7. David Levering Lewis, "Ghana, 1963: A Memoir," *The American Scholar* 68, no. 1 (1999): 59; JSTOR, www.jstor.org/stable/41212832.
8. Vicki Garvin, interview with Les Payne, February 1993.
9. Leslie Alexander Lacy, *The Rise and Fall of a Proper Negro* (New York: Pocket, 1971), 162.
10. Ibid., 182.
11. Alice Windom to Christine Johnson, May 21, 1964, Julian Mayfield Papers, Schomburg Center for Research and Black Culture (Manuscripts and Archives Section), New York.

12. Garvin interview.
13. Windom to Johnson, May 21, 1964.
14. Ibid.
15. Lewis, "Ghana, 1963," 59.
16. Alice Windom, interview with Les Payne, April 2016.
17. Maya Angelou, *All God's Children Need Traveling Shoes* (New York: Vintage, 1991), 141.
18. Windom interview.
19. Malcolm X and Haley, *Autobiography*, 357.
20. Kojo Botsio, interview with Les Payne.
21. Muhammad Ali and Hana Yasmeen Ali, *The Soul of a Butterfly: Reflections on Life's Journey* (New York: Simon & Schuster, 2004), 85.
22. Malcolm X to Earl Grant, October 26, 1964; https://www.historyinink .com/1328401_Malcolm_X_ALS_10-26-1964.htm.
23. FBI Files, SAC, New York, to Director, FBI, "Communist Party, United States of America—Negro Question, Communist Influence in Racial Matters," June 16, 1964; FBI Files, SAC, New York, to Director, FBI, "Malcolm X Little Internal Security—MMI," June 13, 1964.
24. FBI Files, Airtel, SAC, New York, to Director, FBI, and SAC, Philadelphia, "Muslim Mosque, Inc. IS-MMI," June 23, 1964.
25. George Breitman, ed., *Malcolm X Speaks* (1965; repr., New York: Grove Weidenfeld, 1990), 98.
26. Azaria Mbughuni, "Malcolm X, the OAU Resolution of 1964 and Tanzania: Pan-African Connections in the Struggle Against Racial Discrimination," *Journal of Pan-African Studies* 7, no. 3 (September 2014): 184.
27. Herb Boyd and Ilyasah Al-Shabazz, eds., *The Diary of Malcolm X (El Hajj Malik El-Shabazz) 1964* (Chicago: Third World Press, 2013), 218.
28. Ibid., 114 (August 29, 1964, diary entry).
29. Ibid., 99 (August 2, 1964, diary entry).
30. M. S. Handler, "Malcolm Rejects Racist Doctrine," *New York Times*, October 4, 1964, 59.
31. Boyd and Al-Shabazz, eds., *The Diary of Malcolm X*, 30 (November 9, 1964, diary entry).
32. John Lewis and Michael D'Orso, *Walking with the Wind: A Memoir of the Movement* (New York: Simon & Schuster, 1998), 295–97.
33. M. S. Handler, "Malcolm X Seeks U.N. Negro Debate," *New York Times*, August 13, 1964, 22.
34. Dr. Njoroge Mungai, interview with Les Payne, March 2, 1994.
35. Ibid.
36. William Attwood, *The Red and the Blacks* (New York: Harper & Row, 1967), 188.

37. Malcolm X and Haley, *Autobiography*, 371.

38. George Breitman, ed., *The Last Year of Malcolm X: The Evolution of a Revolutionary* (New York: Pathfinder, 1992), 65. The interview also appears in George Breitman, ed., *By Any Means Necessary: Speeches, Interviews, and a Letter by Malcolm X* (New York: Pathfinder, 1970).

39. Breitman, ed., *Malcolm X Speaks*, 91.

40. Dr. Robert Lee, interview with Les Payne, May 1994.

41. Lewis and D'Orso, *Walking with the Wind*, 296–97.

42. "Malik Shabazz (Malcolm X): Some Questions Answered," distributed by the Islamic Centre of Geneva; courtesy of Walter and Linda Evans, Savannah, Georgia.

43. Lewis and D'Orso, *Walking with the Wind*, 295–97.


CHAPTER 17: THE WEEK BEFORE: A DRY RUN

1. Gene Roberts, interview with Les Payne, February 1992.

2. "Malik Shabazz (Malcolm X): Some Questions Answered," distributed by the Islamic Centre of Geneva; courtesy of Walter and Linda Evans, Savannah, Georgia.

3. Luqman Raheem, interview with Les Payne, May 1993.

4. Jeremiah Shabazz (aka Jeremiah X), interview with Les Payne, January 1997.

5. Chuck Stone, interview with Les Payne, February 1995.

6. Raheem interview.

7. Roberts interview.

8. Abdullah Abdur Razzaq (aka James 67X), interview with Les Payne, June 1993.

9. Roberts interview.

10. Ibid.

11. Ibid.

12. Malcolm X, "A Worldwide Revolution," *February 1965: The Final Speeches*, ed. Steve Clark (New York: Pathfinder, 1992), 120.

13. Ibid.

14. "United States Department of Justice Federal Bureau of Investigation, New York, NY, February 16, 1965, Internal Security Report," in Clayborne Carson, *Malcolm X: The FBI File*, ed. David Gallen (1991; repr., New York: Skyhorse, 2012), 351–54.

15. Les Payne interviewed Yusuf Shah (aka Captain Joseph) for many hours in 1992–1993. Captain Joseph called Les Payne directly and made this admission over the phone.

16. Yusuf Shah (aka Captain Joseph), interview with Les Payne, October 1992.
17. Jeremiah Shabazz interview.
18. Roberts interview.
19. Malcolm X, "A Worldwide Revolution," 122.
20. Ibid., 122–23.
21. Roberts interview.

CHAPTER 18: THE HIT

1. Sara Mitchell, interview with Les Payne, May 1992.
2. Malcolm X, "A Worldwide Revolution," *February 1965: The Final Speeches*, ed. Steve Clark (New York: Pathfinder, 1992), 126.
3. Mitchell interview.
4. Ibid.
5. Abdullah Abdur Razzaq (aka James 67X), interview with Les Payne, June 1993.
6. Ibid.
7. Ibid.
8. Ibid.
9. Benjamin Karim (aka Benjamin 2X), interview with Les Payne, May 1992.
10. Gene Roberts, interview with Les Payne, February 1992.
11. Yuri Kochiyama, interview with Les Payne, May 1992.
12. Karim interview.
13. Ibid.
14. Mitchell interview.
15. Karim interview.
16. Thomas Hayer (aka Talmadge Hayer or Thomas Hagan) provided details of this plot in a handwritten affidavit sworn to before William Kunstler, February 25, 1978.
17. Talib (pseudonym), interview with Les Payne.
18. Roberts interview.
19. Ibid.
20. Luqman Raheem, interview with Les Payne, May 1993.
21. Ibid.
22. Alvin Arnoff, interview with Les Payne.
23. Chuck Moore, interview with Les Payne; Gene Simpson, interview with Les Payne.
24. Aubrey Lewis, interview with Les Payne.
25. Kochiyama interview.
26. Ibid.

27. Roberts interview.
28. Ibid.
29. Ibid.
30. Ibid.
31. Ibid.
32. Ibid.
33. Raheem interview.
34. Mitchell interview.
35. Raheem interview.
36. Ibid.
37. Ibid.
38. Ibid.
39. Ibid.
40. Ibid.
41. Ossie Davis, interview with Les Payne, December 1995.
42. Roberts interview.
43. Lewis interview.
44. Ibid.
45. Raheem interview.
46. Shah interview.
47. Raheem interview.
48. Razzaq interview.
49. Charles Kenyatta (aka Charles 37X), interview with Les Payne, July 1992.
50. Roberts interview.
51. Thomas Johnson, interview with Les Payne, June 1993.
52. Ibid.; Norman Butler, interview with Les Payne, April 1993.
53. Agieb Bilal, interview with Les Payne, November 25, 1995.
54. Karim interview.


CHAPTER 19: BACK AT THE MOSQUE

1. Anonymous source (a member of the Newark mosque in 1965), interview with Les Payne.
2. Louis Farrakhan, "The Death of Malcolm X: Its Effects 25 Years Later" (speech given Malcolm X College, Chicago, February 21, 1990); tape recording in author's collection.
3. Jeremiah Shabazz (aka Jeremiah X), interview with Les Payne, January 1997.
4. Anonymous source (on the administrative staff of the Newark mosque in 1965), interview with Les Payne.
5. Ibid.

6. Talib (pseudonym), interview with Les Payne.

7. Agieb Bilal, interview with Les Payne, November 25, 1995.

8. Jeremiah Shabazz interview.

9. Talib interview.

10. Anonymous source (corrections officer with New Jersey state prisons), interview with Les Payne.

11. Talib interview.

12. Ibid.

13. Ibid.

14. Ibid.

15. Thomas Hayer (aka Talmadge Hayer or Thomas Hagan) provided details of the plot in a handwritten affidavit sworn to before William Kunstler, February 25, 1978.

16. Talib interview.

17. Ibid.

18. Johnson interview.

19. Talib interview.

20. Richard Harris, interview with Les Payne, August 5, 1995.

21. Minister James 3X, "Minister Moves New York Mosque to New Heights Warns Muslims Against False Leaders," *Muhammad Speaks,* October 9, 1964, 11.

22. Talib interview.

## EPILOGUE

1. Barack Obama, *Dreams from My Father: A Story of Race and Inheritance* (New York: Times Books, 1995), 86.

2. Hisham Aidi, *Rebel Music: Race, Empire, and the New Muslim Youth Culture* (New York: Pantheon, 2014), 309.

3. Agence France Presse, "Creation of the Indigenous Party," *Le Figaro,* February 3, 2010; http://www.lefigaro.fr/flash-actu/2010/03/02/01011 -20100302FILWWW00730-creation-du-parti-des-indigenes.php; Aidi, *Rebel Music,* 311.

4. Malcolm X, speech in Detroit, February 14, 1965, in *Malcolm X Speaks,* ed. George Breitman (1965; repr., New York: Grove Weidenfeld, 1990), 202.

5. Dr. Azizah al-Hibri, "A Special Fiftieth Anniversary Commemoration of the Assassination of Malcolm X" (panel discussion at the Schomburg Center for Research in Black Culture, New York), February 21, 2015; Les Payne, moderator. No recording of Malcolm's speech in Beirut of September 29, 1964, has been found.

6. American University of Beirut, *Malcolm X Speaks,* video performance

published March 9, 2015, on YouTube; https://www.youtube.com/watch?v=IOEcdkQkEEk, accessed June 28, 2019.

7. "Malcolm X," *New York Times*, February 22, 1965, 20.

8. Wilfred Little, "Our Family from the Inside: Growing Up with Malcolm X," *Contributions to Black Studies* 13, article 2; accessed April 26, 2019.

9. Jean Calmen, "Minister Was Malcolm X's Brother," *Detroit Free Press*, February 8, 1994, 14.

10. "Malik Shabazz (Malcolm X): Some Questions Answered," distributed by the Islamic Centre of Geneva; courtesy of Walter and Linda Evans, Savannah, Georgia.

# SELECTED BIBLIOGRAPHY

## BOOKS AND PAMPHLETS

Aidi, Hisham. *Rebel Music: Race, Empire and the New Muslim Youth Culture.* New York: Pantheon, 2014.

Ali, Muhammad, and Hana Yasmeen Ali. *The Soul of a Butterfly: Reflections on Life's Journey.* New York: Simon & Schuster, 2004.

Anderson, Jervis. *This Was Harlem, 1900–1950.* New York: Farrar, Straus & Giroux, 1982.

Angelou, Maya. *All God's Children Need Traveling Shoes.* New York: Vintage, 1991.

———. *The Heart of a Woman.* New York: Random House, 1981.

———. *A Song Flew Up to Heaven.* New York: Random House, 2002.

Attwood, William. *The Red and the Blacks.* New York: Harper & Row, 1967.

Baldwin, James. *One Day When I was Lost: A Scenario Based on Alex Haley's "The Autobiography of Malcolm X."* New York: Dial Press, 1973.

"The Birth of a Nation" (brochure). New York: Epoch Producing, 1915.

Bontemps, Arna, and Jack Conroy. *Anyplace but Here.* New York: Hill & Wang, 1967.

———. *They Seek a City.* Garden City, N.Y.: Doubleday, Doran, 1945.

Boyd, Herb, and Ilyasah Al-Shabazz, eds. *The Diary of Malcolm X (El Hajj Malik El-Shabazz), 1964.* Chicago: Third World Press, 2013.

Branch, Taylor. *Parting the Waters: America in the King Years, 1954–63.* New York: Simon & Schuster, 1998.

Breitman, George, ed. *By Any Means Necessary: Speeches, Interviews, and a Letter by Malcolm X.* New York: Pathfinder, 1970.

———. *The Last Year of Malcolm X: The Evolution of a Revolutionary.* New York: Pathfinder, 1992.

———. *Malcolm X on Afro-American History.* New York: Pathfinder, 1967.

———. *Malcolm X Speaks: Selected Speeches and Statements.* 1965; repr., New York: Grove Weidenfield, 1990.

———. *Malcolm X: The Man and His Ideas.* New York: Pathfinder, 1965.

———, Herman Porter, and Baxter Smith, eds. *The Assassination of Malcolm X.* New York: Pathfinder, 1976.

Bryer, Jackson R., and Mary C. Hartig, eds., *Conversations with August Wilson.* Jackson: University Press of Mississippi, 2006.

Carew, Jan. *Ghosts in Our Blood: With Malcolm X in Africa, England, and the Caribbean.* Westport, Conn.: Lawrence Hill Books, 1994.

Carson, Clayborne. *Malcolm X: The FBI File.* Edited by David Gallen. 1991; repr., New York: Skyhorse, 2012.

Carson, Clayborne, Ralph E. Luker, and Penny A. Russell, eds. *The Papers of Martin Luther King, Jr.* 7 vols. Berkeley: University of California Press, 1992–2014.

Clark, Kenneth B. *The Negro Protest: James Baldwin, Malcolm X and Martin Luther King.* Boston: Beacon, 1963.

Clark, Steve, ed. *Malcolm X Talks to Young People: Speeches in the U.S., Britain and Africa.* New York: Pathfinder, 1991.

Clarke, John Henrik, ed. *Malcolm X: The Man and His Times.* Trenton, N.J.: Africa World Press, 1990.

Clegg III, Claude Andrew. *An Original Man: The Life and Times of Elijah Muhammad.* New York: St. Martin's,1997.

Collins, Rodnell P., and A. Peter Bailey. *Seventh Child: A Family Memoir of Malcolm X.* Secaucus, N.J.: Birch Lane/Carol Publishing, 1998.

Cone, James. *Martin and Malcolm and America: A Dream or a Nightmare.* Maryknoll, N.Y.: Oris, 1992.

Cronin, E. David, *Black Moses: The Story of Marcus Garvey and the Universal Improvement Association.* Madison: University of Wisconsin Press, 1960.

Cruse, Harold. *The Crisis of the Negro Intellectual: From Its Origins to the Present.* New York: William Morrow, 1967.

Davis, Angela, *Angela Davis: An Autobiography.* 1974; repr., New York: International Publishers, 1996.

DeCaro, Louis A., Jr. *On the Side of My People: A Religious Life of Malcolm X, and Christianity.* New York: New York University Press, 1996.

Dixon, Willie and Don Snowden. *I Am the Blues.* New York: Da Capo Press, 1990.

Douglass, Frederick. *Narrative of the Life of Frederick Douglass: An American Slave.* 1846. Reprint, New York: Signet, 1968.

Du Bois, W. E. B. *The Souls of Black Folks.* New York, Penguin, 1989.

Epps, Archie, ed. *The Malcolm X Speeches at Harvard.* New York, Paragon House, 1961.

Essien-Udom, E. U. *Black Nationalism: A Search for an Identity in America.* Chicago: University of Chicago Press, 1962.

Evanzz, Karl. *The Judas Factor: The Plot to Kill Malcolm X.* New York: Thunder's Mouth, 1992.

Fonda, Henry, and Howard Teichmann. *Fonda: My Life.* New York: New American Library, 1981.

Fox, Stephen R. *The Guardian of Boston: William Monroe Trotter.* New York: Atheneum, 1970.

Friedly, Michael. *Malcolm X: The Assassination.* New York: Carroll & Graf, 1992.

Gallen, David, ed. *Malcolm X: As They Knew Him.* New York: Carroll & Graf, 1992.

Garvey, Amy Jacques, comp. *The Philosophy and Opinions of Marcus Garvey, Or Africa for the Africans.* Dover, Mass.: Majority Press, 1986.

Gentry, Curt, *J. Edgar Hoover: The Man and the Secrets.* New York: Plume, 1992.

Ginzburg, Ralph, *100 Years of Lynchings.* 1962. Reprint, Baltimore: Black Classic Press, 1988.

Goldman, Peter. *The Death and Life of Malcolm X.* Urbana: University of Illinois, 1979.

Gomez, Michael A. *Black Crescent: The Experience and Legacy of African Muslims in the Americas.* Cambridge: Cambridge University Press, 2005.

Hill, Robert A., ed. *The Marcus Garvey and Universal Negro Improvement Association Papers.* 6 vols. Berkeley: University of California Press, 1983–1989.

Hughes, Langston. *I Wonder as I Wander: An Autobiographical Journey.* New York: Fang Hill, 1993.

Ianni, Francis A. J. *Black Mafia: Ethnic Succession in Organized Crime.* New York: Simon & Schuster, 1974.

Jamal, Hakim. *From the Dead Level: Malcolm X and Me.* London: Andre Deutsch, 1971.

Jarvis, Malcolm L. *Myself and I: Malcolm L. Jarvis.* N.p.: Rice Offset Printing, 1979.

Karim, Benjamin, ed. *The End of White World Supremacy: Four Speeches by Malcolm X.* New York: Seaver, 1971.

———, Peter Skutches, and David Gallen. *Remembering Malcolm.* New York: Carroll and Graf, 1992.

Kondo, Zak. *Conspiracys: Unraveling the Assassination of Malcolm X.* Washington, D.C.: Nubia, 1993.

Lewis, David Levering. *W. E. B. Du Bois: The Fight for Equality and the American Century, 1919–1963.* New York: Henry Holt, 2000.

Lewis, John, and Michael D'Orso. *Walking with the Wind: A Memoir of the Movement.* New York: Simon & Schuster, 1998.

Lincoln, C. Eric. *The Black Muslims in America.* Boston, Mass.: Beacon Press, 1961.

Link, Arthur S., et al., eds. *The Papers of Woodrow Wilson.* Vol. 55, *February 8– March 16, 1919.* Princeton, N.J.: Princeton University Press, 1986.

Lomax, Louis E. *The Negro Revolt.* New York: Signet, 1964.

———. *To Kill a Black Man.* Los Angeles: Holloway House, 1987.

———. *When the Word Is Given . . .* Cleveland: World, 1963.

Malcolm X. *February 1965: The Final Speeches.* Edited by Steve Clark. New York: Pathfinder, 1992.

Malcolm X and Alex Haley. *The Autobiography of Malcolm X.* New York: Ballantine, 1992.

Marable, Manning. *Malcolm X: A Life of Reinvention.* New York: Viking, 2011.

McWhirter, Cameron. *Red Summer: The Summer of 1919 and the Awakening of Black America.* New York: Henry Holt, 2011.

Mencken, Henry Louis. *Mencken's America.* Athens: Ohio University Press, 2004.

Milmine, Georgine. *The Life of Mary Baker G. Eddy.* New York: Doubleday, 1909.

Muhammad, Elijah. *Our Saviour Has Arrived.* Chicago: Muhammad's Temple of Islam No. 2, 1974.

Murphy, Larry, ed. *Down by the Riverside: Readings in African-American Religion.* New York: New York University Press, 2000.

Obama, Barack. *Dreams from My Father: A Story of Race and Inheritance.* New York: Times Books, 1995.

"Omaha's Riot in Story and Picture." Omaha: Educational Publishing Co., 1919.

Perry, Bruce. *Malcolm: The Life of a Man Who Changed Black America.* Barrytown, NY: Station Hill, 1991.

Powers, Richard Gid. *Secrecy and Power: The Life of J. Edgar Hoover.* New York: Free Press, 1987.

Price, Joe X. *Redd Foxx, BS (Before Sandford).* Chicago: Contemporary Books, 1979.

Rickford, Russell J. *Betty Shabazz: A Life Before and After Malcolm X.* Naperville, Ill.: Sourcebooks, 2003.

Singely, Bernestine, ed. *When Race Becomes Real: Black and White Writers Confront Their Personal Histories.* Chicago: Lawrence Hill Books, 2002.

Stone, I. F. *In a Time of Torment.* New York: Random House, 1967.

Strickland, William T., and Cheryll Y. Greene, eds. *Malcolm X: Make It Plain.* New York: Viking, 1994.

Talese, Gay. *The Kingdom and the Power.* New York: Random House, 2007.

Turner, Elizabeth Hutton, ed. *Jacob Lawrence: The Migration Series.* Washington, D.C.: Rappahannock Press, 1993.

Tushnet, Mark V., ed. *Thurgood Marshall: His Speeches, Writings, Arguments, Opinions and Reminiscences.* Chicago: Lawrence Hill Books, 2001.

Tyson, Timothy B. *The Blood of Emmett Till.* New York: Simon & Schuster, 2017.

Wade, Wyn Craig, *The Fiery Cross: The Ku Klux Klan in America.* New York: Simon & Schuster, 1987.

Watson, Bruce. *Sacco and Vanzetti: The Men, the Murders, and the Judgment of Mankind.* New York: Viking, 2007.

Wilson, Peter Lamborn. *Sacred Drift: Essays on the Margins of Islam.* San Francisco: City Lights Books, 1993.

Works Progress Administration. *The Negroes of Nebraska.* Lincoln, Neb.: Woodruff Printing Co., 1940.

Wright, Richard. *Black Boy: A Record of Childhood and Youth.* New York: Harper & Brothers, 1945.

## JOURNAL ARTICLES

Abdat, Fathie Ali. "Before the Fez: Life and Times of Drew Ali, 1886–1924." *Journal of Race, Ethnicity, and Religions* 5 (2014): 1–39.

Cunningham, Bill, and Daniel Golden. "Malcolm: The Boston Years." *The Boston Globe Magazine,* February 16, 1992.

Du Bois, W. E. B. "Back to Africa." *The Century* 105, no 4 (February 1923).

———. "Let Us Reason Together." *The Crisis* 18, no. 5 (September 1919).

———. "Lunatic or a Traitor," *The Crisis* 28, no. 1 (May 1924).

———. "Returning Soldiers." *The Crisis* 18, no. 1 (May 1919).

Haley, Alex. "Martin Luther King Jr.: A Candid Conversation with the Nobel Prize Winning Civil Rights Leader." *Playboy,* January 1965, 65–78.

———. "Playboy Interview: Malcolm X; A Candid Conversation with the Militant Major-Domo of the Black Muslims." *Playboy,* May 1963, 53–63.

Huie, William Bradford. "The Shocking Story of Approved Killing in Mississippi." *Look,* January 1956.

Leighton, George Ross. "Omaha Nebraska—The Glory Is Departed: Part Two." *Harper's Monthly Magazine,* August 1938, 309–29.

Levingston, Steven. "John F. Kennedy, Martin Luther King, Jr., and the Phone Call That Changed History." *Time,* June 20, 2017.

Lewis, David Levering. "Ghana, 1963: A Memoir." *The American Scholar* 68, no. 1 (1999): 39–60; JSTOR, www.jstor.org/stable/41212832.

Little, Wilfred. "Our Family from the Inside: Growing Up with Malcolm X." *Contributions to Black Studies* 13, article 2; https://scholarworks.umass .edu/cgi/viewcontent.cgi?article=1123&context=cibs, accessed April 26, 2019.

Menard, Orville D. "Lest We Forget: The Lynching of Will Brown, Omaha's 1919 Race Riot." *Nebraska History* 91 (2010).

Mencken, H. L. "The Aframerican: New Style." *The American Mercury* 7, no. 26 (February 1926).

Payne, Les. "Taking the Measure of Malcolm and Martin." *Newsday*, May 14, 1989.

Randolph, Asa Philip. "A Supreme Negro Jamaican Jackass." *The Messenger* 5, no. 1 (January 1923).

Rotberg, Robert. "Where Can a Negro Live? A Study of Housing Discrimination in Hartford" (7-part series). *Hartford Courant*, August 19–25, 1956.

Schuyler, Michael W. "The Ku Klux Klan in Nebraska, 1920–1930." *Nebraska History* 66 (1985): 234–56.

Terry, Wallace H., II, "Black Muslim Elijah's Lowly Start," in six-part "Cult of Hate" series. *Washington Post*, December 11–16, 1960. Reproduced at the National Archives.

Tygiel, Jules. "The Court Marshall of Jackie Robinson." *American Heritage*, August-September 1984.

Watson, Franklin J. "A Comparison of Negro and White Populations, Connecticut: (1940–1960)." *Phylon Magazine* 29, no. 2 (1968): 142–55.

## FBI FILES

Wallace Farad (file 100-8458)
Wali Fard, W. D. Fard, Wallie D. Ford, W. D. Fard (file 100-9129)
Wallace D. Fard (file 100-32609)
Elijah Muhammad (file 105-24822)
Malcolm X (files MX/NY-2174, 21-73, and MX/NY-3429)
Muslim Mosque, Inc. (file 100-441765)

## GOVERNMENT DOCUMENTS

Earl Little, Death Certificate (register 545). Ingham County, Michigan Department of Health.

Ingham County Circuit Court. *Capital View Land Company and James W. Nicoll v. Earl Little, Louise Little and Cora I. Way.* Docket 14215. October 12, 1929.

Ingham County Probate Court. Michigan State Police Report, by G. W. Waterman, Bureau of Criminal Investigation, case #2155, suspected arson of the Little family home on November 8, 1929, Lansing, Michigan.

Louise Little Mental Health Record (file B-4398), Ingham County Probate Court, State of Michigan.

Malcolm Little, Birth Certificate (#A19357). Douglas County Health Department, Omaha, Nebraska.

Malcolm Little Juvenile Division (file 4053), Ingham County Probate Court, State of Michigan.

Senate, U.S. *Reports of the Immigration Commission: Emigration Conditions in Europe.* 61st Cong., 3d Sess., doc. 748. Washington, D.C.: Government Printing Office, 1911.

*State of Louisiana v. Troy Bland Cade,* Supreme Court of Louisiana. https://law.justia.com/cases/louisiana/supreme-court/1963/244-la-534-0.html.


## NEWSPAPERS

*Boston Herald*
*Hartford Courant*
*Hartford Times*
Lansing *State Journal*
*Montgomery Advertiser*
*New York Post*
*The New York Times*
Omaha *Morning World-Herald*
*The Omaha Daily Bee*
*Pittsburgh Courier*
*The Salt Lake Tribune*


## ONLINE SOURCES

American University of Beirut. *Malcolm X Speaks,* video performance published March 9, 2015 on YouTube: https://www.youtube.com/watch?v=IOEcdkQkEEk, accessed June 28, 2019.

Fields, Tara D., comp. "A Brief Timeline of Georgia Laws Relating to Slaves, Nominal Slaves and Free Persons of Color," published February 14, 2004, http://files.usgwarchives.net/ga/court/lawsfreed.txt.

GPB Education documentary. *Was Lester Maddox the South's Most Racist Gov-*

*ernor?*, published November 21, 2017 on YouTube: https://www.youtube .com/watch?v=sHNR5GRKCqg.

Jim Crow laws on the National Parks Service website: https://www.nps.gov/ malu/learn/education/jim_crow_laws.htm; accessed June 7, 2018.

National Public Radio. "The Boston Red Sox and Racism with New Owners: Team, Confronts Legacy of Intolerance." National Public Radio, 2002; retrieved April 10, 2008.

Swiercek, Nicholas. "Stoking a White Backlash: Race, Violence and Yellow Journalism in Omaha 1919." Paper presented at the 3rd Annual James A. Rawley Graduate Conference in the Humanities, "Imagining Communities: People, Places, Meanings," Lincoln, Neb., April 12, 2008. https:// digitalcommons.unl.edu/historyrawleyconference/31/.

UCLA Athletics. "Jackie Robinson UCLA Biography." Robinson, Jackie (1995); retrieved April 13, 2009.

## INTERVIEWS

(For reasons of space, multiple interviews with a single source are indicated by reference to the date of the first interview only.)

Ali, John (aka John X), February 28, 1998

Alston, Christopher C., September 19, 1993

Arnoff, Alvin

Botsio, Kojo

Brown, Lewis, 1994

Butler, Norman, April 1993

Cotton, Audrey, June 1992

Cotton, James, June 20, 1992

Dart, Rollin, 1992

Davis, John, Jr., September 1, 1993

Davis, Ossie, December 1995

Forrest, Fred, August 8, 1993

Forrest, Rosalie, April 14, 1993

Garvin, Vicki, February 1993

Hamod, Dr. Sam, January 1995

Hassain, Moustafa (aka Robert Hassain), June 8, 1996

Hassain, Raushanah (aka Dorothy Warner), June 16, 1996

Jarvis, Malcolm, December 9, 1992

Johnson, Thomas, June 1993

Jones, Ted, September 1992

Karim, Benjamin (aka Benjamin Goodman; aka Benjamin 2X), May 1992

Kempton, Murray, June 1992

Kenyatta, Charles (aka Charles 37X), July 1992

Kochiyama, Yuri, May 1992

Lee, Dr. Robert, May 1994

Lewis, Aubrey

Little, Philbert, November 15, 1990

Little, Wilfred, April 26, 1991

Mitchell, Sara, May 1992

Moore, Chuck

Muhammad, John, September 18, 1993

Muhammad, Nathaniel, September 27, 2015

Muhammad, Sallid

Mungai, Dr. Njoroge, March 2, 1994

Osman, Dr. Ahmed, August 2016

Peoples, John, August 1993

Perry, Bazeley, February 27, 1993

Raheem, Luqman, May 1993

Razzaq, Abdullah Abdur (aka James 67X; aka James Shabazz), June 1993

Roberts, Gene, February 1992

St. John, Eddie, August 14, 1993

Shabazz, Elizabeth, February 1, 1997

Shabazz, Jeremiah (aka Jeremiah X), January 1997

Shah, Yusuf (aka Joseph Gravitt; aka Captain Joseph), October 9, 1992

Simpson, Gene

Slaught, Audrey, June 7, 1993

Steinberg, Brian, December 1993

Stone, Chuck, February 1995

Talib (pseudonym)

Taylor, Rev. Gardiner C., August 1993

Tisdale, Charles, May 15, 1994

Walker, Wyatt Tee, June 1994

Windom, Alice, April 2016

# INDEX

# ABOUT THE AUTHORS

**Les Payne** (1941–2018), was a Pulitzer Prize–winning journalist, an editor at *Newsday*, and a syndicated columnist. He was a founder of the National Association of Black Journalists and served as the organization's fourth president, where he worked to improve racial fairness and media employment practices, and to expand coverage of black and developing world communities. As an investigative reporter, he won a Pulitzer Prize, along with two fellow reporters, for "The Heroin Trail" series, which traced the flow of illegal drugs from the poppy fields of Turkey, through the "French Connection," and to drug addicts in the New York City area.

In 1976, he cowrote *The Life and Death of the SLA* about the group that kidnapped newspaper heiress Patty Hearst and terrorized the West Coast. He also investigated the Long Island migrant farmworkers' system, involuntary sterilization of indigent women, atomic testing in Nevada, the FBI's surveillance of the Black Panther Party, and the assassination of Dr. Martin Luther King Jr. In addition, Payne covered the 1976 Soweto uprising, as well as the Rhodesia-Zimbabwe guerrilla war that brought the late Robert Mugabe to power.

As an editor at *Newsday*, his news staffs won every major award in journalism, including six Pulitzer Prizes. Payne was the Inaugural Professor for the David Laventhol Chair at Columbia University Graduate School of Journalism. In 2017, he was inducted into the New York Journalism Hall of Fame. Payne was a weekly panelist for *Sunday Edition* on WCBS-TV and appeared frequently on *Bill Moyer's Journal, Nightline, Meet the Press, The Press, Good Morning America, Democracy Now*, and Gil Noble's *Like It Is*.

**Tamara Payne** is a graduate of William Smith College and taught English for two years in the People's Republic of China. For twenty-eight years, she served as her father's principal researcher for *The Dead Are Arising*. She lives in New York.